Teacher Comp

MyMaths for Key Stage 3

1A

Powered by MyMaths.co.uk

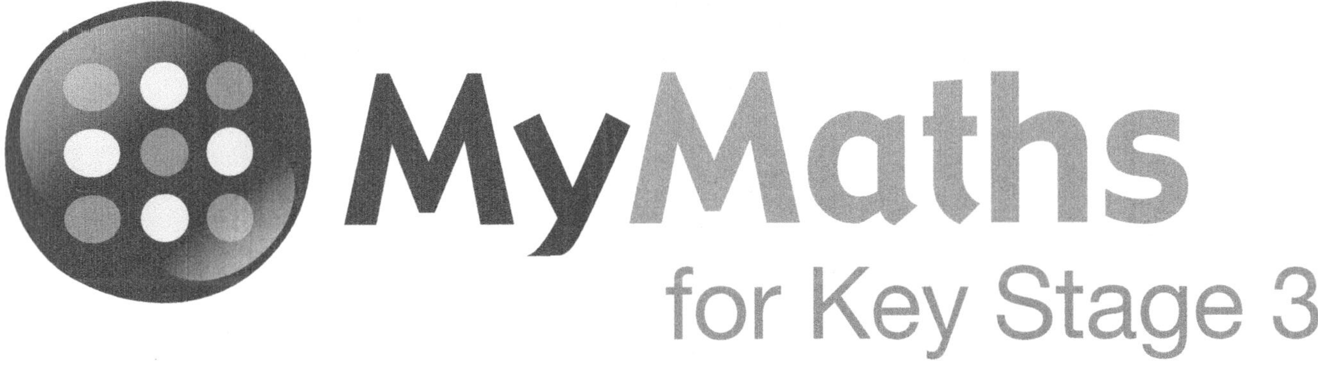

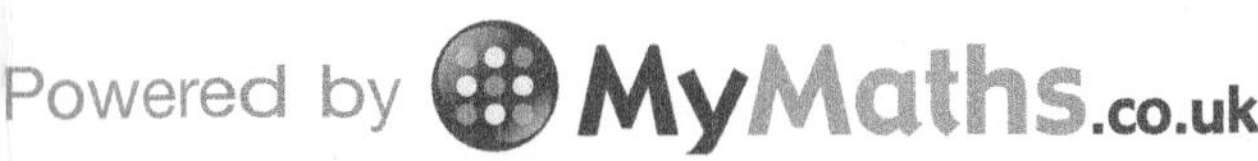

OXFORD UNIVERSITY PRESS

OXFORD
UNIVERSITY PRESS

Great Clarendon Street, Oxford OX2 6DP

Oxford University Press is a department of the University of Oxford.
It furthers the University's objective of excellence in research, scholarship, and education by publishing worldwide in

Oxford New York

Auckland Cape Town Dar es Salaam Hong Kong Karachi
Kuala Lumpur Madrid Melbourne Mexico City Nairobi
New Delhi Shanghai Taipei Toronto

With offices in

Argentina Austria Brazil Chile Czech Republic France Greece
Guatemala Hungary Italy Japan South Korea Poland Portugal
Singapore Switzerland Thailand Turkey Ukraine Vietnam

Oxford is a registered trade mark of Oxford University Press
in the UK and in certain other countries

First published 2014

British Library Cataloguing in Publication Data

Data available

ISBN 978-0-19-830450-0

10 9 8 7 6 5 4 3 2 1

Printed in Great Britain by Bell and Bain Ltd., Glasgow

Paper used in the production of this book is a natural, recyclable product made from wood grown in sustainable forests. The manufacturing process conforms to the environmental regulations of the country of origin.

Acknowledgements

The editors would like to thank Mike Heylings, Katie Wood and Ian Bettison for their excellent work on this book.

Contents

About this book

This Teacher Companion is part of the MyMaths for Key Stage 3 series which has been specially written for the new National Curriculum for Key Stage 3 Mathematics in England. It accompanies Student Book **1A** and is designed to help you have the greatest impact on the learning experience of low ability students at the start of their Key Stage 3 studies.

The author team bring a wealth of classroom experience to the Teacher Companion making it easy for you to plan and deliver lessons with confidence.

The structure of this book closely follows the content of the student so that it is easy to find the information and resources you need. These include for each

Lesson: objectives; a list of resources – including MyMaths 4-digit codes; a starter, teaching notes, plenary and alternative approach; simplification and extension ideas; an exercise commentary and full answers; the key ideas and checkpoint questions to test them; and a summary of the key literacy issues.

Chapter: National Curriculum objectives; any assumed prior knowledge; notes supporting the Student Book introduction and starter problem; the associated MyMaths and InvisiPen resources – including those offering extra support to weaker students; questions to test understanding; and how the material is developed and used.

The accompanying CD-ROM makes all the lesson plans available as Word files, so that you can customize them to suit your students' needs. Also on the CD are full sets of answers for Homework Book **1A** and Practice Book **1**.

The integrated solution

This teacher guide is part of a set of resources designed to support you and your students with a fully integrated package of resources.

MyMaths
Direct links to the ever popular site's lessons and auto-marked homeworks.

Online Student Book
Digital versions of the student books for home and classroom use.

Online Testbank
A complete suite of assessment tests: good to go, formative (including feedback), auto-marked and print based.

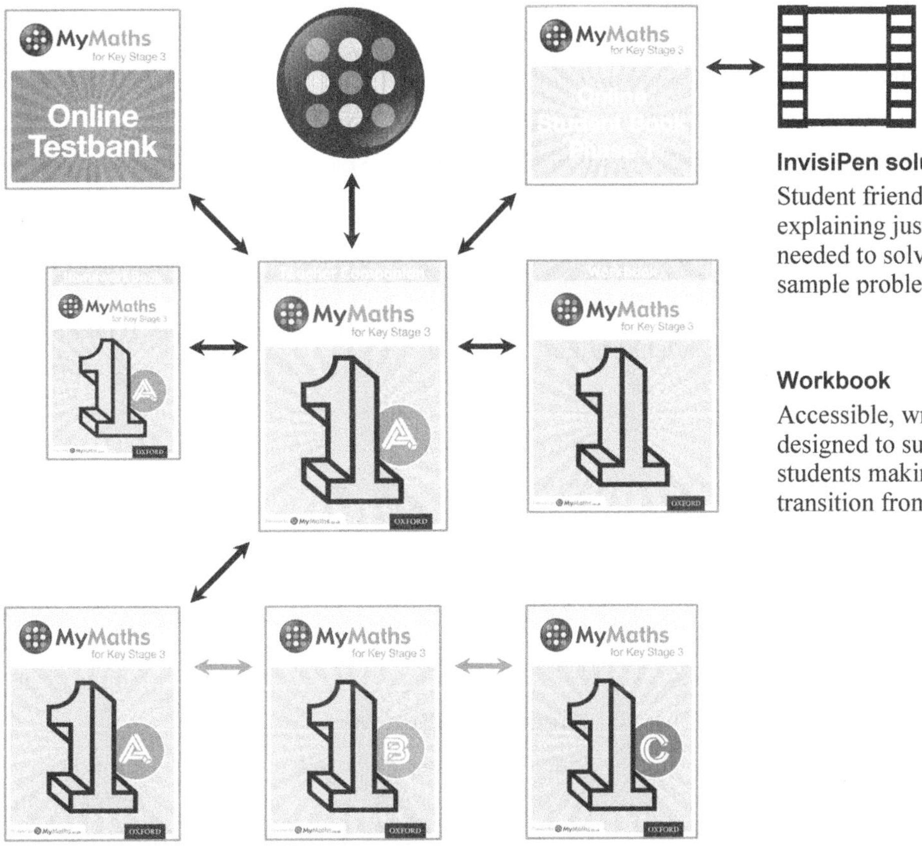

InvisiPen solutions
Student friendly videos explaining just what is needed to solve a sample problem.

HomeworkBook
Handy, pocket-sized books, tailored to the content of each student book lesson.

Workbook
Accessible, write in books designed to support weaker students making the transition from KS2 to KS3.

Student Book
The three books in a phase are organized to cover topics in the same order but at three ability levels.

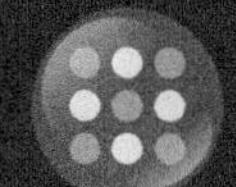

1 Whole numbers and decimals

Learning outcomes	
N1 Understand and use place value for decimals, measures and integers of any size.	(L3)
N2 Order positive and negative integers, decimals and fractions; use the number line as a model for ordering of the real numbers; use the symbols =, ≠, <, >, ≤, ≥.	(L3)
N4 Use the 4 operations, including formal written methods, applied to integers, decimals, proper and improper fractions, and mixed numbers, all both positive and negative.	(L4)

Introduction

The chapter starts by revisiting the idea of place value before going on to consider ordering whole numbers using the concepts of greater than and less than, along with considering the place value of digits. Place value and decimals is then covered before considering decimals in the context of money. Adding decimals is covered before negative numbers are introduced through the idea of temperature. Rounding numbers to the nearest 10, 100 or 1000 is then covered before the final lesson which considers the order of operations.

The introduction discusses the introduction of the number 'zero' in the ninth century by Indian mathematicians in order to help them the write down any number using just the digits 0 to 9. Before this time, written numbers had to stand for something concrete: a number *of* things like goods or people. A brief history of the number 'zero' can be found at

http://www-history.mcs.st-and.ac.uk/HistTopics/Zero.html

The introduction also refers to the prime meridian of longitude, the Greenwich meridian, which is the benchmark for measuring the number of degrees we go around the earth. The prime meridian is so famous that thousands of tourists from around the world visit Greenwich and the Royal Observatory every year. There is even a website dedicated to the Greenwich meridian.

http://www.thegreenwichmeridian.org/tgm/articles.php?article=0

Prior knowledge

Students should already know how to…

- Do basic arithmetic with whole numbers.
- Understand simple place value for integers.
- Use informal mental methods for calculating.

Starter problem

The starter problem is an example of a binary search. Mr Ceero has asked his class to identify the number in 10 moves. It seems obvious that random guessing will not work, since there are 1001 possibilities. Since Mr Ceero can only answer that the guess was too high or too low, the strategy that the children can adopt is to divide the list of numbers successively into two parts. The first guess should therefore be 500. A possible sequence of guesses is shown below. The answers assume Mr Ceero has written 364 on the paper.

500 – too high
250 – too low
375 – too high
313 – too low
344 – too low
360 – too low
368 – too high
364 – YES!

Binary searches can help to find a single item very quickly in a large list, as long as the list has some kind of order. Principles such as the binary search play a very important part in making modern computers very efficient at processing information.

Resources

MyMaths

Rounding to 10, 100	1003	Money calculations	1014	Negative numbers 1	1069
Ordering decimals	1072	Decimal place value	1076	Order of operations	1167
Ordering whole numbers	1217	Introducing money	1226	Place value 100s, 1000s	1352
Solving problems by rounding			1373	Money problems	1377

Online assessment

Chapter test	1A–1
Formative test	1A–1
Summative test	1A–1

InvisiPen solutions

Place value and decimals	111	Rounding	112
Negative numbers	113	Order of operations	124
Written methods of addition and subtraction			131

Topic scheme

Teaching time = 8 lessons/3 weeks

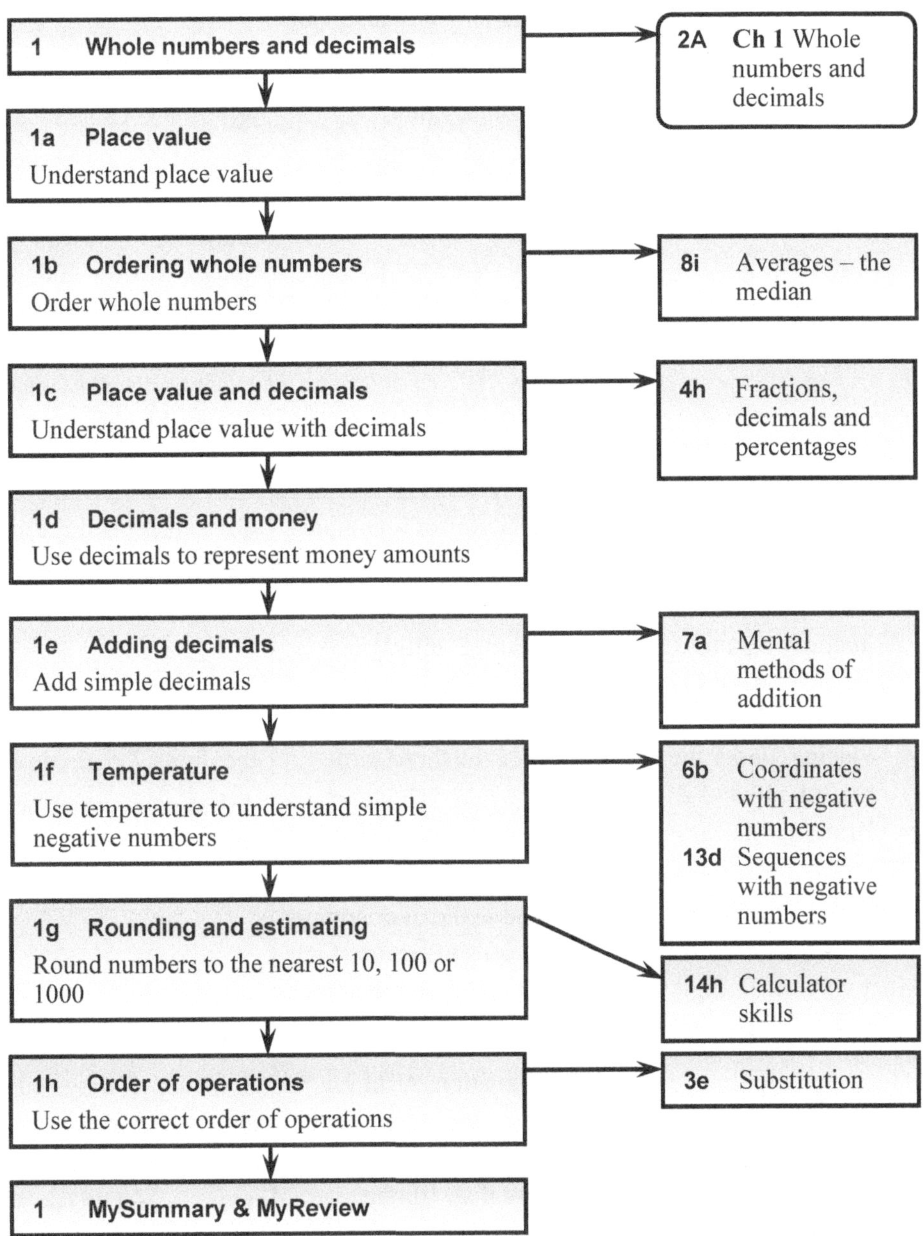

Differentiation

Student book 1A 2 – 23	Student book 1B 2 – 19	Student book 1C 2 – 19
Work with place value in whole numbers Order whole numbers Understand place value in decimals Work with decimals and money Work with temperature Understand simple rounding and estimating Understand the basic order of operations	Work with place value Order whole numbers and decimals Order, add and subtract negative numbers Perform mental and written calculations involving addition and subtraction of whole numbers and decimals Use a calculator efficiently	Work with place value Order whole numbers and decimals Order, add and subtract negative numbers Perform mental and written calculations involving addition and subtraction of whole numbers and decimals Use a calculator efficiently

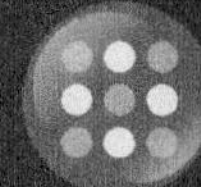

1a Place value

Objectives	
• Understand and use decimal notation and place value. (L3)	
Key ideas	**Resources**
1 The position of a digit determines its value. **2** The values of the positions (or columns) increase from right to left (from U to T, H, Th and beyond).	Place value hundreds thousands (1352) A teacher's set of number cards which can be overlapped to form any four-digit number: single digits showing 1 – 9, tens showing 10 – 90, hundreds showing 100 – 900, and thousands showing 1000 – 9000 Student sets of single-digit cards, 1 – 9 Utility bills showing meter readings Dienes blocks
Simplification	**Extension**
There can be four parallel representations of a number. For example, for 342, they are • Visual representation using Dienes blocks as 3 hundred-squares, four ten-rods and 2 units. • Saying the name of the number: "three hundred and forty two". • Placing, under the Dienes blocks, the three cards for 300, 40 and 2. • Bringing the cards together by overlapping them, so that only the three digits 3, 4 and 2 are visible. Once understanding is secure, abandon the overlapping cards and use only the single digit cards instead, asking what value each digit is and whether the order matters.	Give students three single-digits, such as 7, 9, 2, and ask them to write all the different 3-digit numbers which can be made using each digit just once. Ask them which two of their numbers has the greatest difference and which two have the smallest difference. Repeat the task, allowing 3-digit numbers where one of the digits 7, 9, 2 can be repeated once. Ask students to name the place values (the column headings) to extend beyond, U, T, H, Th, … Can they name them up to a million and beyond?
Literacy	**Links**
The word 'digit' needs careful explanation. A digit is just part of a number. A number can have many digits. The value of a digit depends on where it is placed within the number. For numbers less than 10, the number has just one digit. Ask students which numbers can be 2-digit numbers, (10 to 99) and which can be 3-digit numbers (100 to 999).	Consider readings taken from gas and electricity meters and from car mileometers (for total mileage and trip mileage). The size and distances of planets from the sun can be found on www.bobthealien.co.uk/table.htm Can students name the place values for the digits in some of these distances?
Alternative approach	
A gentle introduction to place value is described above in the **Simplification** section. All students would benefit from this introduction, with the less confident spending more time at this stage until they are secure.	
Checkpoint	
1 What four overlapping cards do you need to make 1632? (1000 + 600 + 30 + 2) For weaker students: Which Dienes blocks do you need to make 1632? **2** What are the values for the two 3s in the number 3235? (3000 and 30)	

Starter – Household bills

Show the students a gas or electricity bill. Ask them to say what the readings are, speaking the numbers in full, at the start and end of the period of the bill. Ask what each digit stands for and what letters (U, T, H,…) might be written above each digit to remind us of its value.
Ask how to find out how much fuel has been used. Take care with using the word 'unit' as a measure of gas or electricity as well as the column heading U.

Teaching notes

Show students the sets of overlapping cards. Ask which cards should be chosen for, say 342. Make the selection and overlap the cards to show 342. Repeat with other numbers, including using the 1000 card.

The teacher now makes a selection and shows the number 624. Ask what the 2 stands for. Withdraw the 20 card and show it. Ask what the 6 stands for (600), withdraw the card and show it. Repeat with other numbers.

Ask for a quicker way of making numbers with cards. Decide on single-digit cards, provided they are in the right order.

Now ask them to show some numbers using their own single-digit cards. First, ask them to show the number 86. Ask them to look at each other's answers. Are any students showing 68? Ask them to explain the difference. Repeat with 3-digit numbers.

Oral work can take the form: 'Add together 300 and 40 and 5. Show me your answer'. 'Add together 100, 100 (pause), 10, 10, 10 (pause), and 1, 1. Show me your answer.'

Later, students' personal mini-whiteboards can be used instead of digit cards. They write down a 3- or 4-digit number and say its name.

Plenary

Give students three single-digit cards, (say) 3, 8 and 5. Ask them to work in pairs and use all three cards to find the largest, the smallest, the number nearest 800, the number nearest 600, etc.

Give the students four single-digit cards, (say) 3, 8, 5 and 7.
In pairs, they find the largest, the smallest using all four cards, the number nearest to 5000, the number nearest to 500 using three cards, etc.

Exercise commentary

Question 1 – It is important for many students to use digit cards to find their answers to this question before they write their answers down.

Question 4 – Many students do not consistently answer this type of question correctly. They should be encouraged, as a first step, to write the letters Th, H, T and U above the digits of each number. They could then be asked to write their answer in two or three ways: for example, the answer to 'What does the digit 6 stand for in the number 164?' could be written as '6 tens', 'sixty' and '60'.

Question 5 – Students will find it helpful to have digit cards when they rearrange the digits. Students should be encouraged to find a systematic way of finding all the possible numbers; e.g. start with the 2 digit in the H column to find 248 and 284, and then have the 4 in the H column, etc.

Answers

1 **a** $(100 + 100 + 100) + (10 + 10 + 10 + 10) + (1 + 1 + 1 + 1 + 1 + 1 + 1)$
or $3 \times 100 + 4 \times 10 + 7 \times 1$
b $1 \times 100 + 2 \times 10 + 3 \times 1$
c $8 \times 100 + 5 \times 10 + 2 \times 1$
d $2 \times 100 + 3 \times 10 + 4 \times 1$
e $7 \times 100 + 2 \times 10 + 7 \times 1$

2 **a** $(1000 + 1000) + (100 + 100 + 100) + (10 + 10) + (1 + 1 + 1 + 1)$
or $2 \times 1000 + 3 \times 100 + 2 \times 10 + 4 \times 1$
b $1 \times 1000 + 3 \times 100 + 5 \times 10 + 4 \times 1$
c $3 \times 1000 + 2 \times 100 + 4 \times 10 + 6 \times 1$
d $2 \times 1000 + 5 \times 100 + 1 \times 10 + 5 \times 1$
e $2 \times 1000 + 4 \times 100 + 0 \times 10 + 8 \times 1$

3 **a** 60 **b** 900 **c** 3000 **d** 0
e 5000 **f** 0 **g** 600 **h** 40

4 **a** 70 + 2 **b** 100 + 20 + 3
c 7000 + 200 + 6 **d** 4000 + 600 + 40 + 2

5 **a** 248 **b** 842
c 428 or 482 or 284 or 824

6 **a** **i** 132 **ii** 232 **iii** 250 **iv** 304
b 221 **c** 1

7 378, 387, 738, 783, 837, 873

8 With repeats, 48; without repeats 18
(Cannot start with 0)

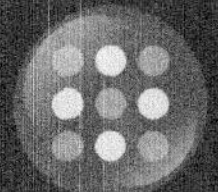

1b Ordering whole numbers

Objectives

- Put numbers up to 1000 in order. (L3)
- Use the symbols > and <. (L3)

Key ideas

1 Use knowledge of both position on a number line and place value to decide the relative sizes of two numbers.

Resources

Ordering whole numbers (1217)

Number lines for different ranges: 0 – 25 labelled in 1s; 0 – 150 labelled in 10s and with 5s marked; 0 – 1200 labelled in 100s and with 50s marked. Use a mixture of horizontal and vertical lines.

Various packs of cards (see **Alternative approach** and **Plenary**)

Simplification

Discuss each number line; decide where the largest numbers are found; ask why. Give two numbers (such as 165 and 245); ask which line is best to show these; decide which is the larger number; ask why?

Repeat with two numbers (such as 362 and 428) without any number line in view; decide which is the larger; ask why. Discuss the place values of the 3 and 4 in 362 and 428. Explore students' understanding of H, T, U to compare two numbers.

When students use < and >, mention that the signs are wider for the bigger number, like a mouth opening to eat a large mouthful. Also, the words 'is greater than' and 'is less than' can be written on triangular cards pointing in the correct direction.

Extension

In problems asking students to order numbers, decimal numbers can be used instead of whole numbers, keeping initially to simple decimals, such as 16.5 and 12.9.

Simple fractions can also be used.

Literacy

Synonyms: 'greater', 'larger', 'bigger'; 'smaller', 'less'

In contexts: 'taller', 'longer', 'shorter'

Comparatives: 'greater', 'greatest'; 'larger', 'largest'; 'smaller', 'smallest'; etc. when there are two or more than two numbers to compare.

Links

The Anno Domini year counting system starts with the birth of Christ and this is called the year AD 1. The year before this is 1 BC. There is no year zero, probably because there was no zero in Roman numerals.

Number lines are used in measurement of length (rulers, tape-measures), temperature (thermometers), and with scales on maps, measuring jugs, etc.

Alternative approach

Ask for (say) six volunteers from the class. Measure their heights in centimetres. Write them down at random. Ask for suggestions to place them in order (either smallest or largest first). Seek explanations for the order. Check by lining up the six volunteers.

Issue packs of 6 cards to the class, with a number (less than 10,000) on each card. Students work in pairs (against the clock) to order them. One (or more) pairs show their results and discuss their reasons for the order.

Checkpoint

1 **a** Which number is larger 869 or 873 (873)

b **i** Which digit in these two numbers has the largest value? (8)

ii What is its value? (800)

c **i** So which digits will tell you which number is the larger? (6 and 7)

ii What are the values of the 6 and 7? (60 and 70)

Starter – Large and small

Ask students to make a 4-digit number using the digits 1, 2, 3 and 4 in any order and to find five more (there are 24 different possibilities).

Ask which is their largest number and why it is the largest. Repeat for the smallest number. Ask for the full names of the chosen numbers (such as 'three thousand', 'two hundred and forty one').

Ask the class to order the numbers with the smallest first, giving reasons for each choice. Discuss the place values of various digits.

Teaching notes

Explore the language of < and >. Ask for different ways of saying '3 is greater than 1' and '1 is less than 3'. (For example, 'greater than', 'more than'; 'bigger than', 'less than', 'smaller than'). To help students use the correct sign, liken the signs to a bird's beak. The open side of the beak holds the larger number, for example, 3 > 1 and 1 < 3.

For a whole-class activity, have 12 numbers on the board with 6 signs (three each of < and >). Students choose two numbers, place the correct sign between them, and say the statement aloud. Note that 5 < 7 and 7 > 5 are both possible. Finally, arrange the 12 numbers is ascending order (smallest first) and then in descending order (largest first) without using the < and > signs.

Another whole-class activity uses 3 numbers (for example, 16, 7, 12). Students find how many correct statements can be made using pairs of these numbers with either the > or < sign.

Plenary

1 Have three numbers on cards, for example. 26, 31, 29.

Ask students to arrange the numbers in ascending order and then in descending order.

Ask them to place the numbers in these boxes to make these statements true:

☐ < ☐ < ☐   and   ☐ > ☐ > ☐

2 Ask students to make the largest 3-digit number from the digits 5, 3 and 8. Ask them to make the smallest 3-digit number. Ask them to make a number which lies between the largest and smallest. Ask how these results can be written as a mathematical statement using < or > (see **1** above).

Exercise commentary

Questions 1 to **5** – These might benefit from having an appropriate number line available; a vertical one would be preferred to a horizontal one.

Questions 3, **4** and **5** – These questions require students to arrange numbers in ascending or descending order and do not require the use of the < and > signs.

Question 6 – This question has several steps. Students have to decide the height of each person. When a student has difficulty in starting, ask 'Which person's height is the easiest to find?' and 'Why is this person the easiest?' Further support can be given by asking the specific question 'Who is the tallest? How tall is this person?' etc.

Answers

1 **a** 9 > 5 **b** 4 < 14 **c** 16 < 25 **d** 38 < 83
  e 101 > 98 **f** 210 > 187

2 **a** 5 is greater than 2 but less than 9
  b 28 is greater than 16 but less than 31
  c 102 is greater than 86 but less than 103
  d 9 is greater than 0 but less than 17

3 **a** **i** 4, 5, 6, 7, 8 **ii** 8, 9, 10, 11, 12
  iii 31, 32, 33, 34, 35 **iv** 18, 19, 20, 21, 22
  v 88, 89, 90, 91, 92 **vi** 98, 99, 100, 101, 102
  vii 234, 235, 236, 237, 238
  viii 996, 997, 998, 999, 1000
  b 1000, 999, 998, 997, 996, 238, 237, 236, 235, 234, 102, 101, 100, 99, 98, 92, 91, 90, 89, 88, 35, 34, 33, 32, 31, 22, 21, 20, 19, 18, 12, 11, 10, 9, 8, 7, 6, 5, 4

4 8, 10, 12, 18, 24, 40, 56, 62

5 30, 25, 23, 18, 14, 11, 8, 3 kg

6 **a** Raj 180 cm, Kelly 170 cm, Nita 150 cm, James 161 cm, Ian 152 cm.
  b Nita 150 cm, Ian 152 cm, James 161 cm, Kelly 170 cm, Raj 181 cm.

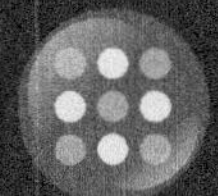

1c Place value and decimals

Objectives	
• Understand and use decimal notation and place value. (L3)	
Key ideas	**Resources**
1 Numbers exist between the whole numbers; they are the fractions and particularly 'decimal fractions' (or just 'decimals' for short). **2** The place values ... H, T, U can extend to the right for decimals with place values t, h, th, ... **3** The decimal point separates the whole number part from the decimal part.	Ordering decimals (1072) Decimal place value (1076) Bamboo sticks 1 metre and 0.1m long Several 10×10cm squares with 1 × 10cm strips A number line labelled 0 – 5 and marked in tenths Four packs of cards: one with multiples of 10 from 10 to 90, another with integers from 0 to 9, a third with decimals from 0.1 to 0.9, a fourth with fractions from $\frac{1}{10}$ to $\frac{9}{10}$ Cards labelled 2.6, 3.2, 4.3, 1.4, 0.7 and 5.1 Cards labelled 0.5, 16.2, 39.1, 6.3, 50.0 and 30.4 Four dice with faces labelled 10 to 60 and 1 to 6 and 0.1 to 0.6 and 0.01 to 0.06
Simplification	**Extension**
We count using whole numbers, but measurement needs the greater accuracy of fractions and decimals. Illustrate this idea using lengths of bamboo cane cut to 1 metre and 0.1 m. Have students estimate and then measure the width of the classroom by placing 1-metre canes end-to-end and then filling the final gap with 0.1m canes. Counting the canes gives the width to the nearest 0.1m and can be written as two digits (labelled U and t) separated by the decimal point. Repeat with other measurements. Even smaller pieces, 0.01m long, can be used to get a more accurate measurement to demonstrate the second decimal place (labelled h).	Students shake three dice (for T, U and t), line them up in order of size (T, U, t) and write down their result. Repeat several times. Now include a fourth dice (for h), shake, line up and write down results.
Literacy	**Links**
A decimal is spoken, for example, as 'two point three' (but not when using money – see later). The decimal 0.3 is not written as .3 but can be spoken as either 'nought point three' or just 'point three'.	The prefix *deci-* means 'tenth', as in December (the tenth month of the Roman calendar), decibel (the measure of noise), decilitre (a measure of wine), decimate (to cut down to a tenth in size). Can students find other words starting with *deci-* or *deca-*?
Alternative approach	
The use of bamboo canes can lead to measurements of length using a ruler marked in mm but labelled in cm. Students can then measure sides of shapes such as irregular triangles and quadrilaterals, writing their answers as decimals. Students can also measure distances between places on maps, again writing their answers as decimals.	
Checkpoint	
1 Write the number $4\frac{3}{10}$ as a decimal. (4.3) **2** Write the number 'seven tenths' as a decimal. (0.7)	

Starter – On the car dashboard

Recap the place values for Th, H, T, U. Write a 4-digit whole number and ask for the values of the digits.

Write down a car's trip meter reading, such as 472.5 with the 5 in colour. Ask what these values mean. Particularly ask what the 5 means and why it might be in colour. Expect the answer 'a half' and ask why 0.5 means 'a half'. After a drive to the shop, the trip meter reads 472.8. Ask what this means and what distance has been travelled.

Teaching notes

As with whole numbers, so also with decimals, a visual representation helps understanding. Use the 10cm-square card to represent 1. Strips of the card are cut to represent tenths. (As a later extension, these strips can be cut into ten pieces to represent hundredths.) Display a selection of squares and strips and ask what number they represent. Say that we separate whole squares (units) and strips (tenths) with a decimal point so that, for example, 1.3 (one point three) is not confused with 13 (thirteen).

Take the packs of cards for tens, units and tenths as decimals, shuffle and withdraw one card per pack. Display them in order, such as 60, 4, 0.3 and ask students to use their mini-whiteboards to write the number as a decimal.

Replace the decimals tenths by fractional tenths and repeat with students writing decimal answers only.

Now use a number line from 0 to 5 with tenths marked (students can use a ruler marked in mm but labelled in cm). Count the tenths in a unit of length to confirm there are ten tenths. An arrow drawn to point at (say) 2.6 as in the Student Book is spoken as 'two point six'.

Plenary

2.6	3.2	4.3	1.4	0.7	5.1

Have six number cards available. You may have these attached to the board, or ask students to hold them. Ask questions such as: 'Can you place these numbers in order, starting with the smallest? How many tenths are there between 2.6 and 3.2?'

Ask students to order cards (with the smallest first) which are labelled 0.5 16.2 39.1 6.3 50.0 30.4
(0.6, 6.3, 16.2, 30.4, 39.1, 50.0)

Exercise commentary

Question 1 – Students should be encouraged, as a first step, to write the letters H T U t above the digits of each number (shown by squares and strips).

Question 2 – Overlapping cards to represent the numbers, as used in the previous exercise, might be a first step here. Labelling the numbers with H, T, U, t is a further help.

Question 4 – Students may need reminding that the 'open beak' of the signs < and > indicates the larger number.

Question 6 – A number line similar to the ruler given in Question 3 could be marked.

Question 7 – Money requires the second decimal place which has not been addressed in this exercise. Discuss with students the need for another column in the grid of Question 5 to hold the hundredths.
A discussion about the 10p coin would bring out that it can be seen either as ten hundredths, that is ten pennies, or as one tenth of a pound.

Answers

1 **a** 1.3 **b** 2.9 **c** 0.5

2 **a** 6 **b** 0.9 **c** 300 **d** 0
e 5 tenths **f** 20

3 **a** 1.2 **b** 1.9 **c** 3.5 **d** 4.1

4 **a** 2.3 < 3.2 **b** 3.1 > 2.9 **c** 5.3 < 6.1 **d** 4.0 > 3.8
e 3.8 < 4.2 **f** 5.0 > 4.9 **g** 3.0 > 0.4 **h** 0.7 < 0.9

5

	1000s	100s	10s	1s	•	$\frac{1}{10}$s
a			1	0	•	6
b			2	4	•	3
c			6	2	•	8
d		1	1	9	•	7
e		6	0	4	•	3
f	7	0	8	5	•	1

6 2.2 (Lara), 2.3 (Anna), 2.9 (Thomas), 3.5 (Liam), 3.7 (Peter)
Fourth

7 **a** They are the same.
b No, because you have 94 p + 15 p = 109p and you need 110p.

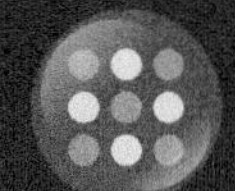

1d Decimals and money

Objectives

- Use decimals to write money. (L3)

Key ideas

1 Money in pounds and pence can be written as a decimal.

2 There are differences in the ways that money as a decimal is spoken and written when compared to decimal measurements of, for example, length, weight and capacity.

Resources

Introducing money (1226)

Selections of coins, especially 1p, 10p and £1

Two packs of five cards each, with denominations written on them: one pack has £10, £5, £2, £1 and 50p; the other pack has 20p, 10p, 5p, 2p and 1p

Simplification

Count real money where possible. In the first instance, use only 10p and 1p coins (a projector is useful for whole-class or large-group counting). First, count sums less than £1 and have students write the totals in pence without a decimal, and also in pounds as a decimal. Then progress to sums above £1 with answers only as decimals. Finally, introduce other coins.

Extension

Measurement of length, weight and capacity provides another another context where decimals are used. In class, measurement of length in metres, cm and mm can be readily undertaken. Ask students to measure various lengths and write the lengths as decimals.

Literacy

Note a difference in spoken language: £1.52 is 'one pound fifty two pence', whereas 1.52m is 'one point five two metres'.

Note the difference in the written language: £1.60 is correct but £1.6 is incorrect, whereas 1.6m and 1.60m are both acceptable.

Also note that, for example, £1.605 does not exist in reality, whereas 1.605 metres, litres or kilograms are all possible measurements.

Links

For every £1 spent on a National Lottery ticket in the UK, £0.28 is distributed to good causes, £0.12 goes to the Treasury in tax, £0.05 goes to the shop which sold the ticket and £0.05 goes to the game operator for operating costs and profit. The rest is spent on prizes. (Source: www.lotterygoodcauses.org.uk)
How much of each £1 goes towards prizes?

In which job do you need a good understanding of decimals? (Examples include builders, joiners, engineers, nurses, doctors, bankers.)

Alternative approach

Instead of taking money as the first contexual use of decimals, the measurement of length can be used as an alternative. Measuring the length of lines in cm and mm and writing decimal answers in cm can be used when finding, for example, perimeters of shapes or distances between places on maps. The general language of decimals (see **Literacy** above) can be reinforced and then compared with the more specific language of money.

Checkpoint

For each scenario ask, How much have I got altogether? Ask students to write and then speak the answers.

1 In my pocket, I've got a one pound coin, a fifty pence coin and a two pence coin. (£1.52)

2 In this pocket, I've got a two pound coin and a two pence coin. (£2. 02)
(Watch for the incorrect £2.20 and £2.2)

3 In my hand, I've got a one pound coin and a twenty pence coin. (£1.20)
(Watch for the incorrect £1.2)

Starter – Pocket money

Have eight 10p coins and six 1p coins in your pocket. Empty your pocket and ask a student to count the coins. Ask how to write down the total. Accept 86p and £0.86. Reject £0.86p.

Repeat with two £1 coins and seven 1p coins. Accept £2.07. Reject £2.7 and £2.70.

Ask why you are rejecting some answers.

Repeat with different values of coins until students are secure in knowing the correct notation.

Teaching notes

These points have already been made in the **Literacy** section but are explored in more detail here.

Students are usually successful with simple problems involving money in pounds and pence. However, there is the potential for confusion between the language, both oral and written, that is used with money and the language that is used with decimals in the context of other measurements. For example, £3.1 is never written whereas 3.1 kg is acceptable. Furthermore, the sum £3.10 is spoken as 'three pounds ten' or 'three pounds, ten pence', whereas 3.1 kg is spoken as 'three point one kilograms'.

Another point of confusion for some students occurs when they write £3.1, instead of £3.01, for 'three pounds and one penny' and particularly when they interpret the display 3.1 on a calculator as £3.01 instead of £3.10.

Furthermore, money does not extend beyond hundredths into thousandths, whereas 3.125 kg is acceptable.

Plenary

Give two students the two packs of cards described in **Resources**, placed face down. Each student selects one card from each pack. All students add the two amounts and write the total on mini-whiteboards. Repeat five times.

Shuffle pack and repeat until answers are secure.

Exercise commentary

Question 2 – Students are asked to add up coins and write the total as a decimal. This should prove an easy task but, if you allow a student to check using a calculator, you can discuss why a calculator shows an answer as 0.6 when, as money, we write £0.60.

Question 4 – Remind students of the idea of 'jumps' on a number line when adding numbers.

Question 7 – Students are asked to find exactly £0.80 from a number of coins. You may like to develop this by asking: How many different ways can you make £0.80? How much money does Stuart have altogether and how much will he have left after paying £0.80?

Question 9 – Students first need to convert all prices to the same format (for example, all prices in pence) before comparing them in order to spot the odd one out.

Answers

1 **a** £0.10 **b** £0.20 **c** £0.50 **d** £0.80
2 **a** £0.20 **b** £0.60 **c** £0.60 **d** £0.90
3 **a** 7.1 **b** 7.5 **c** 7.7 **d** 7.9
4 **a** £0.40 **b** £0.90 **c** £0.90 **d** £1.00
e £1.00 **f** £0.80
5 **a** $3 \times 10p$ or $20p + 10p$
b $50p + 20p$ or $50p + 2 \times 10p$ or $3 \times 20p + 10p$ or $2 \times 20p + 3 \times 10p$ or $3 \times 20p + 10p$ or $7 \times 10p$
c $2 \times 20p$ or $20p + 2 \times 10p$ or $4 \times 10p$
d $50p + 20p + 10p$ or $50p + 3 \times 10p$ or $4 \times 20p$ or $3 \times 20p + 2 \times 10p$ or $2 \times 20p + 4\times 10p$ or $20p + 6 \times 10p$ or $8 \times 10p$
e $50p + 10p$ or $3 \times 20p$ or $2 \times 20p + 2 \times 10p$ or $20p + 4 \times 10p$ or $6 \times 10p$
6 Yes, 10p
7 $50p + 20p + 10p$ or $50p + 3 \times 10p$ or $3 \times 20p + 2 \times 10p$
8 Three, 155 p = £1 + 50p + 5p
9 8 pounds and 5 pence ($\neq$ £8.50)
10 **a** Four, 20p + 20p + 5p + 1p
b Four, 50p + 20p + 2p + 1p
c Four, 10p + 5p + 2p + 2p
d Three, £1 + 5p + 2p
e Four, 20p + 10p + 5p + 1p
f Five, 50p + 10p + 5p + 2p + 2p

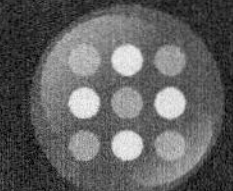

1e Adding decimals

Objectives	
• Use decimals to write sums of money. (L3) • Add decimals. (L3)	
Key ideas	**Resources**
1 A sum in pence can be written in pounds as a decimal to two decimal places. **2** Line up decimal points vertically when using a written method to add decimals.	Money calculations (1014) Money problems (1377) A template of columns labelled T, U, t, h which are wide enough to place coins in A number line labelled from 0 to 1.00 with every 0.10 marked
Simplification	**Extension**
Each student needing specific support can be supplied with their own templates of columns labelled T, U, t, h. The columns can also have diagrams of the appropriate note or coin above each letter of the columns. Students can then match real coins to the correct columns before writing down the amounts. For simple additions of money, the use of a template also helps students to set out their additions accurately.	What is the least number of coins that you need to make each sum of money from £0.01 to £0.99? Which coins do you use for each sum? For example, the least number for 19p is four coins; one 10p, one 5p, two 2p. This task can take some time to complete with much of it done outside lessons. It can be adopted as a class project, with students recording their results on a poster.
Literacy	**Links**
Throughout this exercise, reinforce the correct spoken and written language of decimal money, as described in the previous exercise.	Dewey Decimal Classification is a decimal system used to classify library books according to subject. The classes are listed at www.bpeck.com/references/DDC/ddc.htm Most libraries use this system.

Alternative approach

Create a simple currency converter. A line has its ends labelled 0 and £1. One side of the line is labelled 'Pence' and marks on this side are labelled 10p, 20p up to 90p. The other side of the line is labelled 'Pounds' and the same marks are labelled £0.10, £0.20 up to £0.90. Finding a number of pence on the line gives its equivalent in pounds, and vice versa.

Checkpoint

1 Hold out a small sum of money in your hand, say 6p or 12p.
Ask student to write down the amount (£0.12 or £0.06)

2 Hold out two small sums of money in each hand, say 30p and 23p
Ask how much money is there altogether?
Write your answer a different way (53p or £0.53)

Ask students to read out their answer to check their spoken words.

Starter – Money bags

Show a template with columns labelled T, U, t, h and with a large decimal point between U and t.
Recap what the letters stand for. Say that they will be used for pounds in this lesson. In this case, if T stands for £10, what do U, t and h stand for? (£1, 10p and 1p)

Give two students two bags of money containing £4.31 and £2.53 in £1, 10p and 1p coins. Each student places their sum in the correct columns, one sum underneath the other. Ask the class to write down the total amount of money on the template. (£6.84)

Repeat with other students and other sums, such as £1.52 and £2.04. Keep the additions within the scope of their skills of mental addition.

Teaching notes

Discuss with students whether having columns labelled 'tens (T)', 'units (U)' and 'tenths (t)' are sufficient when we want to write money as a decimal. Ask students if columns for H, Th and th are acceptable on the template. (H and Th are, but th is not.)

Discuss which coin or note we would need if we placed, in turn, a 1 in each column. Discuss that 0.1 is a tenth, but a tenth of a pound is written as £0.10 (which is 10p). Discuss that 0.01 is a hundredth and a hundredth of a pound is written as £0.01, which is 1p.

As in the **Starter**, the template can be used with initial work with addition. When students are confident, the template can be omitted.

Addition of simple sums, as in Question 1, can be done using jumps along a decimal number line, labelled in steps of 0.10 from 0 to 1.00.

Plenary

Plenary exercises can reinforce students' mental number skills. Display two or three sums of money as decimals of a pound, such as £0.30, £0.45 and £0.20. Ask students to add these sums mentally and to explain how they did the addition. For example, it is often useful to start with the largest number.

Ask who starts by adding the 10p column first and who starts with the 1p column. Is one column easier to start with or they equally straightforward?

Exercise commentary

Question 1 – This question does not refer directly to decimals as money. It is a reminder that additions can be seen as 'jumps' along a number line.

Question 2 – Although these amounts of money are all less than £1, the answers should be written as decimals of a pound.

Question 4 – Encourage a mental approach to finding the amounts.

Question 5 – See that answers for **d**, **e**, and **f** are written to two decimal places.

Question 6 – Part **c** can be tackled by using repeated subtraction from the total amount that Martin has or by repeated addition up to Martin's total amount.

Question 7 This can be extended by asking how much change Sangita will get from her £10. (£0.50, £4.05, £7.50, £6.20, £0.25, £1.55, £6.30)

Answers

1 **a** 0.5 **b** 0.8 **c** 0.8 **d** 0.9
e 1.0 **f** 1.0

2 **a** £0.12 **b** £0.19 **c** £0.46 **d** £0.63

3 **a** £0.12 **b** £0.52 **c** £0.48 **d** £0.08
e £3.30 **f** £2.09

4 **a** £1.45 **b** £2.54 **c** £1.46

5 **a** £0.12 **b** £0.25 **c** £0.18 **d** £0.20
e £0.20 **f** £0.30

6 **a** £0.49 **b** £2.40 **c** 30p

7 Any individual item or scarf + diary
or scarf + necklace or diary + necklace

1f Temperature

Objectives	
• Use positive and negative numbers for temperatures. (L3)	
Key ideas	**Resources**
1 Know that a thermometer measures temperatures which can be above, at, or below freezing. **2** When water begins to freeze, its temperature is zero. **3** Numbers greater than zero are positive and numbers less than zero are negative.	Negative numbers 1 (1069) A large vertical number line (to act as a thermometer) from -10 to 10 for whole-class use Small vertical number lines from -10 to 10 for individual use
Simplification	**Extension**
Some students will find it helpful to have their own personal vertical number line, labelled from -10 to 10, to represent a thermometer. They can then count by touching with a pencil point to find (or to use) changes in temperature by counting up or down the line.	For **Exercise 1f**, students could be asked to write the problems in Question 2 as problems in arithmetic. For example, part **a** could be written as -5 + 2 = -3 and part **b** as -2 – 5 = -7. Ask students to invent five similar problems and challenge their partner to answer them.
Literacy	**Links**
The symbol 0 is called 'zero'. Sometimes it may be called 'nought'. It is never called the letter O, as is often the case when saying telephone numbers. In soccer and tennis, 0 is 'nil' and 'love' respectively. Some people think the word 'love' in tennis comes from the French word *l'oeuf* meaning 'egg' which is shaped like a 0. Compare cricket's use of 'duck', for no score, with a duck egg shaped like a 0.	Consider water in a garden pond during the winter. As the water gets colder, it sinks until it reaches 4 °C. Water colder than 4 °C begins to rise again as ice which floats on water. So, ponds freeze over from the top downwards and the water at the bottom stays unfrozen at 4 °C. This effect allows fish to stay alive beneath the ice during the winter. Of course, if the weather is very cold, the pond can freeze completely from the top right down to the bottom!

Alternative approach

Sketch a mountain near the sea, such as on Scotland's west coast or a Pacific island. The base of the mountain is below sea-level. Discuss with students the difference between the overall height of the mountain (distance from base to peak) and the height of the peak above sea-level.

The highest mountain in the world is Mount Everest, but it is not the tallest mountain from base to peak. The tallest is Mauna Kea on the Pacific island of Hawaii. Its peak is 4200 metres above sea-level and its base is 6000 metres below sea-level.

So what is its overall height? (4200 + 6000 = 10 200 metres)

If sea-level is labelled 0, what labels could be given to the peak and base of Mauna Kea? (+4200 and -6000)

Checkpoint

1 Find the rise in temperature from -4 °C to +3 °C by counting it out and pointing with a pencil. (7 °C)

Students should count the jumps between temperatures: -4 to -3 '1', -3 to -2 '2', etc.
Students should not count the temperatures: -4 '1', -3 '2', etc.

Starter – Warmer or colder

You choose a temperature between -10 °C and 10 °C. Students take turns to guess the temperature. After each guess, say whether the next guess should be warmer or colder until the right temperature is found.

Teaching notes

There are four points of potential confusion.

1. Students need to know that -5 has two meanings. When read as 'negative 5', it is the value of a number on the number line. When read as 'subtract 5' or 'take away 5', it is an operation used in a calculation. When it is read as 'minus 5', it can confusingly have either meaning; so saying 'minus 5' is best avoided. Two slightly different signs are often used: -5 for 'negative 5' and – 5 for 'subtract 5'.
2. Students need to know that, for example, -4 is greater than -7. Initial discussion using a vertical number line is useful. For example, mark 3 and -5 on a vertical number line. Ask students to imagine the line as a thermometer and ask which the higher temperature is, and so which is the larger number? Repeat with other pairs of numbers such as -2 and -5 to show that
   -2 is greater than -5.
3. With temperatures, 10°C usually means the value of a temperature on a thermometer. It can also mean a change in temperature of 10 degrees (for example, a change from 13°C to 23°C).
4. Positive numbers can be written with a positive sign but, more often, the positive sign is not written. For example, +3 is written simply as 3.

Plenary

Use a large number line as a thermometer with the whole class. Issue instructions for students to follow. For example, 'Start at 5 °C. Rise 3 degrees. Fall 6 degrees. What is the temperature now?' (2 °C)

Students write answers on their mini-whiteboards.

Exercise commentary

Question 2 – In part **a**, students need to know that '.... rise by 2 °C' indicates a *change* of temperature of 2 degrees. The *actual* temperature of 2 °*C* is not involved in the question. Similarly in parts **b**, **c** and **d**.

Question 3 – The answer can be found by a mental subtraction (or addition), but students might find it easier to touch-count the spaces between the numbers on the number line to find the difference.

Questions 4 and **5** – Students can refer to the vertical number line (which looks like a thermometer) to find the coldest temperatures.

Question 7 – Students need to eliminate the easy pairs first (such as the ice lolly and boiling kettle). Note that 37 °C is the normal body temperature for a healthy person but it rises when the person is unwell.

Answers

1 **a** 20 °C **b** 17 °C **c** 10 °C **d** 0 °C
e 19 °C **f** 1 °C **g** -3 °C **h** -7 °C

2 **a** -3 °C **b** -7 °C **c** -2 °C **d** 0 °C

3 **a** Rise, 5 °C **b** Fall, -11 °C
c Fall, -8 °C **d** Rise, 7 °C
e Fall, -5 °C **f** Fall, -15 °C

4 **a** -7 °C **b** -3 °C **c** -10 °C **d** -7 °C
e 0 °C **f** -14 °C

5 **a** 0 °C, 3 °C, 9 °C **b** -6 °C, -5 °C, -2 °C
c -6 °C, 1 °C, 4 °C **d** -8 °C, -5 °C, 0 °C
e -10 °C, -6 °C, 6 °C **f** -7 °C, 0 °C, 4 °C
g -6 °C, -4 °C, 5 °C

6 6

7 **a** 68 °C **b** 100 °C **c** 3 °C
d -1 °C **e** 37 °C

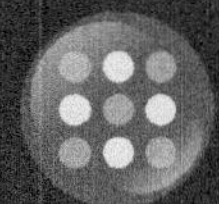

1g Rounding and estimating

Objectives	
• Round positive whole numbers to the nearest 10, 100 or 1000. (L4)	
Key ideas	**Resources**
1 Numbers can be rounded up or rounded down. **2** A number exactly at the midpoint between two numbers is always rounded up.	Rounding to 10, 100 (1003) Solving problems by rounding (1373) Numbers lines labelled in 10s from 0 to 100, from 500 to 600, and for other ranges as needed Number lines labelled in 100s from 0 to 1000
Simplification	**Extension**
Provide enlarged sections of number lines with intermediate unlabelled marks. For example, with labels at 30, 40, 50, all intermediate numbers have unlabelled marks. Students can find exactly where their given number is and then decide which multiple of 10 is nearest. The intermediate marks are then removed and students have to estimate where their given number is, before deciding which multiple of 10 is the nearest. A similar enlarged section can be labelled 300, 400, 500 for numbers rounded to the nearest 100.	**1** Show a calculation to the whole class or group, such as 389 + 118. Students use mini-whiteboards to round each number to the nearest 100, estimate the answer and show their result. Then they repeat by rounding to the nearest 10. Discuss which answer is the more accurate. **2** Provide measuring instruments such as a ruler, a bathroom-type scale, a thermometer, a clock. Students are allocated tasks in which they measure length, weight, temperature and time. They then have to round their measurements to the nearest 1, 10 or 100.
Literacy	**Links**
The word 'estimate' has two senses. • It can be used when gauging a measurement or quantity by direct comparison with a known measurement or quantity, such as estimating the height of the classroom knowing that the door is 2 metres high, or estimating the number of sweets in a jar knowing that you can hold 10 sweets in your hand. • It can also be used when finding an approximate answer to a calculation by rounding the numbers involved. For example, 649 + 197 is approximately 650 + 200, giving an estimated answer of 850.	Justin Gatlin ran 100 m in 9.766 seconds at the Qatar Grand Prix in Doha in 2006. His time was rounded incorrectly to 9.76s and Gatlin thought that he had beaten the World record of 9.77s set by Asafa Powell in 2005. It took five days to correct the error and Gatlin and Powell had to share the record. There is more information about Justin Gatlin here. www.usatf.org/Athlete-Bios/Justin-Gatlin.aspx

Alternative approach

Use measurement of length as an introduction to rounding. Show students a metre rule. Ask them to imagine how many metre rules would be needed end-to-end to cross the classroom and so estimate the width of the room. Check their estimates by using the rule to measure the width to the nearest metre. Explain that this result has been 'rounded'. Repeat with other measurements such as the length of the room and the heights of students.

Checkpoint

1 On a number line labelled in 10s from 0 to 100
  a Point to 68 and ask whether it is closer to 60 or 70 (70)
  b Round these numbers to the nearest 10 **i** 68 **ii** 62 **iii** 65 (70, 60, 70)

2 On a number line labelled in 100s from 0 to 1000
  Round these numbers to the nearest 100 **a** 685 **b** 623 **c** 650 (700, 600, 700)

Starter – Length, weight and capacity

Show students a metre rule, an object weighing 1kg and a container with capacity 1 litre. Now show them a length of string, a different object and a different container. Ask them to estimate the length, weight and capacity. They may wish to hold the two objects to feel their weight. Discuss how they get their answers and whether they are automatically 'rounding' their estimates.

Teaching notes

Knowing how to round a digit up or down is usually understood quickly. Difficulties in deciding which digit of a number to concentrate on can be quickly resolved by using a number line appropriately labelled. When rounding to the nearest 10, the number line should be labelled with multiples of every 10 over a range that includes the number being rounded. Similarly when rounding to the nearest 100, the labels should be multiples of 100.

When rounding to the nearest 10, the questions to ask students are 'Whereabouts on the number line is the number?', 'Which two multiples of 10 does it lie between?' and 'Which of these multiples is it closer to?' The closest multiple of 10 is the rounded value. Similar questions can be asked when rounding to the nearest 100.

Plenary

The use of mini-whiteboards is a productive way to recap and to provide effective assessment of students' understanding. Present the class with various whole numbers, one at a time, which they have to round to the nearest 10 or 100. Questions can be set in context by presenting the class with various measurements, for example integer values of lengths or weights of known objects, which are also to be rounded to the nearest 10 or 100. Questions can then involve a change of unit; for example, lengths such as 184 cm can be rounded to the nearest metre.

Exercise commentary

Questions 2, 3 and **4** – Students should draw their own number lines if they cannot imagine one mentally. In Question 3, watch that students do *not* round the units digit or the tens digit. Drawing a number line labelled only in 100s should encourage students to round the correct digit. Similarly for Question 4, students should not round the units digit, the tens digit or the hundreds digit.

Question 6 – A vertical number line labelled every 10 cm from 120 cm to (say) 180 cm can be used to mark on it the two known heights. The two estimates can then be taken from the number line.

Question 7 – Students need to discuss their thinking. For example, some might see a connection between weight and cost; others might simply halve the cost of the 10 kg bag.

Question 8 – Students should explain their strategy. For example, one starting point would be to give the smallest height to the shortest person. The value of the problem is having students articulate their thinking.

Question 9 – Students could count the top row in the diagram as a start.

Answers

1 **a** 30 **b** 50

2 **a** 10 **b** 30 **c** 40 **d** 70
e 50 **f** 110 **g** 240 **h** 220
i 210

3 **a** 200 **b** 400 **c** 800 **d** 600
e 500 **f** 800 **g** 100 **h** 500
i 1000

4 **a** 6000 **b** 5000 **c** 4000 **d** 1000
e 11 000 **f** 4000 **g** 0 **h** 23 000
i 6000

5 **a** 12 950 **b** 12 900 **c** 13 000

6 Allow reasonable estimates.
a 145 cm **b** 175 cm

7 £5 or any other reasonable estimate.

8 Beth – 165 cm, Fowsia – 154 cm, Craig – 144 cm, Imran – 161 cm, Ian – 185 cm, Karim – 184 cm

9 Sam There are about 10 layers each containing about 25 (5×5) sweets.

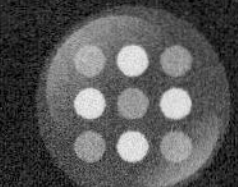

1h Order of operations

Objectives	
• Use the order of operations. (L4)	
Key ideas	**Resources**
1 Know the rule 'Multiply or divide before you add or subtract'. **2** Some calculators do not follow this rule.	Order of operations (1167) Packs of five cards for paired work with the numbers 2, 3 and 4 and the operations × and +
Simplification	**Extension**
If students' mental number skills are weak, then use numbers facts requiring smaller numbers. Have such students use two calculators which give different answers to convince them that 'order matters'. Draw brackets or a circle round the first operation to emphasise it visually; for example 2 + 3 × 4 becomes 2 + (3 × 4).	For students who are confident with this type of problem, challenge them to write four pairs of questions where, for each pair, they use the same numbers and the same signs but get different answers, for example 15 ÷ 5 + 3 × 4 and 5 × 4 + 15 ÷ 3. Ask them to give their questions to a partner to solve.
Literacy	**Links**
Working out a calculation is not like reading a sentence. When we read, we take each word of the sentence in the order that it is written. When we calculate, we have to look for × and ÷ first, no matter where they are, before we look for + and –. 'Doubled' means 'multiplied by 2'.	Doing things in the right order is essential in many everyday events; for example, how do we cross a road safely, how do we bake a cake or pitch a tent? Visit IKEA's website to see how precise the order of instructions can be to assemble a flat-pack. www.ikea.com/ms/en_US/customer_service/assembly_instructions_new.html

Alternative approach

For students who have not understood the need to prioritise the operations, ask them to point to any × or ÷ and to bracket or circle that operation. Ask them to work out what they have inside the bracket or circle and re-write the whole calculation, replacing the bracket or circle with its value. Now continue the calculation.

For example, 2 + 3 × 4 becomes 2 + (3 × 4) which is re-written as 2 + 12 to give the answer 14.

Checkpoint

Show the calculation 3 × 8 + 2

a Ask student to cover the operation which should be performed second (Cover '+ 2')

c How do you work out this calculation? (Multiplication before addition: 24 + 2)

c What does the calculation equal? (26)

Repeat with different numbers and a variety of operations. Check they perform × or ÷ before + or –.

Starter – 1234

1 Ask students to make each of the numbers 1 to 10 using *any* of the digits 1, 2, 3 and 4 with any of the four basic operations. For example, $4 - 3 = 1$.

2 Ask students to make each of the numbers 1 to 10 using *all* of the digits 1, 2, 3 and 4 with any of the four basic operations. For example, $2 \times 1 + 3 + 4 = 9$. This task can be extended by making numbers up to 20.

Teaching notes

This activity provides a good introduction. Give pairs of students three cards for the numbers 2, 3 and 4 and two cards for the operations × and + .

Ask students to find how many different ways they can order these cards and find how many different answers they can make. Set a time limit.

There are 12 possible ways.

$2 + 3 \times 4$	$2 \times 4 + 3$	$3 + 4 \times 2$	$4 \times 2 + 3$
$2 \times 3 + 4$	$3 + 2 \times 4$	$3 \times 4 + 2$	$4 + 3 \times 2$
$2 + 4 \times 3$	$3 \times 2 + 4$	$4 + 2 \times 3$	$4 \times 3 + 2$

But there are only three possible answers: 10, 11 and 14. Explore why some of the students' answers are not allowed; for example, $2 + 3 \times 4 \neq 20$. Lead students to realise that they must multiply before they add.

Do some of these calculations on various calculators to realise that not all calculators obey the rule of 'multiply first, add second'.

It is a straightforward extension to the rule to say 'multiply or divide first, then add or subtract'.

Plenary

The students adopt the role of teacher and are given some marking to do. There are some right answers but there are also mistakes which they need to correct.

For example,

$3 + 5 \times 6 = 48$ × (33)	$4 + 6 \div 2 = 5$ × (7)
$6 \times 4 - 7 = 17$ ✓	$18 \div 3 - 1 = 5$ ✓
$12 - 8 \div 4 = 1$ × (10)	$4 + 20 \div 2 = 12$ × (14)

A whole-class discussion can be used to identify and correct the mistakes.

Exercise commentary

Question 3 – Students should set out their working at each step: for example, $4 \times 5 - 16$ is written as $20 - 16$ before writing the answer 4.

Question 4 – As with Question 1, students should write down the intermediate stages of their working: for example, $16 \times 2 + 4 \times 2 = 32 + 8 = 40$.

Question 5 – Students can discuss in pairs what their strategy will be for each question part: for example, which operations will they perform and in what order?

Question 6 – Students need to take care to make sure they perform the operations in the right order: they need to find out how much each girl earns (multiplying 20×2 and 15×3) before adding the two amounts together.

Answers

1	**a** 19	**b** 40	**c** 5	**d** 46
	e 9	**f** 21	**g** 100	**h** 3
2	**a** 4	**b** 20	**c** 58	**d** 21
	e 47	**f** 74	**g** 39	**h** 10
	i 55	**j** 140	**k** 1	**l** 20
	m 31	**n** 183	**o** 17	**p** 23
	q 6	**r** 19	**s** 39	**t** 7
3	**a** 40	**b** 40	**c** 8	**d** 50
	e 0	**f** 57	**g** 16	**h** 15
	i 22	**j** 20	**k** 8	**l** 0
	m 38	**n** 4	**o** 5	**p** 10
	q 36	**r** 12	**s** 10	**t** 15
4	**a** 25	**b** 4	**c** 20	**d** 3
	e 0			
5	**a** £9	**b** £115	**c** 24	
6	**a** 12	**b** £85		
7	**a** $3 \times 5 - 7 = 8$		**b** $3 - 5 + 7 = 5$	
	c $3 + 5 + 7 = 15$		**d** $3 + 5 \times 7 = 38$	

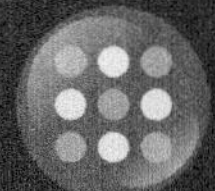

1 Whole numbers and decimals – MySummary

Key outcomes		Quick check
Understand place value for whole numbers.	L3	What is the value of the 3 in these numbers? **a** 132 (30) **b** 301 (300) **c** 3002 (3000)
Compare and order whole numbers.	L3	Put these numbers in order, from largest to smallest. 123, 231, 33,103, 330 (330, 231, 123, 103, 33)
Use place value and decimal notation in different contexts, including money.	L3	**1** Write these numbers in figures **a** Two hundred point three (200.3) **b** One thousand and ten point one (1010.1) **2** Use the symbols > or < to show which number is larger. **a** 3.2 □ 2.3 (3.2 > 2.3) **b** 0.3 □ 1.2 (0.3 < 1.2)
Add decimals using mental and written methods.	L3	Alice has £5. She spends £1.20 on a note pad and buys two 45p pencils. How much money does she have left? (£2.90)
Understand and order negative numbers in the context of temperature.	L3	**1** Write these numbers in figures **a** Two hundred point three (200.3) **b** One thousand and ten point one (1010.1) **2** Use the symbols > or < to show which number is larger. **a** 3.2 □ 2.3 (3.2 > 2.3) **b** 0.3 □ 1.2 (0.3 < 1.2)
Round a number to the nearest 10, 100 or 1000.	L4	Round 1489 to the nearest **a** ten (1490) **b** hundred (1500) **c** thousand (1000)
Use an estimate to check a result.	L4	The weights of three people, rounded to the nearest 10 kg, are Adam 30 kg, Ben 40 kg and Carl 50 kg. The actual weights are 45 kg, 44 kg and 34 kg. Match each person to their actual weight. (Adam, 34 kg, Ben 44 kg, Carl 45 kg)
Use the order of operations.	L4	Work out these calculations **a** 8 – 2 × 3 (2) **b** 24 ÷ 4 – 2 × 3 (0)

Development and links
Ordering whole numbers and decimals is used when sorting data to find the median in chapter **8**. Decimals are related to fractions and decimals and percentages in chapter **4**. Methods for addition and subtraction are further developed in chapter 7. Negative numbers are used in the context of coordinates in chapter **6** and sequences in chapter **13**. Rounding and estimating is used to check calculator results in chapter **14**. The order of arithmetical operations is assumed when substituting into algebraic expressions in chapter **3**. The basic number skills encountered in this chapter will be met repeatedly during this course and throughout later life.

MyMaths extra support

Lesson/online homework			Description
Place value HTU	1216	L2	Revises the meaning of place value for whole numbers and how they are written in words.
Introducing decimals	1378	L3	Introduces the meaning of a decimal number and how pounds and pence are written using decimals.
Introducing money	1226	L5	A series of games used to familiarize students with coins, making amounts using coins and simple sums involving money.

My Review

1 MySummary

Check out You should now be able to ...		Test it ➡ Questions
✓ Understand place value for whole numbers.	3	1
✓ Compare and order whole numbers.	3	2
✓ Use place value and decimal notation in different contexts, including money.	3	3, 4
✓ Add decimals using mental and written methods.	3	5, 6
✓ Understand and order negative numbers in the context of temperature.	3	7
✓ Round a number to the nearest 10, 100 or 1000.	4	8
✓ Use an estimate to check a result.	4	9
✓ Use the order of operations.	4	10

Language	Meaning	Example
Digit	Any of the numbers 0, 1, 2, 3, 4, 5, 6, 7, 8 or 9.	3.65 contains 3 digits
Place value	The value of a digit in a decimal number.	3.65 contains 6 tenths
Decimal	The decimal part of a number occurs to the right of the decimal point.	3.65 has a decimal part of 0.65
Negative number	Any number less than zero.	-7 is a negative number
Round (verb)	To express a number to a given degree of accuracy.	639 is 600 rounded to the nearest 100
Estimate	An approximate answer.	149 + 302 can be estimated as 150 + 300 = 450
Operation	A rule for processing numbers.	In 6 × 4 the operation is ×

1 MyReview

1 What is the value of the 6 in each of these numbers?
a 4630 b 76
c 82.6 d 967.3

2 Write these numbers in order. Start with the smallest number.
208, 820, 88, 280, 802

3 Write each of these numbers in figures.
a Ninety one point six
b Four hundred and eighteen point one
c Seventy point four
d Eight thousand and fifty two point five

4 Place > or < into the boxes to show which number is greater.
a 7.6 □ 6.7 b 5.5 □ 5.6
c 0.9 □ 0.6 d 3.2 □ 8.8

5 Alice has a one pound coin. She buys an eraser for 20p and a pencil for 55p. How much change should she get?

6 Bob has a £2.40 in his pocket. He finds a 50p coin, three 10p coins and four pennies behind the sofa.
a How much money has Bob found?
b How much does he now have?

7 Find the final temperatures.
a Start at -8 °C and rise by 2 °C
b Start at 5 °C and fall by 10 °C
c Start at -7 °C and rise by 7 °C
d Start at -3 °C and fall by 6 °C

8 Round 4467 to
a the nearest ten
b the nearest hundred
c the nearest thousand.

9 Mel is 120 cm tall. Onora is 150 cm tall.

a Give an estimate for Nina's height.
b Give an estimate for Penny's height.

10 Work out each of these calculations.
a 2 + 8 − 7 b 3 × 3 × 4
c 28 − 16 − 5 d 40 ÷ 5 ÷ 4
e 3 + 5 × 6 f 4 × 6 − 16
g 2 × 8 + 4 × 5 h 32 ÷ 4 − 2 × 2

What next?

Score		
0 – 3		Your knowledge of this topic is still developing. To improve look at Formative test: 1A-1; MyMaths: 1003, 1014, 1069, 1072, 1076, 1167, 1217, 1226, 1352, 1373 and 1377
4 – 8		You are gaining a secure knowledge of this topic. To improve look at InvisiPen: 111, 112, 113, 124 and 131
9 – 10		You have mastered this topic. Well done, you are ready to progress!

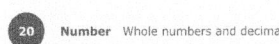

20 **Number** Whole numbers and decimals

MyMaths.co.uk 21

Question commentary

Question 1 – (lessons **1a** and **1c**) For part **a**, accept six hundreds or 600, etc.

Question 2 – (lesson **1b**) Students may write answers in reverse order.

Question 3 – (lesson **1c**) In parts **c** and **d,** check that zeroes are included in the correct places.

Question 4 – (lesson **1c**) Allow struggling students to simply say which number is bigger, rather than use the inequality signs.

Question 5 – (lesson **1d**) Check students get 75p for the cost of the items.

Question 6 – (lesson **1e**) Students could use a column addition method, taking care to line up decimal points. Check they carry over correctly in part **b**.

Question 7 – (lesson **1f**) Students could use a number line to help with this question.

Question 8 – (lesson **1g**) Students may incorrectly round starting from the previous answer; this would give 5000 for part **c**.

Question 9 – (lesson **1g**) In part **a**, check that the answer is in the range 120 – 150 cm, that is between Mel's and Onora's heights. In part **b**, check that the answer is greater than 150 cm, that is, Onora's height.

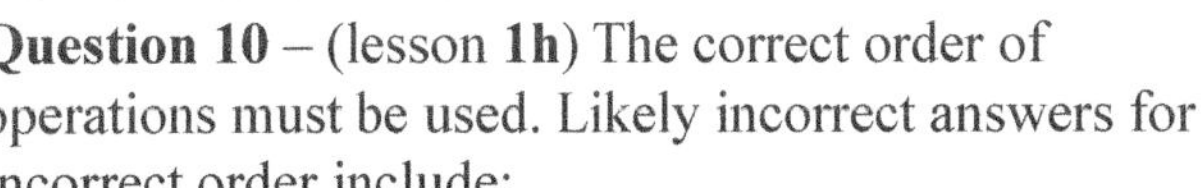

Question 10 – (lesson **1h**) The correct order of operations must be used. Likely incorrect answers for incorrect order include:

c $28 - 16 - 5 \neq 28 - 11 = 17$,
e $3 + 5 \times 6 \neq 8 \times 6 = 48$,
f $4 \times 6 - 16 \neq 4 \times 10 = 40$,
g $2 \times 8 + 4 \times 5 \neq 2 \times 12 \times 5 = 120$
h $32 \div 4 - 2 \times 2 \neq 32 \div 2 \times 2 = 32$

Answers

1	**a**	6 hundreds, 600		**b**	6 units, 6			
	c	6 tenths, 0.6		**d**	6 tens, 60			
2	88, 208, 280, 802, 820							
3	**a**	91.6	**b**	418.1	**c**	70.4	**d**	8052.5
4	**a**	>	**b**	<	**c**	>	**d**	<
5	25p							
6	**a**	84p	**b**	324p = £3.24				
7	**a**	-6 °C	**b**	-5 °C	**c**	0 °C	**d**	-9 °C
8	**a**	4470	**b**	4500	**c**	4000		
9	**a**	135 cm	**b**	165 cm				
10	**a**	3	**b**	36	**c**	7	**d**	2
	e	33	**f**	8	**g**	36	**h**	4

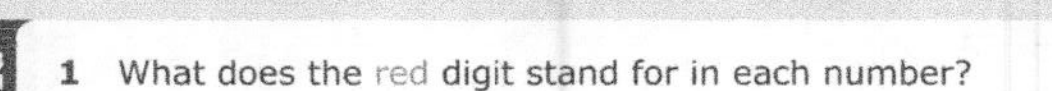

1 MyPractice

1a

1 What does the red digit stand for in each number?

a 427 **b** 6009 **c** 1570
d 716 **e** 3085 **f** 5172

2 Split these numbers into 100s, 10s, and 1s. The first is done for you.

a 224 = 100 + 100 + 10 + 10 + 1 + 1 + 1 + 1
b 344 **c** 431 **d** 136 **e** 201

1b

3 Jamie caught five fish.
He measured the length of each fish:

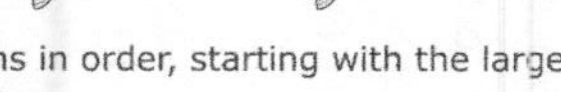

a Write out the lengths in order, starting with the largest.

Next he weighed each fish.

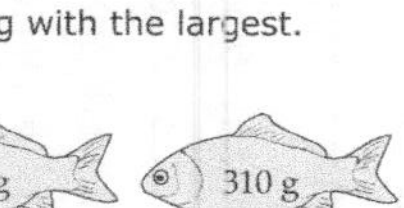

b Write out the weights in order, starting with the smallest.

1c

4 Put these decimal numbers in order, starting with the smallest.

a 5.8, 4.9, 7.2, 6.5 **b** 8.4, 3.2, 6.9, 0.9
c 2.4, 2.1, 2.0, 2.5 **d** 4.1, 3.9, 4.2, 3.8

5 Write each of these as decimals.

a three-tenths **b** seven-tenths **c** nine-tenths

6 Use the number line to help you add these decimals.

0 0.1 0.2 0.3 0.4 0.5 0.6 0.7 0.8 0.9 1

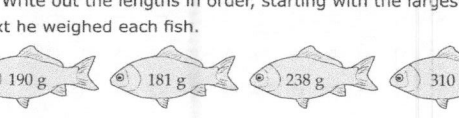

a 0.6 + 0.2 **b** 0.3 + 0.4 **c** 0.9 + 0.1 **d** 0.5 + 0.4

1d

7 Add these amounts.

a £0.20 + £0.50 **b** £0.40 + £0.70
c £0.60 + 80p **d** £0.90 + £0.35 + 65p
e 50p + 21p **f** 40p + £1.20
g £2.50 + £3.20 **h** 60p + £4.20

1e

8 Use the number line to help you add these decimals.

0.30 0.35 0.40 0.45 0.50

a 0.30 + 0.03 **b** 0.45 + 0.01 **c** 0.35 + 0.06 **d** 0.30 + 0.09

1f

9 Use the number line to find each new temperature.

-8 -7 -6 -5 -4 -3 -2 -1 0 1 2 3 4 5 6 7 8

a Start at 7°C and drop by 9 degrees.
b Start at -5°C and go up by 7 degrees.
c Start at -4°C and drop by 4 degrees.
d Start at -8°C and go up by 5 degrees.
e Start at -5°C and go up by 9 degrees.

10 Complete these problems using negative numbers.

a 4 − 7 = ? **b** 8 − 12 = ? **c** 10 − 12 = ? **d** 0 − 7 = ?
e -2 − 6 = ? **f** -2 + 5 = ? **g** -5 − 3 = ? **h** -10 + 6 = ?
i -6 − 11 = ? **j** -12 + 20 = ? **k** -13 + 22 = ? **l** -11 − 17 = ?

1g

11 Round each number to the nearest ten.

a 54 **b** 149 **c** 65 **d** 612
e 98 **f** 185 **g** 102 **h** 3

12 Round each number to the nearest whole number.

a 4.7 **b** 8.1 **c** 5.4 **d** 11.8
e 19.5 **f** 25.4 **g** 0.7 **h** 0.4

1h

13 Work out each calculation and say which of each group has a different answer.

a **i** 360 ÷ 5 ÷ 3 **ii** 840 ÷ 6 ÷ 5 **iii** 200 ÷ 25 × 3
b **i** 155 + 27 − 106 **ii** 133 − 95 + 34 **iii** 250 − 115 − 63

14 Work out each calculation and say which of each group has a different answer.

a **i** 84 ÷ 7 + 12 × 5 **ii** 48 ÷ 3 + 8 × 7
iii 128 ÷ 8 + 300 ÷ 5 **iv** 192 ÷ 4 + 72 ÷ 3
b **i** 450 ÷ 6 − 13 × 3 **ii** 300 ÷ 5 − 8 × 3
iii 360 ÷ 4 − 162 ÷ 3 **iv** 480 ÷ 8 − 84 ÷ 3

22 **Number** Whole numbers and decimals

Question commentary

Questions 1 – In part **e** check that students know that the zero means no hundreds: How would the number change if the zero was missing? (There would be 3 hundreds rather than three thousands)

Question 3 and **4** – Check that students go largest to smallest or vice versa as appropriate. It may help to start by identifying the smallest and lowest values and then sort the remaining numbers, possibly repeating this approach.

Question 5 – Students should write 0.3 rather than .3; this helps avoid confusion with the number 3.

Question 6 – This could also be done by thinking in terms of money. For example, 0.6 + 0.2 = 60p + 20p = 80p = 0.8

Question 7 – Check that in parts **c**, **d**, **f** and **h** students use consistent units, pounds or pence. Encourage the use of a written method with numbers lined up on the decimal point.

Question 9 – Ensure that students count 'jumps' and don't count '1' from the start number: this will give answers that are out by one.

Question 10 – Have available a longer number line, going down to -30.

Question 11 – Suggest students draw sections of the number line to help them decide how to round. For example, place 54 on the line segment 50 – 60 and ask is the number closer to 50 or 60. Parts **c** and **f** end in a 5 and should be rounded up. In part **h** students may need reassuring that the answer is zero.

Question 12 – This goes beyond the content of lesson **1g**. Students could think about the problem in the context of money and ask 'How much money do I have to the nearest pound'. Alternatively they could generalise the method of 'looking at the next digit on the right'.

Question 13 and 14 – Require students to show their workings step by step. For example, 360 ÷ 5 ÷ 3 = 72 ÷ 3 = 24 or 84 ÷ 7 + 12 × 5 = 12 + 60 = 72. As well as good practice it will help to distinguish arithmetic errors from conceptual errors with applying BIDMAS.

Answers

1 **a** 20 **b** 9 **c** 500 **d** 700
e 0 **f** 5000

2 **a** 2 × 100 + 2 × 10 + 4 × 1
b 3 × 100 + 4 × 10 + 4 × 1
c 4 × 100 + 3 × 10 + 1
d 100 + 3 × 10 + 6 × 1
e 2 × 100 + 1

3 **a** 33 cm, 31 cm, 27 cm, 21 cm, 19 cm
b 181 g, 190 g, 218 g, 238 g, 310 g

4 **a** 4.9, 5.8, 6.5, 7.2 **b** 0.9, 3.2, 6.9, 8.4
c 2.0, 2.1, 2.4, 2.5 **d** 3.8, 3.9, 4.1, 4.2

5 **a** 0.3 **b** 0.7 **c** 0.9

6 **a** 0.8 **b** 0.7 **c** 1 **d** 0.9

7 **a** £0.70 **b** £1.10 **c** £1.40 **d** £1.90
e £0.71 **f** £1.60 **g** £5.70 **h** £4.80

8 **a** 0.33 **b** 0.46 **c** 0.41 **d** 0.39

9 **a** -2 °C **b** 2 °C **c** -8 °C **d** -3 °C
e 4 °C

10 **a** -3 **b** -4 **c** -2 **d** -7
e -8 **f** 3 **g** -8 **h** -4
i -17 **j** 8 **k** 9 **l** -28

11 **a** 50 **b** 150 **c** 70 **d** 610
e 100 **f** 190 **g** 100 **h** 0

12 **a** 5 **b** 8 **c** 5 **d** 12
e 20 **f** 25 **g** 1 **h** 0

13 **a** **i** 24 **ii** 28 **iii** 24
b **i** 76 **ii** 72 **iii** 72

14 **a** **i** 72 **ii** 72 **iii** 76 **iv** 72
b **i** 36 **ii** 36 **iii** 36 **iv** 32

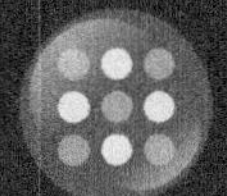

2 Measures, perimeter and area

Learning outcomes

R1 Change freely between related standard units [for example time, length, area, volume/capacity, mass]. (L3)

N12 use standard units of mass, length, time, money and other measures, including with decimal quantities. (L3)

G1 Derive and apply formulae to calculate and solve problems involving: perimeter and area of triangles, parallelograms, trapezia, volume of cuboids (including cubes) and other prisms (including cylinders). (L4)

G2 Calculate and solve problems involving: perimeters of 2D shapes (including circles), areas of circles and composite shapes. (L4)

Introduction

The chapter starts by looking at measuring lines and then reading scales. The basics of time are covered, before moving on to consider naming and recognising 2D shapes. Simple concepts of perimeter and area are then developed before the final lesson on metric units.

The introduction discusses how surveyors set about measuring the area of a country. The example given is that of the United Kingdom, but the methods are appropriate for any large, irregular area. Dividing the shape up into smaller shapes helps the surveyor to get a good, but approximate, value for the area.

If you divide the country into only four or five pieces, your estimate will be very rough. Using more, and smaller, pieces will give a better approximation, but to get the exact area, you would have to divide the area into an infinite number of infinitesimally small shapes!

Similarly, if you wanted to measure the length of the coastline of the UK, you could break the coastline down into a series of straight lines. Using smaller and smaller straight lines would change the answer but in an unexpected way – the coast line gets longer and longer. This is an example of fractal geometry, developed by Benoit Mandelbrot in 1975.

http://en.wikipedia.org/wiki/Coastline_paradox

http://www.ted.com/talks/benoit_mandelbrot_fractals_the_art_of_roughness.html

Prior knowledge

Students should already know how to…

- Use a ruler to measure lengths.
- Tell the time on an analogue clock.
- Categorise units of measurement as length, mass or capacity.
- Multiply and divide by powers of 10.
- Add and subtract whole numbers.

Starter problem

In the starter problem, the students are presented with a giant footprint and asked to consider how this could be used to work out how tall the giant was.

The idea here is that if we can draw a comparison between the length of the giant's footprint and the length of our own foot (or footprint) we can scale the answers and work out an approximate height for the giant.

For example, if our foot measures 20 cm and the giant's footprint measures 30 cm, we can multiply our height by the scale factor, 1.5, to determine how tall the giant may have been. If the students do this themselves, there is also scope to discuss the possibility of variation in the estimates since people of equal height quite often have a range of different foot sizes.

Further questions could be posed such as how big the giant's head was, the length of its hand or arm, or how broad the giant was across the shoulders.

Resources

MyMaths

Area of rectangles	1084	Units of length	1101	Units of capacity	1104
Units of mass	1105	Perimeter	1110	Time and timetables	1124
Measuring lengths	1146	2D and 3D shapes	1229	Measures	1232
Telling the time 2	1234	Describing shapes	1390		

Online assessment

Chapter test	1A–2
Formative test	1A–2
Summative test	1A–2

InvisiPen solutions

Identifying 2D shapes	311	Perimeter	312
Area	313	Length	331
Metric measures	332		

Topic scheme

Teaching time = 7 lessons/3 weeks

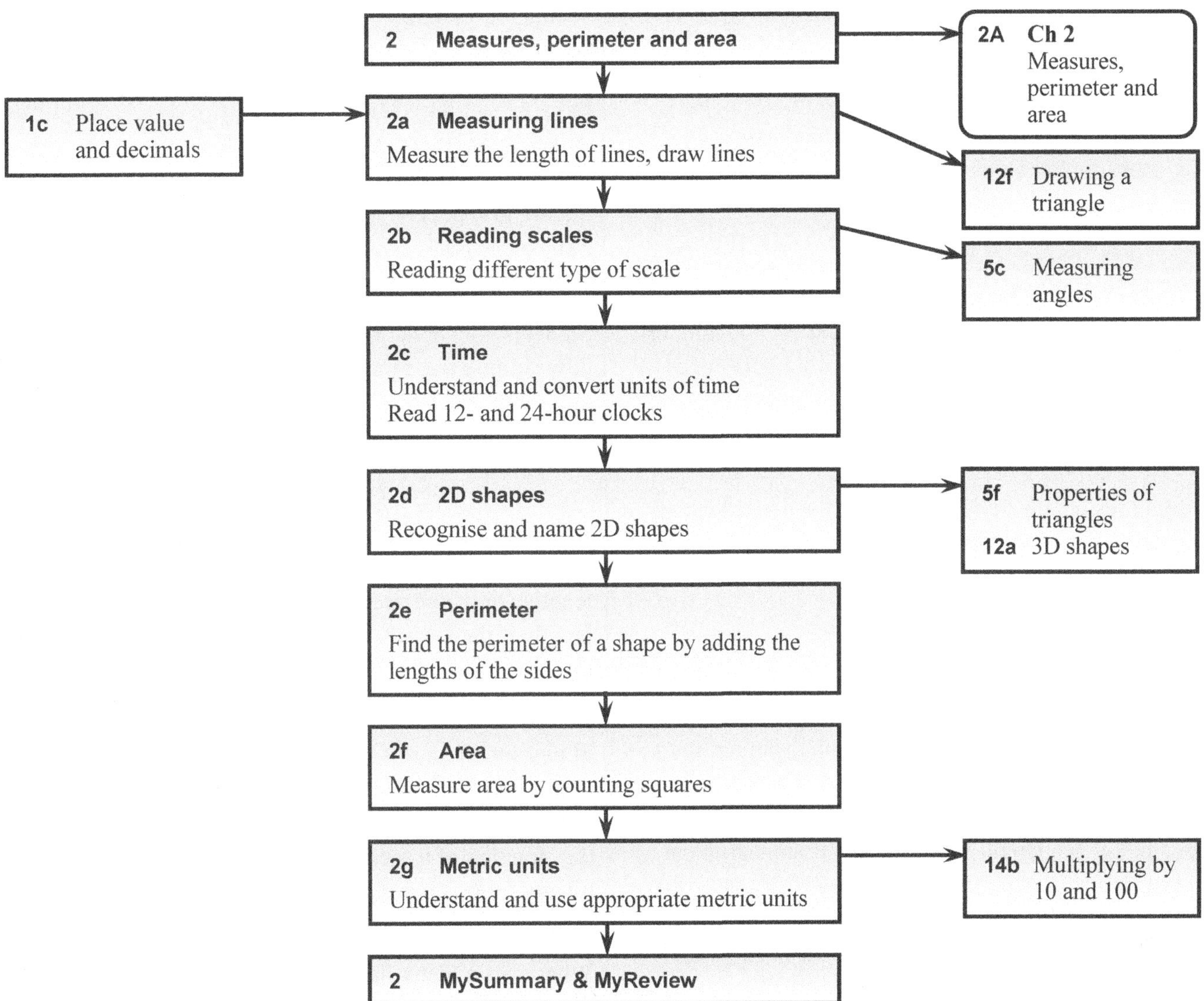

Differentiation

Student book 1A 24 – 43

Measure the lengths of lines
Read scales
Understand units of time
Understand how to find simple areas and perimeters
Understand basic metric units of measurement

Student book 1B 20 – 41

Understand and convert between metric units of length, capacity and mass
Read scales
Find basic areas and perimeters by counting squares and adding lengths
Find the areas of rectangles, triangles and parallelograms

Student book 1C 20 – 39

Find the perimeter and area of rectangles and triangles
Find the area of parallelograms and trapezia
Understand units of measurement and convert between metric units
Find the volume and surface area of a cuboid

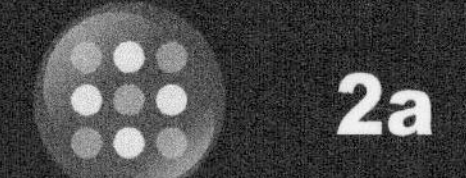

2a Measuring lines

Objectives

- Use a ruler to measure lines to the nearest mm. (L3)
- Use a wider range of measures including standard metric units for length. (L3)

Key ideas

1 Short and long lengths may need different units.
2 There are 10mm in 1cm and a length can be measured in either unit.

Resources

Measuring lengths (1146)

Rulers marked in mm and cm
Sharp pencils
Square grid paper
Tape measure

Simplification

Where edges of a ruler are marked in cm and mm, ask students to measure the same line using both edges of the ruler, writing the answers using the correct units. (Students should be aware that some rulers may still have edges marked in inches.)

Remind students that a sharp pencil is needed when drawing lines accurately.

Extension

Students who are confident with measuring lengths can draw simple diagrams (with right angles) on square grid paper, such as

Students are given all the horizontal and vertical lengths, draw the shape accurately and measure the length of the sloping side.

Literacy

The same units are used for measuring **length** and **distance**. The two words are close in meaning; for example, the length of a line is the distance between its two ends.

A 'metre' is a length, but a 'meter' is an instrument used for measuring, such as a gas meter. In the USA, they use 'meter' for both cases.

The prefixes *kilo-*, *centi-* and *milli-* mean 'thousand', 'hundredth' and 'thousandth', respectively.

Links

France was the first country to adopt a metric system of measurement in 1791. From 1889 to 1960, the metre was defined by the length of a metal bar in Paris, and today it is defined as the distance that light travels in a tiny fraction of a second. More information about the history of the metric system can be found here.

www.ukma.org.uk/what-is-metric

What does a metre have to do with the distance from the equator to the north pole?

What other units of length are based on the metre?

Which countries today have not 'gone metric'?

Alternative approach

This approach draws on students' previous work with place value. Ask them what they understand by the column headings Th, H, T, U, t, h and where a decimal point should be inserted in these headings. Students write the headings on their mini-whiteboards. Measure the height of the teacher or the tallest student to the nearest centimetre. Students write their results under the headings and check with the teacher. Now measure the height in millimetres, write the result and check it. Finally, measure the height in metres, write the result and check it. All three measurements are now together on each mini-whiteboard and can be discussed. Was there a need for an extra column for thousandths (th)?

Checkpoint

Show an object from the classroom: pencil, book, paperclip, desk, whiteboard, etc. Select objects with straight edges and of different sizes.

1 What is the most appropriate unit of measurement [mm, cm or m]?

2 **a** Accurately measure the object using a ruler/tape.
b Convert the measurement to a different unit [m to cm, or cm to mm].

Starter – Lines ancient and modern

Lines can be curved or straight. Discuss the map of Roman roads here.

www.en.wikipedia.org/wiki/Roman_roads_in_Britain

and ask why the Romans tried to build their roads as straight as possible. Ask where straight lines are used today, such as in plans for buildings, in designs for furniture, etc. Ask what measurements are used for lengths and distances. Separate answers into metric and non-metric. Ask which are used for long and which for short lengths and distances.

Teaching notes

To decide which unit is most appropriate, suggest that, when measuring something

- less than the width of your thumb, use mm;
- about the width of your hand, use cm or mm;
- about the length of your arm span, use cm;
- about the length of the classroom, use m;
- about the length of the street, use m;
- about the length of a ride by bus or train, use km.

Ask students to estimate lengths of items in school, using mini-whiteboards to show their answers. Show them a 30 cm ruler and a metre rule to help gauge lengths and widths of, for example, books, tables, doors, corridors, playgrounds.

When measuring and drawing, remind them that they line up the zero mark on the ruler and not the end of the ruler.

Recall what H, T, U, t means when writing a decimal. Ask how they would write 24 mm in cm.

Be aware that simple errors can occur in students' measurements when:

- the end of the ruler is used instead of the zero mark;
- the ruler is read correctly but the wrong units are written;
- the decimal point is omitted after using the ruler to measure in cm but having counting in mm;
- a blunt pencil is used.

Plenary

Display the following six measurements, which have been taken by six people measuring the same line drawn on a sheet of paper. Ask students to use mini-whiteboards to identify the answers they think are correct, giving their reasons.

5.2 cm   5 cm $5\frac{1}{2}$ mm   52 cm $5\frac{1}{2}$ cm   52 mm

Which two of these are the same length? Why?

(5.2 cm = 52 mm; 1 cm = 10 mm)

How long do students think the line is? Why?

Exercise commentary

Question 1 – Tell students that the diagrams in parts **c** to **f** do not show the whole ruler.

Question 2 – Watch for two misuses of a ruler. Some students might line up the very end of the ruler itself with the end of the line. Others might line up the 1 cm mark rather than the 0 mark. Note that not all rulers label the end of the scale with a 0.
A whole-class discussion can make these points efficiently before any measuring is done.

Question 3 – Sharp pencils are needed!

Question 4 – The pairs are formed from one lettered length and one numbered length.

Question 5 – This is an 'optical illusion', as both blue lines are the same length. Other optical illusions can be found on the Internet.

Question 6 – Students should decide first what units of length other than cm and mm there are.

Answers

1 **a** 3.4 cm **b** 4.9 cm **c** 4.2 cm **d** 16.8 cm
e 12.2 cm **f** 9.4 cm

2 **a** 6.6 cm **b** 7.2 cm **c** 5.9 cm **d** 7.5 cm
e 6.3 cm **f** 6.9 cm

3 Check students' work by measuring their lines.

4 **a** 2 **b** 6 **c** 1 **d** 5
e 4 **f** 3

5 They are the same – both are 2.6 cm

6 **a** cm **b** cm **c** m **d** mm

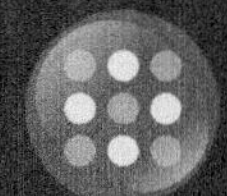

2b Reading scales

Objectives	
• Read and interpret scales on a range of measuring instruments, explaining what each labelled division represents. (L5)	
Key ideas	**Resources**
1 Scales are used in many instruments and meters. **2** The reading on the scale can be found by counting from one marked value to another.	Measures (1232) Two blank number lines: one with two unlabelled end values and ten intermediate subdivisions; the other with several unlabelled values and their intermediate subdivisions
Simplification	**Extension**
Initially, use the scale on the millimetre edge of a ruler. Ask students to count from one labelled number to the next in ones (for example, 30, 31, 32, ...). Point at an intermediate value and ask them what number you are pointing at. Only progress when confident and then use the scale on the centimetre edge of a ruler, with the student now counting in tenths (for example, 5.0, 5.1, 5.2, 5.3, ...). Once confident, use a scale marked from 0 to (say) 200 with subdivisions worth ten and count in tens.	For students who confidently read scales involving intervals worth 1, 10 and 0.1, they can now practise using scales where there are five intervals between numbered labels and each interval is worth 2, 0.2 or 20.
Literacy	**Links**
Many modern measuring instruments and meters no long use scales. Their readings are **digital**. Those instruments and meters which still use scales have **analogue** readings. An analogue instrument measures continuously over a whole range. A digital instrument only measures at certain points across the range. (In the USA, 'analogue' is spelled 'analog'.)	Coin-operated weighing scales were popular during the period from the First World War into the 1950s. They could be found in shops and on street corners. People did not have scales at home so they would pay to weigh themselves. The first coin-operated weighing machine was patented by Percy Everitt, a London engineer, in 1884. You can find some good photos of old scales here. www.pennyscale.com/types-of-scales.html

Alternative approach

Count forwards in ones starting at various starting values, such as 20, 50 or 130, until stopped, and then count backwards in ones to the start. Repeat with counting in 10s from, say 70, 200 or 350, until stopped, and then count backwards in tens to the start. Finally, repeat with counting in tenths from, say 1, 7 or 15, until stopped, and then count backwards in tenths to the start.

These counting exericses can be performed initially with no visual aid, and then with the teacher pointing, in time with the counting, to an appropriately labelled number line.

Checkpoint

Hold up a ruler marked in cm and mm, or a number line where ten subdivisions are marked between each number.

1 Point to 7 and then to 15: count out loud from 7 to 15 in ones. (7, 8, 9, 10, 11, 12, 13, 14, 15)

2 Point to 10 and then to 30: count out loud from 10 to 30 in tens. (10, 20, 30)

3 Point to 2.6 and then to 3.2: count out loud from 2.6 to 3.1 in tenths. (2.6, 2.7, 2.8, 2.9, 3.0, 3.1)

Starter – Arrows and accuracy

Show the whole class a large blank number line with ten subdivisions between two unlabelled marks.

Add labels such as 20 and 30 and position the point of an arrow between them. Students write on their mini-whiteboards the value at the arrow. Repeat several times, before pointing the arrow at a subdivision just outside the range 20 to 30 (say, 31 or 18).

Change the labels to 200 and 300. Repeat.

Change the labels to 2 and 3, or 2.0 and 3.0, and repeat.

Ask students where they might see scales like these, such as a car's speedometer, non-digital bathroom scales.

Teaching notes

All scales in the Student Book have either

- *either* no markings between the labelled values (so intermediate values have to be estimated);
- *or* ten subdivisions, with the middle mark being slightly longer.

  There are no awkward subdivisions in this exercise.

For scales with subdivisions, ask students to look at the labelled values and decide how they will count to get from one label to the other. Will they count in ones (1, 2, 3, …), in tens (10, 20, 30, …), or in tenths (0.1, 0.2, 0.3, …)? Having chosen, count all the way from one label to the next to see if the counts work.

Only now are they ready to read the pointer on the scale.

A blank number line for a wider range of labelled values than used in the **Starter** (and with 10 subdivisions between values) can help whole-class discussion. Choose different start and finish numbers, for example 0 and 30, 400 and 700, 5 and 8, and ask students to read arrows placed by the teacher and then to explain where arrows should point for numbers such as 17, 560 and 7.2 respectively.

Plenary

With this number line subdivided into 10 sections, students discuss in pairs the values for each arrow A to D and write their results on mini-whiteboards to share with the class.

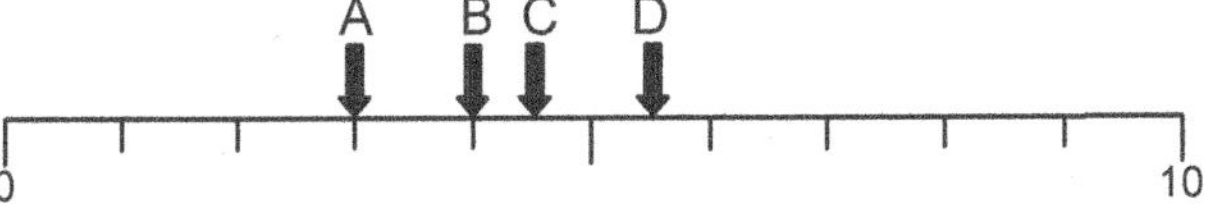

Exercise commentary

Question 1 – Discussion is needed on how the best estimate was achieved. Ask 'How did you decide what the scale was? How did you decide that the scale involved decimals? What is the best way of finding a quick estimate?'

Question 2 – Students may need reminding of the meaning of a decimal as they use the decimal scale.

Question 3 – Students could work in pairs to discuss and agree what each interval is worth.

Question 4 – Students have to look carefully at what the gaps between adjacent marks are worth in order to work out an accurate value for the scale reading.

Answers

1 **a** 28 **b** 4.4 **c** 420

2 **a** 0.4 **b** 0.9 **c** 2.6 **d** 4 **e** 6.2

3 **a** 8 **b** 12 **c** 39 **d** 140 **e** 80 **f** 260

4 **a** 2.9 **b** 18 **c** 39 **d** 140

5 D (1.5), B (2.4), A (3.2), E (3.7), C (4.1)

Objectives

- Use standard units of time. (L3)

Key ideas	Resources
1 Analogue time uses am and pm. **2** Digital time can use the 24-hour clock. **3** In speech, we often use 'past the hour' and 'to the hour'.	Time and timetables (1124) Telling the time 2 (1234) An analogue clock and a digital clock, both of which can have their times easily changed.

Simplification	Extension
Ensure students can tell the time using the words 'o'clock', 'quarter', 'half', 'past' and 'to'. Mark a clock-face with multiples of 5 up to 55 in small print under the numbers 1 to 11. Set a time on a clock-face and say if it is morning or evening. Ask for the time using the words above and then ask for the time using am or pm. When confident, remove the multiples of 5. Only when totally secure, move to the 24-hour clock.	Start with a particular time, for example 11.50 am. Ask students what the time will be after, for example, 1 hour; 45 minutes; 2 h 15 min etc. Set these questions in the context of train and coach journeys.

Literacy	Links
The letters am and pm are abbreviations of the Latin *ante meridiem* and *post meridiem* meaning 'before midday' and 'after midday'. So midday, or noon, and midnight cannot use am and pm. Instead we say '12 noon' and '12 midnight'. The words 'clockwise' and 'anticlockwise' are used in situations that have nothing to do with time, such as opening a screw-top bottle, tightening a nut on a bolt or driving a car round a round-about. Use 'h' and 'min' as abbreviations for 'hour' and 'minute'.	The Mayan people lived in Central America between AD 300 and AD 900, in present-day Mexico and Guatemala. They built great cities with large elaborate pyramid-shaped temples. They were very good farmers and had their own calendar based on their considerable knowledge of astronomy and mathematics. There is more information about the Mayan civilisation here. www.historymuseum.ca/cmc/exhibitions/civil/maya/mmc01eng.shtml

Alternative approach

An introduction to telling the time, using the 24-hour clock and using differences in time, can use simple (maybe, invented) train or coach timetables. Say that the next train from town X to town Y leaves at, say, 8:10 am and the journey takes 1 h 15 min. Turns the hands on an analogue clock, set at 8.10 am, to find the arrival time. Then find the length of the journey, knowing the departure and arrival times.

Checkpoint

1 Adjust or draw an analogue clock to show 6:45.

a If the time shown is after midday, write it two different ways (6:45 pm or 18:45)

b How would you say the time using 'past' or 'to' (Quarter to seven)

2 Jenny leaves her house at 6.45pm. It takes her 30 minutes to walk to the cinema.
At what time does she arrive? (7:15 pm or 19:15 or quarter past seven)

Starter – Times waits for no-one

Display a variety of clocks and clock-faces. Include analogue faces numbered: 1 to 12; I to XII; 1 to 12 and also 13 to 24; 1 to 12 and also 5 to 55. Include digital displays 00:00 to 24:00 and 00:00 to 12:00 and other clocks such as sun-dials, clepsydra (water clocks). Ask who has an analogue watch and who has a digital watch.

Teaching notes

Show an analogue clock on the hour and ask students for the time; for example, four o'clock. Turn clockwise through 5 minutes and ask for the time using the word 'past'. Repeat every 5 minutes, with students taking turns. Accept '15 minutes past 4' but ask for the alternative using 'quarter'. Keep asking in 5 minutes intervals for up to two hours as students take turns. Now set various different times with students responding on their mini-whiteboards.

Show a clock-face with multiples of 5 to 55 alongside 1 to 12. Set a time, say whether it is morning or evening and ask two students for the time: one uses 'past/to'; the other uses am/pm. Repeat with other students. Then all students respond using am/pm on their mini-whiteboards.

Show a clock-face with the numbers 13 to 24 alongside 1 to 12. Set a time, say whether it is morning or evening and ask three students for the time: one uses 'past/to'; one uses am/pm; the third uses the 24-hour clock. Repeat with other students. Then all students respond to a variety of times using the 24-hour clock on mini-whiteboards.

Subsidiary questions could explore other units of time (such as days, weeks, months, years). For example,

- How long have you been at school this week?
- How long have you have been at school this term?
- How long have you been at school since you first started?

Plenary

Show times on a clock-face and ask students to respond on their mini-whiteboards to show the time using one of the methods: 'past/to', am/pm or the 24-hour clock. Change the times on the clock-face and ask for the three alternatives in turn.

Exercise commentary

Many students will be more familiar with digital times than analogue times. Ask the class how many have watches or clocks with analogue or digital faces at school or at home.

Question 2 – Students will need an understanding of the 24-hour clock.

Question 3 – Students need to apply common sense here – for example, realizing that Kim wakes up at 7 am not 7 pm.

Question 4 –'Depart' means 'leave'. The times on the train ticket are given in 24-hour clock.

Answers

1 **a** Seconds **b** Years **c** Hours **d** Weeks
e Seconds **f** Minutes

2 **a** D **b** E **c** A **d** B
e C

3 **a** Watching TV **b** 1 pm
c Maths class **d** Shower
e 9:45 pm

4 **a** 9:35 am **b** 3 hours 30 minutes

2d Shapes

Objectives	
• Identify simple 2D shapes from their properties. (L3)	
Key ideas	**Resources**
1 Shapes can be described by their names and sides. **2** Their sides can be curved or straight. **3** Sides can have the same length or different lengths.	2D and 3D shapes (1229) Describing shapes (1390) A variety of shapes, cut out of card, to include those from the page of the Student Book and also an irregular triangle, pentagon, hexagon and octagon Pre-drawn hexagons A geoboard and rubber bands for the **Alternative approach**
Simplification	**Extension**
Ensure that students first know the names of the circle, square, rectangle and triangle. Ensure that they can describe their sides as curved or straight and that they can recognise whether some sides are equal in length. Only then move to discuss the other shapes.	Extend the range of shapes to various types of triangle, using the names 'isosceles', 'scalene', 'equilateral', and other types of quadrilateral, using the names 'kite', 'parallelogram', 'rhombus'. Discuss whether these shapes can be regular or not. Can the students draw an irregular hexagon and octagon?
Literacy	**Links**
The *tri-* in 'triangle' is also found in the words 'tricycle', 'tripod', triplets' and indicates 'three'. The *pent-* in 'pentagon' is also found in 'pentagram' and indicates 'five'. The Pentagon is a US government building in Washington. The *hex-* in 'hexagon' indicates 'six' and the *octa-* of 'octagon' (as in 'octopus') indicates 'eight'. The word 'trapezium' comes from the Greek meaning 'a little table'. The word 'rhombus' is also from the Greek meaning 'a lozenge' which is a diamond-shaped cough sweet. A *regular* shape has all its sides equal and all its angles equal.If the sides or angles are not equal, then the shape is *irregular*. (Compare a square with a rectangle ir a rhombus.) For some students, this may be a first meeting of the words 'two-dimenional' and 'three-dimensional'.	Can students suggest where these shapes can be found in the 'real world'? For example, circles are used in making tins, plates and roundabouts in roads; squares and rectangles are used in buildings for floors, walls, windows, etc; triangles are used to make certain types of bridges; bees use hexagons for their honeycombs; and many of these shapes are used in patterns for tiling floors and in the design of fabrics and wallpapers. Some examples of tiled patterns can be found here. www.mathsinthecity.com/sites/mathematics-tiling

Alternative approach

Geoboards and rubber bands provide a simple way to create and reconfigure different straight-sided shapes. Can students find all the possible different sized squares, rectangles and triangles that can be made on a 3-by-3 geoboard and then (much more challenging) on a 4-by-4 geoboard?

Checkpoint

Show a selection of basic shapes cut out of card. For each shape, include a variety of sizes and regular and irregular shapes.

1 Name a shape

- **a** Pick out that shape from the selection, (Different sizes should be included)
- **b** Run your finger along the edges of the shape and identify any sides which are equal in length.
- **c** Do all the sides have the same length?

Starter – Quick fire

As this is a straightforward topic, the starter can be used instead to refresh students' understanding of the number work of Chapter 1. Use mini-whiteboards for quick-fire questions such as:

- What does the 2 stand for in the number 425?
- Write 15 mm in centimetres.
- Write three-tenths as a decimal.
- Which is greater, 3.2 or 2.3?
- What temperature is 5 degrees warmer than -1 °C?

Discuss any misunderstandings.

Teaching notes

Ask for the names of shapes that students already know, writing them in two lists: 2D and 3D. Ask why they think you have made two lists: flat shapes and solid shapes. Introduce the words '2-dimensional' and '3-dimensional'. Establish that the focus of this lesson is on 2D (flat) shapes.

With their textbook closed, ask students to sketch, in turn, a circle, square, rectangle, triangle and pentagon on their mini-whiteboards. Ask whether the sides are curved or straight and how many sides each shape has.

Have a variety of shapes cut out of card, including the eight shapes from the page in their textbook and also some irregular shapes. Label each shape with a letter. Introduce the pentagon, hexagon and octagon, both the regular and irregular in each case. Discuss and illustrate what is meant by the words 'regular' and 'irregular' and by the word 'parallel'.

Display the shapes so the class can see them. Define a shape by its properties by saying, for example, 'I am looking at a shape. It has four sides. They are not all equal in length, but its opposite sides are equal in length. Write the letter for the shape on your mini-whiteboard.' Ask if it is regular or irregular.

Plenary

Ask students what new words have they met and what the words mean. Say the numbers 3 to 8 in turn and ask for names of shapes with that number of sides. Now do the reverse; say the name of a shape and students write the number of sides on their mini-whiteboards.

Ask for the main difference between a circle and the other shapes. Introduce the word 'polygon', meaning 'many sides', as the family name for the straight-sided shapes.

Exercise commentary

Question 1 – Some students might say that the rectangle and square are special parallelograms and that a square is a special rectangle. After debate, agree with them.

Question 2 – This involves describing basic properties of shapes, and includes measuring lengths with a ruler. Ensure that students use the correct scale on their ruler and start from zero.

Question 3 – Answering the questions is quite straightforward. But extending the question to ask how many of each shape is problematic if overlapping shapes are allowed. In which case, the hull contains seven trapezia!

Question 4 – It may be helpful to have available pre-drawn hexagons. Encourage students to add one diagonal at a time and think about what shapes they have made.

Question 5 – This should be done as a practical activity. Students can create a pair of parallel lines by using both sides of a ruler. If they are ensure what shape is created encourage students to repeat the construction with a more 'exaggerated' initial shape.

Answers

1 **a** Triangle **b** Circle
c Square **d** Octagon
e Trapezium **f** Rectangle
g Hexagon **h** Pentagon

2 **a** 3; triangle; 1.5 cm
b 6; hexagon; 0.7 cm
c 8; octagon; 0.6 cm
d 4, trapezium; 1.7 cm, 0.85 cm, 1.1 cm, 1.1 cm

3 Circle (pale orange), triangle (red), square, (white), parallelogram (pink), rectangle (pale orange), kite (green), trapezium (brown).

4 **a** 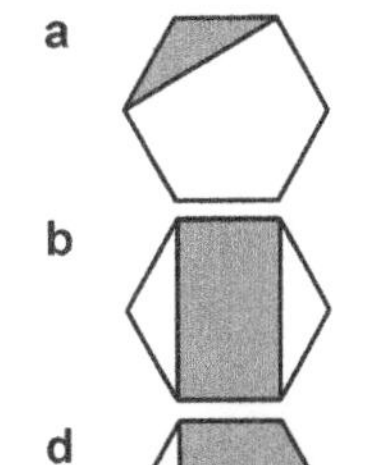 or 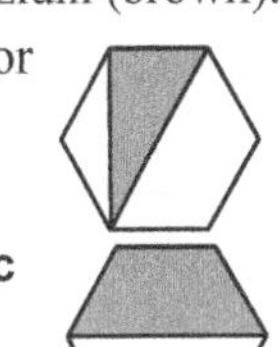 or 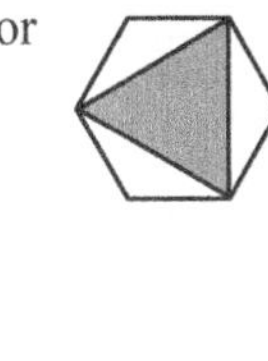
b **c**
d 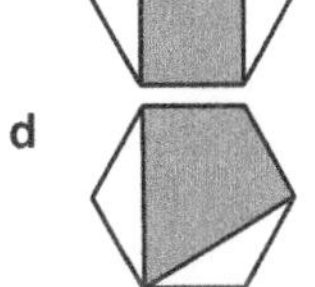 **e**

5 **a** Rhombus **b** Parallelogram
c Rectangle **d** Parallelogram
e Rectangle

2e Perimeter

Objectives	
• Find perimeters of simple shapes.	(L4)

Key ideas	Resources
1 The perimeter is the distance around the edge of a 2D shape. **2** Shapes with curved or straight edges and shapes which are regular or irregular, all have perimeters.	Perimeter (1110) Sets of straws Sets of shapes cut from card Rulers and a tape measure String

Simplification	Extension
The concept of perimeter is more clearly embedded with irregular shapes where a student uses string placed around the edge of the shape. The string is then measured using a ruler. No addition of straight lengths is needed and the notion of 'going right round the shape' is visually more pronounced. Straws of different lengths can make triangles or quadrilaterals and then, when placed end-to-end, measured all in one 'go' to find the perimeter. Again, no addition of lengths is required.	Find perimeters of shapes where not all the sides are given explicitly but where missing lengths can be calculated from known lengths. For example, where two sides of a rectangle are not labelled or where an L-shape has two missing lengths. Give students the perimeter of a rectangle and the length of one side. Ask them to draw the rectangle and explain their method. Ask students to draw a regular pentagon of side 5 cm.

Literacy	Links
The Ancient Greeks were early mathematicians. *Peri-* is Greek for 'around' and a meter is for measuring, so 'perimeter' means 'measuring around'. Compare 'periscope' which means 'seeing around'.	Perimeters are important as they define boundaries. For example, what is a 'perimeter fence' and who might want one? What is the perimeter of a country? Look at a map of Europe and particularly at Norway and Great Britain. What geographical features make perimeters much longer? Look at river estuaries and fjords.

Alternative approach

The concept of perimeter is more firmly embedded if students have the find the perimeter of something more than shapes in a book. Have them use a metre rule or a measuring tape to measure the perimeter of their classroom or the school hall.

Delegate some students to walk round the edge of the school playground or playing field and count the number of paces they take as a measure of perimeter. (Their pace could be measured in centimetres in the clasroom and a calculator used to find the perimeter in cm and metres.) Discuss that a shape, such as a flower bed, can have curved edges and still have a perimeter.

Checkpoint

1 Show a regular pentagon of side 4cm cut from card. State that the shape is regular. Point to one side and say that it is 4cm long.

a Point to each of the other four sides in turn and ask what length they are. (All 4cm)

b How you would calculate the perimeter of the shape and whatis its value?

(4 cm × 5 = 20cm or 4cm + 4cm + 4cm + 4cm + 4cm = 20cm)

2 Repeat for other regular shapes of different side length.

Starter – Quick fire

Ask similar quick fire questions to those in lesson **2d**, ending with the following.

What is the distance right round the edge of

- A square with sides 5 cm long? (20 cm)
- An equilateral triangle with sides 4 cm long? (12 cm)

Teaching notes

The two suggestions under **Simplification** can be useful introductions for the whole class. Further practical tasks are given below.

Give pairs of students four straws of lengths 5 cm, 6 cm, 8 cm and 10 cm. Ask them to make the triangle with the largest perimeter. Ask what the perimeter is and whether they all have the same triangle. Repeat with making a quadrilateral and ask the same two questions: what is the perimeter and are all their quadrilaterals the same? Note that all their triangles have the same shape, but not their quadrilaterals. Note that different shapes can have the same perimeter.

Give pairs of students five shapes, regular and irregular, cut from card and labelled A to E. Ask them to order them from smallest perimeter to largest perimeter, using a ruler to find lengths.

Repeat the previous task with five shapes, labelled V to Z, drawn on paper, using a ruler to find lengths.

A more challenging task for pairs of students is to choose from only six lines with lengths 4 cm, 4 cm, 7cm, 7 cm, 8 cm and 10 cm to make:

- Any rectangle and find its perimeter.
  (4, 4, 7 and 7; 22 cm)
- The triangle with the shortest possible perimeter.
  (4, 4 and 7; 15 cm)
- The triangle with the longest possible perimeter.
  (7, 8 and 10; 25 cm)
- A triangle with a perimeter of 19 cm. (4, 7 and 8)
- As many different triangles as possible.
  (Any triple, except 4, 4 and 8 or 4, 4 and 10)
- A rectangle with a perimeter of 30 cm.
  (Not possible)

Some students can confuse perimeter with previous experiences of area. Have no shapes in this lesson drawn on square grid paper. Only use blank paper or card. They will be less tempted to 'count squares'.

Plenary

Show a selection of polygons, regular and irregular, with sides labelled with their lengths. Ask students to work out the perimeters 'in their heads'.
Show a polygon with the lengths given for all but one side. Give the perimeter and ask for the length of the missing side

Exercise commentary

Question 1 – Take the opportunity to emphasise that students must always include the units in their answers.

Question 2 – Each shape is regular, so all the sides of each shape are equal in length. Students can use the 'multiplication' method here.

Question 4 – Some students may think their answers are wrong just because all three thirds of the court have the same perimeter.

Question 5 – In part **a**, think of crossing the shape from left to right. Think of doing it in two ways. Firstly, cross the whole 9 cm width at one 'go' across the top of the shape. Then cross the shape in two stages, a 2 cm stage and an unknown stage. $2 + ? = 9$ gives the unknown length as 7 cm. Repeat by thinking of going from the top to the bottom of the shape in one and then two stages. $8 = ? + 5$ gives the unknown length as 3 cm.

Answers

1 **a** 30 cm **b** 32 cm **c** 24 cm **d** 26 cm
2 **a** 44 cm **b** 30 cm **c** 39 cm **d** 80 cm
3 **a** 38 cm **b** 50 cm
4 **a** 90 m **b** 50 m
5 **a** 7 cm, 3 cm **b** 9 cm
c 34 cm

Objectives	
• Find the areas by counting squares. (L4)	
Key ideas	**Resources**
1 Area measures the amount of space inside a 2D shape. **2** Shapes with curved sides or straight sides both have areas.	Area of rectangles (1084) Acetate sheets with a square grid Separate small squares of card or plastic Various shapes with straight sides and right-angled corners; various shapes with curved perimeters Sheets of centimetre-squared paper
Simplification	**Extension**
Provide an outline of a square, rectangle or L-shape and a pile of centimetre squares made from card or plastic. The aim is to fill each outline completely with the card or plastic squares. Count the number of small squares used. This number is the area of the shape, measured in square centimetres. If the squares are non-standard, then the area is measured in *square units*.	A further development is to place the acetate grid on an irregular area with a curved perimeter (such as a sketch of a flower bed) and find an approximate value for the area. Agree that, round the edges, it is fair to count more than half a square as a whole square and to ignore less than half a square. The areas of countries taken from an atlas provide a further 'real-life' context. If the area scale factor (the number of km^2 for each 1 cm^2) is known, then the area of the country can be checked from a data bank.
Literacy	**Links**
Students may be meeting the notation cm^2 for the first time. Explain that it is shorthand to remind us of 'centimetre squares' (see **Simplification** above) and that we use the little 2 because we have a 2D shape. Emphasise that it is spoken as 'square centimetres' or 'centimetre squared' and not 'centimetre two'. If the squares are non-standard, then we write $unit^2$ and say 'square units' or 'unit squared'.	Use commercial catalogues or the Internet to find the prices of different styles of paving stone. Which paving is the cheapest? How much would it cost to pave a given area of, for example, 12 m^2? Data showing the population and area of countries can be used, with a calculator, to compare the population densities of contrasting countries. See, for example www.worldatlas.com/aatlas/populations/ctypopls.htm

Alternative approach

If the concepts of area and perimeter are secure, give pairs of students a pile of 24 small squares and ask them to make as many rectangles as possible. For each rectangle, write down the length, width, area and perimeter. Decide how best to tabulate all the results (maybe in order of width). Encourage them to accept that the 2 × 12 rectangle is different from the 12 × 2 rectangle. Which shapes have the smallest perimeter?

Checkpoint

1 On centimetre-squared paper
  a Draw around one square, what is its area? (1cm^2, must include cm^2)
  b Draw around a four squares (creating a 2 × 2 square), what is its area? (4cm^2)

2 **a** Draw shapes of area 6 cm^2, 8 cm^2 and 10 cm^2 – allow rectangles or triangular half-squares.
  b Count out loud the number of squares inside the shape.

Starter – Quick fire

Ask similar quick-fire questions to those in lessons **2d** and **2e**, ending with the following question.
How many squares are inside

- a rectangle with an internal square grid drawn for easy counting;
- an L-shape with a similar internal square grid?

Teaching notes

It is best not to mention the word 'perimeter' in this lesson. The concepts of perimeter and area are often confused and, initially, should be taught separately. A gradual development of the concept of area will avoid misunderstandings. Do not, at this stage, encourage students to multiply length by width to find areas of rectangles and squares. To stress this multiplication too early can lead to some students multiplying any length and width even when the shape is not rectangular.

Provide students with acetate sheets of a centimetre grid of squares. Provide various shapes (squares, rectangles, L-shapes, other shapes with sides at right-angles). Ask students to place the grid over each shape and count the squares to find each area.

As a development, provide similar shapes and, this time, the students use rulers to draw their own centimetre grids within each shape. They count the squares they have drawn to find each area.

A further development is to place the acetate grid on an irregular area which has straight sides and half-squares drawn diagonally (such as sketch of a garden patio) and find the area. Students now count whole squares and half-squares.

Plenary

Ask pairs of students to design a bar of chocolate made up of 24 square pieces. Ask how many different rectangular-shaped bars can be made and get the answers 1×24, 2×12, 3×8, 4×6. Discuss whether, for example, 3×8 is the same as 8×3. What are the areas of these bars? Which bars are more likely to be manufactured? Why?

Exercise commentary

Question 1 –Parts **e** and **f** need students to estimate halves of squares. Use the method of the 50p example on the previous page.

Question 2 – The rounded edges of some shapes will pose more of a challenge when estimating area.

Question 3 – Students are asked to find the areas of rectangles where some of the squares have been obscured. In each case, they will need to find the width and length and use a multiplication to calculate the area.

Question 4 – Precision is needed when adding up all of the whole and part squares. This activity can be made more real by getting students to draw around their, or a partners, hand and finding its area.

Answers

1 **a** 12 cm^2 **b** 12 cm^2 **c** 20 cm^2 **d** 15 cm^2
e 4.5 cm^2 **d** 4.5 cm^2

2 **a** 24 cm^2 **b** 6 cm^2 **c** 15 cm^2 **d** 13 cm^2

3 **a** 20 $units^2$ **b** 25 $units^2$ **c** 21 $units^2$

4 Daniel The hand is roughly a 5×14 rectangle.

2g Metric units

Objectives

- Use a wider range of measures including non-standard units and standard metric units of length, capacity and mass in a range of contexts. (L3)

Key ideas

1. Length, mass and capacity can be measured in metric units. Some units are more appropriate than others in a given case.
2. You can change from one metric unit to another, such as from litres to millilitres.

Resources

Units of length	(1101)
Units of capacity	(1104)
Units of mass	(1105)

A variety of items or packaging with labels given a mass, volume or length

A metre rule, a 1 kg mass, a 1 litre container

A pack of cards with objects written on them

Simplification

It is important for students to relate this work to real-life objects. It is also necessary to build up experience of what 1 metre, 1 kg and 1 litre looks or feels like. Have them hold a metre rule and estimate the width of the room. Have them feel the weight of a 1 kg mass, perhaps from the science department, and estimate the mass of a thick book. Have them hold a hollow 10 cm cube, with a capacity of 1 litre, and estimate the capacity of an empty bottle.

Extension

Students write a short story in which they mention two lengths or distances, two weights and two volumes or capacities. The story could be based, for example, on their school or favourite sport.

Literacy

Length and *distance* are not quite the same but are related. The length of a line is the distance between its ends. Generally, distance is used for longer lengths, as for a journey.

Mass is the amount of matter in an object; *weight* is the force of the Earth on it. We often use the word 'weight' in everyday speech rather than 'mass'.

The *capacity* of a container tells us the volume of liquid it can hold. In commerical containers even when 'full', the volume of liquid is often slightly less than the capacity to avoid spillage when opening.

Links

It takes 3600 litres of paint to cover the surface area of an A380-800 Airbus. How many 5 litre tins of paint would the painters use?

There is more information about the A380-800 Airbus here

http://portal.aircraft-info.net/article8.html

and at

www.airliners.net/aircraft-data/stats.main?id=29

Alternative approach

A more adventurous approach is to use a science laboratory where there is ready access to sets of weights and water – and the means to measure the mass or capacity of objects.

Have students tabulate commercial items, such as groceries, by name and by the length, mass or volume given on the labels, then check by measuring. Have several unlabelled items for which students estimate the length, mass or capacity, and then check by measuring.

Checkpoint

1. Show an object
   - **i** Would you measure it in terms of length, mass or capacity
   - **ii** What would be sensible units to use? Give the iunits name and its abreviation.

   a A skipping rope (Length; metres, m)

   b An apple (Mass; grams, g)

   c A glass of water (Capacity; millilitres, ml)
2. Repeat for other objects, such as a pencil, a heavy bag of flour, and a large bottle of lemonade.

Starter – Quick fire

Continue quick-fire questions to consolidate students' understanding of the number work of Chapter 1. They should write their answers on mini-whiteboards. End by asking students to imagine a 2 litre bottle of lemonade, and ask

- How heavy do you think it is?
- How tall do you think it is?

Check that answers have units and then discuss whether the answers are reasonable.

Teaching notes

Building on the final questions of the **Starter**, have a 1 metre rule, a 1 kg weight and a 1 litre container to show students to help them estimate. A useful starting activity is to have a wide selection of commercial products or their packaging. Each label must have a mass, volume or, less often, a length on it. Have students look at the three standard measures and guess the mass, volume or length printed on each label. If lengths on labels are few, they can estimate distances within the classroom.

Results can be tabulated under three headings: 'Object', 'Estimated value', 'Actual value'. The aim is for students to know which units are used for various measures and which unit is the most appropriate to measure a given object.

As an extension, students offer other units for measuring small or larger masses, volumes or lengths. List them in writing. Have a pack of cards with objects written on them, for example, the height of Blackpool Tower, the capacity of a medicine spoon, the weight of a car. Students, in turn, select a card and read it to the class. All students write the most appropriate units.

If pupils have been taught metric equivalents, such as 1000 m = 1 km, then show them the following measurements:

1 cm	10 cm	1 m	10 m	1 km
10 mm	100 mm	100 cm	1000 cm	1000 m,

and ask them to find equivalent pairs.

Plenary

Find equivalent pairs from this list.

1 litre	1 cm	1 kg	1000 kg	1 m
1 tonne	1000 ml	10 mm	100 cm	1000 g

The teacher selects one value and students use mini-whiteboards to give the paired value.

Exercise commentary

Question 1 – This task could be used as a whole-class activity. Select an abbreviation and ask students to give the full name of the measurement. Then do the reverse.

Question 2 – In parts **a** and **d**, students firstly must decide whether they are measuring a length, weight or volume.

Question 4 – This requires a simple division with no remainder. This could be done by doing 1000 ÷ 10 or repeatedly adding 100.

Question 5 – Parts **a** and **b** require simple multiplications. Parts **c** and **d** need knowledge of two simple fractions: a half and a tenth.

Question 6 – Two double-conversions are needed in each part. Part **a** needs metres converting to cm and then cm to mm. Part **b** needs tonnes converting to kg and then kg to grams.

Question 7 – In part **a** students need to know there are 10 lots of 100 g and 4 lots of 250 g in 1 kg and then find a tenth or a quarter of £6 = 600p. In part **b** students need to divide 750 by 600; it may be easier to think of £7.50 as £6 + £1.50 and ask what fraction of 6 is 1.5 to obtain one and one quarter kilogrammes.

Question 8 – This reqires the division 100 ÷ 8 and identifying the remainder 4 with the fraction a half.

Answers

1 Kilogram – kg, Gramme – g, Metre – m, Litre – *l*, Tonne – t, Millimetre – mm, Millilitre – ml, Centimetre – cm, Kilometre – km

2 **a** mm **b** km **c** kg **d** *l* **e** cm **f** t

3 **a** g **b** m **c** ml **d** km **e** m **f** *l* **g** kg **h** cm

4 10

5 **a** £20 **b** £60 **c** £2 **d** £0.40

6 **a** 1460 mm **b** 50 000 g

7 **a** **i** £0.60 **ii** £1.50
b $1\frac{1}{4}$kg or 1.25 kg

8 $12\frac{1}{2}$ litres or 12.5 litres

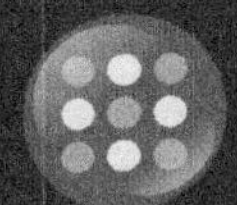

2 Measures, perimeter and area – MySummary

Key outcomes	Quick check
Measure lengths in centimetres and millimetres. L3	Measure the length of these lines in **i** cm **ii** mm. **a** ——— (3.5 cm, 35 mm) **b** ——— (7.3 cm,73 mm)
Read and interpret scales in different contexts including time. L3	**1** What are these arrows pointing at? 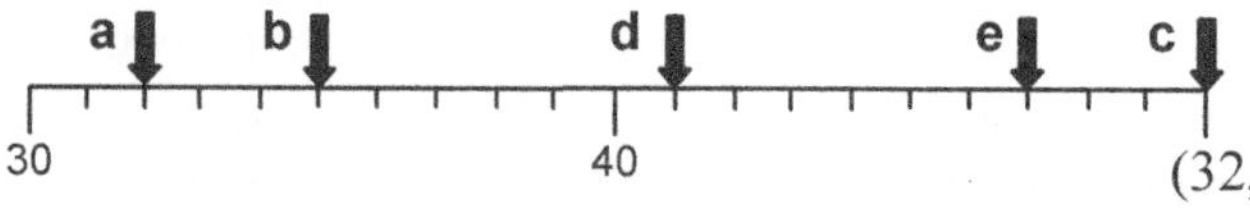 (scale 30 to 40 with arrows a, b, d, e, c) (32, 35, 50, 41, 47) **2** **a** Write 8:35 am using the 24-hour clock (08:35) **b** Write 19:15 using am or pm. (7:15 pm)
Classify 2D shapes by their properties. L3	For each shape give its **i** number of sides **ii** name. **a** 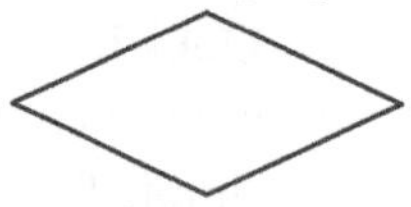 (4, rhombus) **b** 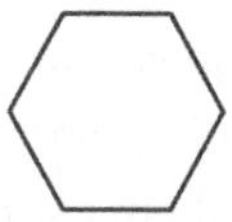 (6, hexagon)
Calculate the perimeter of simple shapes. L4	**1** A regular octagon has sides of length 2 cm, what is its perimeter? (16 cm) **2** What is the perimeter of this shape? 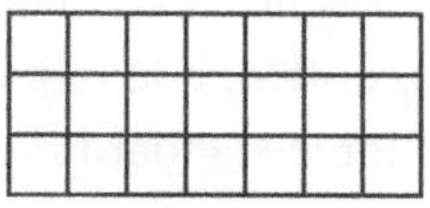 (20 units)
Calculate or estimate the area of a shape by counting squares. L4	**1** What is the area of the shape in question **2** above? (21 units^2) **2** Esitmate the area of this shape. 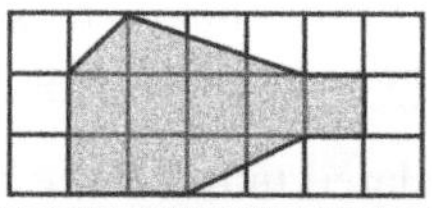 (10 units^2)
Select and use standard metric units of measure. L3	Which metric measure would you use to measure the following? For your chosen unit, give **i** its name **ii** its abreviation. **a** The width of a pencil. (Millimetre, mm) **b** A spoonfull of water. (Millilitre, ml) **c** The mass of a lorry. (Tonne, t)

Development and links
Accurately drawing and measuring lines is required to do constructions in chapter **12**. Reading scales is revisited in the context of measuring angles in chapter **5**. Knowledge of 2D shapes is extended to special properties of triangles in chapter **5** and 3D shapes in chapter **12**. Changing between metric units provides a context for multiplying and dividing by powers of ten in chapter **14**. The basic measure skills encountered in this chapter will be met repeatedly during this course and throughout later life. Formulae for calculating areas are developed in book 2A, whilst decorating – buying paint, wallpaper, carpet, tiles, etc. – uses the ability to estimate areas.

MyMaths extra support

Lesson/online homework			Description
Telling the time 1	1233	L3	The lesson covers how to read the time on an analogue clock and write it in words and numbers; avoids covering am and pm.
Measures	1232	L2	The first part of this lesson covers reading scales. The second half introduces common metric units for length, mass and capacity.

My Review

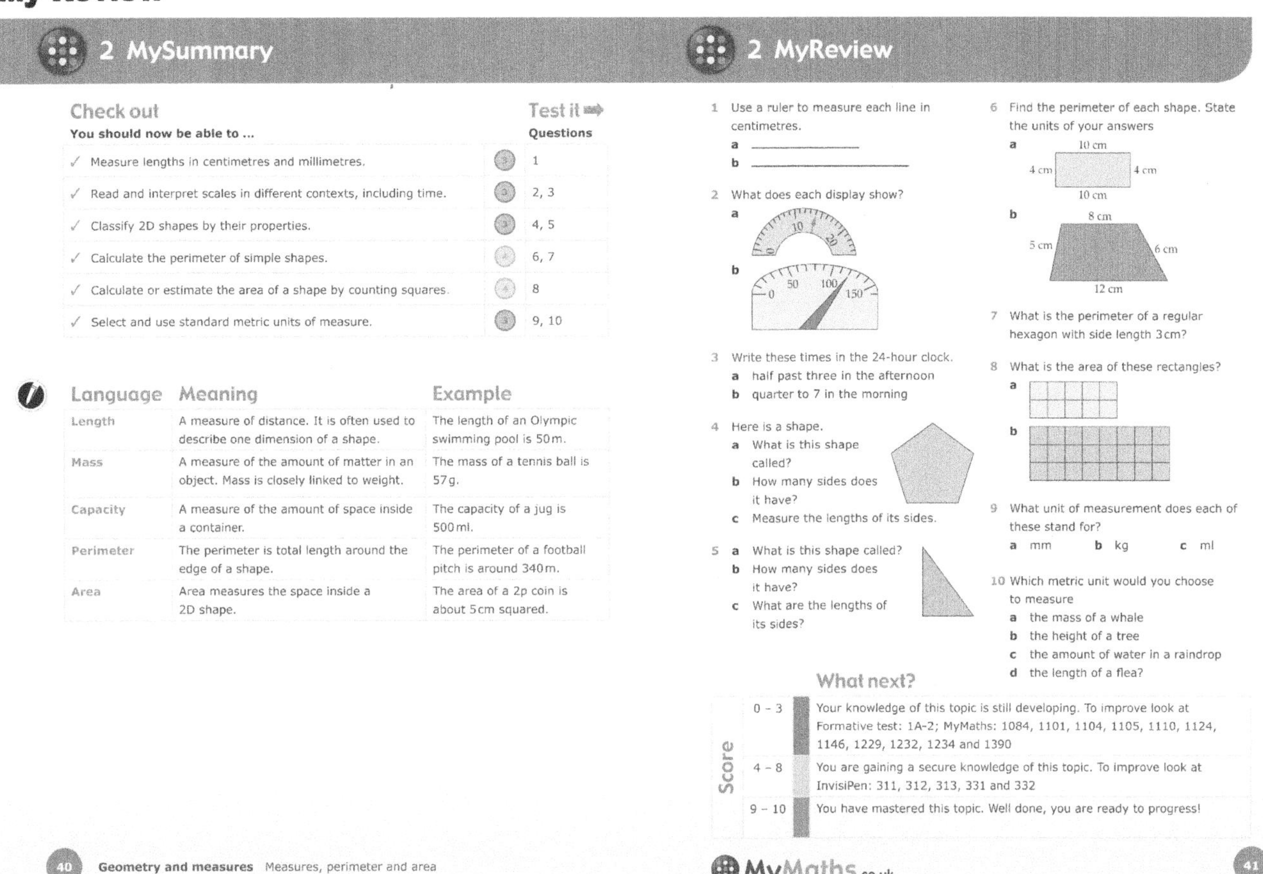

2 MySummary
Check out
You should now be able to ...
Test it
Questions
Measure lengths in centimetres and millimetres. 1
Read and interpret scales in different contexts, including time. 2, 3
Classify 2D shapes by their properties. 4, 5
Calculate the perimeter of simple shapes. 6, 7
Calculate or estimate the area of a shape by counting squares. 8
Select and use standard metric units of measure. 9, 10
Language Meaning Example
Length A measure of distance. It is often used to describe one dimension of a shape. The length of an Olympic swimming pool is 50m.
Mass A measure of the amount of matter in an object. Mass is closely linked to weight. The mass of a tennis ball is 57g.
Capacity A measure of the amount of space inside a container. The capacity of a jug is 500ml.
Perimeter The perimeter is total length around the edge of a shape. The perimeter of a football pitch is around 340m.
Area Area measures the space inside a 2D shape. The area of a 2p coin is about 5cm squared.
2 MyReview
1 Use a ruler to measure each line in centimetres.
2 What does each display show?
3 Write these times in the 24-hour clock.
a half past three in the afternoon
b quarter to 7 in the morning
4 Here is a shape.
a What is this shape called?
b How many sides does it have?
c Measure the lengths of its sides.
5 a What is this shape called?
b How many sides does it have?
c What are the lengths of its sides?
6 Find the perimeter of each shape. State the units of your answers
7 What is the perimeter of a regular hexagon with side length 3cm?
8 What is the area of these rectangles?
9 What unit of measurement does each of these stand for?
a mm b kg c ml
10 Which metric unit would you choose to measure
a the mass of a whale
b the height of a tree
c the amount of water in a raindrop
d the length of a flea?
What next?
Score
0 - 3 Your knowledge of this topic is still developing. To improve look at Formative test: 1A-2; MyMaths: 1084, 1101, 1104, 1105, 1110, 1124, 1146, 1229, 1232, 1234 and 1390
4 - 8 You are gaining a secure knowledge of this topic. To improve look at InvisiPen: 311, 312, 313, 331 and 332
9 - 10 You have mastered this topic. Well done, you are ready to progress!
40 Geometry and measures Measures, perimeter and area
MyMaths.co.uk
41

Question commentary

Question 1 – (lessons **2a**) Allow ±2 mm; units should be given.

Question 2 – (lesson **2b**) Students need to work out what each division represents: 1 in part **a** and 10 in part **b**.

Question 3 – (lesson **2c**) Times given in the 24-hour clock should have 4 digits, so in part **b** 6:45 would not be correct.

Question 4 – (lesson **2d**) You could ask if the shape is regular. (Yes)

Question 5 – (lesson **2d**) You could discuss what type of triangle it is. (Right-angled)

Question 6 – (lesson **2e**) In part **a**, it is possible students could confuse perimeter with area to obtain 40 cm^2.

Question 7 – (lessons **2d** and **2e**) Students may need help recalling the definition of a regular hexagon. (Six equal sides)

Question 8 – (lesson **2f**) Students need to count the squares, units not required, but could put 'units^2'. Discuss a possible 'short-cut' to counting squares. (2 × 5 in part **a** and 8 × 3 in part **b**).

If students confuse area and perimeter they will get 14 units and 22 units as there answers.

Question 9 – (lesson **2g**) You could give students choices to pick from here to help with spelling.

Question 10 – (lesson **2g**) Give students credit for giving a unit of mass, length, capacity and length respectively.

Answers

1 **a** 3.2 cm **b** 4.7 cm
2 **a** 14 **b** 120
3 **a** 15:30 **b** 06:45
4 **a** Pentagon **b** 5 **c** 1.5 cm
5 **a** Triangle **b** 3 **c** 2 cm, 1.5 cm, 2.5 cm
6 **a** 28 cm **b** 31 cm
7 18 cm
8 **a** 10 units^2 **b** 24 units^2
9 **a** Millimetres **b** Kilograms **c** Millilitres
10 **a** Tonne **b** Metre **c** Millilitre **d** Millimetre

2 MyPractice

2a

1 Draw a line of each length.
Write the measurement beside each line that you draw.

a 10 cm **b** 9 cm **c** 13 cm
d 10.5 cm **e** 11.4 cm **f** 8.2 cm

2 Measure the length of each line.

a ________________________
b ______________________
c __________________
d ________________________________
e ___
f ____

2b

3 What numbers are the arrows pointing to on each sca e?

a °C 34 35 36 37 38 39
B DA E F G CH

b volts 0 50 100
G E F C B D A

2c

4 Write these times as 24-hour clock times.

a p.m. **b** p.m. **c** a.m. **d** a.m.

e p.m. **f** p.m. **g** a.m. **h** p.m.

2d

5 List the shapes you can see in this picture.

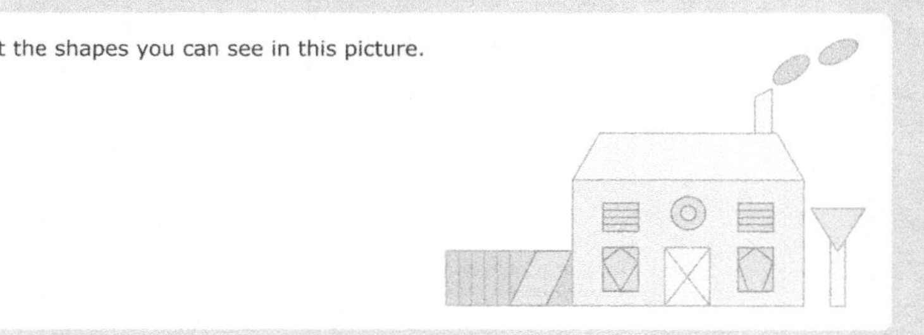

2e

6 Find the perimeter of each shape.

a 5 cm, 5 cm, 10 cm, 7 cm

b

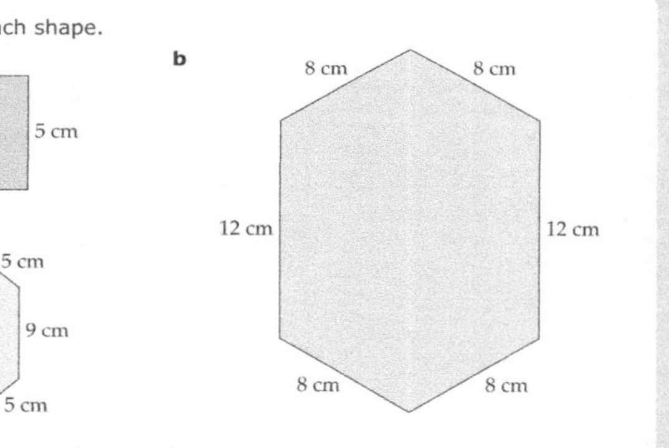

c 9 cm, 5 cm, 9 cm, 5 cm, 9 cm, 5 cm, 9 cm, 5 cm

2f

7 Find the area of each rectangle by counting squares.

a

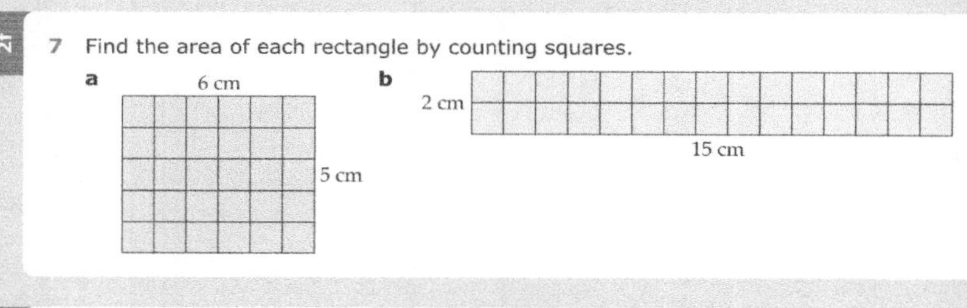

b

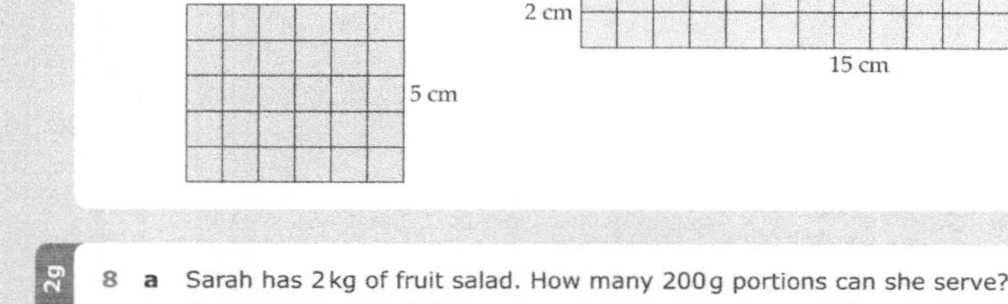

2g

8 **a** Sarah has 2 kg of fruit salad. How many 200 g portions can she serve?
b Farmer Jones has 4000 kg of seeds. How many tonnes of seeds does he have?

42 Geometry and measures Measures, perimeter and area

Question commentary

Questions 1 – Ensure students use a sharp pencil. If students are paired they can check each other's lines, which should be accurate to ±1 mm. In the case of a mistake can the students explain how they went wrong? As well as labelling their lines with the measurement in centimetres, students could also be asked to give the measurement in millimetres.

Questions 2 – Answers should be accurate to ±1 mm. They can be given either in centimetres to one decimal place or millimetres.

Question 3 – In part **a**, students should be confident that the ten intervals between integer values represent tenths, which are written as a decimal as 0.1, 0.2 etc. In part **b**, for A – C students should agree that the main intervals are tens whilst in D-G the subintervals are fives.

Question 4 – As necessary the answer can be done in two steps: first, write the time using am or pm and then for pm convert to the 24-hour clock.

Question 5 – This question could be done as an against the clock activity. For shapes such as triangles there are multiple instances in the picture; students can be asked to find more than one, triangle, rectangle, trapezium, etc.

Question 6 – Ensure that students give the units with their answers.

Question 7 – Check that students do not confuse perimeter with area. As well as finding the answer by counting ask students to write down the multiplication that also gives the area. ($6 \times 5 = 30$ cm^2, $2 \times 15 = 30$ cm^2) Ask students to find the other two rectangles that have the same area. (3×10 or 1×30)

Question 8 – In part **a**, students can either work out how many 200 g portions are in 1 Kg = 1000 g and then multiply by two or they can evaluate $2000 \div 200$. In part **b**, ask students which is the bigger unit a kilogramme or a tonne.

Answers

1 Check student's drawings by measuring. Lines should be accurate to ±1 mm.

2 **a** 6.4 cm **b** 5.9 cm **c** 4.7 cm **d** 8.9 cm
e 0.8 cm **f** 12.4 cm

3 **a** All answers are in °C.
A 35.5 B 34.3 C 38.6 D 35.2
E 36.1 F 36.8 G 37.9 H 38.9

b All answers are in Volts.
A 90 B 60 C 45 D 75
E 15 F 25 G 5

4 **a** 14:00 **b** 19:30 **c** 6:30 **d** 0:00
e 20:00 **f** 22:15 **g** 3:45 **h** 19:25

5 Circle (blue), triangle (green), square, (upper windows), parallelogram (blue), rectangle (fence),
kite (lower left window), trapezium (roof, chimney),
pentagon (lower right window).

6 **a** 27 cm **b** 56 cm **c** 56 cm

7 **a** 30 cm^2 **b** 30 cm^2

8 **a** 10 **b** 4 t

Learning outcomes

A1 Use and interpret algebraic notation, including:

- ab in place of $a \times b$
- $3y$ in place of $y + y + y$ and $3 \times y$
- a^2 in place of $a \times a$, a^3 in place of $a \times a \times a$; a^2b in place of $a \times a \times b$
- coefficients written as fractions rather than as decimals
- a/b in place of a ÷ b
- brackets. (L5)

A2 Substitute numerical values into formulae and expressions, including scientific formulae. (L5)

A3 Understand and use the concepts and vocabulary of expressions, equations, inequalities, terms and factor. (L5)

A4 Simplify and manipulate algebraic expressions to maintain equivalence by:

- collecting like terms
- multiplying a single term over a bracket. (L5)

A6 Model situations or procedures by translating them into algebraic expressions or formulae and by using graphs. (L4)

Introduction

The chapter starts by looking at how we use letters to stand for unknown numbers before moving on to simplifying algebraic expressions by collecting like terms. Substitution into formulae is covered before the skill of writing formulae from given information.

The introduction considers the use of algebraic formulae in everyday life. Converting between currencies, costing mobile phone tariffs and working with recipes are the examples given but students could be asked to think of other examples as well.

While algebraic representations have been used since ancient times, the general principles of algebra were first written down in detail by an Arabic mathematician named Muḥammad ibn Mūsā al-Khwārizmī in the ninthcentury AD. He wrote a very famous book called '*Al-kitāb al-mukhtaṣar fī ḥisāb al-ğabr wa'l-muqābala*' which outlined the use of the symbols and techniques we still use today. The words 'algebra' and 'algorithm' both come directly from this work. A history of al-Khwārizmī can be found here.

http://www-history.mcs.st-and.ac.uk/Mathematicians/Al-Khwarizmi.html

It is worth emphasising to students that a good grasp of basic algebra is essential for solving more complex problems later on in their mathematical journey.

Prior knowledge

Students should already know how to…

- Carry out arithmetic operations in the correct order.
- Extract information from a written description.

Starter problem

The starter problem is a classic example of a number trick. No matter which number you start with, the answer will always be 2. You can see how the trick works by considering the algebra that underpins it.

Let the number you first think of be x. The steps then lead to the following sequence of algebraic expressions: $2x$, $2x + 4$, $x + 2$, 2. So it doesn't matter which number you start with. In fact, you could start with *any* number, not just one between 1 and 10, since the algebra shows the general structure of the problem.

Popularisers of mathematics have used these tricks for many years to engage students in the structures of mathematics and you can make up other examples by considering the algebra first. Able students may even be able to develop their own once they have completed the work in this chapter.

Resources

MyMaths

Rules and formulae	1158	Simplifying 1	1179	Substitution 1	1187

Online assessment		**InvisiPen solutions**			
Chapter test	1A-3	Expressions	211	Collecting like terms	212
Formative test	1A-3	Formulae and expressions	251	Substitution	254
Summative test	1A-3				

Topic scheme

Teaching time = 6 lessons/2 weeks

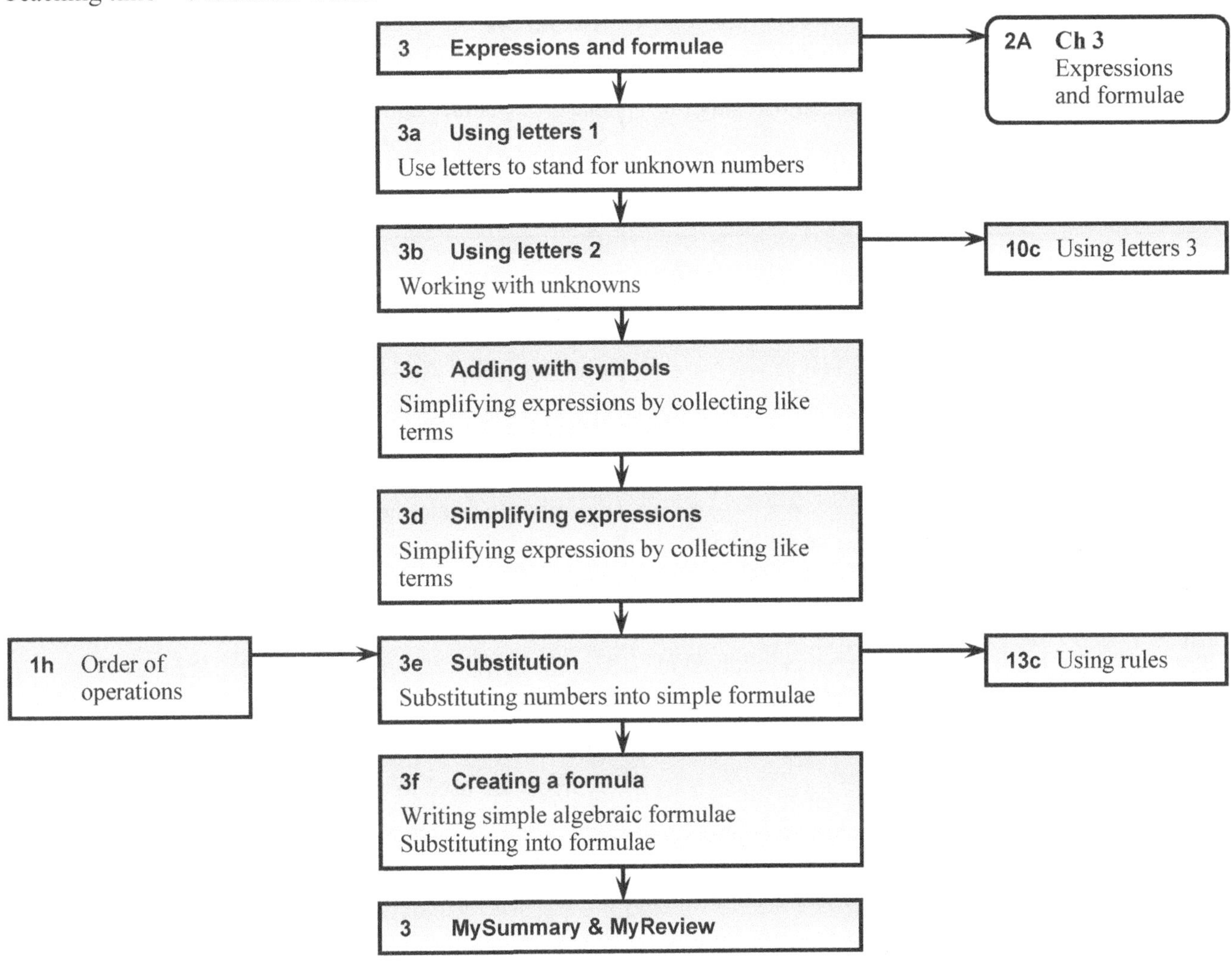

Differentiation

Student book 1A	44 – 61
Using letters Adding with symbols Simplifying symbols Basic substitution Creating a formula	

Student book 1B	42 – 59
Writing algebraic terms and expressions Collecting like terms Substituting into given formulae Writing and using simple formulae	

Student book 1C	40 – 61
Using letter symbols Collecting like terms Expanding brackets Using and deriving formulae Substituting into formulae Further algebraic simplification	

Objectives	
• Use letter symbols to represent unknown numbers or variables. (L5)	
Key ideas	**Resources**
1 A letter can stand for an unknown number. **2** An unknown number can be changed by using the basic operations of +, –, × and ÷.	A cloth bag containing a collection of items such as marbles, pebbles and sweets Several identical cloth bags holding the same number of items Two dice
Simplification	**Extension**
Have the same starting point for several questions. Show a packet of biscuits but don't count how many are in it. Decide there are n biscuits in it. If I find two extra biscuits, how many have I now? $(n + 2)$ If I eat three from the packet, how many are left in it? $(n - 3)$ If I have two identical packets, how many have I altogether? $(2n)$	Explore the idea of function machines further in pairs. One student draws a function machine on their mini-whiteboard but does not show their partner. The other student gives an input number and receives an output number. They have to guess what the function machine is doing. Together they agree the expression that best describes the function machine.
Literacy	**Links**
Often we do not know the actual numbers involved in these questions. We write **expressions** instead. Each expression uses a **symbol** (in our case, a letter) to stand for the unknown number. Centuries ago, the Arabs were excellent at mathematics. The word 'algebra' comes from the Arabic *al-jabr* and was first used in AD 825 to mean 'rejoining separate parts'. We join letters and numbers in our expressions.	Use the activity 'Your number was…' at the nrich website. www.nrich.maths.org/7216 Symbols are used to represent various things. For example, the Royal Air Force has its red, white and blue concentric circles. Can the students think of other symbols and, particularly, any letters which are used as symbols commercially, such as the letter M for a famous fast-food eatery?

Alternative approach

Instead of using bags and dice as in the **Teaching notes**, the idea of a function machine, see Chapter **10**, can be used here. A carboard box has two holes in it on opposite faces. Cards can be passed through both holes. Students are told that, inside the box, there is a machine that adds 6 to the number that enters it. A number, unknown to the students, enters one hole on a card and reappears out of the other hole. Discuss how to write the input and output numbers.
Repeat by saying that the machine now subtracts 3 from the input.
Repeat again by saying the machine doubles the input.

Checkpoint

1 A bag contains n items.
How many items the bag will contain if
- **a** 3 items are added. $(n + 3)$
- **b** 2 items are taken out. $(n - 2)$
- **c** The number of items is trebled. $(3n)$
- **d** Half the items are removed from the bag. $(n \div 2)$

Use a bag containing items, such as marbles, plus have extra to hand to illustrate this scenario.

Starter – Bags of stuff

Act out a scene similar to that on p46 of the Student Book. Have a bag of marbles, pebbles, sweets, cubes or other small items. Hold it up and say that you have no idea how many items are in it. Take out, say, 4 items. Ask for ideas about how you can write the number left in the bag. Suggest that symbols on a keyboard might have the answer. Agree that a letter can be used for an unknown number. Choose a letter to stand for the original number in the bag. Have them write, on their mini-whiteboards, how many are in there after the 4 have been taken out.

Teaching notes

Continue the **Starter** by putting the four items back. Now add some extras to the bag. On their mini-whiteboards, students write how many are now in the bag. Remove the extras.

Have a different bag with a different unknown number in it. Choose a different letter. Add extra items and use mini-whiteboards to record how many are in the bag now. Remove the extras. Write how many are now in the bag. Take several more items out. Record how many are in the bag now.

Show three new identical bags containing the same (but unknown) number of items. Choose a new letter. Is it the same letter for each bag? Discuss how to write the total number of items in all three bags.

Take two dice. Roll them. Refuse to say what the score is on the first dice. Tell the students the score on the second dice. They use their mini-whiteboards to write the total score, using a letter to represent the score on the first dice. Roll again and repeat.

Roll both dice but refuse to say what either score is. Just say that the scores are the same. They write the total score. (Accept answers such as $s + s$ and $2 \times s$.)

If you had b items in a bag, ask what you have done if you now have $b + 7$ items or $b - 8$ items or $4 \times b$ items.

Plenary

Imagine a bag holding n sweets. Ask students what you have done to the bag if it now holds $n + 7$ sweets. Ask students to write their answers on mini-whiteboards. Repeat for the expressions $n - 3$ (eaten three sweet), $2 \times n$ (two bags), $2 \times n + 5$ (two bags plus five sweets), $2 \times n - 6$ (two bags less six sweets).

Exercise commentary

Questions 1 to **5** –Ask students to find the letter which tells them how many objects they have at the start before the situation changes. Then, they need to read the question to find the key words that tell them how the starting value changes. For example, in Question 2, the key words are 'caught' and 'left' because these words indicate that the starting value will reduce by subtraction. In short, we start with s fish, we reduce by 20 fish, and we have $s - 20$ fish left.

Question 6 – The answer for part **a** is $g - 100$. But the answer for part **b** could $5 \times g$ for the number before any trees are cut down or $5 \times g - 100$ after the 100 trees are cut down in the first forest. However, the forests are no longer the same size if only one forest has its trees cur down. So the answer could be $5 \times g - 500$ to make all forest of equal size after cutting. There needs to be a discussion.

Question 7 – It may help students to understand what to do if they take a specific value for P (≥ 25) and start by treating it as a numerical problem. For example, if $P = 40$ then the number wrong = 40 – 25 (= 15).

Question 7 – Encourage a step-by-step approach. How much did Kat raise? ($2P$) What is $P + 2P$? ($3P$)

Answers

1 $m + 5$

2 $s - 20$

3 $\frac{m}{2}$ or $m \div 2$

4 **a** $n + 12$ **b** $n + 19$ **c** $3n$ **d** $n \div 6$

5 $j + 7$

6 **a** $g - 100$ **b** $5g$

7 $p - 25$

8 $3p$

3b Using letters 2

Objectives

- Use letter symbols to represent unknown numbers or variables. (L5)

Key ideas	Resources
1 An expression uses both numbers and letters. **2** Different letters can stand for different numbers in the same expression.	A cloth bag containing a collection of items Several identical cloth bags holding the same number of items Two dice

Simplification	Extension
Revise the previous exercise where the same starting point is used for several questions. Extend by having two different packs of biscuits. Say 'If there are 10 biscuits in this pack and 8 in this other pack, what do you do to get the total number of biscuits?' However, if the numbers are not known, agree that two different letters can be added to give the total. This can be extended further by imagining eating, say, four biscuits and writing an expression for the number left.	An empty bus collects n passengers at its first stop. It makes another four stops. Students work in pairs with their mini-whiteboards. Both write the letter n. One student tells the story of the journey (how many times the bus stops, and how many passengers get on or off the bus) and writes an appropriate expression. The partner also writes an expression. They do not see each other's boards. After all the stops, they compare what they have written and explain any differences.

Literacy	Links
The points made for the previous lesson apply here too.	A common symbol for a number is the asterisk * or the bullet •. These symbols are displayed onscreen when entering pin numbers or passwords into a computer. Unlike when performing algebra, we cannot +, –, × or ÷ them. Use the nrich website again and try the activity called 'Your number is…'. www.nrich.maths.org/2289

Alternative approach

Recap the use of a function machine as in the previous exercise. Now extend the use. The carboard box now has three holes in it, two on the same face and the third on the opposite face. Two cards are passed, one each through the two holes on the same face, and one card is withdrawn from the hole on the opposite face. Students are told that, inside the box, the function machine adds the two input numbers together and gives their total as the output. Without showing what is on any card, ask what the output will be if the input numbers are, for example, 6 and 4. If the inputs are unknown numbers, discuss how the output could be written.

Checkpoint

1 A bag contains n items.
How many items would you have in total if

- **a** You have 5 bags containing n items. $(5n)$
- **b** You also have another bag with m items inside. $(n + m)$
- **c** You remove p items from the bag. $(n - p)$
- **d** You added s items to the bag. $(n + s)$

Use a bag containing items, such as marbles, plus have extra to hand to illustrate this scenario.

Starter – Number machines

Show a diagram of a simple number machine labelled with the operation 'add 3'. Ask what happens to an input number that enters to machine. Give various input numbers and have students use their mini-whiteboards to give answers (outputs). Now ask what happens if an unknown number enters the machine. Agree the symbol, that is the letter, to use and they write the output.

Change the operation to 'subtract 5' and then change again to 'double'. In each case, use inputs of known numbers and then letters for unknown numbers.

Teaching notes

Use the teaching notes from the previous exercise to recap the various scenarios used so far and write expressions for the number of items and the total scores; namely:

- one bag with an unknown number of items to which extra items are added or from which some items are taken out;
- several identical bags containing the same number of unknown items;
- two dice, one of which has an unknown score, the other of which has a known score;
- several dice, all with the same unknown score.

Now introduce new scenarios. Have two different bags with different numbers of unknown items or two dice with neither score known. Decide that two different letters are needed to stand for the unknown numbers. Write expressions for the number of items and the total score. This is the first time that expressions will contain two different letters.

Students now work in pairs. Tell them that there are several identical packets of sweets and that there are n sweets in each packet. Each student chooses three of the following expressions and writes a sentence to explain what they do to have the numbers of sweets in each chosen expression. They exchange whiteboards to check their partner's answers.

$2 \times n$	$n - 6$	$4 \times n + 3$
$n + 2$	$3 \times n - 4$	$5 \times n - 2$

Plenary

Describe various scenarios with bags or dice and ask students to write appropriate expressions on their mini-whiteboards. For example, I roll two dice, get the same score on each of them and then subtract 1 from my total score. (They write $2 \times n - 1$.)

Exercise commentary

Question 1 – This question follows on naturally from the previous page in the Student Book. Each part starts afresh with m strawberries.

Question 2 – This question is potentially confusing. Each part does not stand alone. The four parts follow on, as if in a story. Nick in part **b** starts with the cakes that Susan leaves him from part **a**, so he finishes with $(x - 6) + 20 = x + 14$. Parts **c** and **d** follow on from Nick and Susan.

Question 3 – Students need to beware that expressions do not always start with a letter. In this question, the string starts with a length of 30 cm. A length of p cm is then cut off to leave $30 - p$ cm.

Question 4 – Part **b** in this question refers only to one row. It does not ask for the new total number of soldiers in 12 rows.

Question 5 – This is the first question to use two letters for two different unknowns. Part **b** follows on from part **a** in the sense that the 10 kg are taken away from the *total* number of Jack's and Derek's apples.

Question 6 – Part **a** requires a n equation to be set up and part **b** requires it to be solved. At this stage an informal method of solution is acceptable, though students should be able to explain what they did. The important point is for students to realize that they can write the problem as an equation in an unknown.

Question 7 – Students should have the correct strategy before they begin to deal with the numerical detail. They could discuss it in pairs.

Answers

1 **a** $m + 1$ **b** $m + 3$ **c** $m - 6$ **d** $m - 12$
e $m + 50$ **f** $\frac{m}{2}$ **g** $3m$ **h** $m + p$
i $m - s$

2 **a** $x - 6$ **b** $x + 20$ **c** $3x$ **d** $4x + 20$

3 **a** $(30 - p)$ m **b** $(30 - 2p)$ m

4 **a** $12b$ **b** $b + 3$

5 **a** $(x + y)$ kg **b** $(x + y - 10)$ kg

6 **a** $b + 5$ **b** 15

7 18

3c Adding with symbols

Objectives	
• Simplify linear algebraic expressions by collecting like terms. (L5)	
Key ideas	**Resources**
1 Know the difference between *like terms* and *unlike terms*. **2** Know that expressions can be simplified by adding like terms.	Simplifying 1 (1179) A cardboard box which can serve as a function machine Two types of bead which can make a necklace
Simplification	**Extension**
Add together only terms in one variable, such as $x + x + x$, $2x + x$ and $2x + 5x$. Then add together similar terms using a letter other than x such as $2b + 4b + b$. Progress to two-letter expressions such as $x + x + x + y + y$, $3x + x + 5y + y$, $2x + 3x + 5y + 4y$ and $2x + 5y + 3x + 4y$.	Mixtures of algebraic and numerical terms could be added together, such as $3x + 7 + 5x + 4$. The additions could then involve two unknowns, such as $3x + 2y + 6 + 3y + 4 + 5x$. Students could be given an expression, such as $3a + 5b$, and the answer, $7a + 6b$, after a second expression has been added. The problem is to find the second expression.
Literacy	**Links**
The multiplication sign is never omitted when placed between two numbers, such as 2×3. However, when a number is multiplied by a unknown value represented by a letter, then the multiplcation sign can be left out without any ambiguity. Students should know that, for example, $2n$ means $2 \times n$ and $2n + 3$ means $2 \times n + 3$ with $\times$ taking priority over $+$. Mention that $1 \times n$ is written simply as just n. You can exploit a play on words. If you *like* terms, then you can add them together. If you *don't like* terms, you can't.	Symbols need not just be letters representing unknown numbers. A symbol can be any image which conveys a meaning associated with what it is representing. For example, a pair of scales is a symbol used to represent the balance of justice. Many court buildings throughout the world have a statue showing Lady Justice holding a pair of scales to show that justice weighs opposing evidence to give a fair trial. She also carries a sword to represent the power to punish. There is more information about Lady Justice at www.commonlaw.com/Justice.html

Alternative approach

The notion of a function machine can be used. As previously used, a cardboard box has two holes in one face and a third hole in the opposite face. Two cards on which expressions such as $3x$ and $5x$ are written are placed into the box through the two holes. Students are told that the machine adds these together and are asked what should appear through the hole in the opposite face. Later expressions can involve two unknowns, such as $3x$ and $5y$.

A third approach is to use a string of beads of two different types. Let x and y be the respective masses of one bead of each type. Ask for the total mass of a necklace of different lengths.

Checkpoint

1 For $2x + 3x$
- **a** How many xs are there in total? (5)
- **b** Write the expression as simply as possible. ($5x$)

2 For $2x + 3y$
- **a** How many xs are there in total? (2)
- **b** How many ys are there in total? (3)
- **c** Write the expression as simply as possible. ($2x + 3y$, it cannot be simplified further)

3 Starting with $2x + 3y$ what do you get if you add
- **a** x ($2x + 3y + x = 3x + 3y$)
- **b** $2y$ ($2x + 3y + 2y = 2x + 5y$)
- **c** $x + y$ ($2x + 3y + x + y = 3x + 4y$)
- **d** z ($2x + 3y + z$)

Starter – Quick fire

Have students respond on mini-whiteboards to a series of quick questions which recap previous work on number and shape. For example, for place value and shape, ask students to

- Identify the value of the digit 2 in the numbers 3256 and 15.2 (200, two-tenths)
- Write 26 mm in centimetres. (2.6 cm)
- Write the value indicated by an arrow pointing to 3.2 on a scale.
- Write the time 'ten past eight in the evening' using am or pm and also using the 24-hour clock. (8:10 pm and 20:10)
- Find the perimeter of a triangle with given integer sides.
- Find the area of an L-shape drawn with an internal square grid.

Discuss answers when necessary.

Teaching notes

Discuss the meaning of 'like' and 'unlike'. Students can respond to questions on their mini-whiteboards. Build up complexity gradually, starting with expressions such as: $x + x + x + x$, $y + y + y$ and extend to such as $2x + x + x$, $3y + 2y$, $x + x + x + x + z + z$, $3x + 2z$, $4x + 2x + 3y + 2y$ and $5x + 6z + 2x + 3z$, including some expressions which cannot be simplified, such as $3x + 2z$. If students write the wrong answer $5xy$ to the addition $2x + 3y$, discuss why it is incorrect.

Set some questions in context by asking, for example

You have 6 beads on a string. Each bead weighs w grams. How much do the six beads weigh?

and

A van delivers two parcels. One weighs $3w$ kg and the other $2w$ kg. What is their total weight?

Plenary

Ask students to simplify additions such as $3m + 2m$, $4m + 2m + 3n + 2n$ and $3m + 4n + 2m + 3n$. Students respond on mini-whiteboards.

Extend the problems by saying

I am now giving you the answer and I want you to find the missing digits that should be written in the two boxes

$3a + 4b + \square a + \square b = 5a + 7b$ (2 and 3)

Extend further by having students write the missing expression in, for example

$3a + 4b + \square + \square = 7a + 6b$ ($4a$ and $2b$)

Exercise commentary

Question 2 – The diagrams could be written, for example, as $k + k + k + k + k$. Indeed, students could be asked to write them as an addition before writing their final answer.

Question 3 – This is similar to Question 2 but it is set in a simple context of a pan on a weighing scale. There is no intention for these diagrams to represent equations.

Question 4 – This question only includes expressions with like terms.

Question 5 – Students need to distinguish between like and unlike terms. A whole-class discussion of this question would be useful.

Question 6 – A brief reminder of the meaning of 'perimeter' may be needed (lesson **2e**): part **a**, which is purely numerical, should allow this. The answer could be written out in full as 2 + 2 + 3 + 3 + 4 (in centimetres) before any addition. Part **b** is purely algebraic and part **c** is 'mixed'.

Question 7 – This follows on from question **6**. Encourage students to be systematic. Ask them to explain why shapes have the same or different perimeters: check that they are comparing the numbers and the coefficients in front of a with each other

Answers

1	**a**	8	**b**	11	**c**	15	**d**	31
	e	38	**f**	30	**g**	32	**h**	30
	i	47	**j**	57				
2	**a**	$5k$	**b**	$6f$	**c**	$7d$	**d**	$9n$
3	**a**	$2a + 3b$	**b**	$4x + 2y$	**c**	$4m + 3n$	**d**	$3p + q + 5$
4	**a**	$7m$	**b**	$75f$	**c**	$34d$	**d**	$15k$
	e	$21y$	**f**	$24z$	**g**	$20g$	**h**	$10q$
	i	$39y$	**j**	$34w$	**k**	$22b$	**l**	$65j$
5	**a**	$9m$	**b**	Unlike	**c**	Unlike	**d**	$3x$
	e	$5s$	**f**	Unlike				
6	**a**	14	**b**	$8a$	**c**	$2m + 2m + 8$		
7	A	$4a + 5$	<u>B</u>	<u>$4a + 4$</u>	C	$5a + 4$	<u>D</u>	<u>$4a + 4$</u>

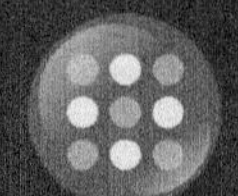

3d Simplifying expressions

Objectives	
• Simplify linear algebraic expressions by collecting like terms. (L5)	
Key ideas	**Resources**
1 Know that expressions can be simplified by adding and subtracting like terms.	Simplifying 1 (1179) Two sets of cards; one set with terms such as $3x$, $5x$, x, and the other with + and – signs
Simplification	**Extension**
Use the same strategy and progression as in the previous exercise. Introduce subtraction, sometimes alone and sometimes with addition; for example, ask students to simplify $5x - 2x$ and $5x + 3x - 2x$. Use only one variable before introducing two variables.	For students who are competent at simplifying expressions, introduce a third variable. Include expressions which, when simplified, have a negative answer for one of the variables. Point out that, for example, $3y - 4y$ is written as $-y$ and not $-1y$. Blank pyramids (see question **6**)
Literacy	**Links**
Throughout this exercise, the sign – is spoken as 'subtract' or 'take away' and never as 'minus'. The word 'negative' is used only in questions late in the exercise. For example, when using a number line to simplify the *y*s in $2x + 3y + 2x - 5y$, 'negative two' is spoken for $-2y$ from reference to a number line.	Letters and numbers are not just symbols found in algebra. The combination 'MP3' is not an algebraic expression. It is an abbreviation for 'Motion Picture Expert Group (Layer 3)' invented in the 1990s. The format of recorded music has changed many times since Thomas Edison first recorded sound using tin foil wrapped around a cylinder in 1877. For much of the 20th century, records were flat discs made of black plastic. Compact cassette tape was introduced in 1963, the first CD player in 1982 and DVD discs in 1997.

Alternative approach

A game can be played with two sets of cards; one set with terms such as $3x$, $5x$, x; the other set with + and – signs. Students make expressions with a combination of cards which they then have to simplify. Alternatively, they are given an answer and have to find the cards that will give the answer.

Checkpoint

1 For $5x - 4x$

a How many *x*s are there in total? (1)

b Write the expression as simply as possible. (x)

2 For $5x - 4y$

a How many *x*s are there in total? (5)

b How many *y*s are there in total? (4)

c Write the expression as simply as possible. ($5x - 4y$, it cannot be simplified further)

3 Starting with $5x - 4y$ what do you get if you add

a y ($5x - 4y + y = 5x - 3y$) **b** $x - y$ ($5x - 4y + x - y = 6x - 5y$)

c z ($5x - 4y + z$) **d** $x + y + z$ ($5x - 4y + x + y + z = 6x - 3y + z$)

Starter – Quick fire

Continue to recap previous work. Students respond as usual on mini-whiteboards. For example, for place value and shape, ask students to

1 Identify the value of the digit 2 in the numbers 5126 and 36.2 (20, 2 tenths)
2 Add together 28 mm and 13 mm and write the total in centimetres. (4.1 cm)
3 Write the value indicated by an arrow pointing to 12.9 on a scale. (12.9)
4 Write the time 'ten to nine in the evening' using am or pm and also using the 24-hour clock. (8:50 pm and 20:50)
5 Find the perimeter of a square with sides of 6 cm. (24 cm)
6 Find the area of a square with sides of 6 cm. (36 cm^2)

Discuss answers when necessary.

Teaching notes

This exercise builds naturally on the previous exercise. The notion of 'like terms' and 'unlike terms' is revisited. Subtraction of 'like terms' is undertaken as well as addition. The process is known as *simplifying*.

Students practise the gradual progression of the exercise of the textbook, responding on mini-whiteboards. That is,

$p + p + p + q + q$ $(4p + q)$
$3p + q + 2p + 4q$ $(5p + 5q)$
$8m - 3m$ $(5m)$
$8m - 3m + 5m$ $(10m)$
$6s - 2s + 4t - 4s + 5t$ $(9t)$

Ensure that some answers need students to understand that, for example, $1x$ is written simply as x and that $0x$ is not written at all, unless it is the only answer in which case it is written simply as 0. For example,

$6x - 5x = x$ $8x - 5x - 3x + 2y + 4y = 6y$
$8x - 5x - 3x = 0$

These answers do not contain negative terms. Once confident, introduce negative terms.

Plenary

Give pairs of students these questions to mark and correct.

$5a - a = 5$ $(4a)$
$3a + 7b + 5a - 3b = 8a - 4b$ (Correct)
$14b - 5a - 5b + 7a + 3a = 9b + 5a$ (Correct)
$5a + 7b - 2a - 5b + 3a = 8ab$ $(8a + 8b)$
$4b - 7a + 15b + 3a + 4a = 19b + 0a$ $(19b)$

Discuss the outcomes with the whole class.

Exercise commentary

Question 1 – This question practices addition and subtraction within one calculation but without any use of algebra.

Question 2 – Students could write this question out in full as, for part **a**, $m + m + m + n + n$, before writing their final answer.

Question 3 – This question uses only one letter at a time. There are no questions using unlike terms. The later parts include two operations.

Question 4 – For the first time in this exercise, two different letters are used together. Students have to distinguish between like and unlike terms.

Question 5 – This is similar to Question **4** but students have to decide how best to set out their work.

Question 6 – It may be helpful to supply students with pre-drawn pyramids so that they can focus on he algebra. Part **c** requires students to 'work backwards', they should check their answer by 'working forwards'.

Answers

1	**a** 11		**b** 44		**c** 29		**d** 17	
	e 52		**f** 20					
2	**a** $3m + 2n$		**b** $4s + 2p$		**c** $5t + 6r$		**d** $7d + 3e$	
3	**a** $3t$		**b** $5g$		**c** $5h$		**d** $9x$	
	e $13p$		**f** $9q$		**g** $3m$		**h** $5b$	
	i $23c$		**j** x		**k** $4y$		**l** $19u$	
4	**a** $9a + 11b$				**b** $17x + 12y$			
	c $15f + 4h$							
5	**a** $6x + 3p$				**b** $20t + 6k$			
	c $26c + 2h$				**d** $60g + 13d$			
	e $7y + 6t$				**f** $20z + 24y$			

6 a

$3m + 10$
$2m + 5$ $m + 5$
$2m$ 5 m

b

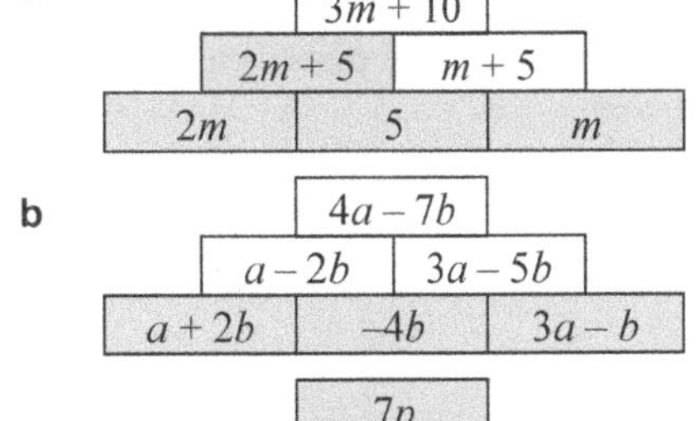

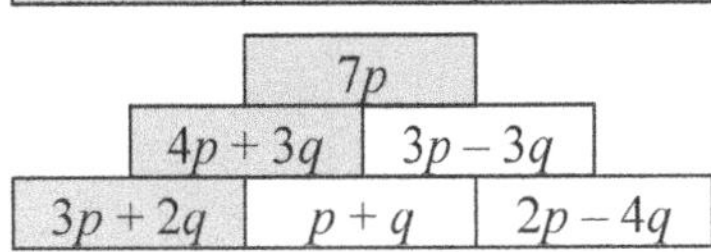

3e Substitution

Objectives	
• Substitute positive integers into linear expressions. (L5)	
Key ideas	**Resources**
1 Know that letters, which represent unknown numbers, can be given values when the number becomes known.	Substitution 1 (1187) Digit cards and cards showing addition and multiplication signs A spreadsheet program
Simplification	**Extension**
Have expressions such as $x + 3$ written large enough so that the x can be covered by small digit cards. Say that x is to be replaced by the number 4. Use the word 'substitute'. Place the digit card 4 on top of the x to produce the calculation $4 + 3$. Find its value. Repeat with other expressions.	Provide students with a list of six expressions involving several variables. Provide a list of the values of the variables and the values of the expressions. The task is to match the expressions to their correct values. Several lists could be available involving increasing levels of difficulty.
Literacy	**Links**
Explore situations where the word 'substitute' could be used. One context is in soccer. Others could be supply teachers in schools; locums in GP surgeries; sugar or sweeteners in food.	Bring in some newspapers with reports of football matches, either local or national. Substitution is used in football and other sports when an existing player is replaced by another after the match has begun. Find the details of a few matches that involved substitutions. For how long did each substituted player play?

Alternative approach

Set up a simple spreadsheet with cells labelled n and $n + 3$. Insert a value for n and check the value for $n + 3$. Contextualise the spreadsheet by saying that n is the number of miles travelled on a taxi ride and that $n + 3$ is the cost of the ride in £.

Checkpoint

1 Tom have a box containing pencils.
Sam has two more pencils than Tom. How many pencils does Sam have if Tom's box contains

- **a** n pencils ($n + 2$ pencils)
- **b** 4 pencils (6 pencils)
- **c** 12 pencils (14 pencils)

2 Sam now has twice as many pencils as Tom. How many pencils does Sam have if Tom's box contains

- **a** m pencils ($3m$ pencils)
- **b** 7 pencils (14 pencils)
- **c** 10 pencils (20 pencils)

Starter – Substitution bingo

Ask students to draw a 3×3 grid and fill it with nine numbers between 1 and 20.

Write $a = 1$, $b = 2$, $c = 3$ on the board. Students substitute the values of a, b and c into expressions you give them such as $a + b$, $5b + c$, $6b$, $5c - a$.

(3, 8, 12, 14)

If students have the answer in their grid, they cross it out. The winner is the first to cross out all nine numbers.

Teaching notes

So far, students have used a letter for the value of a number which is not known. They have used letters to stand for numbers in different contexts. They have simplified expressions involving letters. In this exercise, for the first time, we use a letter to stand for a number and then assign a value to the number. This process is known as 'substitution'.

The analogy with football where one player (a letter) is substituted by another player (a number) is worth making.

A whole-class approach has students using their mini-whiteboards. A gradual progression could be to find the values of expressions of these types

$n + 6$, $n - 2$, $3n$, when $n = 10$ (16, 8, 30)
$2x + 3$, $3x - 2$, when $n = 5$ (13, 12)
$x + y$, $2x + 3y$, when $x = 10$ and $y = 2$ (12, 26)
$2p + q - 1$, when $p = 10$ and $q = 5$ (24)

At this stage, no negative answers are included.

Questions in context can be asked, such as

A marathon runner weighs a kg at the start and b kg at the end of a run.
What does $a - b$ tell you? (The weight loss)
If $a = 70$ and $b = 66$, what is the value of $a - b$? (4)
How much does the runner lose during the run? (4 kg)

Plenary

Reinforce the short-hand notations, such as $3c$ for both $3 \times c$ and also $c + c + c$. Then, give c a value and ask for the value of $3c$. Write the values for (say) c, d and e on the board. Then present students with various expressions, such as $c + d$, $3c + d$, $3c - d$, $3c - d + e$. Students respond using their mini-whiteboards.

Exercise commentary

Question 1 – Answers to parts **a**, **b** and **c** can be written in terms of m and n before being calculated numerically.

Questions 2 – This question has algebraic answers for parts **a i** to **v** and numeric answers for part **f**.

Question 6 – In part **c**, you buy either green packs or red packs. Can students argue the case for not buying a combination of red and green packs? (There is no combination of 20 and 15 that will give 60.)

Answers

1 **a** 40 **b** 44 **c** 41 **d** 13
e 10 **f** 37

2 **a** **i** $h + 13$ **ii** $h + 14$ **iii** $4h$ **iv** $2h + 5$
v $3h + 5$
b **i** 43 **ii** 44 **iii** 120 **iv** 65
v 95

3 **a** 15 **b** 26 **c** 7 **d** 0
e 20 **f** 50 **g** 5 **h** 100

4 **a** 48 **b** 11 **c** 30 **d** 12
e 36 **f** 54 **g** 3 **h** 1

5 **a** 14 **b** 2 **c** -2 **d** 22
e 20 **f** 28

6 **a** $k + j$ **b** 35
c Either 3 large green or 4 small red

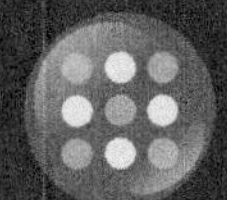

3f Creating a formula

Objectives	
• Substitute positive integers into linear expressions and formulae and, in simple cases, derive a formula. (L5)	
Key ideas	**Resources**
1 A formula is an expression into which values can be substituted. **2** A formula can be used many times with different values.	Rules and formulae (1158) Year 7 science book for looking up scientific formulas
Simplification	**Extension**
Begin with formulas involving just one operation. For example, your neighbour pays you £4 an hour for weeding his garden. Find how much the student earns for different lengths of time. Build up to the formula which is written as 'Earnings = 4 × Time'. Repeat with similar one-step formulas before introducing formulas needing two operations.	Ask students how they might make the formulas more compact to write, using ideas from algebra. Introduce letters to represent words. Explore pricing structures for mobile phones and express them as formulas.
Literacy	**Links**
The word 'formula' means a rule which is followed, rather like a recipe when baking a cake, to achieve a desired aim. In mathematics, a formula is used to find the value of something that needs to be known.	Formulas are used in science. For example, when changing temperatures from Fahrenheit to Celsius the formula is $F = \frac{9C}{5} + 32$ Formulas are also used in medicine when mixing different ingredients and 'formula milk' is a manufactured baby food made from various ingredients. 'Formula 1' is the highest class of car-racing where the word 'formula' refers to the set of rules which all the cars must comply with.

Alternative approach

Consider an example where a taxi driver charges a basic fare of £2 and then, in addition, there is a cost of £3 for every mile of the journey. A box with one hole in each of two opposite faces can be used, where a card with the mileage enters one hole and a card giving the fare exits the other hole. The machine inside the box uses a formula to work out the fare.

This example can transfer to a simple spreadhseet with two columns labelled 'Distance in miles' and 'Fare in £'.

Checkpoint

In Ellie's café, the blueberry muffins each contain 8 blueberries.

1 Use words to write a formula for the number of blueberries eaten in the café in a day.
(number of muffins ordered × 8 blueberries each = total number of blueberries)

2 Use symbols to write the formula in a shorter way. ($m \times 8 = b$)

3 How many blueberries are eaten if 7 people order muffins? ($7 \times 8 = 56$)

4 How many blueberries are eaten if 10 people order muffins? ($10 \times 8 = 80$)

5 Ellie has a punnet containing 100 blueberries.
Does she have enough blueberries to make a batch of 12 muffins? (Yes, since $12 \times 8 = 96$)

Starter – Quick fire

Continue the periodic use of **Starters** to revise and consolidate previous learning. For example

1 Add together 19 mm and 8 mm and write the total in centimetres. (2.7 cm)
2 Write the value indicated by an arrow pointing to 13.5 on a scale. (13.5)
3 A train leaves a station at 14:20. What time is this using am or pm? (2:20 pm)
4 Find the area of an L-shape containing a grid of squares. If each square is a carpet tile costing £2, what is the cost of all the tiles?
5 What is the value of $2x + 6$ when $x = 5$? (16)

Discuss answers when necessary.

Teaching notes

A formula can be thought of an expression which gives the value of one thing if we know the value of another. A formula can be expressed in words (as in the students' book where 'Number of tea bags = 2 × number of pots of tea made'.) Later, a formula can also be expressed in symbols such as '$n = 2 \times p$'.

A whole-class introduction can present various problems (in written form) which are discussed in detail. For example, a taxi driver charges a basic fare of £2 and then, in addition, there is a cost of £3 for every mile of the journey. Discuss how much the fare is for 5 miles, 10 miles, 20 miles and then any number of miles. Write a formula (in words) for the total cost using the signs +, × and = to give:

'Fare (£) = 2 + 3 × distance (miles)'.

Ask how the formula is changed if the taxi charges an extra £1 for luggage regardless of the length of the trip.

Finally, Ellie's work in the café needs discussing as a lead-in to the exercise.

Plenary

As a whole class, discuss the solutions to Questions **3**, **4** and **5**. Find a formula for a new situation; for example, the cost (in £) of making a picture frame if the charge is 40p per centimetre for each centimetre of its length and its width.

Exercise commentary

The whole exercise develops the scenario in the Student Book about Ellie working in a café.

Question 1 – Students simply write out the worded formula and replace the box by the number 3.

Question 2 – This question uses the formula in Question 1 and asks the students to substitute various values into it.

Questions 3 and **4** – These develop the scenario further and each question requires a new formula. Much discussion is useful for both questions.

Question 5 – This uses the formula created in Question **4** and asks students to substitute various values.

Question 6 – This question could usefully be repeated giving different values for the numbers of sandwiches and tomato slices. For example

14 sandwiches, 43 slices (43 – 3 × 14 = 1)
9 sandwiches, 25 slices (25 – 3 × 9 = -2)

Answers

1 Number of sandwiches × 3 = number of tomato slices
$3s = t$

2 **a** 12 **b** 9 **c** 21 **d** 27
e 30 **f** 45

3 **a** Number of customers × 2 = Number of plates
$2c = p$
b **i** 6 **ii** 8 **iii** 16 **iv** 20
v 14 **vi** 18 **vii** 40 **viii** 26

4 Number of customers × 3 = Number of items washed up
$3c = w$

5 **a** 9 **b** 12 **c** 36 **d** 42
e 75 **f** 90 **g** 150 **h** 0

6 **a** No **b** 1 fewer (= 3 × 18 – 53 = 54 – 53)

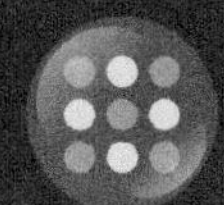

3 Expressions and formulae – MySummary

Key outcomes	Quick check
Use letters to represent unknown numbers. L5	Jenny has apacket of biscuits, it contains x biscuits. Write an expression for the number of biscuits in each situation. **a** Jenny eats 5 biscuits. $(x-5)$ **b** Karen has two packets of biscuits. $(2x)$ **c** Laura has three packets and 7 loose biscuits. $(3x+7)$ **d** Mandy has four biscuits left, how many did she eat? $(x-4)$
Simplify algebraic expressions by collecting like terms. L5	Simplify these expressions. **a** $3a+5a-6a$ $(2a)$ **b** $5b-3c+4b+4c$ $(9b+c)$ **c** $12d-4+6d$ $(18d-4)$ **d** $9e+9f$ $(9e+9f)$
Substitute whole numbers into expressions and formulae. L5	**1** Work out these expressions given $p=6$. **a** $p+5$ (11) **b** $3p$ (18) **c** $d\div 2$ (3) **d** $p\times p$ (36) **2** Work out these expressions given $s=2$ and $t=5$. **a** $s+t$ (7) **b** $t-s$ (3) **c** $2s+t$ (9) **d** $2t-3s$ (4)
Derive a simple formula. L4	In a café each customer uses a knife a fork and a spoon. **a** Write a formula for the number of pieces of cutlery used. $(c=3n)$ **b** If there were 25 customers, use the fomula toi find how many pieces of cutlery were used (75)

Development and links
Letters are used to stand for an unknown in an equation in chapter **10**. Algebra is a basic mathematical skill that will be used and developed throughout this course. Algebra is used throughout the sciences to write down laws of behaviour. Using variables allows the law to be written in a simple way that works for any numerical value. It is also used in computing to code the rules for how to perform calculations.

My Review

3 MySummary

Check out

You should now be able to ...

Check out		Test it ➡ Questions
✓ Use letters to represent unknown numbers.	5	1 - 4
✓ Simplify algebraic expressions by collecting like terms.	5	5, 6
✓ Substitute whole numbers into expressions and formulae.	5	7, 8
✓ Derive a simple formula.	6	9, 10

Language	Meaning	Example
Symbol	A letter that is used to represent a number.	In $2a + 3b$ a and b are symbols
Expression	A collection of numbers and symbols linked by operations.	$2a + 3b$ and $13q - 4q$ are expressions
Term	A group of symbols in an expression that are separated by plus or minus signs.	In $2a + 3b$ the terms are $2a$ and $3b$
Substitute	Replace a symbol with a numerical value.	In $n + 16$ If $n = 10$, $n + 16 = 26$
Formula	A statement that links quantities.	number of sandwiches × 2 = number of slices of bread

3 MyReview

1 There are n biscuits on a plate. Two biscuits are eaten, how many are left?

2 Grace has £m. Tim has twice as much money as Grace. Write an expression for the amount of money Tim has.

3 There are 15 sweets in a packet, how many sweets are there in
- **a** 8 packets
- **b** p packets
- **c** q packets plus r loose sweets?

4 A swimming pool is 25 m long. Bethany is swimming the length of the pool. How much further has she got left to swim after swimming d metres?

5 Simplify these expressions.
- **a** $a + a$
- **b** $2b + 5b$
- **c** $14c + 5c + c$

6 Simplify these expressions.
- **a** $5f - 3f$
- **b** $24g - 8g$
- **c** $18h - 6h - 7h$
- **d** $10i + 3i - 8i$

7 If $t = 5$, work out these calculations.

a $t + 4$ **b** $t - 3$
c $3 \times t$ **d** $t \times t$

8 If $v = 12$ and $w = 4$ work out these calculations.

a $v \div 2$ **b** $v + w$
c $w \times v$ **d** $w \div v$
e $v - w$ **f** $w - v$

9 Two spoons are required for every person at a dinner.
- **a** Copy and complete the formula

  number of spoons = ... × number of people
- **b** Write your formula in a shorter way, use s for the number of spoons and p for the number of people
- **c** Use your formula to calculate the number of spoons required for 12 people.

10 The length of a rectangle is 2 cm more than its width.
- **a** Write a formula for the length of rectangle. Use W for the width and L for the length in cm.
- **b** Use your formula to find the length of the rectangle if its width is 7 cm.

What next?

Score		
0 - 3		Your knowledge of this topic is still developing. To improve look at Formative test: 1A-3; MyMaths: 1158, 1179 and 1187
4 - 8		You are gaining a secure knowledge of this topic. To improve look at InvisiPen: 211, 212, 251 and 254
9 - 10		You have mastered this topic. Well done, you are ready to progress!

MyMaths.co.uk

Question commentary

Students need to understand the difference between an expression – a collection of terms with not including an equals sign – and a formula – a collection of terms including an equals sign.

Question 1 – (lessons **3a**)

Question 2 – (lesson **3b**) Accept $2 \times m$ but ask if this can be written in a shorter way.

Question 3 – (lesson **3b**) Accept $15 \times p$ in part **b** and $15 \times q + r$ in part **c**.

Question 4 – (lesson **3b**) If students answer $d - 25$ ask them to do the calculation with numbers.

Question 5 – (lesson **3c**) Only like terms are involved.

Question 6 – (lesson **3d**) Again only like terms are involved but students must now correctly handle negative coefficients.

Questions 7 and **8** – (lesson **3e**) Students should first write out the calculations.

Question 9 – (lesson **3g**) In part **b**, accept $s = 2 \times p$.

Question 10 – (lesson **3g**) Students could first write the formula in words before writing it in symbols.

Answers

1 $n - 2$

2 $2m$

3 **a** 120 **b** $15p$ **c** $15q + r$

4 $25 - d$

5 **a** $2a$ **b** $7b$ **c** $20c$

6 **a** $2f$ **b** $16g$ **c** $5h$ **d** $5i$

7 **a** 9 **b** 2 **c** 15 **d** 25

8 **a** 6 **b** 16 **c** 48 **d** 3
e 8 **f** -8

9 **a** Number of spoons = 2 × number of people
b $s = 2p$ **c** 24

10 **a** $W = L + 2$ **b** 9

3 MyPractice

3a

1 In a match box there are 50 matches.

How many matches are there in

a 2 boxes b 3 boxes c y boxes?

2 A bottle contains 100 tablets. How many tablets are there in

a 3 bottles b 4 bottles c t bottles

3b

3 Liam has m sweets.

a He gives y sweets to Sharon. How many does Liam have now?

b Then Ben gives Liam 10 sweets. How many does Liam have now?

4 Rebekah is cooking breakfast for herself, her parents and two brothers.

a She has bought q sausages, r eggs and s rashers of bacon. If everyone has one sausage, two eggs and three rashers of bacon, how many of each will she have left over?

b There were z slices of bread in the loaf and the loaf was finished after breakfast. Rebekah and her brothers each had two slices and Rebekah's parents each had one slice. What was z?

3c

5 Simplify each of these expressions.

a $2a + a$ b $5b + 2b$ c $13c + 11c$

d $10d + 6d$ e $9e + 2e + e$ f $8f + 4f + 2f$

g $4g + 4g + 4g$ h $12h + 10h + 7h$ i $19i + 6i + 5i$

6 Say if these expressions have like or unlike symbols. Simplify them if you can.

a $3p + 4q$ b $9m + 2m$ c $x + 4$

d $3y + 6 + y$ e $10 + t + 1$ f $4a + 4b$

3d

7 Collect like terms in each of these expressions.

a $3u + 7v + 5u$ b $6x + 4y + x$

c $3p + 7q + 2p + 5q$ d $3a + 5b + 2a + 4b$

e $2a + 3b + 3a + 4b + 4a$ f $12m + 6n + 7m + n + 3m$

g $9x + 3y + 7x + 2y + 5x + y$

8 Collect like terms in each of these expressions.

a $7x + 9y - 5x$ b $8u + 6v - 3u$

c $2d + 7e + 3d - 4e$ d $5q + 9r + 2q - r$

e $9p + 7q - 4p - 3q$ f $12m + 10n - 7m - 3n$

g $20c + 11d - 8c - 7d$ h $8p + 6q - 3p - 2q + 4p$

3e

9 Find the value of each expression if

★ = 4, ☺ = 3, □ = 2

a ★ + □ b ★ − ☺ c ☺ − □

d ★ + ☺ − □ e 2 × ★ f 2 × □

g 4 × ☺ h 4 × □ i 6 × ☺

j 10 × ☺

10 If $v = 4$ and $w = 6$, work out these expressions.

a $v + w$ b $2v + 3$ c $w - v$

d $2w - 2v$ e $3v - w$ f $2w - 3v$

3f

11 A gate is made from five pieces of wood, all the same length.

a Write a formula connecting the number of pieces of wood required, w, with the number of gates made, g.

b Find the number of pieces of wood needed to make

i 4 gates ii 8 gates iii 15 gates iv 20 gates.

12 The distance around your neck (n) is about seven times the distance around your thumb (t).

a Use the formula $n = 7t$ to estimate the neck measurements of people with these thumb measures.

i 5 cm ii 8 cm iii 10 cm

b Carmen has a neck measurement of 35 cm. Estimate the distance around her thumb.

MyMaths.co.uk

Question commentary

Questions 1 and **2** – These are designed to lead students towards using a variable for the number of matches or tablets respectively. Further similar examples could be used to strengthen this key idea.

Question 3 – It may be helpful to start by doing a few examples with numerical values for the number of sweets Liam starts with and gives to Sharon. Once students are confident in moving to the formula they should go back to the numerical examples and check that their formula works. part **b** uses the answer from part **a**.

Question 4 – In part **a**, first check how many people have breakfast $(1 + 2 + 2 = 5)$ and then check how many sausages, eggs and rashers of bacon are used $(1 \times 5 = 5, 2 \times 5 = 10, 3 \times 5 = 15)$. If these numbers are correct then move to finding the formulae. In part **b**, check that students are correctly calculating the number of slices of toast. $(3 \times 2 + 2 \times 1 = 8)$ The question can be extended by changing the size of the family, the number of rashers etc. eaten by adults and children or adding new ingredients.

Question 5 – This is a simple addition of like terms.

Question 6 – This requires students to identify like terms. In parts **d** and **e** you can say that there are unlike terms but that it is still possible to simplify the expressions.

Question 7 – This develops question **6**.

Question 8 – This involves subtracting terms but there are no negative numbers in the answers.

Question 9 – This is simply algebra using unconventional symbols. For parts **e** to **j** ask students how they could write the expression in a shorter way. (for example, $4 \times \square = 4\square$). To make a connection with questions **10**, ask students to rewrite the expressions using the variables x, y and z.

Question 11 – To develop confidence it may be useful to find the number of pieces of wood required to make a given number of gates before making use of a formula. Students could start by first writing the formula in words and then in symbols.

Question 12 – Part **b** requires an equation to be solved which could be done informally; equations are covered in chapter **10**.

Answers

1 **a** 100 **b** 150 **c** $50y$

2 **a** 300 **b** 400 **c** $100t$

3 **a** $m - y$ **b** $m - y + 10$

4 **a** $q - 5$ sausages, $r - 10$ eggs, $s - 15$ rashers
b 8

5 **a** $3a$ **b** $7b$ **c** $24c$ **d** $16d$
e $12e$ **f** $14f$ **g** $12g$ **h** $29h$
i $30i$

6 **a** Unlike **b** $11m$ **c** Unlike **d** $4y + 6$
e $t + 11$ **f** Unlike

7 **a** $8u + 7v$ **b** $7x + 4y$ **c** $5p + 12q$ **d** $5a + 9b$
e $9a + 7b$ **f** $22m + 7n$ **g** $21x + 6y$

8 **a** $2x + 9y$ **b** $5u + 6v$ **c** $5d + 3e$ **d** $7q + 8r$
e $5p + 4q$ **f** $5m + 7n$ **g** $12c + 4d$ **h** $9p + 4q$

9 **a** 6 **b** 1 **c** 1 **d** 5
e 8 **f** 4 **g** 12 **h** 8
i 18 **j** 30

10 **a** 10 **b** 11 **c** 2 **d** 4
e 6 **f** 0

11 **a** $w = 5g$
b **i** 20 **ii** 40 **iii** 75 **iv** 100

12 **a** **i** 35 cm **ii** 56 cm **iii** 70 cm
b 5 cm

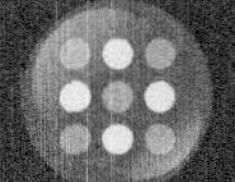

Case study 1: Dairy farm

Related lessons		Resources
Ordering whole numbers	1b	Ordering whole numbers (1217)
Decimals and money	1d	Websites on running a dairy farm, see links.
Metric units	2g	

Simplification	Extension
Students will need to build confidence in their problem solving skills. Encourage weaker students to work in pairs and share ideas with one another and then with you. The first two tasks involve simple maths and are largely an exercise in learning to find the necessary information and confidence building. Task **3** uses further information from the cowshed doors in multiplication and addition calculations. This can be broken down into the amounts eaten by individual breeds before finding the total. Avoid task **5**.	Students could explore the effect on the daily profit of changing the mix of breeds in the fifty cows in the farm's herd. This provides an opportunity to set up and use a spreadsheet: can they maximise profits whilst being constrained to fifty cows? The costs shown in the case study are not all the costs that will be incurred in reality: what other costs do students think would be involved in running a dairy farm? (Land rental, vet bills, fertilizer, etc.) Students could research some of these costs and include them in their calculations of profit or loss

Links

A useful, if US-centric, source of information on cattle breeds is http://www.ansi.okstate.edu/breeds/cattle/

There are a number of websites providing information about dairy farming in Britain. The first site is for a more general audience, the second site is more focussed on farmers.

http://www.thisisdairyfarming.com/ http://www.dairyco.org.uk/

In Hinduism, Jainism and Zoroastrianism the cow is a sacred animal that is associated with wealth, strength and abundance. Historically this may have arisen from how economically useful cattle were for providing dairy products, meat, fertilizer, fuel and tilling fields. It is still illegal to kill cows in several Indian states.

Case study 1: Dairy farm
A dairy farm is a business. The farmer sells the cows' milk to make a profit, so they must be well looked after.
Task 1
Put the cows in order by weight, lightest first.
Perfect for drinking
1st Class Butter
The best cheese
HOLSTEIN
Weight: 650 kg
Food: 24 kg per day
Number on farm: 25
JERSEY
Weight: 450 kg
Food: 18 kg per day
Number on farm: 10
BROWN SWISS
Weight: 585 kg
Food: 23 kg per day
Number on farm: 15
Task 2
How many cows are there in total in the herd?
Task 3
How much does the herd eat per day?
Task 4
How much does the food cost per day
a in summer
b in winter?
*** FARM FOOD ***
Grass ... Free (April-Sept only)
Silage ... £10 per 100 kg
PLEASE RETAIN RECEIPT
THANK YOU.
We pay
Holstein Jersey Brown Swiss
18 p 22 p 20 p
per litre
ONE COW: HOLSTEIN JERSEY BROWN SWISS
GIVES 20 LITRES 10 LITRES 16 LITRES
NUMBER IN HERD
HERD GIVES LITRES LITRES LITRES
Task 5
If the farmer sells all the milk does he make a profit each day?
Profit = Sales - Cost
62
63

Teaching notes

Many students probably give little thought to all the things that happen before milk gets to a supermarket. This case study looks at the beginning of the process – the dairy farm. Running a dairy farm, like any other business, means considering income and outgoings. Students explore some of these issues by considering the cost of feeding cattle and the returns achieved selling their milk. Students can also explore the profitability of different breeds of cow by comparing the information for each breed.

Ask the students if they have been shopping in a supermarket recently. Ask questions about the milk that was on sale: What different size containers of milk can you buy? Do you know what they cost?

Discuss how the prices might vary depending on the size of the container and also the different units of capacity that might be used - pints and litres. Determine an average price that a supermarket might charge for 1 litre of milk. Then ask, how much do you think the dairy farmer got paid for each litre of milk?

Look at the case study and ask do you think that the farmer makes a profit selling milk at that price? Discuss the meaning of profit in this case and explain that the students are going to answer this question for the farmer.

Since this is the first case study it may be useful to adopt a collective or group work approach to understanding what to do, finding the necessary information and agreeing what to calculate.

The main, technical skill required is basic arithmetic; discourage the use of a calculator unless the calculations impede developing problem solving skills.

Tasks 1 and 2

Give students the opportunity to find for themselves the information about weights and numbers on the cow shed doors, offering pointers only as necessary.

Task 3

Ask students to talk to a partner about how they would work out the total weight of food eaten per day by the herd. Hear student's ideas and then give them time to calculate the answer. Discuss the different strategies students used when calculating their answers.

Task 4

Look at information about the cost of the food, white receipt at the bottom of the page. Discuss how the cost of buying silage (moist, fermented grass; often seen as plastic wrapped round bales) is only incurred for the six months from October to March, or half a year.

Take this opportunity to ask, how do you calculate the average daily cost of feeding the cattle? Hear students' ideas and as necessary remind them that the average is for the whole year before giving them time to calculate their answers.

Task 5

This is a more complicated task and suitable questions can be used to break it into sub-tasks. Ask how much milk is produced by the herd and direct them to the churns. The total yield is 840 litres per day but they will need this broken down by breed of cow. There is opportunity to discuss mental methods for doing some of the calculations. For the Brown Swiss, 15 × 16 can be done as 10 × 16 plus half as much again.

Ask how much money do you make selling the milk from the Holstein cows. Allow students to find the price per litre on the side of the tanker. Since the price is in pence students should consider converting their answers to pounds. Once students have successfully done this calculation ask them to repeat it for the Jersey and Brown Swiss cows before checking their total income from sales.

Finally ask if the farm makes a profit or a loss each day. Students should treat summer months and winter months separately and also consider a daily average over a whole year.

Answers

1 Jersey, Brown Swiss, Holstein

2 50

3 25 × 24 + 10 × 18 + 15 × 23
= 600 + 180 +345
= 1125 kg

4 **a** Free **b** £112.50

5 Yields table

	Holstein	Jersey	Brown Swiss
Yield per cow	20	10	16
No in herd	25	10	15
Litres	500	100	240

Sales = 500 × 0.18 + 100 × 0.22 + 240 × 0.20
= 90 + 22 + 48
= £160

Profit (Summer) = £160

Profit (Winter) = 160 – 112.50 = £47.50

Average daily profit = £103.75

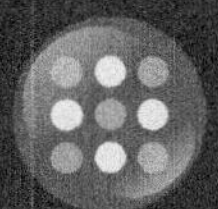

4 Fractions, decimals and percentages

Learning outcomes	
N4 Use the 4 operations, including formal written methods, applied to integers, decimals, proper and improper fractions, and mixed numbers, all both positive and negative.	(L4/5)
N9 Work interchangeably with terminating decimals and their corresponding fractions (such as 3.5 and $\frac{7}{2}$ or 0.375 and $\frac{3}{8}$.	(L5)
N10 Define percentage as 'number of parts per hundred', interpret percentages and percentage changes as a fraction or a decimal, interpret these multiplicatively, express 1 quantity as a percentage of another, compare 2 quantities using percentages, and work with percentages greater than 100%.	(L4)

Introduction

The chapter starts by looking at simple fractions of the whole before moving on to equivalent fractions, improper fractions and fractions of an amount. Percentages are introduced with two different aspects covered: finding percentages of amounts and converting between percentages, decimals and fractions.

The introduction discusses how the use of fractions developed over time. Since the very first fractions can be traced back to ancient Egypt, they have obviously been in use for thousands of years. With a few exceptions ($\frac{1}{2}, \frac{2}{3}, \frac{3}{4}$) Egyptian fractions were always given as unit fractions in the form 'one over'. All other fractions were written as a sum of unit fractions.

For example: 'two fifths' of a quantity was written as 'one third' plus 'one fifteenth'.

A detailed and interesting article on the history of Egyptian mathematics can be found here.

http://www.maths.surrey.ac.uk/hosted-sites/R.Knott/Fractions/egyptian.html

Prior knowledge

Students should already know how to…

- Interpret place value for decimals
- Carry out basic arithmetic including division

Starter problem

The starter problem requires students to divide up a 3 cm by 4 cm rectangle into four fractions which together make up the whole rectangle. This idea of 'unit fractions' summing to a whole follows on from the introduction where Egyptian fractions are considered.

Students are invited to draw different sized rectangles and repeat the process, deriving different unit fraction sums which add to a whole. Examples might include a 3 cm by 6 cm rectangle which can be divided up using $\frac{1}{2}, \frac{1}{3}$ and $\frac{1}{6}$.

Generally, areas which have lots of factors, such as 12 and 18, are easier to divide up. A 3 cm by 5 cm rectangle, for example, cannot be divided up without repeating unit fractions of the same amount.

Resources

MyMaths

Fractions of amounts	1018	Improper and mixed fractions			1019
Fractions, decimals and percentages 1			1029	Percentages of amounts 1	1030
Simple fractions	1220	More fractions	1370	Simple equivalent fractions	1371

Online assessment		**InvisiPen solutions**			
Chapter test	1A–4	Fractions	141	Fraction of a quantity	142
Formative test	1A–4	Percentage of an amount	151	Percentages	162
Summative test	1A–4				

Topic scheme

Teaching time = 8 lessons/3 weeks

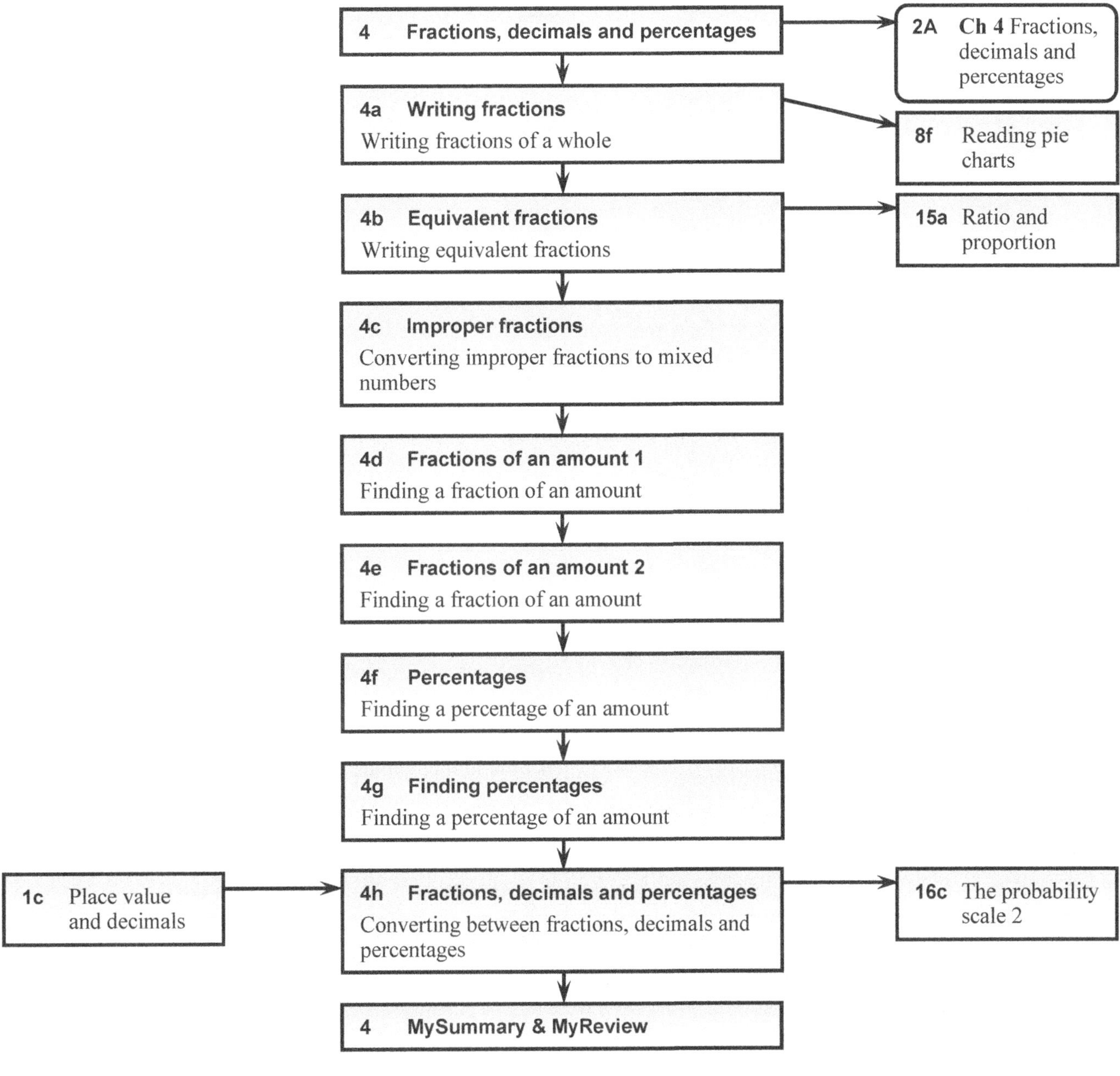

Differentiation

Student book 1A 64 – 85

Writing fractions
Equivalent fractions
Improper fractions
Fractions of an amount
Percentages
Finding percentages
Converting fractions, decimals and percentages

Student book 1B 62 – 83

Finding fractions of amounts
Using equivalent fractions
Adding and subtracting fractions
Converting from decimals to fractions
Percentages
Converting fractions, decimals and percentages
Finding percentages of amounts

Student book 1C 64 – 81

Fraction notation
Adding and subtracting fractions
Decimals and fractions
Finding fractions of amounts
Percentages
Converting fractions, decimals and percentages

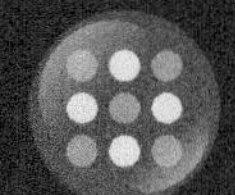

4a Writing fractions

Objectives	
• Use simple fractions that are several parts of a whole. (L3)	
Key ideas	**Resources**
1 Make sure a shape is divided into equal pieces before finding at fraction of it. **2** Count how many pieces there are (the denominator) and how many you want (the numerator) before writing the fraction.	Simple fractions (1220) More fractions (1370) Sheets showing rectangles made up of small squares Square grid paper or mini-whiteboards
Simplification	**Extension**
To find a fraction, ask the questions which give the numerator and denominator: that is, 'Into how many pieces has the shape been divided?' and 'How many of these pieces are shaded?' Check that the pieces are all the same size. The further question 'What fraction of the shape is *not* shaded?' can be used to test the depth of a student's understanding.	A giant pizza is cut into 12 equal pieces and shared between four friends. One person has three pieces and two others have two pieces each. What fraction of the pizza is left for the fourth friend? Ask a similar question for a chocolate bar marked into 12 pieces. Students work in pairs to invent similar problems and give them to their partners to solve.
Literacy	**Links**
The words 'numerator' and 'denominator' should be known. The prefix *de-* often indicates 'down' or 'under' as in the words 'decrease', 'deflate', 'dethrone'. It is even more important, however, to name fractions correctly. For example, the name of $\frac{3}{5}$ is 'three-fifths' and not 'three over five' or 'three out of five'.	Modern pizza is often served whole but cut into pieces which are fractions of the whole. You can also buy a single piece. The pizza is descended from types of flat bread eaten with olive oil and spices by the Greeks, Romans and Egyptians. Tomatoes were introduced to Europe from America in the 16th century and the people in the Naples area of Italy started to put tomatoes on their bread. The colours on a Margherita pizza are thought to represent the Italian flag: red (tomatoes), white (mozzarella cheese) and green (basil).

Alternative approach

Use MyMaths lesson 1220 ('Simple fractions') to introduce and begin to use fractions.

Checkpoint

1 Show a rectangle divided up into eight equal squares.
- **a** How many equal parts are there? (8)
- **b** Shade one square.
  - **i** How many squares are shaded? (1)
  - **ii** What fraction of the shape is shaded? ($\frac{1}{8}$, one-eighth)

2 Shade three squares
- **a** **i** How many squares are shaded? (3)
  - **ii** What fraction of the shape is shaded? ($\frac{3}{8}$, three-eighths)
- **b** What fraction of the shape remains unshaded? ($\frac{3}{8}$, five-eighths)

Starter – Unit fractions

Ask students to

- Draw a 3×4 rectangle.
- Colour in one half of the rectangle.
- Colour in one quarter of the rectangle.
- Colour in one sixth of the rectangle.

What fraction of the rectangle is left uncoloured? ($\frac{1}{12}$)

Teaching notes

Some students may meet fractions written as a numerator and denominator when their work is marked as, for example $\frac{7}{10}$.

Other more visual examples use 2D shapes, parts of which are shaded – such as a square divided into four equal parts with one part shaded and identified as $\frac{1}{4}$.

Students need to practise the appropriate vocabulary for everyday fractions, particularly one-half, one-third, two-thirds, one-quarter, three-quarters, one-fifth, one-tenth. Students may incorrectly say, for example, 'one over five' instead of the correct 'one-fifth'.

Plenary

Give students a sheet showing six rectangles divided into 3, 4, 5, 6, 8 and 10 small squares or rectangles. Ask them, in pairs, to shade in $\frac{2}{3}, \frac{3}{4}, \frac{2}{5}, \frac{1}{6}, \frac{5}{8}, \frac{3}{10}$, respectively.

Ask them which of the rectangles have more than half of the rectangle shaded. ($\frac{2}{3}$, $\frac{3}{4}$ and $\frac{5}{8}$)

Compare these three fractions with the fractions for those rectangles that have less than a half shaded. Can you explain how you can tell simply by looking at the fractions which are more than a half and which are less than a half? (The numerator is more than or less than half the denominator.)

Exercise commentary

Question 1 – Students are asked to write the fraction shaded. In all these questions, the numerator is 1.

Question 2 – Numerators are greater than 1. Point out that the amount eaten added to the amount left, that is $\frac{3}{8}$ and $\frac{5}{8}$, gives $\frac{3}{8}$.

Question 3 – As in Question **2**, it can be pointed out that each pair of answers should add to give 1.

Question 4 – It may be helpful to ask pairs of students to explain to each another how they decide which fraction and diagram formed pairs and any strategies they used to find all the pairs.

Question 5 – This question reiterates the point that all parts in earlier questions have been *equal parts*. Students to look carefully at the diagram and realise that Lydia has not cut the pizza into equal pieces.

Answers

1	**a** $\frac{1}{6}$	**b** $\frac{1}{2}$	**c** $\frac{1}{5}$	**d** $\frac{1}{12}$
2	**a** $\frac{3}{8}$	**b** $\frac{5}{8}$		
3	**a** $\frac{2}{5}$	**b** $\frac{3}{10}$	**c** $\frac{4}{9}$	**d** $\frac{5}{6}$
4	**a** $\frac{1}{8}$	**b** $\frac{2}{3}$	**c** $\frac{1}{4}$	**d** $\frac{1}{10}$
	e $\frac{4}{7}$	**f** $\frac{3}{4}$	**g** $\frac{1}{6}$	**h** $\frac{3}{5}$
	i $\frac{3}{8}$	**j** $\frac{1}{5}$		

5 No There are four pieces but they are not equal in size.

Objectives	
• Recognise when two simple fractions are equivalent. (L3)	
Key ideas	**Resources**
1 The same fraction can be written with different numerators and denominators. **2** Multiplying or dividing the numerator and denominator by the same number creates an equivalent fraction.	Simple equivalent fractions (1371) Cards containing pairs of diagrams showing two equivalent fractions
Simplification	**Extension**
Base much of the early work around the $\frac{1}{2}$, $\frac{1}{4}$, $\frac{1}{8}$ family and the $\frac{1}{3}$, $\frac{1}{6}$ family. Make the work practical by drawing fractions, of rectangles or circles, so that students are clear on the meaning of numerator, denominator and equivalence.	Ask students to use numbers less than 36 and 48 to find as many fractions as they can which are equivalent to the fraction $\frac{36}{48}$. ($\frac{3}{4}$, $\frac{6}{8}$, $\frac{9}{12}$, $\frac{12}{16}$, $\frac{15}{20}$, $\frac{18}{24}$, $\frac{21}{28}$, $\frac{24}{32}$, $\frac{27}{36}$ $\frac{30}{40}$ and $\frac{33}{44}$)
Literacy	**Links**
The word 'equivalent' is close in meaning to the word 'equal'. We can say that, if two fractions are equal, then they are equivalent fractions. When finding equivalent fractions by multiplying or dividing the 'top' and 'bottom' of a fraction, the use of two curved arrows, as in the Student Book, labelled by the operation, such as × 2, is a useful visual support.	Musical notation uses fractions. If a crotchet is taken as a whole note or a single beat, then the semibreve lasts for four beats and the minim for two beats. Fractions are used for the quaver (half of a beat) and a semiquaver (a quarter of a beat). A dot after a note means that it lasts for half as long again. How many different lengths of note can the class find using the above information? The musical notation for each of the notes is given at in the 'Rhythm and metre' section her. www.bbc.co.uk/schools/gcsebitesize/music/musicalelements/rhythmandmetrerev3.shtml

Alternative approach

In addition to the cards used in the **Teaching notes,** a useful approach is found in MyMaths lesson 1029 'Fractions, Decimals and Percentages Intro'.

Checkpoint

1 Show a rectangle divided up into eight equal squares.

a Shade two squares.

i How many squares are shaded? (1)

ii How many eights are shaded? (2)

iii What fraction is shaded? ($\frac{2}{8}$, two-eights)

b **i** How do you turn the fraction $\frac{2}{8}$ into quarters?

(Multiply the numerator (top) and denominator (bottom) by 2)

ii What is the equivalent fraction? ($\frac{1}{4}$)

c Find another fractions equivalent to $\frac{2}{8}$? ($\frac{3}{12}$, $\frac{4}{16}$, $\frac{5}{20}$ …)

Starter – How big?

Pose the situation where you are making a patio in your garden and you can choose between two sizes of paving stones. Show two rectangles to represent the patio: one is divided into four smaller equal rectangles; the other into eight smaller equal rectangles.

Shade a quarter of the first rectangle and two-eighths of the second. Ask which of the two larger rectangles is shaded the most. Agree that both are shaded the same, so that $\frac{1}{4} = \frac{2}{8}$.

Repeat with other pairs of equivalent fractions.

Teaching notes

Without a visual approach, some students may say, for example, that $\frac{4}{10}$ appears larger than $\frac{2}{5}$. So it is important that this work is approached visually using diagrams. The pairs of equivalent fractions of the **Starter** make the point that fractions can have different names and be written using different numerators and denominators, but they can still have the same value. Stress the words 'equivalent fractions' rather than 'equal fractions'.

Give pairs of students a pack of cards in which pairs of cards show diagrams of equivalent fractions. Students match the pairs. They then write the equivalent fractions that they have found.

Discuss that equivalent fractions can be found by multiplying the numerator and denominator by the same number, for example, doubling or trebling them. Once confident, discuss that they can also be found by dividing the numerator and denominator.

Plenary

The teacher has a pack of cards similar to the pack used by the students: it has pairs of cards showing diagrams of similar fractions. The teacher holds up a matching pair and the students write the equivalent fractions on their mini-whiteboards.

Exercise commentary

Question 1 – This provides an opportunity to test students' basic understanding.

Question 2 – Students should first write the fraction from each diagram and then find an equivalent fraction.

Question 3 – Emphasise that whatever multiplication or division is performed on the 'top' should also be performed on the 'bottom'.

Question 4 – As an initial strategy, if the pies are drawn on separate pieces of tracing paper as equal rectangles, students can overlay to compare them. The method needs careful drawing. A second method uses equivalent fractions with a denominator of 35.

Answers

1	**a** $\frac{1}{3}$	**b** $\frac{1}{2}$	**c** $\frac{1}{4}$	**d** $\frac{1}{4}$
	e $\frac{1}{2}$	**f** $\frac{1}{3}$	**g** $\frac{1}{4}$	**h** $\frac{1}{3}$
2	**a** $\frac{1}{2}$	**b** $\frac{1}{3}$	**c** $\frac{1}{4}$	
3	**a** 3	**b** 1	**c** 2	**d** 9
	e 3	**f** 1		
4	Apple pie			

Objectives	
• Change improper fractions to mixed numbers.	(L4)
• Change mixed numbers to improper fractions.	(L4)

Key ideas	Resources
1 An improper fraction has a numerator greater than its denominator. **2** A mixed number contains a whole number and a fraction. **3** An improper fraction can be writted as a mixed number.	Improper and mixed fractions (1019) Cards representing whole pizzas and fractions of pizzas

Simplification	Extension
The visual use of diagrams is essential throughout this exercise. Initially, keep the fraction 'families' restricted to halves, thirds and quarters. Students should initially have diagrams where circles and rectangles (representing pizzas, pies or bars of chocolate) are already divided into equal pieces. Much discussion is essential to relate diagrams to fractions.	Students who are competent with improper fractions are asked to design a challenge for a friend. They choose, say, four improper fractions, find their equivalents as mixed numbers, and draw appropriately shaded diagrams. The challenge is for the friend to match each improper fraction with a mixed number and a diagram.

Literacy	Links
Words beginning with *im-* often (but not always) mean 'not'. For example, with 'immature', 'immobile', 'immoral', 'imperfect', 'improper', *im-* means 'not'. But with 'important', 'image', 'impact', 'improve' it does not have the same meaning. To make an improper fraction 'proper', it is changed to a mixed number. An improper fraction is sometimes called a 'top-heavy' fraction.	In the game 'Trivial Pursuit', players answer questions to collect coloured wedges. Each plastic wedge fits into a circular 'pie'. The first player to complete his or her pie with six different coloured wedges and answer a final question wins the game. Each wedge is $\frac{1}{6}$ of the pie. How many pies would 15 wedges fill? There is more information about the history of Trivial Pursuit here. www.inventors.about.com/library/inventors/bl_trivia_pursuit.htm

Alternative approach

A computer-based approach can be found in MyMaths lesson 1019 'Improper and mixed fractions'.

Such an approach should be reinforced with the physical manipulation of pieces which make wholes.

Checkpoint

1 Draw two circles, they could be pizzas, both divided into quarters.

a Shade a quarter.

i What fraction is this piece? ($\frac{1}{4}$)

ii How many pieces are there like this one? (8)

iii Write the total number of pieces as an improper fraction. ($\frac{8}{4}$)

b Shade two quarters.

i How many pieces are left? (6)

ii Write the number of pieces left as an improper fraction? ($\frac{6}{4}$)

iii Write the improper fraction as a mixed number? ($1\frac{2}{4} = 1\frac{1}{2}$)

Starter – Pieces of pizzas

Show students five semicircles, all the same size, and say that they represent halves of pizzas. Ask how you can write five halves as a fraction. ($\frac{5}{2}$)

A fraction with a numerator larger than the denominator is called an 'improper fraction' because it is 'top heavy'.

Ask how many whole pizzas can be made and rewrite it as $2\frac{1}{2}$. This fraction is called a 'mixed number' because it is partly a whole number and partly a fraction.

Teaching notes

Repeat the **Starter** with other fractions of pizzas cut from card – such as seven quarters and eight thirds. Discuss making whole pizzas from the fractions. Write each fraction as both an improper fraction and a mixed number.

The reverse process can be discussed. For example, you show three pizzas to students. You cut one of them into quarters and eat three of the quarters. Ask students to draw the pizzas that you have left on their mini-whiteboards. Ask them to write a mixed number to label what they have drawn. Ask them to cut the pizzas into quarters on their mini-whiteboards and write an improper fraction next to their mixed number. Point out that, for example, $\frac{4}{4}$ is equivalent to one

whole and we can write $\frac{4}{4} = 1$.

Plenary

Students work in pairs with their mini-whiteboards. Each student draws a diagram of a mixed number of pizzas and writes a mixed number. They exchange whiteboards and write the equivalent improper fractions. They discuss their results and then repeat.

Exercise commentary

Question 1 – Students have to visualise (or draw) five pieces being removed and then count the pieces left.

Question 2 – Remind students that $\frac{3}{3}$ and $\frac{4}{4}$ are both equal to 1.

Question 3 – See that students write the figure for the whole number part of a mixed number in larger script than the figures used in the fractional part.

Questions 5 and **6** – For some students, diagrams can be used to explain the method.

Question 7 – As a further problem, ask students 'If you had four cakes, into how many pieces would you need to cut each cake into so that all students in the class get one piece each? How many pieces would be left over?'

Answers

1	**a**	$\frac{7}{4} = 1\frac{3}{4}$						
2	**a**	6	**b**	12	**c**	$\frac{8}{2}$	**d**	$\frac{15}{5}$
3	**a**	$3\frac{1}{2}$	**b**	$4\frac{2}{3}$	**c**	$2\frac{5}{6}$	**d**	$1\frac{3}{5}$
4	**a i**	$\frac{11}{4}$	**ii**	$2\frac{3}{4}$				
	b i	$\frac{47}{10}$	**ii**	$4\frac{7}{10}$				
5	**a**	$2\frac{1}{2}$	**b**	$3\frac{1}{3}$	**c**	$4\frac{1}{2}$	**d**	$2\frac{1}{4}$
	e	$2\frac{3}{5}$	**f**	$2\frac{3}{4}$	**g**	$2\frac{4}{5}$	**h**	$6\frac{1}{3}$
	i	$2\frac{2}{7}$						
6	**a**	$\frac{3}{2}$	**b**	$\frac{5}{4}$	**c**	$\frac{5}{2}$	**d**	$\frac{8}{3}$
	e	$\frac{19}{5}$	**f**	$\frac{24}{7}$	**g**	$\frac{17}{6}$	**h**	$\frac{28}{9}$
	i	$\frac{35}{8}$						
7	**a**	5	**b**	$3\frac{3}{5}$				

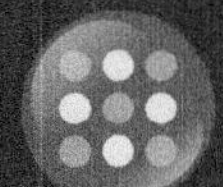

4d Fractions of an amount 1

Objectives

- Calculate simple fractions of quantities and measurements. (L4)

Key ideas

1. Appreciate the visual link between a fraction of a shape and a fraction of a number.
2. The link between finding a fraction of a number and division.

Resources

Fractions of amounts (1018)

Pairs of rectangular cards: the one showing a fraction of the area; the other showing the fraction of a number
Digital scales and some rice
Small objects such as counters

Simplification

Use counters to share a number equally into parts. The line of questioning is "How many sweets do you have altogether? Can you share them equally between two (three, four) people? How many will each person have? What is a half (third, quarter) of …?"
Write down a division and a fraction calculation and link them with the action of 'sharing'. Emphasise that finding a fraction is the same as doing a division.

Extension

More able students are given questions with non-integer answers. For example, find $\frac{1}{2}$ of 15 ($7\frac{1}{2}$), $\frac{1}{4}$ of 13 ($3\frac{1}{4}$), $\frac{1}{3}$ of 10 ($3\frac{1}{3}$). None of these answers have multiple-fractions, that is, the numerators in fractional parts of the answers are always 1. Questions can be set in context; for example, 'If a recipe requires a third of a 100 gram tube of tomato puree, what weight of puree is needed?'

Literacy

The words 'divide' and 'share' are interchangeable. These three statements are different ways of expressing the same process of 'sharing' or 'dividing:

$\frac{1}{3}$of 21 = $\frac{21}{3}$ = 21 ÷ 3

Links

Bring in some used postage stamps for the class to use. Before 1840, the person receiving a letter had to pay the postage cost. In 1840 postage stamps were introduced and the sender paid one penny to post a letter anywhere in the UK. Pictures of postage stamps from the 1840s can be found here

http://en.wikipedia.org/wiki/Penny_Black

and at

www.postalheritage.org.uk/page/gbstamps

How much did it cost to post a letter in the past? When were half-pennies used? Compare with modern designs and today's cost of postage.

Alternative approach

Use weight rather than area as the measure to be divided. Use digital scales to weigh 36 grams of rice. Ask students how the rice can be shared amongst three people. Measure the amount three times to check that their method is correct. Write $\frac{1}{3}$of 36 = $\frac{36}{3}$ = 36 ÷ 3 = 12 grams each. Repeat by sharing the rice among 4 people and then between 2 people.

Checkpoint

1. There are 24 counters
   - **a** How many counters would each person get if they were divided equally amoung three people? (8)
   - **b** What fraction of the 24 counters each person has received ($\frac{1}{3}$)
   - **c** Complete the statement: $\frac{1}{3}$ of 24 = □ = □ = □ ($\frac{1}{3}$ of 24 = $\frac{24}{3}$ = 24 ÷ 3 = 8)

This can be illustrateded by dividing out 24 counters or other small objects.

Starter – Quick fire

This lesson requires division, so students practise recall of multiplication and division facts. They use their mini-whiteboards to respond to calculations such as 6×5, $30 \div 5$ and $30 \div 6$.

Questions can also be asked in context, such as "How many tins are packed in a box of 4 rows with 8 tins in each row?" and "If there are 32 tins in a box with 8 tins in each row, how many rows are in the box?"

Teaching notes

Fractions can be set in two contexts: fractions of shapes and fractions of a number or quantity. Fractions of shapes have already been studied in earlier lessons. This lesson begins to explore fractions of a number or quantity.

Show students a rectangle divided into equal parts with some parts shaded. Ask them for the total number of parts (the denominator), the number of shaded parts (the numerator), and the fraction of the shape which is shaded.

Now present them with a rectangle of the same size on which is drawn an array of (say) 12 'hollow' dots. Shade half the dots. Ask students for the total number of dots, the number of shaded dots, and the fraction of dots which are shaded. If the answer $\frac{6}{12}$ is given, agree that this is $\frac{1}{2}$. Ask them for $\frac{1}{2}$ of 12. Also ask them how many dots each person would have if shared equally between two people. Write two statements:

$\frac{1}{2}$ of $12 = 6$ and $12 \div 2 = 6$.

Agree that these two statements are different ways of writing the same fact.

Repeat with the same 12 dots split into 4 equal groups by shading one quarter of them. Establish that $\frac{1}{4}$ of $12 = 3$ and $12 \div 4 = 3$. Repeat with $\frac{1}{3}$ of 12 to establish $\frac{1}{3}$ of $12 = 4$ and $12 \div 3 = 4$. Emphasise that finding a fraction of a number is the same as dividing by the denominator.

Write, for example, $\frac{1}{2}$ of 8 and $8 \div 2$ and ask for the answers without a diagram. Ask students for $\frac{1}{3}$ of 15, $\frac{1}{4}$ of 8 and $\frac{1}{2}$ of 18 without providing diagrams.

It is important for students to see the questions written as well as to hear them asked. Students can write their answers on mini-whiteboards.

Plenary

Students write three questions to find fractions of quantities on their mini-whiteboards. They exchange boards with a partner and work out the answers. They change back and discuss their answers. Repeat.

Exercise commentary

Question 1 – These divisions have no remainders. You could ask students to use their answers to find $\frac{1}{2}$ of 8, $\frac{1}{3}$ of 9 etc.

Question 2 – This question reinforces, yet again, that finding a fraction requires a division.

Question 4 – Some students might need copies of these diagrams so that they can group the sweets into three groups for part **a**, four groups for part **b**, etc. Great care is needed: 'making four groups' is not the same as 'making groups of 4'. In part **b**, 'making four groups' finds quarters of 12, whereas (in this case) 'making groups of 4' makes thirds of 12.

Extreme care needs to be taken when phrasing questions and giving instructions.

Question 5 – Part **a** involves a fraction. Part **b** does not involve fractions.

Question 6 – This question can be interpreted two ways. It could be said that Harry has not eaten a whole cake; he only eats one fifth of a cake each time. However, it can be interpreted in terms of Harry eating the equivalent of whole cakes. In this case, students have to work out 40 fifths as a whole number.

Answers

1 **a** $8 \div 2 = 4$ **b** $9 \div 3 = 3$
c $10 \div 5 = 2$ **d** $12 \div 4 = 3$
e $15 \div 3 = 5$ **f** $18 \div 6 = 3$

2 **a** 5 **b** 10 **c** 2 **d** 8

3 2

4 **a** 3 **b** 3 **c** 3 **d** 4
e 4 **f** 4

5 **a** $\frac{1}{8}$ **b** 8

6 8

4e Fractions of an amount 2

Objectives

- Use division to calculate multiple fractions of a quantity. (L5)

Key ideas	Resources
1 Find a unit fraction of a quantity by dividing. **2** Find a multiple fraction of a quantity by multiplying the unit fraction.	Fractions of amounts (1018) A selection of similar objects Rectangular cards with various sizes grids on them, such as 3×4 and 3×5 Digital scales and some rice Small objects such as counters

Simplification	Extension
Use the same strategy and line of questioning as in **Exercise 4d**. When sharing among, say, three people, extend the process by asking how many sweets two people will have. When students use fractions beyond halves, quarters and thirds, use fifths and tenths before those fractions requiring the more awkward 'times tables'. Having a 10×10 multiplication grid to hand will be useful for the more awkward number facts.	As with **Exercise 4d**, more able students are given questions requiring non-integer answers. Both questions and answers can now have multiple-fractions. For example, find $\frac{3}{4}$ of 20, $\frac{3}{4}$ of 21, $\frac{3}{4}$ of 19. ($15, 15\frac{3}{4}, 14\frac{1}{4}$) Questions can also be set in context; for example, if a recipe requires two-thirds of 40 ml of olive oil, what is the volume of oil needed?

Literacy	Links
A 'unit fraction' is a fraction having a numerator of 1. A 'multiple fraction' is thus a multiple of a unit fraction.	Different varieties of bird lay eggs of different sizes; usually the larger the bird, the larger the egg. A chicken egg weighs about 55 g. An ostrich egg weighs about 1400 g, while some hummingbird eggs weigh only 0.5 g. How many hummingbird eggs would equal the weight of an ostrich egg? Students could research the weight of eggs from different birds and express them as fractions.

Alternative approach

Again, weight rather than area can be used as the measure to be divided. Use digital scales, as before, to weigh 36 grams of rice. Ask students how the rice can be shared among three people. Measure the amount three times to check that their method is correct. Write $\frac{1}{3}$ of $36 = \frac{36}{3} = 36 \div 3 = 12$. Now continue by saying that two people combine their shares. Ask what two-thirds of 36 will be. Write $\frac{2}{3}$ of $36 = 2 \times 12 = 24$.

Checkpoint

Give the student 12 counters, or other small objects, and ask them to place the counters into 3 equal groups.

How many counters are in each group? (4)
What is one-third of 12? Write the answer as a statement. ($\frac{1}{3}$ of $12 = 4$)
What is two-thirds of the counters? Write the answer as a statement. ($\frac{2}{3}$ of $12 = 8$)

Repeat for quarters of 12, finding $\frac{1}{4}$ and $\frac{3}{4}$ of 12 in turn. ($\frac{1}{4}$ of $12 = 3$; $\frac{3}{4}$ of $12 = 9$)

Starter – Quick fire

Recap work of previous chapters and this chapter so far. Ask rapid response questions. Ask students to reply by writing on their mini-whiteboards. Discuss questions when their answers indicate a need.

Teaching notes

This exercise consolidates and extends the work of **Exercise 4d**. The link between finding a fraction and doing a division is reinforced.

Initially, students see a collection of, say, 15 objects, see them divided into, say, 3 groups (to find thirds), and see the sharing process recorded as $15 \div 3$, $\frac{15}{3}$ and $\frac{1}{3}$ of 15. These equivalents represent the words spoken during the act of sharing.

Extend the discussion to find multiple fractions. Having established that $\frac{1}{3}$ of $15 = 5$, ask how many groups are needed to find two-thirds and how many objects are there in two-thirds. Establish that $\frac{2}{3}$ of $15 = 2 \times 5 = 10$. Repeat, for example, with finding three-quarters of 16.

A rectangle divided into 4 rows of 5 squares can be used to find fractions such as $\frac{3}{4}$ of 20 (15) and $\frac{2}{5}$ of 20 (8). Students shade the relevant fractions of the rectangle, (for example, firstly $\frac{1}{4}$ and then $\frac{3}{4}$) and then count the relevant squares. Students will find it useful to have several diagrams where the grid is already drawn without any shading.

Plenary

Students are shown diagrams of objects in groups; for example, 15 dots divided into 3 groups. They are asked to find $\frac{1}{3}$ of 15 and $\frac{2}{3}$ of 15 and write answers on their mini-whiteboards. (5, 10)

Diagrams of rectangular arrays can then be shown and similar questions asked.

Questions can be asked (both orally and in writing) without any diagrams; for example, find $\frac{1}{4}$ of 20 and find $\frac{3}{4}$ of 20. Finally, questions are given only orally. (5, 15)

Exercise commentary

Questions 1 to **4** all make the link between finding a fraction and doing a division. Some students may need a multiplication grid on hand for some of the number facts required.

Question 2 – This question assumes that you may support neither team but you certainly won't support both teams!

Question 3 – For part **a**, the way the diagram is drawn lends itself to easily visualising three groups of buttons with four buttons in each group. So $\frac{1}{3}$ of all the buttons is 4. This visual method does not rely on counting the total number of buttons. Counting and dividing is an alternative method. However, for part **b**, it is difficult to visualise this diagram sub-divided into four equal groups to find quarters. The best method here is to count all 12 and divide by 4.

Question 5 – A preliminary discussion needs to establish that there were three different ways of voting, that every one of the 21 people voted, and that there were no spoiled ballot papers. References to voting in UK local and general elections would be appropriate.

Question 6 requires a blank copy of the diagram for the second part.

Answers

1 **a** $\frac{1}{3}$ of $9 = 3$ **b** $\frac{1}{3}$ of $27 = 9$
c $\frac{1}{4}$ of $16 = 4$ **d** $\frac{1}{5}$ of $40 = 8$
e $\frac{1}{4}$ of $24 = 6$ **f** $\frac{1}{5}$ of $25 = 5$
g $\frac{1}{4}$ of $28 = 7$ **h** $\frac{1}{3}$ of $30 = 10$

2 **a** 5 **b** 4 **c** 11

3 **a** 8 **b** 9

4 **a** £8

8 1

9 $\frac{1}{2}$ of $24 = 12$ $\frac{1}{4}$ of $24 = 6$
$\frac{2}{3}$ of $24 = 16$ $\frac{3}{4}$ of $24 = 18$
$\frac{1}{6}$ of $24 = 4$ $\frac{1}{3}$ of $24 = 8$

Objectives

- 'Understand percentages as the number of parts per 100'. (L4)
- Calculate simple percentages. (L4)
- Recognise the equivalence of fractions, decimals and percentages. (L4)

Key ideas

1 A percentage is a type of fraction.
2 A percentage is a number of hundreths which is written using the % sign

Resources

Percentages of amounts (1030)

Large squares divided into 10 equal strips or into 100 equal small squares

A metre rule marked in cm but not mm

Simplification

There are two simplified approaches.

Restrict students initially to seeing 50%, 25%, 75% as fractions (half, quarter, three-quarters) of the whole 100%, followed by 10% and its multiples. Given a sound understanding of the fractions, these percentages can become secure. However, the notion of 'percentage' as 'hundredth' is not central to this approach.

The other approach is to take the line developed later in these notes, where 1% is the first major focus and other percentages are built up from 1%.

Extension

Referring to the squares divided into 10 strips or 100 small squares, extend the discussion to finding the fraction, decimal and percentage of that part of the square which is not shaded. Emphasise that the percentages which are shaded and not shaded add together to make 100%; that is, the whole square.

Challenge the more able students with problems in various contexts, such as paying 25% tax on an income or making a profit of 20% on an investment.

Literacy

The **Starter** for this lesson explores the derivation of the word 'percentage'. An outline of the origins of the English language might be useful: that the invasions of the Angles and Saxons brought a new language to England ('Angle-land') called Anglo-Saxon English. The Norman invasion of 1066 brought French and Latin which mixed with the Anglo-Saxon. So now we have many words in modern English from both sources: for example, 'house', 'mansion', 'man', 'person', 'percentage', 'hundredth'.

Links

The packaging of food lists the composition of the food by weight and often gives the percentage of the Recommended Daily Allowance (RDA). Which foods contain the most fat and the most sugar?

The different coins of the USA, where cents can be thought of as percentages of dollars, and the years of last century on the Chinese calendar, begging questions about the percentages for each animal, can be found here

www.immihelp.com/newcomer/usa-currency-coins.html

and here

www.pinyin.info/chinese_new_year/cny1900-1999.html

Alternative approach

Show a metre rule marked in centimetres, but not millimetres. Agree than 1 cm is one-hundredth of a metre. Offer the new name 'percentage' for 'one hundredth', saying that 'percentage' is the Latin equivalent for the English 'a hundredth'. So we can write $1\% = \frac{1}{100}$, which are two ways, Latin and English, of writing the same thing.

Checkpoint

1 Tahir has a bag of marbles. Some marbles are red the remainder are blue.

a What is the percentage of red marbles if the percentage of blue marbles is

i 50% **ii** 60% **iii** 70% (50%, 40%, 30%)

b Tahir has 50 marbles in total. How many marbles are the following percentages

i 50% **ii** 10% **iii** 20% **iv** 100%? (25, 5, 10, 50)

Starter – Words ancient and modern

Show pictures of a 1 cent coin from the USA, a centipede, a ruler marked in centimetres, a Roman centurion, and a calendar showing all years from 1900 to 1999. Ask what the connection between them might be.

(The names of each contain the letters *cent* which comes from the Latin word *centum* meaning 'a hundred'.)

Teaching notes

This is a long chapter. If students' motivation is beginning to flag, then this a suitable point to visit another chapter on a contrasting topic, such as Chapter **6** (Graphs) and return to percentages later.

Show students two squares: one divided into 10 equal parallel strips, the other divided into 100 small squares in 10 rows of 10. Shade one small square and agree it is one hundredth ($\frac{1}{100}$) of the whole square. Give this fraction a new name, 'percentage' (from two Latin words, *per centum*, meaning 'by a hundred') which is written 1%. So $1\% = \frac{1}{100}$.

Shade one strip and the equivalent 10 small squares. Ask for the fraction of the whole square which is shaded. Discuss why $\frac{1}{10} = \frac{10}{100} = 10\%$.

Repeat for other strips and squares, such as $\frac{3}{10} = \frac{30}{100} = 30\%$. Now repeat for shaded small squares which do not make whole strips, such as $\frac{3}{100} = 3\%$ and $\frac{21}{100} = 21\%$.

Once students are confident with fractions as percentages, remind them of their earlier work with decimals where $0.1 = \frac{1}{10}$, $0.01 = \frac{1}{100}$ and $0.21 = \frac{21}{100}$.

Now present them with more partly-shaded squares and ask for the shaded part in three ways: as a fraction, as a decimal and as a percentage. For example, write the three equivalences together: $\frac{5}{100} = 0.05 = 5\%$ and $\frac{13}{100} = 0.13 = 13\%$.

Finally, ask questions such as 'If 10% is one-tenth, what is 10% of £40?' Extend the questions to finding 20%, 30%, 50% (and, later, 25% and 75%) of £40.

Plenary

Students use their mini-white boards to answers questions given to the whole class, such as:

- Write $\frac{3}{100}$ as a percentage and as a decimal. (3%, 0.03)
- Write 23% as a fraction and as a decimal. ($\frac{23}{100}$, 0.23)
- What is 10% of £30 and what is 20% of £30? (£3, £6)
- What is 1% of £200? (£2)

Exercise commentary

Question 1 – A reference to the 100 square would quickly remind pupils that, for part **a**, if 40% is shaded, then 60% is not shaded.

Question 2 – Students readily give correct answers for red as it starts at 0%, but not for blue as it starts higher up the scale. Touch-counting in 10s to find the percentages for blue can confirm the students' mental subtractions.

Question 3 – Some students will count each 10% in 3s. Those who count in 1s should adopt a more efficient method. Some students might realise that, as 10% is 3 marbles, then they can use their 3-times table. This final method is worth a whole-class discussion.

Questions 4 and **5** – Students should know that 50% and 10% are $\frac{1}{2}$ and $\frac{1}{10}$ respectively and so find answers by dividing by 2 and 10.

Question 6 – For part **a**, the people in the diagram have to be counted. Beware to check students' thinking. If they get their answer by multiplying by 10, it should be because they know that there are ten 10%s in 100%.

Question 7 assumes that what isn't juice must be water. A discussion can explore what else might be in the fruit drink and refer to 'real-life' commercial products. Any additives will be soluble in the water, so it could be said that the only liquids in the drink are likely to be pure juice and water. A simple subtraction from 100% is reasonably all that is required.

Answers

1 **a** 60% **b** 65%

2 **a** Red 60% Blue 40%
b Red 80% Blue 20%

3 **a** 3 **b** 9 **c** 15 **d** 24
e 18 **f** 30

4 **a** 4 kg **b** 8 kg **c** 2 kg **d** 10 kg
e 4.5 kg

5 **a** £6 **b** 15 kg **c** 45 days **d** 25p
e 11 minutes **f** 60 litres

6 **a** 90 (= 10 × 9) **b** 18

7 87%

Objectives	
• Calculate simple percentages. • Find the outcome of a given percentage increase or decrease.	(L4) (L6)

Key ideas	Resources
1 50% and 10% of a quantity can be found by dividing by 2 and 10 respectively. **2** Some other percentages of a quantity can be found mentally by first finding 50% or 10%.	Percentages of amounts 1 (1030) Calculators with different methods for finding a percentage of a number Templates for a spider diagram
Simplification	**Extension**
Make sure that students know that a quarter is 'a half of a half' and that three-quarters can be found from 50% + 25% or from 3 × 25%. Other percentages in this lesson can now be found by linking them to 50%, 25% or 10%. Ask questions firstly about amounts which are less than £100 and are *either* easily divisible by 4 *or* multiples of 10.	Extend the percentages being used beyond multiples of 10% to include 5%, 15%, 35%, …, where students work out, for example, 35% from 30% and 5%. They can draw a new spider diagram to give the methods for these various new percentages. When confident, a new central leg to the spider diagram can be added with 1% being a third alternative to 50% and 10%.
Literacy	**Links**
A **spider diagram** is a useful visual aid which has many applications beyond mathematics. Use a search engine to look for 'Images for spider diagrams' to find its many uses.	Auction websites usually charge a fee for selling an article at an auction. The charge is usually a fixed 'listing fee' depending on the starting price, plus a percentage of the selling price. For example, if it costs 20 pence to list an item and then 10% of the selling price, how much would you actually receive if you sold a set of CDs for £30 on the auction website?

Alternative approach

Calculators invariably have a [%] key. But different calculators have different ways of using these keys. There is potential for much confusion. The teacher can provide several calculators requiring different approaches and students can attempt to find a known answer to, say, 25% of £40, on each calculator. The end result may well be that students are advised to ignore the [%] key and, instead, use the [÷] key to divide by 100 (to find 1%) and then the [×] key to multiply by the required percentage. This method reinforces the concept of 'percentage' as a hundredth.

Checkpoint

1 A shop sells a coat for £40.

a In the first week of a sale, 10% is taken off the price.
What is the saving? (£4)

b In the second week of the sale, the saving is increased to 30%.
What is the new saving? (3 × £4 = £12)

2 The same shop sells a pair of trainers for £60.

a i Find 50% of this price (£30)

ii Use previous your answer to find 25%. (£30 ÷ 2 = £15)

b If 25% is taken off the price of the trainers, what is the new price? (£60 – £15 = £45)

Starter – Quick fire

Revise the essential elements of previous work using quick fire questions and quick responses on mini-whiteboards. Include questions such as:

- write 3% as a fraction ($\frac{3}{100}$)
- write 12% as a decimal (0.12)

Teaching notes

Students can readily find 50% of an amount by halving. Explore finding 25% by 'halving the half' and finding 75% by *either* trebling 25% *or* adding 50% and 25%. Ask questions requiring answers on mini-whiteboards, such as 'Find 50% of £60, 25% of £60 and 75% of 60', asking how they worked out 75%.

Similarly, once students appreciate that 10% is $\frac{1}{10}$, then the relation with 20%, 30% etc can be made explicit. Ask questions such as 'Find 10% of £60, 20% of £60, 30% of £60', asking how they worked out 30%.

A good visual aid to have is a spider diagram. The diagram makes clear the importance of first finding 50% or 10%.

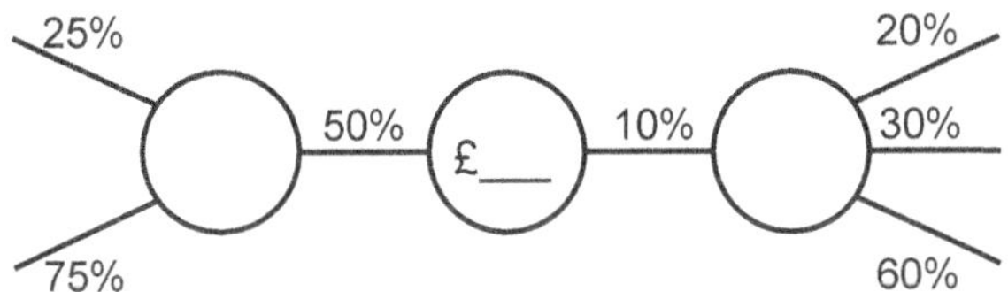

Copy and complete the spider diagram by inserting an amount in the centre and writing five amounts (in £) on the five outer legs. After work as a whole class, ask students to create their own spider diagrams for different amounts.

When confident, a new central leg to the spider diagram can be added with 1% being a third alternative to 50% and 10%.

Plenary

A sale offers different percentage discounts on different articles. Use mini-whiteboards and discuss answers where appropriate to questions such as the following.

Find the discount in £s when there is

- 25% off a coat costing £80 (£60)
- 75% off a pair of trousers costing £40 (£10)
- 10% off a mobile phone costing £60 (£54)
- 20% off a holiday costing £300 (£240)
- 5% off a computer costing £400 (£380)

Exercise commentary

Question 1 – Remind students to include units in their answers.

Question 2 – Note that units are not required here. Answers are found from multiples of 10%.

Question 4 – This builds on Question **3**. After finding how much is saved in the sale, students have to subtract the saving to find the sale price of the various objects. There should be no need to use a calculator.

Answers

1 **a** 5 m **b** 3 hours **c** 9 kg **d** £15
e 25 votes **f** 11 litres

2 **a** 8 **b** 48 **c** 18 **d** 28
e 21 **f** 5

3 **a** £10 **b** £7 **c** £12 **d** £45

4 **a** £54 **b** £96 **c** £30 **d** £11
e £12

4 **a** 75% of 12 = 9 Other calculations give 10
b 10% of 200 = 20 Other calculations give 12
c 10% of 120 = 12 Other calculations give 21
d 25% of 32 = 8 Other calculations give 9

6 70% of 150 = 105 20% of 105 = 21
20% of 150 = 30 70% of 30 = 21
The same because $\frac{3}{4}\times\frac{1}{5}\times$ is the same as $\frac{1}{5}\times\frac{3}{4}\times$. The order of multiplication does not matter, even for fractions.

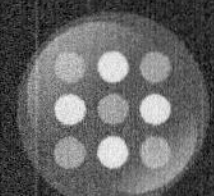

4h Fractions, decimals and percentages

Objectives	
• Write decimals using tenths and hundredths. (L4) • Change fractions to decimals and decimals to fractions. (L4)	
Key ideas	**Resources**
1 A fraction, a decimal and a percentage are three equivalent ways of writing the same number.	Fractions, decimals and percentages 1 (1029) Large squares divided into 10 equal strips or into 100 equal small squares (a 100-square) A number line labelled from 0 to 1 in tenths and subdivided into hundredths
Simplification	**Extension**
The use of partly-shaded squares with 10 strips and with 100 small squares provides a strong visual aid to the concepts of this lesson. Have partly-shaded squares for which students write equivalent decimals and fractions, with percentages included later. Once confident, they do the reverse by shading unshaded squares, prepared with strips and small squares, to represent decimals, fractions and percentages given to them.	The square with 100 squares is used to make a mosaic using various colours for the small squares. When fully coloured, students write down, as fractions, decimals and percentages, how much of the whole square is given to each colour. Ask how they can check their answers. (Add all together to get 1.00 or 100%.)
Literacy	**Links**
Part of being 'mathematically literate', that is, 'numerate' is to be confident in knowing and using the various equivalences of fractions, decimals and percentages. Re-visiting the equivalences as part of the **Starter** to a lesson is a routine which, if not daily, is sufficiently regular to establish and maintain understanding and confidence.	In the USA, measurements are made in fractions of inches. So a drill bit size might be $\frac{7}{16}$ inches. There is an online chart to convert fractional inches to decimal inches and to find the metric equivalent at www.edsebooks.com/paper/inchmetric.html

Alternative approach

Another visual aid offers an alternative approach and uses a number line from 0 to 1. The line is labelled in tenths from 0.1 to 0.9 and then sub-divided into hundredths. Place a pointer at various positions and express the reading as a decimal and as a fraction, both orally and in writing. Start with decimals such as 0.3 before moving to 0.31. The readings can also be given as percentages, in which case all three, fractions, decimals and percentages, can be required for a given position of the pointer.

Checkpoint

1 Shade 25 squares on a hundred square (see example in the student book)

- **a** **i** What percentage of the squares are shaded? (25%)
  - **ii** What fraction are shaded? ($\frac{1}{4}$)
  - **iii** What is this as a decimal? (0.25)
- **b** **i** What percentage of the squares are not shaded? (75%)
  - **ii** What fraction are not shaded? ($\frac{3}{4}$)
  - **iii** What is this as a decimal? (0.75)

2 Repeat question **1** for other shapes, such as a circle or rectangle, divided into equal parts.

Starter – Fraction bingo

Ask students to draw a 2×2 grid and write four one-digit decimals between 0.1 and 0.9 (inclusive) on the grid. Give fractions equivalent to the decimals – for example, one-tenth, seven-tenths, a half. The winner is the first student to cross out all their four decimals.

Repeat the game by writing four one-digit decimals between 0.01 and 0.09 (inclusive).

Repeat using a mixture of one-digit decimals, both tenths and hundredths, such as 0.2 and 0.02

Teaching notes

Two squares, one divided into ten parallel strips to indicate tenths, and the other divided into 100 small squares to indicate hundredths, are powerful visual aids for the link between fractions, decimal and percentages. Refer to the **Teaching notes** for **Exercise 4f** which are also pertinent to this lesson.

The lesson falls into two parts. Shade part of the large square with the 100 small squares and write the shaded part both as a fraction and as a decimal. Firstly, shade fewer than 10 small squares and write, for example, $\frac{3}{100} = 0.03$. Then, shade more than 10 small squares and write, for example, $\frac{17}{100} = 0.17$. The discussion can extend to percentages and hundredths and, in these two cases, 3% and 17% can be added as equivalents.

Now turn to the other large square and shade some of the strips. Write the shaded part both as a fraction and as a decimal as, for example, $\frac{3}{10} = 0.3$.

The discussion can now extend to 0.17 being thought of as '1 strip and 7 squares', leading to $\frac{1}{10} + \frac{7}{100} = \frac{17}{100} = 0.17 = 17\%$.

Another visual aid offers an alternative approach using a number line from 0 to 1. See details in the **Alternative approach.**

Plenary

A regular re-visiting of equivalences is important to drive home these essential basic forms. For example, $\frac{7}{10} + \frac{3}{100} = \frac{73}{100} = 0.73 = 17\%$ and also $0.7 = \frac{7}{10} = \frac{70}{100} = 70\%$

Prepared squares with various shaded parts can be shown to the whole class to provide a brisk recap with answers written on mini-whiteboards. A fully-shaded square with no divisions can be shown together with a partly shaded square to gives answers such as 1.2 and 1.23.

Discuss where answers show the need.

Exercise commentary

Question 1 – Once the student realises that each red slice is 10%, the answers are found simply by counting and multiplying by 10.

Question 2 – Converting multiples of 10% to fractions as tenths is straightforward if they are left as tenths. This may be sufficient to make the point, when Questions 1, 2 and 3 are taken together, that fractions, decimals and percentages are readily interchangeable. However, students could be reminded that some of these fractions do have equivalent fractions.

Question 3 – Students may need a reminder that the first decimal place is for tenths. Writing U and t may be useful a headings. It is important to draw Questions **1**, **2** and **3** together, as mentioned in Question **2** above.

Question 4 – Further emphasises the equivalence of the three forms. The blue and yellow areas need hundredths. The green and red can be worked as tenths or hundredths (or both).

Question 5 – This question provides an opportunity for students to work in pairs and discuss their methods and approach to finding pairs.

Answers

Placeholder

1	**a**	10%	**b**	20%	**c**	30%	**d**	50%	
	e	90%	**f**	30%	**g**	40%	**h**	70%	
	i	60%	**j**	80%	**k**	0%	**l**	100%	
2	**a**	$\frac{9}{10}$	**b**	$\frac{8}{10} = \frac{4}{5}$	**c**	$\frac{7}{10}$	**d**	$\frac{5}{10} = \frac{1}{2}$	
	e	$\frac{1}{10}$	**f**	$\frac{7}{10}$	**g**	$\frac{6}{10} = \frac{3}{5}$	**h**	$\frac{3}{10}$	
	i	$\frac{4}{10} = \frac{2}{5}$	**j**	$\frac{2}{10} = \frac{1}{5}$	**k**	$\frac{10}{10} = 1$	**l**	0	
3	**a**	0.9	**b**	0.8	**c**	0.7	**d**	0.5	
	e	0.1	**f**	0.7	**g**	0.6	**h**	0.3	
	i	0.4	**j**	0.2	**k**	1	**l**	0	
4	**a**	**i** $\frac{7}{100}$			**ii**	0.07	**iii**	7%	
	b	**i** $\frac{20}{100} = \frac{2}{10} = \frac{1}{5}$			**ii**	0.2	**iii**	20%	**c**
	c	**i** $\frac{10}{100} = \frac{1}{10}$			**ii**	0.1	**iii**	10%	
	d	**i** $\frac{25}{100} = \frac{1}{4}$			**ii**	0.25	**iii**	25%	
	e	**i** $\frac{30}{100} = \frac{3}{10}$			**ii**	0.3	**iii**	32%	
	f	**i** $\frac{32}{100} = \frac{8}{25}$			**ii**	0.32	**iii**	32%	
	g	**i** $\frac{38}{100} = \frac{19}{50}$			**ii**	0.38	**iii**	38%	
5	**a**	$\frac{3}{4}$ (=0.75 = 75%)							
	b	$\frac{1}{2}$ and 0.5				30% and $\frac{7}{10}$			
		0.25 and $\frac{3}{4}$				0.6 and 40%			

Key outcomes	Quick check
Use fractions to describe parts of a whole, including improper fractions. L4	**1** What fraction of this shape is shaded? ($\frac{3}{8}$) **2** **a** Write $\frac{11}{8}$ as a mixed number? ($1\frac{3}{8}$) **b** Write $2\frac{4}{5}$ as an improper fraction? ($\frac{14}{5}$)
	What is the missing number in these pairs of equivalent fractions? **a** $\frac{2}{3}=\frac{?}{9}$ (6) **b** $\frac{3}{4}=\frac{9}{?}$ (12) **c** $\frac{4}{?}=\frac{8}{10}$ (5)
Find fractions of a quantity. L5	Find **a** $\frac{1}{4}$ of 24 (6) **b** $\frac{1}{3}$ of 24 (8) **c** $\frac{2}{3}$ of 24 (16)
Calculate simple percentages, including problems involving money L4	**1** Find **a** 10% of £30 (£3) **b** 30% of £30 (£9) **c** 60% of £40 (£24) **2** A jacket normally costs £50. In a sale it is reduced by 20%. How much does it cost now? (£40)
Express a proportion as a fraction, a decimal or a percentage L5	**1** Write the shaded areas as a **i** fraction **ii** decimal **iii** percentage **a** Black **b** Whte **c** Grey ($\frac{1}{10}$, 0.1, 10%) ($\frac{1}{2}$, 0.5, 50%) ($\frac{2}{5}$, 0.4, 40%)

Development and links
Using fractions to describe a proportion is used when interpreting pie charts in chapter **8**. Finding equivalent fractions shares common features with simplifying ratios and fractions are used to describe proportions in in chapter **15**. Fractions, decimals and percentages provide the natural language for quantifying probabilities in chapter **16** Fractions, decimals and percentages form part of the basic language of numbers and are used throughout this course and in life. For example, stores often use special offers such as 'one third extra free' or '25% off'; road signs may describe a slope as a '10% gradient'; a project may be '40% completed'; your homework might be 'nine out of ten'. Students may be able to suggest many more examples.

MyMaths extra support

Lesson/online homework			Description
Introducing fractions	1369	L2	Introduces the meaning of the fractions one half and one quarter.
Finding fractions	1062	L3	The first part of this lesson allows students to test their understanding of the meaning of a fraction.
Fractions to decimals	1016	L3	The first part of this lesson strengthens the recall of simple fractions and decimals.

My Review

4 MySummary

Check out

You should now be able to ...

	Test it ➡ Questions
✓ Use fractions to describe parts of a whole, including improper fractions.	1 – 3
✓ Identify equivalent fractions.	4
✓ Find fractions of a quantity.	5, 6
✓ Calculate simple percentages, including problems involving money.	7, 8
✓ Express a proportion as a fraction, a decimal or a percentage.	9

Language	Meaning	Example
Fraction	A fraction is a part of a whole.	$\frac{1}{2}$ is half of a whole
Denominator	The bottom number in a fraction. It tells you how many equal parts the whole has been divided into.	In $\frac{3}{4}$, the denominator is 4: the whole has been divided into 4 equal parts – quarters.
Numerator	The top number in a fraction. It tells you how many equal parts of the whole you have.	The numerator is 3: you have 3 quarters.
Equivalent fractions	Fractions with the same value.	$\frac{1}{2}=\frac{2}{4}=\frac{3}{6}$
Mixed number	A fraction with a whole number part and a fraction part.	$1\frac{2}{3}$
Improper fraction	A fraction with a numerator larger than the denominator.	$\frac{5}{3}$
Percentage	A fraction out of 100.	$20\% = \frac{20}{100}$

4 MyReview

1 Write the fraction of the shape which is shaded.

a

b

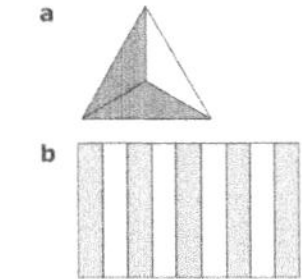

2 Convert these improper fractions to mixed numbers.

a $\frac{3}{2}$ b $\frac{7}{3}$ c $\frac{15}{4}$

3 Convert these mixed numbers to improper fractions.

a $2\frac{2}{3}$ b $1\frac{1}{4}$ c $7\frac{1}{2}$

4 Copy and complete these pairs of equivalent fractions.

a $\frac{3}{9}=\frac{\square}{3}$ b $\frac{1}{4}=\frac{\square}{20}$

c $\frac{1}{\square}=\frac{10}{20}$ d $\frac{6}{24}=\frac{1}{\square}$

5 Find

a $\frac{1}{2}$ of 10 b $\frac{1}{3}$ of 12

c $\frac{1}{4}$ of 40 d $\frac{1}{5}$ of 30

6 Find

a $\frac{2}{3}$ of 24 b $\frac{3}{4}$ of 16 c $\frac{3}{5}$ of 10

7 Find

a 10% of 40 b 20% of 40

c 30% of 40 d 50% of 40

e 60% of 40 f 25% of 40

8 Find

a 10% of 60 b 30% of 60

c 40% of 60 d 50% of 60

e 70% of 60 f 100% of 60

9 This hundred square is divided into 100 equal parts

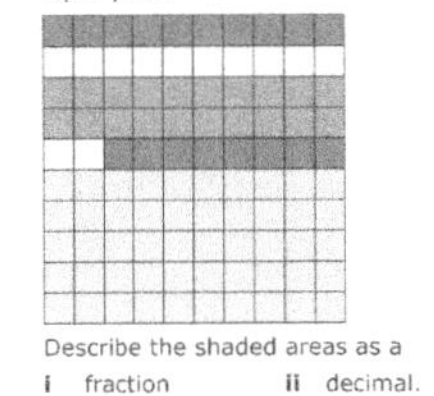

Describe the shaded areas as a

i fraction ii decimal.

a red b green

c blue d yellow

What next?

Score	
0 – 3	Your knowledge of this topic is still developing. To improve look at Formative test: 1A-4; MyMaths: 1018, 1019, 1029, 1030, 1220, 1370 and 1371
4 – 7	You are gaining a secure knowledge of this topic. To improve look at InvisiPen: 141, 142, 151 and 162
8 – 9	You have mastered this topic. Well done, you are ready to progress!

MyMaths.co.uk 83

Question commentary

Question 1 – (lesson **4a**) If students answer '2 out of 3', and '5 out of 9' press them to use fraction notation.

Questions 2 and **3** – (lesson **4c**) Encourage the use of diagrams to visualise the conversions.

Question 4 – (lesson **4b**) Students need to work out what to multiply or divide the top and bottom by: part **a** $\div 3$, in part **b** $\times 5$, in part **c** $\times 10$ and in part **d** $\div 6$

Question 5 – (lesson **4d**) To find unit fractions, remind students to divide by the denominator.

Question 6 – (lesson **4e**) Students should solve the problems in two steps: first find the unit fraction by dividing by the denominator, second multiply by the numerator. In part **a** $\frac{1}{3}$ of 24 = 8 in part **b** $\frac{1}{4}$ of 16 = 4 and in part **c** $\frac{1}{5}$ of 10 = 2.

Questions 7 and **8** – (lessons **4f** and **4g**) Students can either convert the percentage to a fraction and proceed as in question **6** or find 10% and multiply. As a minimum students should know that $10\% = \frac{1}{10}$, $50\% = \frac{1}{2}$ and $25\% = \frac{1}{4}$; this is a good opportunity for discussion.

Question 9 – (lesson **4h**) Fractions should ideally be simplified. Un-simplified the answers are: part **a** $\frac{10}{100}$, part **b** $\frac{20}{100}$, part **c** $\frac{8}{100}$ and part **d** $\frac{50}{100}$.

Answers

1	**a** $\frac{2}{3}$		**b** $\frac{5}{9}$					
2	**a** $1\frac{1}{2}$		**b** $2\frac{1}{3}$		**c** $3\frac{3}{4}$			
3	**a** $\frac{8}{3}$		**b** $\frac{5}{4}$		**c** $\frac{15}{2}$			
4	**a** $\frac{1}{3}$		**b** $\frac{5}{20}$		**c** $\frac{1}{2}$		**d** $\frac{1}{4}$	
5	**a** 5		**b** 4		**c** 10		**d** 6	
6	**a** 16		**b** 12		**c** 6			
7	**a** 4		**b** 8		**c** 12		**d** 20	
	e 24		**f** 10					
8	**a** 6		**b** 18		**c** 24		**d** 30	
	e 42		**f** 60					
9	**a i**	$\frac{1}{10}$	**ii** 0.1		**b i**	$\frac{1}{5}$	**ii** 0.2	
	c i	$\frac{2}{25}$	**ii** 0.08		**d i**	$\frac{1}{2}$	**ii** 0.5	

4 MyPractice

4a

1 What fraction of each shape is shaded?

a b c

d e f

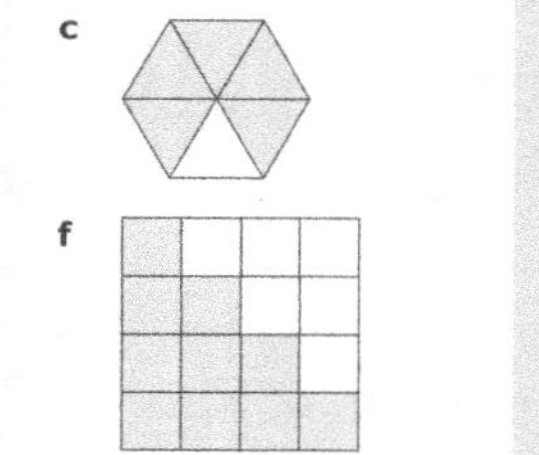
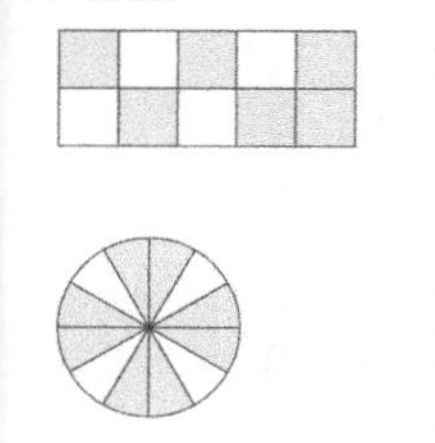
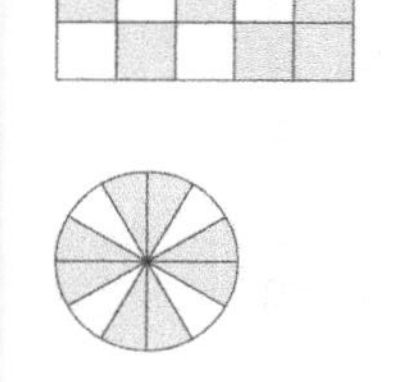
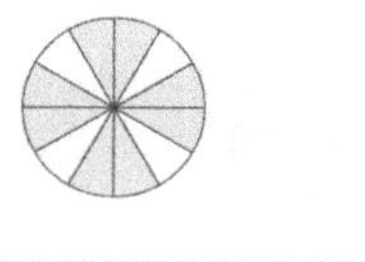
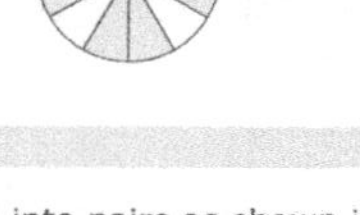
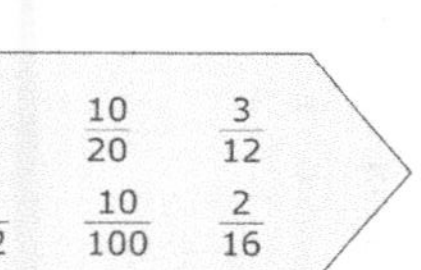

4b

2 Put these equivalent fractions into pairs as shown in the example.

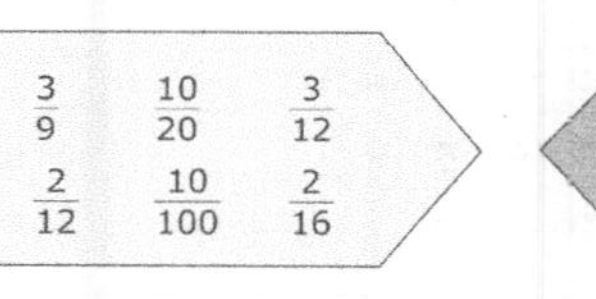

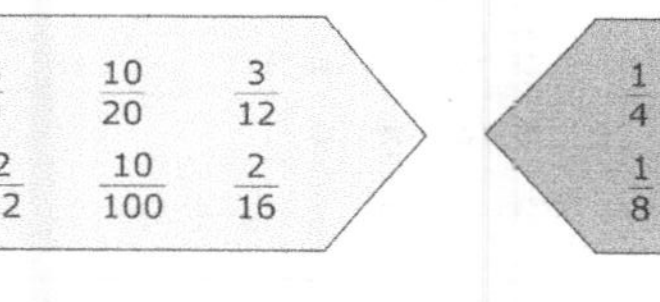

$\frac{3}{9}$ $\frac{10}{20}$ $\frac{3}{12}$
$\frac{2}{12}$ $\frac{10}{100}$ $\frac{2}{16}$

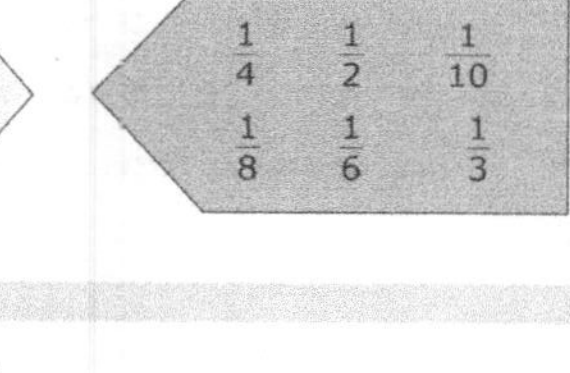

4c

3 Write these whole numbers as improper fractions.

a $4 = \frac{\square}{2}$ b $3 = \frac{\square}{3}$ c $6 = \frac{\square}{2}$

d $2 = \frac{8}{\square}$ e $5 = \frac{15}{\square}$ f $5 = \frac{20}{\square}$

4 Write these improper fractions as whole numbers.

a $\frac{6}{2}$ b $\frac{8}{4}$ c $\frac{10}{2}$

d $\frac{15}{3}$ e $\frac{12}{3}$ f $\frac{28}{7}$

5 Write these improper fractions as mixed numbers.

a $\frac{7}{2}$ b $\frac{8}{3}$ c $\frac{9}{2}$

d $\frac{9}{4}$ e $\frac{11}{3}$ f $\frac{17}{5}$

6 Convert these mixed numbers into improper fractions.

a $2\frac{1}{2} = \frac{\square}{\square}$ b $3\frac{1}{2} = \frac{\square}{\square}$ c $2\frac{1}{4} = \frac{\square}{\square}$

d $3\frac{1}{3} = \frac{\square}{\square}$ e $2\frac{2}{5} = \frac{\square}{\square}$ f $3\frac{2}{7} = \frac{\square}{\square}$

4d

7 Divide these counters into 2 equal groups.

a There are ____ counters in each group.

b What fraction is each group of the total?

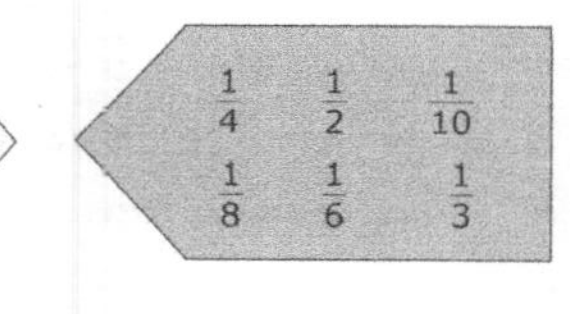

8 What is

a $\frac{1}{10}$ of 30 b $\frac{1}{2}$ of 24 c $\frac{1}{5}$ of 30 d $\frac{1}{4}$ of 24 e $\frac{1}{8}$ of 24

9 Divide these counters into 4 equal groups.

a There are ____ counters in each group.

b What fraction is each group of the total?

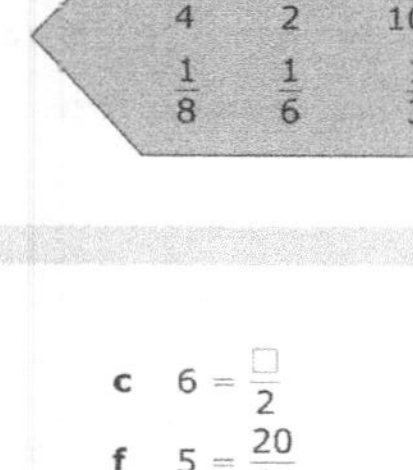

4e

10 A bag of 25 counters is divided into 5 groups.

a How many counters are there in $\frac{1}{5}$ of the bag?

b How many counters are there in $\frac{3}{5}$ of the bag?

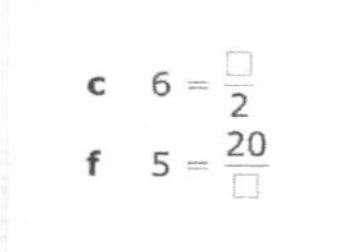

11 Find

a $\frac{2}{5}$ of 10 b $\frac{2}{3}$ of 15 c $\frac{2}{3}$ of 12 d $\frac{3}{10}$ of 20 e $\frac{3}{5}$ of 20

4f

12 40 teachers are surveyed about the time that school starts each morning. Use the percent strip below to help you.

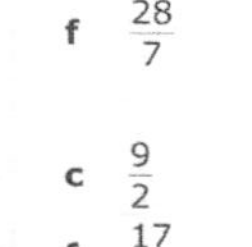

a 40% vote for an earlier start. How many vote for this?

b 30% vote to keep the same start time. How many vote for this?

c 20% vote for a later start. How many vote for this?

d 10% vote 'Don't Know'. How many vote for this?

4g

13 These items are 10% off in a sale. Find their sale price.

a Skirt costing £40 b Blouse costing £30 c Trousers costing £35

4h

14 Copy and complete this equivalence table.

Fraction	Decimal	Percentage
$\frac{1}{10}$		
	0.2	
		60%

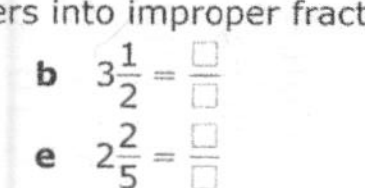
MyMaths.co.uk

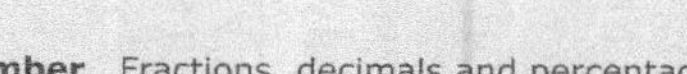

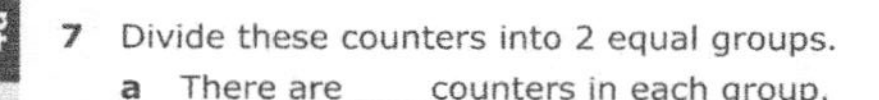

Question commentary

Questions 1 – This provides an opportunity to test students basic understanding of what a fraction represents: number of (shaded) parts over number of parts in the whole.

Question 2 – This question can be done as a paired activity allowing students to explain methods and pairing strategies.

Question 3 – For example in part **a**, students could think of 4 as $\frac{4}{1}$ and apply the method of multiplying top and bottom by the same number.

Question 4 – By 'cancelling top and bottom', these fractions can be reduced to integers, in a reverse of question **3**.

Question 5 and **6** – As well as an arithmetic approach, students could be given tokens, such as part circles, to physically manipulate. Question **5** requires assembling parts into wholes with part remainders. Question **6** requires counting the number of parts in a given number of wholes and parts.

Question 7, **8** and **9** – These questions aim to test and strength the idea of rearranging tokens into equal groups, division by an integer and multiplying by a unit fraction. None of the questions involve remainders.

Question 10 and **11** – Supply students with counters so that they can physically make the connection between dividing by the denominator – partitioning into equal sized groups- and multiplying by the numerator – taking a given number of groups.

Question 12 – The key is for students to understand that if 100% equals 40 then 10% equals 4. Then for example, in part **a**, they can find 40% as 4 lots of 10% equivalent to 4 × 4 =16.

Question 13 – Students should solve this question in two stages: first find 10% and then subtract this number from the original price. As well as being good practice this should help to isolate arithmetical errors, division or subtraction, from conceptual errors.

Question 14 – This question can be extended by adding more rows with other simple entries.

Answers

1 **a** $\frac{2}{5}$ **b** $\frac{6}{10} = \frac{3}{5}$ **c** $\frac{5}{6}$ **d** $\frac{1}{8}$
e $\frac{8}{12} = \frac{2}{3}$ **f** $\frac{10}{16} = \frac{5}{8}$

2 $\frac{3}{9} = \frac{1}{3}$ $\frac{10}{20} = \frac{1}{2}$ $\frac{3}{12} = \frac{1}{4}$ $\frac{2}{10} = \frac{1}{5}$
$\frac{10}{100} = \frac{1}{10}$ $\frac{2}{16} = \frac{1}{8}$

3 **a** 8 **b** 9 **c** 12 **d** 4
e 3 **f** 4

4 **a** 3 **b** 2 **c** 5 **d** 5
e 4 **f** 4

5 **a** $3\frac{1}{2}$ **b** $2\frac{2}{3}$ **c** $4\frac{1}{2}$ **d** $2\frac{1}{4}$
e $3\frac{2}{3}$ **f** $3\frac{2}{5}$

6 **a** $\frac{5}{2}$ **b** $\frac{7}{2}$ **c** $\frac{9}{4}$ **d** $\frac{10}{3}$
e $\frac{12}{5}$ **f** $\frac{23}{7}$

7 **a** There are 4 counters in each group. **b** $\frac{1}{2}$

8 **a** 3 **b** 12 **c** 6 **d** 6
e 3

9 **a** There are 4 counters in each group. **b** $\frac{1}{4}$

10 **a** 5 **b** 15

11 **a** 4 **b** 10 **c** 9 **d** 6
e 12

12 **a** 16 **b** 12 **c** 8 **d** 4

13 **a** £36 **b** £27 **c** £31.50

14

Fraction	Decimal	Percentage
$\frac{1}{10}$	0.1	10%
$\frac{1}{5}$	0.2	20%
$\frac{3}{5}$	0.6	60%

MyAssessment 1

These questions will test you on your knowledge of the topics in chapters 1 to 4.
They give you practice in the types of questions that you may see in your GCSE exams.
There are 70 marks in total.

1 a Write down the value of the 4 in words in each of these numbers.
  i 24 **ii** 476 **iii** 984 **iv** 341 (4 marks)
b Write these numbers in order from smallest to largest.
  347, 162, 971, 437, 734, 612, 791 (1 mark)
c Write down these decimal money amounts from smallest to largest.
  £4.32, £3.42, £4.23, £2.43, £2.34, £3.24 (1 mark)

2 Find the total of each of these. Do not use a calculator.
a £0.60 + £0.27 **b** £3.27 + £9.30 + £7.41 (2 marks)

3 The recorded temperatures during seven consecutive days in a UK city were
1°C, -3°C, -2°C, 2°C, -4°C, -1°C, 3°C
a Write these in order from coldest to warmest. (2 marks)
b What was the difference in temperature between the coldest and warmest days? (1 mark)

4 Round these numbers to
a the nearest 10 **i** 12 **ii** 44 **iii** 63 (3 marks)
b the nearest 100 **i** 235 **ii** 626 **iii** 967 (3 marks)
c the nearest whole number. **i** 3.88 **ii** 9.65 **iii** 23.54 (3 marks)

5 What are the readings given on these scales?
a **b**

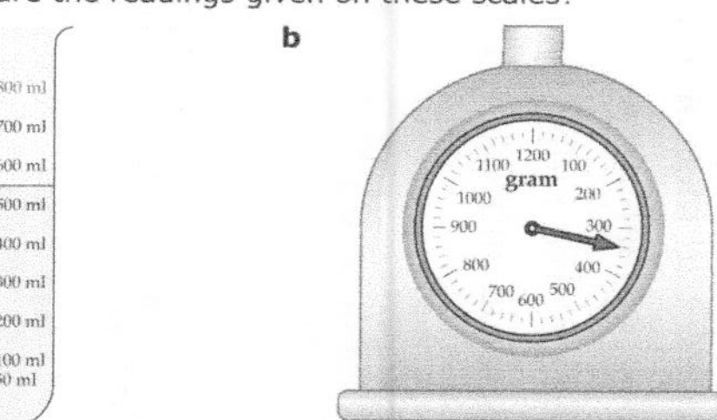

(2 marks)

6 The times shown are taken from different clocks.
Give the equivalent time in the clock given in brackets.
a 9.30 pm (24-hour clock) **b** 3.30 am (24-hour clock)
c 13.45 (am/pm clock) **d** 18:15 (am/pm clock) (4 marks)

7 A tennis court is 78 feet long by 36 feet wide.
a What is the perimeter of a tennis court? (1 mark)
b What is the name of the shape of a tennis court? (1 mark)

8 For the irregular pentagon shown find
a the perimeter (1 mark)
b the area. (2 marks)

4.5 cm, 4.5 cm, 3.5 cm, 2.5 cm, 3 cm

9 Express each metric quantity in terms of the new metric unit given in brackets.
a 3.7 m (cm)
b 195 g (kg)
c 500 ml (litres)
d 3.4 litres (cl) (4 marks)

10 I have picked 2 boxes of strawberries at a fruit farm.
Each box contains x strawberries.
a How many strawberries in total do I have?
  Write your answer in terms of x. (1 mark)
b On the way home I eat 5 strawberries.
  How many strawberries do I now have? (1 mark)
c If each box initially contains 42 strawberries, how many remain when I reach home? (2 marks)

11 Simplify these expressions by adding or subtracting like terms.
a $4p + p$ **b** $5w + 12w - 1$
c $6x + 4y - 3x$ **d** $9t - 2s + 6t - s$ (4 marks)

12 If $a = 3$, $b = 4$ and $c = 2$ work out the value of these expressions.
a $3b$ (1 mark) **b** $2c + a$ (2 marks)
c $ac - b$ (2 marks) **d** abc (2 marks)

13 There are 14 animals waiting to be seen by a vet. Seven are cats, four are dogs, two are rabbits and one is a hamster.
a What fraction of the animals are
  i dogs **ii** cats **iii** rabbits **iv** hamsters? (4 marks)
b Write each fractions as another equivalent fraction. (4 marks)

14 Convert these fractions to either mixed numbers or improper fractions.
a $\frac{8}{3}$ **b** $2\frac{2}{3}$ **c** $\frac{15}{2}$ **d** $4\frac{1}{4}$ (4 marks)

15 Find
a $\frac{2}{5}$ of £25 **b** 50% of £30 **c** $\frac{1}{4}$ of 1200 g **d** 30% of 240 litres (4 marks)

16 a Change these fractions to decimals **i** $\frac{4}{5}$ **ii** $\frac{7}{10}$ (2 marks)
b Change these decimals to percentages **i** 0.6 **ii** 0.75 (2 marks)

Mark scheme

Questions 1 – 6 marks (lessons **1a** and **1b**)

a i 1 Four
ii 1 Four hundred
iii 1 Four
iv 1 Forty
b 1 162, 347, 437, 612, 734, 791, 971
c 1 £2.34, £2.43, £3.24, £3.42, £4.23, £4.32

Questions 2 – 2 marks (lesson **1e**)

a 1 £0.87**b** 1 £19.98

Questions 3 – 3 marks (lesson **1f**)

a 2 -4 °C, -3 °C, -2 °C, -1 °C, 1 °C, 2 °C, 3 °C
b 1 7 °C

Questions 4 – 9 marks (lesson **1g**)

a i 1 10 **ii** 1 40
iii 1 60
b i 1 200 **ii** 1 600
iii 1 1000
c i 1 4 **ii** 1 10
iii 1 24

Questions 5 – 2 marks (lesson **2b**)

a 1 550 ml; accept ±10 ml
b 1 350 g; accept ±10 g

Questions 6 – 4 marks (lesson **2c**)

a 1 21:30 **b** 1 15:30
c 1 1:45 pm **c** 1 6:15 pm

Questions 7 – 2 marks(lessons **2d** and **2e**)

a 1 228 feet
b 1 Rectangle

Questions 8 – 3 marks (lessons **2e** and **2f**)

a 1 18 cm
b 2 $19\frac{1}{2}$ cm^2; accept $\pm\frac{1}{2}$ cm^2

Questions 9 – 4 marks (lesson **2g**)

a 1 3700 cm
b 1 0.195 kg
c 1 0.5 litres
d 1 340 cl

Questions 10 – 4 marks (lessons **3a** and **3b**)

a 1 $2x$
b 1 $2x - 5$
c 1 79

Questions 11 – 4 marks (lessons **3c** and **3d**)

a 1 $5p$
b 1 $17w - 1$
c 1 $3x + 4y$
d 1 $15t - 3s$

Questions 12 – 4 marks (lesson **3e**)

a 1 12 **b** 1 7
c 1 2 **d** 1 24

Questions 13 – 8 marks (lessons **4a** and **4b**)

a i 1 $\frac{4}{14}$ **ii** 1 $\frac{7}{14}$
iii 1 $\frac{2}{14}$ **iv** 1 $\frac{1}{14}$
b 4 $\frac{2}{7}$, $\frac{1}{2}$, $\frac{1}{7}$, $\frac{2}{28}$
or any other equivalent fraction.

Questions 14 – 4 marks (lesson **4c**)

a 1 $2\frac{2}{3}$
b 1 $\frac{8}{3}$
c 1 $7\frac{1}{2}$
d 1 $\frac{17}{4}$

Questions 15 – 4 marks (lessons **4d**, **4e**, **4f** and **4g**)

a 1 £10
b 1 £15
c 1 300 g
d 1 80 litres

Questions 16 – 4 marks (lesson **4h**)

a i 1 0.8 **ii** 1 0.7
b i 1 60% **ii** 1 75%

Levels

	Q1 – 4	Q5 – 9	Q10 – 12	Q13 – 16
	N	G & M	A	N
M 5			13 – 15	
S 5			9 – 12	17 – 20
D 5			5 – 8	13 – 16
M 4				9 – 12
S 4		13 – 15		5 – 8
D 4	17 – 20	9 – 12		
M 3	13 – 16	5 – 8		
S 3	9 – 12			
D 3	5 – 8			
FA	0 – 4	0 – 4	0 – 4	0 – 4

D developing S secure M mastery FA further assessment needed

Learning outcomes

G3 Draw and measure line segments and angles in geometric figures, including interpreting scale drawings. (L4/5)

G7 Derive and illustrate properties of triangles, quadrilaterals, circles, and other plane figures [for example, equal lengths and angles] using appropriate language and technologies. (L4)

G10 Apply the properties of angles at a point, angles at a point on a straight line, vertically opposite angles. (L5)

G12 Derive and use the sum of angles in a triangle and use it to deduce the angle sum in any polygon, and to derive properties of regular polygons. (L5)

Introduction

The chapter starts by discussing the terminology associated with angle measure and asking students to classify and match angles. Measuring angles and angles on straight-lines are then covered before the chapter moves on to using simple angle rules to calculate unknown angles at a point. Properties of triangles and angles in a triangle are then covered, followed by a spread dealing with compass turns.

The introduction describes the Leaning Tower of Pisa and the efforts made both in its construction and restoration in order to prevent it falling down. The angle of lean is not very big, but the weight and height of the tower mean that it is in danger of falling. This website provides a good introduction to the history and heritage of Pisa and its famous leaning tower.

http://www.opapisa.it/en/home-page.html

In a more general sense, the need to construct buildings with right-angled corners, vertical walls and stable roofs has occupied mankind for thousands of years. When the Egyptians built the pyramids, they needed to ensure the angles of the sloping faces were consistent and also that they had right-angles at each corner. They used knotted ropes to accurately measure right-angles using principles closely related to Pythagoras and his famous theorem. The fact that the pyramids were built around 2400BC, nearly 2000 years before Pythagoras, makes this principle all the more remarkable!

Prior knowledge

Students should already know how to…

- Describe turns using clockwise and anticlockwise
- Order angles according to size
- Read scales
- Perform basic arithmetic with whole numbers

Starter problem

The starter problem is an investigation into toppling angles. While this topic is more likely to be covered in technical detail as part of an A level mathematics course, the general principles can be discussed with younger students. The activity could be carried out in class, or set as an investigation for homework.

The key concept is that of the centre of mass. An object will topple when its centre of mass passes the pivot point of the plane. Generally, taller (or thinner) objects will fall more quickly since their centre of mass passes the pivot sooner as the plane is raised.

It is also interesting to consider how rough the surface of the plane is. Some objects may not topple since they will slide *down* the plane before their centre of mass reaches the critical point of the pivot.

Resources

MyMaths

Measuring angles	1081	Angle sums	1082	Properties of triangles	1130
Position and turning	1231				

Online assessment

Chapter test	1A–5
Formative test	1A–5
Summative test	1A–5

InvisiPen solutions

Angle measure	341	Calculating angles	342
Angles in a triangle	343		

Topic scheme

Teaching time = 8 lessons/3 weeks

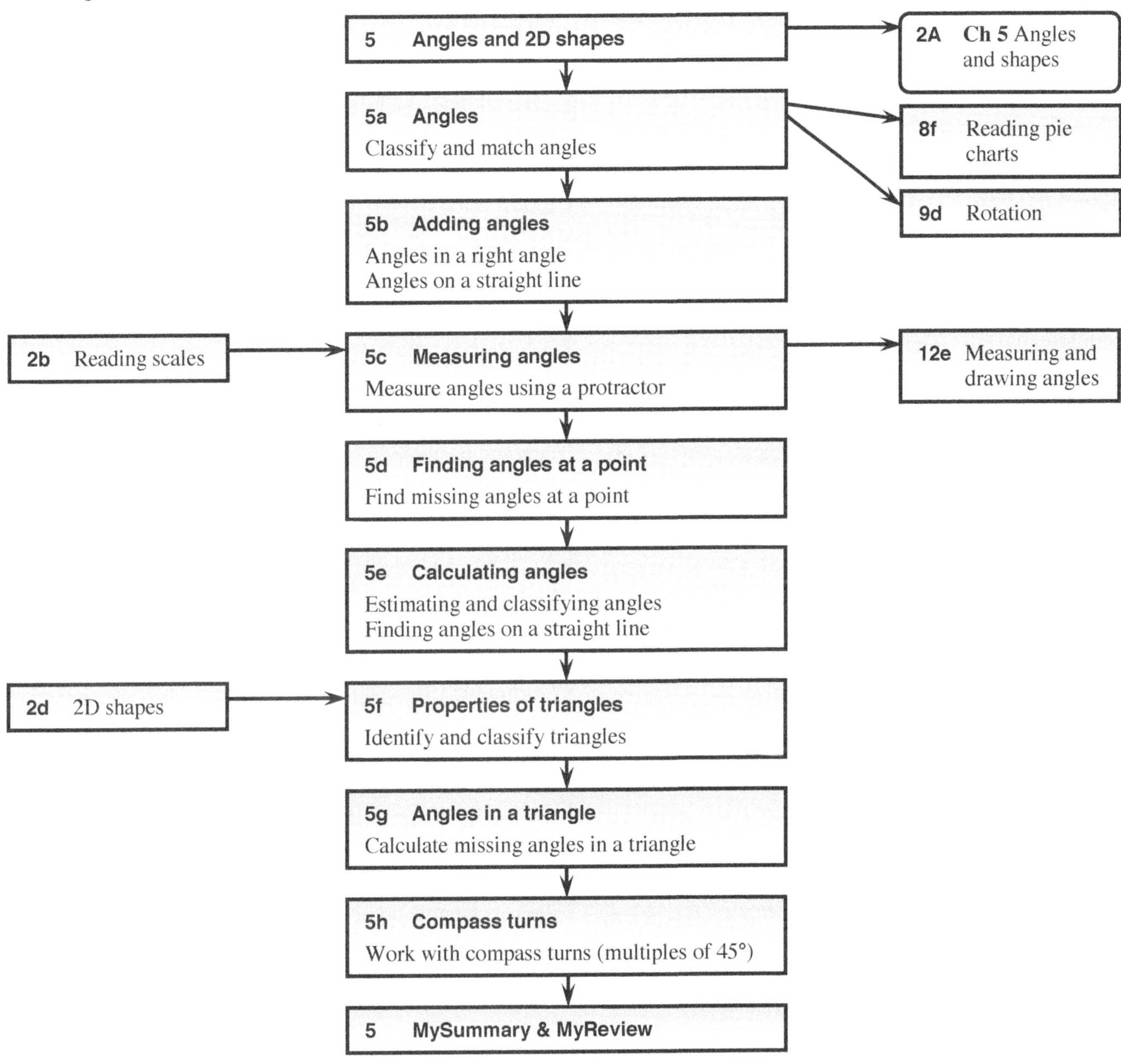

Differentiation

Student book 1A 88 – 109

Introduction to angles
Adding angles
Measuring angles
Angles at a point
Calculating angles
Properties of and angles in a triangle
Compass turns

Student book 1B 86 – 107

Describe and measure angles
Accurately draw angles and straight lines
Calculate with angles at a point and on a straight line
Calculate angles in a triangle
Describe the properties of triangles, quadrilaterals and simple polygons

Student book 1C 84 – 101

Calculate angles
Work with angles and parallel lines
Work with angles in triangles and quadrilaterals
Describe the properties of triangles, quadrilaterals and polygons

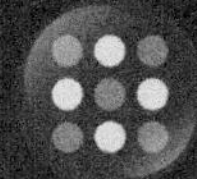

5a Angles

Objectives	
• Distinguish between and estimate the size of acute and obtuse angles. (L4/5)	
Key ideas	**Resources**
1 An angle can measure the amount of turn and a change in direction. **2** An angle can be measured in 'turns' and 'degrees'. **3** Different sizes of angle have different names.	Measuring angles (1081) An analogue clock face where the hands can be moved independently Compasses
Simplification	**Extension**
On introducing degrees, work with only acute and right angles in the first instance, both naming them and estimating their size. Then introduce obtuse angles and straight angles.	Extend these activities to include reflex angles. Having met rotations of more than one full turn; introduce the idea that angles can be more than 360°.
Literacy	**Links**
Take care with spelling: an 'angle' is not an 'angel'. The words 'clockwise' and 'anticlockwise' derive from hands turning on a clock face, but they are often used where not clock is involved, such as when opening a bottle or turning a screw.	How many days are there in a year? How many degrees are there in a full turn? Why do the Ancient Babylonians provide a link beteen the answers to these two questions? (base 60, sexagessimal, numbers) What angle does the Earth rotate about the sun between March and June and between June and December? Students could draw a diagram to help find the answers. (90°) During the fifth century, tribes that invaded Britain were known as the Angles. The French name for England is *Angleterre*, which means 'Angle Land' or 'The Land of the Angles'. Students could use the Internet to discover if this name has any connection with mathematical angles. (Geometric angles come from the latin word for bend, the tribes name comes from Angeln an area in northern Germany. However both words may derive from the same root.)

Alternative approach

The clock face and the use of N, S, E and W provide two approaches. A class set of magnetic compasses, particularly those for orienteering and map-reading, can be used to exploit the second of these two approaches more fully. It combines the notions of an angle as a turn, from north, and an angle as a change in direction. Ask students to point the compass north and to face north. Turn the rotating part of the compass to point in a given direction, say, 120°, and then rotate yourself to that direction, while keeping the compass pointing north.

Checkpoint

Use an analogue clock, or two pencils to mimic the hands of a clock. Keep the 'hour' hand fixed and rotate the 'minute hand' through one half turn, stopping periodically.

1 Name the angle turned through. (acute, right angle, obtuse, straight line)

2 Show a full turn, half turn and quarter turn.
How many degrees are in each type of turn? (360°; 180°; 90°)

3 Draw several angles in turn (such as 45°, 60°, 120°).
Estmate the size of the angle in degrees.

Starter – Spinning around

Have the students stand up and face the front of the room. Give them a turning instruction, such as 'Turn to face the right wall/back wall/left wall)'. Discuss whether they turned clockwise or anticlockwise and whether they could they have turned in the opposite direction to end up facing the correct wall.

Teaching notes

The notion of 'angle' has two aspects. Angles can have a dynamic aspect, as described in the **Starter** above where turning takes place. Angles can also have a static aspect where there is a difference in direction, such as an angle between two roads at a junction.

Display an analogue clock face with hands that can be moved independently. Leave the hour hand at 12. Start with the minute hand at 12 and slowly rotate it clockwise. Have students tell you when it has rotated a quarter turn, a half turn, three-quarters of a turn and a full turn. Ask how many turns a minute hand rotates in, say, one-and-a-half hours.

Label walls of the classroom N, S, E and W. Give instructions for students to face a certain direction and rotate an amount of a turn clockwise or anticlockwise, such as 'Face north and rotate a quarter turn clockwise'. Ask what direction they now face.

Discuss that a more accurate measure of angle needs smaller units than 'turns'. Introduce degrees. Return to the minute hand of the clock and ask how many degrees the hand rotates in a quarter, a half and three-quarters of a turn. Let a student turn the minute hand by following instructions, such as 'Start at 12 and rotate 90° anticlockwise'. Have a student turn by following instructions using the N, S, E and W signs.

Define the different types of angle (acute, right, obtuse and straight) in terms of degrees and illustrate with appropriate visual aids. Show different angles and ask students to name them and estimate their size in degrees.

Plenary

Use the analogue clock face. Keeping the hour hand fixed at 12, turn the minute hand from 12 through an angle. Students use their mini-whiteboards to give the size of angle both as a fraction of a turn and in degrees.

Draw an angle with one line of the angle vertical to mimic the minute hand at 12. Students write the type of angle and an estimate of its size in degrees on their mini-whiteboards.

Exercise commentary

The exercise focuses on describing angles by naming them and by allocating them a size in degrees. Students often find it harder to interpret an angle where one of the sides is not horizontal or vertical (for example in **1d**, **2e** and **2f**). Emphasise that it is the position of the two lines in relation to each other that matters; not whether one side is horizontal. As necessary, suggest that students rotate their books to make one side horizontal or vertical.

Question 1 does not include reflex angles. They are introduced in lesson **5d**.

Questions 2 and **3** – It may help to name the angle first. Naming an angle provides a range within which the correct size is found.

Question 4 – All four angles can be found in the diagram, and students should be encouraged to look closely. The cables form a curve and it may be interesting to discuss whether it is possible to define an angle between a curve, or its tangent, and a straight line.

Answers

1 **a** Obtuse **b** Right **c** Acute **d** Acute
e Straight line **f** Obtuse **g** Right
h Straight line

2 **a** 40° **b** 120° **c** 130° **d** 65°
e 115° **f** 160°

3 **a** 90° **b** 75° **c** 120° **d** 30°
e 180° **f** 155°

4 The triangular pylons define acute, right and obtuse angles. Reflex angles appear at the ends of the bridge.

Objectives

- Know and use the angle sum in a right angle and on a straight line. (L5)

Key ideas	Resources
1 The size of a straight angle is 180°. **2** When a straight angle is divided into smaller angles, you can calculate the size of one if you know the sizes of all the others.	Angle sums (1082) A pair of class-size compasses for displaying at the front of the classroom Cards cut into pairs of acute and obtuse angles which make straight angles A semicircular scale labelled from 0° to 180° in 10° intervals

Simplification	Extension
By placing a pencil so that it points along one line of an angle and turning it to point along the other line of the angle, the two notions of angle –'turn' and 'difference in directions' – are brought together. Discussion about the pencil turning leads to whether it turns through an acute, right or obtuse angle. When adding two angles, students could have both angles cut out of card. They place them together to form one angle before adding them numerically.	Have straight angles split into more than two pieces, and students find the size of the unknown angle with all other angles being known. Extend the sets of cards of paired angles so that some pairs make straight lines and other pairs make right angles.

Literacy	Links
The first known recorded modern use of the degree symbol, °, in mathematics is in 1569. The same symbol is used for degrees when measuring temperature rather than angles. Common units of temperature are degrees centigrade, °C, and degrees Fahrenheit, °F. There are special words for pairs of angles with a given sum. Angles that add to 90° are complementary 180° are supplementary 360° are explementary.	A half-pipe is a structure used for stunts in extreme sports such as snowboarding, skateboarding and freestyle BMX. Originally, the half-pipe cross-section was a semicircle, containing 180°, but over time the design was changed and since the 1980s it has had a flat bottom with two quarter-circles, containing 90°, at each side. Search online for 'half-pipe' to find suitable images to show the class.

Alternative approach

Have sets of labelled angles cut from card. The angles are chosen so that pairs of them can be placed together to make straight lines. Students have to find the pairs and positions the cards to make the straight lines.

Checkpoint

1 Draw a semicircular scale labelled from 0° to 180° in 10° intervals. Place two pencils together along the 0° line with their ends at the centre of the scale. Rotate one pencil through a multiple of 10°, say 50°

a By reading the scale, how many degrees the pencil has rotated? (50°)

b Is this angle acute or obtuse? (Acute)

c How many degrees the pencil still needs to turn through in order to reach

i 90° (40°)

ii 180°? (140°)

Repeat for a range of angles.

Starter – Naming, estimating and using

Revise the names of different angles. Open a pair of class-size compasses, or use two rulers, to each type of angle in turn: acute, right, obtuse and straight. Draw each angle. Ask students to use mini-whiteboards to name the type of angle and estimate its size in degrees.

Ask what type of angle is involved in practical tasks such as opening a door, opening a book, using a pencil-sharpener, putting a nut on a bolt. Estimate the size of the angle in each scenario.

Teaching notes

Ask a student to face north and then to turn half a turn clockwise. Ask what direction they now face and how many degrees they have turned through.

Ask a student to face north and then turn clockwise 90°. Ask how many *more* degrees they should turn to face south. Repeat for other angles. Ask how they work out their answers.

Draw diagrams to represent the turning from north to south. Have the first line drawn vertically up the board, the second line at a given angle (labelled, say, 100°), and the third line vertically down the board. Ask for the size of the second angle (say, 80°). Repeat for other angles.

Repeat with angles for anti-clockwise turns from the north.

Repeat with angles starting from the horizontal and then from sloping positions. In all positions, emphasise that straight angles, or half turns, have 180°.

Plenary

Ask students to use mini-whiteboards to draw each type of angle: acute, right, obtuse, straight. Ask students to draw a straight angle of 180° split into two parts, with one of the angles labelled with a given number of degrees. Ask them to find the size of the other angle and label it.

Exercise commentary

Question 1 – Did students notice that **c** and **d** form a complementary pair or that in part **e**, 45°, is its own complement and therefore half a right angle.

Question 2 – Students should notice that in part **c**, 90°, is its own supplement and therefore half a straight line.

Question 3 – Each answer can be found by looking *either* at the shape of the angle *or* at the numerical size of the angle. Discuss both methods.

Question 4 – Ensure that students calculate which pairs of angles add to 180° rather than try to judge by eye; though the later method provides a good check of the calculation. Students should be systematic so that once one pair has been found they should eliminate the two angles from further considerations.

Questions 5 and **6** – Imagine that the pink line has already turned through the angle with the given size. It now continues on its journey to turn through an overall angle of 90° or 180°.

Questions 7 and **8** – After discussing and solving the questions using the idea of a straight angle of 180°, ask the students if these diagrams remind them of any mathematical instrument that they may have already met; namely, the protractor. Look at the two scales on a protractor and note that the pairs on numbers on the two scales add together to give 180° in each case. Can any student explain why?

Answers

1	**a**	50°	**b**	60°	**c**	15°	**d**	75°
	e	45°	**f**	85°				
2	**a**	60°	**b**	150°	**c**	90°	**d**	75°
	e	135°	**f**	165°				
3	**a**	Acute	**b**	Acute	**c**	Obtuse	**d**	Acute
	e	Obtuse	**f**	Acute	**g**	Obtuse	**h**	Obtuse

4 40° and 140°; 80° and 100°; 70° and 110°; 30° and 150°

5	**a**	25°	**b**	15°	**c**	70°	**d**	5°
6	**a**	30°	**b**	80°	**c**	85°	**d**	85°

7 57°

8 Marie by 40° = 74° – 34°

5c Measuring angles

Objectives	
• Measure angles, up to 180°, to the nearest degree. (L5)	
Key ideas	**Resources**
1 Line up the protractor correctly on the angle. **2** Choose the correct scale and measure the angle by counting upwards from the correct 0°.	Measuring angles (1081) A large class-size protractor (0° to 180°) Smaller student-size protractors (0° to 180°) An example of a 360° protractor Sheets of angles drawn appropriately for measuring
Simplification	**Extension**
Draw a simplified protractor on tracing paper. It should have a radius of 5 cm and only one scale, the outer clockwise scale, labelled in 10s but with no 1° divisions. Draw a selection of acute, right and obtuse angles, with sizes only multiples of 10°, with their lines, or 'arms', just over 5 cm long. Have students name the angle first (acute, right, obtuse), say what the name means numerically, for example, less than 90°, estimate the angle size, and only then use the simplified protractor to measure each angle accurately.	Provide angles where both lines of the angle slope, where the angles point 'upwards' and 'downwards', where the lines of the angle are less than 5 cm long, and where angles are reflex, that is, greater than 180°.
Literacy	**Links**
Words containing the letters *–tract* are usually connected with 'drawing', either drawing as with a pencil or drawing as with a horse and cart. A tractor draws a plough, a contractor draws a project together (*con* = together), a subcontractor works under a contractor (*sub* = under). The word 'protractor', first used with angles in the 1650s, comes from Latin words meaning 'draw forward'.	Protractors can be used to plot the position of a ship on a navigational chart. The type of protractor used is called a 'three-arm protractor' or 'station pointer' and was invented in 1801 by Joseph Huddart of the US Navy. There is more information about station pointers at www.americanhistory.si.edu/collections/search/object/nmah_904347
Alternative approach	
Use an overhead projector with overlapping acetate sheets to demonstrate the correct use of a protractor. There is some good computer software available to develop the correct use of the protractor. For example, visit www.nrich.maths.org/1235	
Checkpoint	
1 Draw the angles 42°, 90°, 117°, 180° on a piece of paper, use the same style as those in Question **2**. **a** Estimate the size of the angle. **b** Using a protractor, rmeasure the angle. (Check the correct scale is used) **c** How does the estimate compare with the measurement? If they do not agree what should you do? Repeat for other angles if more practice is needed with measuring or estimating.	

Starter – 180

Give two numbers to add together, with students showing their answers on mini-whiteboards. Repeat using other pairs of numbers that always add together to give 180. Start with numbers which are multiples of 10.

Give one number and ask for another number to give a total of 180.

Teaching notes

All angles provided for students to measure should have both lines, arms, at least 5 cm long, the usual radius of student-sized protractors.

When using a 180° protractor, students need to

- Place the protractor correctly on the angle.
- Use the correct scale and read it accurately.

Initially, provide only angles which have one line horizontal, rather than sloped, and the other line sloped so that, when using the protractor, the angle is measured using the *outside scale*; that is, measured clockwise from the horizontal. These angles avoid the potential confusion of reading the inner scale.

To place the protractor correctly, firstly ask students to position the cross-line of the protractor on the vertex of the angle. Then ask students to turn the protractor so that one of the 0s lies on one of the lines of the angle. For angles as drawn above, this will be the left-hand zero and the horizontal line.

To choose the correct scale, ask students to start counting from the 0, zero, that they have lined up and to ignore the other zero. To read the scale accurately, ask students to move their finger around the protractor from the correct 0, counting in 10s, until they reach the other line of the angle. Vigilance by the teacher is essential.

Plenary

Give pairs of students up to ten angles drawn on paper, with the lines, arms, of the angles at least 5 cm long. Firstly, ask students to rank the angles in ascending order of size by estimating their sizes. The students then check their order by measuring the angles with a protractor.

Ensure that one pair and one threesome of angles add together to make two straight angles. Ask students to find them.

Exercise commentary

Question 1 – Note that there are two zeros. Discuss that the correct 0 is the one that lies on one of the pink lines of the angle. Count up from the correct 0 to the other pink line of the angle – this is on the inner scale for parts **a** and **b** and the outer scale for parts **c** and **d.** In each case, firmly ignore the other 0 and its scale. The arrows give very strong hints at which way to read the scales.

Question 2 – The angles are chosen so that the scales are easy to read. Ideally, the arms of each angle should be 5 cm long to fit the standard school protractor. Ensure the protractor is placed correctly; that

- The black diameter of the protractor, not its edge, lies on a pink line,
- A zero lies on top of this pink line of the angle.
- The radial centre of the protractor lies on the point of the angle.

Note the common misconception that longer lines of an angle would increase its size – but angle is a measure of turn, not length. If a pencil placed on one line is rotated, it doesn't matter how long the pencil is.

Question 3 – Having two other angles nearby can cause visual confusion when measuring the third angle. Covering the two angles with a blank sheet of paper leaves just the third angle in view.

Students could be encouraged to draw their own triangles and measure the three angles in them. Suggest that they add the angles: are their answers always within a few degrees of 180°?

Answers

Angles should be measured to at least ±2° or better ±1°.

1 **a** Obtuse, 145° **b** Acute, 70°
c Obtuse, 115° **d** Acute, 45°

2 **a** 110° **b** 30° **c** 90° **d** 140°

3 Purple 49°, Orange 70°, Yellow 61°

5d Finding angles at a point

Objectives	
• Know and use the angle sum at a point. (L5)	
Key ideas	**Resources**
1 The size of a full turn is 360°. **2** When a full turn is divided into two or more angles, you can calculate the size of one if you know the sizes of all the others.	Angle sums (1082) A class-size pair of compasses Sets of labelled cards which fit together to make a full turn A circular scale labelled from 0° to 360° in 20° intervals
Simplification	**Extension**
Only use angles that require straightforward calculations. Ask students to choose between two methods when finding the answers mentally: subtraction by 'taking away', such as for 360 – 120 and subtraction by 'adding on', such as for 360 – 290.	Provide diagrams where there are three or more angles making full turns, of which one angle in each case is not known.
Literacy	**Links**
Links can be made with algebra in the way that problems can be written. For example, when making a straight angle, write $120 + 40 + a = 180$ $160 + a = 180$ So $a = 20$	The first traffic roundabout was built in 1901 around the Arc de Triomphe in Paris, although traffic did not become one-way around the roundabout until 1907. Today it has eight lanes of traffic. There is a bird's eye view of the Arc de Triomphe and the Etoile at www.maps.google.co.uk/maps?t=k&hl=en&ie=UTF8&ll=48.873013,2.294683&spn=0.00645,0.019956&z=16&om=1 For a diagram showing traffic flow around a modern roundabout, see www.en.wikipedia.org/wiki/File:UK_Roundabout_8_Cars.gif

Alternative approach

Have sets of labelled angles cut from card. Choose angles so that pairs of them can be placed together to make a full turn. Ask students to find the pairs and position the cards to make full turns.

Checkpoint

1 Draw a semicircular scale labelled from 0° to 360° in 20° intervals. Place two pencils together along the 0° line with their ends at the centre of the scale. Rotate one pencil through a multiple of 20°, say 260°.

a By reading the scale, how many degrees the pencil has rotated? (260°)

b What is the name for this type of angle? (Reflex)

c Ask the student to rotate the pencil to complete a full turn.

i How many degrees has the pencil turned through? (100°)

ii Write this as a mathematical statement. (260° + 100° = 360°)

Repeat for a range of angles.

Starter – 360

Ask students to use mini-whiteboards and give them two or three numbers to add together, where all the totals are 360. For example,

310 + 50, 200 + 160, 290 + 10 + 60

Give them a number, such as 340, 310, 270, 90, 180, 250, and ask what other number must be added to give a total of 360. (20, 50, 90, 270, 180, 110)

Teaching notes

These notes progress from the dynamic notion of 'angle', through a static but tactile angle in card, to a diagram of an angle.

Remind students of quarter turns, half turns and full turns; ask how many degrees are in each of them.

Use a class-size pair of compasses, or two parallel rulers, and open up an angle of, say 260°. Ask how many more degrees are needed for a full turn. (100°) Repeat for other 'easy' angles, such as 300°, 200°, 250°. (60°, 160°, 110°)

Have an angle of, say 260°, cut out of card and ask what other angle is needed to make a full turn. Fit an angle of 100° to make the full turn. Repeat with other cards.

Sketch an angle labelled, say 290°. Label the other angle with a letter. Ask for the size of the lettered angle. Ask how it was calculated. Repeat with other angles.

Refer to the Student Book and discuss Rory on his roundabout.

Plenary

Give pairs of students up to ten angles drawn on paper, with the lines, arms, of the angles at least 5 cm long. Firstly, ask students to rank the angles in ascending order of size by estimating their sizes. The students then check their order by measuring the angles with a protractor.

Ensure that one pair and one threesome of angles add together to make two full turns. Ask students to find them.

Exercise commentary

Questions 1 – This tests the number bond arithmetic required to do subsequent questions. Discourage the use of a calculator.

Questions 2 and **3** – These link to the calculations done in Question **1** and to the example of Rory's roundabout, with Question **3** being more abstract. Students should not use a protractor.

Question 4 – Encourage students to be systematic as they work through the possibilities. There is a unique solution. It is possible to approach this question be drawing and cutting out appropriately sized angles and fitting them together.

Question 5 – The easiest way to measure the angle is to use a 360° protractor. Two other ways use a 180° protractor which is placed over the obtuse angle. *Either* measure the obtuse angle and subtract it from 360° *or* measure that part of the coloured angle under the protractor and add it to the remaining 180° part of the coloured angle.

Question 6 – See question 5 for suggestions. This question can be extended by asking for the largest obtuse angle. (170° = 110° + 60°)

Answers

1	**a** 160		**b** 240		**c** 130		**d** 110	
	e 260		**f** 100		**g** 300		**h** 115	
	i 180		**f** 270		**g** 150		**h** 230	
2	**a** 270°		**b** 130°		**c** 205°		**d** 85°	
3	**a** 245°		**b** 180°		**c** 110°		**d** 225°	

4 **b**, **c** and **e** (150° + 100° + 110°)

5 Measure the acute (explementary) angle and subtract it from 360°.

or

Place the protractor along one ray but in 'reverse' so as to measure the angle beyond 180° and add this to 180°.

6 185° = 110° + 15° + 60°

5e Calculating angles

Objectives	
• Know and use the angle sum in a right angle, on a straight line and at a point. (L5)	
Key ideas	**Resources**
1 The number of degrees in right angles, straight angles and full turns. **2** These three types of angle can be divided into smaller parts.	Angle sums (1082) A set of angles made from card which can be paired to make other angles Sheets of plain paper which can be folded and drawn on
Simplification	**Extension**
When asking students to name an angle, provide them with the list: 'acute', 'right', 'obtuse', 'straight', 'reflex'. When asking students to estimate the size of an angle, have them name the angle first.	Provide a list of angle sizes, including values such as 75°and 15°, which can be paired to make right angles, straight angles and full turns. Students are to pair them and say what type of angle they make.
Literacy	**Links**
The word 'acute' can mean 'sharp', so think of an acute angle as a sharp one. If something is 'upright', then it is at 90° to the ground. A 'right' angle is the angle between the horizontal and vertical. The word obtuse can mean 'not sharp or pointed', which is a good way of describing an obtuse angle. The word 'reflex' comes from Latin and means 'bend back' which is how a reflex angle looks.	Angles are applied, for example: • to create wedges to force things apart; • to pull objects up an inclined plane as when Stonehenge and the Pyramids were built; • to design the camber on a road round a bend; • when aeroplanes take off and land. Can students suggest other applications of angles?

Alternative approach

Provide a pack of angles made from card. The angles can be paired to make right angles, straight angles and full turns. The students' task is to pair them, measure them with a protractor, and write a statement using their results, such as 55° + 35° = 90°.

Checkpoint

Show the six angles: 35°, 96°, 132°, 55°, 264°, 46°. The angles can be drawn on a piece of paper or cut out of card. The numerical values should be given.

1 name the type of angle (Acute, Obtuse, Obtuse, Acute, Reflex, Acute)

2 For the angles given above

- **a** Which pair fit together to make a right angle? (35° and 55°)
- **b** Which pair fit together to make a straight line? (132° and 48°)
- **c** Which pair fit together to make a complete turn? (96° and 264°)

3 Write a statement for each pair of angles in question **2**.
(35° + 55° = 90°, 132° + 48° = 180°, 96° + 264° = 360°)

Starter – Quick fire

Continue to consolidate previous learning by asking students to use mini-whiteboards to respond to questions from all of Chapters **1** to **4** and Chapter **5** so far, such as:

- A straight angle is made from two angles. One of the angles is 110°. What is the size of the other angle? (70°)
- What is the name of a triangle with two equal sides? (Isosceles)
- What is the name of a triangle with two equal sides and one right angle? (Right angle, isosceles)

Discuss answers when necessary.

Teaching notes

Ensure that students know the names and meanings of the different kinds of angle. Introduce the reflex angle to those who may not have met it before. Draw various angles, including reflex angles, and discuss, as a whole class, their names and approximate sizes. Refine students' skills at estimating sizes of angle but be willing to accept broad approximations.

Take a sheet of paper and mark one angle as a right angle. Ask how many degrees are in a right angle. Fold the right angle so only part of it is visible to students. Ask for an estimate of the visible angle and, from the answer, what the size of the other angle is likely to be. Open the paper and draw along the crease to highlight the two angles.

Repeat with an edge of paper. Ask how many degrees are in a straight angle. Fold it into two angles, etc.

Now draw a right angle and divide it into two parts. Ask "If this angle is 60°, what is the size of this angle?", expecting the answer 30°. Repeat with other right angles, straight angles and full turns. In each case, give the size of one angle and ask for the size of the other. You could also ask students to name the type of angle for each of their answers; for example, '30° and acute'. Divide angles into three parts, give the size of two angles and ask for the size of the third angle. Explore how the answers are calculated. Answers can be written on mini-whiteboards.

Plenary

Ask students to compile an 'angle fact' revision sheet with vocabulary definitions and an example of calculations of angles which make right angles, straight angles and full turns. This task can be undertaken as a whole class with the teacher acting as the scribe.

Exercise commentary

Question 1 – No reflex angles are given. Students should imagine a right angle and then decide whether the given angle is almost a right angle or not. This line of thought helps them make the correct choice.

Question 2 – Students will most likely find this question easier than Question **1**.

Question 3 – Some students may need a calculator to find the correct pairs.

Question 4 – The angles add up to give a right angle, a straight line or a full turn. Some students may need a calculator for some of these questions. Students could imagine cutting away the known angles to emphasise that a subtraction is involved. Parts **e** to **h** require two angles to be added before subtracting from 180° and 360° respectively.

Question 5 – Students can use angles **a** to **g** more than once as they work through the list of angles A to G. Students should use their mental addition skills before they resort to a calculator. The question can be extended by having students make their own combinations and then asking a partner to pair angles together.

Answers

1	**a**	80°	**b**	110°	**c**	90°	**d**	155°
2	**a**	Acute	**b**	Obtuse	**c**	Obtuse	**d**	Acute
	e	Obtuse	**f**	Obtuse	**g**	Acute	**h**	Acute

3 **a** and **f**, **b** and **d**, **c** and **h**, **e** and **g** make a straight line.

4	**a**	57°	**b**	113°	**c**	309°	**d**	113°
	e	64°	**f**	225°	**g**	98°	**h**	58°
	i	120°						
4	**A**	**a** and **e**	**B**	**b** and **e**	**C**	**a** and **c**	**D**	**d** and **e**
	E	**f** and **g**	**F**	**e** and **f**	**G**	**b** and **f**		

5f Properties of triangles

Objectives	
• Identify triangles using their angle and side properties. (L5)	
Key ideas	**Resources**
1 Triangles can be named by looking at their angles. **2** Triangles can be named by looking at their sides.	Properties of triangles (1130) Cards of different shapes: triangles and non-triangles; different types of triangles Geoboard and rubber bands
Simplification	**Extension**
Sets of cards of different shapes can be used to collate shapes into groups of 'triangles' and 'not triangles'. Sets of cards of different triangles can be used to group the cards into three groups either by the lengths of their sides, or by the sizes of their angles. Rulers and protractors can be used to check the results.	Students can be asked to draw isosceles, equilateral and scalene triangles and measure their angles. Ask them the question, if some sides are equal, does that mean that some angles are equal?
Literacy	**Links**
The word 'equilateral' comes from two Latin words meaning 'equal sides'. The word 'isosceles' comes from two Greek words meaning 'equal legs'. The word 'scalene' comes from a Greek word meaning 'uneven'. A triangle can also be called 'equiangular' which means it has 'equal angles'. Is an equiangular triangle also equilateral? (Yes)	A triangle is the name of a percussion instrument, consisting of a steel tube bent into a triangle shape. It is played by striking it with a steel rod. The triangle first became an orchestral instrument in the 18th century. One could be borrowed from the music department and shown to the class. The triangle is the basis for the construction of many bridges. It has a rigid structure, unlike the quadrilateral. Various designs can be found online; use a search engine and look for 'Images of truss bridges'.

Alternative approach

Show the class straws of various lengths and several of the same length. Straws of different colours help to distinguish different lengths. Arrange the straws into different triangular shapes. Discuss the sides and angles of the triangles and categorise them.

Use rubber bands on a 3-by-3 geoboard to make different types of triangle. Are there any types that cannot be made on this geoboard? (Equilateral triangle). How many different triangles of each type can be made?

Checkpoint

1 Draw an isosceles, right-angled, equilateral and scalene triangle; include the symbols for equal sides or right angles where necessary.

Do not allow students to refer to the Student Book.

2 For each of the following descriptions, identify which triangle the description refers to.

a Two sides equal, two angles equal. (Isosceles)
a One angle 90°. (Right-angled)
a All sides equal, all angles equal. (Equilateral)
a All sides different, all angles different. (Scalene)

Starter – Quick fire

Continue to consolidate previous learning by asking students to use mini-whiteboards to respond to questions from all of Chapters 1 to 4 and Chapter 5 so far, such as:

- Write the size of any acute angle in degrees.
- Draw any obtuse angle.
- After turning through 150°, how many more degrees to you have to turn to complete a half turn?
- A full turn is made from two angles. If one angle is 250°, what is the other angle?

Discuss answers when necessary.

Teaching notes

Draw an acute-angled triangle. For each angle in turn, ask students to say what type of angle it is. Give this type of triangle the name 'acute-angled triangle'.
Repeat for a right-angled triangle. Note that one angle is a right-angle. Give the triangle its name.
Repeat for an obtuse-angled triangle. Note that one angle is an obtuse angle. Give the triangle its name.

Draw an isosceles triangle, an equilateral triangle and a scalene triangle. Ask students to now concentrate on the lengths of the sides, not the sizes of the angles.

Ask what is special about the isosceles triangle (two sides are equal), about the equilateral triangle (all three sides are equal) and about the scalene triangle (all sides are different).

Draw a triangle. Ask students to look at its angles and give the triangle a name (acute-angled, right-angled or obtuse-angled). Ask them now to look at the sides and give the triangle a name (isosceles, equilateral or scalene). Students should respond by writing on their mini-whiteboards.

Mention that equal sides have short dashes on them to show that they are equal in length.

Plenary

Provide pairs of students with three straws of length 10 cm, 8 cm and 5 cm respectively. How many different triangles can they make with these three straws? Ask them to draw as many different triangles as they can find. Ask questions about the types of angles in the triangles that they make. Introduce the word 'congruent' to discuss congruent triangles. Discuss rotations and reflections of triangles. Show that only one unique triangle is possible. Appropriate computer software could be used to draw and move lines and triangles.

Exercise commentary

Questions 1 and **2** – These are straight forward, and test students' ability to identify triangles both by sight and by description.

Question 3 – Students can record the lengths in cm, using a decimal point, or in mm. Measuring angles consolidates their skills with a protractor and, if needed, two angles can be covered up with another sheet of paper to focus more easily on the angle being measured.

Question 4 – Some larger triangles are formed from two, or even three, smaller adjacent triangles. This question is not as easy as it appears at first glance. Students may need reminding that triangles must have straight edges, this excludes all the 'triangles' with a base on the curved line.

Answers

1 **a** Right-angled, Scalene **b** Isosceles
c Scalene **d** Equilateral

2 Check students 'drawings of triangles
a Equilateral **b** Right-angled
c Scalene

3 **a** **i** 43 mm (all 3 sides)
ii 35 mm, 35 mm, 50 mm
b **i** 60° (all 3 angles) **ii** 45°, 45°, 90°
c **i** Equilateral **ii** Right-angled, isosceles

4 17; Scalene (6), Isosceles (3), Right-angled (8)

Objectives

- Know and use the angle sum in a triangle. (L5)

Key ideas	Resources
1 The three angles of any triangle can be re-arranged to make a straight line of 180°. 2 The three angles of any triangle add up to 180°.	Angle sums (1082) Card on which large triangles can be drawn Protractors Pictures of different types of triangle

Simplification	Extension
When finding angles in triangles, ensure that the calculations are straightforward by involving, for example, only multiples of 10°. For more awkward calculations, allow the use of a calculator but insist that the calculation as well as the answer is written down.	More problems similar to those problems in question **4**, which require two or more angles facts, can be given to students.

Literacy	Links
Connections with algebra can be reinforced by setting out the written work as, for example: $40° + 80° + x = 180°$ $120° + x = 180°$ $x = 180° - 120°$ $x = 60°$	It is often claimed that there is a mysterious area west of the tip of Florida called the Bermuda triangle where planes and ships disappear. There is claimed to be another mysterious area called the devil's triangle somewhere south of Tokyo, Japan. Students could try to find these areas, using an atlas or the internet, and then discuss how they could really decide if the area was unusual or not. Neither area is listed as particularly dangerous to shipping by the insurers Lloyd's of London.

Alternative approach

Before dissecting the triangle and re-assembling its three angles as a straight line, students could draw large triangles, each one different, and use protractors to measure the three angles. Ask them to add the three angles together and collect the totals from all the class. Decide whether each of the totals should be the same and ask why they are not. If all measurements had been accurate, what would the totals have been? Decide that a proof is still needed.

Checkpoint

1 Draw or, for more able students describe, the following triangles and ask students to find the missing lettered angle in each case.

- **a** Right-angled triangle with angles 90°, 60°, a. ($a = 30°$)
- **b** Scalene triangle with angles 70°, 50°, b. ($b = 60°$)
- **c** Isosceles triangle with angles 80°, c, c. ($c = 50°$)
- **d** Equilateral triangle with three angles labelled as d. ($d = 60°$)

Starter – Dissecting triangles

Ask each student to draw a large triangle, cut it out and tear (not cut) it into three pieces so that each angle is separated. They should label the three angles using an arc and a letter. The three angles are then re-arranged at the same point to make a straight line. Ask if all students can make a straight line. Ask them how many degrees make a straight line and ask them what total the three angles of the triangle add up to.

Teaching notes

When calculating the third angle of a triangle from two known angles, students should set out their work by writing, for example, $40° + 80° + x = 180°$ as a first line to reinforce the total of all three angles as 180° and then follow this line with $120° + x = 180°$ and $x = 60°$ to reinforce links with algebra. See the exemplar working-out in the **Literacy** section.

Students should use mental methods in the first instance when calculating their answers. Written computation may be needed for some problems. The use of a calculator should be a last resort, although the weakest students' use of a calculator would help them succeed with the geometry without struggling with the arithmetic.

Plenary

Ask students to sit in pairs back to back. Give one of the pair a picture of an isosceles, equilateral, right-angled or scalene triangle. The second student is allowed to ask questions about the sides and angles but neither student is allowed to use the key words 'isosceles', 'equilateral', etc. The aim is to identify the type of triangle with as few questions as possible. To make for greater challenge, include two angles of the triangle and ask for the size of the third angle.

Exercise commentary

Questions 1 and **2 –** Students generally find this early work with triangles straightforward. Question **1** involves only scalene triangles. Students should use their mental number skills. They should write the final subtraction as part of their answer; for example, $a = 180 - 90 - 40 = 50°$. Indeed, they could reinforce writing algebraic expressions by setting out their work as in the **Literacy** section.

Question 3 – This could be posed as a 'real' problem using an actual paper triangle with a corner torn off.

Question 4 – Part **a** involves a straight angle and a right-angle triangle. The triangle is redundant and most of it can be covered up so that the student only sees the straight angle. Part **b** builds on part **a**. Parts of the diagram can be covered up so that each straight angle in turn is seen alone to find angles a and b. The focus then moves to just the triangle with the 120° and 130° covered up if necessary.

Question 5 – Students are likely to say all angles must be equal 'by symmetry'. A variant is to consider the triangle as isosceles and use this fact to argue that all pairs of angles are equal.

Question 6 – Beware of students who use the argument 'by looking'. Often angles and diagrams will be misdrawn to stop people measuring them.

Answers

1 **a** 60° **b** 75° **c** 60° **d** 45°
e 55° **f** 30°

2 **a** $a = 50°$ **b** $b = c = 70°$
c $d = e = 60°$ **d** $f = 65°, g = 50°$
e $h = 35°$ **f** $i = 25°, j = 130°$
g $k = 35°$

3 60°

4 **a** $k = 35°, l = 56°$
b $m = 60°, n = 50°, o = 70°$

5 All angles, always 60° (180° ÷ 3)
Accurately draw and measure the angles in several equilateral triangles.

6 $c = 40° < b = 45° < a = 50°$

5h Compass turns

Objectives	
• Use the eight compass points to describe direction.	(L4)

Key ideas	Resources
1 Specify directions using the names of the eight compass points	Position and turning (1231) Compasses 360° protractor Printed direction instructions Clear transparencies

Simplification	Extension
Give students a transparency and ask them to copy and label the 8 point compass rose. This can either either be done by tracing the example at the top of p104 of the Student Book, or by measuring angles with a protractor as appropriate. Use the transparency as an overlay to help with the questions. As students become more confident at remembering the directions reduce the reliance on the transparency. Initially avoid Questions **2** and **4** of **Exercise 4h** which mix directions and angles.	Invite students to create their own set of instructions for going between two places in the school based on compass bearings and distances. Students could work in pairs to create the instructions and then swap with another pair to test them. Alternatively students could make their own versions of Question 5, either using the same town layout or inventing their own layout, and providing a set of instructions for a partner to follow.

Literacy	Links
Students may need help to remember the eight compass points. Start with the opposite pair 'north' and 'south', with north placed at the top. The second pair 'west' and 'east' spell out the word WE. The four intermediate directions are then composites of the main directions on each side with N/S coming before W/E. The Student Book suggests the mnemonic 'Naughty Elephants Splash Water' for the cardinal points. Students might like to invent their own mnemonics or share their own ideas for how to remember the compass points.	The Student Book introduces the four cardinal compass points (N, E, S, W) and the eight principal compass points (N, NE, E, SE, S, SW, W, NW). However in earlier times, sailors would be expected to memorise the names of more directions. The 16-point compass uses N, NNE, NE, ENE, E, ESE, SE, SSE, S etc. The 32-point compass uses N, NbE, NNE, NEbN, NE, NEbE, ENE, EbN, E etc. (where 'b' stands for 'by'). If you could remember all 32 names you could 'box the compass'.

Alternative approach

Adopt a practical approach to covering this material. Start by asking for a volunteer. Place them at a 'starting' point and give them a compass and a set of straightforward instructions: directions and distances (number of paces). Ask the volunteer to read out the first instruction, say, 'travel 10 paces east' and discuss with the class what the volunteer should do before they carry out the instruction. Repeat with more instructions based on N, E, S, W directions before including NE,SE, SW, NW directions. Once the class understands how to proceed, organise them into groups and issue them with there own instructions. This is likely to work best in a more open space than a classroom where there may be more than one 'stopping' point.

After this practical activity adopt a more abstract approach and do some exercise questions collectively, including covering the idea of an anti/clockwise turn through a specified angle. Using **Exercise 5h**, do Question 1 parts **a** and **c** together while students do parts **b** and **d** on mini-whiteboards. Likewise do Question **2** parts **a** and **c** together while students do parts **b** and **d** on mini-whiteboards. Once secure students should work on their own.

Checkpoint

1 For Amy in Question **1**	**a**	What does she see to the north-west?	(Cinema)
	b	What direction is New Road?	(South-east)
2 If you are facing east	**a**	What direction is 45° clockwise?	(South east)
	b	What direction is 180° anticlockwise?	(West)

Starter – Simon says turn

Ask students to stand up and clear a little space around them. Issue the instructions 'Simon says quarter turn clockwise', 'Simon says turn 180° anticlockwise' etc. As soon as the command is issued the students must act; those that are too slow or wrong must sit down. Increase the speed of instructions and introduce less obvious angles 45°, 60° etc. until one winner remains.

Teaching notes

Ask students to imagine that they are at sea, in fog, with only a compass to point in the direction of north and that they need to give directions. How should they do it? The compass should hint at directions such as east or south-west. Give students a compass and ask them to identify the direction a particular classroom feature is in (such as the door, window or whiteboard). Then reverse the question by giving them a direction and asking what feature it leads to. For consistency students should imagine themselves to be in the centre of the classroom.

Ask a student to suggest an angle and a direction from north (for example, 90° anticlockwise). Check that students are confident deciding between clockwise and anticlockwise. Then ask the class what classroom feature is at the point 90° anticlockwise. It may help to use a 360° protractor, oriented so that 0° is in the initial direction.

Finally mix the two approaches and ask questions such as 'Suppose you were facing west, what direction would be 90° anticlockwise?' (south)

Plenary

Use mini-whiteboards and questions to check students' understanding. The **Checkpoint** gives examples.

As time permits, discuss situations where giving compass directions is important, such as navigating in boats and planes, when walking or orienteering, etc. Suggest that in the future students might have to give even more accurate directions and then they will learn how to give three-figure bearings using angles.

Exercise commentary

Questions 1 – This tests students' understanding of the basic language for directions; parts **a** to **c** match features to directions while parts **d** and **e** match directions to features. Point out the compass rose to help students remember the directions.

Question 2 – It may help students to place a sketch of the compass rose in front of them, pointing east or south-west, and then to imagine doing the turn through 90° or 180°. The compass rose must not be turned! Mixing up clockwise and anticlockwise will give the *wrong* answers of N in part **a** and SE in part **d**. In order to answer parts **b** and **d** correctly, parts **a** and **c** first have to be answered correctly.

Question 3 – This is a more abstract version of Question 1. Check that students understand that only the direction and not the distances are important.

Question 4 – Confusing clockwise and anticlockwise will result in the *wrong* answers of 1 in part **a** and 3 in part **b**. As necessary remind students that there are three lots of 30° in a right angle (quarter turn).

Question 5 – Students need to understand that they should follow the instructions at any junction that they cross or reach. Early finishers could be asked to copy the road layout and provide their own set of instructions for a partner to follow.

Answers

1 **a** High road **b** Museum
  c Station **d** East
  e North-East
2 **a** South **b** North
  c North-East **d** North-West
3 **a** North **b** West
  c South-East **d** North-East
4 **a** 7 **b** 9
5 Ray, Swimming pool Liz, Cinema

Key outcomes	Quick check
Estimate angles and use a protractor to measure them. L5	Measure these angles. **a** (25°) **b** (145°)
Distinguish between acute, obtuse and reflex angles. L3	**1** How do you describe the angles in question **1** above? (Acute, Obtuse) **2** What other words are used to describe angles? (Right, Reflex)
Use the sum of angles at a point, on a straight line and and in a right angle. L5	Find the missing angles in these diagrams. 42°, *a*, *b* — ($a = 48°$, $b = 25°$) 122°, *c* — ($c = 238°$)
Classify triangles by there properties. L4	**1** Find the missing angle(s) in these triangles. **2** Give the mathematical name for the type of triangle?
Find missing angles in a triangle. L5	*a*, 38°, 52° — ($a = 90°$, Right angle) *b*, *c*, 60° — ($b = c = 60°$, Equilateral)
Understand and use the points of a compass. L5	**1** What direction is opposite south-east? (North-west) **2** You are facing East and turn 90° anticlockwise, what direction are you now facing?. (North)

Development and links
The ability to estimate the size of angles is assumed when interpreting pie charts in chapter **8**. The language of angles is used to describe rotations in chapter **9** and geometry in general. Accurately drawing angles is revisited in chapter **12**, where the skill is used to draw SAS triangles. Much of this material is revisited and extended in book **2A**: calculating angles includes opposite angles and more complex configurations of lines, constructions include ASA triangles, and classification of 2D shapes includes quadrilaterals. Accurately drawing angles is also used when creating pie charts. The use of compass points is regularly used in Geography and when giving directions.

MyMaths extra support

Lesson/online homework			Description
Position and turning	1231	L2	The first part of this lesson covers understanding clockwise and anticlockwise and identifying right angles.

My Review

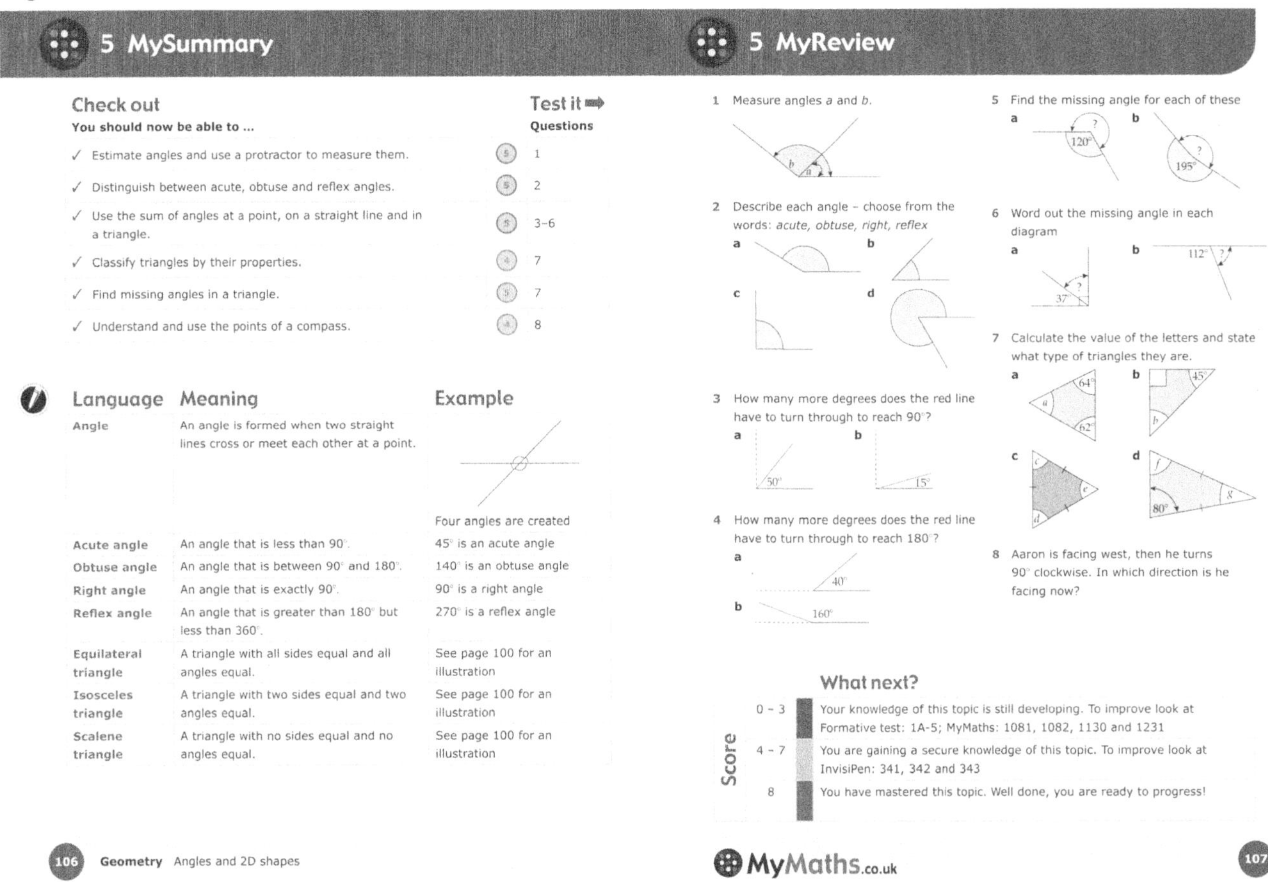

5 MySummary

Check out
You should now be able to ...

	Test it ➡ Questions
✓ Estimate angles and use a protractor to measure them.	1
✓ Distinguish between acute, obtuse and reflex angles.	2
✓ Use the sum of angles at a point, on a straight line and in a triangle.	3–6
✓ Classify triangles by their properties.	7
✓ Find missing angles in a triangle.	7
✓ Understand and use the points of a compass.	8

Language	Meaning	Example
Angle	An angle is formed when two straight lines cross or meet each other at a point.	Four angles are created
Acute angle	An angle that is less than 90°.	45° is an acute angle
Obtuse angle	An angle that is between 90° and 180°.	140° is an obtuse angle
Right angle	An angle that is exactly 90°.	90° is a right angle
Reflex angle	An angle that is greater than 180° but less than 360°.	270° is a reflex angle
Equilateral triangle	A triangle with all sides equal and all angles equal.	See page 100 for an illustration
Isosceles triangle	A triangle with two sides equal and two angles equal.	See page 100 for an illustration
Scalene triangle	A triangle with no sides equal and no angles equal.	See page 100 for an illustration

106 **Geometry** Angles and 2D shapes

5 MyReview

1 Measure angles *a* and *b*.

2 Describe each angle – choose from the words: *acute, obtuse, right, reflex*
a b c d

3 How many more degrees does the red line have to turn through to reach 90°?
a 50° b 15°

4 How many more degrees does the red line have to turn through to reach 180°?
a 40° b 160°

5 Find the missing angle for each of these
a 120° ? b 195° ?

6 Work out the missing angle in each diagram
a 37° ? b 112° ?

7 Calculate the value of the letters and state what type of triangles they are.
a 64° 62° *a* b 45° *b* c *c* *d* *e* d *f* 80° *g*

8 Aaron is facing west, then he turns 90° clockwise. In which direction is he facing now?

What next?

Score	
0 – 3	Your knowledge of this topic is still developing. To improve look at Formative test: 1A-5; MyMaths: 1081, 1082, 1130 and 1231
4 – 7	You are gaining a secure knowledge of this topic. To improve look at InvisiPen: 341, 342 and 343
8	You have mastered this topic. Well done, you are ready to progress!

MyMaths.co.uk 107

Question commentary

Question 1 – (lesson **5c**) Allow ±2°, though ±1° accuracy would be exam standard. Students should estimate the angles first as an aid to using the correct scales; likely misreadings are **a** 135° and **b** 40°.

Question 2 – (spread **5a**) As a follow up to question **1**, consider asking students to measure the angles: **a** 150°, **b** 45°, **c** 90° and **d** 300°. Part **d** will be tricky, particular if students only have a semi-circular protractor. Likely misreadings are **a** 30°, **b** 135° and **d** 60°/240°.

Questions 3 – **7** Check that students are aware that diagrams may not be drawn accurately and therefore these questions should be done by calculation and not by measurement.

Question 3 – (lesson **5b**) Students need to know that angles forming a right angle add up to 90°.

Question 4 – (lesson **5b**) Students need to know that the angles on a straight line add up to 180°.

Question 5 – (lesson **5d**) Students need to know that the angles around a point add up to 360°.

Question 6 – (lesson **5e**) This mixes two cases and requires students to recognise the symbol for a right-angle.

Question 7 – (lessons **f** and **g**) Students should be able to spell correctly the names of triangles. They may miss **b** being isosceles.

Question 8 – (lesson **h**) It would be both helpful and good practice to draw a four-point compass. An anticlockwise turn gives the answer South.

Answers

1 **a** 45° **b** 140°

2 **a** Obtuse **b** Acute
c Right-angle **d** Reflex

3 **a** 40° **b** 75°

4 **a** 140° **b** 20°

5 **a** 240° **b** 165°

6 **a** 53° **b** 68°

7 **a** $a = 54°$, scalene
b $b = 45°$, right-angled and isosceles
c $c = d = e = 60°$, equilateral
d $f = 80°$, $g = 20°$, isosceles

8 North

5 MyPractice

5a

1 What kind of angle is each of these?

a b c d

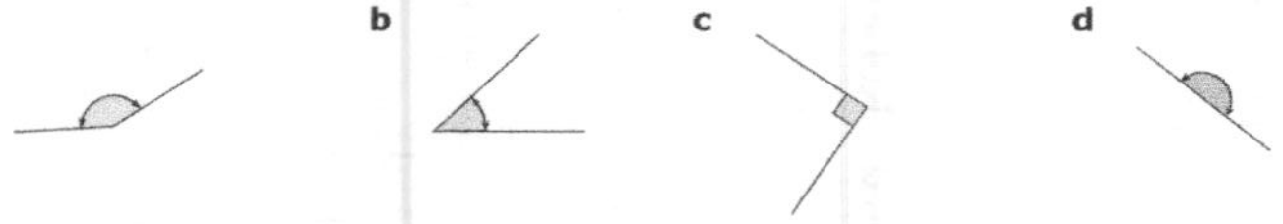

5b

2 Find the other angle on the straight line in each diagram.

a 35° 75° ?

b 55° ? 90°

c 45° 40° ?

d 35° 25° ?

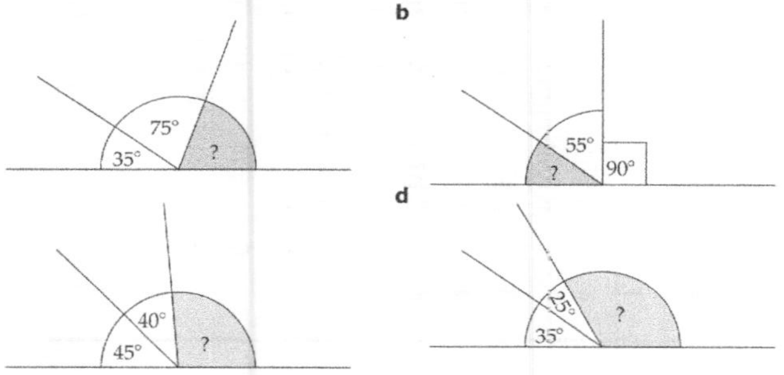

5c

3 Measure each of these angles.

a b

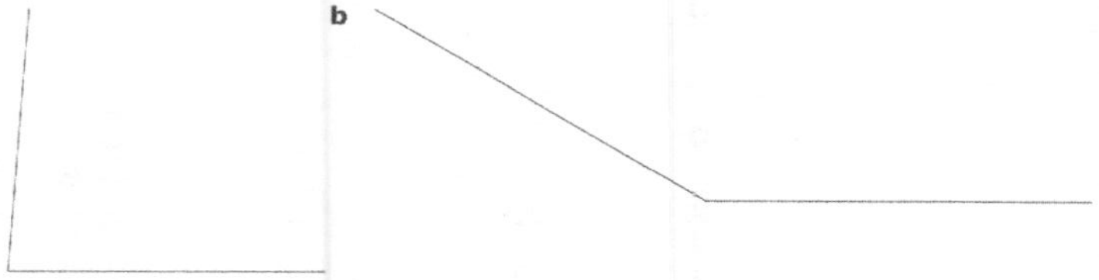

5d

4 Find the missing angle in each diagram.

a 140° 115° ?

b 120° 130° ?

c 175° ? 90°

d 135° 145° ?

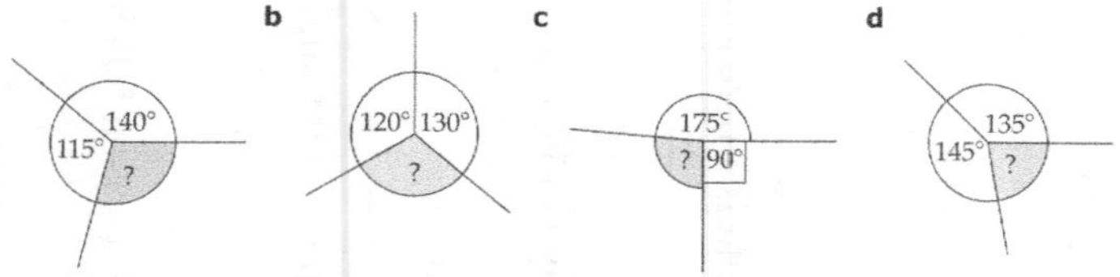

5e

5 Find the missing angles.

a *a* 38°

b 310° *b*

c *c* 63°

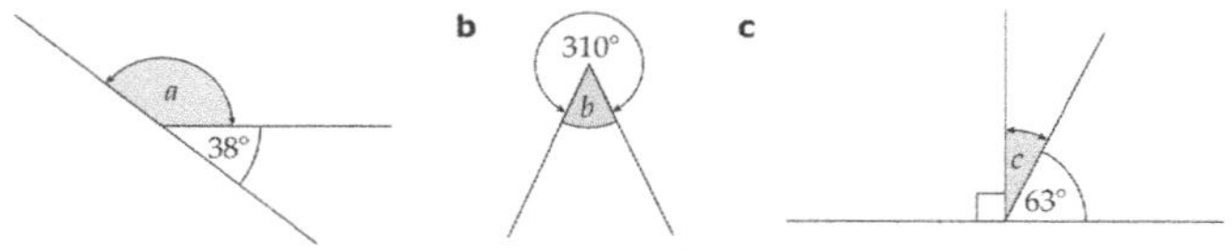

5f

6 Match the triangle to its name and description.

a Right-angled

b Equilateral

c Isosceles

d Scalene

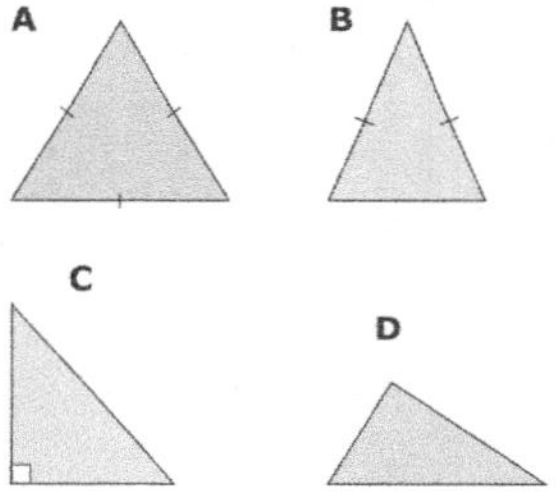

A B C D

1 All sides different
All angles different

2 One angle 90°

3 Two sides equal
Two angles equal

4 All sides equal
All angles equal

5g

7 Find the missing angles in these triangles.

a *a* 60° 50°

b *b* 80° 80°

c 43° 102° *c*

d 40° *d* 50°

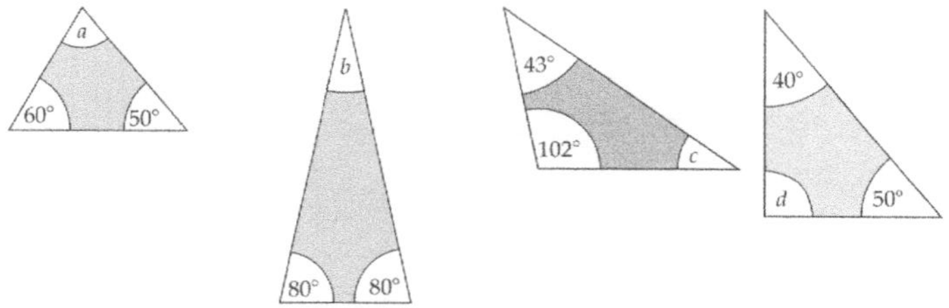

5h

8 Vicky is facing North. She turns 135° clockwise, then 180° anticlockwise, then 90° clockwise, then 225° anticlockwise. Which direction is Vicky facing now?

MyMaths.co.uk

Question commentary

Questions 1 – Students can do this question by eye. Discuss what ranges of angles in degrees make up acute (0°, 90°) and obtuse (90°, 180°) angles. This knowledge is essential for checking that an angle has been measured correctly.

Questions 2 – These questions are a little harder than in lesson **2b** as they involve three angles on a line; this type of situation is covered in lesson **5e**.

Encourage students to write simple equations as a way of capturing their thinking. For example for part **a**: 'what do the angles on a straight line add up to?' – 35 + 75 + ? = 180, 'what do the two given angles add up to?' – 110 + ? = 180, 'What do you add to 110 to make 180?' – ? = 180 – 110 = 70°.

Question 3 – After correctly lining up their protractors the most important thing is that students use the correct scale. Insist that students check their answer by asking themselves is the angle acute or obtuse and therefore in what range should the answer lie?

Question 4 – These questions are a little harder than in lesson **2d** as they involve three angles at a point; this type of situation is covered in lesson **5e**.

Encourage students to write simple equations as a way of capturing their thinking. For example for part **a**: 'what do the angles at a point add up to?' – 115 + 140 + ? = 360, 'what do the two given angles add up to?' – 255 + ? = 360, 'What do you add to 255 to make 360?' – ? = 360 – 255 = 105°.

Question 5 – Straightforward questions that mix up angles on a straight line and at a point. In part **c**, check that students understand the significance of the right angle symbol: its use is much more common than labelling with 90°.

Question 6 – This question can usefully be done in small groups with students encouraged to explain their reasoning and approaches.

Question 7 – Encourage students to write simple equations as a way of capturing their thinking. For example for part **a**: 'what do the angles in a triangle up to?' – 60 + 50 + a = 180, 'what do the two given angles add up to?' – 110 + a = 180, 'What do you add to 110 to make 180?' – a = 180 – 110 = 70°. The question encourages the explicit use of a variable to represent the unknown angle.

Question 8 – This question is hard. Encourage students to draw a diagram as a way to understand what is going on. Two approaches are: one, make an accurate drawing using a protractor; two, do the sum 135 – 180 + 90 – 225 = -180 and realise 180° (anticlockwise) from north is south.

Answers

1 **a** Obtuse **b** Acute **c** Right angle
d Straight line

2 **a** 70° **b** 35° **c** 95° **d** 120°

3 **a** 85° **b** 150°

4 **a** 105° **b** 110° **c** 95° **d** 80°

5 **a** 142° **b** 50° **c** 27°

6 **a** C, 2 **b** A, 4 **c** B, 3 **d** D, 1

7 **a** 70° **b** 20° **c** 35° **d** 90°

8 South

Learning outcomes	
A8 Work with coordinates in all 4 quadrants.	(L5)
S2 Construct and interpret appropriate tables, charts, and diagrams, including frequency tables, bar charts, pie charts, and pictograms for categorical data, and vertical line (or bar) charts for ungrouped and grouped numerical data.	(L4)

Introduction

The chapter starts by reviewing the plotting of coordinates on a set of axes before looking at coordinates in all four quadrants. The remaining sections covers real-life graphs, in particular time series-type graphs (line graphs) which are used to model real-life situations.

The introduction discusses how satellite navigation systems use principles of coordinates to locate your position, accurate to a few metres. Global Positioning Systems or GPS are now found on a wide range of devices, not just satellite navigation systems in cars. Most modern smartphones use GPS to locate your position and there are wide ranging uses in both industrial and military operations.

The origin of our standard coordinate system can be traced back to a famous French mathematician, Rene Descartes (hence 'Cartesian coordinates'). Descartes was born in 1596 and was famous not only as a mathematician, but also a philosopher. He worked in several fields of mathematics but is most famous for his work on position and geometry. He came up with his system of coordinates when he was lying in bed watching a fly crawl across the ceiling. A good biography of Descartes can be found here.

http://www-history.mcs.st-andrews.ac.uk/Mathematicians/Descartes.html

Prior knowledge

Students should already know how to…

- Work with coordinates in the first quadrant
- Name standard geometrical shapes

Starter problem

The starter problem looks at how one might complete a drawing in 2D coordinate space. The problem set is to complete the third corner of a right angled triangle, given the other two points. Students should be encouraged to look at the slope of the line between these two points and consider how a right angle could be made. It is important also to emphasise that the right angle could be at any of the three corners of the triangle.

Possible solutions (although not exhaustive) could be (2, 6), (4, 2), (4, 1) or (0, 8). More able students could be invited to find additional solutions in other quadrants, or to develop their own problem along similar lines.

The problem could be further extended by asking students to find two additional points such that the resulting shape is a rectangle or parallelogram, for example.

Resources

MyMaths

Coordinates 2	1093	Line graphs and two-way tables	1198

Online assessment

Chapter test	1A-6
Formative test	1A-6
Summative test	1A-6

InvisiPen solutions

Coordinates	261	Real life graphs	275
Line graphs data	277		

Topic scheme

Teaching time = 5 lessons/2 weeks

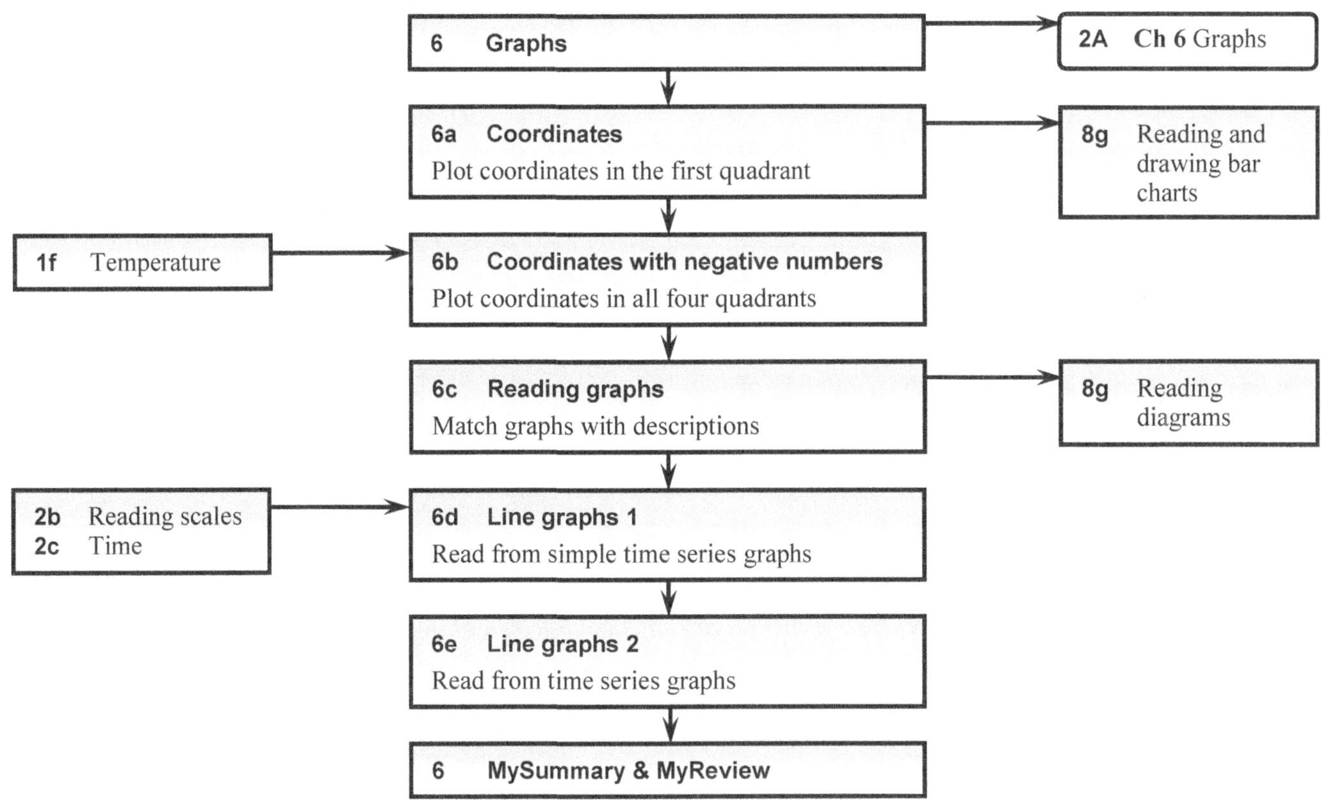

Differentiation

Student book 1A 110 – 125	Student book 1B 108 – 121	Student book 1C 102 – 119
Coordinates, including negative coordinates Reading graphs Basic straight-line graphs	Plotting coordinates in all four quadrants Recognising quadrilaterals Creating tables of values Plotting simple straight-line graphs Using real life graphs in context	Plotting coordinates in all four quadrants Plotting horizontal and vertical lines Plotting straight line graphs Equation of a straight line Using real life graphs in context Time series

6a Coordinates

Objectives	
• Use and interpret coordinates in the first quadrant.	(L4)

Key ideas	Resources
1 A grid needs two labelled axes, the x-axis and the y-axis, and an origin. **2** The coordinates (x, y) give the position of the point on the grid.	Coordinates 1 (1092) Sets of cards, each showing six or eight letters OS maps and road maps
Simplification	**Extension**
A game to practise reading coordinates is 'Coordinate Bingo'. On a grid with both axes labelled from 0 to 8, write twenty letters at twenty intersections of the grid. Students are given Bingo cards with six or eight of these letters written on them. You read out the coordinates of the numbered intersections and the students play Bingo.	Provide a map with significant places labelled at points having decimal or zero values of x or y. Students write the coordinates of these places and add their own. A further extension is to learn how to write six-figure grid references for places on Ordnance Survey (OS) maps, ideally of the local area.
Literacy	**Links**
Words starting with *co-* (or *con-* or *col-*) usually mean 'together' as in 'cooperate', 'congregate', 'college'. So 'coordinate' has a meaning related to 'ordering together'.	You can give the coordinates of any place on Earth using latitude and longitude. The latitude and longitude of any town can be found at the following sites: www.satsig.net/maps/lat-long-finder.htm www.confluence.org/search.php

Alternative approach

Draw an island with an indented coastline on a grid with both axes labelled from 0 to 8. Label a grid intersection, *not* the middle of a square, on the coast with the letter H for 'harbour'. Students imagine a fishing boat leaving H to circumnavigate the island square by square. Each student in turn gives the coordinates of the next leg of the journey. The teacher draws the route on the grid.

Checkpoint

Give students a copy of a grid with axes labelled from 0 to 8, or ask them to draw one on squared paper.

1 Label the x-axis and the y-axis. (x-axis horizontal, y-axis vertical)

2 **a** Plot these following points.

A (1, 2) **B** (1, 6)
C (7, 6) **D** (7, 2)

b Join the four points and name the shape that is formed. (Rectangle)

Starter – Meter reading

Draw a horizontal axis with major and minor tick marks. Label the major tick marks 0, 10, 20, etc. Add an arrow and ask, what value is it pointing to. Repeat with different labels on the major tick marks: 0, 100, 200, 300, etc.; 0, 50, 100, 150 etc.; 1, 2, 3 etc. Then repeat use labelling where values are missing, for example, * 10 * 30, *, *.

Teaching notes

A coordinate grid is used to fix a point on a 2D plane.

Emphasise that the numeric labels on the axes number the lines of the grid and not the gaps between the lines.

Emphasise that a coordinate pair is always written inside curved brackets with a comma between the two coordinates. The x-coordinate is written first and the y-coordinate second.

Emphasise that, when using whole numbers, the position of a point is always drawn on the intersection of the grid lines. It is better to use a pencil rather than a pen.

Plenary

Ask students to draw an 8 ×8 grid and then work in pairs. One student draws three corners (but not the sides) of a quadrilateral: a square, rectangle, parallelogram, rhombus, or kite. The student names the shape and exchanges it with their partner. Each student has to complete the drawing of their partner's quadrilateral and write the coordinates of all four of its corners.

Exercise commentary

Questions 1, 2 and 3 – All require students to read coordinates or plot points using given coordinates. The only major error is students may have the incorrect order for the x- and y-coordinates. Three common ways of ensuring the correct order for (x, y) are: first, to say that x and y are written alphabetically inside the brackets; second, to say that you go *in* a house before going *up* the stairs (that is: across before up); third, note that the letter x is 'a cross' – across.

Question 4 – Students need to plot and draw in pencil, as it can be rubbed out. See that the axes are labelled correctly, especially that both the labels 1 are correct, and that the labels are on the grid lines, not in the spaces between the lines.

Question 5 – This question is quickly done by using the given map of Scotland. However, if students have access to road atlases of the UK, they can compare them with this map and notice that, in most road atlases, it is the spaces between grid lines that are labelled (often using letters as well as numbers) and not the grid lines themselves. If students look at OS maps, however, they will see that, as in mathematics, it is the lines and not the spaces which are labelled. Discussion about the two ways of labelling maps is essential to avoid potential confusion. Cross-curricular references to the use of maps in geography lessons can be made.

Questions 6 and 7 – The grid lines might be imagined to find a solution or squared paper can be provided.

Answers

1 **a** (3, 4) **b** (8, 2) **c** (5, 3) **d** (1, 7)
e (5, 8) **f** (8, 9)

2 A (3, 4 B (1, 6) C (5, 1) D (8, 5)
E (2, 7) F (6, 3)

3

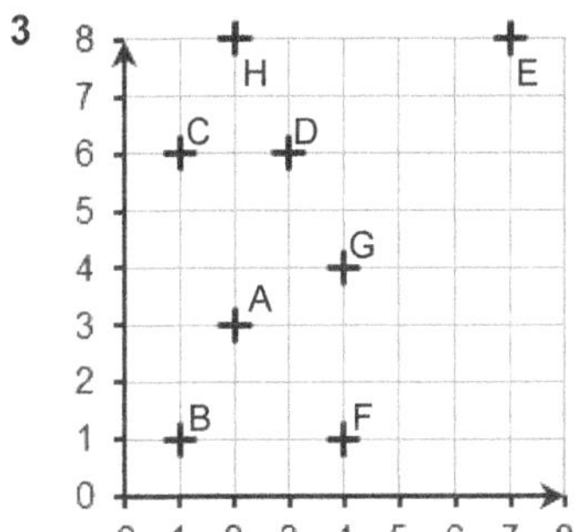

4 **a, b** **c** Pentagon

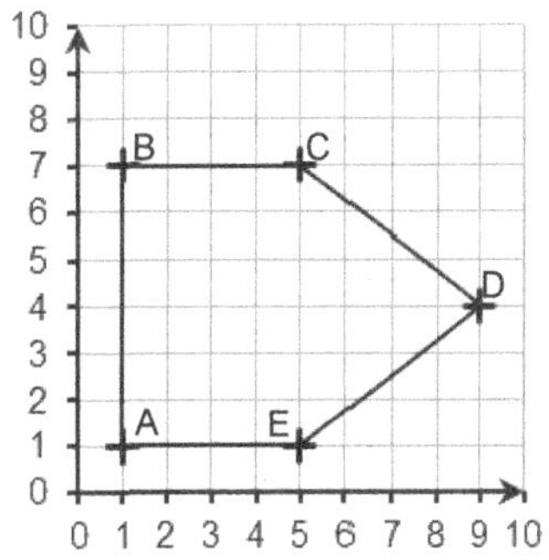

5 **a** (5, 2) **b** (4, 2) **c** (2, 5) **d** (5, 5)
e (5, 3)

6 (4, 1)

7 (2, 8)

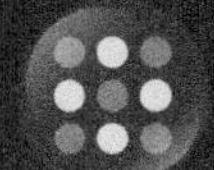

6b Coordinates with negative numbers

Objectives	
• Use and interpret coordinates in all four quadrants. (L5)	
Key ideas	**Resources**
1 Extending the number line using negative numbers allows coordintaes to be defined for all points on a grid. 2 Negative x-coordinates indicate points to the left of the origin and negative y-coordinates indicate points below the origin.	Coordinates 2 (1093) Pre-drawn axes, labelled -5 to 5 A grid, from -5 to 5, with the 26 letters of the alphabet placed at grid crossings; see question **3**
Simplification	**Extension**
For question **2** provide students with pre-drawn axes so that they can first concentrate on plotting the points. Have available sets of points for squares and rectangles with horizontal and vertical sides which may help to give students confidence in where to plot points.	A harder variant of question **2** is to give three of the four vertices for a symmetric quadrilateral such as a square, parallelogram or rhombus and challenge the students to find the fourth vertex. A harder version of question **4** is to give students the coordinates of point A and of the midpoint M and challenge them to find B. A graphical approach is likely to be most successful.
Literacy	**Links**
Coordinates on a square grid are sometimes called Cartesian coordinates after the French mathematician and philosopher René Descartes. The story, probably untrue but fun, is that as he lay in bed one morning he noticed a fly walking across the ceiling and after a while thinking he realised that he could describe where the fly was by specifying its distance from two walls. It is true that Descartes spent a lot of time in bed.	A game in which students have to navigate a robot through a mine field by giving coordinates can be found here http://www.shodor.org/interactivate/activities/MazeGame/ Whilst this application is simply for fun students might like to think of real world situates where coordinates could be used to specify a path.

Alternative approach

Draw a vertical number line, including the negative numbers, and use questions to test students understanding. Point at positive and negative numbers and ask what the values are, which number in a pair is larger, what do you add to one number to get another, etc. See lesson **1f**. Repeat the exercise with a horizontal number line.

Next, draw an island with an indented coastline on a grid with both axes labelled from -8 to 8. Ensure that the island straddles all four quadrants and label a grid intersection, *not* the middle of a square, on the coast in the first quadrant with the letter H for 'harbour'. Students are to imagine a fishing boat leaving H to circumnavigate the island, clockwise, going square by square. Each student in turn gives the coordinates of the next leg of the journey. The teacher draws the route on the grid. See lesson **6a**. At the transition between coordinates emphasis that nothing changes: you read the x-coordinate off the horizontal axis and the y-coordinate of the vertical axis and identify a point by giving (x, y).

Checkpoint

1 Ask students to draw a coordinate grid from -5 to 5. (Check labelling)

  a Put an 'X' at (-2, 3), ask students to give its coordinates. (Check correct x-y order)

  b Plot the point (-1, -4) (Check correct x-y order)

  Repeat for different points in different quadrants.

Starter – Join up!

Draw two axes and a grid labelled from 0 to 8. Divide the class into two teams. Each member of each team, in turn, gives the coordinate of a point. The teacher plots the points using two colours. Where points are adjacent, they are joined along the grid in that team's colour. The aim is to be the first team to plot their way across the grid, with one team working from top to bottom and the other from left to right.

Teaching notes

The main ideas concerning how to specify a point in the 2D plane carry over from lesson **6a**. The only new ingredient is the introduction of negative numbers and their interpretation. Negative numbers, in the context of temperature, are covered in lesson **1f**.

On the board draw and label a grid, placing the origin near the centre; this could be carried over from the starter activity. Start by indicating a few points and checking, using mini-whiteboards, that students can correctly give the coordinates of the points. Vary this by asking students to give you the coordinates of a point to plot. Deliberately indicate the wrong point, say swap the x- and y-coordinates or go between grid lines, and see if students correct you.

Next place a cross to the left of the y-axis on what would be the negative x-axis, say (-3, 0), and pose the question, how should we describe where this point is? Take suggestions then ask if students can do better than 'left of the origin'. Suggest or select, '3 units to the left' as a possible answer. Extend the x-axis to the left marking off units to show this. Now ask if this reminds students of something that they have seen before. As necessary, guide them to the idea of the number line including negative numbers and add axis labels showing the point at (-3, 0). Develop this idea by plotting further points in the second quadrant $(-x, +y)$ and asking students for their coordinates.

Repeat this procedure for a point on the negative y-axis and agree how to plot points below the x-axis. Test the students' understanding using first points in the fourth quadrant $(+x, -y)$ and then points in the third quadrant $(-x, -y)$.

Plenary

Plot points in all four quadrants and ask students for their coordinates. Then ask students to give you the coordinates of points to plot but in doing so make a series of deliberate mistakes focussing on misinterpreting negative numbers. Ask students to explain where you have gone wrong and where the point should be.

Exercise commentary

Questions 1 – There are two things to check. That students understand how to use negative coordinates and that they write them in the correct order. If students need reminding of the importance of writing (x, y) and not (y, x) then ask them to consider their answers to parts **b** and **e** or parts **c** and **f** which would be swapped if the coordinates were the wrong way round.

Questions 2 – Before students start to plot the points ask then to check that their axes are correctly labelled. Do the numbers go … -2, -1, 0, 1, 2 …? Are they evenly spaced? Are the labels aligned with the grid lines? Lesson **2d** introduces the names for special quadrilaterals.

Questions 3 – Students could be asked to use coordinates to create a 'secret message' which a partner then has to decode. The grid in the question is missing the letters F, H, J, M, N, P, Q, U, V, W, X, Y and Z; these can either be added or a new grid showing all 26 letters created.

Questions 4 – As necessary, suggest students draw the points on a graph and then use a ruler to find the mid-point. This could be repeated for 'vertical' pairs of points, such as (3, 4) and (3, 8) – midpoint (3, 6), 'mixed' pairs, such as (1, 2) and (5, 4) – midpoint (3, 3), or pairs with negatives, such as (-2, 4) and (4, -6) – midpoint (1, -1). Given enough examples perhaps students could find a rule for how to find the midpoint without using a diagram?

Answers

1 **a** (1, 3) **b** (1, -2) **c** (-4, 3) **d** (-2, -3)
e (-2, 1) **f** (3, -4) **g** (4, 3) **h** (4, -2)

2 **a, b, c**

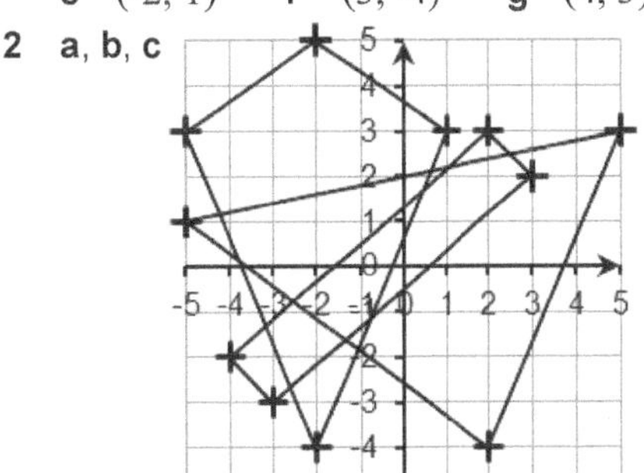

d **i** (Scalene) Triangle **ii** Rectangle
iii Kite

3 The big bald blokes back brake block broke.

4 (7, 1)

Objectives

- Interpret simple time series graphs. (L4)

Key ideas

1 Many variables change with time.

2 Changes with time can be shown on a sketch graph.

Resources

A list of scenarios, involving a variable changing in time, with graphs that match them.

Simplification

Tell a simple 'story' where the variable only increases or stays constant. For example, leaving home by bus which stops four times before arriving at the town centre. Draw the graph of distance against time as the story unfolds.

Once confident, tell the story of going by bus to the town centre and returning home later.

Extension

Ask students to draw and explain graphs for more complex scenarios. For example, students draw a graph for the level of water in a bath where the person runs hot water into the bath, finds it too hot and so adds cold water before getting into the bath. Students write a commentary, or 'story', of why the level of water is changing. If students work in pairs, they can tell their 'story' and have their partner draw the graph by listening to the 'story'.

Literacy

The words 'sketch', 'draw', 'plot' have different uses.

Point out the distinction between 'drawing a graph' and 'sketching a graph'. In this exercise, the graphs are sketches because the axes are not labelled numerically and the graph is not drawn accurately.

Also make the distinction between *drawing* a graph but *plotting* a point.

Links

The activity at the website

www.nrich.maths.org/4802

will draw a graph as the student moves a farmer in a field with his sheep.

Information on the safety aspects of fireworks can be found here

www.saferfireworks.com/statistics/gb/stats1997_2002.htm

Students could sketch (but not draw accurately) graphs to show some of the accident statistics.

Alternative approach

Provide pairs or small groups of students with both a list of scenarios where variables change with time and sketch graphs of how the variables are likely to change. Students match the list to the graphs and explain their decisions to the whole class.

Checkpoint

1 Show this graph of brightness for a rocket.

Brightness

Time

Ask students to point to the origin and then move their finger along the graph as you tell this 'story'.

It is dark when the rocket is lit. There is a streak of light as the rocket climbs in to the sky. It then goes dark before a large burst of light. The star burst quickly fades leaving a dim ember that fades away.

2 Show this graph of brightness for a roman candle.

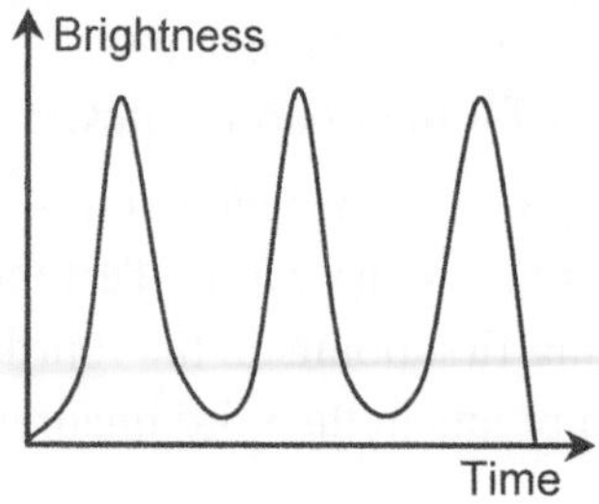

Move your finger along the graph and ask students to describe the story as trace out the graph.

(It is dark when the roman candle is lit. It quickly grows very bright as a star shoots into the sky and then fades to a faint glow. The process repeats two more times.)

Starter – Quick fire

Ask students to respond on mini-whiteboards to a series of quick questions which recap previous work on algebra and graphs. For example

- If I add 7 counters to a bag containing n counters, how many counters are there in total? (n +7)
- What is $3x + 4y + 2x$? ($5x + 4y$)
- If $f = 3$, what is the value of $4f$? (12)
- On a graph, which axis is horizontal? (x-axis) Which axis is vertical? (y-axis)

Teaching notes

Many students are likely to find interpreting graphs which represent real-life contexts quite challenging. Provide several examples for the whole class to consider and talk about.

For example, draw two axes with the horizontal axis labelled 'Time' and the vertical axis labelled 'Number of children'. Ask students to imagine a primary school with three classes. Each class arrives in the school hall for morning assembly at slightly different times. When all are in the hall, the assembly takes place and then all the classes depart at the same time. Sketch a graph of the number of children in the hall over time. Ask students what is happening at each part of the graph. Ask why the graph cannot have a section going from right to left. (Time cannot go backwards.)

Other examples are can be used.

- A temperature–time graph for a radiator in a centrally-heated room. The temperature rises quite rapidly, reaches a maximum, falls slowly, and then repeats the same cycle. Students should discuss what is happening and why.
- A distance–time graph for a short car journey. Have students discuss when the car is at rest and when it is travelling at its slowest and fastest speeds.
- A graph showing how the money in a person's bank balance changes over a month.

Plenary

Ask all students to sketch a distance–time graph for their journey to school in the morning and then compare it to a similar graph for them returning home in the afternoon. Discuss their graphs with their partner. Ask whether the graphs area a mirror image of each other and discuss why they are not. (The distance travelled runs from 0 each time.)

Exercise commentary

Questions 1 and **2** – In both these questions students have to match a statement in words with a graph. Question **1** could be discussed as a whole-class before students try Question **2** singly or in pairs. For example, ask, what is the variable on all the x-axes on these graphs and why is it there? What does the steepness of the graph tell you about the change that is happening?

It will be useful to have students discuss their strategies for identifying pairs. Suggest that it is a good idea to look at all the descriptions and graphs before making any pairs. In question **2** part **a**, both graphs A and F meet the description. However in part **d**, you are told that one of the graphs has a horizontal section, so that the answer to part **a** must be F. Another useful strategy is to start with the easiest cases and then remove them from further discussion.

Question 3 – Several underlying points need discussing as a whole class first, such as

- Where is the distance measured from? For example, the starting point might be the cyclist's home.
- What does the graph tell you about the shape of the route taken by the cyclist? (Nothing!)

It is a common misconception to think the graph gives the shape of the route. The graph tells us about the distance from the start, not about what shape that distance takes. It can be useful to draw a winding route for the whole class to see and then tell the 'story' of the journey as the cyclist (cut from card) travels along the route.

Answers

1 **a** B **b** D **c** C **d** A

2 **a** F **b** E **c** B **d** A
e C **f** D

3 The cyclist rides away from his starting point cycling steadily. He takes a short break and then rides home again at the same speed.

6d Line graphs 1

Objectives	
• Interpret and read data from simple line graphs where the intermediate values have meaning. (L4)	
Key ideas	**Resources**
1 A line graph tells the 'story' of a scenario. **2** The lines on a line graph may provide data at intermediate points or they may just indicate the rise and fall of the data over time.	Line graphs and two-way tables (1198) Computer software for drawing graphs Square grid paper
Simplification	**Extension**
Give students line graphs with axes which are straightforward to read. For example, take the scenario of a hiker walking for 8 hours in one day. The time axis might be labelled in hours from 0 to 8 and the vertical axis in miles from 0 to 16. The line graph would have all its points plotted at intersections of the grid, making any readings from the grid at these points straightforward.	For more able students, give a written description of changes over time. For example, the depth of oil in the school's oil tank during a week when the heating is on for four days and there is an oil delivery during the week. Ask students to show this information on an appropriate line graph.
Literacy	**Links**
A *line graph* uses points connected by lines to show how something changes in value, usually over time. Students should take care when drawing their own line graphs, making sure they have the axes the right way round, and that they have use an appropriate scale with correct labels. Refer to the line graph only as a graph, and not as a chart. Avoid confusion with *bar charts*, which are introduced in Chapter **8**.	Line graphs are used to show temperature changes over time. An example is at www.bbc.co.uk/schools/gcsebitesize/geography/geographical_skills/graphs_rev4.shtml Temperatures across the world are vastly different. For example, Al'Aziziyah in Libya is a place on the edge of the Sahara desert where the highest temperature ever recorded (57.7°C) was taken. It might have been hotter still in some places in the middle of the desert, so why isn't one of these places recorded as the hottest place on Earth? (There is no weather station there to record the temperature.)
Alternative approach	
Computer software is available to draw a variety of graphs. Alternatively, there are free online tools such as the graph plotter at www.mathsisfun.com/data/data-graph.php Take the data collected in the **Starter** and use a computer to draw a line graph.	
Checkpoint	
Refer to the temperature–time graph given in Question **2**. **1** Describe briefly (out loud, in words) what the graph shows. **2 a** What was the lowest temperature recorded, and when was it recorded? (12°C; 8 a.m.) **b** For how many hours was the temperature recorded? (11 hours) **c** For how many hours was the temperature higher than 20°C? (3 hours) Other graphs can be used to test the soundness of students' understanding.	

Starter – How warm is it?

Collect data before this lesson by taking the temperature (in °C) of the classroom every hour over an entire school day. Draw axes labelled with the hours of the day, on the horizontal axis, against temperature. Ask students to read out the data and plot the graph as they do so. Discuss the result.

Teaching notes

For each line graph drawn, ask students if values read from the line *between* the points plotted from the known data make any sense.

For example, in the student book, the line graph of people on a bus for each day of the week has no meaning *between* the days. The line shows the general rise and fall over the week.

However, the next graph in the student book showing temperature in an oven over 3 hours does have meaning between the plotted points, as time on this graph is continuous.

Invite students to suggest other data that might be most appropriately represented using a line graph.

Some students may join the first point which is plotted to the origin of the axes. Discuss and agree that this would be incorrect.
(The temperature is unlikely to be 0 °C at 14:15)

Plenary

Give six or seven examples of data collection. For example, the numbers of cars of different colours in a car park, the growth of a baby over six months, the distance of a cyclist from home measured every 15 minutes, the number of goals scored each week by a football team during a season. Ask students to decide whether a line graph would be a suitable way to represent the set of data and why.

Exercise commentary

Questions 1, 2 and **3** – These all require students to answer questions by extracting information from a line graph. Some questions need students to take readings from the graphs for intermediate values between the points that are plotted.

When appropriate, check that students include the correct units.

Question 4 – Students should take care when drawing the line graph; in particular they should choose a sensible scale for each axis.

Question 5 – This question provides a good assessment activity of students' understanding. Note that some times have to be estimated as most points are not plotted at intersections of the grid.

It may help some students to say that Ruby got into the bath at 18:00, so that the times become 18:05, 18:10, etc.

Answers

1 **a** 9:15 **b** 300 m **c** 2 hours

2 These answers are approximate.
a 18 °C **b** 22 °C **c** 9:10 and 18.00

3 **a** 13 m **b** 1965 **c** 17.5 m

4

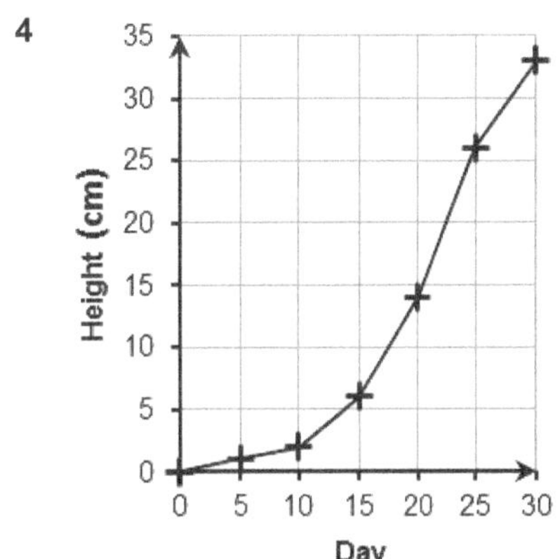

5 The bath was filled to a depth of 25 cm in the first 4 minutes.
Two minutes later Ruby got into the bath and the depth went up to 35 cm.
Ruby stayed in the bath for 10 minutes before letting out some water and refilling it with hot water. The water went down to 20 cm, which took 3 minutes, and it took 3 minutes to top it up.
Ruby stayed in the bath for another 3 minutes before emptying the water out, which took 4 minutes.

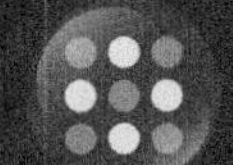

6e Line graphs 2

Objectives

- Interpret and read data from line graphs where the intermediate values have meaning. (L4)
- Compare two sets of data shown on the same line graph (L4)

Key ideas	**Resources**
1 More than one line graph can be drawn on the same axes. **2** The data from two lines graphs can be compared directly when drawn on the same axes.	Line graphs and two-way tables (1198) Atlases
Simplification	**Extension**
Give students line graphs with axes which are straightforward to read, like those in Question **1**. The questions here are answered by points which, being on intersection of the grid, are easy to read. Provide other simple graphs with these features before moving students on to other graphs.	Use atlases from the geography department and ask more able students to choose two temperature graphs for contrasting regions of the world. Draw them on one set of axes and compare the main features.
Literacy	**Links**
As in the previous lesson, reiterate that a line graph uses points connected by lines to show how something changes over time. Avoid confusion with a bar graph (or bar chart), which uses rectangular bars to show the value of each piece of data.	The highest tides in the world are at the Bay of Fundy in Canada. The water rises and falls up to 16 metres between high tide and low tide. There is an interactive picture of tides at the Bay of Fundy here. www.bayoffundytourism.com/tide/ Britain's Severn Bore has the world's third highest tide which can be viewed here. www.severn-bore.co.uk/videos.html

Alternative approach

A variety of scenarios involving line graphs, including ready-made graphs to manipulate, are available in MyMaths lesson 1198 ('Line Graphs and 2 Way Tables').

Checkpoint

Refer to the graph given in Question **3**. Ask students to use the graph to answer further questions until it is clear that their understanding is sound.

1 Describe the main features of the graph (out loud, in words).

2 **a** During which months might the temperature in both cities be the same? (April and August)

b For how many months of the year might you expect the temperature in Sydney to be above 20°C? (7 – 8 months)

c During June, what is the difference between the temperatures in each city? (≈ 23 – 17 = 6 °C)

Other graphs can be used to test the soundness of students' understanding.

Starter – Pollsters

Carry out a poll in class to find each student's birthday month. Create a tally and frequency table for the results, and ask how best to present the data as a graph. Decide on a line graph.

Teaching notes

Discuss the kind of data that is best represented as a line graph and why this is the case. (Usually, the data changes over time.)

Students choose appropriate scenarios for use with line graphs from examples such as: the temperature of a sick child; the distance from home on a journey; students' shoe sizes; the amount of hot water in the tank at home; students' ages; the different makes of car in the school car park. Ask students to decide which of these sets of data could be represented by a line graph and, if not a line graph, what other graph could be used.

Emphasise aspects such as accurate labelling of the axes and how the points are marked. Mention that some line graphs are curved but other line graphs use short straight lines.

Ask students to give the advantages of showing more than one set of data on the same line graph.

Plenary

Ask students to suggest two examples of data that they would represent on the same line graph. Ask them to explain the reasons for their choice.

Exercise commentary

Cross-curricular links can be made with line graphs in geography and science.

Question 1 – The first day, Day 1, is on the line graph even if it is not labelled on the horizontal axis. The height on Day 15 can be estimated by eye or students can place a ruler on the line to make their reading.

Question 2 – Many students will have little knowledge of tides. This question could usefully provoke much discussion about the nature and timing of tides and about the need for deep water for ships to dock. Students need to read intermediate values on both axes. A final whole-class discussion would be valuable.

Question 3 – Discuss the labelling on the horizontal axis and whether the months are labelling the grid lines or the gaps between them. Ask students to talk through the annual cycle of temperatures in Moscow and then Sydney. Note that Moscow's highest temperatures are in June, July and August, and ask why this is not the case in Sydney. (It is in the southern hemisphere.) Ask students how they know that the line graph does not give the temperatures for each day of each month and then discuss the meaning of 'average monthly temperature'.

Question 4 – Al'Aziziyah is on the edge of the Sahara Desert near Tripoli. Students can estimate where 57.7° is on the vertical axis. Knowing that this temperature was reached on 13th September 1922 can lead them to finding a point on the grid. However, it is not known if this graph is for Al'Aziziyah, only that it is for a part of Libya. Also, the individual temperature of 57.7°C would not be plotted on this graph as it shows average, not individual, temperatures. Indeed, if the 57.7°C is already included in the average, then the line of this graph would not be affected.

Answers

1 **a** 70 mm **b** 80 mm **c** day 6 **d** 48 mm

2 **a** 02:00 and just after 14:00
b Just before 08:00 and 20:00
c 8 metres
d 05:30 and 10:00 *or* 18:00 and 22:15

3 **a** Moscow -4 °C, Sydney 27 °C
b Mid-April to the start of August
c 4.75 months

4 The point would be close to the top and probably in July or August.
It would pull the line up; however because the line plots averages it would not pull the line up to the point.

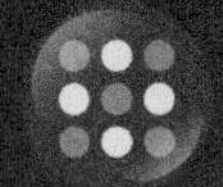

6 Graphs – MySummary

Key outcomes		Quick check
Identify and plot coordinates in all four quadrants.	L5	**1** Give the coordinates of the labelled points. (A (1, 6) B (5, 1) C (7, 3) D (2,5) E (1, 2) F (7, 7) G (3, 3) H (5, 6) 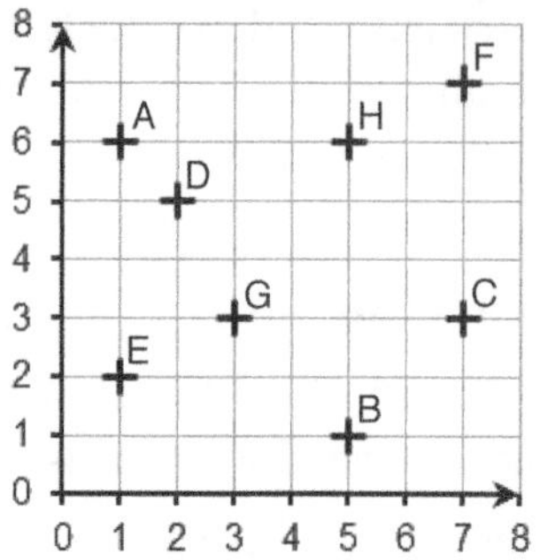) **2** **a** Draw and label a set of axes from -5 to 5. **b** Plot these sets of points, join them with straight lines and give the mathematical name of the shape. **i** (1, 4) (3, 1) (1, -2) (-1, 1) (1, 4) (Rhombus) **ii** (-2, -4) (-4, -2) (1, -1) (3, -3) (-2, -4) (Parralelogram) **iii** (-4, -1) (-4, 3) (-2, 1) (-4, -1) (Isosceles, right-angle triangle) 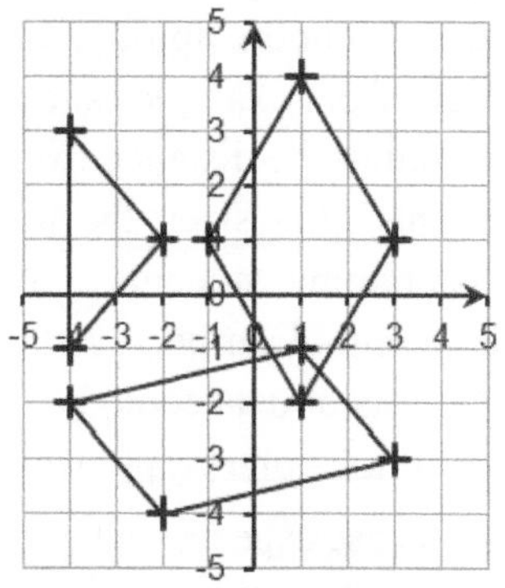
Construct and interpret line graphs in context.	L4	**1** Charlie goes on a bike ride. Use the data provided to plot a graph of distance against time for her journey. Time (mins) 0 5 10 30 40 60 Dist. (km) 0 3 3 5 5 0 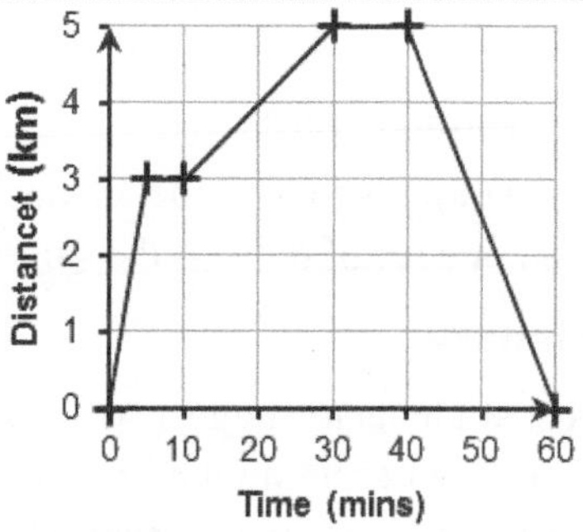 **2** Describe Charlie's journey above. (She start out very fast but stops after 5 mins at 3 km and rests for 5 mins. She then cycles more slowly for another 20 mins. After resting 10 mins, she travels 5 km back to her starting point.)

Development and links

Drawing a coordinate grid and plotting points is a basic skill that is assumed whenever a graph of a function is required. In book **2A** students will learn how to plot graphs of linear functions. Interpreting graphs and reading off scales is revisited in the context of bar charts and line graphs in chapter **8**.

Coordinates are the standard way to specify the location of a place in Geography. Students may be familiar with using coordinates in applications like Google Maps or GPS devices. Coordinates are also often used in road atlases, though here the convention is to label the squares and not the grid line intersections.

Line graphs often appear whenever someone wants to show how data changes – often against time. It is not hard to find lots of examples in newspaper reports, technical documents, weather reports, etc. Knowing how to make sense of such graphs is a life skill.

My Review

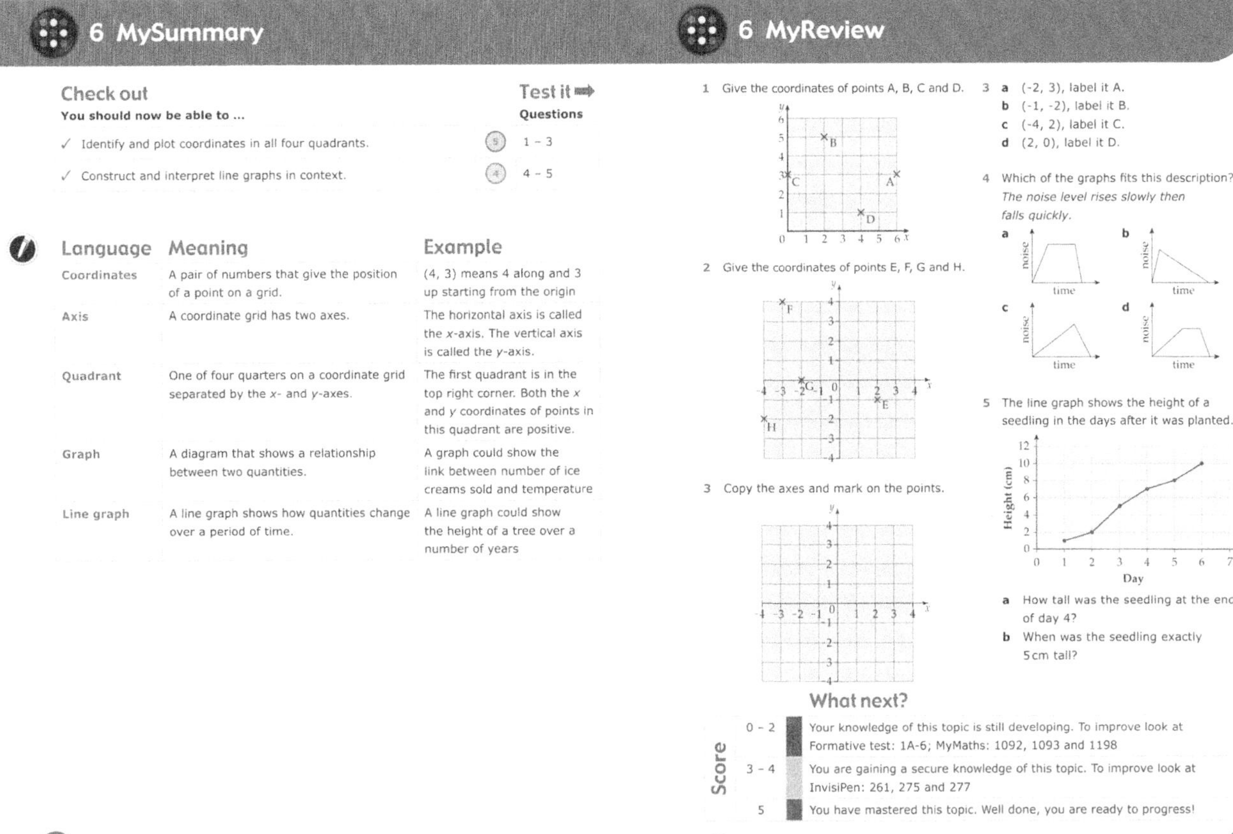

6 MySummary
Check out
You should now be able to ...
Identify and plot coordinates in all four quadrants.
Construct and interpret line graphs in context.
Test it
Questions
1 - 3
4 - 5
Language
Meaning
Example
Coordinates
A pair of numbers that give the position of a point on a grid.
(4, 3) means 4 along and 3 up starting from the origin
Axis
A coordinate grid has two axes.
The horizontal axis is called the x-axis. The vertical axis is called the y-axis.
Quadrant
One of four quarters on a coordinate grid separated by the x- and y-axes.
The first quadrant is in the top right corner. Both the x and y coordinates of points in this quadrant are positive.
Graph
A diagram that shows a relationship between two quantities.
A graph could show the link between number of ice creams sold and temperature
Line graph
A line graph shows how quantities change over a period of time.
A line graph could show the height of a tree over a number of years
122 Algebra Graphs
6 MyReview
1 Give the coordinates of points A, B, C and D.
2 Give the coordinates of points E, F, G and H.
3 Copy the axes and mark on the points.
3 a (-2, 3), label it A.
b (-1, -2), label it B.
c (-4, 2), label it C.
d (2, 0), label it D.
4 Which of the graphs fits this description?
The noise level rises slowly then falls quickly.
5 The line graph shows the height of a seedling in the days after it was planted.
Height (cm)
Day
a How tall was the seedling at the end of day 4?
b When was the seedling exactly 5 cm tall?
What next?
Score
0 - 2 Your knowledge of this topic is still developing. To improve look at Formative test: 1A-6; MyMaths: 1092, 1093 and 1198
3 - 4 You are gaining a secure knowledge of this topic. To improve look at InvisiPen: 261, 275 and 277
5 You have mastered this topic. Well done, you are ready to progress!
MyMaths.co.uk
123

Question commentary

Question 1 – (lesson **6a**) Students sometimes swap the *x* and *y* coordinate around and may be confused in particular with point C.

Questions 2 – (lesson **6b**) Extends question **1** to all four quadrants. Again beware of students swapping the *x* and *y* coordinate around or being confused by the negative numbers.

Questions 3 – (lesson **6b**) Check that students draw and label both axes correctly. Also check that they get the *x* and *y* coordinates the correct way round.

Question 4 – (lesson **6c**) Ask students to explain their reasoning; use prompts as necessary. Why can't it be **a** or **d**? What does the flat section represent? How did you decide between **b** and **c**?

Students could also be asked to explain what the other graphs represent.t

Question 5 – (lesson **6d**) In part **a,** students will need to interpolate between 6 and 8 when reading off the scale. Check that they give the units with their answer. In part **b**, students will need to 'draw' a line carefully to avoid inaccuracy.

If students read the graphs the wrong way round they will get 2.6 and 8 as their answers.

Answers

1 A (6, 3) B (2, 5) C (0, 3) D (4, 1)

2 E (2, -1) F (-3, 4) G (-2, 0) H (-4, -2)

3

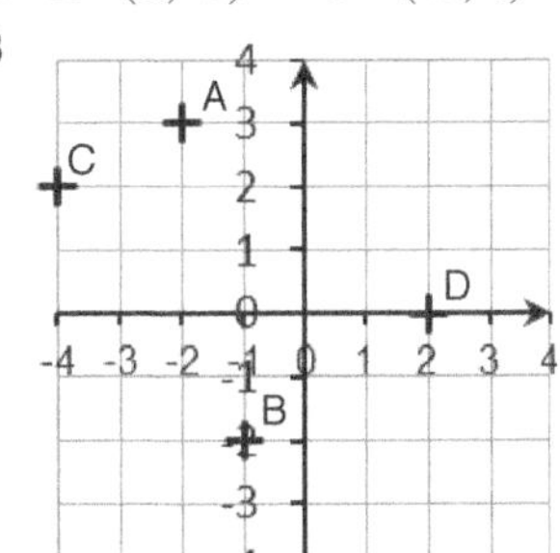

4 Graph **c**

5 **a** 7 cm **b** day 3

6 MyPractice

6a

1 Write the coordinates of each point.

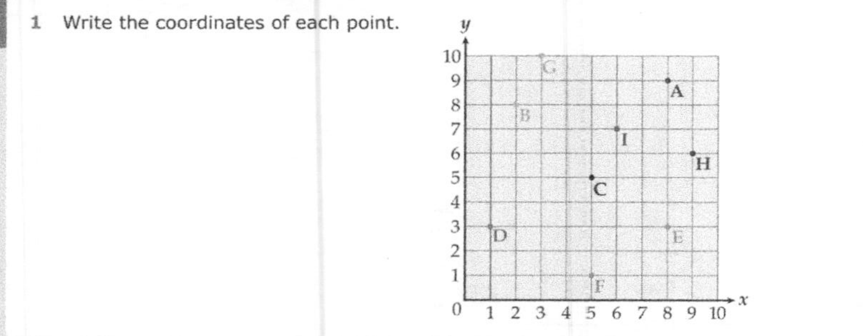

6b

2 For each part, plot the points given on a grid with axes labelled -5 to 5. Join each point to the next with a straight line.

a (0, -4) (0, -2) (-5, 0) (-5, 1) (0, -1) (0, 0) (5, 0) (5, -4) (0, -4)

b (-4, -3) (-4, -1) (-5, -1) (-5, 0) (2, 0) (3, 2) (4, 2) (5, 0) (5, -1) (4, -3) (3, -3) (2, -1) (-2, -1) (-2, -3) (-4, -3)

6c

3 The graphs show the relationship between time and the number of people in a theatre during a play. Match each of the descriptions with a possible graph.

a The play had no interval.

b Relatively few people went to the play and nearly all of them left the theatre during the interval. Most didn't come back.

c The second half of the play was much longer than the first half.

d Relatively few people left the theatre during the interval.

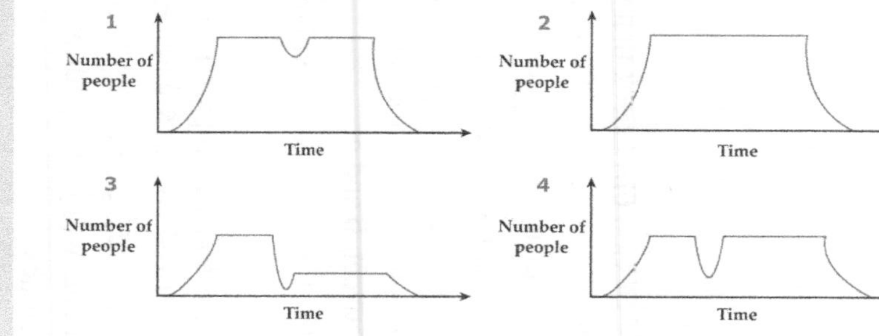

6d

4 This line graph shows how the temperature in a room changed.

a At what time was the temperature 18 °C?

b What was the temperature at 10:00?

c How many hours did it take for the temperature to drop from 21 °C to 15 °C?

d At what time was the temperature the same as it was at 10:00?

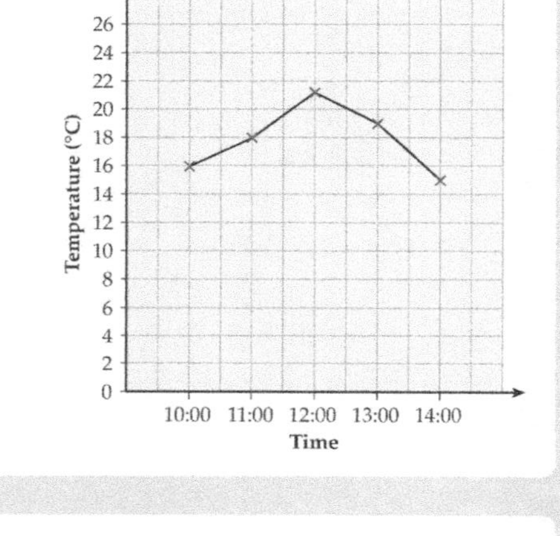

6e

5 A group of hikers walked 20 km between 10 a.m. and 2:30 p.m. The line graph shows details of their progress.

a What distance had they walked by

i 10:45 a.m.

ii 11:15 a.m.

iii 12:15 p.m.

b How far did they walk during the first half hour?

c During which half hour interval did they walk the furthest? How far was this?

d Between which times did they stop for lunch?

Question commentary

Questions 1 – Check that students know the correct order of coordinates (x, y) not (y, x). As a class it may be useful to discuss the various ways in which students remember the correct order.

More able students could be asked to see if they can give a geometric meaning to swapping the x and y coordinates. Points on the line $y = x$, (x, x), may help them to see that it is the same as a reflection in the diagonal line.

Question 2 – As a preliminary it may be helpful to pick points on the grid and ask students to give their coordinates. Include points that are outside the first quadrant to test the students understanding of negative coordinates. Also include points that appear on one of the two axes as these will not have been previously seen in lessons **6a** or **6b**.

Question 3 – To help set the context, as a class, discuss what happens when you go to the theatre to see a play; ensure that the meaning of interval, as a break in the performance when people main leave the main auditorium, is understood.

If students are organized into small groups, each group could discuss how they made their choices before reporting back to the whole class. Focus the discussion on the meaning of the heights of the 'plateaus' and their lengths.

Question 4 – The graph's horizontal scale assumes students can use the 24-hour clock, this is discussed in lesson **2c**.

Encourage students to place rulers or a set square over the graph to help them read off values accurately. In part **a**, the first time is easy to read off. The second time is a quarter of the way between 13:00 and 14:00 and quarter of an hour is 15 minutes. In discussing part **c** check that students understand why the graph shows the temperature is rising before 12:00 and falling afterwards.

Question 5 – In part **c** encourage students to think about the slope of the line segments. When accuracy is needed this must be done by reading off the initial and final distances from the graph but often 'by eye' is sufficient. In part **d** student should understand that a flat line segment means that time is changing but distance is not.

Answers

1 A (8, 9) B (2, 8) C (5, 5) D (1, 3)
E (8, 3) F (5, 1) G (3, 10) H (9, 6)
I (6, 7)

2 **a**

b

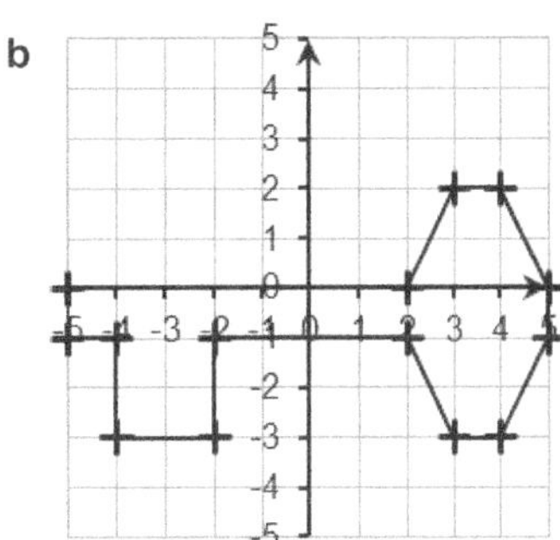

3 **a** 2 **b** 3 **c** 4 **d** 1

4 **a** 11:00 and 13:15 **b** 16 °C
c 2 hours **d** 13:45

5 **a** **i** 6 km **ii** 8 km **iii** 13 km
b 5 km
c 10:00 – 11:30, 5 km
d 12:30 – 13:30

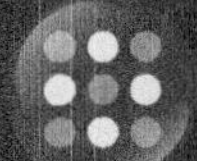

Case study 2: Recycling and energy

Related lessons		Resources	
Rounding and estimating	1g	Multiply double digits	(1025)
Metric units	2g	Division chunking	(1021)
Fractions, decimals and percentages	4h	Leaflets on recycling	
Multiplication and division	14a-h		

Simplification	Extension
The calculations require only basic aritmetic, principally multiplication and division, so the main difficulty is likely to be understanding the language and then realising what needs to be done. Paired work can help with language difficulties. It may also help to use discussion to contextualize the scenario and then pose the questions orally. Calculators can be made available.	Ask students to carry out further research on recycling which they could use to make a simple poster for a display. They could investigate different usage equivalents or recycling other materials. For example, how many trees are used to make paper and how many could be saved by recycling? The UK government recycling website is www.recyclenow.com/

Links

Aluminium makes up about 8% of the earth's crust; is the most abundant element after oxygen and silicon. However it is a very reactive metal and is almost always found combined with other elements in minerals, the most common of which is bauxite. To extract aluminium requires lots of energy. First the ore is purified to give aluminium oxide, Al_2O_3, which is then melted, at 960 °C, before an electric current is passed through it to separate the aluminium from the oxygen. Before this electrolytic process made aluminium cheap, it was very expensive and was considered a precious metal. As a show of wealth the Washington monument in Washington DC, America was given a cap/lightening rod made of aluminium. The statue of Anteros (brother of Eros) in Piccadilly circus is also made of aluminium. Needless to say this makes recycling aluminium very cost effective.

More information about producing aluminium can be found at the World Aluminium web site.

www.world-aluminium.org/

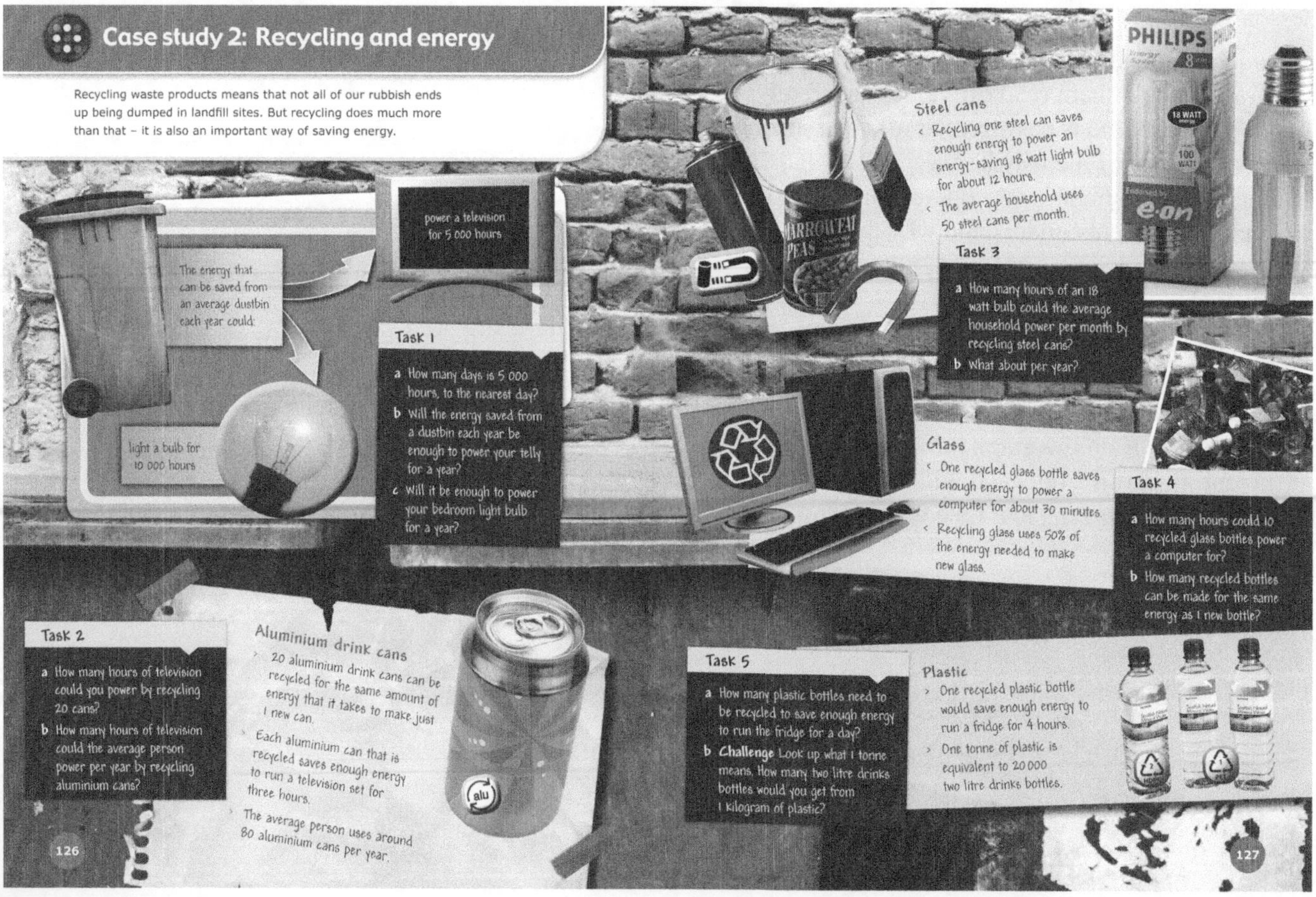

Case study 2: Recycling and energy

Recycling waste products means that not all of our rubbish ends up being dumped in landfill sites. But recycling does much more than that – it is also an important way of saving energy.

The energy that can be saved from an average dustbin each year could:

power a television for 5 000 hours

light a bulb for 10 000 hours

Task 1

a How many days is 5 000 hours, to the nearest day?
b Will the energy saved from a dustbin each year be enough to power your telly for a year?
c Will it be enough to power your bedroom light bulb for a year?

Steel cans

- Recycling one steel can saves enough energy to power an energy-saving 18 watt light bulb for about 12 hours.
- The average household uses 50 steel cans per month.

Task 3

a How many hours of an 18 watt bulb could the average household power per month by recycling steel cans?
b What about per year?

Glass

- One recycled glass bottle saves enough energy to power a computer for about 30 minutes.
- Recycling glass uses 50% of the energy needed to make new glass.

Task 4

a How many hours could 10 recycled glass bottles power a computer for?
b How many recycled bottles can be made for the same energy as 1 new bottle?

Task 2

a How many hours of television could you power by recycling 20 cans?
b How many hours of television could the average person power per year by recycling aluminium cans?

Aluminium drink cans

- 20 aluminium drink cans can be recycled for the same amount of energy that it takes to make just 1 new can.
- Each aluminium can that is recycled saves enough energy to run a television set for three hours.
- The average person uses around 80 aluminium cans per year.

Task 5

a How many plastic bottles need to be recycled to save enough energy to run the fridge for a day?
b **Challenge** Look up what 1 tonne means. How many two litre drinks bottles would you get from 1 kilogram of plastic?

Plastic

- One recycled plastic bottle would save enough energy to run a fridge for 4 hours.
- One tonne of plastic is equivalent to 20 000 two litre drinks bottles.

126 127

Teaching notes

Many of the calculations in this case study involve multiplication and division which is not covered formally until Chapter 14. However the calculations are straightforward and assume only basic prior knowledge from primary school; as necessary calculators can be made available.

Many areas have recycling schemes as part of the refuse services. Whilst students might play their part in sorting the rubbish, they may not be aware of the potential energy savings to which they are contributing. By exploring the energy savings made by recycling, expressed in hours of use of common household appliances, students might better appreciate the implications of recycling and also become more aware of energy usage.

Ask the students to think about what they throw away at home. (Packaging, tins, food, ...) Do you recycle any of the items and if so what? How do you recycle the items: do you go to a centre or do you have recycling bin(s)/box(es)?

Having established that some things can be recycled ask further questions. Why do you think that we are being encouraged to recycle waste products? What does recycling achieve? Discuss things such as cutting down on landfill and then look together at the information about the dustbin at the start of the case study. Focus on the idea of recycling saving energy, discussing how recycling reduces energy usage by, for example, cutting down on the need for raw materials. Ask students to think about what the figures mean.

Task 1

Discuss how to convert 5000 hours into days. The division by 24 is relatively hard but a good approximation is obtained by dividing by 25, which gives 200 days. Students could use a calculator to get a more accurate answer which they will then need to round (down) to get to the nearest number of days. Ask students to convert 10 000 hours into days on their own. Do any of them think to double their previous answer? A rounding error means they will be out by one but this is not important here. A related question is how much more energy does a television use than an 18 Watt light bulb. (Two times)

More able students could be asked to think what ‘average’ dustbin means and why averaging over a year is a good idea. (Evens out fluctuations: empty during holidays, very full at Christmas, etc.)

Task 2

The first point, about the energy used to recycle a can or make from new, is not relevant to answering the questions in the task panel.

To set the context ask students how much television they watch a week and how many aluminium cans they use a week. Once they have answered the questions they could be asked, how many hours of power for a t.v. could you save if you recycled all your aluminium cans? Or how many cans would you need to recycle to get to your number of hours of t.v. watching?

Task 3

Encourage students to try these questions on their own or in small groups/pairs. The first question requires 50×12 and the second $50 \times 12 \times 12$.

Again it might be helpful to ask students to think about how many steel cans their family use a week or a day. The average quoted suggests 12 cans per week or a little fewer than two cans per day.

Task 4

The second questions needs students to recognise that 50% is the same as one half and then if one recycled glass is equivalent to half a new glass then two recycled glasses are equivalent to one new glass. The maths is not hard but students may need help with the reasoning.

Task 5

These are two division problems. For the first question it may help to do it by repeated addition/multiplication. That is one bottle ~ 4 hours, two bottles ~ 8 hours, …, 6 bottles ~ 24 hours. This could then be related to $24 \div 4 = 6$. The second question involves division by 1000.

Answers

1 **a** 208 days **b** No (208 < 365)
c Yes (417 > 365)
2 **a** 60 hours **b** 240 hours (10 days)
3 **a** 600 hours (25 days) **b** 7200 hours (300 days)
4 **a** 5 hours **b** 2
5 **a** 6
b 1 tonne = 1000 kg, 20 bottles

7 Adding and subtracting

Learning outcomes	
N1 Understand and use place value for decimals, measures and integers of any size.	(L3)
N4 Use the 4 operations, including formal written methods, applied to integers, decimals, proper and improper fractions, and mixed numbers, all both positive and negative.	(L4)

Introduction

The chapter starts by looking at mental methods for addition and subtraction before covering written methods for addition and subtraction.

The introduction discusses the importance of being able to calculate things in real life. The importance of calculating with money, for example when working out your change in a shop, is the key point that is made. However it is equally important when working with bus and train timetables, recipes, and a whole manner of other things we might encounter in our day to day lives. Students could be invited to come up with their own examples of where carrying out accurate calculations is important.

The use of a calculator in modern society reduces the need for formal methods for carrying out calculations, but it is worth pointing out to students that while today, we have access to a wide range of calculating devices, both in the classroom and also about our person (most smartphones will do now complex calculations), it was not until the late 1970s that portable, personal calculators became widely available.

http://www.thecalculatorsite.com/articles/units/history-of-the-calculator.php

Prior knowledge

Students should already know how to…

- Carry out basic arithmetic
- Understand place value

Starter problem

The starter problem is a simple dice game where the objective is to create the largest possible sum for yourself, while restricting your opponent's total. An obvious strategy is to place large numbers in your own tens column, while putting smaller numbers in your opponent's tens column or your own units column. Since both players will be doing the same thing (assuming sensible strategies!) then the game might get quite tactical and interesting.

Similar games can be developed with single digit multiplication, or subtraction-style problems. Students could also be invited to develop the addition version to include more numbers, or three and four digit numbers.

Resources

MyMaths

Adding in columns	1020	Subtraction columns	1028	Mixed sums all numbers	1345

Online assessment

Chapter test	1A–7
Formative test	1A–7
Summative test	1A–7

InvisiPen solutions

Mental methods of addition and subtraction	121
Written addition and subtraction	125

Topic scheme

Teaching time = 4 lessons/2 weeks

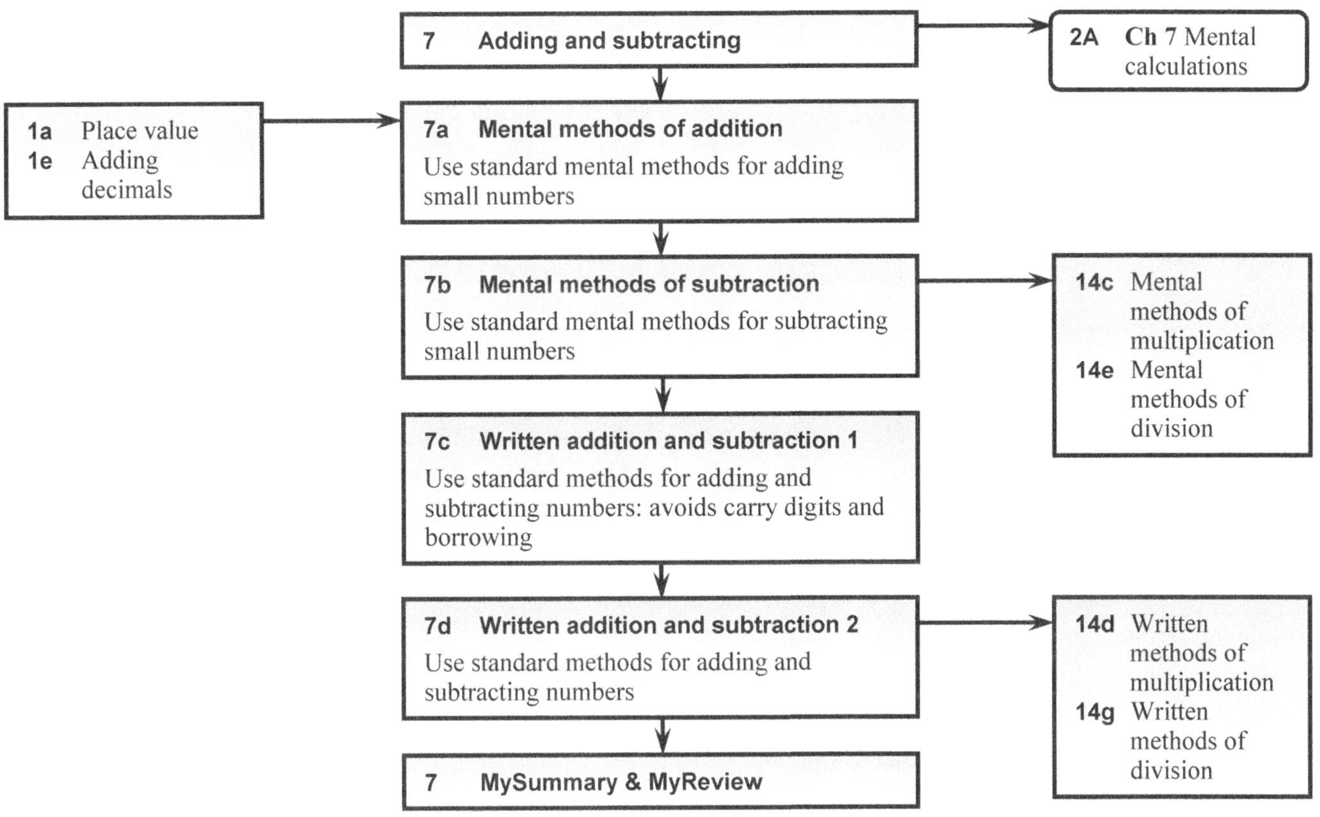

Differentiation

Student book 1A 128 – 141

Mental methods of addition and subtraction
Written methods of addition and subtraction

Student book 1B 124 – 141

Rounding
Order of operations
Mental methods of multiplication and division
Written methods of multiplication
Written methods of division
Calculator methods

Student book 1C 122 – 139

Rounding
Order of operations
Mental methods of multiplication and division
Written methods of multiplication
Written methods of division
Calculator methods

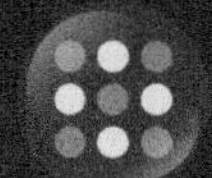

7a Mental methods of addition

Objectives

- Recall number facts including positive number compliments to 20. (L3)
- Add two-digit integers mentally. (L3)

Key ideas

1 A number line is one of several ways of representing a number.
2 Drawing jumps on a number line is a useful step on the way to a totally mental method for adding numbers.

Resources

Mixed sums all numbers (1345)

Two six-sided dice, labelled 1 – 6 and 10 – 60
Number lines with various labels
Overlapping 'place value' cards
A 100-square
Dienes blocks

Simplification

Students who have difficulty using a number line could first use a 100-square to add two 2-digit numbers. An initial progression would be:

- start at the larger number;
- add the multiples of 10 of the smaller number;
- add the units of the smaller number.

While the student uses the 100-square, the teacher could be using overlapping 'place value' cards simultaneously to match what the student does.

The student could then progress to using a blank number line, labelled in 10s.

Extension

For students competent at adding two 2-digit numbers, ask them to add three or more 2-digit numbers or to add a 2- or 3-digit number to a 3-digit number, such as 243 + 36 (279).

Literacy

To become numerically literate, students should develop mental subtraction skills in parallel with mental addition skills, seeing subtraction as the inverse of adding. So a number 'trio', such as 3, 5, 8, is seen equally for subtraction bonds and addition bonds and, later, when using the number line, addition and subtraction receive equal emphasis.

Mental methods of subtraction are covered in the next lesson.

Links

The Student Book shows Kia practising her mental addition in various scenarios: following a recipe, downloading music, shopping. Discuss other situations where the ability to add quickly and accurately in your head is useful.

For example, use the context of consumer arithmetic, such as adding up the cost of items in a supermarket basket to make sure you have enough money to pay before reaching the checkout.

Alternative approach

Three approaches have been suggested above: the 100-square, overlapping 'place value' cards and the number line. A more tactile approach is to use Dienes blocks where 2- and 3-digit numbers are represented by cubes, rods and squares in columns labelled T and U (and later H, T, U). Manipulation of this apparatus can be undertaken simultaneously with any or all of the other three approaches.

Checkpoint

1 Add the following numbers in your head
- **a** 5 + 4 (9)
- **b** 15 + 4 (19)
- **c** 5 + 40 (45)
- **d** 5 + 40 + 3 (48)

Repeat using pairs of single and double digit numbers, adding multiples of ten and adding three numbers.

Starter – Dicey

Take two dice, one labelled 1 to 6, and the other labelled 10 to 60 in tens. Throw both dice together and record both numbers. Ask students to add the two numbers and show their results on mini-whiteboards.

Repeat by throwing both dice twice and recording two 2-digit numbers.

Teaching notes

Extend students' skills at adding two single-digit numbers. Include

- Doubles and near-doubles, such as 6 + 6 (12) and 6 + 7 (13).
- Adding 1, 2 and 3 by counting on/back in their heads, such as 16 + 1 (17) and 12 – 3 (9).
- Using smaller bonds, such as 13 + 5 = 10 + 8 (18) demonstrated with 'place value' cards.
- Crossing 'ten', such as 9 + 4 (13) and 12 – 5 (7).

A blank number line labelled only in 10s from 0 to 100 is a useful aid for adding two 2-digit numbers. Work towards seeing 23 + 14 as one jump of 10 and one jump of 4, rather than four jumps of 1, and, later, seeing 56 + 25 as one jump of 20 and one jump of 5 from a start at 56. As a whole class, discuss students' different methods. For example, for 56 + 25, accept adding 10s first (70) and units next (11) to get 70 + 11 and 81.

Later, a blank number line labelled from 0 to 500 in 100s can be used with the whole class. Multiple copies of all number lines should be available for students to draw their own methods. The ultimate aim is for a totally mental method, which students can articulate on request.

Plenary

Ask individual students to explain their mental methods to the whole class. Ask some questions in various contexts. All students should use their mini-whiteboards to answer questions, either with diagrams of 'jumps' or by totally mental methods.

Exercise commentary

Question 1 – Students pair numbers to total 20. This task could be done as a whole-class activity with the numbers on cards on the board and students asked to find a pair that total 20. Can students find further pairs of numbers that total 20? (2 + 18, 4 + 16, 6 + 14 and 7 + 13)

Question 2 – Remind students to start with the bigger number when adding. Parts **g** to **j** should be done in two steps. It may be useful to discuss the order in which the additions are done. For example 10 + 6 + 8 = 10 + 14 = 24 may be easier than = 16 + 8 = 24. It may help some students to know that the numbers can be commuted: 10 + 6 + 8 = 18 + 6 = 24.

Question 3 – This question lends itself to using overlapping 'place value' cards simultaneously with a labelled number line. In part **g**, check that students handle the carry digit correctly.

Question 4 – Mention that students will look at sequences again in chapter **13** where they will be expected to be able to count on in fixed steps.

Question 6 – As with Question **2**, remind students to start with the bigger number.

Question 7 and **8** – In a whole-class session, ask students to articulate their method. List the methods on offer. Discuss which method is the most efficient, the quickest and the one likely to give fewest errors.

In question **7** it may be useful to add the numbers in a different order. For example, starting with 35 + 45 = 80, which is easy to add to 120, also means that all remaining numbers are multiples of ten.

Answers

1 1 + 19, 12 + 8, 9 + 11, 17 + 3, 10 + 10, 15 + 5

2 **a** 16 **b** 18 **c** 12 **d** 17
e 19 **f** 20 **g** 10 **h** 24
i 24 **j** 43

3 **a** 29 **b** 37 **c** 40 **d** 48
e 65 **f** 73 **g** 94 **h** 100
i 110 **j** 134

4 **a** 110, 210, 310, 410, 510, 610
b 243, 343, 443, 543, 643, 743
c 76, 176, 276, 376, 476, 576

5 **a** 23 + 24 = 47 **b** 48 + 33 = 81
c 101 + 34 = 135 **d** 94 + 42 = 136

6 **a** 45 **b** 73 **c** 47 **d** 89
e 46 **f** 75 **g** 59 **h** 89
i 76 **j** 52 **k** 107 **l** 167
m 377 **j** 213

6 **a** 55p **b** 65p **c** 150p = £1.50

7 32 kg

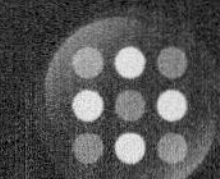

7b Mental methods of subtraction

Objectives	
• Subtract two-digit integers mentally. (L3)	
Key ideas	**Resources**
1 You can subtract by 'taking away' from the larger number or 'adding on' to the smaller number. **2** The difference between two numbers can be found by 'taking away' or by 'adding on'.	Mixed sums all numbers (1345) Number lines with various labels Overlapping 'place value' cards A 100-square Dienes blocks Dice labelled 1 – 6 and 10 – 60 in tens
Simplification	**Extension**
Knowing bonds within 10 and 20 is a basic requirement. Then, as with addition, various tactile and visual representations can be used: Dienes blocks, the 100-square, overlapping 'place value' cards and various number lines. For example, with a 100-square, a progression such as 46 – 10, 46 – 20, 46 – 30; then 46 – 11, 46 – 12, 46 – 21, 46 – 22 is useful.	Pairs of students individually devise four or more ways to work out 82 – 37. They should then compare their methods and explain them. Feedback to the whole class can take place.
Literacy	**Links**
The word 'difference' is often associated with subtraction. But, in some cases, it can be found more easily by addition. For instance, the difference between 59 and 62 is best found by 'adding on 3' to 59, whereas the difference between 32 and 85 can easily be found either 'adding on' to 32 to reach 85 or by 'taking away' 32 from 85.	As in the previous lesson, discuss situations where the ability to subtract quickly and accurately in your head is useful. Even in the age of technology, mental arithmetic skills are useful. For example, bus drivers, waiters and market stall traders all need to be able to perform quick calculations when giving change for cash payments. They may not always have access to a computer or calculator.

Alternative approach

The same four approaches for addition also apply to subtraction: namely, Dienes blocks, the 100-square, overlapping 'place value' cards and the number line. When using any of these approaches, discussing the action as it takes places assists understanding.

Checkpoint

1 **a** 10 – 7 (30) **b** 15 – 7 (8)
c 25 – 11 (14) **d** 25 – 3 – 2 (20)
e 25 – 4 – 4 (17)

Ask students to discuss which methods they chose for the calculations and the reasons for their choice.

Further series of mental calculations can be asked following the progression: subtracting single and double digits; calculations with two numbers then three numbers.

Starter – Bonds up to 10 and beyond

Revise the essential early number bonds using quick-fire questions and quick responses on mini-whiteboards. These bonds include both addition and subtraction. For bonds of 10, ask 10 – 7 and 10 – 3 as well as 7 + 3 and 3 + 7; set some questions in context. For earlier bonds, ask 5 + 3 and also 8 – 3. Beyond 10, ask 14 – 4 as well as 10 + 4 and demonstrate with overlapping 'place value' cards. Ask for the trio of numbers 3, 6, 9 to be written as four different bonds. Discuss answers where they show a need.

Teaching notes

Continue to emphasise subtraction and addition as inverse operations. Continue to practise number bonds up to 20 with subtraction alongside addition; for example, 8 + 9 = 17 with 17 – 8 = 9.

Subtraction can be done mentally in two different ways. Students need to be skilled not only with both methods, but also in choosing when one method is clearly better than the other.

One way to subtract is to start with the larger number and 'take away' the smaller number by counting backwards; for example 64 – 12 is best done this way.

The other way to subtract is to start with the smaller number and 'add on' by counting forwards to reach the larger number. This method is called *complementary addition*. For example, 42 – 29 is best done this way.

Sometimes, there is little to choose between these two methods; for example, 54 – 26 could be done either way.

Finding the 'difference' of two numbers can be done by either of these methods; that is, using subtraction by 'taking away' or using complementary addition by 'adding on'.

Plenary

As a whole-class session, ask students to use a + or – sign and a 2-digit number to fill in the gaps in the problems below.

27 ☐ = 52		29 ☐ = 43	
36 ☐ = 49		64 ☐ = 31	
73 ☐ = 15			

Exercise commentary

Questions 1, 3 and **5** – If students don't know the answers to some of the simpler questions by instant recall, they can choose between adding on to the smaller number and taking away from the larger one. In Question **5**, the 100-square is a useful visual aid.

Question 2 – Students should look for bonds of 10, such as 4 + 6 in part **c**, before making the choice of methods listed above. This could be made into a more hands on activity using three dice. Insist that students write down the three individual scores as well as their answer.

Question 4 – Overlapping 'place value' cards are a useful visual aid in parts **a** to **e**.

Questions 6 – As in earlier questions, students should decide on the most sensible method for subtraction before beginning the calculation in their heads.

Answers

1	**a** 13	**b** 8	**c** 15	**d** 9
	e 11	**f** 3		
2	**a** 11	**b** 9	**c** 7	**d** 11
	e 5	**f** 13		
3	**a** 3	**b** 3	**c** 11	**d** 11
	e 4	**f** 0	**g** 85	**h** 99
	i 63	**j** 24		
4	**a** 9	**b** 21	**c** 30	**d** 58
	e 65	**f** 70	**g** 90	**h** 97
5	**a** 10	**b** 34	**c** 12	**d** 55
	e 37	**f** 22	**g** 53	**h** 35

6 Charlie 9 kg, Howda 8 kg, Kia 4 kg, Jake 7 kg

7c Written addition and subtraction 1

Objectives

- Use efficient written methods for addition and subtraction (L3)

Key ideas	Resources
1 Written methods use different stategies from mental methods. **2** The standard written method uses columns for hundreds, tens and units.	Adding in columns (1020) Subtraction columns (1028) Dice Number lines with various labels Overlapping 'place value' cards A 100-square Dienes blocks

Simplification	Extension
Revisit the 100-square and number lines to remind students of the various mental methods. Some students may find the written method using columns easier than the methods using a number line. Early work with the written method will be more successful where smaller digits are carefully chosen; for example, 123 + 212 rather than 423 + 576.	Students who find this work easy could be given an example of some working-out where the answer given is deliberately incorrect; such as the examples given below. The students are to mark the questions, highlighting the errors. 274 + 245 = 4119 (Incorrect carry) 426 − 231 = 215 (Subtracted the tens-digits the wrong way around.)

Literacy	Links
Using the written methods effectively requires students to organise their written calculations. The use of square grid paper with the digits of numbers each having their own square is helpful. Labelling columns with H, T, U may only be necessary for a few pupils.	The abacus is a counting tool made of a frame with beads sliding on wires or rids. It was used by ancient civilisations, such as the Egyptians and Greeks, for complicated calculations. In some countries, the abacus is still used to help young children with their arithmetic. If one is available, an abacus could be shown to the class, or there is a virtual one to try out at www.mathsisfun.com/numbers/abacus.html

Alternative approach

The same alternative representations of number which have been listed and used in lessons **7a** and **7b** still apply here. When students are confident with the written approach in columns, they could be given calculations in a horizontal format which they re-write vertically.

Checkpoint

1 Use a standard column method to do these calculations.

a 234 + 142 (376)

b 384 – 262 (122)

Ask students to label the H, T and U columns and then to explain out loud how they did the calculation. Check that they are adding the units, then the tens, and then the hundreds.

2 Which is greater 33 + 16 or 59 – 14? (33 + 16 = 49 > 59 – 14 = 45)

Starter – Dicey returns

Choose two rules, such as 'add 20' and 'subtract 5' and throw a dice labelled 1 to 6. Ask the students to apply the rule to the dice score. Repeat.

Change the rules. Possible rules are 'double and add 32' or 'double and subtract 5'.
Ask students to respond on mini-whiteboards. Discuss answers were necessary.

Teaching notes

In this lesson most of the calculations do not involve interchanges between place values. That is, the additions don't involve 'carry digits' and the subtractions don't involve 'decomposition/borrow digits'. How to handle these situations is covered in the next lesson, **6d**.

Revise using jumps on a number line, or the 100-square to add and subtract for numbers less than 100. Revise using jumps on a number line for numbers greater than 100. Encourage a fully mental approach.

Remind students that there are two methods to subtract: jumping forward from the smaller number, as for 62 – 29, and jumping backwards from the larger number, as for 68 – 21.

Setting the work out in columns avoids the need for drawing a number line and can be used where the numbers are too difficult for mental methods. Ensure that students use the columns in the order U T H from right to left, even though it is not essential in this exercise.

Whole-class examples could be: 245 + 614 (859) and 768 – 356 (423).

Plenary

Ask students, in pairs, to complete these four calculations: 236 + 423 (659), 236 + 424 (660), 265 – 134 (131), and 265 – 136 (129). They can use any method of their choice. Ask them to share their working out with the class. The variety of possible methods for each calculation is recorded.

Exercise commentary

Questions 1 – Make the answers clearly different from by the given numbers by entering them in a different colour.

Question 2 – The usual first step when subtracting applies here: subtract by adding on to the smaller number or taking away from the larger number.

Question 3 – All the additions can be completed without any 'carrying' from one column to the next. All the subtractions can be completed without any transfer from one column to the next.

Questions 4 and **5** – Some students might benefit from a brief refresher of addition and subtraction methods before attempting these questions.

Answers

1

+	34	43	14
23	57	66	37
63	97	106	77
52	86	95	66
17	51	60	31

2 **a** 21 **b** 31 **c** 36 **d** 16
e 15

3 Addition **a** 39 **b** 58 **c** 69
d 374 **e** 539 **f** 897
Subtraction **a** 31 **b** 44 **c** 36
d 311 **e** 350 **f** 60

4 **a**

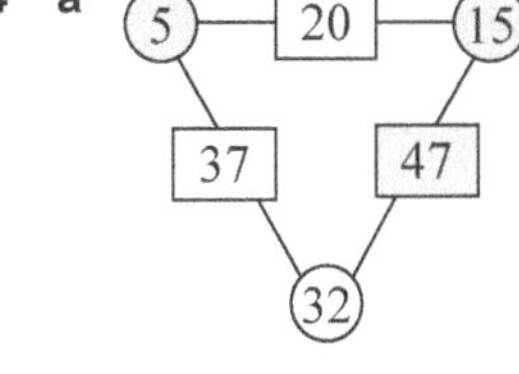

b

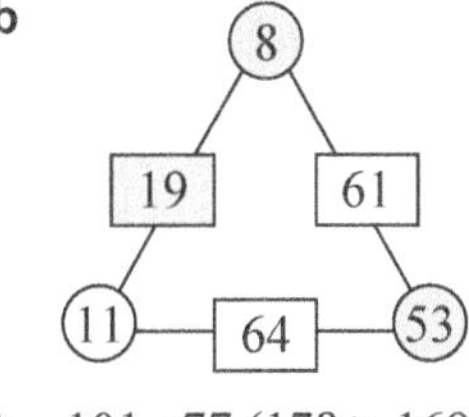

5 **a** 88 – 14 (74 > 37) **b** 101 +77 (178 > 169)
c 98 – 53 (45 > 39) **d** 87 – 26 (61 > 30)
e 108 + 144 ((252 > 237) **f** 88 + 120 (208 > 202)

7d Written addition and subtraction 2

<table>
<tr><th colspan="2">Objectives</th></tr>
<tr><td colspan="2">• Use efficient written methods for addition and subtraction. (L4)</td></tr>
<tr><th>Key ideas</th><th>Resources</th></tr>
<tr><td>1 Column arithmetic is an efficient way of adding or subtracting two numbers.
2 In some calculations, digits have to be 'carried' between columns.</td><td>Adding in columns (1020)
Subtraction columns (1028)
Number lines with various labels
Overlapping 'place value' cards
A 100-square
Dienes blocks</td></tr>
<tr><th>Simplification</th><th>Extension</th></tr>
<tr><td>Help student to gain confidence with additions of two 3-digit numbers, before moving to subtractions. Work with
• additions which require no 'carrying';
• additions which 'carry over' just one digit between two columns;
• additions which 'carry over' two digits across three columns.
Allow students to check their answers using a calculator before attempting a further question.
Only when confident, move to subtractions of two 3-digit numbers with a similar progression: those that require no decomposition and then those needing just one decomposition. Do not give questions requiring two decompositions across three columns at this stage.</td><td>Ask students how they could use an addition to check the answer to a subtraction. Ask them to check their subtraction answers by adding their answer to the 'bottom' number of the subtraction. In short,
to check a
$-b$
c show that $c + b = a$.
A further extension is to offer some word problems which are set in context.</td></tr>
<tr><th>Literacy</th><th>Links</th></tr>
<tr><td>The calculations in the exercise require students to be organised and methodical in their working.
Ensure students have a correct understanding of the words 'column' and 'vertical'.</td><td>Nelson's Column is a monument in Trafalgar Square in London. It was built as a tribute to Lord Nelson who fought and died at the Battle of Trafalgar in 1805. The granite column is 46 metres high and has a 5.5 metre tall statue of Lord Nelson on the top. How high is the top of Lord Nelson's hat from the ground?
There is more information about Trafalgar Square at
www.projectbritain.com/london/attractions/trafalgar.htm</td></tr>
<tr><th colspan="2">Alternative approach</th></tr>
<tr><td colspan="2">Again, the alternative representations of number used in previous lessons can still be used here, namely the 100-square, overlapping 'place value' cards, the number line and Dienes blocks.</td></tr>
<tr><th colspan="2">Checkpoint</th></tr>
<tr><td colspan="2">1 Use a written method to alculate
a 129 + 283 b 261 – 134 (412; 127)
Ask student to explain their calculations out loud.
(Check that they are looking at the units first, then the tens, and then the hundred.)
Repeat with further additions and subtractions of three-digit numbers that test transfering digits between columns.</td></tr>
</table>

Starter – Quick fire

Recap work of previous chapters and this chapter so far, especially number topics. Include questions on place value for integers and decimals, measuring and scales, changing between fractions, decimals and percentages, and mental methods of computation. Ask rapid response questions with students using mini-whiteboards. Discuss answers when there is a need.

Teaching notes

This lesson extends the previous lesson **7c**, to include additions and calculations that require transfers between place values. That is, the additions involve 'carry digits' and the subtractions involve 'decomposition/borrow digits'.

In developing the formal written methods of computation in this and later exercises, ask students what methods they used in primary school. Note that even identical ways of setting out the work on paper can have different oral explanations. Students may not recognise a method that they have met before because it is not explained in the same way.

As with mental methods, students' proficiency is more quickly gained with addition than with subtraction. When adding, students readily appreciate the need to 'carry over' into the next column. The method of subtraction by 'decomposition' is undertaken in this exercise; be aware that students may have previously met other methods. If a student is competent with an alternative method of subtraction, it is a moot point whether to let them continue with it or change them to the 'decomposition' method.

When subtracting, watch for the common error of finding the difference of two digits regardless of their order. A good oral explanation, linked as necessary to appropriate use of Dienes blocks, is essential for students' success.

Plenary

In a whole-class session, ask students to articulate their thinking as they work through an addition and a subtraction problem using the formal written methods.

Write two other calculations which they carry out on their mini-whiteboards and then discuss their methods in pairs.

Exercise commentary

The use of squared paper might help some students to line up the columns when working through the calculations in this exercise. Writing one digit per square is also good practice.

Questions 1, **2** and **3** – No 'carrying' or 'decomposition' is required here.

Question 4 – Having been told that there are errors in the working shown, students can do some quick mental reasoning to locate them. Encourage them to look at the units column first and to realise that subtraction gives you a smaller number than the one you start with. In part **c**, rounding 699 up to 700 quickly shows that the answer of 129 is wrong.

Question 5 – Each of these calculations requires the carrying of digits between one or two columns.

Question 6 – Remind students that 1 kg = 1000 g, which leads to a calculation with a 4-digit number in part **a**. For part **b**, the calculation should be done as a 3-tiered addition (adding three lots of 750 ml).

Question 7 – These two calculations are truly a challenge! Students might want to work by themselves but check their progress periodically with a partner. Ask them if their calculator would help them with these calculations.

Answers

1 **a** 93 – 17 = 76 **b** 49 + 39 = 88
c 152 – 61 = 91 **d** 235 + 67 = 302

2 **a** 678 **b** 477 **c** 896 **d** 795

3 **a** 214 **b** 332 **c** 138 **d** 320

4 Workcard 1 **a** 672 **b** 572 **c** 631 **d** 529 **e** 705 **f** 927
Workcard 2 **a** 425 **b** 327 **c** 466 **d** 470 **e** 129 **f** 270

5 **a** 750 g **b** 2250 ml = 2.25 litres

6 **a** 1111111110111111111100
That is, 9 ones, 1 zero, 9 ones, 2 zeroes
b 7406740674067406
That is, 7406 repeated 4 times

<table>
<tr><th>Key outcomes</th><th>Quick check</th></tr>
<tr><td>Strengthen and extend mental methods of addition and subtraction. L3</td><td>Do these calculations in your head.
a i 75 + 20 ii 63 + 47 iii 88 + 64 iv 124 + 55
(95, 110, 152, 179)
b i 94 – 23 ii 83 – 48 iii 101 – 44 iv 387 – 236
(71, 35, 57, 151)</td></tr>
<tr><td>Use efficient written methods to add and subtract whole numbers. L4</td><td>1 Use a standard written method to do these calculations.
a i 37 + 61 ii 933 + 245 iii 77 + 55 iv 867 + 567
(98, 1178, 132, 1434)
b i 76 – 45 ii 684 – 503 iii 120 – 47 iv 555 – 366
(21, 181, 73, 189)
2 You buy a magazine for £2.55 and some chewing gum for 78p.
a How much have you spent in total? (£3.33)
b If you pay with £5 how much change should you get? (£1.67)</td></tr>
</table>

Development and links

The ability to add and subtract numbers is a precursor skill to being able to multiply and divide numbers, which can be viewed as repeated addition and subtraction respectively; this is treated in chapter **14**.

In book **2A**, multiplication and division is extended to handling larger numbers, contextual settings and some decimals. The emphasis is placed on using standard column procedures for written methods.

Arithmetic is fundamental to mathematics and wherever numbers appear it is almost certain that some form of arithmetic will be required. As in maths, as in life – arithmetic is a basic life skill. In an age of calculators the ability to perform written calculations may not be as important as it was but the ability to (approximate and) do mental arithmetic remains important as a way of checking more accurate calculations.

MyMaths extra support

Lesson/online homework	Description
Adding two-digit numbers 1225 L3	This lesson revises adding and subtracting two-digit numbers by splitting them into tens and units.
Mixed sums over 100 1344 L3	A set of games that require you to add and subtract numbers in your head against the clock.
Number facts and doubles 4 1338 L4	A set of activities that require you to find number bounds for 100 and 1000 and number doubles.
Sums using 10s, 100s and 1000s 1342 L4	Addition and subtraction techniques based on rounding to a multiple of ten and adjusting: $+19 \equiv +20-1$ or $-98 \equiv -100+2$

My Review

7 MySummary

Check out

You should now be able to ...

	Test it ➡ Questions
✓ Strengthen and extend mental methods of addition and subtraction. (3)	1, 2
✓ Use efficient written methods to add and subtract whole numbers. (4)	3 - 6

Language	Meaning	Example
Addition	The act of summing two numbers.	12 + 7 is an addition of 12 and 7
Sum	The result of an addition.	19 is the sum
Subtraction	The act of taking away one number from another.	12 − 7 = 5 is the subtraction of 7 from 12
Column arithmetic	An efficient method of adding or subtracting two numbers.	$\begin{array}{r} 43 \\ +69 \\ \hline 112 \end{array}$ $\begin{array}{r} {}^{6}\not{7}{}^{1}1 \\ -23 \\ \hline 48 \end{array}$

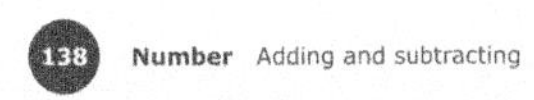

7 MyReview

1 Work out these additions in your head.

a 50 + 30 **b** 75 + 20
c 15 + 35 **d** 40 + 38
e 7 + 0 **f** 23 + 7
g 14 + 21 **h** 18 + 51
i 47 + 35 **j** 97 + 23
k 235 + 144 **l** 99 + 99

2 Work out these subtractions in your head.

a 50 − 9 **b** 67 − 20
c 41 − 21 **d** 65 − 30
e 87 − 32 **f** 73 − 38
g 56 − 18 **h** 177 − 116
i 257 − 129 **j** 408 − 212

3 Copy and complete these calculations.

a $\begin{array}{r} 57 \\ +21 \\ \hline \end{array}$ **b** $\begin{array}{r} 816 \\ +171 \\ \hline \end{array}$

c $\begin{array}{r} 65 \\ -24 \\ \hline \end{array}$ **d** $\begin{array}{r} 574 \\ -163 \\ \hline \end{array}$

4 Copy and complete these calculations.

a $\begin{array}{r} 63 \\ +29 \\ \hline \end{array}$ **b** $\begin{array}{r} 335 \\ +718 \\ \hline \end{array}$

c $\begin{array}{r} 83 \\ -65 \\ \hline \end{array}$ **d** $\begin{array}{r} 304 \\ -185 \\ \hline \end{array}$

5 Work out these calculations using a written method.

a 46 + 123 **b** 316 − 202
c 478 + 767 **d** 553 − 47

6 You buy a chocolate bar for 84p and a magazine for £2.50

a How much money have you spent?
b If you pay with a £5 note how much change should you get?

What next?

Score	
0 - 2	Your knowledge of this topic is still developing. To improve look at Formative test: 1A-7; MyMaths: 1020, 1028 and 1345
3 - 5	You are gaining a secure knowledge of this topic. To improve look at InvisiPen: 121 and 125
6	You have mastered this topic. Well done, you are ready to progress!

MyMaths.co.uk

Question commentary

Question 1 – (lesson **7a**) Allow students to use a number line if they need one, they can add the 10s first then the units. In parts **f**, **i**, **j** and **l** check that the carry digits are handled correctly; failure to do so would give the wrong answers: 20, 72, 110 and 188. Ask if students can see an 'easy' way to do part **l** by thinking of 99 as 100 – 1.

Question 2 – (lesson **7b**) Again allow students to use a number line if they need one, they can count back in 10s first then units.

Question 3 – (lesson **7c**) These are straightforward additions and subtractions not requiring any carrying or borrowing

Question 4 – (lesson **7d**) These additions require carry digits and the subtractions require borrowing. Part **d** is particularly tricky as they have to borrow from the hundreds column for the units. A common mistake would be as follows.

$$\begin{array}{r} {}^{1}\not{2}\not{3}{}^{1}\not{0}{}^{1}4 \\ -\ 1\ 8\ 5 \\ \hline 2\ 9 \end{array}$$

Question 5 – (lesson **7d**) This requires students to write the calculations into columns themselves, taking care to line up correctly. Lining up from the left instead of the right could give the wrong answers **a** 583 and **d** 83.

Question 6 – (lessons **7d** and **1e**) Check that students have written down the correct calculations based on the information given in the question. This will require them to convert between numbers given in pounds and numbers given in pence. In part **a** the calculation is 84 + 250 and in part **b** it is 500 – 334. The answer to part **b** depends on that for part **a**.

Answers

1	**a**	80	**b**	95	**c**	50	**d**	78
	e	7	**f**	30	**g**	35	**h**	69
	i	82	**j**	120	**k**	379	**l**	189
2	**a**	41	**b**	47	**c**	20	**d**	35
	e	55	**f**	35	**g**	38	**h**	61
	i	128	**j**	196				
3	**a**	78	**b**	987	**c**	41	**d**	411
4	**a**	92	**b**	1053	**c**	18	**d**	119
5	**a**	169	**b**	114	**c**	1245	**d**	506
6	**a**	334p = £3.34			**b**	166p = £1.66		

7 MyPractice

7a

1 Calculate these additions.

a 54 + 16 **b** 48 + 22
c 53 + 17 **d** 51 + 19
e 65 + 39 **f** 79 + 13

2 A lorry of length 25 m is towing a trailer of length 15 m. What is the total length?

3 Use the method of 'adding tens and then units' to find each answer.

a 54 + 31 **b** 70 + 14 **c** 62 + 22 **d** 79 + 12

4 Use a number line to find the answer if you need to.

a 77 + 35 **b** 88 + 26 **c** 60 + 54 **d** 83 + 28

5 In these pyramids, each number is found by adding the two numbers below it. Copy the pyramids and fill in the missing numbers.

a

b

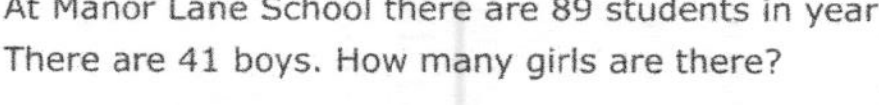

7b

6 Calculate these.

a 74 − 31 **b** 47 − 32 **c** 54 − 12
d 64 − 19 **e** 62 − 48 **f** 84 − 8

7 At Manor Lane School there are 89 students in year 7. There are 41 boys. How many girls are there?

8 Use the method of 'subtracting tens and then units' to find each answer.

a 89 − 43 **b** 68 − 22 **c** 96 − 51 **d** 81 − 39

9 Find the answers. Use a number line if you need to.

a 102 − 57 **b** 110 − 65 **c** 91 − 48 **d** 102 − 43

10 In these pyramids, each number is found by subtracting the two numbers below it. Copy the pyramids and fill in the missing numbers.

a

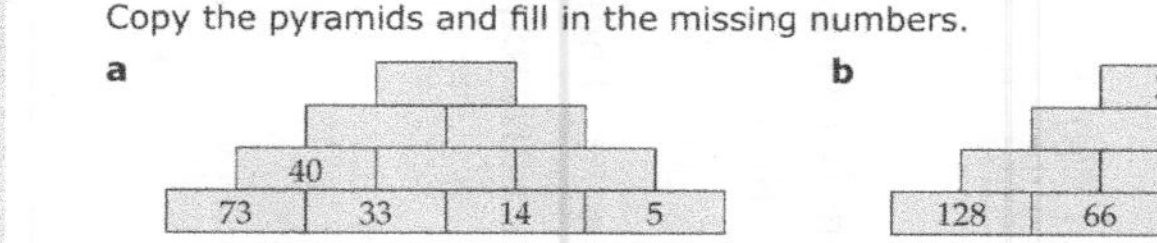

b

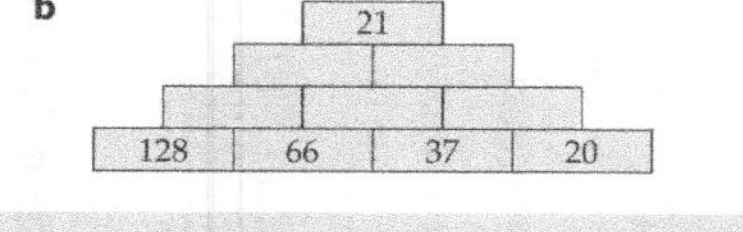

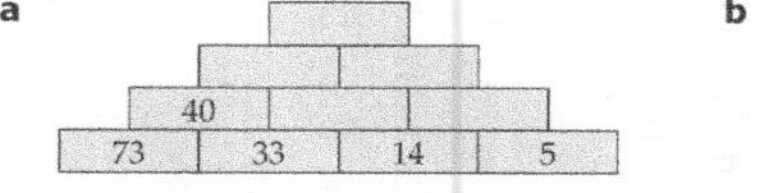

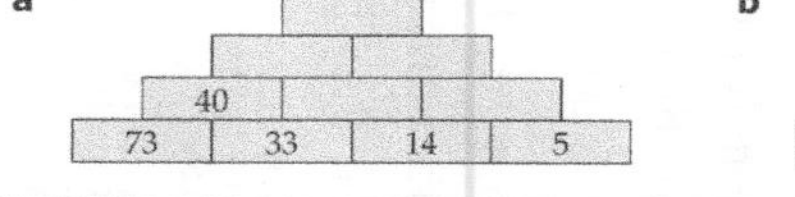

7c

11 Complete these column additions and subtractions.

a 43 + 25 **b** 72 + 26 **c** 66 − 32 **d** 95 − 73

12 Work out these using column arithmetic.

a 245 + 352 **b** 628 + 371 **c** 307 + 651 **d** 273 + 516
e 356 − 134 **f** 728 − 617 **g** 856 − 35 **h** 764 − 560

7d

13 Complete these column additions and subtractions.

a 464 + 318 **b** 218 + 302 **c** 584 − 380 **d** 670 − 235

14 Add or subtract using columns.

a 596 + 327 **b** 641 + 239 **c** 452 − 106 **d** 817 − 280

15 Write these problems in columns and then add or subtract.

a 539 + 254 **b** 107 + 448 **c** 472 − 209 **d** 703 − 362

16 The passenger numbers for a train service are: Monday 562, Tuesday 703, Wednesday 481

a Find the total number of passengers for the three days.

b Find the difference between the number of passengers on Tuesday and the number of passengers on Wednesday.

Question commentary

Questions 1 to **10** – Allow students to use jottings to support doing the working out in their heads.

Questions 1 – If the method of 'adding tens then units' is used check that the carry digit is handled correctly.

Question 2 – Ask students to write out the calculation that needs to be done, 25 + 15, and ensure the answer includes the units.

Question 3 – Part **d** involves a carry digit; ignoring it gives 81 not 91.

Question 4 – A ruler can be used as a number line.

Question 5 – Parts of these questions can be done together as a class to help ensure students understand what is required.

Questions 6 – If the method of 'subtracting tens then units' is used check that any borrowed digit is handled correctly.

Question 7 – Ask students to write out the calculation that needs to be done, 89 – 41.

Question 8 – Part **d** involves a borrow; not changing the 8 to a 7 would give 52 not 42.

Question 9 – A ruler can be used as a number line.

Question 10 – Parts of these questions can be done together as a class to help ensure students understand what is required. It is intended that the number on the right is subtracted from the number on the left.

Questions 11 – No carry or borrow digits are involved. Ask students to explain what they are doing and why to check understanding.

Question 12 – Again no carry or borrow digits are involved. The important point to check is that students write out the calculations using the correct columns. Particular attention should be paid to part **g** which could be confused with 856 – 350 = 506.

Question 13 – Parts **a** and **b** both involve a carry digit whilst part **d** involves a borrow digit. Ask students to explain what they are doing and why to check understanding.

Question 14 – Part **a** involves multiple carry digits.

Question 15 – Check that students correctly write out the calculations using columns.

Question 16 – Part **a** involves adding three numbers. Either the standard written method can be used or the calculation can be done in two stages:
562 + (703 + 381) = 562 + 1084 = 1646 or
(562 + 703) + 381 = 1265 + 381 = 1646

Answers

1 **a** 70 **b** 70 **c** 70 **d** 70
e 104 **f** 92

2 40 m

3 **a** 85 **b** 84 **c** 84 **d** 91

4 **a** 112 **b** 114 **c** 114 **d** 111

5 **a**

126
60 | 66
31 | 29 | 37
17 | 14 | 15 | 22

b

247
132 | 115
68 | 64 | 51
23 | 45 | 19 | 32

6 **a** 43 **b** 15 **c** 42 **d** 45
e 14 **f** 76

7 48 girls
a 46 **b** 46 **c** 45 **d** 42

9 **a** 45 **b** 45 **c** 43 **d** 59

10 **a**

11
21 | 10
40 | 19 | 9
73 | 33 | 14 | 5

b

21
33 | 12
62 | 29 | 17
128 | 66 | 37 | 20

11 **a** 68 **b** 98 **c** 34 **d** 22

12 **a** 597 **b** 999 **c** 958 **d** 789
e 222 **f** 111 **g** 821 **h** 204

13 **a** 782 **b** 520 **c** 204 **d** 435

14 **a** 923 **b** 880 **c** 346 **d** 537

15 **a** 793 **b** 555 **c** 263 **d** 341

16 **a** 1646 **b** 222

Learning outcomes

S1 Describe, interpret and compare observed distributions of a single variable through: appropriate graphical representation involving discrete, continuous and grouped data; and appropriate measures of central tendency (mean, mode, median) and spread (range, consideration of outliers). (L4)

S2 Construct and interpret appropriate tables, charts, and diagrams, including frequency tables, bar charts, pie charts, and pictograms for categorical data, and vertical line (or bar) charts for ungrouped and grouped numerical data. (L3/4)

Introduction

The chapter starts by looking at how we can collect and organise data. Reading from lists and tables is then covered before work on pictograms bar charts and pie charts. Reading from more general statistical diagrams is then covered. The next two sections cover the mode and median. The final spread is on comparing data using the mode, median and range.

The introduction discusses the use of market research in retail and business. It is important for businesses to find out information about their customers in order that they can provide the appropriate products and services.

In 2012, it is estimated that $18.9 billion was spent globally on marketing and market research. In the US alone, spending was $6.7 billion and this accounted for 10.4% of total business revenue in that year. As you can see, marketing and market research is BIG business and therefore a thorough understanding of statistical methods is extremely important.

Prior knowledge

Students should already know how to…

- Carry out simple arithmetical operations
- Estimate the size of angles, including as fractions of a whole

Starter problem

In the starter problem asks students to compare the 'average' boy with the 'average' girl in their class. This is very open-ended but the students could be directed to consider what we mean by 'average' in this context.

Data can be collected from the class. This could take the form of biometric data (height, hand span, etc.) or more general data such as hair colour, eye colour and number of siblings.

Calculations should be kept relatively simple, or a computer programme used, in order for the students to get a sense of the 'average', rather than relying on complex calculation methods not covered in this chapter.

Resources

MyMaths

Frequency tables and bar charts	1193		
Line graphs and two-way tables	1198	Mean and mode	1200
Median and range	1203	Pictograms and bar charts	1205
Reading pie charts	1206	Introducing data	1235

Online assessment

Chapter test	1A–8
Formative test	1A–8
Summative test	1A–8

InvisiPen solutions

Tally charts and frequency tables	411		
Collecting data	415	Pictograms	421
Reading and interpreting pie charts	423		
Line graphs data	424	Averages of a list	441

Topic scheme

Teaching time = 10 lessons/4 weeks

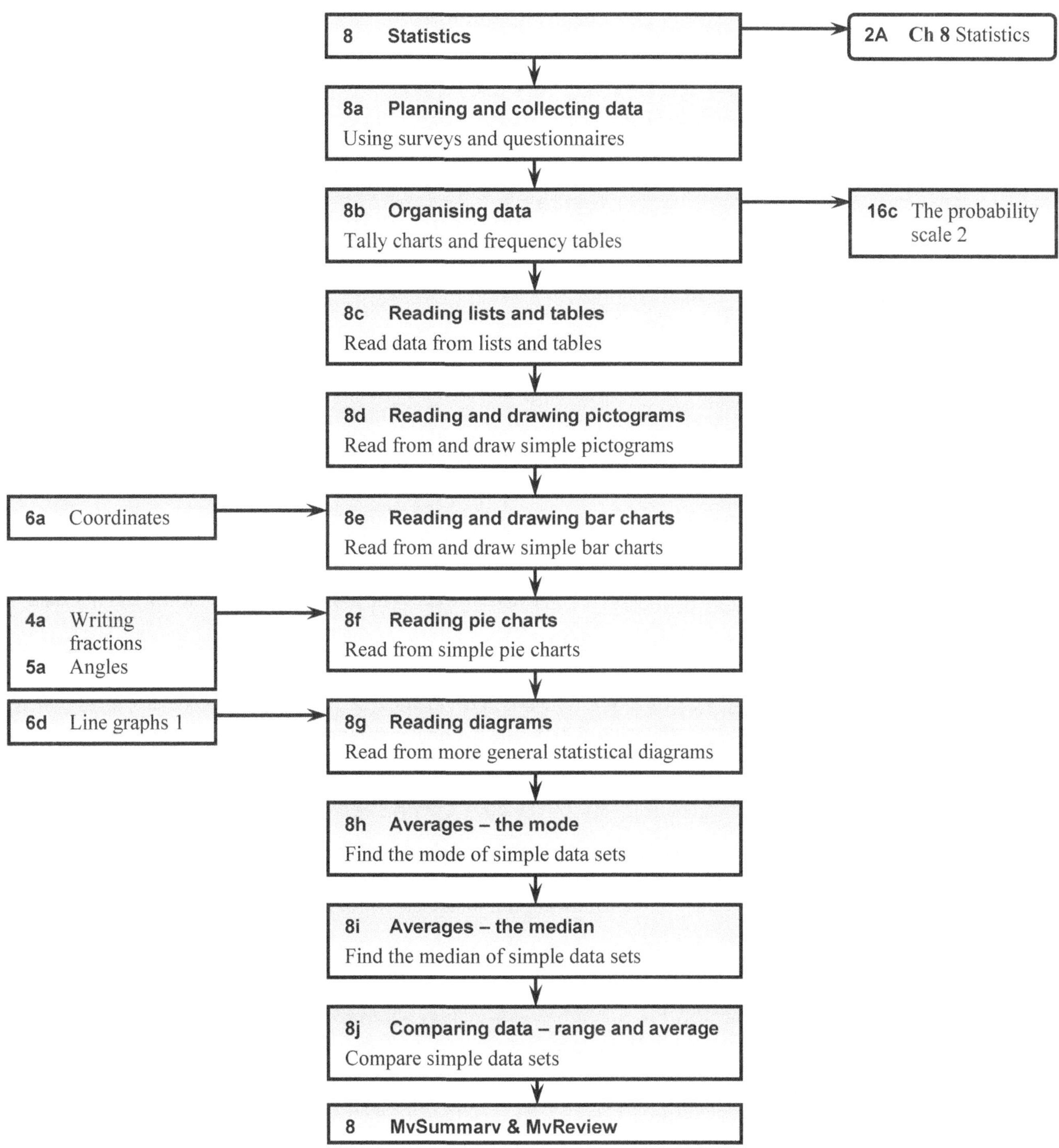

Differentiation

Student book 1A 142 – 167

Planning, collecting and organising data
Reading statistical diagrams such as pie charts, bar charts and pictograms
Draw bar charts
Finding the mode and median
Comparing data sets

Student book 1B 142 – 167

Draw, read and interpret bar charts, pie charts and line graphs
Find the mean, median, mode and range of a set of data
Understand the data-handling cycle and methods for collecting data
Draw tally charts and frequency tables
Compare data sets

Student book 1C 140 – 165

Understand types of data
Calculate the mean
Construct frequency tables and diagrams
Read and interpret pie charts
Understand the data-handling cycle and plan a statistical enquiry
Collect data and design questionnaires
Group and compare data

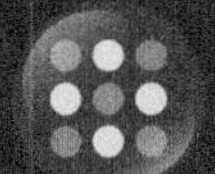

8a Planning and collecting data

Objectives	
• Design questionnaires to use in a simple survey.	(L3)

Key ideas	Resources
1 Data can be gathered in different situations, such as experiements and questionnaires. **2** Questionnaires must be written in ways which provide good-quality data.	Examples of badly-written questions for a questionnaire Examples of the outcomes of good questionnaires
Simplification	**Extension**
To help with creating a questionnaire, offer students various questions to use to get the same information. They can discuss the strengths and weaknesses of each question and decide on the best.	Students can create a questionnaire for a more wide-ranging investigation on a topic of their choice. They can create it by hand or by using a computer.
Literacy	**Links**
Theexercise requires good writing skills. When creating questions for a questionnaire, the writing needs to be clear, unambiguous, concise and allowing a range of responses that are easy to collate.	Bring in some newspapers for the class to use, or look at online news bulletins. Ask students to find any reference to the results of *opinion polls*. An opinion poll is an estimate of the opinion of the public as a whole, based on questioning a sample of people. They are often used to try to predict the winner of a forthcoming election. Opinion polls can be conducted in the street, on people's doorsteps, using the Internet, by telephone or by post.

Alternative approach

Rather than create questions from scratch for a questionnaire, provide instead the results of a questionnaire which have already been collected, organised and analysed to produce a final commentary. Ask the students what questions would be necessary to obtain the information necessary to produce that analysis and commentary.

MyMaths lesson 1249, 'Questionnaires', provides commentary on designing questionnaires and carrying out surveys.

Checkpoint

1 Ask students what is wrong with each of the following questions taken from a questionnaire.

a What is your favourite colour?

Blue ☐ Red ☐ Yellow ☐ Green ☐ (There are many other colours!)

b How many pets do you have at home?

1 ☐ 2 ☐ 3 ☐ More than 3☐ (There is no option for 0 pets)

c What time do you get up in the morning?

Before 7 a.m. ☐ 7 – 7.30 a.m. ☐

7.30 – 8 a.m. ☐ After 8 a.m. ☐ (This will vary depending on the day)

Can students suggest a way to improve each of the questions?

Starter – Today's number is ... 39

This starter revises number work of previous chapters. Ask students to respond on mini-whiteboards to a series of quick questions based on today's number, 39. Discuss answers where there is a need.

- What is half of 39? (19.5)
- What is one third of 39? (13)
- What is 19 more than 39? (58)
- Give a multiple of 39. (39, 78, 117, ...)

Teaching notes

Ask students for situations in which information is collected and analysed. Data can be collected by

- the students themselves;
- other people and organisations.

Categorise the situations as

- an experiment, as done in a science lesson;
- an observation, as in a traffic survey;
- a census, as when all the population is involved;
- a sample, as when a questionnaire is used with few people involved.

Provide a list of scenarios and ask which category of data-collection is required. For example, the temperature of a cooling chemical requires a science experiment; the income of the school's 16-year-olds with Saturday jobs needs a sample of some teenagers or a census of all the 16-year-olds in the school.

Before constructing their own questionnaires, students should learn the common pitfalls. Issue students with four or five badly constructed questions that might be used in a questionnaire and ask why these questions are not suitable. For example, where did you go for your last holiday? or which is your favourite kind of pet: dog, horse, budgie, other?. A poor question could be too broad or too specific; it might only allow certain answers and exclude valid answers.

Students can work in pairs to construct a questionnaire and then exchange with another pair to get critical suggestions for improvement. Discuss suggestions as a whole class and agree the best types of questions.

Plenary

Ask pairs of students to list the most important points that they would give as advice to someone who was about to write questions for a questionnaire. The pairs can share their best findings in a whole-class discussion.

Exercise commentary

Much in this exercise lends itself to paired work linked with whole-class discussion.

Question 1 – Anna's question links directly with Tracy's work in the introduction to the lesson. Students could discuss each question in pairs before making their own decision.

Question 3 – When improving questionnaires students need to remember that a question must allow a range of responses which cover all possibilities, but the answers to the question must be easy to collate and analyse.

Question 4 – It is not difficult to invent questions for these answers. However, finding good questions is the real task for students.
The task can be extended to considering the ways that questions are phrased in advertising so as to get a desired response. Examples from the media can be examined.

Answers

1 **c** It gives a choice of types and includes 'other'. Add 'If other please give details ___________'
 a Too restrictive, only asks about one type of music.
 c Too open, results will be hard to analyse.

2 Students' answers; a possible question is
'How do you listen to music?
Radio ☐ Phone ☐ Internet ☐
Other ☐ If other, please give details _______'

3 **a** Include the names of other popular DJs and include an 'other' option.
 b Include an 'other' option.
 Consider asking about the DJ's level of popularity; could rank the options1, 2 3.
 c The results from this question will not answer the question posed. Replace with an improved version of question **b**.

4 Students' answers; possible answers are
 a What is your favourite time of year?
 b Which is your favourite season?
 c What is your favourite food?
 d What motivates you?
 e What is your favourite girl's name?
 f Where is your favourite place to go on holiday?

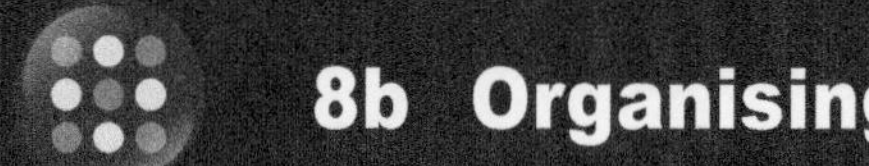

8b Organising data

Objectives	
• Collect and record discrete data. (L3) • Construct frequency tables for gathering discrete data. (L3)	
Key ideas	**Resources**
1 A tally chart helps in the collection of data. **2** A frequency table is a concise way of presenting the data.	Introducing data (1235) Pre-drawn blank tally charts and frequency tables
Simplification	**Extension**
Students can use pre-drawn blank tally charts and frequency tables to complete.	Ask students to think through the process of gathering and presenting data using a tally chart and frequency table. They can then create an annotated flow diagram showing the process that they went through.
Literacy	**Links**
Tally marks are used for counting. They are particularly useful for keeping track of ongoing results, such as the score in a game or sport. We usually record tally marks in groups of five, which look likt five-bar gates as found in the countryside.	The RSPB has been carrying out its annual Big Garden Birdwatch since 1979, and the results for 2014 are given at www.rspb.org.uk/birdwatch/index.asp The bird seen most frequently in gardens across England, Scotland, Wales and Northern Ireland was the house sparrow, and in total 7 274 159 birds were counted.

Alternative approach

Schools regularly survey opinions of students and parents. A larger-scale task for students would be to have the school delegate the use of a questionnaire to the class to gather and analyse information on a topic such as school uniform or school trip destinations.

MyMaths lesson 1235, 'Introducing Data', gives an interactive demonstration of using tallies to create a frequency table for car colours.

Checkpoint

1 **a** What numbers do these tally marks represent.

i 𝍸 **ii** 𝍸 ||| **iii** 𝍸 𝍸 || **iv** 𝍸 𝍸 𝍸 |||| **v** 𝍸 𝍸 𝍸 𝍸 ||| (5, 8, 12, 19, 23)

b Write these numbers using tally marks.

i 3 **ii** 7 **iii** 15 **iv** 18 **v** 25

(|||, 𝍸 ||, 𝍸 𝍸 𝍸, 𝍸 𝍸 𝍸 |||, 𝍸 𝍸 𝍸 𝍸 𝍸)

Starter – Pollsters

Carry out a poll in class for responses to questions such as 'What is your favourite vegetable?' or 'How did you get to school this morning?' Create tally charts to display the results. Discuss any significant findings and ask if there is a better way to represent the data.

Teaching notes

Gather data on favourite colours across the class. Record data using a tally. Ask students how this data might be presented more clearly, and agree that a frequency table summarises the results clearly.

Draw the distinction between data that is

- descriptive, such as colour ;
- counted, such as goals in a soccer match;
- measured, such as a person's temperature when they are ill.

Invite students to suggest another area to investigate where the data is counted, such as the number of the siblings each student has. Collect the data, one student at a time, using a tally chart to organise responses. Time how long it takes to collect responses. Compile a frequency table for the whole class.

Repeat for other data that is counted (for example, the number of pets each student has). This time, collect data by asking for a show of hands, working upwards from 'no pets'. Time how long it takes to collect the data and compare it with the previous method. Compile another whole-class frequency table.

Plenary

Ask students to summarise the three most important points they have gained from the lesson that will help them to collect and analyse data using tally charts and frequency tables correctly and efficiently.

Exercise commentary

Question 1 – Students construct their own frequency table here. A blank frequency table could be provided for those students who need extra support.

Question 2 – Students could either copy the given table and add an extra column for the frequencies, or replace the 'Tally' column by a 'Frequency' column.

Question 3 – Remind students that they should write out the names of each bird rather than trying to draw them!

Question 4 – Ronnie's tallies can be counted in fives or in lots of 25, as one row is worth 25. We presume that Johnny kept a running total in his head, which could have led to error. Discuss the advantages and disadvantages of the different methods of keeping tally.

Question 5 – This question shows students the importance of being clear and accurate when recording data. If students are struggling to find errors in the chart, they should be encouraged to check that the values in the 'Tally' and 'Frequency' column match and that the frequency total is correct. Ask them if they can tell you what the chart is supposed to show.

Answers

1

Fruit	Frequency
Banana	7
Apple	8
Orange	5
Total	20

2

Club	Frequency
Art club	16
Netball club	22
Computer club	13
Total	51

3

Bird	Tally	Frequency
Sparrow	卌 卌 卌 |	16
Robin	卌	5
Magpie	卌 |	6
Pigeon	|||	3
	Total	30

4 Ronnie with 104

5 In row 3, frequency for Guaymi should be 7
In row 9, Guaymi appear a second time. Total frequency for Guaymi should be 11.
In row 10, total from listed frequencies should be 45.
Correcting error in row 2, total should be 46.

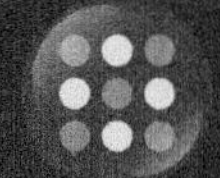

8c Reading lists and tables

Objectives

- Extract and process data presented in simple tables and lists. (L3)

Key ideas

1 Data in lists is usually listed item by item.

2 Data in tables is often collected into a fequency table.

Resources

Frequency tables and bar charts (1193)

Sources of listed and tabulated data, such as, furniture catalogues

A calculator

Simplification

Provide students with further examples of simple lists and tables of data about which simple questions can be asked.

Any calculations based on the data, such as finding the total money spent in a corner shop, should be straightforward and, in some cases, can be done using a calculator.

Extension

As an extension, students could think of a situation requiring the tabulation of data; for example, the purchase of food and drink for a school fete. Students can generate their own data (or research the prices of grocery items) for their scenario and write it as a table.

Literacy

Ensure students are confident with the vocabulary surrounding consumer arithmetic, as they look at examples and questions involving prices and the addition of amounts of money.

In a restaurant, a *bill* shows how much money you owe in total for a meal, and also often lists each item separately. Prices are usually shown on the *menu*, so you know in advance what you will need to pay.

Shops, such as, furniture stores sometimes produce a *catalogue* or *price list* for customers to take home and look at. In fact, nowadays, many shops also have an online catalogue showing all of the items they have for sale

Links

Bring in some furniture catalogues for the class to use. Draw up a shopping list for a basic set of furniture for a living room, dining room or bedroom. Ask the class to find prices for the items on the list. Who can furnish the room for the least money? Who has spent the most money?

Alternative approach

Several alternative approaches have been mentioned. They include using and understanding data from other sources as well as gathering and processing your own data.

Checkpoint

Refer to the bill from Carla's Restaurant in the student book.

1 **a** How many desserts did the group have? (Three)

b What was the price of the cheapest maincourse? (£7.95)

c If an extra two drinks, each costing £2.50, were added to the bill, what would the new total be? (£69.00)

Starter – Today's number is ... 100

This starter revises number work of previous chapters Ask students to respond on mini-whiteboards to a series of quick questions based on today's number, 100. Discuss answers where there is a need.

- What is half of 100? (50)
- How many centimetres are there in 100 mm? (10)
- What is 2.7×100? (270)
- Write five factors of 100. (1, 2, 4, 5, 10, 25, 50, 100)
- Subtract 21 from 100. (79)
- What does the number 3 stand for in 0.13? (0.03)

Teaching notes

To show that data is more clearly understandable in list or table format, gather some simple information from each student in the class. For example, ask each student which month their birthday is in. Write the responses in the order they are given and then ask students how the responses could be organised. Compare both the list and table format and discuss which is the easier to access.

Display a table of school-based data; for example, the numbers of different items of stationery sold in a month in a school shop or a table of one of the divisions of the football league. Hold a whole-class discussion to decide the kinds of information that can be found in the table. For the stationery, ask about the most popular items, the cost of items, the income from selling pens, etc.

Plenary

Show students a supermarket receipt. In pairs, ask each student to write three questions that can be answered using the receipt. Students should take it in turns to answer their partner's questions.

Exercise commentary

Questions 1 and **2** – Students need to refer to the tables in the examples on the opposite page.

Question 3 – Students need to calculate the cost of two or three items, which involves addition of money, using whole numbers only.

Question 4 – Discuss with students how to convert the total time in minutes to hours and minutes.

Question 5 – Students can draw on Question **4** to present the information in a table. They should convert the total time in minutes to a time in hours and minutes. Discuss whether an answer in minutes or hours is preferable.

Answers

1 **a** 2 **b** £4.75
c They are all different prices. **d** £6

2 **a** 4 **b** Stuffed Courgette
c Dover Sole

3 **a** £180 **b** £265 **c** £225

4 **a** Sunday
b Friday and Saturday
c 235 min = 3 hours 55 min

5 **a**

Day	Mon	Tue	Wed	Thu	Fri	Sat	Sun
Mins	30	30	60	75	15	90	0

b 300 mins = 5 hours
c $\frac{5}{24}$

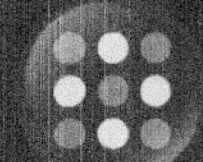

8d Reading and drawing pictograms

Objectives

- Extract and understand information presented in pictograms. (L3)
- Construct pictograms, where the symbol represents a group of units. (L3)

Key ideas

1 A pictogram is a visual way of representing data in a table.

2 The key of the pictogram can represent one or more items.

Resources

Pictograms and bar charts (1205)

Data from the school and local area

Atlases which contain pictograms.

Simplification

Students should avoid overly artistic symbols. Initially, use a key of one symbol for one item. Where additional practice is needed, choose data carefully where one symbol represents more than one item.

Extension

Ask students to draw their own pictogram of a scenario of their choosing. The pictogram could incorporate quarter, half and three-quarter symbols. Ask student to write a paragraph about what the pictogram represents.

Literacy

The word 'pictogram' comes from two words, one meaning the same as 'picture' and the other a Latin word meaning 'to write or draw'.

Outside mathematics, a pictogram is simply an image or icon representing something. It is not a numerical table.

Students should avoid the incorrect spelling 'pictagram'.

Links

Refer students to a choice of atlases. As well as maps, some atlases also show numerical data in different forms that often include pictograms. See if students can find any pictograms, perhaps giving information about populations, the use of land, etc.

The following web page gives a table and pictogram for population of large countries.

www.jaconline.com.au/downloads/sose/2004-09-pictogram.pdf

Alternative approach

Pictograms can be drawn electronically. Use MyMaths lesson 1205 ('Pictograms and Bar Charts') to investigate and draw pictograms (note that the page also uses bar charts, which are introduced in lesson **8e**).

In addition, there are games and worksheets involving pictograms at

www.softschools.com/math/data_analysis/

Checkpoint

Refer to Question **3** in the student book.

1 Redraw the pictogram using a new key in which each symbol represents

a 5 houses (▯▯▯▯/▯▯▯▯▯▯▯▯▯▯▯▯/▯▯▯▯▯▯)

b 20 houses. (▯/▯▯▯/▯□)

2 **a** What is the total number of houses in Apton and Bapton? (80)

b What is the total number of houses in Bapton and Capton? (90)

Starter – Doubling

Ask students for the answers to the following calculations.

- 4 × 7 (28)

(suggest they double 2 × 7 if necessary)

- 4 × 14 (56)

  (suggest doubling the previous answer)
- 4 × 28 (112)
- 4 × 3.5 (14)

Discuss how this method of doubling, or halving, can help students with calculations they find difficult.

Teaching notes

Make links with previous work on lists and tables and discuss the advantages of the visual nature of pictograms. As a whole-class, construct a pictogram for the number of computers in classrooms in your school (see also the example in the students' book) and agree the symbol to represent one computer.

Make some of the basic errors commonly encountered in drawing pictograms, such as a disorganized diagram with symbols of erratic sizes with uneven spacing between them. Ask students to criticise your pictogram and suggest how it can be corrected.

Now consider an example where one symbol no longer represents an individual item. For example, construct a pictogram for the number of students is each Year 7 class in school. Ensure, initially, that the data requires students to use only complete symbols. At a later stage, introduce half-symbols or other parts of a symbol. Ask students 'What if one symbol represents 10 children and there are 25 or 27 in the class?'

Plenary

Give pairs of students some written text containing information that has been displayed in a pictogram. Ensure that the pictogram contains errors and ask each pair to discuss and identify the mistakes and to redraw the pictogram correctly.

Exercise commentary

Question 1 – This question is straightforward as they key shows each symbol representing just one person.

Question 2 – Students need to decide on a suitable key, representing the numbers 2 and 5 clearly, and should choose sensible symbols for a can.

Questions 3 and **4** – These questions involve extracting information from pictograms where a key is used. In Question **3**, only whole symbols are used in the key. In Question **4**, part symbols are used. It may be a good opportunity to discuss how symbols can be used to clearly show a 'half' or a 'quarter'.

Question 5 – Again, students need to decide on a suitable key. Using one symbol for 2 items involves only whole symbols in the pictogram, but using one symbol for 4 items would involve some half-symbols in the pictogram.

Question 6 – The information on the completed pictogram needs to agree with the information in the completed table. The paw prints should not be counted.

Answers

1 **a**

House number	Number of people
1	6
2	4
3	4

b 14

2

Flavour	No of cans
Beef	□ □
Tuna	□ □
Chicken	□ □ □ □ □

Key: □ = 1 can

3 **a** Apton 20, Bapton 60, Capton 30

b 110

4 **a** 60 **b** 35 **c** Wednesday

d 355

5

Bird	No of birds
Chaffinches	□ □
Pigeons	□ □ □
Starlings	□ □ □ □ □ □
Sparrows	□ □ □ □ □ □ □ □ □

Key: □ = 2 birds

6 Pictogram: cat 3 smiley faces; fish 2 smiley faces

Table: dog 7; other 3

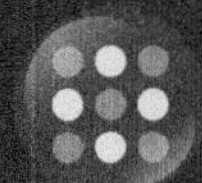

8e Reading and drawing bar charts

Objectives

- Extract and understand information presented in bar charts. (L3)
- Construct bar charts. (L3)

Key ideas

1. Bar charts can represent data which are collected about various attributes of a scenario.
2. Both axes of a bar chart need labelling.

Resources

Frequency tables and bar charts (1193)
Pictograms and bar charts (1205)

Partially-drawn bar charts
Square grid paper

Simplification

Initially, have axes drawn and labelled in advance. Students then simply draw the bars of the bar charts. When students progress to drawing their own axes, let them use square grid paper

Extension

Give students a written description of a scenario and data from the scenario presented in three forms – as table, a pictogram and a bar chart. Invite them to comment on the advantages and disadvantages of the different representations.

Literacy

Bar charts can have their bars drawn horizontally rather than vertically. They are sometimes called 'bar graphs' or 'column graphs'.

When drawing their own bar charts, students should follow the instructions given in the student book.

- Leave gaps between the bars.
- Make sure all the bars are the same width.
- Write a label on each axis.
- Make sure that the vertical axis has a clear scale.

Links

Tea is made from the leaves of the tea bush. Tea-drinking originated in China but most tea drunk in Britain comes from India. This website

www.tea.co.uk

has a counter showing how many cups of tea have been drunk in Britain so far today. Read the counter every minute for five minutes, work out the number of cups drunk each minute and draw a bar chart of the results.

Alternative approach

Discuss the use of bar charts with the geography and science teachers of this class of students. Ask if there is any recent or imminent work in these subjects that involves bar charts. If so, exploit the opportunity for some cross-curricular co-operation.

Refer again to MyMaths lesson 1205, 'Pictograms and Bar Charts'.

Checkpoint

1 Refer to the bar chart given in the student book example.

a What is shown on the vertical axis, and what is shown on the horizontal axis? (Number of computers; Room number)

b How many computers are there in Room 23? (5)

c Which room has the fewest computers? (22)

d How many rooms are shown in the bar chart? (4)

Starter – Cats and dogs

This starter revises fractions, decimals and percentages in context.

Count the number of students who have cats at home and write the fraction of the class with cats. Ask if the fraction can be simplified. Ask how to use a calculator to change the fraction to a decimal (rounded to 2 dp). Write the decimal as a percentage.

Repeat by for the number of students with dogs at home or with brothers and sisters. For each find the fraction, decimal and percentage.

On mini-whiteboards, have students write $\frac{79}{100}$ as a decimal (0.79) and as a percentage (79%). Repeat for $\frac{4}{7}$ using a calculator. (0.57, 57%)

Teaching notes

Initially, present students with a bar chart with no title, no labels and no scales on the axes. Ask what kind of graph it is and what it shows. Most students will be able to identify it as a bar chart. Use their inability to say what it shows to emphasise the importance of appropriate and accurate labelling.

Also emphasise that the scale on the vertical axis increases in regular steps and that the numbers labelling this axis lie on the grid lines and not in the gaps between them.

Compile a table using students' birth months. Ask students to represent this data in a bar chart. Discuss the advantages and disadvantages of the table and the chart for giving the clearest representation.

Plenary

Give pairs of students two bar charts. Without talking to each other, each student should write three questions that can be answered from their bar chart. They should then swap bar charts and answer their partners' questions and finally discuss their answers together.

Exercise commentary

Question 1 – Parts **b** and **c** can be done by looking at the heights of the bars.

Questions 2 and **3** – The questions require students to convert between representations. They should take care wto count accurately and use an appropriate scale.

Question 4 – Ensure that students have their axes the right way round and correctly labelled.

Question 5 – This is a good, comprehensive question as it requires the use of three stages of data processing: collection, tabulation and representation.

Question 6 – Constructing a bar chart for both sets of data together on the same axes would help students draw their conclusions about the data. Alternatively, they could draw one graph directly below or next to the other to make comparisons easier.

Answers

1 **a** 5 **b** 7D **c** 7B **d** 18

2

Frequency: 0, 1, 2, 3
Mon Tue Wed Thu Fri
Day

3

Frequency: 0, 10, 20, 30, 40, 50
7A 7B 7C 7D
Class

4

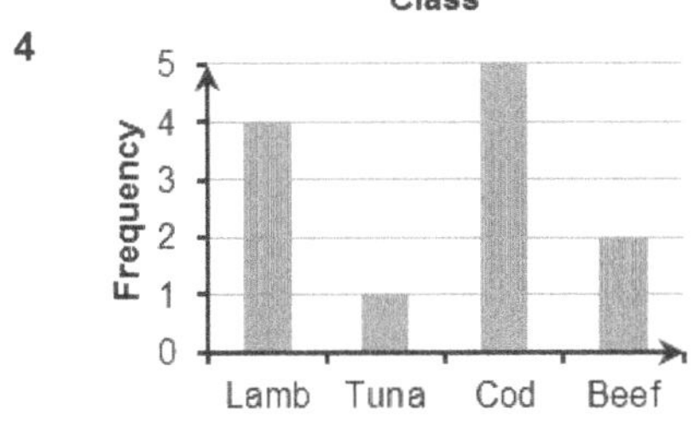

5 **a**

Activity	Tally	Frequency
Hockey	卌 卌	10
Football	卌 |	6
Netball	||||	4
	Total	20

b

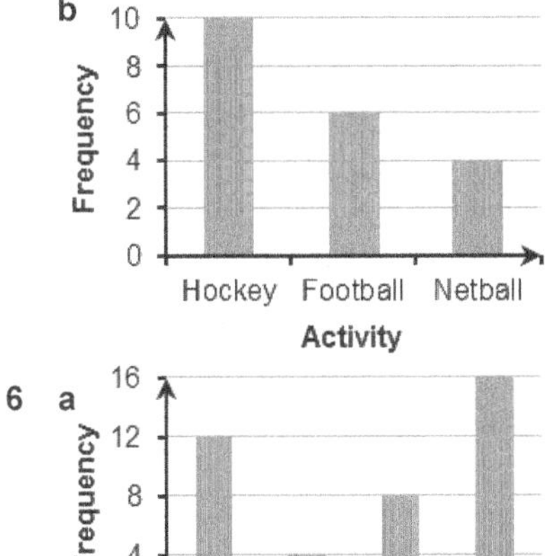

6 **a**

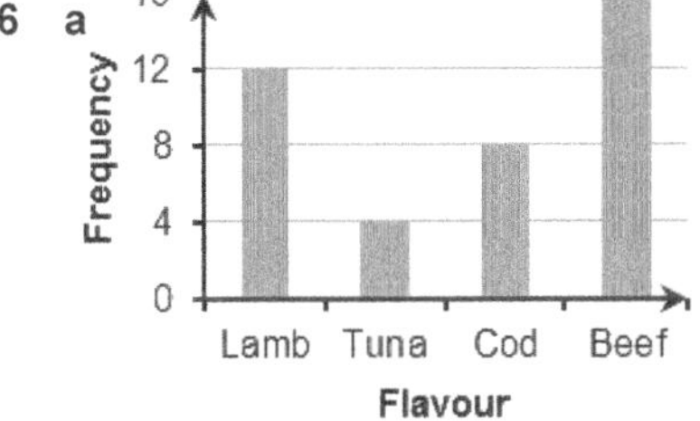

b The same: tuna is the least popular flavour and lamb is the second most popular flavour.
Different: The relative popularity of cod and beef (first and third) have swapped. There are over three times as many entries in the month graph.

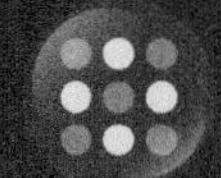

8f Reading pie charts

Objectives	
• Interpret pie charts and draw conclusions. (L4)	
Key ideas	**Resources**
1 A circle can be divided into sectors to represent the various categories of data.	Reading pie charts (1206) Circles of different colours divided into sectors Various shapes cut out of card with fractions of them marked and coloured 360° protractor Selection of simple pie charts, similar to those in the student book
Simplification	**Extension**
Show students a circle divided into four quarters, another (in a different colour) into eight eighths, and another (in yet another colour) into three thirds. Ask them to discuss how they would recognise a particular fraction of a circle such as $\frac{3}{4}$ or $\frac{2}{3}$.	For the first time, begin to calculate the fraction of the total for a given sector. Show two pie charts illustrating the same type of data, for example, eye colour as in Question **1**, but involving different numbers of students for each pie chart. Show fractions such as 9 students out of 36 with brown eyes and 6 out of 18 students in the two pie charts. Ask students which class has more students with brown eyes. Discuss how pie charts can be used to compare data and consider the common mistakes.
Literacy	**Links**
The *pie chart* is sometimes known as a 'circle diagram'. It is divided into *sectors* of a circle, which are parts of a circle bounded by two radii (the plural of 'radius') and an arc. Words which include *sect-* such as 'bisect', 'disect', 'insect', and 'section' all come from a Latin word *sectus* meaning 'cut'.	Statistics showing the number of pet-owning households in the UK in 2013 can be found at http://www.pfma.org.uk/pet-population/ An estimated 45% of households in the UK in 2013 owned a pet. What percentage of pet-owning households owned a cat? What about guinea pigs?

Alternative approach

Suppose that a student spends 6 hours at school each day; that is 360 minutes. List the number of minutes spent in each activity through the day (for example, time in lessons, time getting to lessons, lunchtime, etc.) and ensure they total 360 minutes. Take a circular protractor of 360°, draw a circle round it and, starting at 0, mark off the degrees for each time on an activity. Draw the radii of the sectors to make a pie chart. Label it. Discuss the fraction for each activity as multiples of $\frac{1}{360}$.

Checkpoint

1 Refer to the pie chart given in Question **4** in the student book.

a How many different fruits are shown in the pie chart? (4)

b What fraction of the class chose pears? ($\frac{1}{12}$)

c Which fruit did $\frac{1}{4}$ of the class choose? (Bananas)

Starter – Pieces of pies

Pies are usually baked in circular dishes, but they can also be made in other shapes of dish. Cut various shapes out of card (circles, squares, rectangles and a regular pentagon) with simple fractions shaded to represent pieces of pie. Label each piece of pie with a letter. Ask students to identify the size of each piece, writing their answers as a letter matched to a fraction. They should write their answers on mini-whiteboards.

Teaching notes

This work on pie charts can be initially linked to lesson **8e** on bar charts. Pie charts are an alternative representation to bar charts. Some time has been spent in the **Starter** with students recognising, on sight, simple fractions of the 'pie' such as $\frac{1}{2}$, $\frac{1}{4}$, $\frac{1}{8}$, $\frac{1}{3}$ and $\frac{2}{3}$. None of the questions in the exercise requires students to work out a fraction of a quantity. Instead, they practise recognising fractions in various contexts.

As a paired activity, students can be given a selection of simple pie charts suitably labelled for different contexts. Each student writes four questions about their chosen example, exchanges their pie chart and questions with their partner, answers their partners' questions, and then discusses with their partner all the answers to see if they agree.

Plenary

Show students a pie chart, for example the favourite desserts that a family enjoys, with labels on it and a key beside it. Ask questions about the data and ask students to answer using their mini-whiteboards.

Exercise commentary

Question 1 – This requires only a simple interpretation of the pie chart. No knowledge of fractions is needed.

Question 2 – Students need to recognise on sight the fraction that each sector is of the full circle.

Question 3 – In part **b**, students should recognise that the pink ('Bills') sector looks to be about a quarter; there is no need to add up the total amount and divide by 4.

Question 4 – Some fractions can be simplified into their lowest terms. Part **c** will need discussing, as there is no information about *numbers* of people.

Question 5 – One approach to this question is to ask students to imagine that they go on a family trip to the cinema and that they must estimate what they think they will spend on various items: tickets, popcorn, parking, etc. Given these numbers they can then try to match them to the variously sized sectors in the pie chart.

Answers

1 **a** 4 **b** Green **c** Brown

2 **a** $\frac{1}{4}$ **b** $\frac{1}{4}$ **c** $\frac{3}{8}$ **d** $\frac{1}{8}$

3 **a** £200 **b** Bills **c** Rent

4 **a** **i** $\frac{1}{4}$ **ii** $\frac{1}{3}$ **b** $\frac{7}{12}$ **c** No

5 Students' answers, one possibility is
Purple – tickets, Orange – baby-sitting,
Blue – parking, Yellow – popcorn

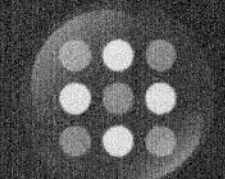

8g Reading diagrams

Objectives	
• Interpret frequency diagrams, including pie charts, and simple line graphs. (L4)	
Key ideas	**Resources**
1 The same data can be represented using different charts and tables. **2** Some charts and tables are better than others for a particular set of data.	Line Graphs and Two-way Tables (1198) Pictograms and Bar Charts (1205) Reading Pie Charts (1206) The same data represented using different charts and graphs A selection of pre-answered questions containing errors
Simplification	**Extension**
Some students will be likely to need support particularly with reading pie charts. They should spend additional time estimating fractions and need to be encouraged to talk through, clarify and explain how they make an estimate.	Ask students to list the types of statistical diagrams that they have been learning about, and to suggest an example of the kind of data that is most easily 'read' from each type of representation. They must be able to justify their opinions and work in pairs to convince each other.
Literacy	**Links**
Once students have mastered the skills of answering particular questions using data presented in different ways, they can hone their general communication skills in speech and writing. For example, a debate could be held on an issue where data in various forms is used to justify different debating positions. Students become skilled in arguing their case based on the data.	Download speeds vary according to the type of internet connection. An old-fashioned dial-up connection could transfer information at a rate of 56 Kbps (kilobytes per second). The transfer rate for standard Broadband is 512 Kbps (about ten times faster). At the time of writing, many Broadband providers offer 2 Mb Broadband (about 40 times faster than dial-up). Broadband speeds can be 4Mb, 8Mb or even 24Mb. How much faster is 24Mb broadband than 2Mb Broadband?

Alternative approach

As suggested in lesson **8e**, investigate the topics students are currently studying in other subjects, particularly in geography, history and science. Represent any data from other subjects in ways that best suit those subjects. Ensure that all subject teachers agree on a consistent approach to naming and labelling graphs and charts.

Ask students keep a diary to collect data over time to investigate an issue (such as rain fall over a month, or the number of students absent each day for a fortnight). Use various (suitable) representations of data when drawing up conclusions. Students could present their findings to the class.

Checkpoint

Ask students to close their copies of the student book, so that they can't see Sarah's 'top tips'.

1 Explain what each of these types of diagram is used to show

a bar charts (Compare totals)

b pictograms (Compare totals)

c line graphs (How things change over time)

d pie charts (How big are the parts of a total)

Starter – Graph words

Write the words 'bar chart', 'pie chart', 'pictogram', 'axes', 'tally', 'frequency table', 'frequency', 'frequencies', 'compare', 'data' on the board. Ask students to give sentences using the vocabulary. Each piece of vocabulary correctly used in a sentence scores a point.

For example, 'A *pie chart* is used to *compare* the *frequencies* of *data*' scores four points.

Teaching notes

This lesson brings together all that has been covered in the chapter so far. Students have to extract and interpret information from pictograms, bar charts, line graphs and pie charts. Dual bar charts (where two bars are placed side-by-side to represent one category on a chart) are introduced and discussed.

Give pairs of students a selection of lists, tables, graphs and charts together with pre-answered questions, some of which have been wrongly answered through 'misreading' of the charts and graphs. Ask them to work together to identify the errors, account for them and correct them. Ask students to give feedback to the whole class to ensure that all common errors are discussed and corrected.

Plenary

Give students the same set of data represented in a variety of different ways. Also give them four questions to answer using each representation in turn.

As they write their answers, ask them to consider, in pairs, the comparative merits of each type of representation.

As a whole-class plenary, ask, which representation do you think is easier to read and interpret? Why?

Exercise commentary

Question 1 – This is the first introduction to a dual bar chart, with two adjacent columns representing each Year 7 class.

Questions 2 – This provides a straightforward revision of line graphs, which were met in Chapter **6**.

Question 3 – Recall Question **4**, about favourite fruits, in lesson **8f** and the lack of information about numbers of people. The same lack applies here, where the numbers of trees are never mentioned. The two pie charts show proportions within each wood, not actual numbers.

Question 4 – If students are unable to think of the best type of diagram to use, they could consider each type in turn and discuss its merits and disadvantages.

Answers

1 **a** 14 **b** 7D **c** 7C **d** 7A (31)

2 **a** 20 **b** August **c** 30, December

3 **a** Cantor wood, Ash; West wood, Oak

b You only know the fraction is bigger but you do not know how many trees are in each wood so not the absolute numbers.

c The fraction for oak trees is larger than the fraction for birch trees in the *same* wood.

4 Students' answers, these should include a reason. A standard choice would be a line graph.

8h Averages – the mode

<table>
<tr><th colspan="2">Objectives</th></tr>
<tr><td colspan="2">• Understand and use the mode to describe sets of data. (L3)</td></tr>
<tr><th>Key ideas</th><th>Resources</th></tr>
<tr><td>1 The mode is one of several kinds of average.
2 The mode is the most common value in a set of data.
3 A set of data may have no mode or may have more than one mode.</td><td>Mean and mode (1200)
Sets of cards with non-numeric data on one set and numeric data on the other</td></tr>
<tr><th>Simplification</th><th>Extension</th></tr>
<tr><td>Present students with a set of non-numeric data with each element of the set written on separate cards. Ask, which is the most common result in this data? and what is the mode of this data?
Repeat the task with numeric data on the separate cards. Ask the same questions.
Repeat again with data where two elements of data have the same frequency. Ask the same questions.</td><td>Ask the more able students to link this exercise to their previous work on surveys. Ask them to conduct a survey in class, using a topic of their choosing. They should decide the questions to ask the class, conduct the survey and find the modal response to each question.</td></tr>
<tr><th>Literacy</th><th>Links</th></tr>
<tr><td>The word mode comes from a Latin word meaning ‘measure or quantity’.
The word is also used to mean ‘fashion’ and the French phrase à la mode means ‘in fashion’.
The associated adjective is ‘modal’, so that in mathematics we talk of ‘the modal score’ or ‘the modal result’.
Remembering that ‘mode’ means ‘the most common’ is helped by the letter o being the only vowel used in ‘mode’, ‘most’ and ‘common’.</td><td>Continental shoe sizes differ from traditional UK shoe sizes. There is an interactive conversion chart at www.onlineconversion.com/clothing_shoes_womens.htm
The continental or European shoe-size equivalents for the shoe sizes in the example on p 158 of the Student Book are:
size 3 = $35\frac{1}{2}$, size 4 = 37, size 5 = 38, size 6 = 39.
What is the most common continental shoe size for the data given? What would it be if Japanese shoe sizes were used?</td></tr>
<tr><th colspan="2">Alternative approach</th></tr>
<tr><td colspan="2">A dynamic approach for a whole class has students responding to ‘Stand up and be counted!’. Ask, for example, all students with no siblings to stand up and be counted; then those with one sibling; then with two siblings, and so on. Keep a record of each answer, and find the mode.
Repeat for students who have blue eyes, green eyes, brown eyes, and so on for other colours. Find the modal colour. Make the point that one data set was numeric and the other was not.</td></tr>
<tr><th colspan="2">Checkpoint</th></tr>
<tr><td colspan="2">1 What is the mode of a set of data?. (The most frequent value in a set of data.)
2 For this set of data: 7 3 4 6 7 6 5 7
a How would you write the data in order? (3 4 5 6 6 7 7 7)
b Which number appears with the highest frequency? (7)
c What is the mode? (7)</td></tr>
</table>

Starter – Quick fire

Ask students to respond on mini-whiteboards to a series of quick questions which recap previous work on this chapter on statistics.

Teaching notes

Gather data from students about their shoe size and eye colour. Construct two frequency tables using the data.

Ask for the most common eye colour of students in the class. Compare the answer with the most common eye colour given in the student book (brown). State that the most common result in a set of data is the *mode*. Ask for the mode of both sets of data on eye colour.

Repeat for shoe sizes, comparing the class data with the data in the student book and asking for the two modes. Beware of a common error: some students might give the *frequency* of the most common shoe size rather than the most common size itself.

Adjust one of the frequency tables so that the highest frequency occurs twice. Ask students to find the mode of this table. Note that a distribution can have more than one mode, or, indeed, no mode at all.

Ask them to look at Questions **1** and **2** and ask how the data has been given differently in the two questions. Ask whether it is easier to find the mode if the data is already in order of size, as in Question **1**, or not in any order at all, as in Question **2**. Which of these two ways applies to data collected in a tally chart?

Plenary

Ask students to write the mode (or modes) on mini-whiteboards for each set of data for the ages of primary school children on a school trip.

a

Age	6	7	8	9	10
Freq	1	3	2	4	2

b

Age	6	7	8	9	10
Freq	1	3	7	5	7

c 6 7 7 7 8 8 9 9 9 9 10 10

d 7 8 6 9 10 7 9 7 9 10 9 8

Note that **a**, **c** and **d** are the same data.

Discuss the easiest format for finding the mode(s).

Exercise commentary

Question 1 – The numerical data is in order of size to make the mode easier find.

Question 2 – This data is not in order, so students need to order it.

Question 3 – The modal number of goals is 2, so discuss carefully with those students who give the answer 6, which is the *frequency* of the modal number.

Question 4 – This question shows the data-handling process as a sequence: collection (shown in the diagram), collation and tabulation (in tally chart and frequency table), conclusion (finding the mode). Again, check that students give the mode, not the frequency of the mode.

Question 6 – The mode is 10 seconds and the mode is one possible average. So it can be said that the average time is 10 seconds. But it is not a 'good' average, as most of the readings are in the 40s and 50s. So, to truly represent this distribution, a different average should be used: see lessons **8i** and **8j**.

Answers

1 **a** 5 **b** 6 **c** 17 **d** 1 and 5

2 **a** 8 **b** 18 **c** 3.4 **d** None

3 2

4 **a, b**

No in car	Tally	Frequency
1	||||	4
2	𝍸 |||	8
3	𝍸 𝍸 ||	12
4	𝍸	5
5	|	1
	Total	30

c 3

5 **a**

No of calls	Tally	Frequency
2	|	1
3		0
4	||||	4
5	|||	3
6	𝍸 |	6
7	𝍸 |	6
8	𝍸 |||	8
9	𝍸 𝍸 |||	13
10	|||	3
11	|||	3
12	||	2
13		0
14		0
15	|	1
	Total	50

b

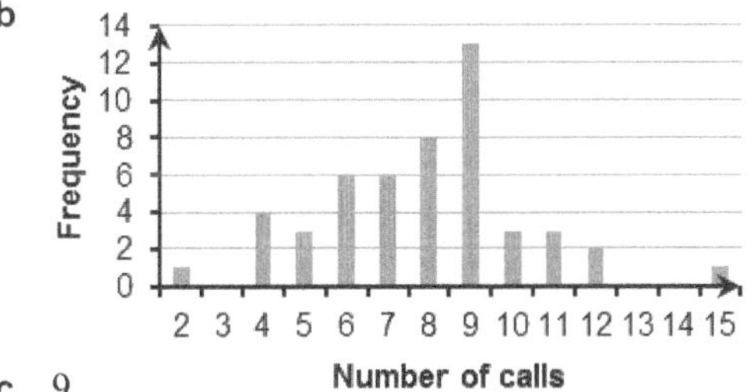

c 9

6 Students' answers.

The data appears in two groups with the second group centred around 46; which is not represented by 10.

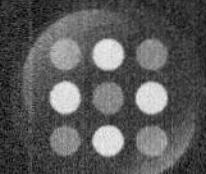

8i Averages – the median

Objectives

- For small sets of discrete data find the median. (L4)

Key ideas

1 The median is one of several kinds of average.
2 The median is the middle value when the data set is arranged in order of size. Where two values are in the middle, the median is 'the middle of the middle'.
3 For a data set which is not numeric, the median does not exist.

Resources

Median and range (1203)

Equipment to measure the heights of students, the mass of objects and the capacity of containers
Sets of cards with each card showing a numerical item of data

Simplification

Provide sets of cards with each card showing a numerical item of data. The data might relate to a context such as the number of pupils in local primary schools. Students arrange the cards in order of size, smallest first, and select the middle card (for an odd number of cards) of the middle two cards (for an even number of cards).

Extension

Ask students to construct a flow diagram which gives instructions for finding a median of a set of data. The instructions should deal with both an odd and even data set.

As a further activity, ask students to suggest situations where the mode is the more useful average to find (for example, the owner of a shoe shop wanting to stock the shelves with new shoes) and where the median is more useful (for example, the average age of a group of tourists where all the tourists have different ages and thus there is no mode).

Literacy

The word *median* comes from a Latin word meaning 'in the middle'. The words 'media', 'mediate', 'mediator', 'medium', and 'Mediterranean' all have something to do with being in the middle.

The word 'median' can be both a noun and an adjective, so mathematicians can say 'median height'. Compare with 'modal height'.

Links

Countries collect statistics about their people. The following website gives the median household income for many countries. Half the households have more than the median value of income, and half the households have less.

www.en.wikipedia.org/wiki/Median_household_income

Median income for the UK, separated by age group, gender and job type, is given here

www.en.wikipedia.org/wiki/Income_in_the_United_Kingdom
Again, half of the people in each category are above the median and half are below.

Alternative approach

A more practical approach is to undertake the activity in the **Teaching notes** using students' heights, and to follow it with two more approaches requiring measurements.

Ask a student to feel the weight of an odd number of objects and order them by weight. Ask other students to check and come to agreement. Choose the middle object, weigh it, and declare it as the median weight of the group. Repeat with an even number of objects, where the middle two objects have median weight. Repeat with bottles or tins of varying capacity.

Checkpoint

1 For this set of data: 13 5 25 17 38 36
  a How would you write this data in order? (5 13 17 25 36 38)
  b What are the middle values, and what is the median? (17 and 25; 21)

Starter – Middles

Ask a student for a number between 1 and 29 inclusive; write the number on the board.

Ask four other students for numbers and write them on the board. Ask students to put them in order of size and work out the middle one. This can be extended to six numbers.

Teaching notes

Gather data from the students by taking a sample of an odd number of students and measuring their heights. Arrange both the students and their heights in order of size, with the smallest first. Ask the class, who is in the middle and what is their height? The height of the middle student is the median height of this group or sample.

Take another sample of a different odd number of students. Repeat the activity and ask the same questions. The height of the middle student when lined up in order is the median height.

Now consider another data set containing an *odd* number of values. Write them in random order, then rearrange them in order of size. Mark off the values, one pair at a time, from both ends of the line, and so find the central value. This central value is the median.

Repeat with a data set containing an *even* number of values where the two central values are consecutive integers. Again, mark off pairs in turn from both ends and so find the central pair. Discuss what the median will be in this case. Agree that it will be 'the middle of the middle pair', resulting in a median which has a half-value. Repeat with a data set of an even number of values where the two central values are not consecutive integers. Discuss the median in this case.

Provide a data set of non-numeric data, for example, eye colour. Ask for the median and agree that no median exists.

Mention to students that they have now met two different kinds of average, the mode and the median. The purpose of an average is to give some idea of the general value of the whole data set. There are different ways of doing this, of which the mode and median are just two.

Plenary

Give some small data sets to students from which to find the median: some sets already ordered by size, and some not. Ask students to respond on mini-whiteboards. Where appropriate, also ask for the mode.

Exercise commentary

Question 2 – Note that part **c** is the only part of this question with an even number of data and two central values.

Question 3 – There is potential confusion because the ordering is listed as 'places' from 1 to 8, so some students may say that the median is between 4 and 5. Remind them that the question asks for median finishing time.

Question 4 – Students have to order the data first and then take particular care when there is an even number of data items.

Question 5 – This is easier than Question 4 once students realise that the large numbers present no particular difficulty.

Question 6 – The final question encourages students to consider the appropriateness of the median as an average. Indeed, if students also find the mode of these sets of data, they can compare the values and decide which is most appropriate. This is a discussion well worth having in class.

Answers

1 **a** 4 **b** 9 **c** 7

2 **a** 5 **b** 4 **c** 7

3 9.84 secs

4 **a** 3, 4, 4, 5, 6, 6, 6, 6, 7 — 6

b 10, 14, 16, 18, 18, 21, 26, 30, 35, 48 — $19\frac{1}{2}$

c 9, 10, 11, 12, 12, 13 — 11.5 cm

d 2, 2, 3, 3, 3, 4, 4, 4, 5, 6 — 3.5

5 **a** 248 000, 280 000, 305 000, 422 000, 449 000

b 305 000

6 Students' answers for whether the median is representative. Suggestions are given.

a 6 — No, the data has 'two centres'.

b 4. 5 — Yes

c 110 — No, but ignoring the outlier 906 it is okay.

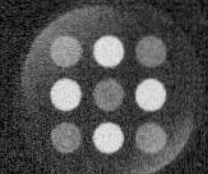

8j Comparing data – range and average

Objectives

- For small sets of discrete data find the range. (L4)
- Compare two simple distributions using the range and one of the mode or median. (L5)

Key ideas

1. The range is the difference between the largest value and the smallest value in a set of data.
2. The mode and the median are different types of average, which can both be used to compare the size of values in two data sets.

Resources

Mean and mode (1200)
Median and range (1203)

Square grid paper
Equipment to measure students' heights and hand spans

Simplification

Provide students with the two essential questions written down.

- Which is the most common value?
- What is the difference between the largest and smallest values?

They can refer to these written questions when they meet the words 'mode' and 'range'. When comparing two data sets, students can discuss their findings with a partner and produce a collaborative answer.

Extension

Ask the more able students to construct a flow diagram to give instructions, in the correct order, for collecting raw data, analysing the results and drawing a comparison.

Literacy

The word 'average' is used frequently in relation to data and statistics, which can lead to confusion. Make it clear that in this context, we refer only to the median and the mode. Avoid introducing the mean as another average at this stage.

The word 'range' can have many meanings. It could refer to a selection of items, such as in a shoe shop, a series of mountains or hills, or a place with targets for shooting practice.

Links

The Burj Khalifa in Dubai is currently the world's tallest building. It was built in 2010. It has 163 floors and it 828 metres tall. If this building is added to the list in Question **2**, what is the new range of heights? (407 m)

There are diagrams comparing the heights of the world's existing tallest buildings and proposed new buildings at

www.skyscraperpage.com/diagrams

Alternative approach

A task can be set for students to find and analyse their own data. Ask them to look up the end of season results online for their local or favourite football team. They record the data and then work out the modal number of goals scored, as well as the range. Does the mode or the range give a better idea of how the team did?

Organising the data systematically is essential for a large data set. Discuss how students might organise it, and how they might set it down on paper. Discuss whether the use of a tally chart and a frequency table might be useful. The task can be extended to a second football team and then a comparison can be made between the two sets of results.

Checkpoint

1 What is the definition of range? (The difference between the largest value and the smallest values)

2 The shoe sizes of a seven women are: 8 6 5 4 6 7 6

a How would you write the data in order? (4 5 6 6 6 7 8)

b What is the range? (8 – 4 = 4)

c What is the mode? (6)

d What is the median? (4th entry in the list = 6)

Starter – Range bingo

Ask students to draw a 3×3 grid and fill it with numbers less than 20. Give two numbers (such as 9 and 16). If students have the difference between the two numbers in their grid (7, in this case), they cross it out. Continue by giving more pairs of numbers. The winner is the first student to cross out all of the numbers in their grid.

Teaching notes

Students will accept the notion of range and calculate the value of the range with little difficulty. Ordering the data to find the smallest and largest data item can be linked with finding the median in lesson **8i**. Ask whether the students think that the range is yet another average (in addition to the mode and the median). Ask them what they think the range is useful for. Agree that, while averages give us a value that tells us something about the general value of the whole data set, the range gives us an idea of how spread out the data is.

Collect some numeric data from the students themselves, such as their heights. Arrange the values in order on the board. Ask the class if there is a mode, if the median is easy to find and how to find it, and whether they can work out the range.

Next, take two sets of numeric data. For example, measure the hand span of each boy and girl, making sure that a mode will exist for each data set! Order the data on the board. Discuss and find the values for the mode and range for each data set. Use the mode and range to describe and compare the two data sets. Use key words such as 'average', 'most common', 'spread out'.

Summarise the findings by writing two or three sentences. The idea is to write a brief but accurate comparison of these two data sets in relation to each other. Refer to the example about leaves in the student book. Discuss the example and the way that the final comparison is written.

Plenary

Ask students to make a list of all the key words that they have used in this chapter so far. Ask them to explain the meaning of 'mode', 'median' and 'range'. Ask them what they understand by the word 'average' and 'spread'. Ask them how they would find the mode, the median, with an odd and even data set, and the range.

Exercise commentary

Question 1 – Students are required to re-arrange the data. They could also be asked to find the median (and mode, if one exists)

Question 2 – The data has already been ordered here. Students could also ask the median height. See **Links** for a suggestion of how to extend the question.

Question 3 – Parts **c** and **d** require students to give written explanations. Merely stating which class is not sufficient.

Question 4 – Again, written explanations are required, which some students may be reluctant to provide. Discuss their answers with them and then suggest how they might write them down.

Question 5 – It would be useful to discuss this question as a class, and to compare the merits of the mode and the median.

Question 6 – Students need to work 'backwards' in both parts of this question. For part **b**, there are many different possible answers. Students could compare their answers with a partner or with the rest of the class.

Answers

1 **a** 4, 6, 11 7
b 3, 6, 7, 8, 9 6
c 1, 5, 5, 9 8
d 5, 6, 8, 12 7

2 87 m

3 **a** 7A 9 7B 10
b 7A 6 7B 8
c 7B They had a higher mode (10 > 9) and their marks were more consistent (less spread).
d 7B They had a greater range (8 > 6).

4 **a** **i** 7 and 8 **ii** 11
b Girls Their mode is higher (11 > 7 or 8)
c **i** 2 **ii** 9
d Girls They had a far greater range (9 > 2).

5 **a** 7A 9 7B 5
b 7A They had a higher median (9 > 5) and their marks were more consistent (less spread).
c No
Students' answers.
More students in 7A get high marks.

6 **a** 4, 11
b Students' answers.
There is no need for the medians to be the same.

<table>
<tr><th>Key outcomes</th><th>Quick check</th></tr>
<tr><td>Plan how to collect and organise small sets of data from surveys and experiments. L3</td><td>You have been asked to find out peoples' favourite icecream.
Write a suitable question for a survey.
(What is you favourite flavour of icecream?
vanilla □ strawberry □ chocolate □ mint □ other □
If other please give details: _______________)</td></tr>
<tr><td>Solve problems by interpreting data in lists and tables L3</td><td>The table shows the number of people visiting a library over one week.
<table>
<tr><th>Mon</th><th>Tue</th><th>Wed</th><th>Thu</th><th>Fri</th><th>Sat</th><th>Sun</th></tr>
<tr><td>0</td><td>35</td><td>15</td><td>20</td><td>40</td><td>30</td><td>20</td></tr>
</table>
a Which was the busiest day? (Friday)
b How many people visited at the weekend? (50)
c On which day is the library closed? (Monday)</td></tr>
<tr><td>Construct and interpret statistical diagrams, including pictograms, bar charts, pie charts and line graphs. L4</td><td>Using the data above for the number of people visiting a library draw a
a pictogram b bar chart.
<table>
<tr><th>Day</th><th>No of visitors</th></tr>
<tr><td>Mon</td><td></td></tr>
<tr><td>Tue</td><td>▯ ▯ ▯ ▫</td></tr>
<tr><td>Wed</td><td>▯ ▫</td></tr>
<tr><td>Thu</td><td>▯ ▯</td></tr>
<tr><td>Fri</td><td>▯ ▯ ▯ ▯</td></tr>
<tr><td>Sat</td><td>▯ ▯ ▯</td></tr>
<tr><td>Sun</td><td>▯ ▯</td></tr>
</table>
Key: ▯ = 10 people
 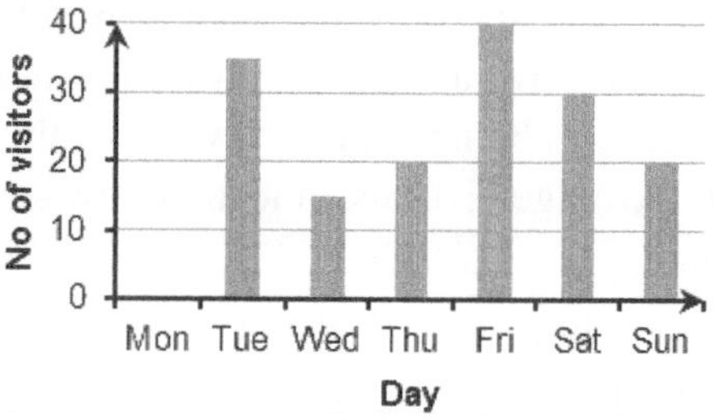
</td></tr>
<tr><td>Calculate statistics for small sets of data, including the mode, median and range L4</td><td>For each set of data find the i mode ii median iii range.
a 8 6 5 3 6 (6, 6, 5)
b 11 23 15 12 11 17 16 10 19 24 15 18 (11 and 15, 15.5, 14)</td></tr>
</table>

Development and links
In the discussion of probability in chapter **16** there is a practical opportunity to collect, organise and display data on the frequencies of the number obtained in the roll of a dice. Data analysis is developed in book **2A** to include: the data handling cycle, grouped frequency tables, the mode, median and range for frequency tables, the mean, drawing pie charts and comparing data sets. In several ways modern life is 'data driven' with businesses and governments increasingly using statistics to decide what to do and how. As a result the news media are full of the results of surveys, quoting statistics, showing graphs and drawing conclusions. Perhaps one of the most useful skills you can have is knowing when to be suspicious of a result and when a conclusion is not supported by the data or how the data might not have been collected fairly.

MyMaths extra support

Lesson/online homework			Description
List and tables 1	1385	L2	This lesson allows students to build confidence in creating very simple tables.

8 MySummary

Check out | **Test it ➡**

You should now be able to...		Questions
✓ Plan how to collect and organise small sets of data from surveys and experiments.	3	1, 2
✓ Solve problems by interpreting data in lists and tables.	3	3
✓ Construct and interpret statistical diagrams, including pictograms, bar charts, pie charts and line graphs.	4	4, 5
✓ Calculate statistics for small sets of data, including the mode, median and range.	5	6, 7

Language	Meaning	Example
Questionnaire	An organised list of questions, often with options for answers.	Examples of questionnaires are on page 144
Frequency table	A table that shows how often a particular item of data occurs. It often includes a tally column.	Examples of frequency tables are on page 146
Pictogram	A diagram that shows data as a series of pictures.	Examples of pictograms are on page 150
Bar chart	A diagram that uses rectangles to represent frequency.	Examples of bar charts are on page 152
Pie chart	A diagram that uses a circle to display data in proportion.	Examples of pie charts are on page 154
Average	A representative value for a set of data.	The average 12-year old girl in the UK is around 1.5 m tall
Mode	The data value that occurs most often.	2, 3, 4, 4, 5, 6, 7, 8, 9 The mode is 4
Median	The middle value when the data are sorted into numerical order.	The median is 5
Range	The difference between the highest and lowest values in a set of data.	The range is 9 − 2 = 7

164 **Statistics and probability** Statistics

8 MyReview

1 You have been asked to find out about the people who go to see films at a local cinema. Write two questions you could use on a questionnaire.

2 A number of different shaped counters are as shown.

Draw a frequency table for this set of data.

3 The table shows how many hours Dave spends driving in a week.

M	T	W	Th	F	Sa	Su
2.5	1.5	2	2	3.5	5	0

a On what day does he drive most?
b How long did he drive for on Friday?

4 The pictogram shows how many books people borrowed from a library in a week.

Number of Books	People
0	
1	
2	
3	
4	

key: = 10 people

4 **a** How many people borrowed exactly 2 books?
b How many people borrowed no books?
c How would you represent 40 people on this pictogram?
d Draw a bar chart for the data in this pictogram.

5 Students in year 8 at a school can bring a packed lunch, go to the canteen, or go home for lunch.

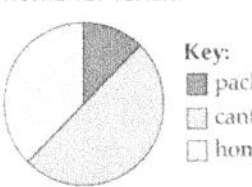

a What is the least popular lunch choice?
b What fraction of the students go to the canteen for lunch?

6 Find the mode for each set of numbers, if there is one.

a 3 5 7 3
b 12 14 16 18 14 15 16 19
c 27 29 26 28 28 27 24 26 29 24 28
d 3 5 7 5 3 7 5 5 7 3 7 3

7 For the data in question **6** find
i the medians **ii** the ranges.

What next?

Score		
0 – 3		Your knowledge of this topic is still developing. To improve look at Formative test: 1A-8; MyMaths: 1193, 1198, 1200, 1203, 1205, 1206 and 1235
4 – 6		You are gaining a secure knowledge of this topic. To improve look at InvisiPen: 411, 415, 411, 421, 423, 424, 441 and 445
7		You have mastered this topic. Well done, you are ready to progress!

MyMaths.co.uk 165

Question commentary

Question 1 – (lesson **8a**) Look for options to choose from including an 'other' option.

Question 2 – (lesson **8b**) Ask students to check if their total comes to 14 and if not what this means.

Question 3 – (lesson **8c**) Ask students further questions as necessary to test understanding.

Question 4 – (lessons **8d** and **8e**) If the answers to parts **a** and **b** are 1 and 5 ask students to explain the key to you. In part **d**, the bar graph could be vertical or horizontal but must be correctly labelled.

Question 5 - (lesson **8f**) As a possible extension say there are 200 students and ask how many are in each category: canteen 100, packed 25 and home 75.

Question 6 - (lesson **8h**) Part **b** is bimodal and in part **d** students may write '3, 5 and 7' if they do not realize 'No mode' is an acceptable answer.

Question 7 - (lesson **8i** and **8j**) Not ordering the data first will give the likely *wrong* answers for the median: **a** 6, **b** 16, **c** 27 and **d** 6. Calculating three of the medians require these averages: **a** $(3 + 5) \div 2$, **b** $(15 + 16) \div 2$ and **d** $(5 + 5) \div 2$. For the range do not accept answers such as '3~7' etc.

Answers

1 Possible questions include

- How often do you come to the cinema in a year: 1 / 2 – 12 / 13 – 48 / more?
- What is your favorite type of film: comedy / thriller / horror / other?
- What age group are you in: 0 – 10 / 11 – 18 / 18 – 30 / older?
- How many miles have you travelled to get to the cinema: 0 – 1 / 2 – 5 / 6 – 20 / further?

2

Shape	Frequency
Square	6
Circle	3
Triangle	5

3 **a** Saturday **b** 3.5 hours

4 **a** 10
b 50
c 4 people
d

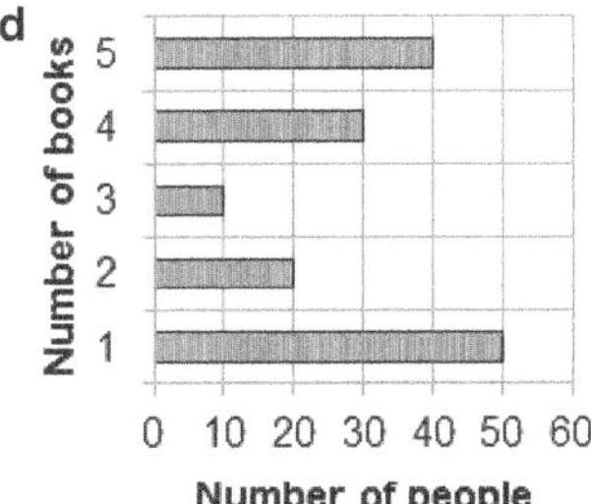

5 **a** Packed lunch
b $\frac{1}{2}$

6 **a** 3
b 14 and 16
c 28
d No mode

7 **a** **i** 4 **ii** 4 **b** **i** 15.5 **ii** 7
c **i** 27 **ii** 5 **d** **i** 5 **ii** 4

8 MyPractice

8a

1 Eva decides to ask all of the students in her group at college how they get to college each day.

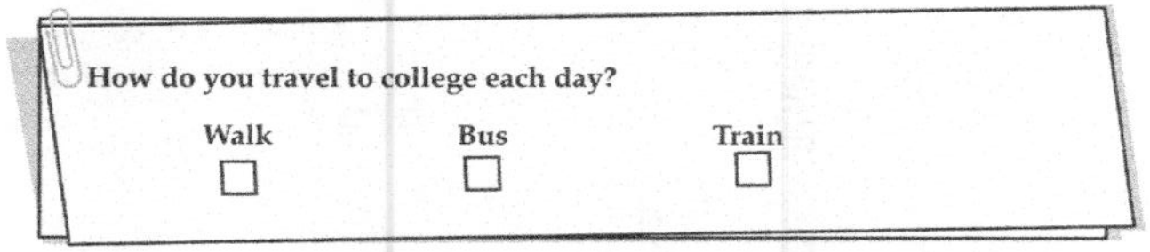

How do you travel to college each day?

Walk ☐ Bus ☐ Train ☐

Suggest any improvements that might be made to Eva's questionnaire.

8b

2 A dice is rolled 30 times. The scores are:

2 5 1 3 1 3 4 1 6 4 4 4 4 2 5
5 5 3 5 4 3 5 2 3 4 2 3 2 6 6

a Make a tally chart for this set of data.

b Use your tally chart to produce a frequency table.

8c

3 Ben recorded the number of times his computer crashed. It crashed three times on Monday, and twice on Tuesday. On Wednesday his computer crashed five times, but on Thursday it did not crash at all. On Friday there were four crashes.

a Draw a table to show this information.

b Write down the total number of crashes.

8d

4 The table shows the number of credits awarded to students in Year 7 at Hollybank High School.

Class	7W1	7W2	7W3	7W4
Credits	8	7	4	6

Draw a pictogram to show this information.
Make sure you choose a suitable symbol.

8e

5 This table shows the number of pieces of homework that Kelly was set each day.

Day	Monday	Tuesday	Wednesday	Thursday	Friday
Pieces of homework	2	3	2	4	5

Draw a bar chart to represent this set of data.

8f

6 This pie chart shows the methods used to generate electricity in the USA.

a What method is $\frac{1}{4}$ of the total?

b What method is $\frac{1}{2}$ of the total?

c What two methods together make up $\frac{1}{4}$ of the total?

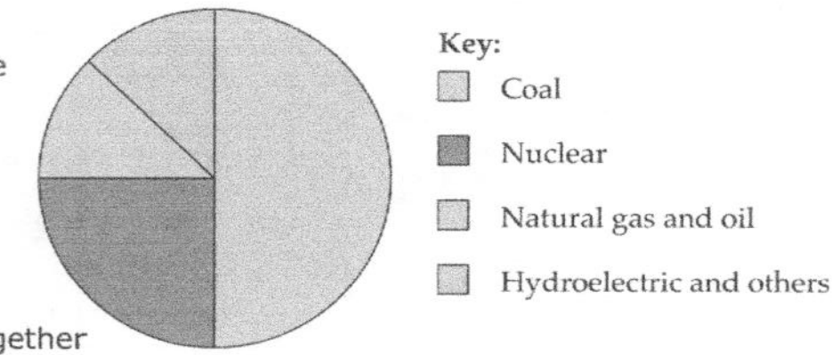

8g

7 The bar chart shows the number of boys and girls in five year groups.

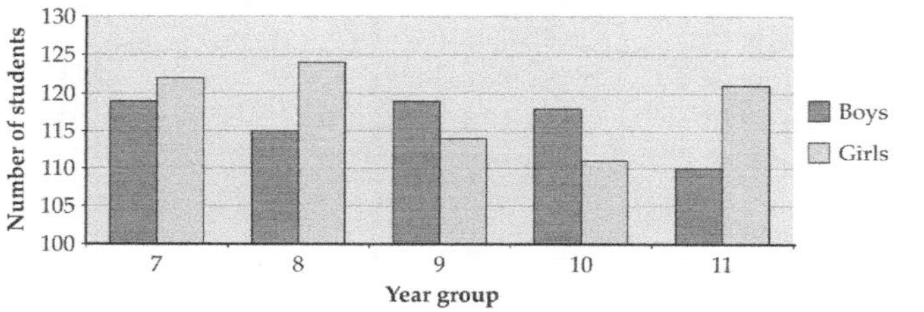

a List the year groups that had more boys than girls.

b Estimate the total number of girls in each of the five year groups.

c Estimate the total number of students in all five year groups combined.

d Say which year group had the largest total number of students.

8h, i, j

8 Near to where Shani works there are two cafés. She timed how long in minutes it took the waitress to bring her lunch on 10 different occasions at both cafes.

Cafe A 5, 3, 3, 6, 6, 8, 3, 5, 3, 8

Cafe B 8, 8, 6, 4, 6, 3, 8, 8, 5, 4

a For each of the two data sets find

i the mode

ii the median

iii the range.

b Describe two differences between the two cafés.

Question commentary

Questions 1 – Make the question a practical one by asking the class how they, or other people they know, get to school – can they give this answer using the questionnaire?. If not how could they change it? Is there a problem if you include lots of possibilities?

Question 2 – To make the question more real, give the students dice so that they can create their own data sets.

Question 3 – The difficulty in this question is identifying the relevant information amongst all the text. The meaning of the word twice may cause difficulties for some students.

Question 4 – Ensure that students chose a simple symbol that can easily be drawn multiple times, such as a rectangle. If the symbol is to be used to represent two credits also ensure that it can be easily recognized when divided in two. Potential problems can be anticipated by asking students to first draw their key. In any case a pictogram must always be accompanied by a key.

Question 5 – This is quite an involved question and it may be useful to work through it as a class. Students will need to choose and correctly label appropriate scales. Bars need to be drawn to the correct height above the axes labels and be evenly spaced with gaps between them.

Questions 6 – Tis is a straightforward question. It may be reversed for more able students. Supply students with a circle with eights marked out and ask them to draw a pie chart using similar data to that in the question. This goes beyond the content of lesson **8f**.

Question 7 – Part **a** should be done by eye. As a precursor to reading values off the vertical scale, which goes up in fives, ask students to say where they think the values 121, 122, 123, and 124 should appear on the axis. (Just above 120, just below halfway, just above halfway, just below 125) In part **c** it may be helpful to discuss what needs to be done to calculate the total number of students in year 7 as a class. Then individual or small groups of students could repeat the calculation for the remaining years. Part **d** could be extended by asking for the years to be ordered by total size.

Question 8 – In part **a**, the calculation for café A could be done as a class before asking students to do café B on their own. Start by emphasizing the need to order the data before agreeing how to calculate the means and range. For part **b** it may help to discuss possible differences as a class but insist that students write answers as full sentences.

Answers

1 Add other options: bicycle, car, etc.
Add an 'other' option plus space for details.
Could be extended to collect information on how often.

2 a

Score	Tally	Frequency
1	III	3
2	卌	5
3	卌 I	6
4	卌 II	7
5	卌 I	6
6	III	3
	Total	30

b

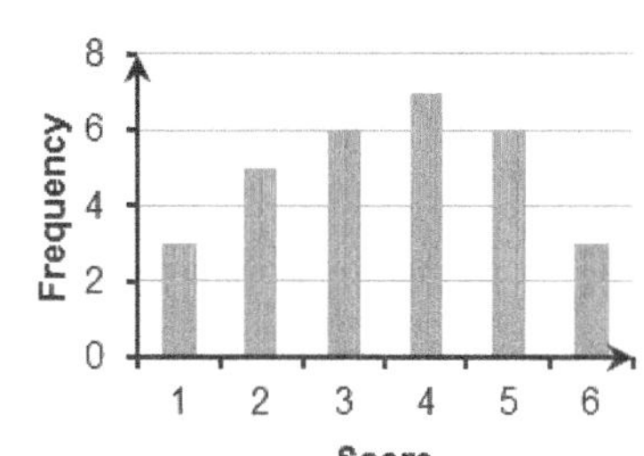

3 a

Day	Mon	Tue	Wed	Thu	Fri
No of crashes	3	2	5	0	4

b 14

4

Class	No of credits
7A	▯▯▯▯▯▯▯▯▯
7B	▯▯▯▯▯▯▯▯
7C	▯▯▯▯
7D	▯▯▯▯▯▯▯

Key: ▯ = 1 credit

5

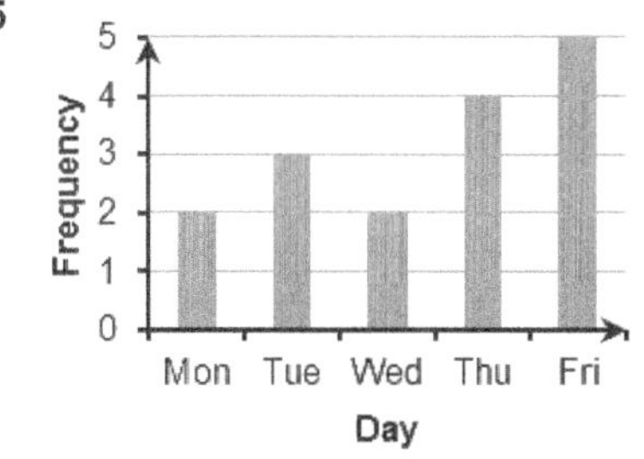

6 a Nuclear **b** Coal
c Natural gas an oil and Hydroelectric and others

7 a 9 and 10
b 7: 122, 8: 124, 9: 114, 10: 111, 11: 121
c 7: 241, 8: 239, 9: 233, 10: 228, 11: 231
d Year 7

8 a Café A **i** 3 **ii** 5 **iii** 5
Café B **i** 8 **ii** 6 **iii** 5
b The service is quicker in café A (modes 3 < 8, medians 5 < 6). There is about the same variation in waiting times (both ranges 5).

MyAssessment 2

These questions will test you on your knowledge of the topics in chapters 5 to 8.
They give you practice in the types of questions that you may see in your GCSE exams.
There are 55 marks in this test.

1 For each angle
  - **i** use a protractor to measure its size (2 marks)
  - **ii** give its mathematical name. (2 marks)

a **b**

2 For each diagram
  - **i** calculate the size the missing angle (2 marks)
  - **ii** give the mathematical name of the angle. (2 marks)

a **b**

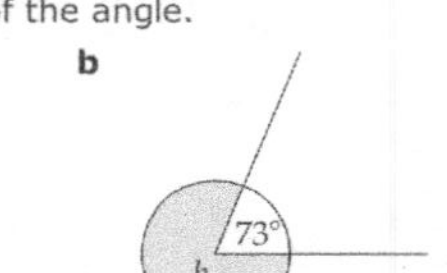

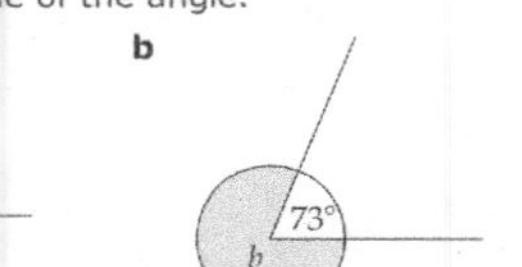

3 **a** What is the name given to a triangle that has all sides of a different length and all angles of a different size? (1 mark)
b What is the name given to a triangle that has all sides of equal length? (1 mark)
c For the triangle in part **b**, what is the common angle? (1 mark)

4 Find the missing angles in these triangles. (4 marks)

a **b**

5 **a** In the diagram write down the coordinates of the points marked A, B, C and D. (4 marks)
b Connect the points with straight lines. What is the name of the shape? (1 mark)

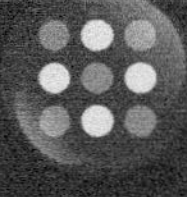

6 This line graph shows how the outside temperature changed during a particular week.
a What day was the lowest temperature recorded? (1 mark)
b What day(s) was the temperature 22°C? (2 marks)
c What was the difference in temperature between **i** Sunday and Thursday and **ii** Sunday and Wednesday? (2 marks)

7 Work these out in your head.

a $29 - 14$ (1 mark) **b** $17 + 14$ (1 mark)
c $85 - 9$ (1 mark) **d** $63 + 15$ (1 mark)
e $103 - 30$ (1 mark)

8 Use a number line or columns to work out these problems.

a $38 + 62$ (1 mark) **b** $87 - 35$ (1 mark)
c $197 + 28$ (1 mark) **d** $492 - 275$ (1 mark)
e $852 - 394$ (1 mark) **f** $321 + 213$ (1 mark)

9 Use columns to work out these problems.

a $608 + 154$ (1 mark) **b** $762 - 387$ (1 mark)
c $569 - 256$ (1 mark) **d** $346 + 861$ (1 mark)

10 The following table shows the sales of canned drinks from a school canteen.
Draw a pictogram to represent these sales.
Use the symbol of a can to represent 5 drinks. (4 marks)

Drink	Sales
Cola	35
Diet Cola	26
Orange	11
Water	4

11 The table shows the frequency of vowels in the first four lines of a well-known play.
a Draw a bar chart for this data. (4 marks)

Vowel	a	e	i	o	u
Frequency	9	16	11	9	5

b What was the mode for the vowels found? (1 mark)

12 Eleven boys and eleven girls have had their height measured to the nearest centimetre as follows.
Boys: 126, 131, 147, 153, 154, 154, 156, 159, 160, 163, 175
Girls: 124, 129, 133, 135, 135, 142, 151, 153, 153, 164, 167
a Find the mode and median of these heights
  - **i** for the boys only (2 marks)
  - **ii** for the girls only. (2 marks)

b **i** What was the range for the boys data? (1 mark)
  - **ii** What was the range for the girls data? (1 mark)

Mark scheme

Questions 1 – 4 marks (lessons **5a** and **5c**)

a **i** 1 64°; allow ±1°
ii 1 125°; allow ±1°
b **i** 1 Acute
ii 1 Obtuse

Questions 2 – 4 marks (lessons **5a**, **5d** and **5e**)

a **i** 1 $a = 125°$; allow ±1°
ii 1 $b = 287°$; allow ±1°
b **i** 1 Obtuse
ii 1 Reflex

Questions 3 – 3 marks (lesson **5f**)

a 1 Scalene
b 1 Equilateral
c 1 60°

Questions 4 – 4 marks (lesson **5g**)

a 2 $u = 67°$, $v = 67°$
b 2 $w = 124°$, $x = 18°$

Questions 5 – 5 marks (lessons **2d**, **6a** and **6b**)

a 1 A (5, 4)
1 B (2, -4)
1 C (-6, -4)
1 D (4, -3)
b 1 Quadrilateral

Questions 6 – 5 marks (lessons **6c**, **6d** and **6e**)

a 1 Tuesday
b 2 Monday and Thursday
c **i** 1 2 °C
ii 1 3.5 °C

Questions 7 – 5 marks (lessons **7a** and **7b**)

a 1 15
b 1 31
c 1 76
d 1 78
e 1 73

Questions 8 – 6 marks (lesson **7c**)

a 1 100
b 1 52
c 1 225
d 1 217
e 1 458
f 1 534

Questions 9 – 4 marks (lesson **7d**)

a 1 762
b 1 375
c 1 31.3
d 1 120.7

Questions 10 – 4 marks (lesson **8d**)

1 Coke
1 Diet Coke
1 Orange
1 Water

Questions 11 – 5 marks (lesson **8h**)

a 4 2 marks for correct axes
2 marks for correct bar heights
–1 mark each error/omission

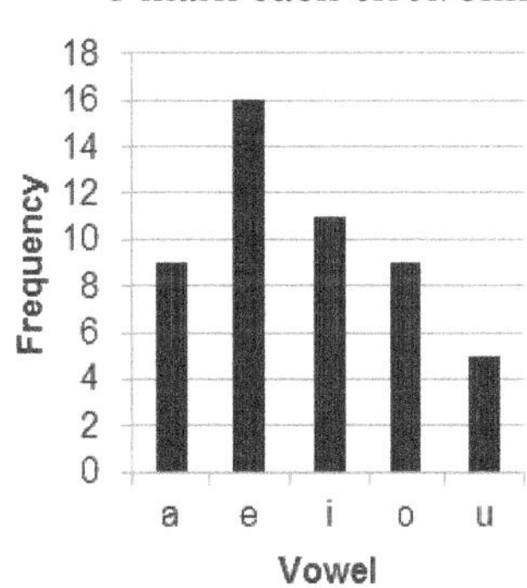

1 vowel ‘e’

Questions 12 – 6 marks (lessons **8h**, **8i** and **8j**)

a **i** 2 Mode = 154 cm
median = 156 cm
ii 2 Mode = 135 cm
Median : 142 cm
b **i** 1 49cm
ii 1 43cm

Levels

	Q1 – 4	Q5 – 6	Q7 – 9	Q10 – 12
	G & M	A	N	S & P
S 5	13 – 15			13 – 15
D 5	9 – 12	7 – 10		9 – 12
M 4	5 – 8	3 – 6		5 – 8
S 4			13 – 15	
D 4			9 – 12	
M 3			5 – 8	
FA	0 – 4	0 – 2	0 – 4	0 – 4

D developing S secure M mastery FA further assessment needed

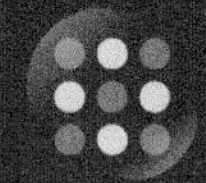

9 Transformations and symmetry

Learning outcomes	
G5 Describe, sketch and draw using conventional terms and notations: points, lines, parallel lines, perpendicular lines, right angles, regular polygons, and other polygons that are reflectively and rotationally symmetric.	(L3/4)
G8 Identify properties of, and describe the results of, translations, rotations and reflections applied to given figures.	(L4/5)

Introduction

The chapter starts by looking at the principle of line symmetry before transforming by reflection. Translations and rotations are covered before the final part of the chapter considers simple tessellations.

The introduction discusses how dance has simple mathematical principles of transformation as one of its key underlying ingredients. By combining several of these, the structure of the dance can be worked out (choreography) before the emotional aspects are added later.

Both art and music are also underpinned by principles of mathematics. Art uses symmetry and ideas of perspective to create pleasing paintings, sculptures and other 'installation' pieces. Often, geometrical shapes are used as well as other mathematical objects. A famous mathematical painting is Albrecht Dürer's *Melancholia 1* which contains a magic square as well as a sphere and other mathematical solids.

http://www.britishmuseum.org/explore/highlights/highlight_objects/pd/a/albrecht_dürer,_melancholia.aspx

The principle of a musical scale is worked out using the ratios between frequencies when strings are plucked in order to make a harmonious sound.

Prior knowledge

Students should already know how to…

- Draw simple geometric shapes on a square grid
- Describe shapes using coordinates

Starter problem

The starter problem asked students to produce a short dance routine for robots. Since robots move according to mathematical rules, the language we need to use has to have the right elements. If, for example, we wish the robot to move along a line, we must specify how far, in which direction and at which speed. If we wish the robot to perform a turn, we must specify the angle through which it turns and the direction, clockwise or anti-clockwise. Encourage students to be precise in their instructions and perhaps even map out the moves using a piece of squared paper. The robot could be represented by a simple square or rectangle.

Resources

MyMaths

Lines of symmetry 1114

Online assessment		InvisiPen solutions			
Chapter test	1A–9	Symmetry	361	Reflection	362
Formative test	1A–9	Translation	363	Rotation	364
Summative test	1A–9	Tessellations	365		

Topic scheme

Teaching time = 5 lessons/2 weeks

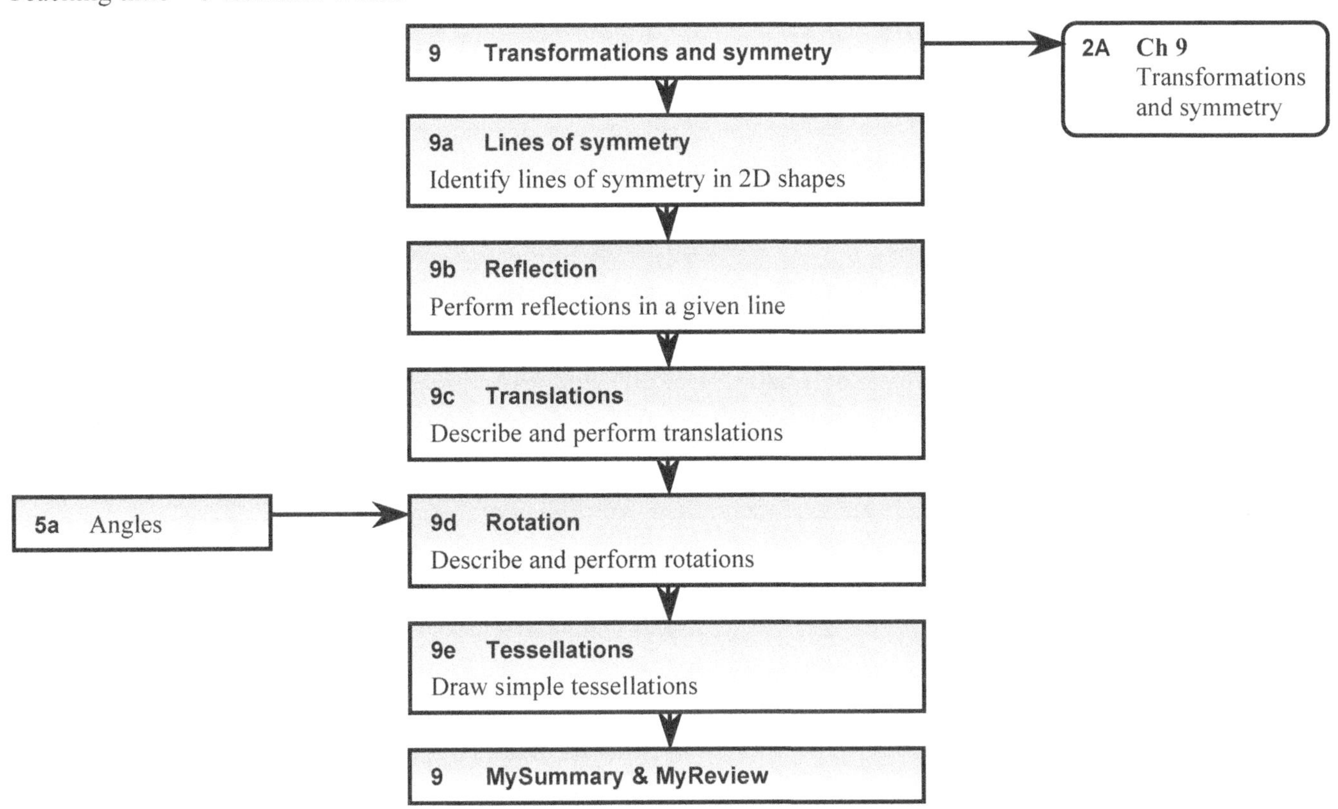

Differentiation

Student book 1A 170 – 185	Student book 1B 170 – 187	Student book 1C 166 – 185
Perform reflections using a mirror line Draw lines of symmetry Perform rotations using an angle and centre Describe rotational symmetry Describe translations Perform simple tessellations	Perform reflections using a mirror line Draw lines of symmetry Perform rotations using an angle and centre Describe rotational symmetry Describe translations Perform simple tessellations	Perform reflections using a mirror line Draw lines of symmetry Perform rotations using an angle and centre Describe rotational symmetry Describe translations Perform simple tessellations Enlargement

9a Lines of symmetry

Objectives	
• Identify reflection symmetry in 2D shapes. (L3)	
Key ideas	**Resources**
1 A shape has line symmetry if it can be folded in half to fit exactly on top of itself. **2** A shape may have more than one line of symmetry or may have none at all.	Lines of Symmetry (1114) Pins, scissors and small mirrors Square grid paper Tracing paper
Simplification	**Extension**
Shapes which are already cut out and can be folded are useful to explore symmetry before mirrors are used. Students can complete shapes which are only half drawn, on square grid paper, so that they have one line of symmetry when fully drawn.	Extend the **Starter** and **Plenary** activities to pentominoes, which are shapes made from five squares touching edge to edge. Ask students to design an original logo for the front cover of a new mathematics textbook that has exactly three lines of symmetry.
Literacy	**Links**
The word *symmetry* comes from two Greek words *sym-* and *-meter* which mean 'equal measure'.	There are many examples of symmetry in nature, such as in animals, insects and plants. There are inspiring images and some ideas for classroom at www.misterteacher.com/symmetry.html Students could be encouraged to find their own examples of symmetry in nature by looking in a garden, park or school playground, and recording their findings, either by taking photographs or making detailed drawings.

Alternative approach

The various approaches offered in **Teaching notes** should be sufficient to provide engaging introductions to line symmetry.

Where a student has difficulty recognising a line of symmetry, an alternative approach is to trace the shape onto transparent paper and repeatedly fold the paper until the line is found.

Checkpoint

1 Name or draw a shape with

a 1 line of symmetry (Isosceles triangle, kite, arrowhead,…)

b 2 lines of symmetry (Rectangle, square, rhombus, …)

c 3 line of symmetry (Equilateral triangle, …)

d No line of symmetry

Discuss student answers — Many other answers are possible

Starter – Tetromino symmetry

Ask students to find as many *tetrominoes*, that is, shapes made from four squares touching edge to edge as they can. Provide

- four squares already cut out for students to rearrange
- square grid paper on which they can record their results.

Discuss whether to classify tetrominoes as 'different' if they are identical when turned over.
(There are five basic tetrominoes., see below.)

Teaching notes

There are several activities which create symmetrical shapes.

The first is to fold a sheet of paper, draw a shape along the crease, pin-prick through the corners of the shape, unfold the paper and join the pin-holes.

The second is to fold a sheet of paper, cut across the crease to cut out a shape, and unfold the shape.

The third is to repeat the first two activities with a sheet of paper folded twice into quarters making two perpendicular creases. Explore what happens if the creases are not at right-angles.

Discuss symmetry and lines of symmetry. Note that a shape can have more than one line of symmetry.

For pre-drawn shapes, students can use a mirror to find lines of symmetry. Students can design their own shapes on square grid paper so that they have one or more lines of symmetry, checking their work with a mirror.

Ask if a shape can have no lines of symmetry and ask for examples. Provide a mixture of shapes with 0, 1, 2 or more lines of symmetry and ask students to sort them into groups, again checking their work with mirrors.

Plenary

Return to the tetrominoes first met in the **Starter**. Classify them by the number of lines of symmetry they have.

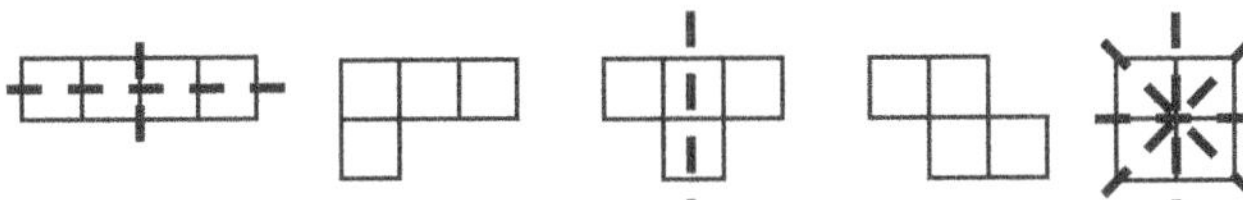

Exercise commentary

Several of the shapes possess rotational symmetry, even if they possess no line symmetry. Students may need reminding that they should only look for mirror symmetry.

Questions 1 to **4** – Students can use a small mirror to check. The answers to Question **1** are 'Yes' or 'No'.

Question 4 – This could be extended by asking students to investigate other examples of symmetrical logos that they can find in daily life.

Question 5 – Any fold which goes through the geometric centre of each shape will result in two identical halves. However not all these folds will correspond to a line of symmetry. Only for the square are the two diagonals lines of symmetry.

Answers

1 **a** Yes, vertical line **b** Yes, 45° line
c No **d** No
e No (rotationally symmetric)
f No **g** Yes, horizontal line
h No (rotationally symmetric)

2 **a**

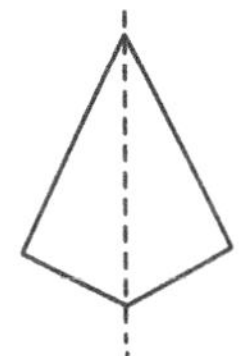

b

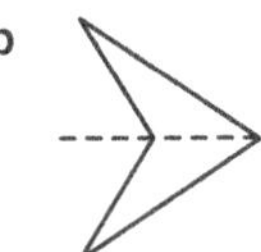

c

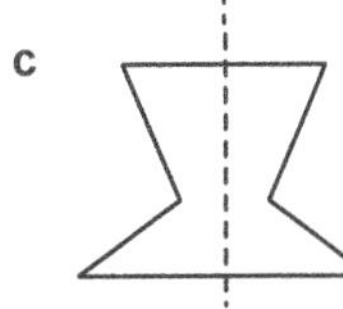

d

2 **a**

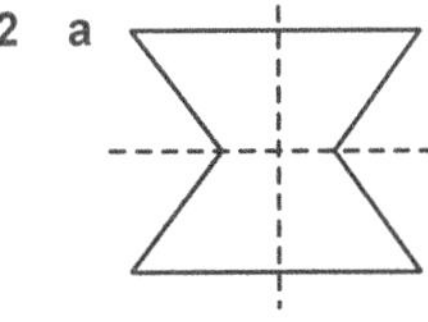

b

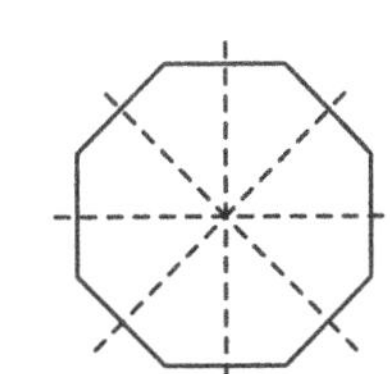

c

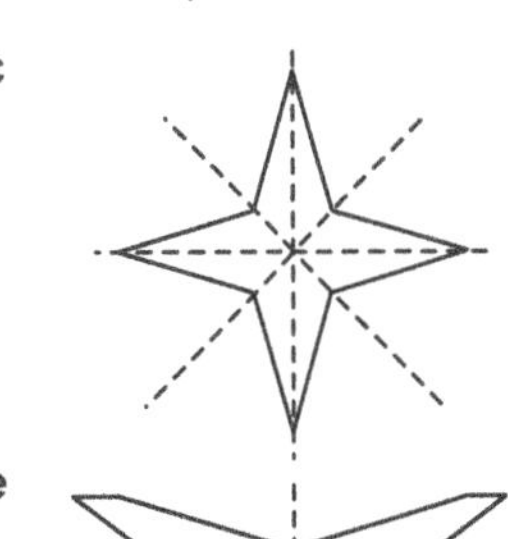

d

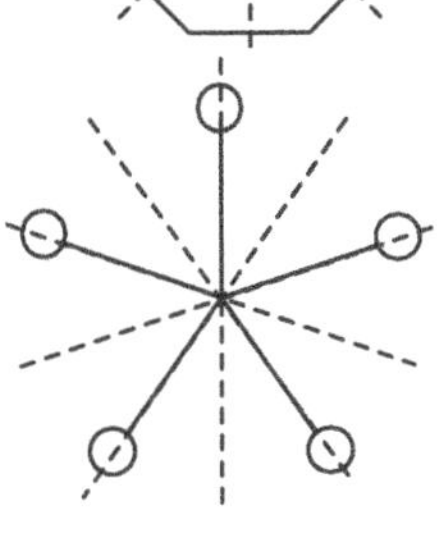

e

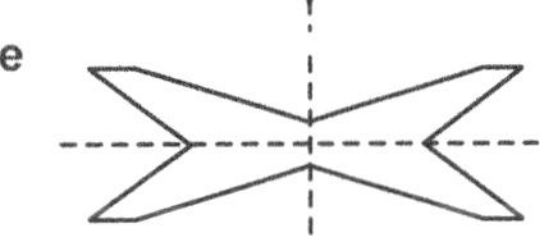

4 **a** **i** 1 **ii** 2 **iii** 1 **iv** 3
e Possible answers include: Audi, 2; Bentley, 1; Infinity, 1; Mazda, 1; Renault, 2; Toyota, 1

5 Rectangle, two ways – horizontally and vertically. Square, four ways – horizontally, vertically and both diagonals.

9b Reflection

Objectives

- Reflect shapes, presented on a grid, in a vertical or horizontal mirror line. (L3)

Key ideas

1. The object and image shapes are on opposite sides of the mirror line.
2. Corresponding points on the object and image are equidistant from the mirror line.
3. The line joining corresponding points on the object and image is at right-angles to the mirror line.

Resources

Lines of symmetry (1114)

Mini-whiteboards with grids

Partially completed diagrams

Mirrors

Square grid paper

Simplification

Give students who need additional support diagrams of objects with mirror lines and partially-completed images. Ask the students to complete the images. Practise reflecting regular shapes before reflecting irregular shapes. Students can use mirrors to check their answers.

Extension

Opportunities for extension include:

- finding an image when a mirror line slopes at 45° on a square grid;
- finding the mirror line where the object and image are both given;
- identifying letters of the alphabet with reflection symmetry.

Choose from them to draw half-letters and so write a coded message.

Literacy

Students should already know the words 'horizontal' and 'vertical' in a mathematical context. They should now know the words 'object' and 'image' and should label their diagrams with these two words.

Note that 'a mirror line' is also called 'a line of reflection'.

Links

When sound is reflected, it creates an echo instead of a visual image. Sound reflects best from hard flat surfaces. Sound echoing around a room causes reverberation which distorts what you hear if you are listening to music or a speech. Reverberation can be reduced by using soft materials around the room, such as curtains, carpets and cushions, as these are much better at absorbing sound than reflecting it.

Alternative approach

Provide pairs of students with axes, labelled from 0 to 10, on which a mirror line is drawn. Give one student a series of points which defines a shape when plotted on the coordinate grid. They should plot the first point. The second student plots its image in the mirror line. The object and image points are plotted one at a time until the object shape and its image are complete. Coordinates are covered in lesson **6a.**

Checkpoint

1. If I hold an object in front of a mirror, what will I see in the mirror? (The image)
2. Reflect these shapes in the mirror line

a

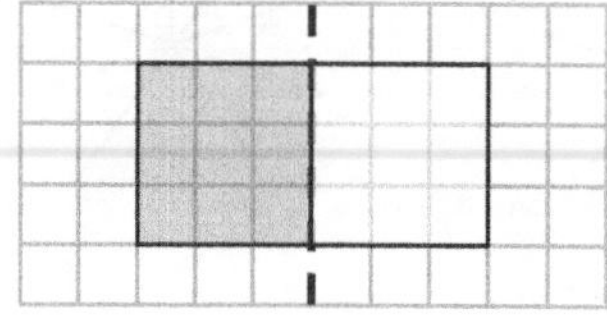

b

Do not include the reflexted shape when posing the question..

Repeat for other shapes if necessary to ensure students' understanding is secure.

Starter – Emergency!

Some emergency vehicles have written sign printed back-to-front in them. Ask students why this might be.

Ask students to write the mirror images of AMBULANCE, POLICE and MATHEMATICS as if they were printed on the front of a vehicle. Students check their results with a mirror.

Ask if there is any other way they could reflect the words; for example, in a vertical or sloping line.

Teaching notes

Provide object shapes drawn on square grid paper with a mirror line for each shape. Ask students how they will draw the reflection of the shape in its line. Probe their answers until three facts are established:

- the image is on the opposite side of the mirror to the object;
- a point on the image is as far from the mirror as the object point;
- the line joining the object and image points is at right-angles to the mirror line.

Draw two or three examples of an object, image and mirror line on square grid paper. The mirror lines are horizontal, vertical and, perhaps, sloping at 45° and none of them intersects the object. As a whole-class activity, have students in turn reflect their chosen corner in the mirror.

This activity can also be undertaken using mini-whiteboards with square grids drawn on them.

Plenary

Get students to work in pairs. Ask each student to draw two objects and two mirror lines, and then swap with their partner who then locates and draws two images. Discuss and agree the outcomes.

Exercise commentary

Questions 1 and **2** – Counting squares to place corners of the images is necessary. If the horizontal mirror line in question **2**, part **c** causes problems then suggest students rotate their diagram by 90°.

Question 3 – The hair shows that part **a** is not the answer. The correct reflection is found by looking at the design on the T-shirt.

Question 4 – Drawing directly onto the squares is one method for completing the letters. Another is to trace and turn over the tracing paper.

Answers

1 a

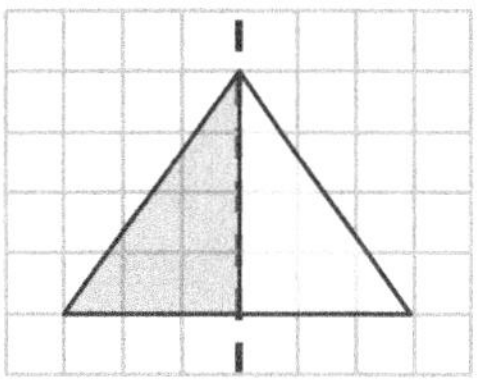

b

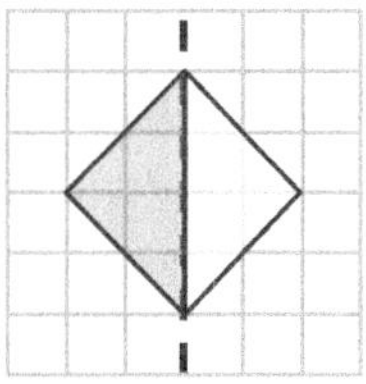

c

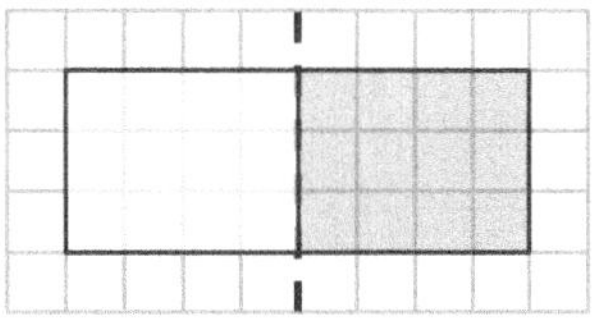

d

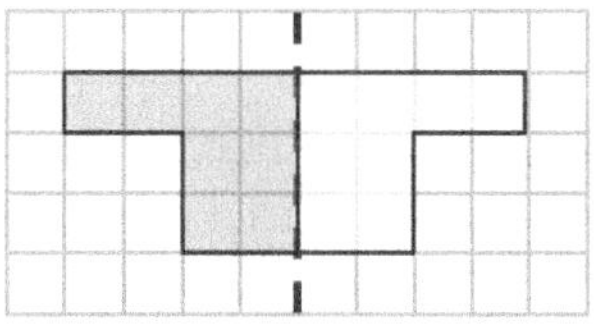

2 a

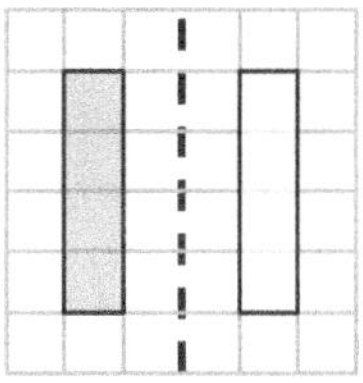

b

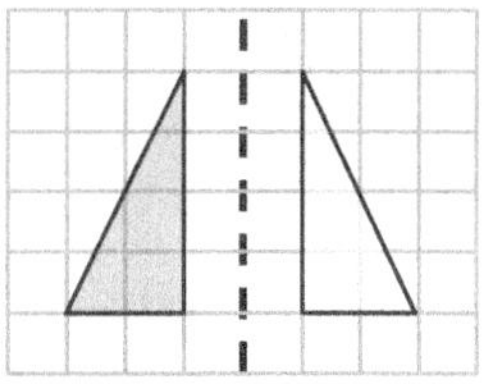

c

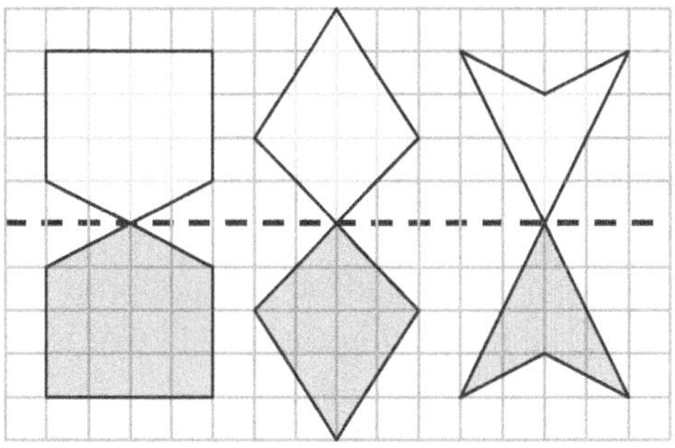

3 c Look at writing and fringe.

4 BED, DOCK

Check student's answers by turning the page upside–down.

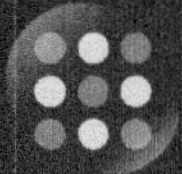

9c Translation

Objectives	
• Translate shapes horizontally or vertically. (L4)	
Key ideas	**Resources**
1 A translation is a sideways shift without reflection or rotation. **2** A translation is described by how far the object moves right/left and up/down.	Coloured card shapes Word examples containing errors Street map on square grid paper
Simplification	**Extension**
Provide students with pairs of shapes, for object and image, similar to those in Question **2**. Initially, have a translation without any up/down component and others without any right/left component. Students describe each translation by counting squares and giving the correct direction. Once students are confident, introduce translations which require both components. A further activity is to provide students with simple shapes made from card. They are to translate one card using a given translation. They draw round the card on squared paper to outline the positions of the object and image.	Draw a street map on squared paper with streets arranged in a grid formation as in New York. Ask students to describe movements between landmarks as a series of translations. A further task is to work in pairs to describe a journey from place to place.
Literacy	**Links**
The two words *translation* and *transformation* are easily confused. Compare the word 'translation' with the move sideways from one language to another. Compare the word 'transformation' with the complete change undergone when a person has a particular experience. Make a poster with the overall title of 'Transformation' above a list of three, 'reflection, rotation, translation'.	Tetris is a video game that was invented in the Soviet Union (now Russia) in the 1980s. It became very popular among adults and children alike in video arcades and on home computers. By 2010, more than 170 million copies of Tetris had been sold worldwide. In the game, players stack shapes together neatly by translating them. A free online version of Tetris can be played at www.freetetris.org

Alternative approach

Ask a student to follow instructions to move about the classroom. Likely instructions are, 'move four steps forwards', 'move four steps to your right'. No rotation is allowed. The aim is have the student return to their place by only undergoing translations.

Checkpoint

1 Place a shape, such as a triangle or rectangle, cut out of card on a grid, draw round it and label it 'object'. Move the shape around the grid performing the following translations.
Describe the translation out loud in words.

a (2, 4) (2 to the right, 4 up)
b (3, -2) (3 to the right, 2 down)
c (-2, 0) (2 to the left, 0 up or down)
d (0, -3) (0 to the left or right, 3 down)

Starter – Quick fire!

Ask students to respond on mini-whiteboards to a series of quick questions which recap previous work on geometry. For example:

- How many sides does a pentagon have? (5)
- How many degrees are there in a full turn? (360°)
- How many lines of symmetry does a rectangle have? (2)

Teaching notes

Ask students how a shape can change its position. Reflection and rotation should be ready answers. Demonstrate them using an object such as book. Ask if there can be an answer that involves no reflection or rotation. Establish that a simple movement in any direction, without reflection or rotation, is a possibility. Give it the name 'translation'. We say that we can 'transform' a shape using a reflection, rotation or translation.

Have a shape drawn on a square grid and labelled 'object'. Also have the shape cut from card and place it on the object. Translate the card and label to its new position 'image'. Ask students how they could describe the translation. Accept right/left and up/down; accept counting squares as a good method. Discuss that a translation has two parts: a right/left part and an up/down part. Arrows can be used to show a translation: use one arrow, by joining an object point to an image point; use two arrows in different colours, with one arrow for right/left and the other for up/down. Describe a translation as, for example, 'two squares right, one square down'.

As a whole-class activity, use cards of different shapes on a squared grid. Draw round the card to give the object. Translate the card and draw round the card to give the image. Discuss the size of the translation. Introduce an example where one of the components of the translation is zero.

Plenary

Show pairs of object shapes and their images under various translations. Ask students to describe the translations on their mini-whiteboards.

Students should agree the key points for translating shapes: namely,

- there is no reflection or rotation;
- the shape may move right or left;
- the shape may move up or down.

Exercise commentary

Question 1 – Remind the students that the dancer always starts from the same position as shown on the diagram.

Question 2 – This only requires students to count the correct number of squares.

Question 3 –Point out to students that the dotted corners, at the right angles, are the best corners to concentrate on. These are the object and image corners. Links can be made with map-work in geography and also with routes planned for orienteering courses.

Question 4 – Students should note that the image point must be the image of the *corresponding* point on the object and not simply the closest point on the object to the image. As in Question **3**, the dotted corners are the best corners to concentrate on.

Answers

1 **a** C **b** I **c** A **d** J
  e H **f** D **g** G **h** B
  i E **j** F

2 **a** 3 to the right, 2 up **b** 4 to the left, 2 down
  c 6 to the left, 0 down

3 **a** 3 **b** 1 **c** 4 **d** 2

4 **a** 6 right, 5 up
  b 3 left, 7 down
  c 6 left, 4 up
  d 8 right, 0 up

9d Rotation

Objectives

- Begin to rotate a simple shape or object about its centre or a vertex. (L4)

Key ideas	Resources
1 A rotation about a fixed point needs three items of information to describe it fully. **2** The items are a centre of rotation, an angle of rotation and a direction of rotation.	Shapes drawn on card, on plain paper and on square grid paper Tracing paper

Simplification	Extension
Provide a shape on plain paper with at least one side horizontal or vertical. Trace the shape onto tracing paper. If the shape is to be rotated 90° one way or the other, ask students to watch this side change from, say, horizontal to vertical, so that they can tell when the 90° turn is complete. Similarly, watch a horizontal or vertical side for turns of 180°.	Find letters of the alphabet which will rotate through 180° so that their image and object coincide. Find the centre of rotation in each case. Find whole words such as 'MOW' which read the same when rotated a half turn about the centre of rotation of the whole word.

Literacy	Links
The word *reflect* comes from Latin words which mean 'bend back'. Students have already met the 'reflex' angle. The word *translate* comes from Latin words which mean 'move across'. The word *rotate* comes from a Latin word meaning 'turn in a circle'.	Wind turbines generate electricity using the energy of the wind. Wind energy is converted into mechanical energy as the vanes turn and the movement is used to generate electricity. The first wind farm in the UK was built in Cornwall in 1991. Wind energy is renewable and does not produce carbon dioxide, but some people criticise wind farms as they think that they spoil the landscape and are a danger to birds. Use this activity at the nrich website to stimulate interest in rotations. www.nrich.maths.org/6987

Alternative approach

Use MyMaths lesson 1115, 'Rotating Shapes', for a more detailed approach.

Checkpoint

1 Place a rectangle, cut out of card, on square grid paper, draw round it and label it 'object'. Mark a centre of rotation at one corner. Ask students to

- **i** perform the rotation by moving the rectangle.
- **ii** say whether the rectangle has gone through a $\frac{1}{4}$ turn, a $\frac{1}{2}$ turn, $\frac{3}{4}$ of a turn, or a full turn.

a Clockwise 90° ($\frac{1}{4}$ turn)

b Anticlockwise 180° ($\frac{1}{2}$ turn)

c Clockwise 270° ($\frac{3}{4}$ of a turn)

d Clockwise 360° (full turn)

e Anticlockwise 360° (full turn)

Starter – Spinning around

Have the students stand up and follow a series of instructions to turn clockwise and anticlockwise at a point in quarter and half turns. See who ends up looking in the correct direction.

Teaching notes

Students have transformed shapes in two different ways: reflection and translation. Ask them for another way to transform a shape; accept 'rotation'.

In a whole-class session, fix, but not yet with a pin, a shape made from card to a board. Ask for a volunteer to describe a rotation of the shape so the teacher can follow instructions. Discuss what information is needed, namely: an angle, in degrees or fractions of a turn, a direction, clockwise or anticlockwise, and a centre of rotation. Draw round the shape before the rotation and then carry out the rotation. Label the object and image positions. Repeat with other shapes and other rotations.

On plain paper, provide shapes, labelled 'object', each with a centre of rotation. Provide a direction and angle of rotation for each object. Students use tracing paper to trace each object and find the positions of the images.

Plenary

Show pairs of object shapes and their images under various rotations. Ask students to write the angle and direction of each rotation on their mini-whiteboards.

Students should agree the key information needed for rotating shapes, namely:

- a centre of rotation;
- an angle of rotation;
- a direction of rotation.

Exercise commentary

Question 1 – For those students who cannot imagine the rotation, they should trace the given shape on tracing paper, place a pencil point on the dot, and turn the tracing paper as necessary. For a 90° turn, watch the rotation of a horizontal side until it becomes vertical; the 90° rotation is then complete.

Question 2 – Students can use the grid to help them decide when the rotation is complete. As in Question **1**, a side which starts vertically on the grid becomes horizontal after a 90° turn.

Question 3 – The diagram in the student book shows the shapes close together. When students copy these shapes, they will need to leave more space between them to make room for the images.

Question 4 – Either imagine the rotation or use tracing paper. The 'f' shape is the most awkward as the image lies partly on the object.

Answers

1 **a** **b** **c**

2

d
a
c
b

3

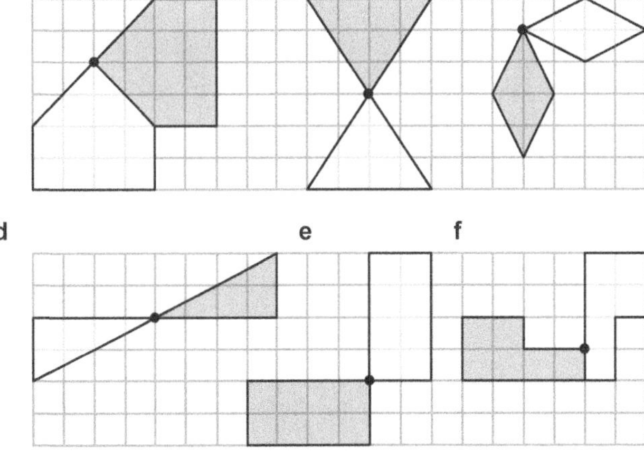

4 Check student's answers.
They should look like: 'an n', 'the same s', 'a backwards p', 'a backwards t' and 'a w'.

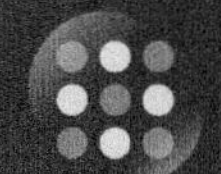

9e Tessellations

Objectives	
• Reason about position and movement and transform shapes (L5)	
Key ideas	**Resources**
1 A tessellation is a repeated pattern of a shape which covers an area without any gaps. **2** Some tessellations can use more than one repeated shape.	Multiple copies of shapes Dotted square grid paper or isometric paper Rubber bands and large geoboards Materials to make posters Software to produce tessellations
Simplification	**Extension**
Multiple copies of a shape can be provided so that students can create a tessellation without the need to draw. Alternatively, one card can be used as a template to draw around as it is placed in each new position.	Ask students to produce a tessellation electronically; see **Alternative approach**. See if they can explain why all triangles and quadrilaterals will tessellate by looking at the angles of these shapes.
Literacy	**Links**
The words *tessellate* and *tessellation* comes from the Latin word 'tessella' which was a small square piece of stone or pottery used as a tile in mosaics. The Romans made many beautiful mosaic floors and pictures which can still be seen today.	The Dutch graphic artist M.C. Escher was very skilled at creating works of art using tessellations. A gallery of his drawings can be found at www.mcescher.com/ For further inspiration, use a search engine to find 'Images of Roman mosaics'.

Alternative approach

Students can use computers to make tessellations. Investigate at

www.nrich.maths.org/6069

There is a tessellation tool on the MyMaths website. Find the 'Toolkit' and use the menu to navigate to 'Shape' and 'Constructions'.

Checkpoint

1 Which three transformations can you perform to make shapes tessellate? (Reflection, translation, rotation)

2 If a shape pattern is a tessellation, can it contain any gaps? (No)

Starter – Triangular doubles

Ask students to describe the shapes formed when congruent pairs of the following triangles are joined edge to edge.

- Two equilateral triangles (Rhombus)
- Two right-angled isosceles triangles (Square, larger right angled triangle)
- Two right-angled triangles which are not isosceles (Rectangle; kite)
- Two isosceles triangles which are not right-angled (Parallelogram; rhombus)

Extend by asking if any of these pairings have more than one possible solution.

Teaching notes

This lesson lends itself to students making posters for displays in classrooms or corridors. There are strong links to work in art and textiles.

Students can create tessellations using:

- plastic shapes or shapes cut from card;
- shapes draw on dotted square grid paper or isometric paper;
- rubber bands on a large geoboard.

Tessellations can involve just one repeated shape, such as any triangle or quadrilateral, an L-shape, a C-shape or a cross, or two repeated shapes, such as hexagons or squares with equilateral triangles of the correct size. Some tessellations have shapes which are translated; other tessellations have shapes which are reflected or rotated.

Some regular polygons will tessellate; some will not. Investigate for regular polygons up to six sides.

Computer software packages can be used to create tessellations using one or more basic shapes.

Plenary

Show a simple shape and ask students to tessellate it on their mini-whiteboards. Repeat for other simple shapes.

Exercise commentary

Question 1 – In part **a**, the basic shape is a rectangle and the tessellation has already been started. In parts **b** and **c**, however, only the basic shape is shown.

Question 2 – Remind students that they have three transformations to call on: reflection, translation and rotation. For example, a reflection or rotation will be needed in parts **c** and **d**.

Question 3 – A honeycomb is an example of a tessellation in the natural world. Students can suggest where else they see tessellations in 'real life'.

Question 4 – If the original shape tessellates, then this method produces other shapes that also tessellate. The work of M. C. Escher offers examples; see **Links**.

Answers

In most instances several different tessellations are possible.

1 **a** **b** **c**

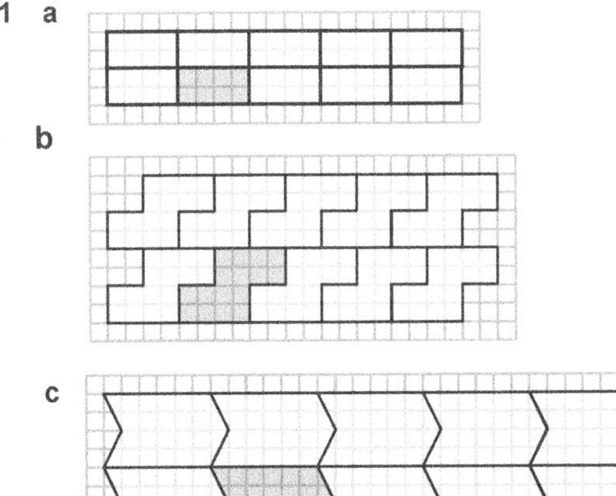

2 **a** **b** **c** **d** **e** **f** **g** **h**

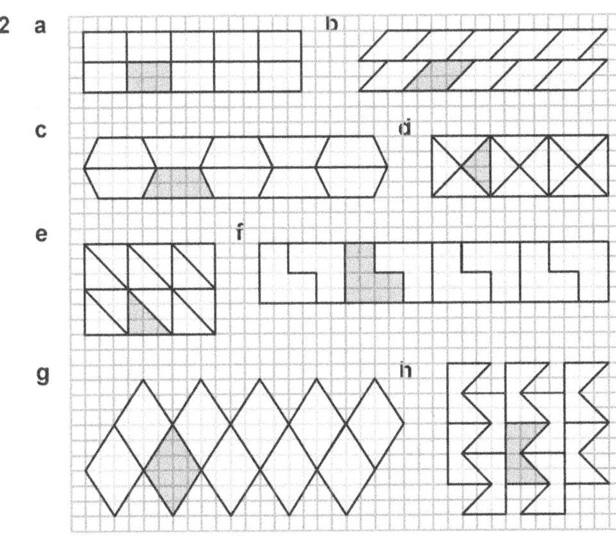

3

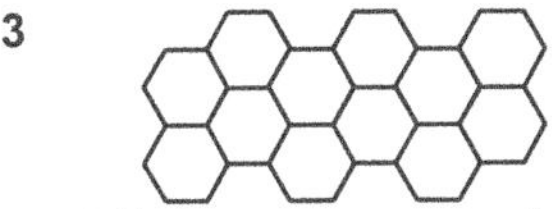

4 All shapes constructed this way should tessellate.

Key outcomes	Quick check
Identify lines of symmetry in a 2D shape. L3	Draw any lines of symmetry on these shapes. **a** 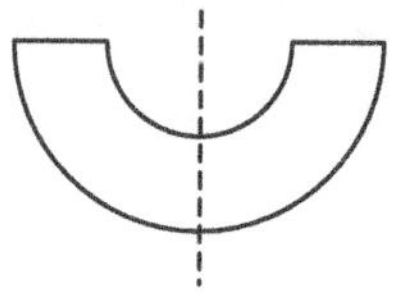 **b** 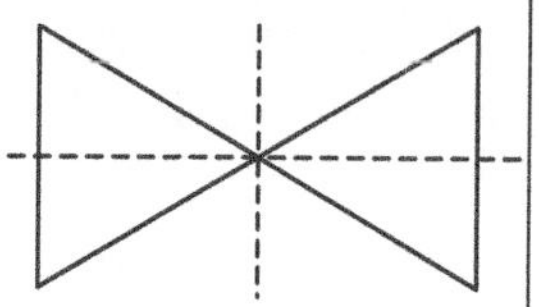 (Shapes should not be shown with lines of symmetry added.)
Transform a shape by reflection in a mirror line. L4 Transform a shape by translation and describe a translation. L5 Transform a shape by rotation about a point. L4	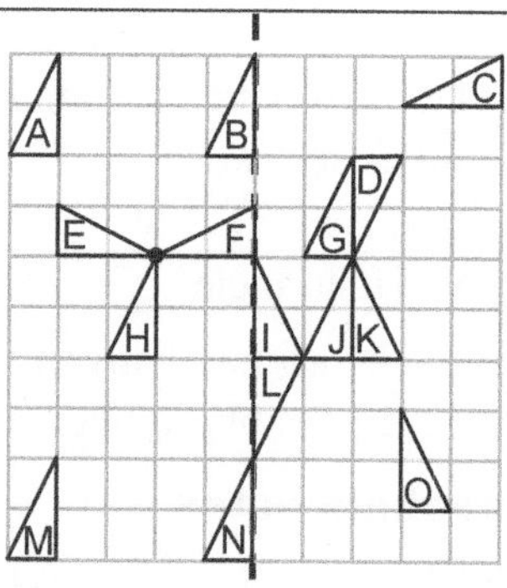 **1** **a** Shape H is reflected in the dashed line. Which shape does it move to? (K) **b** Describe the translation that takes shape H to shape M. (left 2, down 4) **2** Shape H is translated 4 units right and 2 units up. Which shape does it move to? (G) **b** Describe the translation that take shape H to shape M. (left 2, down 4) **3** **a** Shape H is rotated about the black dot 90° anticlockwise. Which shape does it move to? (F) **b** Shape A is rotated about the black dot 90°clockwise. Which shape does it move to? (L)
Create tessellations using reflections, rotations and translations. L4	Does this shape tessellate? If it does show how. 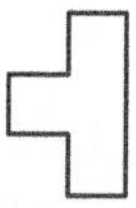 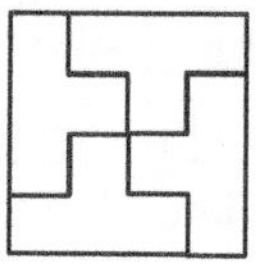 or 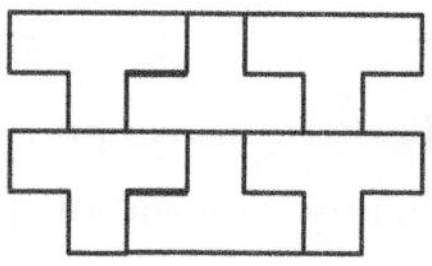

Development and links
Some of the skills developed in visualizing the transformations of 2D shapes will help in chapter **12** when thinking about 3D shapes. The study of transformations is continued in book 2A where transformations on coordinate grids and rotational symmetry are introduced together with harder examples of reflections and rotations. Humans have a strong appreciation of symmetry and it is used frequently in art and design, for example in textiles, wall paper and tilling patterns. Knowing how to transform objects also proves indispensable in programing robotic machinery and video games.

MyMaths extra support

Lesson/online homework			Description
Symmetry	1230	L3	A simple introduction to recognizing reflection symmetry and reflecting square-based shapes in vertical and horizontal lines.

My Review

9 MySummary

Check out

You should now be able to ...

		Test it ➡ Questions
✓ Identify lines of symmetry in a 2D shape.	3	1
✓ Transform a shape by reflection in a mirror line.	4	2
✓ Transform a shape by translation and describe a translation.	5	3
✓ Transform a shape by rotation about a point.	4	4, 5
✓ Create tessellations using reflections, rotations and translations.	4	6

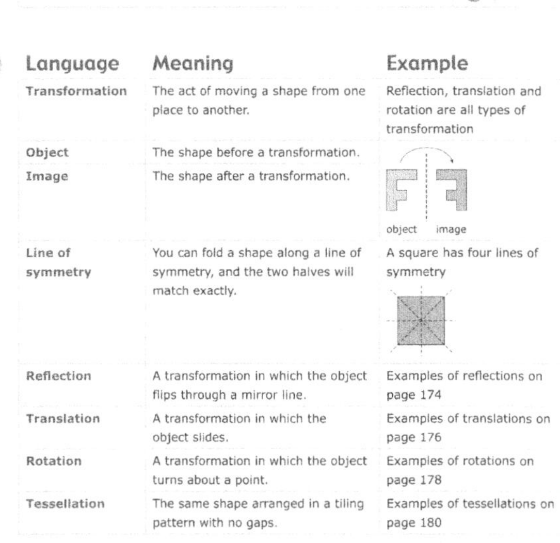

Language	Meaning	Example
Transformation	The act of moving a shape from one place to another.	Reflection, translation and rotation are all types of transformation
Object	The shape before a transformation.	
Image	The shape after a transformation.	object image
Line of symmetry	You can fold a shape along a line of symmetry, and the two halves will match exactly.	A square has four lines of symmetry
Reflection	A transformation in which the object flips through a mirror line.	Examples of reflections on page 174
Translation	A transformation in which the object slides.	Examples of translations on page 176
Rotation	A transformation in which the object turns about a point.	Examples of rotations on page 178
Tessellation	The same shape arranged in a tiling pattern with no gaps.	Examples of tessellations on page 180

9 MyReview

1 Copy or trace each shape and draw all the lines of symmetry. How many lines of symmetry do these shapes have?

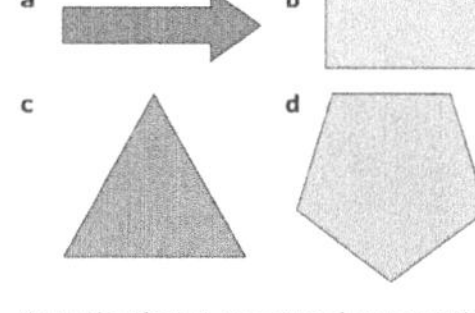
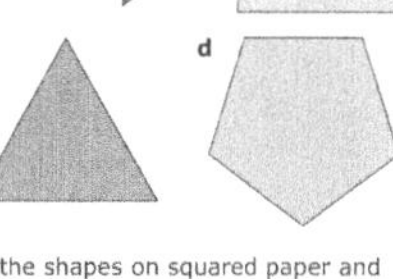

2 Copy the shapes on squared paper and reflect the shapes in the mirror lines.

3 Describe the translations of

a A to B
b B to A
c A to C
d C to A
e B to C
f C to B.

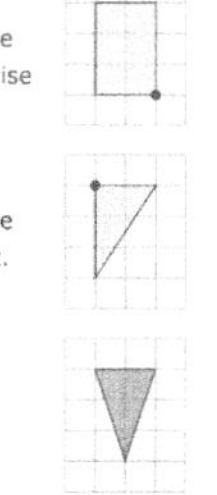

4 Copy the rectangle on squared paper and rotate the rectangle 90° clockwise about the red point.

5 Copy the triangle on squared paper and rotate 180° about the red point.

6 Copy the triangle on square grid paper and tessellate it six times.

What next?

Score	
0 – 2	Your knowledge of this topic is still developing. To improve look at Formative test: 1A-9; MyMaths: 1114
3 – 5	You are gaining a secure knowledge of this topic. To improve look at InvisiPen: 361, 362, 363, 364 and 365
6	You have mastered this topic. Well done, you are ready to progress!

MyMaths.co.uk 183

Question commentary

Students should be using a sharp pencil and ruler and will require squared paper.

Question 1 – (lesson 9**a**) Beware of students who think the diagonals of the rectangle are lines of symmetry (as in a square).

Question 2 – (lesson 9**b**) Students can use a mirror to check their answers if they are unsure.

Question 3 - (lesson 9**c**) Student sometimes confuse the term 'translation' with 'transformation'. The preferred order should be left-right before up-down.

Questions 4 and **5** - (lesson 9**d**) Students need to know which direction is clockwise. They can use tracing paper to do the rotations if necessary.

Question 6 - (lesson 9**e**) There must be at least six shapes, not just in a straight line.

Answers

1 a 1 **b** 2 **c** 3 **d** 5

2 a

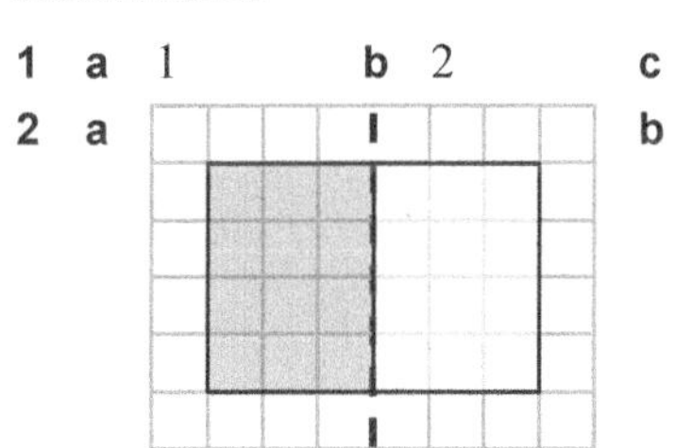

b

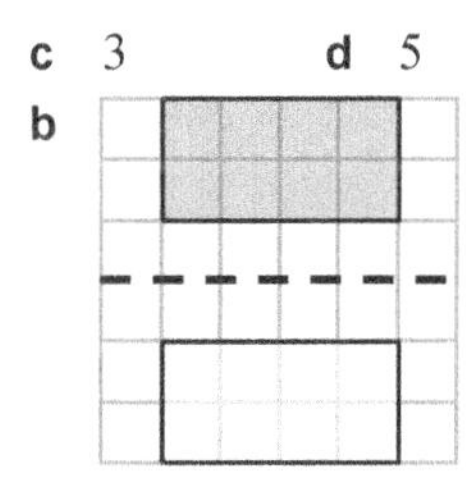

c

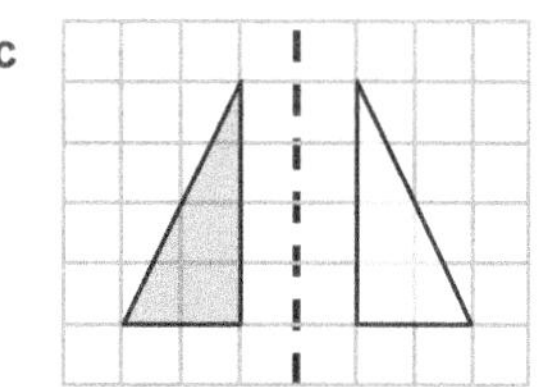

d

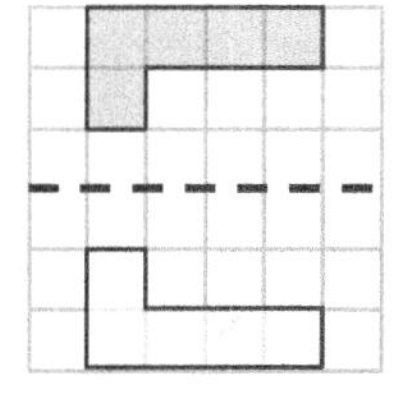

e

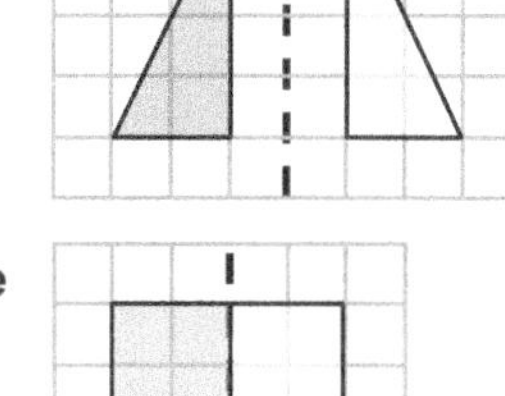

f

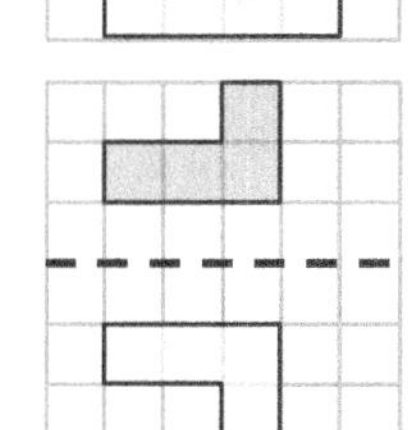

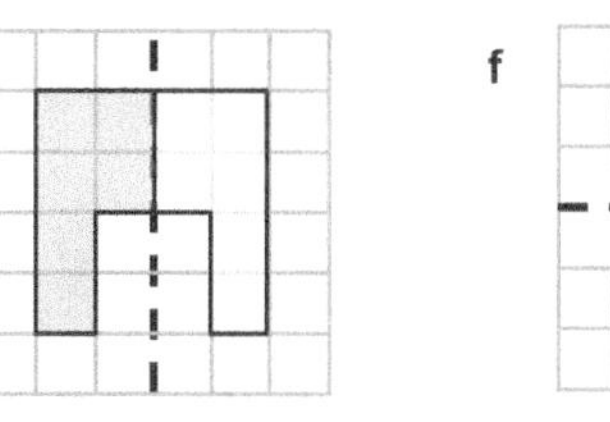

3 a 6 right, 3 down **b** 6 left, 3 up
c 2 right, 4 down **d** 2 left, 4 up
e 4 left, 1 down **f** 4 right, 1 up

4

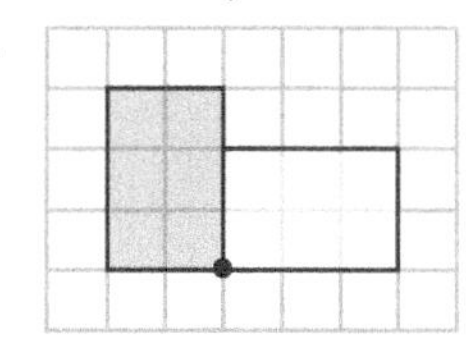

5

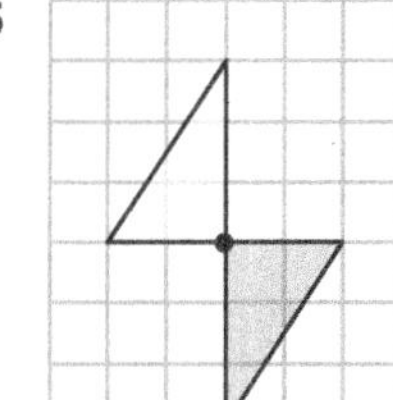

6 For example

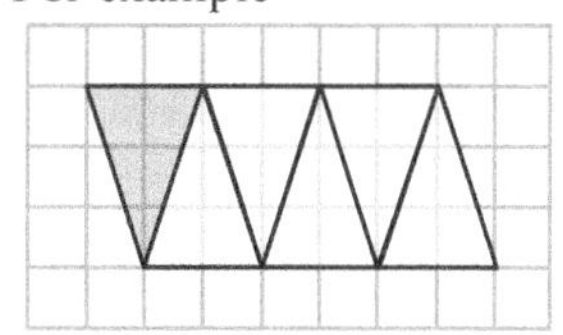

9 MyPractice

9a

1 Each shape has only one line of symmetry.
Copy each shape and draw the line of symmetry on your copy.

a b c d e

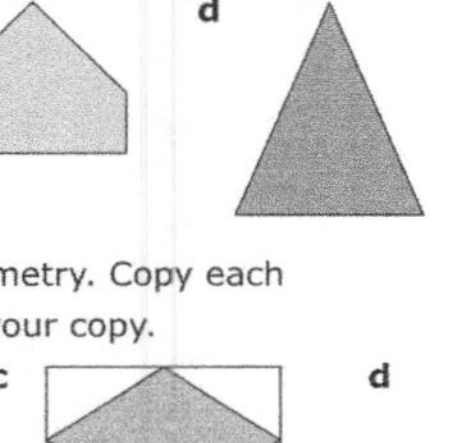
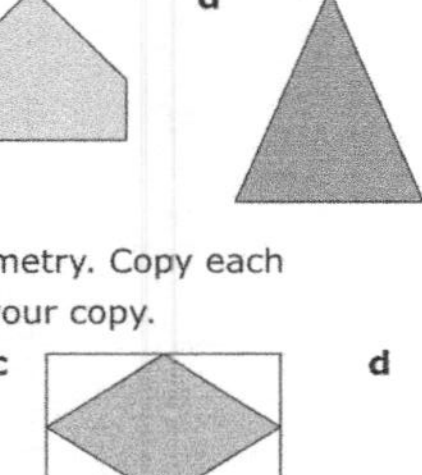

2 Each shape has more than one line of symmetry. Copy each shape and draw the lines of symmetry on your copy.

a b c d

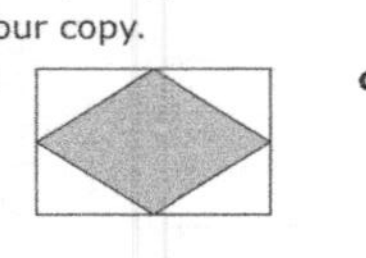
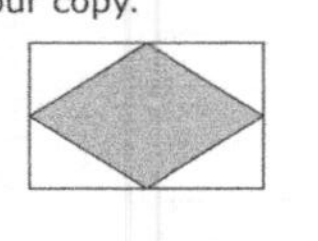
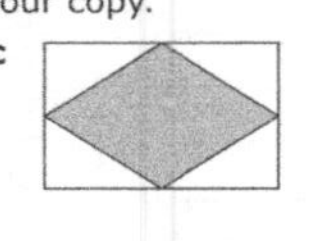
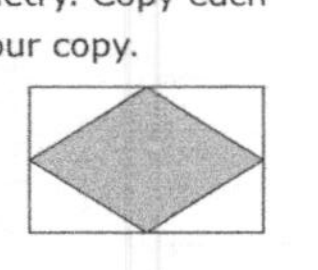
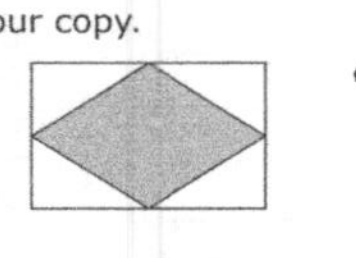
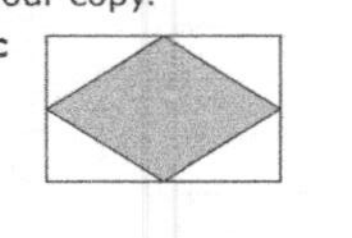
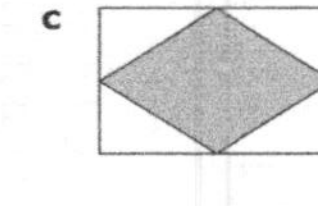
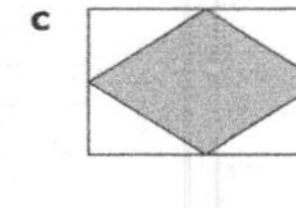
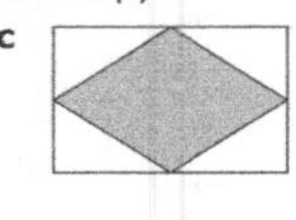
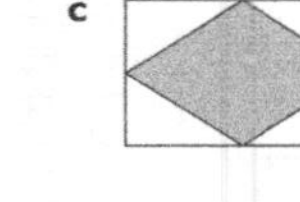
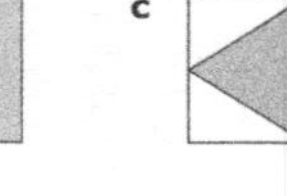
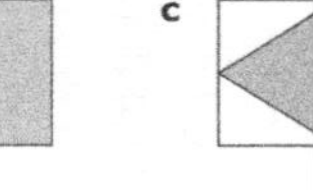

9b

3 Copy each shape onto squared paper and reflect it in the mirror lines.

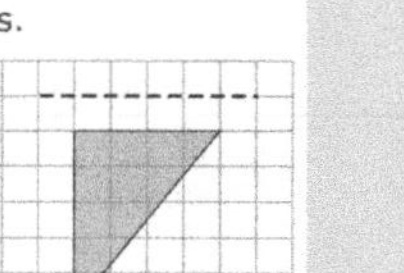
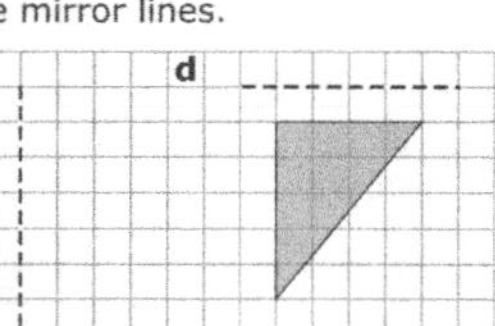
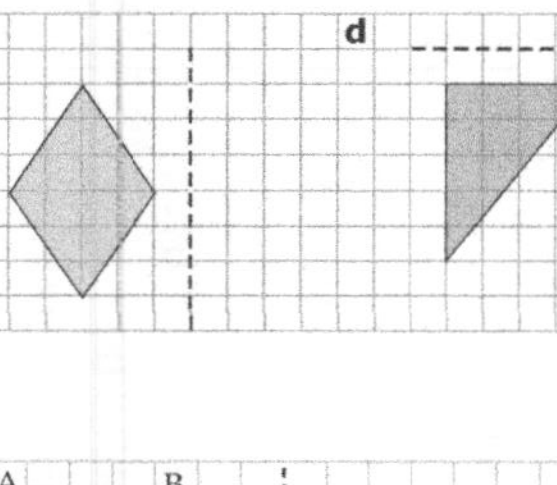

< p.112

4 **a** Copy this shape onto squared paper and reflect it in the mirror line.
b Give coordinates for the corners of the image.

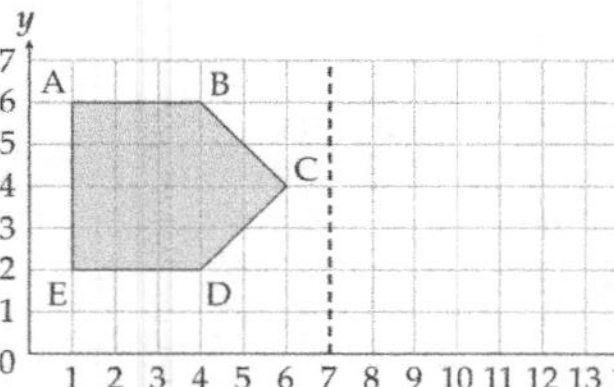

9c

5 Copy this shape onto squared paper and translate it.
a 4 left, 3 up
b 3 right, 3 down
c 5 left, 2 down
d 1 right, 4 up

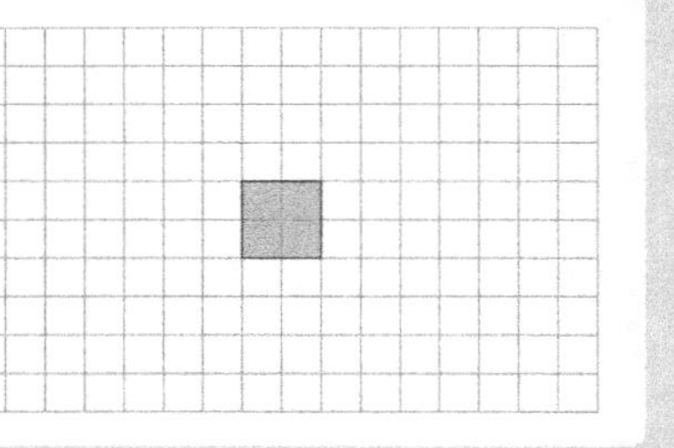

9d

6 Copy the diagram onto squared paper.
Draw the images of the object after following each of these transformations.
a A reflection in the mirror line.
b A translation by 4 to the right and 4 down.
c A clockwise rotation about the red dot of
i 90 degrees
ii 180 degrees and
iii 270 degrees.

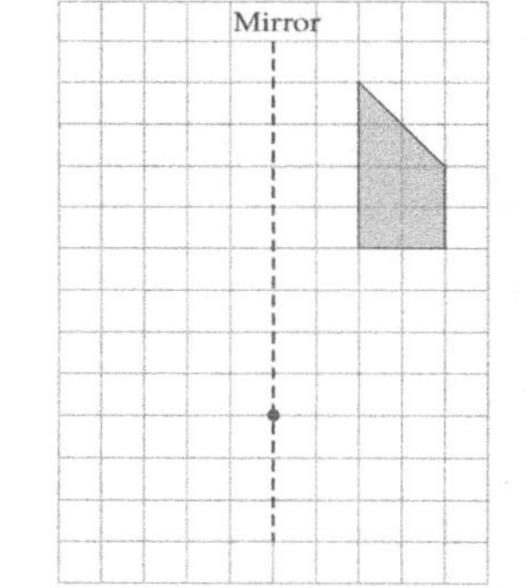

9e

7 Test each shape to see if it will tessellate.
(Remember there must be no gaps or overlaps.)

a b c

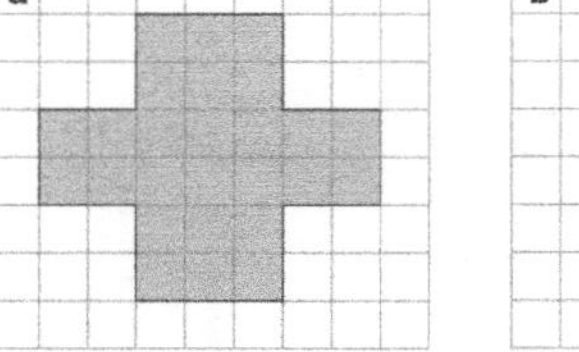
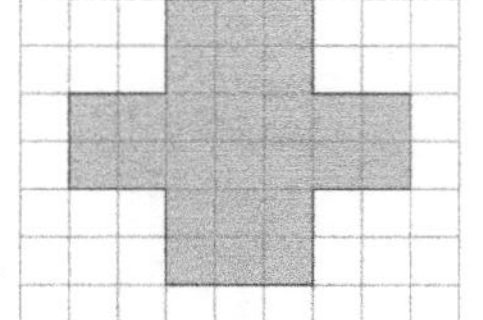
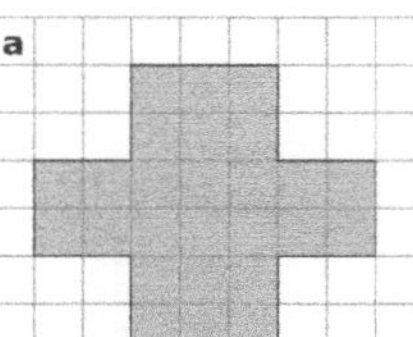
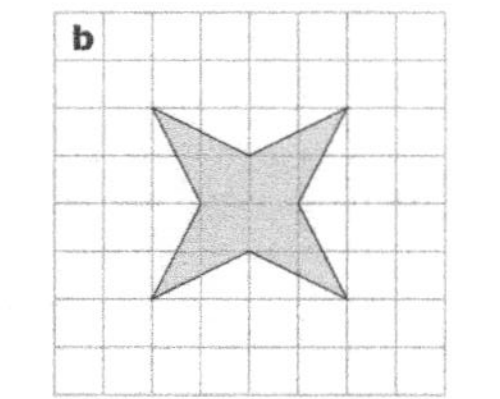
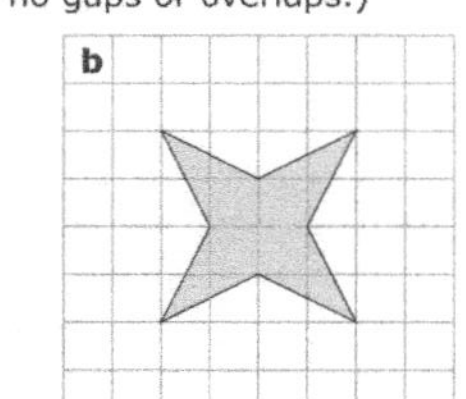
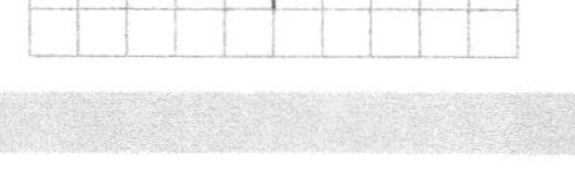

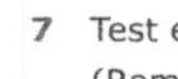

Question commentary

Questions 1 and **2**– It may help to draw these shapes on 1 cm square grid paper, or provide them pre-drawn. Once students have added their lines of symmetry they can then be cut out and folded to test their answers.

Question 2 – In part **d**, if students fail to spot that there are three lines of symmetry, once they have drawn one, suggest that they rotate the shape. This should help them spot the other two.

Question 3 – If students have more success drawing the correct reflection with a vertical than a horizontal line, or visa versa, then suggest they turn the page through 90°. This strategy is also useful when 45° mirror lines are encountered.

Question 4 – Once students have found the coordinates of the reflected vertices ask them what they notice about the y-coordinates: they are the same. The rule for the x-coordinates is $x' = 14 - x$, but it would be optimistic to expect anyone to notice this. The question could usefully by repeated for a horizontal mirror line, in which case the x-coordinates do not change.

Question 5 – The most likely error is confusing left and right. Also beware of students apply the translation in part **b** to the answer to part **a**; they should always start from the original square.

Stronger students could be asked to carry out successive translations and to see if they can make a connection between the total translation and the two component translations: they add. In order to avoid complications with negative numbers keep the two translations in the same direction (left, up) and (left up) or (left, down) and (left, down) etc.

Another variant of this question is to reverse it and give students two squares drawn on a grid and ask them what is the translation that takes one to the other? Here the likely error is mis-pairing corresponding vertices when counting squares; typically students will want to count between closest vertices.

Questions 6 – This will require a large piece of square grid paper. Part **c** goes further than lesson **9d**, in that the centre of rotation is not a vertex of the shape. Students may need reassuring that the standard tracing paper technique will work.

Question 7 – The shapes in parts **a** and **b** do not tessellate, ask students to try and explain why not. In part **c**, ensure students draw sufficient shapes to convincingly show that a tessellation is possible.

Answers

1

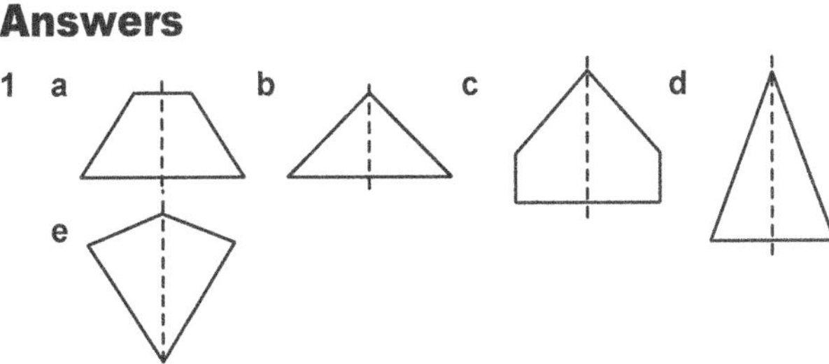

2

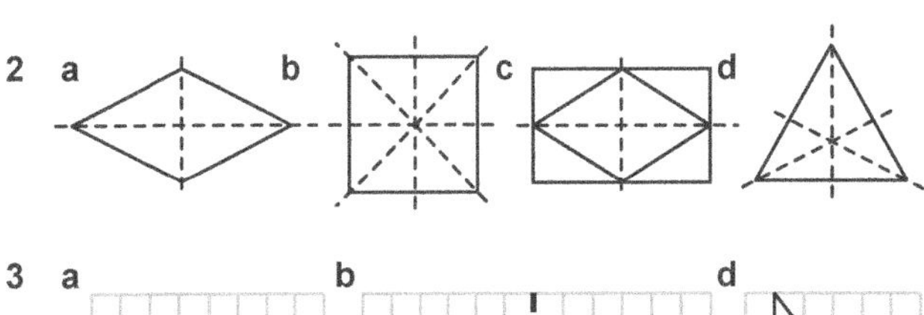

3

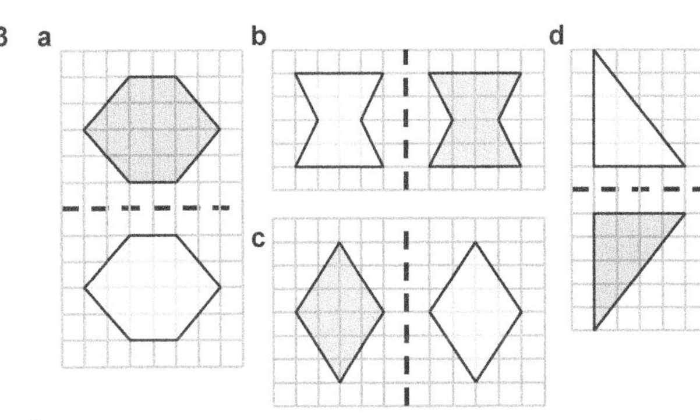

4

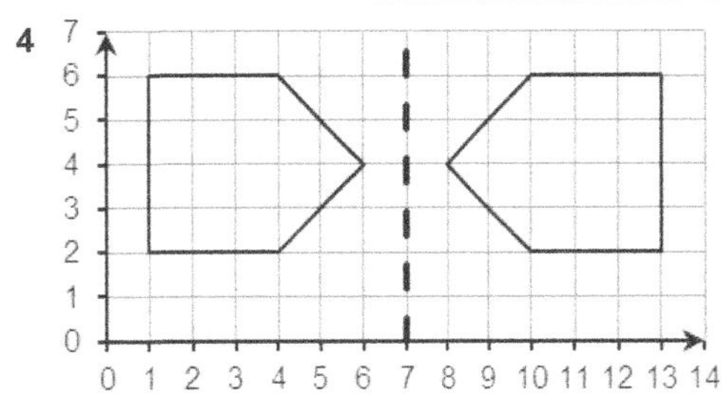

5

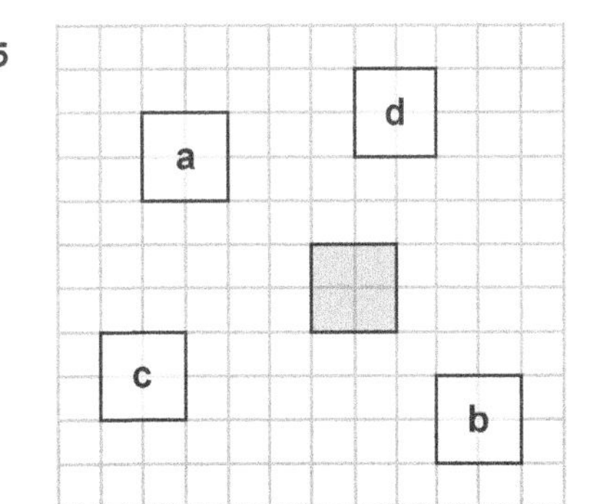

6

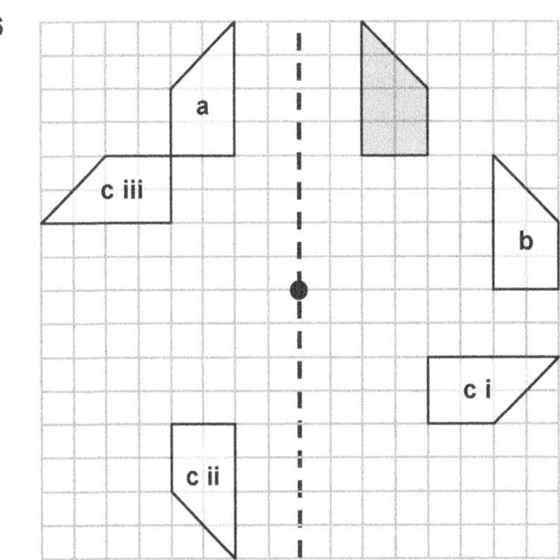

7 **a** No **b** No **c** Yes

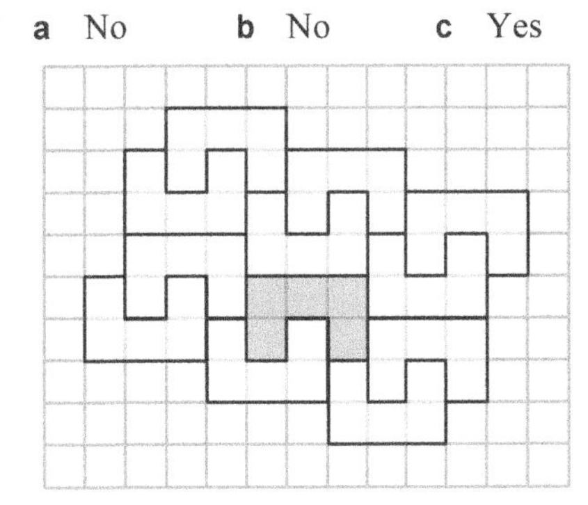

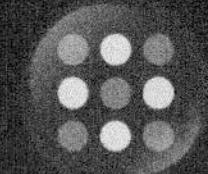

Case study 3: Rangoli

Related lessons		Resources	
Lines of symmetry	9a	Lines of symmetry	(1114)
Reflection	9b	Rangoli designs	
Rotation	9d	Dotted paper	
		Mirrors	

Simplification	Extension
Some students may find it hard to make accurate drawings for task 2. Encourage them to fold their dotted paper in half along the lines of symmetry to test their diagrams after each reflection. This should help to reduce the propagation of errors and provide a concrete check of accuracy. Do not include task 3.	Students can draw further rangoli patterns. They should follow the same basic instructions given in the case study, but you should encourage them to try drawing at least one pattern where the shape that they draw for the diagonal lines of symmetry is different to the shape they drew in step 1. This will give the patterns more variation. Some could also be encouraged to include curved lines.

Links

There are many websites featuring Rangoli designs, two useful sites are

www.rangoliworld.org/index.html   www.tutivaanavil.com/

The first is a good source of information and lots of images of Rangoli designs, including geometric patterns. The second focuses on geometric patterns and includes lots of instructions for creating designs.

Rangoli patterns offer the opportunity to make cross-curricular links.

- Art and design – fabric and tile designs.
- History – where cultural aspects can be explored.
- Religious studies –understanding the religious beliefs behind the Rangoli patterns.
- Geography – looking at areas where Rangoli designs are commonly found.

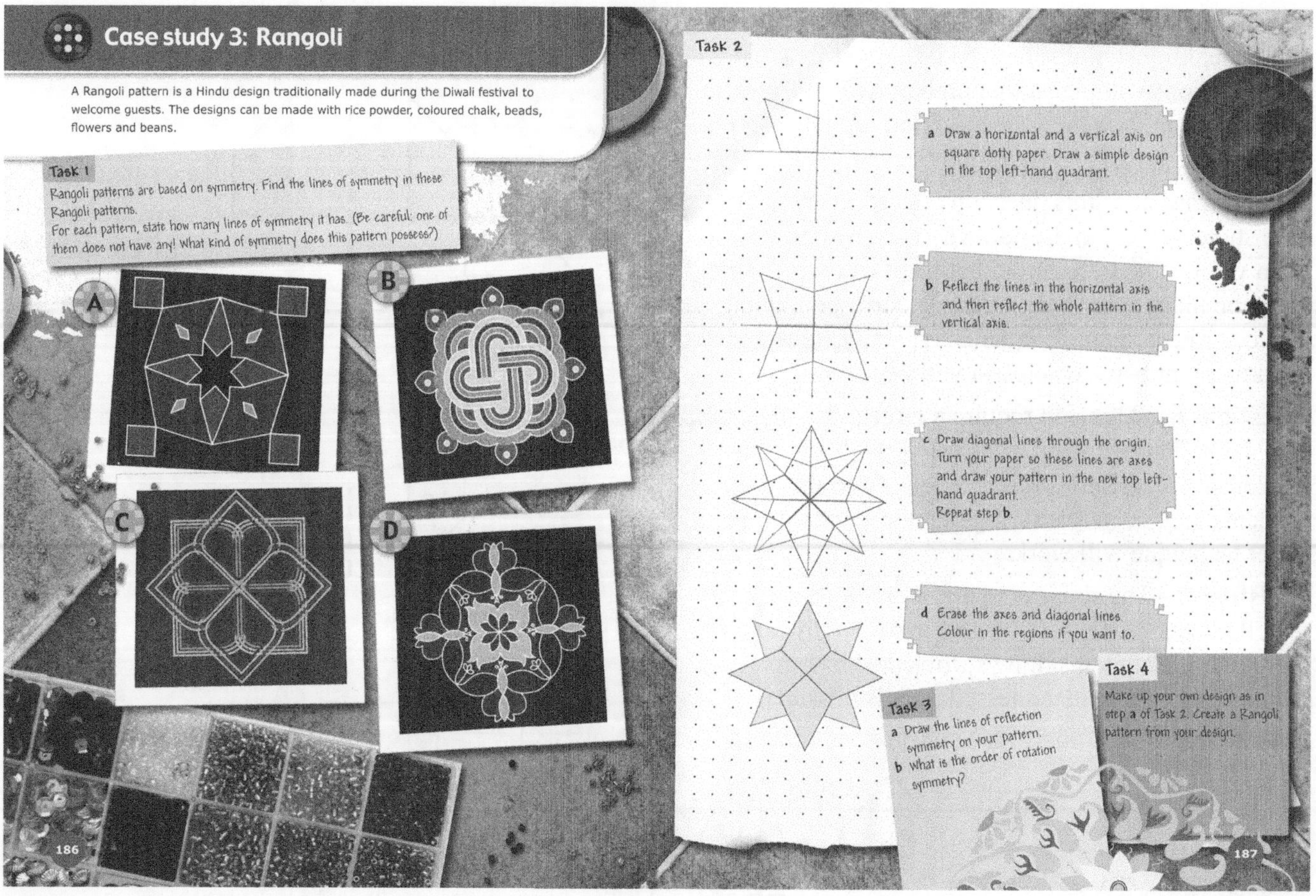

Case study 3: Rangoli

A Rangoli pattern is a Hindu design traditionally made during the Diwali festival to welcome guests. The designs can be made with rice powder, coloured chalk, beads, flowers and beans.

Task 1

Rangoli patterns are based on symmetry. Find the lines of symmetry in these Rangoli patterns.
For each pattern, state how many lines of symmetry it has. (Be careful: one of them does not have any! What kind of symmetry does this pattern possess?)

A B C D

186

Task 2

a Draw a horizontal and a vertical axis on square dotty paper. Draw a simple design in the top left-hand quadrant.

b Reflect the lines in the horizontal axis and then reflect the whole pattern in the vertical axis.

c Draw diagonal lines through the origin. Turn your paper so these lines are axes and draw your pattern in the new top left-hand quadrant.
Repeat step b.

d Erase the axes and diagonal lines. Colour in the regions if you want to.

Task 3

a Draw the lines of reflection symmetry on your pattern.
b What is the order of rotation symmetry?

Task 4

Make up your own design as in step a of Task 2. Create a Rangoli pattern from your design.

187

Teaching notes

Rangoli is an ancient form of Indian folk art in which patterns are created on the floor, or occasionally walls, using coloured rice powder or similar materials. The designs often involve geometric shapes and symmetry. They are intended to sacred welcoming spaces for Hindu deities that bring good luck. As such they are often placed at the entrances to homes at Hindu festivals such as Diwali or at weddings.

A variant, found in southern India, are Kolam patterns. These are like Rangoli patterns but tend to use fewer colours and involve more complex, symmetric designs based on line drawings.

Depending on your class, you may have students who have seen Rangoli patterns or know about them: their history, how they are made and why.

This case study looks at the symmetry properties of Rangoli patterns and involves a practical activity creating one.

Task 1

Look at the first Rangoli pattern, A, and discuss how it has symmetry. Restrict this initial discussion to reflection symmetry. Ask, can you show me where one of the lines of symmetry is? You can check each suggested line by placing a mirror along the line and seeing if the reflection matches the pattern.

Give students time to find the positions of the lines of symmetry in the other three Rangoli patterns. Some students might find it helpful to use a mirror when doing this.

Once the students have found the lines of symmetry discuss what the patterns have in common. Ask, do you notice anything the same about the patterns? How many lines of symmetry are there altogether in each pattern? What can you say about the lines of symmetry?

Agree that each pattern has four lines of symmetry: a horizontal and vertical pair of lines of symmetry that are at right angles to each other and a 'diagonal' or 45° pair that are also at right angles to each other. Explain that they are going to use this type of symmetrical arrangement to make their own Rangoli patterns.

Task 2

Issue students with dotted paper and explain that the four steps give instructions for one way to create a Rangoli pattern. It may be useful to work through the instructions as a whole class with you building up the picture on the board in order to help students understand what needs to be done.

At step **b**, make sure that students understand that when they have reflected the first shape in the horizontal axis, they then reflect everything that is to the left of the vertical axis in the vertical axis, not just the original shape.

At step **c**, advise students to turn their design to make the new lines of symmetry vertical and horizontal before repeating the whole process.

Task 3

Students are likely to have encountered the idea of rotational symmetry before but this is not covered in the course until book **2A**.

The key idea is that the pattern looks the same when it is turned through a particular angle such as a half turn (180°) or a quarter turn (90°). This can be demonstrated by turning a cut out version of the pattern and asking students to say when it looks the same as it first did. Counting the number of times that this happens during one full turn gives the order of rotational symmetry.

Use the four Rangoli patterns in the student book to test students' understanding. Discounting the small asymmetries in shape D, then they all have order of rotational symmetry 4.

If you just consider the shape and not the colouring – look at it as a silhouette – then shape C has order of rotational symmetry 8. When you include the colouring, the 'top' section of the original is drawn over the sections either side of it but, when turned through 45°, the new 'top' section is below the sections either side of it, which is not the same.

Task 4

It may help to keep students focussed if this task is done immediately following task **2**.

Answers

1 **a** 4 Horizontal, vertical and diagonals 45°
b 0 Rotational symmetry (order 4)
c 4 Horizontal, vertical and diagonals 45°
d Strictly no lines of symmetry (the centre is slightly asymmetric as are the green leaves).
4 Horizontal, vertical and diagonals 45°

2 Check student's drawings for accuracy and symmetry.

3 **a** Check accuracy **b** 4

4 Check student's drawings for accuracy and symmetry.

Learning outcomes	
A1 Use and interpret algebraic notation, including: • ab in place of $a \times b$ • $3y$ in place of $y + y + y$ and $3 \times y$ • $\frac{a}{b}$ in place of $a \div b$.	(L5)
A3 Understand and use the concepts and vocabulary of expressions, equations, inequalities, terms and factors.	(L5)
A7 Use algebraic methods to solve linear equations in 1 variable (including all forms that require rearrangement).	(L5)
N6 Recognise and use relationships between operations including inverse operations.	(L4/5)

Introduction

This chapter starts by looking at the concepts of operations and inverse operations in the context of arithmetic. Simple equations are then introduced and developed through the next three spreads.

The introduction discusses the history of the word *algebra*. The history of algebra is very interesting. There are lots of twists and turns. A brief primer can be found here.

http://www.ucs.louisiana.edu/~sxw8045/history.htm

Ancient peoples tended to solve problems geometrically rather than use formulas with variables or solve equations with unknowns.

At its heart 'classical' algebra is about doing calculations with numbers that are not known or numbers that can change. However 'modern' algebra now describes non-numeric objects.

It is maybe worth discussing with pupils how algebra is often the best method for solving problems and to do this they first need to learn the rules for working with letters.

Prior knowledge

Students should already know how to…

- Use basic algebraic notation
- Apply operations in the correct order
- Carry out simple arithmetic

Starter problem

Pupils should enjoy trying to spot magic squares and will be solving lots of intuitive mathematical equations along the way, for example, $a + 3 + 4 = 15$. They need to know that the sum of digits in any row or column must be the same, 15. Additionally the diagonals should also be made to sum to 15.

You might need to give the pupils some partially completed magic squares to get them going.

2	9	4
7	5	3
6	1	8

They should spot that the number 5 appears in the middle and that the different magic squares are essentially rotations and reflections of the one given.

They could investigate a 4×4 magic square and see if they could identify the magic number.

Resources

MyMaths

Simple equations	1154	Function machines	1159

Online assessment

Chapter test	1A–10
Formative test	1A–10
Summative test	1A–10

InvisiPen solutions

Symbols and values	211	Algebraic fractions	233
One-step equations	234	Inverse function machines	239
Function machines	253		

Topic scheme

Teaching time = 5 lessons/2 weeks

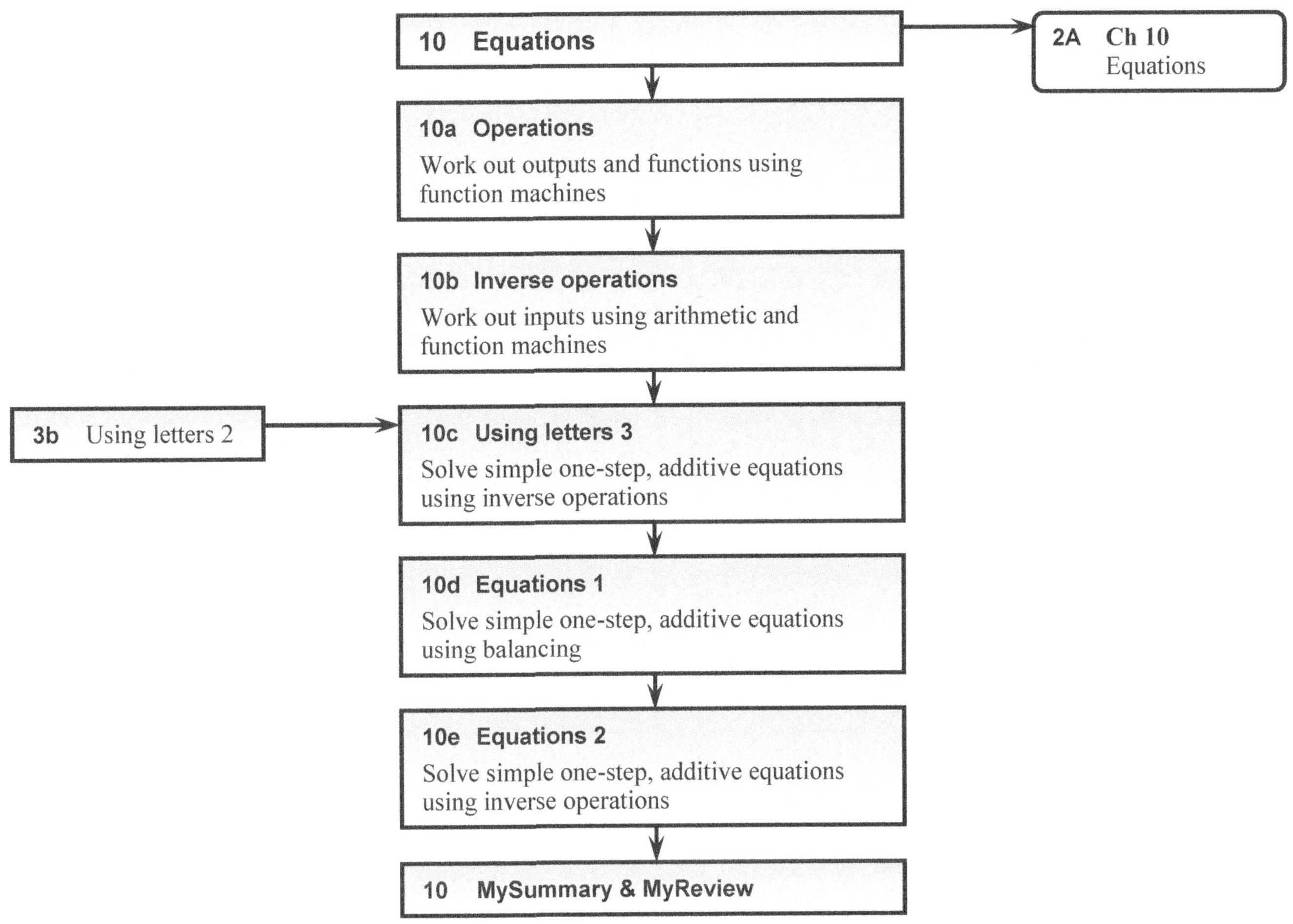

Differentiation

Student book 1A 188 – 203

Treating +, −, ×, ÷ as operations and finding outputs to up to two successive function machines.
Using inverse operations to find inputs to function machines.
Using letters for unknowns.
Solving one-step equations using semi-formal reasoning.
Constructing simple one-step equations.

Student book 1B 190 – 205

Multiply algebraic expressions and divide terms by an integer.
Relate balances to equations and check arithmetic equality.
Use inverse operations to solve one-step additive and multiplicative equations.
Solve two-step equations using sequences of inverse operations.

Student book 1C 188 – 201

Solving multi-step equations including: x on both sides; expanding brackets; and negative x terms.
Use formal methods including collecting like-terms, rearrangement and inverse operations.
Constructing 'real life' equations.

Objectives	
• Express simple functions in words then using symbols.	(L4)

Key ideas	Resources
1 An operation is a rule for processing numbers. The basic operations are addition, subtraction, multiplication and division. **2** A function takes an input, applies an operation, and produces an output. **3** A two-stage function has two operations. The order of the operations may or may not affect the output.	Function machines (1159) Square grid paper

Simplification	Extension
Use functions with only one operation until students are secure in finding an output for a given operation and input. Repeat by changing the input but not the function. A tables of values headed 'Input' and 'Output' can be created. For a two-stage function, write the intermediate value after the first operation in the space between the two stages.	Students who are successful with two-stage functions could be given the task of creating two functions of their own with three inputs and three outputs. They then remove the two operations and exchange their examples with a partner. The partners have to find the two missing operations. Note that there are usually at least two answers to two-stage function problems of this kind, so the two students may end up with different answers, which can be discussed.

Literacy	Links
Addition, subtraction, multiplication and division are all *operations*. The word *function* has a specific mathematical meaning which is not explored in this lesson. It can be thought of in its more general meaning as an action designed to do a specific job.	The control of machinery is often undertaken automatically by computer. In industry, the device controlling a piece of machinery is called a *control system*. The design of control systems involves diagrams which look like complicated function diagrams. Use a search engine to find 'Images of control systems'. Can students find examples of branches of industry which use them?

Alternative approach

Discuss operations in the context of everyday life.

For example, for every birthday you have, you could think of the operation '+ 1' being applied to your age. So a student who is 11 would have an input age of 11 on their next birthday, with an output age of 12.

The theme of age could be extended with other operation. Ask, Tim is twice as old as his cousin Matthew. If Matthew is 9 years old, how old is Tim? Students should recognise that the input here is 9, the operation is × 2, and the output, Tim's age, is 18.

Repeat for other real-life examples using subtraction and division.

Checkpoint

1	If the input is 5 and the operation is + 7, what is the output?	(12)
2	If a function has an input of 2 and an output of 10, what is the operation?	(× 5 or + 8)
3	The input is 20. The first operation is ÷ 2 and the second operation is – 5. What is the output?	(5)

Starter – Substitution bingo

Ask students to draw a 3 × 3 grid and fill it with nine numbers between 1 and 20 inclusive.

Write $a = 1$, $b = 3$, $c = 5$. Write expressions, one at a time, on the board: for example, $2c$, $3b + c$, $3b$, $c - b$, $a + c$. Students should substitute the values of a, b and c into each expression. They cross out the value of the expression if they have it on their grid. (10, 14, 9, 2, 6)

The winner is the first student to cross out all their numbers.

Teaching notes

As a whole-class activity, draw a diagram for a simple operation such as + 5 or × 3. Choose different inputs and ask students to show their outputs on mini-whiteboards. This activity can be changed by giving students an output and asking them to find the input. A further change is to remove the operation, provide students with both input and output and have them suggest the operation. There may be several possible operations, but providing further inputs and outputs will give a unique operation.

An extension is to use a two-stage function machine. The teacher provides both operations and an input; the students show the output on their mini-whiteboards.

Change the order of the operations and explore whether there is any change to the output for the same input. Discover that, when one operation is + or – and the other is × or ÷ , then the order of the operations affects the output.

The exercise can be contextualised by having the two operations as, for example, × 3 and + 2 respectively and saying that, if the input represents the mileage of a taxi ride, the output give the cost in £s.

Plenary

As a whole-class plenary session, draw the diagram for a two-stage function. List four operations that may be used, for example, × 3, × 2, – 1, + 2. Give students an input and the corresponding output.
Students have to select two of the four operations, so that the given input produces the given output. For example, an input of 4 and an output of 9 would have – 1 as the first operation and × 3 as the second operation. Repeat for other inputs and outputs.

Exercise commentary

Questions 1 and **2** – These questions test students' understanding of basic function machines. Do not allow a student to progress until they can do this type of question.

Question 3 – Students can use multiplication and division here as well as addition and subtraction. In some cases there may be more than one answer (for example, part **b** could be '× 10' or '+ 18'). Indeed, students could be asked, as a class, for suggestions for alternative operations.

Question 4 – This is the first question with a two-stage function and multiple inputs. Three answers are required for the one diagram.

Question 5 – This question is more challenging. It would help to write down the intermediate value after one operation and use it to find the second operation.

Question 6 – Make sure the wording is understood. Does Bradley get £10 back on each week's ticket or on the total of all four weeks? It's the latter.

Question 7 – A clue that suggests a strategy is that all the outputs are larger than the inputs. The choices are usually between + and – and then between × and ÷. But which box has which choice? Students need to be systematic in their search.

Answers

1 **a** 7 **b** 12 **c** 16 **d** 30

2 **a** 9 **b** 2 **c** 18 **d** 3

3 **a** + 2 **b** × 10 or + 18
c + 6 **d** – 9 or ÷ 2
e × 6 or + 20 **f** – 14 or ÷ 3
g ×12 or + 33 **h** ÷ 3 or – 16
i ÷ 3 or – 30

4 10, 24, 18

5 **a** – 2 **b** × 3

6 £110

7 × 3 then + 1

10b Inverse operations

Objectives

- Understand and use the rules of arithmetic and inverse operations. (L4/5)

Key ideas

1 An inverse operation will undo the original operation.
2 Subtraction is the inverse of addition, and vice versa; similarly for multiplication and division.

Resources

Calculators

Simplification

Students who are finding the concept of 'inverse' difficult can be more systematic with basic function diagrams like this.

? → + 7 → ?

Input the number 1 and find the output 8. Increase the input in steps of 1 and find the output each time. Tabulate the results in two columns. Continue the pattern by asking, what will be the next output? What will the input have to be? What do you do to get from the output to the input?

Repeat with an operation such as $\times 4$.

Extension

Students can change miles to kilometres using a two-stage function machine and then devise the inverse operations which change kilometres back to miles. They can construct a table with headings 'Miles' and 'Kilometres' to summarise their results.

miles → ÷ 5 → × 8 → km

miles ← × 5 ← ÷ 8 ← km

Literacy

The words *opposite* and *inverse* have similar meanings, but 'inverse' is the word used in mathematics. In this chapter, the words 'inverse operation' are used in an arithmetic setting. In Chapter **9**, the words 'inverse transformation' could have been used for a reflection, rotation or translation which returns the image to the position of the object.

Links

The student book talks about turning a light bulb on and off. Unwanted light can be a nuisance and is called *light pollution*. Artificial lighting can reflect from water vapour and dust in the air and make the night sky brighter, especially above towns and main roads. In a dark sky, it is usual to see about 50 stars in the constellation Orion but 54% of people taking part in a survey in the UK in 2006–7 could see fewer than ten stars. There is more information about light pollution at

www.darksky.org/assets/documents/PG1-light-pollution.pdf

Alternative approach

Discuss inverse operations in context. For example, what are the inverse operations for turning a tap on, spending money, leaving home, or climbing up a ladder? Show how operations also appear naturally in real-life contexts. For example, £1 can be changed into 90 Indian rupees. Construct a table to show the rupees for £2, £3, £4, ... and show the process as a function with the operation $\times 90$. Ask how we find the number of pounds if we change 540 rupees back into pounds. (£6)

Repeat with the cost of hiring a pedal bike if each hour of hire costs £2.

Checkpoint

1 What is the inverse operation of $\times 5$? $(\div 5)$
2 I think of a number and add 6. The answer is 14. What was the number? (8)
3 If $18 \div 3 = 6$, what operation takes 6 back to 18? $(\times 3)$

Starter – 1 2 3 4

Ask students to make the numbers 1 to 10 using the digits 1, 2, 3 and 4 with any operations.

Students score a point for every number they can make using all four digits. For example, $2 \times 1 + 3 + 4$ (= 9) scores 1 point.

This can be extended by making numbers up to 20.

Teaching notes

As a whole-class activity with students responding on mini-whiteboards, ask, I am thinking of a number. I add 6 and my answer is 11. What number am I thinking of? Repeat with subtraction, multiplication and division. Discuss how students found the answers. Use the words 'inverse', 'inverse operation' and 'opposite'.
As further reinforcement, ask students to put any number into a calculator and multiply it by a number of their choice. Ask them to do just one operation to return the display back to the original number. Thus division is shown to be the inverse of multiplication. Repeat for addition and subtraction.

Now draw the diagram for a function with a given operation and a given input and ask for the output. Remove the input and output and now provide an output but no input. Ask how the input could be found. Again, use the words 'inverse' and 'inverse operation'.

Apply a function in the context of thunderstorms. Input the number of seconds between the thunder and lightning and output the distance of the storm away from you in miles. Use the operation ÷ 5. Find the distance for different times and, in reverse, find the times for different distances.

Plenary

On a map of England, 1 cm stands for 6 kilometres. Draw the diagram of a function with 'Distance on the map (cm)' as the input and 'Actual distance on land (km)' as the output. Ask students to respond on mini-whiteboards to questions such as, two towns are 5 cm apart on the map. How far apart are they on land in km? (30 km) and, in reverse, it is 60 km from Manchester to Liverpool. How far apart are they on the map? (10 cm)

Scale drawings are covered in lesson **15d**.

Exercise commentary

Question 1 – Students need to understand that two things are required for the operation to be an inverse. It must be the correct inverse arithmetical operation, + ↔ – and × ↔ ÷, and it must be the same numeric value.

Question 2 – Each square represents either a missing number or a missing operation. The answer of the first operation becomes the starting point of the inverse operation.

Questions 3 and **4** – Again, emphasise that the answer of the first operation becomes the starting point of the inverse operation.

Question 5 – Students could draw the diagram of the function for each part, then use it in reverse or draw another diagram for the inverse function.

Question 6 – Remind students that subtraction is the opposite of addition, not division.

Answers

1 + 3 and – 3 × 12 and ÷ 12
÷ 3 and × 3 – 12 and + 12

2 **a** 6 **b** 5 **c** 4 **d** 4
e + **f** 3 **g** 2 **h** ×
i × **j** ×

3 **a** ÷ 4 **b** ÷ 6

4 **a** 7, 7 **b** 31, +9, 31
c 17, – 10, 17 **d** 32, +7, 32
e 80, × 2, 80 **f** 30, +12, 30

5 **a** 28 **b** 9

6 Harry has divided (25 ÷ 5 = 5)
25 – 5 = 20

Objectives	
• Construct and solve simple linear equations with integer coefficients (unknown on one side only) using an appropriate method (eg inverse operations). (L5)	
Key ideas	**Resources**
1 Know that an unknown number in an equation can be represented by a letter. **2** Know that inverse operations allow you to solve an equation	Simple equations (1154)
Simplification	**Extension**
Avoid questions **3** to **5**. Instead use quite repetitive 'think of a number' questions. This means that the context only has to be understood once allowing students to focus on writing the equation, choosing the correct inverse operation and finally doing the arithmetic.	Introduce one-step equations that involve the unknown being multiplied or divided by another number, say, $2 \times x = 8$ or $y \div 3 = 6$. This can be extended further by placing the equation in a context. For example, four people give the same amount of money to a fund that is worth £24. How much did they each give? ($4 \times x = 24, x = 6$) Or, a prize is shared equally between five people who each get £6. How much was the prize? ($x \div 5 = 6, x = 30$)
Literacy	**Links**
We can describe situations using letters as they are short and make expressions easier to work with. Often, any letter can be chosen to represent an unknown number. Ensure students understand that their choice of letter will not affect the outcome of the problem or calculation. Two students who choose different letters in Question **3** should (ideally) still produce the same answers to Question **4**.	Marbles is an old-fashioned game played by two or more people who roll small glass marbles along the ground and aim to hit their opponents' marbles in order to win them. The game was particularly popular during the late 19th and early 20th centuries – and is even thought to have been played as long ago as 4000 BC in ancient Egypt – but is still played today. The marbles themselves can be very pretty and often become collector's items. The British World Marbles Championship is played every year at Tinsley Green in West Sussex. There is also an annual National Marbles Tournament held on Jersey. There is more information about marbles at www.imarbles.com/howtoplaymarbles.php

Alternative approach

Give students three numbers that are related by addition, such a, 13, 17 and 30. Ask students for a calcukation that connects all three numbers and keep asking for more suggestions until all possibilities have been found: $13 + 17 = 17 + 13 = 30$, $30 - 13 = 17$, $30 - 17 = 13$. It may need a prompt to include subtraction calculations. Repeat with other numbers and emphasise that addition and subtraction are connected as *inverse operations*.

Tell your students, I have a number, I add 4, the answer is 7. What is my number? Show how this can be written as an equation, $n + 4 = 7$, and encourage students to link the answer, 3, with the calculation $7 - 4$. Work through further examples, including those in the student book, and encourage students to use substitution to the check their answers.

Checkpoint

1 I had £25 in my wallet. I have £15 left.

a If m stands for the amount I spent, how can you describe the situation? ($m + 15 = 25$)

b How much did I spend? ($m = 15$ means I spent £15)

Starter – Fruit

Ask students questions that involve simplifying. For example

- You have 3 apples. You are given another 6 apples and give away 4 apples. How many apples do you have left? $(3 + 6 - 4 = 5)$
- You promise to give a friend 2 bananas and are given 7. How many bananas do you have left once you have seen your friend? $(7 - 2 = 5)$
- You have 4 apples and 2 bananas. You are given another 3 apples and give away a banana. What do you have left? (7 apples, 1 banana)

This can be extend by discussing the use of the letters a and b to represent the fruit.

Teaching notes

Ask a simple 'think of a number' question. I think of a number add two to the number and now I have 7. What number was I thinking of? Use questioning to unpick how the students arrived at the right answer, writing the reasoning on the board. Guide them towards

'something' + 2 = 7	$x + 2 = 7$
'something' = 7 –2	$x = 7 - 2$
'something' = 7	$x = 5$

Next suggest that it would be easier and more professional to use x rather than 'something' for the unknown number and show how this is written.

Work through a second 'think of a number' question that involves a subtraction. I think of a number subtract three from the number and now I have 5. What number was I thinking of? Ask students to write an equation and then agree what inverse operation should be used to find the unknown.

$$x - 3 = 5$$
$$x = 5 + 3$$
$$x = 8$$

Repeat with other examples in different contexts and with slightly harder numbers but keep to addition and subtraction problems. Avoid questions where the unknown itself is subtracted.

As appropriate, take the opportunity to show how the answers can be checked by substituting them back into the original equation and checking that the left hand side gives the right hand side.

Plenary

Ask students to write and then solve an equation for this problem using mini-whiteboards.

Eddie pays for £14 worth of shopping and gets £6 change. What did he pay with?
$(x - 14 = 6; x = 6 + 14; x = 20)$

Exercise commentary

Question 1 – The equations given use only addition, requiring students to perform the inverse operation of subtraction in each case. The calculations are straightforward, but students will most likely need to jot down their working rather than performing all subtractions mentally.

Question 2 – This question is much the same as Question **1**, except that it requires students to perform addition to find the value of each letter.

Questions 3 and **4** – Remind students that they can choose any letter to represent the unknown quantity, but to avoid confusion, they should choose a different letter in each case. They need to make it clear what the letter stands for. For example, in part **a**, the letter stands for the *total* amount of money Deepak had originally, but in part **b**, it stands for the *increase* in Katie's weight. This is the context for the answers to Question **4**.

Question 5 – This is a simple problem provided students recognise that the aliens have different weights, and that 'together' means the two weights add up to 30 kg. They need to choose a letter to represent Alien 2's weight and perform the inverse operation of subtraction.

Answers

1 **a** 3 **b** 4 **c** 1 **d** 4
e 0 **f** 4 **g** 10 **h** 5
i 5 **j** 8 **k** 4 **l** 5
m 8 **n** 25 **o** 15 **p** 99

2 **a** 11 **b** 11 **c** 18 **d** 9
e 7 **f** 10 **g** 25 **h** 30
i 28 **j** 20 **k** 37 **l** 60
m 15 **n** 20 **o** 20 **p** 101

3 Students could use another letter for the variable, x.
a x = Original amount of money $x - 5 = 10$
b x = Increase in weight $30 + x = 45$
c x = Extra pages read $30 + x = 55$
d x = Number of broken CDs $14 + x = 30$

4 **a** 15 **b** 15 **c** 25 **d** 16

5 18 kg

Objectives

- Construct and solve simple linear equations with integer coefficients (unknown on one side only) using an appropriate method (eg inverse operations). (L5)

Key ideas

1. A balance can be represented as an equation.
2. A balance is maintained when the same amount is taken away from both sides.

Resources

Simple equations (1154)

Old-style kitchen scales or a metre rule with weights

Grocery items with weights printed on the packaging, such as bags of flour and sugar

Simplification

The old style of kitchen scales with two pans is useful to illustrate objects in balance becoming unbalanced when something is 'taken away' from one side. Show that the balance returns when the same amount is taken away from the other side. Use the method of 'taking away', rather than 'counting on', as it derives naturally from using kitchen scales and lays a surer foundation for future work with equations. Another useful form of words is 'What I do to one side, I must also do to the other'.

Extension

Students who understand the notation $2x$ could be asked to solve equations such as $2x + 3 = 15$. ($x = 6$) They could even progress to solving equations involving 'half of an object' such as $\frac{1}{2}x + 3 = 4$. ($x = 2$)

Literacy

The words 'bicycle', 'bisect', 'biannual', and 'biscuit' start with the letters *bi-* meaning 'two' in Latin ,with 'biscuit' meaning 'twice-baked'. The word *balance* comes from two Latin words *bi-* and *lanx* meaning 'two dishes' or 'two scales' and, over time, the *bi-* became a *ba-*.

Links

Equations are used in chemistry to describe reactions between molecules. The letters represent atoms of different elements and the equation describes the changes that occur during the reaction. The first ever chemical equation was written by the Frenchman Jean Beguin in 1615. Examples can found at

www.newworldencyclopedia.org/entry/Chemical_equation

Notice they use an arrow rather an 'equals' sign.

Alternative approach

The idea of an equation as a balancing set of scales can be explored further. The use of a more modern weighing scale can be found in MyMaths lesson 1154, 'Simple equations'.

Students could look at grocery items whose weights are printed on the packaging, such as bags of flour and sugar. They could experiment with scales, or draw diagrams to help them form and solve equations. For example, if a package weighing 750 g is on one side of the scale and another weighing 1000 g is on the other side, what weight needs to be added to make the scales balance? Can students find a package of suitable weight (250 g)?

Checkpoint

1. look at the equation $x + 14 = 20$.
   - **a** What is on the left-hand side of the equation, and what is on the right-hand side? ($x + 14$; 20)
   - **b** If you want the x to be by itself on the left, what has to be taken away from it? (14)
   - **c** What value of x makes the equation balance? ($x = 6$)

Starter – Balancing the books!

Say to students, you have £20 in your bank account. This is called your balance. You put another £5 into your account. What is your new balance? (£25) Students should respond using mini-whiteboards. Now ask, you spend £3, what is your new balance? (£22) Continue with this scenario or change to a more demanding one. Tell students that this process of keeping track of income and spending is known as 'balancing the books'.

Teaching notes

Use an old-style kitchen balance with two pans and a set of weights. Alternatively, a metre rule resting at its centre on a crude pivot can suffice. Borrow a set of weights from the science department. Discuss how a balance can be achieved by adding more weights or more objects but don't mention adjusting the distance from the pivot! If there isn't a balance, discuss which side is the heavier and the lighter.

Draw a simple picture of two scales on a pivot and say that we can represent this picture with an equation where the equals sign stands for the pivot when both sides of the equation balance. We use a letter for any unknown weight.

There are two ways of thinking to find a missing number. If $18 + x = 20$, we can ask, what do I add to 18 to make 20? or what is left if I take 18 from both sides? These two methods are equivalent to jumping forwards from 18 or backwards from 20 on a number line. Both methods are valid but 'taking away from both sides' provides a better introduction to solving equations.

Plenary

On a simple picture of two scales on a pivot, draw the weight 10 kg balancing an x and 6 kg. Ask for the value of x. Repeat for different values.

Replace the picture with an equation such as $x + 5 = 9$. Ask for the value of x.

If students show a good understanding, extend the equations, such as $x + x + 10 = 16$ but do not use the notation $2x$ for $x + x$ at this stage.

Exercise commentary

Question 1 – Each equation can use the question mark or, expecting what is to come, can use the letter x from the start.

Question 2 – This question uses only addition on the left-hand side of the equations.

Question 3 – This question may require some whole-class groundwork before pupils attempt it. Parts **a** to **d** develop readily from previous work. Part **g** is the only part that involves subtraction rather than addition. Drawing a diagram of weights is redundant due to the – 10. Instead, use the language of inverse functions: I need to get rid of the – 10. What is the inverse of 'subtracting 10'? Then I must do the same to both sides to keep the balance. Another approach, which is less reliant on 'balancing', is to say, think of a number, p, which, after subtracting 10, leaves you with 10.

Question 4 – As a footnote, ask students how they can write the problem down as an equation. ($x + 200 + 25 + 50 + 50 + 25 = x + 350 = 425$)

Question 5 – This requires some simplification and collection of 'like terms' before solving an equation.

Answers

1 **a** **i** $x + 10 = 15$ **ii** $x + 7 = 14$
iii $3 + x = 18$ **iv** $37 + x = 52$
b **i** 5 kg **ii** 7 kg **iii** 15 kg **iv** 15 kg

2 **a** 5 **b** 4 **c** 11 **d** 6
e 5 **f** 7

3 **a** 6 **b** 2 **c** 14 **d** 12
e 2 **f** 6 **g** 20 **h** 8
i 0 **j** 13 **k** 4 **l** 11

4 75 g

5 **a**

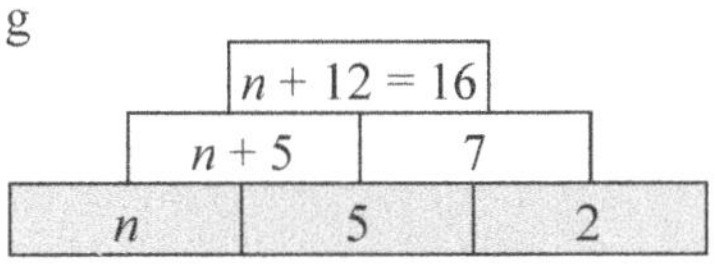

$n + 12 = 16$	
$n + 5$	7

n	5	2

$n = 4$

b

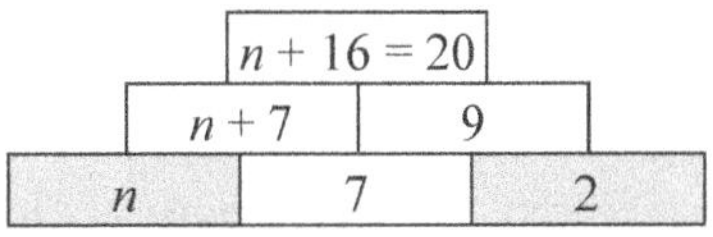

$n + 16 = 20$	
$n + 7$	9

n	7	2

$n = 4$

Objectives	
• Construct and solve simple linear equations with integer coefficients (unknown on one side only) using an appropriate method (eg inverse operations). (L5)	
Key ideas	**Resources**
1 A function with an input x and a known output can be represented by an equation. 2 The inverse operations of a function can be used to solve the equation.	Simple equations (1154)
Simplification	**Extension**
Make sure that students can find an output given an input and an operation. Establish that students understand that, to reverse the process or 'work backwards', they have to 'do the opposite'. Provide an output and ask for the input. Repeat for other outputs. Only when students understand how to perform an operation 'forwards' and 'backwards' should an equation be used to represent the function.	Give students two-stage functions that lead to more complicated equations. For example, the two-stage function which has × 3 for the first operation, + 2 for the second operation, and with 14 as the output can be used to solve the equation $3x + 2 = 14$. The two inverse operations (– 2 and ÷ 3) must be used in the correct order.
Literacy	**Links**
The word *inverse* comes from a Latin word meaning 'turn'. Compare the word 'inverse' with the words 'revert', 'divert', 'subvert', 'vertical', 'introvert', all of which can be connected with 'turning'.	Many so-called magic tricks begin with 'Think of a number'. Here is one example. Ask each student to think of a number between 1 and 10, multiply the number by 9, add the digits of the result and subtract 5. Then, taking A = 1, B = 2, C = 3, etc., find the letter of the alphabet that corresponds to the current answer. Ask the students to think of • a country that begins with this letter • an animal that begins with the second letter of the country • the colour of that animal. Now tell the class that there aren't too many grey elephants in Denmark and see if they are astounded. There are examples of some more 'Think of a number' tricks, along with the mathematics behind them, at www.nrich.maths.org/1051

Alternative approach

Set an example in context. When a length of cloth is cut from a roll, the cost depends on the length. Suppose each metre costs £4. Discuss a function with the operation × 4 and what the input and output represent. Use it, for example, to find the cost of a 6 metre length of cloth (£24) and, in reverse, to find the length of cloth which costs £32 (8 m).

Repeat for different types of cloth with varying prices, or items bought by weight, such as sweets in a sweet shop which charges per 100 g.

Checkpoint

1 I had £15 in my wallet but now I only have a third of the money left. How much do I have? (£5)

2 I think of a number and add 25. Now I have 45. What was the number? (20)

3 What is the value of w in the equation $w \div 4 = 4$? (16)

Starter – Think of a number

Ask students to respond to questions using mini-whiteboards.

Say, I'm thinking of a number. I add 6 and get 10. What number am I thinking of? (4). Ask further questions, including all four basic operations, such as

- I subtract 6 and get 4 (10)
- I multiply by 3 and get 15 (5)
- I divide by 2 and get 8 (16)

Teaching notes

The **Starter** leads to the question, what is an 'inverse operation?' Ask for examples. Establish the inverses of each of the basic operations, +, –, × and ÷. Use the words 'opposite' and 'doing the opposite' where appropriate.

Show the whole class an equation such as $x + 4 = 9$ and illustrate it by drawing the diagram of a function with an input x and the operation + 4. Ask students what the output is, what the inverse operation is, and what the value of x is. Repeat with similar equations until students are confident and then progress to equations such as $x - 5 = 1$ ($x = 6$), $2 \times x = 16$ ($x = 8$) and $x \div 2 = 6$ ($x = 12$). At all times, ask students to say what the inverse operation is and discuss how they will use it.

Plenary

Draw the diagram of a function for the whole class to see. Specify the operation, such as + 4. Label the input with the letter x and give the output a numeric value, such as 6. Ask students to write

- the equation for the function machine ($x + 4 = 6$)
- the value of the input x (2)

Students should respond on mini-whiteboards.

Repeat for function diagrams representing equations such as $x - 5 = 11$ ($x = 16$), $2 \times x = 18$ ($x = 9$) and $x \div 3 = 5$ ($x = 15$). In each case, ask for the equation and the value of x. Discuss any misconceptions as a whole class.

Exercise commentary

Question 1 – This should by now offer familiar problems that use inverse operations which students can solve mentally.

Questions 2 to **4** – These are the symbolic equivalent to Question **1**. Students may be able to perform inverse operations mentally, or they may need to write down their working. Question **3** makes explicit the link between the written form of Question **1** and the symbolic form of Question **2**.

Question 5 – Students needs to convert the information given in the diagram into an equation. You could suggest that they use the letter c to stand for the total cost, forming an equation which starts with '$c = \ldots$' Part **b** could be extended by changing the number of rides Mark goes on, or giving the scenario where Mark visits the fair with a friend, and working out the total cost for both people.

Answers

1 **a** 7 **b** 10 **c** 11 **d** 2
e 30

2 **a** $x = 8$ **b** $m = 25$ **c** $d = 24$ **d** $h = 0$
e $p = 8$ **f** $r = 30$ **c** $m = 4$ **d** $y = 27$

3 **a** $x + 17 = 42$ **b** $x = 25$

4 **a** 1 **b** 15 **c** 65 **d** 23
e 12 **f** 8 **g** 30 **h** 21

5 **a** Total cost $= 3 + 2n$ **b** £9

Key outcomes	Quick check
Represent functions as sequences of operations. L4	**1** Find the missing outputs. 3, 5, 7 → $+3$ → $\times 4$ → ?, ?, ? (24) (32) (40) **2** Find the missing operation. 2, 6, 12 → -2 → ? → 0, 2, 5 (÷ 2)
Understand and use inverse operations. L5	Write down the inverse of the given operations. **a** $+4$ (– 4) **b** -7 (+ 7) **c** $\times 4$ (÷ 4) **d** $\div 12$ (× 12)
Use letters to represent unknown numbers. L5	Solve these equations. **a** $w + 7 = 15$ (8) **b** $x \times 4 = 24$ (6) **c** $y - 12 = 7$ (19) **d** $z \div 4 = 16$ (64)
Construct and solve simple equations. L5	For each of these puzzles **i** write an equation for the starting number **ii** find the starting number. **a** I think of a number and add 22. I now have 33. ($x + 22 = 33$, 11) **b** I think of a number and subtract 12. I now have 2. ($x - 12 = 2$, 14) **c** I think of a number and multiply it by 7. I now have 21. ($x \times 7 = 21$, 3) **d** I think of a number and divide it by 3. I now have 3. ($x \div 3 = 3$, 9)

Development and links
Solving equations is a recurrent theme in algebra. In book **2A**, students learn how to solve equations in which the unknown occurs on both sides of the equals sign, two-step equations and how to formulate equations from a scenario. Finding an unknown value is a common problem in many situations and equations provide the natural language. For example you may want to know how much money to change into dollars at a given exchange rate, £1 = \$1.75 in order to have \$350 dollars: the equation is $x \times 1.75 = 350$ with solution x = £200. If there is a fixed £14 commission then the equation becomes more complicated: $(x - 14) \times 1.75 = 350$ with solution x = £214.

My Review

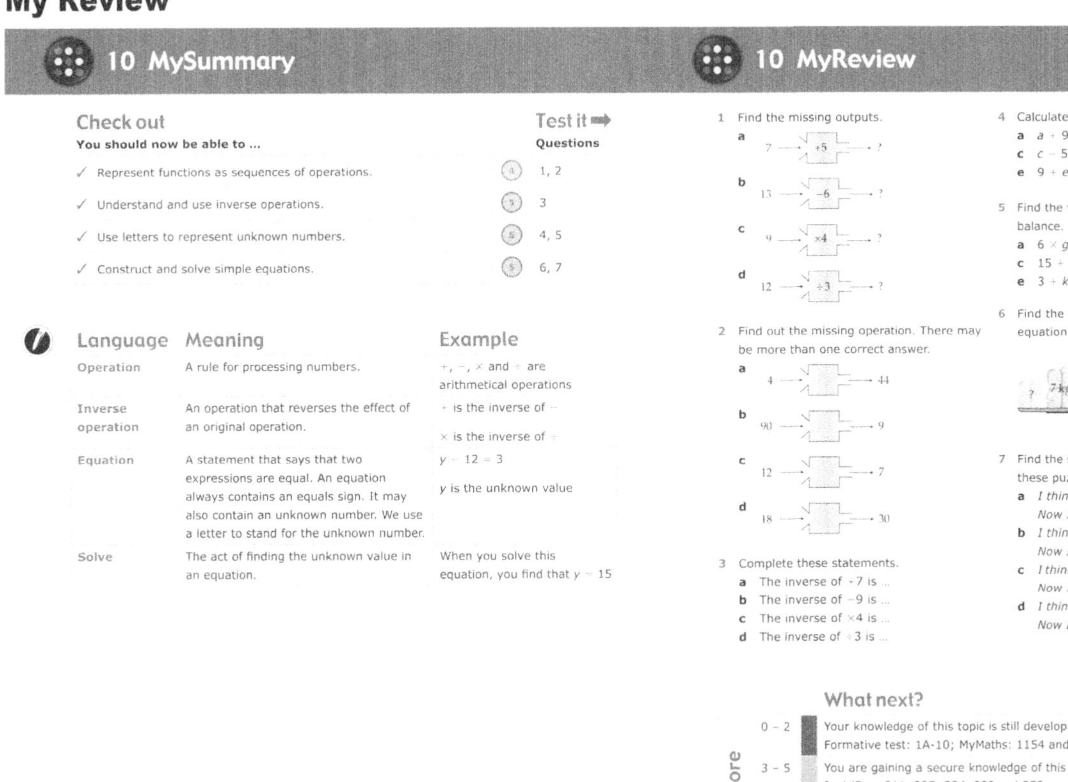

Question commentary

Questions 1 and **2** – (lesson **10a**) For question **2** there is more than one possible answer for each part. Only those for parts **a** and **b** are likely to be given as parts **c** and **d** involve fractional multipliers.

Question 3 – (lesson **10b**)

Question 4 – (lesson **10c**) Students can use inverse operations to answer these, neglecting to use the inverse will give the incorrect answers **a** 24, **b** 34, **c** 4, **d** 4, **e** 34, and **f** 24.

Question 5 – (lesson **10d**) Students could use inverse operations here. Part **e** may confuse some students. In part **f**, students should work out the left hand side of the equation first (8).

Question 6 – (lesson **10d**) Suggest students think about removing 7 kg from both sides, what is left? Or write as an equation: ? + 7 = 12

Question 7 – (lesson **10e**) Students may incorrectly apply the operation instead of the inverse, giving the incorrect answers **a** 20, **b** 15, **c** 99 and **d** 2.

.

Answers

1 **a** 12 **b** 7 **c** 36 **d** 4

2 **a** × 11 or + 40 **b** ÷ 10 or – 81
c – 5 **d** + 12

3 **a** – 7 **b** + 9 **c** ÷ 4 **d** × 3

4 **a** 6 **b** 18 **c** 14 **d** 12
e 16 **f** 50

5 **a** 4 **b** 5 **c** 9 **d** 7
e 0 **f** 11

6 12 kg

7 **a** 6 **b** 35 **c** 11 **d** 32

10 MyPractice

10a

1 Calculate the input in each case.

a ? → +9 → 30
b ? → −11 → 15
c ? → ×7 → 56
d ? → ÷5 → 12

2 Work out the missing operations. There may be more than one answer.

a 3 → ? → 33
b 4 → ? → 7
c 4 → ? → 8
d 4 → ? → 2

3 Find the missing operations.

a 6, 12, 4 → +4 → ? → 5, 8, 4
b 7, 4, 3 → ? → ×3 → 12, 3, 0

10b

4 Use inverse operations to find the missing inputs.

a ? → +5 → 20
b ? → −7 → 11
c ? → ×8 → 40
d ? → ÷9 → 8
e ? → ÷7 → 4
f ? → −17 → 30

10c

5 Work out the value of these letters.

a $4 + a = 10$	**b** $12 = b + 10$	**c** $c + 6 = 15$
d $14 = 7 + d$	**e** $15 + e = 20$	**f** $f - 4 = 2$
g $g - 10 = 10$	**h** $20 = 16 + h$	**i** $9 - i = 9$
j $j - 15 = 5$	**k** $23 + k = 30$	**l** $l - 8 = 12$

10d

6 Write equations using letters for these drawings. Do not give a value for ?.

a

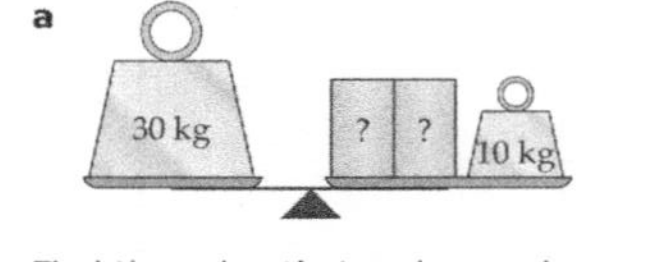

b

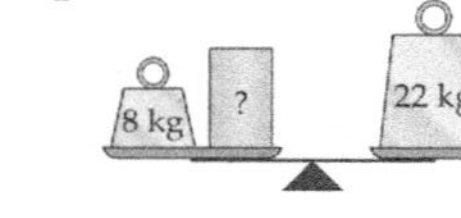

7 Find the value that makes each equation balance.

a $3 + 6 = 4 + a$	**b** $7 + 5 = b + 10$
c $18 + 2 = c + 8$	**d** $20 - 5 = 10 + d$
e $20 - 7 = 1 + e$	**f** $6 \times 2 = 9 + f$
g $15 - 6 = 5 + g$	**h** $30 - 11 = h + 2$

8 Find the value of the letter in each of these equations.

a $t + 6 = 10$	**b** $y + 8 = 12$	**c** $x + 9 = 14$
d $g + 19 = 23$	**e** $m - 4 = 7$	**f** $n - 10 = 6$
g $v + 23 = 25$	**h** $r - 4 = 16$	**i** $g + 5 = 21$
j $q - 14 = 6$	**k** $t + 16 = 20$	**l** $h - 5 = 1$

10e

9 Find the value that makes each equation balance.

a $y - 9 = 15$	**b** $5t = 75$	**c** $60 \div v = 12$
d $n \div 6 = 3$	**e** $p + 11 = 26$	**f** $50 - r = 39$
g $m \div 4 = 12$	**h** $t + 21 = 30$	**i** $6a = 60$

10 Find the value of the letter in each equation.

a $y + 35 = 60$	**b** $t - 39 = 15$	**c** $5 \times m = 90$
d $7 \times p = 224$	**e** $r \div 12 = 8$	**f** $6a = 24$
g $9b = 63$	**h** $c \div 4 = 32$	**i** $p \div 10 = 10$

11 For each puzzle **i** write an equation
ii find the unknown starting number.

a I think of a number and divide it by 6. Now I have 8.
b I think of a number and multiply it by 6. Now I have 36.
c I think of a number and add 19. Now I have 47.
d I think of a number and subtract 23. Now I have 38.
e I think of a number and multiply it by 7. Now I have 49.
f I think of a number and add 22. Now I have 55.
g I think of a number and subtract 15. Now I have 12.
h I think of a number and divide it by 4. Now I have 9.

Question commentary

Questions 1 – Encourage students to write down the equivalent calculation as well as the answer. For example, in part **a**, $\underline{21} + 9 = 31$.

Question 2 – As necessary ask students to work in pairs to find second operations. In part **b**, it is unlikely that students will suggest $\times \frac{7}{4}$.

Question 3 – It may help to organise thinking if the two-step function machine is first reduced to a one-step machine: in part **a**, 10, 16, 8 → ? → 5, 8, 4 and in part **b**, 7, 4, 3 → ? → 4, 1, 0. Knowing multiple inputs and outputs makes it very hard for there to be more than one possible operation.

Question 4 – Students could formalise their thinking by writing down what they are given and how they calculate the answer. for example, in part **a**, given $? + 5 = 20$, answer $? = 20 - 5 = 15$

Question 5 – Students may be unsettled by the order in which the equations are written, for example in part **b**, they should be reassured that $12 = b + 10$ can also be written as $b + 10 = 12$.

Questions 6 – If students do solve the equations they should get **a** 10 kg and **b** 14 kg.

Question 7 – Students should be encouraged to write out their workings as a series of steps on separate lines. Beware of students mis-using the equals sign. For example in part **a**, $3 + 6 = 4 + a$, $9 = 4 + a$ (or $4 + a = 9$), $a = 9 - 4 = 5$.

Question 8 – Take the opportunity to discuss how students can check their answers. In addition to substituting back into the original equation they can use reasoning/common sense. For example, in part **a** ask why 16 must be wrong (something added to 6 to make 10 must be less than 10) or in part **e** why must 3 be wrong (something take away 4 to give 7 must be bigger than 4).

Questions 9 – Continue to emphasise the use of inverse operations + ↔ – and now × ↔ ÷. For example in part **b**, first establish students understand that $5t$ means $5 \times t$, that is, the given equation is $5 \times t = 75$ and so $t = 75 \div 5 = 15$.

Questions 10 – The question's parts involve all four operations. Make minimal interventions so that the question can be used as a test of basic understanding.

Questions 11 – The first few parts could be done collectively as a class with the aim of establishing how to solve the problem and then how to write down the solution more formally. Ask the class to answer part **a** in their heads and discuss how they arrived at their answer. Then try to capture the method in equations: 'let me call the number x, so $x \div 6 = 8$, then you multiply to undo the division so $x = 8 \times 6 = 48$' etc.

Answers

1 **a** 21 **b** 26 **c** 8 **d** 60

2 **a** × 11 or + 27 **b** + 3
c × 2 or + 4 **d** ÷ 2 or – 2

3 **a** ÷ 2 **b** – 3

4 **a** 15 **b** 18 **c** 5 **d** 72
e 28 **f** 47

5 **a** 6 **b** 2 **c** 9 **d** 7
e 5 **f** 6 **g** 20 **h** 4
i 0 **j** 20 **k** 7 **l** 20

6 **a** $2x + 10 = 30$ **b** $x + 8 = 22$

7 **a** 5 **b** 2 **c** 12 **d** 5
e 12 **f** 3 **g** 4 **h** 17

8 **a** 4 **b** 4 **c** 5 **d** 4
e 11 **f** 16 **g** 2 **h** 20
i 16 **j** 20 **k** 4 **l** 6

9 **a** 24 **b** 15 **c** 5 **d** 18
e 15 **f** 11 **g** 48 **h** 9
i 10

10 **a** 25 **b** 54 **c** 18 **d** 32
e 96 **f** 4 **g** 7 **h** 128
i 100

11 **a** **i** $x \div 6 = 8$ **ii** 48
b **i** $x \times 6 = 36$ **ii** 6
c **i** $x + 19 = 47$ **ii** 28
d **i** $x - 23 = 38$ **ii** 61
e **i** $x \times 7 = 49$ **ii** 7
f **i** $x + 22 = 55$ **ii** 33
g **i** $x - 15 = 12$ **ii** 27
h **i** $x \div 4 = 9$ **ii** 36

11 Factors and multiples

Learning outcomes
N3 Use the concepts and vocabulary of prime numbers, factors (or divisors), multiples, common factors, common multiples, highest common factor, lowest common multiple, prime factorisation, including using product notation and the unique factorisation property. (L4)
N7 Use integer powers and associated real roots (square, cube and higher), recognise powers of 2, 3, 4, 5 and distinguish between exact representations of roots and their decimal approximations. (L4)

Introduction

The chapter starts by looking at the basics of factors and multiples before work on divisibility tests. Square numbers are then covered in the final section of the chapter.

The introduction discusses the use of very large numbers to describe computer storage and memory. The use of prefixes such as giga- and mega- allow us to describe very large numbers in terms of smaller units such as 'bytes'. 1 gigabyte, for example, if equal to one billion bytes. Similar ideas are also used for standard units of measurement. The kilometre, for example, is 1000 metres and the the kilotonne is 1000 tonnes.

The use of prime numbers, multiples and factors is far more widespread in the real world than simply defining large and small numbers. The product of large primes plays an important role in modern day encryption methods (coding), particularly since we now transmit enormous amounts of information such as credit card numbers and other sensitive details over the internet. Public Key Encryption uses the product of two extremely large prime numbers to encode data so it can be transferred securely on line.

http://computer.howstuffworks.com/encryption3.htm

Prior knowledge

Students should already know how to…

- Find factors of small numbers
- Find multiples of small numbers
- Work with times tables up to 12

Starter problem

The starter problem is a logical exercise. The rules are fairly simple and students can experiment by trying different combinations. This activity is best done in pairs and students need to have a basic understanding of factors in order to play it.

The optimum strategy would be to take the largest prime number card first (11) so the computer takes only the card with 1 on it. If the player then takes the number 9 card, the computer can only take the 3. The player takes the 10, leaving the computer to take 2 and 5, then takes the 8 leaving the computer to take the 4. This leaves only to 6, the 7 and the 12. If the player takes the 12, the computer takes the 6 and then the 7 (since it is left remaining) and the player wins:

$9 + 10 + 8 + 12 = 39$

$1 + 3 + 2 + 5 + 6 + 7 = 24$

The game could also be played between two players who take a card in turn and their opponent takes the factors of that number before selecting their own card. This might make an interesting variation if students pick up the strategy for the computer version quite quickly.

Resources

MyMaths

Factors and primes	1032	Multiples	1035	Squares and cubes	1053
Odds, evens, multiples	1218				

Online assessment

Chapter test	1A–11
Formative test	1A–11
Summative test	1A–11

InvisiPen solutions

Factors and multiples	171	Square numbers	181

Topic scheme

Teaching time = 4 lessons/2 weeks

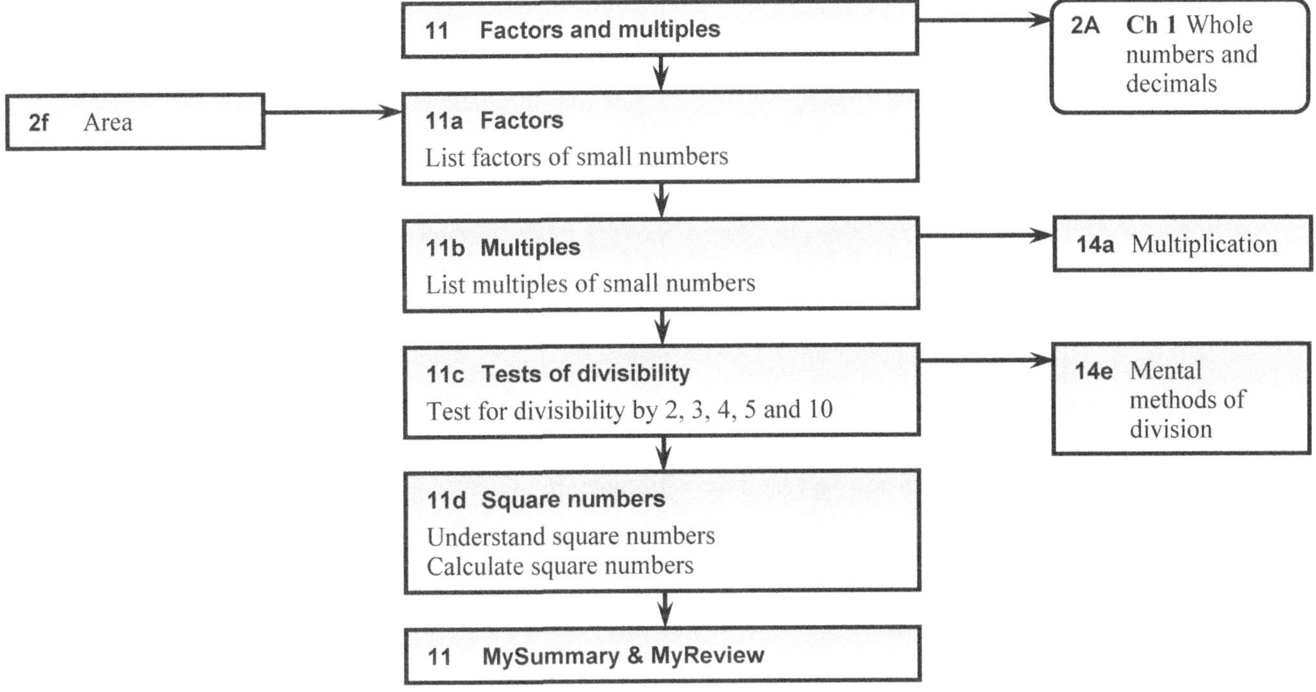

Differentiation

Student book 1A 204 – 217

Factors and multiples
Square numbers
Tests for divisibility

Student book 1B 206 – 221

Find factors and multiples
Understand and calculate square numbers
Understand and calculate square roots
Understand and identify prime numbers
Find lowest common multiples and highest common factors

Student book 1C 200 – 215

Understand and calculate square numbers
Understand and calculate square roots
Find factors and multiples
Understand and identify prime numbers and prime factors
Divisibility tests
Find lowest common multiples and highest common factors

11a Factors

Objectives	
• Recognise and describe number relationships including factor. (L4)	
Key ideas	**Resources**
1 A factor of a number divides into the number exactly. It gives an integer answer which is also a factor. **2** A factor pair of a number is made of two factors which multiply together to give the number.	Factors and primes (1032) 10× 10 multiplication table Counters A calculator
Simplification	**Extension**
Early work making rectangular arrays of counters is useful to find factor pairs. It provides a tactile experience which links with the multiplication table. Encourage students to be systematic by trying to make an array with 1 row, 2 rows, 3 rows etc. Check that every array found with counters can also be found in the multiplication table.	Give pairs of students two numbers, such as 18 and 24. Ask them to find, for each number separately, all the factor pairs and to list all the factors for each number. Then ask them to list all the factors that are common to both numbers and to find the highest factor that is common. Repeat this process with other pairs of numbers.
Literacy	**Links**
The word *factor* has several meanings. For example, in Scotland, a factor is a land agent on a highland estate. The word comes a Latin word meaning 'to make'. In mathematics, factors of a number can make the number by multiplication. Compare the word 'factory' which is a place where things are made.	The word 'factor' is also used to describe the ability of sunscreen to block the harmful rays of the sun. Sun tan lotions are labelled with a 'Sun Protection Factor' or SPF. The higher the SPF, the more protection the lotion gives. The SPF is the number of times longer that the treated skin can be exposed to the sun before it will burn compared with untreated skin.

Alternative approach

An approach using counters to make rectangular arrays provides a practical introduction. A blank multiplication table for numbers up to only (say) 6 can be filled in with the results from each rectangual array which is made. For example, an array of 4 rows of 5 counters leads to two entries of 20 in the multiplication table for 4× 5 and 5×4.

Checkpoint

1 Ask students to look at the 10×10 multiplication table in the student book.
- **a** Which multiplications give 10? (1×10, 10×1, 2×5, 5×2)
- **b** What are the factor pairs? (1 and 10, 2 and 5)
- **c** What are the factors of 10? (1, 2, 5 and 10)

2 Ask students how they can tell, without looking at the multiplication table, that 8 is not a factor of 10. (10 ÷ 8 = 1 r 2, it is not exact)

Starter – Factor circles

Draw two overlapping circles. Ask students to give numbers less than 25. Write the factors of 20 in the left circle, factors of 24 in the right circle, and factors of 20 and 24 in the overlap. Challenge students to explain what rules you are using to place the numbers.

This can be extended using different starting numbers.

Teaching notes

Draw two overlapping circles labelled 12 and 18. Ask students to give you whole numbers less than 18. Write factors of 12 in one circle, factors of 18 in the other, and factors of both, namely, 1, 2, 3 and 6, in the overlap. Students should try to discover the rules you are using. Use the word 'factor' to describe the numbers in the circles.

Provide a 10×10 multiplication table for the whole class to see. Instruct students use it to find products, such as $6 \times 8 = 48$, $4 \times 9 = 36$, and to do divisions, such as $36 \div 4 = 9$, $32 \div 8 = 4$. Develop this activity by asking a series of questions. Which two numbers multiply to give 24? (4 & 6 and 3 & 8 in the table) Is there more than one possible pair of numbers? Is 4×6 the same pair as 6×4? (Yes) Are there any factor pairs for 24 not in the multiplication table? (2 & 12 and 1 & 24) Develop the language of factors and factor pairs.

A good strategy to find all the factors of a number is by listing all the factor pairs. Start with 1 multiplied by the number itself. Then consider 2, then 3, then 4, etc. For example, for the number 28, the factors pairs are

1 × 28,	2 × 14,	3 × no factors,
4 × 7,	5 × no factors,	6 × no factors,
7 × 4,	14 × 2,	28 × 1.

The factor pairs for 28 are (1, 28), (2, 14) and (4, 7). The factors of 28 are thus 1, 2, 4, 7, 14 and 28. Point out that there is always a symmetry in the results using this method.

Plenary

Ask students to write any factor pair for the number 20 on their mini-whiteboards. Ask for another factor pair and then a third pair. Students do not rub off their earlier answers. Now ask for a list of all the factors of 20. Repeat with other numbers.

Exercise commentary

Questions 1 and **2** – Pairs of students can work with counters. Students can then record their rectangular arrays as drawings and using numbers.

Question 3 – Students should look carefully at the 10×10 multiplication table to find factor pairs of the numbers given. Note that not all the pairs will appear in the finite table.

Question 4 – A good strategy for solving this problem would be to find all the factors of the numbers in the green boxes. These can then be matched to the lists of numbers and the 'odd one out' factors identified. To find the mystery number it may help to remind students that 1 and the number itself are always a factor pair and that the number itself will therefore be the largest factor.

Question 5 – The question is solved quickly by counting the squares to find that all the rectangles have equal areas. Extend this to finding three rectangles and a square all with the same area. Area is covered in lesson **2f**.

Questions 6 – This provides an introduction to prime numbers and square numbers.

Answers

1 **a** Students drawings: six rectangular patterns with dimensions given in **b**.
  b 1×12, 2×6, 3×4, 4×3, 6×2, 12×1
  c All products give 12 (1×12 and 12×1 not shown in student book table).
  d 1, 2, 3, 4, 6, 12

2 **a** 1×20, 2×10, 4×5, 5×4, 10×2, 20×1
  b 1, 2, 4, 5, 10, 20
  c All factor pairs are in the multiplication table but 1×20 and 20×1 require a larger table to be shown.

3 **a** 1, 3, 9 **b** 1, 2, 3, 4, 6, 12
  c 1, 3, 5, 15 **d** 1, 2, 4, 8, 16
  e 1, 2, 3, 6, 9, 18 **f** 1, 3, 7, 21
  g 1, 2, 3, 4, 6, 8, 12, 24 **h** 1, 3, 9, 27
  i 1, 5, 25

4 **a** 30 **b** 27 **c** 60 **d** 13
  Non-factors are 28, 7, 14 and 4; the fifth number is 28.

6 They are all the same (18 square units)

7 7 and 13
  Any prime number squared: 4, 9, 25, 49, 121, etc.

Objectives

- Recognise and describe number relationships including multiple. (L4)

Key ideas

1 A multiple of a number is that number multiplied by any whole number.
2 Multiples of a number are the answers in the multiplication table for that number.

Resources

Multiples (1035)

10× 10 multiplication table

Simplification

Students use the 10 × 10 multiplication table in two ways for a given number, say, 8.

First, to find multiples, they locate row 8 and write the answers from row 8, that is, 8, 16, 24, 32, …

Second, to find factors, they search the body of the grid to find all the 8s, write the factor pairs, in this case, 1 × 8, 2 × 4, 4 × 2 and 8 × 1, and, from the pairs, write the list of factors, in this case, 1, 2, 4, 8.

These two activities can be repeated for other numbers up to 10.

Extension

Write a list of the first ten multiples for each of the numbers 4 and 10. From these two lists, write down the multiples that 4 and 10 have in common. Which of these common multiples is the lowest? This introduces the idea of the *lowest common multiple*.

Find the lowest common multiple of 9 and 12. (36)

Find the lowest common multiple of 15 and 18. (90)

Literacy

The prefix *multi-* is used in many words, such as 'multiple'and 'multiply', in mathematics, and also 'multiflora', a stalk with many flowers on it, 'multilingual', speaking many languages, 'multitude', a crowd of many people, 'multimillionaire', a very rich person, 'multiracial', of many races, 'multiplex', a cinema with many screens.

Links

A multiple birth is when two or more babies are born to the same mother at the end of the same pregnancy. In humans, the normal incidence of twins, two babies, is about 1 in 90 pregnancies, but modern fertility treatments increase the chances of multiple births.

Three babies born from the same pregnancy are called triplets, and four babies are called quadruplets.

In 1983, a set of sextuplets, 6 babies, was born to parents Janet and Graham Walton in Liverpool.

Alternative approach

A calculator can generate the multiples of number by repeated additions of the number, because multiplication is a shorthand for repeated additions. For example, 3 + 3 + 3 + 3 + 3 + 3 + 3 is 7 × 3 and adding another 3 gives the multiplication 8 × 3.

Checkpoint

1 Complete these calculations

a **i** 7 + 7 = ? **ii** 2 × 7 = ? (14)

b **i** 7 + 7 + 7 = ? **ii** 3 × 7 = ? (21)

c **i** 7 + 7 + 7 + 7 = ? **ii** 4 × 7 = ? (28)

etc.

2 What calculation could be added at the top of these two columns? (7 = 7 and 1 × 7 = 7)

Understanding can be checked using other multiplication tables.

Starter – Quick fire

Ask students to respond on mini-whiteboards to a series of quick questions which recap previous work on number. For example:

- What is £0.25 + £0.30 + £0.50? (£1.05)
- Which is colder, -3°C or -5°C? (-5°C)
- What is 762 – 435? (327)
- What is $\frac{8}{3}$ as a mixed number? ($2\frac{2}{3}$)

Teaching notes

Ask students to draw a 3 × 3 grid and write nine answers from the 3 times table up to 3 × 12, such as 9, 12, 21, 33, in the grid. Say a number between 1 and 12. Students should multiply it by 3 and cross out their answer if it is written in their grid. Repeat with other numbers up to 12. The winner is the first student to cross out all nine of their numbers.

Ask for the answers to 1 × 3, 2 × 3, 3 × 3, … up to 10 × 3. Write down the answers and ask if any student knows the name for this group of numbers; introduce the word 'multiple'. Ask for the next multiple of 3 after 10 × 3, and the next several multiples. Ask students where they could quickly find all the multiples of 3 up to 30. Refer to a 10 × 10 multiplication square. Ask them which number is the smallest multiple of 3, namely, 3 itself.

Ask students for the first few multiples of 4, then, for the first few multiples of 5, etc. until they are confident. Ask other questions such as, what is the second smallest multiple of 4? (8) What is the third smallest multiple of 6? (18) Initially, students will need sight of a 10 × 10 multiplication square.

Plenary

Some students may confuse factors and multiples. Draw the distinction by asking for the first four multiples of 6 and then asking for all the factors of 6. Students should use their mini-whiteboards to reply. Discuss the results. Remind them that multiples come from multiplication tables and factors come from factor pairs.

Ask students to write the first five multiples of 4 on their whiteboards. Then ask them for all the factors, or factor pairs, for 4. Write both lists for all students to see: 4, 8, 12, 16, 20 and 1 × 4, 2 × 2, giving the factors 1, 2 and 4.

Repeat with numbers such as 10, 12 and 20.

Exercise commentary

Questions 1 and **2** – Students are asked to enter multiples of 5, 3 and 6 on a spider diagram. There should be no or limited access to a 10 × 10 multiplication grid.

Question 3 – Ask students if they can see what all the numbers in their answer to part **c** have in common: they are the multiples of 6 = 2 × 3. This could be repeated with the common multiples of 2 and 5 (multiples of 10) or 3 and 5 (multiples of 15). This is straightforward because 2, 3 and 5 are primes.

Question 4 – At each point on each route, students have a choice of two ways to go. Only one way is correct; students should pay attention to their starting number.

Question 5 – In part **a**, searching the multiplication grid will quickly give students the answer 6. However, students should persevere to find the answers 2 and 3 and, with further thought, the answer 1.

Question 6 – This question give a taste of the divisibility rules which are studied later in this chapter. It might amuse students to realise that they can apply the divisibility test to the sum of the digits. For example in part **c**, 1 + 7 + 4 = 12 and to test 12 for divisibility by 3 you can look at 1 + 2 = 3.

Answers

1 Clockwise from the top: 10, 15, 20, 25, 30, 35, 40, 45

2 **a** 6, 9, 12, 15, 18, 21, 24, 27
b 12, 18, 24, 30, 36, 42, 48, 54

3 **a** 2, 4, 6, 8, 10, 12, 14, 16, 18, 20, 22, 24, 26, 28, 30
b 3, 6, 9, 12, 15, 18, 21, 24, 27, 30
c 6, 12, 18, 24, 30

4 5–15–35–40–25–45–C 3–15–34–21–12–30–A
7–14–35–21–28–49–B 4–16–24–40–28–32–E

5 **a** 1, 2, 3, 6 **b** 30 or other multiple of 6

6 **a** Yes **b** No **c** Yes **d** Yes
e No **f** Yes

11c Tests of divisibility

Objectives	
• Use simple tests of divisibility (L4)	
Key ideas	**Resources**
1 The tests for divisibility by 2, 3, 4, 5 and 10 are straightforward.	Odds, evens, multiples (1218) 100-square showing numbers from 1 to 100 A calculator Materials to make small posters
Simplification	**Extension**
Some students may only be able to cope with divisibility rules for 2, 5 and 10. Make sure that extra practice, especially using smaller numbers, is available for these students. It may be possible to introduce the divisibility rule for 4 but, in this case, much practice with halving will be required.	Students could devise their own divisibility test for 11. Ask them to add the pairs of digits for each of the multiples of 11 as an initial step in their investigation.
Literacy	**Links**
Encourage the correct pronunciation of the word 'divisibility' by saying it slowly and clearly. It is unlikely that students will ever have to spell this word.	A number that can only be divided by one and itself is called a prime number. The largest prime number discovered so far has over seventeen million digits. The first person to find a prime number with more than ten million digits will win a prize of \$100 000. All prime numbers discovered since 1951 have been found using computers. A list of the first thousand prime numbers can be found here. www.primes.utm.edu/lists/small/1000.txt

Alternative approach

On a 100-square, that is, a square lisiting nunbers up to 100 in ten rows of ten, shade all numbers that are divisible by 2. Repeat on other 100-squares for all numbers that are divisible by 10, by 5, by 3 and by 4. Do the multiples form patterns in each case?

Checkpoint

1 For the number 457
- **a** What are the three digits of this number? (4, 5, 7)
- **b** What is the total when you add these three digits together? (4 + 5 + 7 = 16)
- **c** Does 3 divide exactly into your total? (No)
- **d** What does it tell you if 3 doesn't divide exactly into the total? (457 is not divisible by 3)

2 For the number 320
- **a** What are the last two digits of this number? (20)
- **b** Are these two digits divisible by 4? (Yes, 20 ÷ 4 = 5)
- **c** What does this tell you? (320 is divisible by 4: 320 ÷ 4 = 80)

3 Give a number less than 100 that is divisible by 2, 5 and 10. (10, 20, 30, 40, 50, 60, 70, 80 or 90)

Starter – Table time

Since the tests for divisibility by 3 or 4 require knowledge of whether the digits of the number are divisible by 3 or 4 respectively, it is useful to test students' memory of the 3 and 4 times tables. Ask them a series of quick questions, or ask them to recite the multiples of 3 and 4 (up to 12×3 and 12×4).

Teaching notes

Discuss each test in turn as a whole class and practise each test before moving to the next.

Ask how students recognise even numbers. Offer a list such as 24, 86, 125, 206, 679, 1794 and ask, with reasons, which numbers are even and hence divisible by 2. Students can check mentally or use a calculator. Ask students to provide other numbers to test and check.

Ask how students recognise multiples of 10. Offer a list such as 30, 120, 145, 206, 679, 1790 and ask, with reasons, which numbers are divisible by 10. Students can check mentally or use a calculator. Ask students to provide other numbers to test and check. Use the same list to explore and check for divisibility by 5.

To test for divisibility by 3, ask students to add together the individual digits of the number, for example, to test 531, add $5 + 3 + 1 = 9$, and if the total, 9, is divisible by 3, then so is the original number. In this case, 9 and so 531 are both divisible by 3. Ask students to suggest numbers to test and check with a calculator.

Repeat this approach to test and check for divisibility by 4.

Now use each of the five tests in succession on one number, such as 345.
(345 is divisible by 5 and 3 but not by 2, 10 or 4)

Plenary

Give all students a number and ask them to carry out the five tests. Students should write 'yes' or 'no' on their mini-whiteboards for each test. Chosen students are asked to justify one of their answers.

Create a poster for the classroom wall to display these five divisibility rules.

Exercise commentary

Question 1 – This can provide a whole-class discussion. Point out that, if 10 divides into a number, then both 2 and 5 will also divide into it because they are factors of 10.

Questions 2 and **3** – These practise students' skills at applying the two tests which only involve looking at the final digit of the given numbers.

Question 4 – Students need to realise that the question is asking, is there a remainder when 94 is divided by 3. The divisibility test shows that 94 is not a multiple of 3 so there is a remainder. To find the actual remainder you have to do the division, $94 \div 3 = 31$ r 1, so the dog get one biscuit.

Question 5 – Students will need to use various tests or, at times, other methods. Part **f** needs two tests, (or 2 and 3, or a more common-sense method.

Question 8 – The answer depends on whether the shares must be whole pounds or not. If not then £416 = 41600p which is divisible by 5 (£83.20).

Question 9 – The language used here might need explaining to some students. Students can use a two-way table having columns labelled with the four large numbers and rows labelled with the five tests to help them be systematic.

Answers

1 **a** Yes **b** Yes **c** No
d They end in 0

2 31, 109, 15

3 58, 103

4 Yes, $94 = 3 \times 31 + 1$

5 **a** 120, 300 or 360
b 28, 120, 168, 300 or 360
c 28, 120, 168, 300 or 360
d 120, 168, 255, 300 or 360
e 120, 255, 300 or 360
f 120, 168, 300, 360

6 **a** Yes **b** No **c** Yes **d** Yes
e No **f** No **g** Yes **h** No
i No **j** Yes

7 **a** 105, 120 or 135 **b** 160 or 180
c 420, 450, 480

8 **a** No **b** Yes (£104)
c Yes (£83.20)

9 229

11d Square numbers

Objectives

- Recognise and describe number relationships including square. (L4)

Key ideas	Resources
1 A square number is a number multiplied by itself. **2** A square number can be written using the index 2.	Squares and cubes (1053) A large collection of counters Square grid paper Multiplication grids A calculator

Simplification	Extension
Initially, concentrate on the square numbers up to 6^2. Use square grid paper to draw all squares from 1×1 to 6×6. Count the number of small squares inside each large square and so find the first six square numbers. Underneath each large square, write, for example, $4 \times 4 = 4^2 = 16$. Extend to square numbers greater than 6^2. Ask students to learn the first ten square numbers by heart.	List the numbers 10 to 30. Ask students to write each number in the list as a sum of two or more square numbers $10 = 3^2 + 1^2$ $11 = 3^2 + 1^2 + 1^2$ $12 = 2^2 + 2^2 + 2^2$ $13 = 3^2 + 2^2$ etc.

Literacy	Links
The notation 5^2 is spoken is two different ways. It is spoken as 'five squared' or as 'five to the power 2'. The first of these is the more popular, but the second is the only way used for higher powers, other than the power 3. The number 2 is called an *index* or *power*.	A square dance is a type of folk dance in which four couples face each other to form a square. It can be similar to some Scottish dances and is very popular in the USA, although it originated in Europe. There is more information about square dancing and animations of dance moves at www.squaredancecd.com/sdance.htm

Alternative approach

An electronic approach to creating and exploring square numbers can be found in MyMaths lesson 1053, 'Squares and cubes'.

Checkpoint

1 On square grid paper, draw a 7×7 square

a Without counting, how many small squares are inside the large square? (49)

b Fill in the missing values in this calculation: $7 \times 7 = \square^2 = \square$ ($7 \times 7 = 7^2 = 49$)

Starter – Square subtractions

Ask students to subtract the odd numbers 1, 3, 5, … in turn from 16 until they reach 0. Ask how many subtractions were made. Repeat for 25 and 49, and ask students what they notice.
(The number of subtractions is the square root of the number: for example, $16 - 1 = 15$, $15 - 3 = 12$, $12 - 5 = 7$, $7 - 7 = 0$ gives $4 = \sqrt{16}$ subtractions.)

Teaching notes

Get students to work in pairs with a collection of counters. They are to arrange the counters into squares and enter their results into a table with headings 'Size of square' and 'Number of counters'. For example, one entry line will be '3 by 3' and '9'. Agree that the name for the numbers of counters used is 'square numbers'. Agree that the smallest square is a '1 by 1' square, even though the counter might be circular!. The squares can also be generated on square grid paper by shading, in which case a '1 by 1' square is square!

Refer to a 10 × 10 multiplication table, and find all the square numbers on it. Ask what pattern the students notice. Can they find any square numbers *not* in the multiplication table, such as 12 × 12 or 20 × 20?

Introduce the notation for a square number and for higher powers too, so that students appreciate the pattern. That is, for example, $5 \times 5 = 5^2$, $5 \times 5 \times 5 = 5^3$, $5 \times 5 \times 5 \times 5 = 5^4$ and so on. Mention that, in algebra, we can write $x \times x$ in short as x^2.

Plenary

The number 40 can be written as the sum of two square numbers, 36 and 4, because
$6^2 + 2^2 = 36 + 4 = 40$.

Ask students to work in pairs and list all the square numbers up to 100.Then ask them to write each of the numbers 50, 85, 25, 34, 100 as the sum of two square numbers. (1 + 49; 36 + 49; 9 + 16; 9 + 25; 36 + 64)

Exercise commentary

Questions 1 to **3** – The simple activity in Question **1** reinforces the geometrical derivation of square numbers and leads into Questions **2** and **3**.

Question 4 –This is a simple maze that requires students to recognise square numbers by sight.

Question 5 – The total value, in pence, of each square is simply the double of the appropriate square number. The exercise could be repeated with 5p and 10p coins.

Answers

1 A 4 × 4 pattern of crosses labelled 4 × 4 = 16
and a 5 × 5 pattern of crosses labelled 5 × 5 = 25

2 **a** $3^2 = 3 \times 3 = 9$ **b** $1^2 = 1 \times 1 = 1$
c $6^2 = 6 \times 6 = 36$ **d** $4^2 = 4 \times 4 = 16$
e $9^2 = 9 \times 9 = 81$ **f** $2^2 = 2 \times 2 = 4$
g $10^2 = 10 \times 10 = 100$ **h** $8^2 = 8 \times 8 = 64$
i $5^2 = 5 \times 5 = 25$ **j** $7^2 = 7 \times 7 = 49$

3 121, 144, 169, 196, 225, 256, 289, 324, 361, 400, etc.

4 CORRECT

5 **a** 32p **b** £2 **c** 4 × 4

Key outcomes		Quick check
Recognise and list factors and multiples	L4	**1** List all the factors of thses numbers. **a** 14 (1, 2, 7, 14) **b** 24 (1, 2,3, 4, 6, 8, 12, 24) **c** 17 (1, 17) **d** 50 (1, 2, 5, 10, 25, 50) **2** List the first ten multiples of these numbers. **a** 4 (4, 8, 12, 16, 20, 24, 28, 32, 36, 40) **b** 7 (7, 14, 21, 28, 35, 42, 49, 56, 63, 70)
Use simple tests of divisibility	L4	123 250 325 402 555 613 704 856 910 1001 Which of these numbers is excatly divisible by **a** 5 (250, 555, 910) **b** 2 (250, 402, 704, 856, 910) **c** 3 (123, 402, 555) **d** 4 (704, 856)
Recognise the squares of numbers.	L4	Calculate **a** 3^2 (9) **b** 9^2 (81) **c** 8^2 (64) **d** 10^2 (100)

Development and links
Familiarity with factors, multiples and squares, together with the easy recall of multiplication tables will help students with their work on multiplication and division in chapter **14**. Knowing factors can help with (mental) division, for example ÷ 6 is equivalent to ÷ 2 ÷ 3, and simplifying fractions by cancelling down. Knowing multiples can help when adding fractions with different denominators. These skills are developed in book **2A**; where also the triangular numbers are introduced. The difficulty in finding the factors of a number when it becomes very large is behind a number of encryption systems used on the internet to pass secure information such as credit card details.

My Review

11 MySummary

Check out
You should now be able to...

	Test it ➡ Questions
✓ Recognise and list factors and multiples.	1 – 6
✓ Use simple tests of divisibility.	7 – 10
✓ Recognise the squares of numbers up to 10 × 10.	11

Language	Meaning	Example
Factor	A number that divides exactly into another number.	1, 2, 5 and 10 are factors of 10
Factor pair	Two factors of a number which give the number when multiplied together.	1 and 10, and 2 and 5 are the factor pairs of 10.
Multiple	A number *A* is a multiple of another number *B* if *B* divides into *A* exactly. *A* is a multiple of *B* if *A* appears in the times table for *B*.	10, 15, 20 and 25 are all multiples of 5
Square number	A whole number multiplied by itself.	$5^2 = 5 \times 5 = 25$ 25 is a square number
Divisible	If a number *A* divides exactly into another number *B*, then *B* is divisible by *A*.	3 divides exactly into 9 9 is divisible by 3

11 MyReview

1 List all the factors of
 a 4 b 6
 c 20 d 25
 e 26 f 30
 g 36 h 44

2 a List all the factors of 12.
 b List all the factors of 15.
 c Which numbers are factors of both 12 and 15?

3 a List the first 15 multiples of 3.
 b List the first ten multiples of 5.
 c Which of these numbers are multiples of both 3 and 5?

4 Write a list of multiples of 7 up to 70.

5 Which numbers have all these as multiples?
 10, 20, 30, 40, 50

6 Write down all of the multiples of 10 between
 a 101 and 137 b 212 and 262
 c 509 and 545 d 1011 and 1089

7 Which of these numbers can you divide by 2 without leaving a remainder?
 a 87 or 88 b 146 or 147
 c 1001 or 1002 d 1010 or 1011

8 Which of these numbers can you divide exactly by 4?
 a 70 or 72 b 238 or 240
 c 158 or 160 d 442 or 444

9 Which of these numbers are multiples of 3?
 a 86 or 87 b 363 or 364
 c 588 or 589 d 675 or 676

10 a Write down a number between 201 and 280 that is divisible by 3 and 10.
 b Write down a number between 401 and 450 that is divisible by 4 and 5.
 c Write down a number between 301 and 350 that is divisible by 3 and 5.

11 Calculate
 a 5^2 b 7^2
 c 1^2 d 11^2

What next?

Score	
0 – 4	Your knowledge of this topic is still developing. To improve look at Formative test: 1A-11; MyMaths: 1032, 1035, 1053 and 1218
5 – 9	You are gaining a secure knowledge of this topic. To improve look at InvisiPen: 171 and 181
10 – 11	You have mastered this topic. Well done, you are ready to progress!

MyMaths.co.uk

Question commentary

Questions 1 and **2** – (lesson **11a**) Students sometime forget that 1 and the number itself are always factors.

Questions 3 and **4** – (lesson **11b**) Students may forget that the number itself is the first multiple.

Questions 5 – (lesson **11b**) This is equivalent to finding common factors. Students may forget to include 1.

Question 6 – (lesson **11b**) Check that students find all the multiple of ten.

Question 7 – (lesson **11c**) Use a divisibility test: is the number even/does the number end in 0, 2, 4, 6, or 8?

Question 8 – (lesson **11c**) Use a divisibility test: is half the number even?

Question 9 – (lesson **11c**) Use a divisibility test: is the sum of the number's digits a multiple of three?

Question 10 – (lesson **11c**) Students will need to use two divisibility tests. This is equivalent to finding multiples of 30, 20 or 15.

Question 11 – (lesson **11d**) Students sometimes multiply by 2 instead of the number itself. This will give the *incorrect* answers **a** 10, **b** 14 and **d** 22.

Answers

1 **a** 1, 2, 4 **b** 1, 2, 3, 6
 c 1, 2, 4, 5, 10, 20 **d** 1, 5, 25
 e 1, 2, 13, 26 **f** 1, 2, 3, 5, 6, 10, 15, 30
 g 1, 2, 3, 4, 6, 9, 12, 18, 36
 h 1, 2, 4, 11, 22, 44

2 **a** 1, 2, 3, 4, 6, 12 **b** 1, 3, 5, 15
 c 1, 3

3 **a** 3, 6, 9, 12, 15, 18, 21, 24, 27, 30, 33, 36, 39, 42, 45
 b 5, 10, 15, 20, 25, 30, 35, 40, 45, 50
 c 15, 30, 45

4 7, 14, 21, 28, 35, 42, 49, 56, 63, 70

5 1, 2, 5 and 10

6 **a** 110, 120, 130
 b 220, 230, 240, 250, 260
 c 510, 520, 530, 540
 d 1020, 1030, 1040, 1050, 1060, 1070, 1080

7 **a** 88 **b** 146 **c** 1002 **d** 1010

8 **a** 72 **b** 240 **c** 160 **d** 444

9 **a** 87 **b** 363 **c** 588 **d** 675

10 **a** 240 or 270 **b** 420 or 440
 c 315, 330 or 345

11 **a** 25 **b** 49 **c** 1 **d** 121

11 MyPractice

11a

1 **a** Arrange 6 counters in equal rows in as many ways as you can.
b For each diagram, write down a multiplication.
c Write down all the factors of 6.
Check your answers in the multiplication table.

2 Find all the factors of the number 8. Use counters to help you.
Check yours answers in the multiplication table.

3 List as many factors as you can for these numbers:
a 8 **b** 10 **c** 20 **d** 22 **e** 28 **f** 30 **g** 36 **h** 50

11b

4 **a** The numbers that belong in the circles are multiples of 4.
Copy the diagram. Start at the top and work clockwise to fill in the circles.

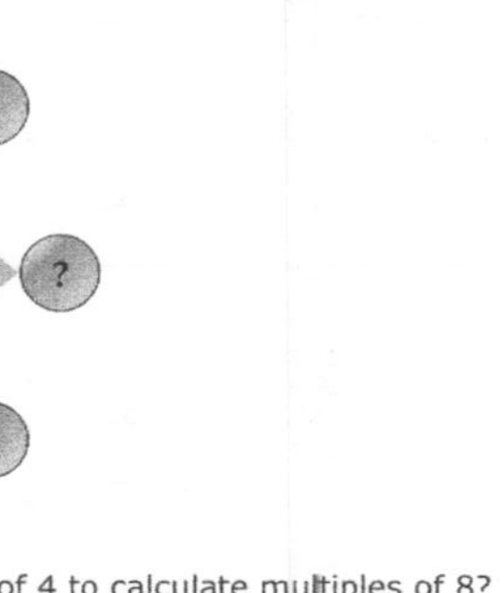

b How could you use multiples of 4 to calculate multiples of 8?

5 **a** Write a list of the multiples of 3 up to 30.
b Write a list of the multiples of 5 up to 30.
c Which of these numbers are multiples of both 3 and 5?

6 **a** Which numbers have all the numbers in the ring as multiples?
b What is the next number that would go into the ring?

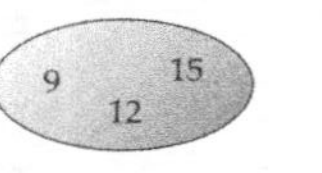

7 24 is a multiple with eight factors. Find as many of these factors as you can.

8 Which numbers are factors of all the numbers in the ring?

9 15 12

11c

9 Copy and complete the table. Write *yes* or *no* in all the spaces on your copy.

Number	Divisible by 2?	Divisible by 3?	Divisible by 4?	Divisible by 5?	Divisible by 10?
154					
315					
364					
990					
1008					

11d

10 Square numbers can be arranged into a square pattern. Which of these groups of tiles can be arranged in a square pattern? Answer **Yes** or **No**.

a **b** **c**
d **e** **f**
g **h**

The number of tiles in a row will be the same as the number of tiles in a column.

11 Use a multiplication table to write as many square numbers as you can.

12 Which of these calculations have a square number as their answer?
Answer 'Square' or 'Not square'.

a 7×7 **b** 9×8 **c** 12×12
d 6×4 **e** 20×3 **f** 3×3
g 11×10 **h** 15×10 **i** 6×6

13 Find as many factors as you can for each of these numbers.
Use a multiplication table to help you.

a 2 **b** 4 **c** 10 **d** 16
e 30 **f** 24 **g** 35 **h** 40

Question commentary

Questions 1 and **2** – Take a little time over these questions to make sure that students make the connection between the length and width of a rectangle, a factor pair and an entry in the multiplication table. The student book has a suitable multiplication table on page 206.

Question 3 – Students need to be systematic in finding factor pairs. Since the answer to part **a** has already been found, with the help of counters, use it to check that students can work more abstractly. Students should start by testing 1 (which will always be a factor), then 2, then 3, etc. Since one factor gets larger and the other smaller there is a natural point, the square root of the number, at which students can stop testing; ask them to explain where this point is.

Question 4 – Beware of students assuming that the entries are in the 'natural' multiplication table order.

Question 5 – Ask students to try to find more numbers which are multiples of both 3 and 5. Can they find a pattern to these numbers: they are multiples of 15.

Questions 6 – For part **a** students may miss 1 and 2.

Question 7 – Once students have found the factors, it may be helpful to ask them to write out their multiples as far as say 30. They should find that 24 is the smallest number that appears in all 8 lists (48 is the next smallest).

Question 8 – Encourage students to make a list of all the factors of 9, 12 and 15 and then look for numbers which appear in all three lists.

Questions 9 – There are quite a few parts to this question so it may help to do (part of) it as a whole class or organise students into small groups or pairs. Encourage students to explain their reasoning.

Questions 10 and **11** – Ideally students should memorize the square numbers: can they do these questions in their heads? Afterwards they can check their answers by arranging the tiles and looking on the leading diagonal of a multiplication table. Students may need reassuring that $1 = 1^2$ is a square number.

Questions 12 – There are no 'trick' questions, such as $4 \times 9 = 36 = 6^2$, here. The aim is to strength the understanding that $n^2 = n \times n$, which corresponds to a rectangle with the same length and width.

Questions 13 – Students should realise that the multiplication tables they have available will only contain entries where the two factors are about the same size. For example they won't show $1 \times 40 = 40$ or $2 \times 20 = 40$ so they will need to use a mixed strategy.

Answers

1 **a** Students drawings: four rectangular patterns with dimensions given in **b**.
b $1 \times 6,\ 2 \times 3,\ 3 \times 2,\ 6 \times 1$
c 1, 2, 3, 6

2 1, 2, 4, 8

3 **a** 1, 2, 4, 8 **b** 1, 2, 5, 10
c 1, 2, 4, 5, 10, 20 **d** 1, 2, 11, 22
e 1, 2, 4, 7, 14, 28 **f** 1, 2, 3, 5, 6, 10, 15, 30
g 1, 2, 3, 4, 6, 9, 12, 18, 36
h 1, 2, 5, 10, 25, 50

4 **a** Clockwise from the top: 20, 40, 12, 24, 36, 48, 28
b Double the multiples of four: $\times 8 = \times 4 \times 2$

5 **a** 3, 6, 9, 12, 15, 18, 21, 24, 27, 30
b 5, 10, 15, 20, 25, 30
c 15, 30

6 **a** 1, 2, 4
b 24 or other multiple of 4.

7 1, 2, 3, 4, 6, 8, 12, 24

8 1, 3

9

No	÷ 2	÷ 3	÷ 4	÷ 5	÷ 10
154	Yes	No	No	No	No
315	No	Yes	No	Yes	No
364	Yes	No	Yes	No	No
990	Yes	Yes	No	Yes	Yes
1008	Yes	Yes	Yes	No	No

10 **a** Yes (2^2) **b** No **c** No **d** No
e Yes (3^2) **f** Yes (4^2) **g** Yes (1^2) **h** No

11 1, 4, 9, 16, 25, 36, 49, 64, 81, 100, 121, 144, 169, 196, 225, 256, 289, 324, 361, 400, etc.

12 **a** Square (49) **b** Not square
c Square (144) **d** Not square
e Not square **f** Square (9)
g Not square **h** Not square
i Square (36)

13 **a** 1, 2 **b** 1, 2, 4
c 1, 2, 5, 10 **d** 1, 2, 4, 8, 16
e 1, 2, 3, 5, 6, 10, 15, 30 **f** 1, 2, 3, 4, 6, 8, 12, 24
g 1, 5, 7, 35 **h** 1, 2, 4, 5, 8, 10, 20, 40

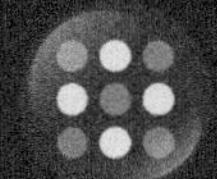

12 Constructions and 3D shapes

Learning outcomes	
G3 Draw and measure line segments and angles in geometric figures, including interpreting scale drawings.	(L5)
G15 Use the properties of faces, surfaces, edges and vertices of cubes, cuboids, prisms, cylinders, pyramids, cones and spheres to solve problems in 3D.	(L3/4)

Introduction

The chapter starts by looking describing 3D shapes. This work includes naming and describing different solid shapes. Nets of cubes and other 3D shapes are then covered before a section on the representation of 3D shapes using 2D drawings. Measuring and drawing angles is then covered before this is used to draw triangles accurately. Circles are introduced in the final spread.

The introduction discusses how a football is constructed from a 2D plan, or net. The basic design of a standard football is one where there are pentagonal faces, each surrounded by hexagons. The overall design uses 20 hexagons and 12 pentagons. The geometrical name for the shape is a truncated icosahedron, or Buckyball. This was so named after the inventor and futurist Richard Buckminster Fuller since it resembles the structure of his famous geodesic domes. A new carbon atom in the same shape was discovered in 1985 and named Buckminsterfullerine for the same reason. For a brief biography of Buckminster Fuller and a link to the institute named after him, visit

http://www.bfi.org/about-bucky

Prior knowledge

Students should already know how to…

- Measure straight lines using a ruler
- Identify simple geometric shapes

Starter problem

The starter problem is an opportunity for the students to be creative and design a model house using combinations of 3D shapes. They could be instructed to sketch out the design and write down the types of 3D shape that they would need.

As a more basic task, this could be discussed as a class as to what 3D shapes would be needed, for example a cuboid for the main body of the house and a triangular prism for the roof.

If the task is taken much further, it might be necessary to cover the lessons on nets (**12b** and **12c**) or provide students with prepared nets to cut out and construct.

Resources

MyMaths

3D shapes	1078	Measuring angles	1081	Constructing triangles	1090
Plans elevations	1098	Nets of 3D shapes	1106		

Online assessment

Chapter test	1A–12
Formative test	1A–12
Summative test	1A–12

InvisiPen solutions

Properties of 3D shapes	321	Nets of 3D shapes	325
2D representations	326	Constructing triangles	371

Topic scheme

Teaching time = 7 lessons/3 weeks

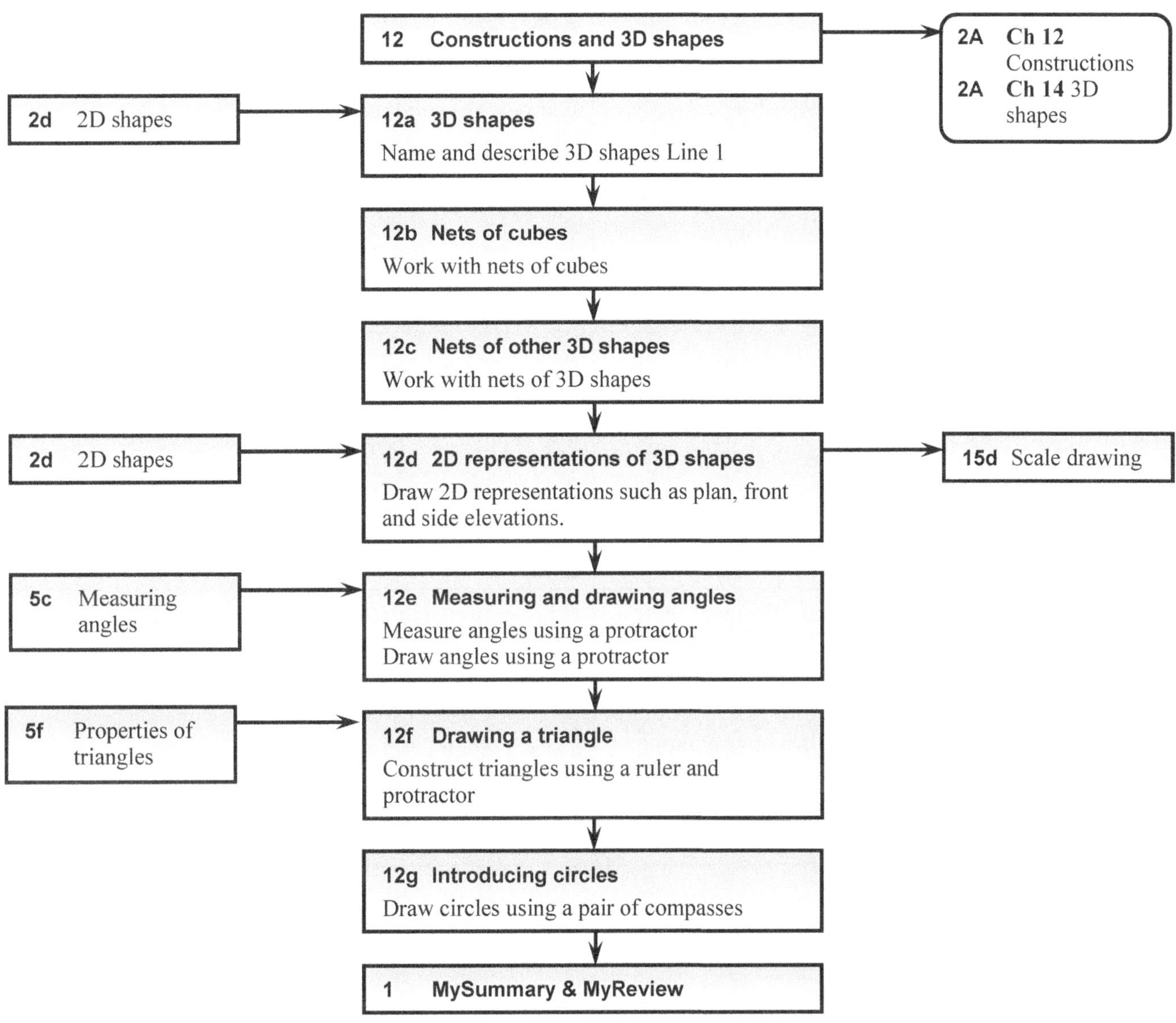

Differentiation

Student book 1A 218 – 237

3D shapes
Nets of cubes and other 3D shapes
2D representations of 3D shapes
Measuring and drawing angles
Drawing triangles
Introducing circles

Student book 1B 222 – 241

Constructing triangles
Scale drawings
Properties of 3D shapes
Isometric drawings
Nets
Volume of a cuboid

Student book 1C 216 – 235

Constructing bisectors
Constructing triangles
Simple loci
Scale drawings
2D representations of 3D shapes
Plans and elevations
Nets

12a 3D shapes

Objectives	
• Classify 3D shapes in various ways using mathematical properties. (L3)	
Key ideas	**Resources**
1 3D shapes can be solid or hollow. **2** 3D shapes have faces, edges and corners.	3D Shapes (1078) Examples of solid or hollow 3D shapes Cards giving names of 3D shapes and cards giving descriptions of the same 3D shapes Pictures of 3D shapes Triangles and quadrilaterals cut from card Isometric paper
Simplification	**Extension**
Students can discuss solid or hollow 3D shapes which are everyday objects, such as tins and boxes from a kitchen, and asked to give them mathematical names. Only after experience with actual 3D shapes should pupils be asked questions based on pictures of 3D shapes.	As an extension, students can develop the plenary activity by drawing the 3D shapes described by their partner on isometric paper. They can then use isometric paper to draw their own 3D shapes of varying complexity.
Literacy	**Links**
In addition to the common names of 3D shapes, note that there are *rectangular-based pyramids* and *hemispheres* where *hemi-*, like *semi-*, means 'half'. Make the distinction between *edge*, for 3D, and *side*, for 2D. Another word for 'corner' is 'vertex', plural 'vertices', which students may sometimes encounter. When ask to draw a shape, the word 'sketch' means that the drawing need not be accurately done.	Bring in some table salt and a magnifying glass and allow the class to view the crystals. A crystal is a solid substance in which the atoms are arranged in regular geometric patterns. Salt crystals are cube-shaped. Use a search engine to find images of 'mineral crystal shapes'.

Alternative approach

Discuss more real-life examples of 3D shapes, looking on a larger scale than groceries and kitchen items. Thinking of local buildings or landmarks they might have seen on holiday or on TV, can students suggest examples for each of the 3D shapes given in the student book? Is there an interesting fact they can associate with each example?

Start with the following

- Outside the Louvre Museum in Paris, there is a large square-based glass pyramid, which was built in 1989. It contains over 600 panes of glass.
- The Earth, and other planets, is in the shape of a sphere. In ancient times, it was thought that the Earth was flat.
- Nelson's Column is a monument in Trafalgar Square in London. It is shaped like a cylinder. There is also a cube at the base of the cylinder, and a statue of Lord Nelson at the top.

In each case, reiterate the features of the 3D shape, using the words 'faces', 'edges' and 'corners', asking students to describe the shapes accordingly.

Checkpoint

1 How many faces does a cuboid have? (6)

2 A shape has four triangular faces and a square base. What is it called? (Square-based pyramid)

3 Sketch a cone.

Starter – What is my shape?

Prepare large cut-out shapes of different triangles and quadrilaterals. Slide each shape out from behind a large piece of card to reveal a small part. Ask students what the shape could be. Ask if there could more than one possibility. Continue revealing the shape as necessary. Encourage students to use the correct terminology.

Teaching notes

Invite students to contribute the names of any 3D shapes, solid or hollow, that they know. Have some examples to show. Introduce the terms 'face', 'edge' and 'corner'. Ask if they know any 3D shapes with curved faces and any with curved edges. Ask if it possible for a 3D shape to have no edges. Is it possible to have no corners? Ask if the word 'side' has any meaning for a 3D shape and agree that it is best only used for 2D shapes. Name the faces of some of the 3D shapes; for example, a cube has square faces.

As a first step towards understanding plan views, ask what various 3D shapes look like when placed on a horizontal surface and viewed from above.

Provide two sets of cards to pairs of students: one set with the name of a 3D shape on each card; another set with a description of a 3D shape on each card. The pairs should work together to match the cards from the two sets.

Note that pyramids do not always have square bases, prisms do not always have an equilateral triangle as a cross-section, and that pyramids and cones need not always have axes at right-angles to their bases.

When drawing 3D shapes, agree that edges that can be seen will be drawn with solid lines, but edges which are not seen, being 'behind' the shape, are drawn with dashed lines.

Plenary

Sit students in pairs back to back. Each one of the pairs takes a turn to describe a 3D shape that they have been given on a card as a picture. The task is to describe the shape so that their partner can sketch it accurately and name it. A student must not use the name of the shape in their descriptions, but they can use terms such as 'face', 'edge' and 'corner' to describe their shape.

Exercise commentary

Question 1 – Students need to know the names of common 3D shapes and should follow the example of part **a**. Students could also try recreating the models shown.

Question 2 – This question is more challenging, and it would be helpful to have 3D shapes to hand for students to look at. This question is a taster for lesson **12d** later in this chapter.

Question 3 – If students find it difficult to visualise the shapes described, they could refer back to the diagrams of shapes given in the student book, counting the number of faces in turn and checking the shape against the descriptions in parts **a** and **b**.

Answers

1 **a** Cone, cylinder, prism, cuboid
b Cuboid, cube, pyramid
c Cuboid, prism
d Cube, cuboid, cylinder
e 2 cuboids, prism
f 2 cuboids
g 2 cuboids, pyramid
h Cube, cuboid, prism
i 2 cuboids
j 2 cuboids, pyramid

2 **a** 8 **b** 10 **c** 2 **d** 9
e 3 **f** 1 **g** 6 **h** 7
i 5 **j** 4

3 **a** Square-based pyramid or triangular prism
b Cone or half a sphere (hemisphere)

12b Nets of cubes

Objectives

- Begin to recognize nets of familiar 3D shapes, eg cube (L3)
- Make 3D models by linking given faces or edges. (L4)

Key ideas	Resources
1 A net of a cube is the flat 2D shape which, when folded, makes a hollow cube. **2** A cube has several different nets.	Nets of 3D Shapes (1106) A selection of empty boxes Pre-cut nets of cubes and cuboids Square grid paper and card Scissors and sticky-tape or glue

Simplification	Extension
Give initial priority to students disassembling packaging and then folding nets already cut out for them. Leave designing nets until later.	Hand students an object from the classroom with an irregular shape and ask them to design a cuboid (or box) to package it so that it just fits inside the box. A *hexomino* is the 2D shape made by six equal squares placed edge to edge. As an investigation, students could be asked to find the eleven different hexominoes which are nets of a cube.

Literacy	Links
The word *net* is taken from fishing where a net is laid out flat on land and then closes up when catching fish. The *hex*- in 'hexomino' is from a Greek word meaning 'six'. Compare the name of the 2D shape 'hexagon'.	Rubik's cube is a puzzle in the shape of a cube with each side divided into nine squares of different colours. It was invented by Erno Rubik in 1974. The puzzle is solved by turning the sides until each face of the cube is a solid colour. There are 43 252 003 274 489 856 000 possible positions for the coloured squares! There is an online Rubik's cube puzzle here. www.agame.com/game/rubix-cube

Alternative approach

There is no real alternative to disassembling packaging and assembling pre-cut nets. However, there are commercial construction kits of plastic pieces that clip together easily to make 3D shapes.

Checkpoint

1 Identify the edge which will join withthe marked edge when the net is folded to make a cube.

a

b

Do not show students a version with the arrows identifying the answer.

Can be avried by using different nets of a cube.

Starter – Quick fire

Ask students to respond on mini-whiteboards to a series of quick questions which recap previous work on geometry.

For example

- What is 230 mm in cm? (23cm)
- How many minutes are there in an hour? (60)
- How many sides does a hexagon have? (6)
- How many degrees are there in a right angle? (90°)

Discuss answers were there is a need.

Teaching notes

Give students cube-shaped packaging from everyday items. The students should disassemble them, unfold them and lay them flat. In this position they are called 'nets'. Investigate how nets of cubes are constructed and establish the difference between a cube and a cuboid. Mention that tabs are used to glue a net together, but that tabs are not strictly part of the net.

Give students square grid paper to design, draw and make nets of cubes of different sizes. Provide some 'nets' that do not 'work' and let students discover why not. They will need scissors and sticky-tape or glue.

Before folding a net into a cube, ask students to practise imagining the cube being made. They should then use different colours to mark pairs of sides that come together to make the same edge. Lastly, they can check the colouring by folding the net to make the cube.

Plenary

Present students as a whole class with a variety of labelled nets. Ask whether each net will make a cube, a cuboid or neither. Students should answer using their mini-whiteboards. Their answers are checked and discussed by folding each net.

Exercise commentary

This topic gives much scope for practical work which develops manipulative and visual skills. Class projects and paired work could both be features. This is time well spent.

Question 1 – For some students, being able to visualise what happens when a net is folded only comes with plenty of practice. Students should either draw these nets and cut them out, or use nets already prepared by the teacher. Construction kits could also be used.

Question 2 – Square grid paper is needed with squares that are at least 1cm^2 in size.

Question 3 – Dots drawn in pencil are easier to alter. Check answers with all three pairs of opposite faces. Ask students if there is just one way of solving this problem. In fact, different possibilities do exist.

Creating nets can be developed further by designing commercial packaging, such as a cereal box, so that the faces of the finished product are in the correct positions.

Answers

1 c and g
2 Practical work
3 Check students' work to ensure opposite faces add to 7.
There are 11 possible nets for a cube.

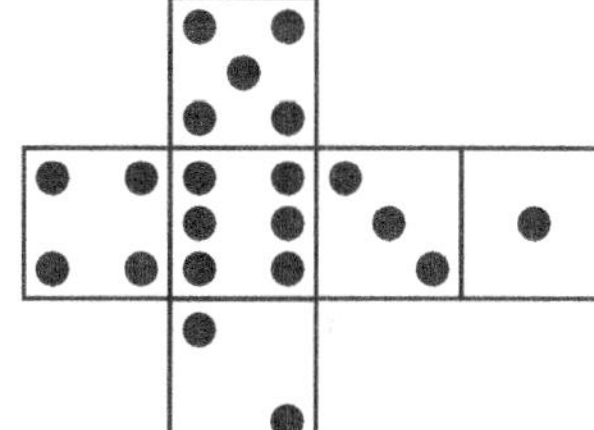

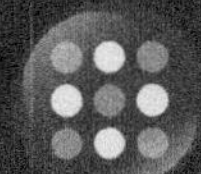

12c Nets of other 3D shapes

Objectives	
• Begin to recognize nets of familiar 3D shapes, eg cube, cuboid, triangular prism, square-based pyramid. (L3)	
Key ideas	**Resources**
1 3D shapes have many names and different properties. **2** 2D nets can be used to make three-dimensional shapes.	Nets of 3D shapes (1106) Various types of packaging to disassemble Square grid paper and pre-cut nets Scissors and sticky-tape or glue Commercial construction kits Dictionaries
Simplification	**Extension**
Students can investigate 3D shapes by using • nets already made for them; • commercial construction kits which click together; • transparent 3D shapes which allow students to see the back from the front; • commercial cartons and packaging which they can disassemble. Introduce all the relevant names of 3D shapes as appropriate and identify and count faces, edges and vertices.	Students can use square grid paper to draw the net of a specified 3D shape with given measurements. Give students several circles of the same size and ask them to cut sectors with different angles at the centre. They can then make hollow cones and measure their heights. Ask students to note how the angle affects the height and to tabulate their results. What is the best angle for making an ice-cream cone?
Literacy	**Links**
The names of shapes introduced in this chapter include 'prism', 'cylinder', 'cone', 'tetrahedron', meaning 'four-faces', and 'pentonimo' where *pent-* means 'five'.	Provide some dictionaries for students to use. See how dictionaries define the names of 3D shapes. Look for the etymologies of the names. Next, ask students to look up the word 'net', which has many meanings and can be used as a noun and a verb. Ask students to list all of the meanings they can find. In which school subject would each of the meanings be most used?

Alternative approach

Consult the book *Mathematical Models* by Cundy and Rollett (Tarquin Publications, 1981) to get ideas for making more complicated nets and 3D shapes. Look for the complicated names that some shapes have, such as rhombicosidodecahedron. Search online for a picture of this shape and make it rotate.

Alternatively, search online for 'Nets Cundy Rollett' and click on 'Images' to find other pictures of complex shapes.

Checkpoint

1 Refer to Question **1** and cover up the green shapes (labelled **a** – **f**).
What 3D shapes are made by each of the nets shown in yellow (labelled **1** – **6**)?
(Cylinder, Square-based pyramid, Cone, Cuboid, Triangular-based pyramid, Cube)

2 **a** How many vertices does a cuboid have? (8)
b How many faces does a triangular-based pyramid have? (4)
c How many edges does a triangular prism have? (9)

Starter – Pentominoes and boxes

A *pentomino* is a 2D shape made by placing five equal squares so that they touch edge to edge. Ask each student to draw a pentomino on their mini-whiteboard which would fold to make an open-topped cube. How many different pentominoes are there that do this? (There are 12 pentominos, eight of which fold to make an open cube.)

Teaching notes

Prepare several pre-cut nets for the class, which students can make into 3D shapes. They will need scissors and sticky-tape or glue. Ask students to name each shape and to describe its properties. How many faces, edges and vertices does each shape have?

In particular, note that pyramids do not all have square bases: their bases can, for example, be rectangular, triangular, hexagonal, or circular. What special names are given to circular-based pyramids (cones) and triangular-based pyramids (tetrahedrons)? Also, prisms can have cross-sections of different shapes. What special name is given to a prism with a circular cross-section (cylinder) and a rectangular cross-section (cuboid)?

Ask students what 2D shape is made when a cylindrical tube is slit along its length and flattened (rectangle). Ask what other 2D shapes are needed to make a closed cylindrical tube or cylinder (2 circles).

Repeat for a hollow cone with no base which, when slit open and flattened, gives a sector of a circle. Ask what else is needed to make a closed or solid cone (a circle for the base). Show how cones change in size as the angle of the sector from which they are made is reduced.

Make the distinction between pyramids and prisms. Discuss their cross-sections and discover that a pyramid has a cross-section which narrows gradually to a point, whereas a prism has the same cross-section throughout its length.

Discuss if it is possible to make a net for a sphere. (It is not.)

Plenary

Present the class with a 3D shape. Ask students to use their mini-whiteboards to give its name and the numbers of faces, edges and vertices it has. Repeat with other 3D shapes. Next, present the class with nets of 3D shapes and ask students to name the shapes.

Finally, describe a 3D shape without showing or naming it. Ask students to write its name on their mini-whiteboards.

Exercise commentary

This topic is one of the most practical that students meet in KS3. Make the most of it by exploring, making and discussing a variety of shapes and nets using different resources. This exercise is then a resumé of previous practical work.

Question 1 – This question introduces several new nets. It can be done collectively and the reasoning behind the choices of answer discussed.

Question 2 – Students need sheets of square grid paper, with squares of length 1 cm or more, on which to draw their net full size. Some students may need to experiment with loose squares of card or squares from a commercial construction kit. Compare different solutions as a class.

Question 3 – The information should be found from the drawings rather than the 3D shapes themselves. Discuss 'hidden' edges which are not always drawn or sometimes drawn as dashed lines. Ask which method the students prefer and why.

Extend the task to other 3D shapes without providing any drawings. Students have to visualise the shapes. Answers can be given on mini-whiteboards.

Answers

1 **a** 3 **b** 2 **c** 4 **d** 1
e 6 **f** 5

2 There are 11 possible solutions, but every face in the net must be 3 × 3 squares in size.

3 **a** Faces = 6, Edges = 12, Vertices = 8
b Faces = 5, Edges = 9, Vertices = 6
c Faces = 5, Edges = 8, Vertices = 5

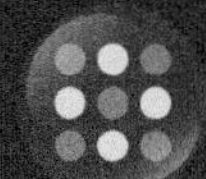

12d 2D representations of 3D shapes

Objectives	
• Use 2D representations to visualize 3D shapes.	(L4)

Key ideas	Resources
1 3D objects can be represented as 2D shapes. **2** The top view and the side view are two common 2D representations of 3D objects.	Plans elevations (1098) Various construction materials and kits, including multi-link cubes Everyday objects of various shapes Bag or cloth to cover items

Simplification	Extension
As described in lesson **12c**, students can construct and investigate 3D shapes using a variety of means. Rather than rotating a 3D shape to get a bird's-eye view by looking horizontally at it, you can place the object on the floor and look directly down on it.	Students can build 3D shapes using multi-link cubes and draw the views from the top and from the side. Working in pairs, one student could provide the top and side view of a shape for their partner who builds it using multi-link cubes. In pairs, students could use a 'feely-bag' to hide items from view. One student describes the 3D shape without naming it or seeing it. Their partner has to give the name of the shape.

Literacy	Links
Students need to be very precise in their oral descriptions of what they see, as they have to reject what they know about the three-dimensionality of the shape and just describe it using the language of 2D.	The largest square-based pyramid in Egypt is the Great Pyramid of Giza which was built for the Pharaoh Cheops over 4000 years ago. It was the tallest building in the world until Lincoln cathedral in England was built around AD 1300. The Pyramids of Giza can be viewed at www.mylivestreams.com/webcam/pyramids-of-giza-live-hd-webcam-cairo-egypt/10728.html

Alternative approach

Rather than simply pointing a 3D shape directly at students, use a piece of cloth to hide all of the shape except for what can be seen from the top or from the side. Ask the students to describe what they now see using their vocabulary of 2D shapes, such as 'rectangle', 'square', 'circle' etc.

Discuss how the language of 3D can become the language of 2D. For example, the word 'vertex' becomes the word 'point' and a 'rectangular face' becomes just a 'rectangle'. The use of a cloth as described above is particularly useful in helping to choose appropriate language.

Checkpoint

1 Show students a cube or a diagram of a cube.

a What shape is the side view? (Square)

b What shape is the top view? (Square)

Repeat for other shapes such as a cuboid and a square-based pyramid.

Starter – Name the 3D shape

Ask students to identify solids from the following clues.

- I have 6 square faces and 8 vertices. (a cube)
- I have no edges and no vertices. (a sphere)
- I have one edge and one vertex. (a cone)
- I have just one face. (a sphere)
- I have four faces and four vertices. (tetrahedron)

Students should display their answers on mini-whiteboards.

Teaching notes

The overall aim of the lesson is to have students readily describe the plan view and the side elevation of various 3D shapes. It is not intended to adopt the formal language of 'elevations' and 'plan views'.

A whole-class approach can be used initially. Ask what students understand by the words 'a bird's-eye view' of something. Can they describe the bird's-eye view of their home, the school or some other place or building?

Now show students, for example, a square-based pyramid and point it, base first, directly towards them. Ask them to describe and then draw what they see on their mini-whiteboards (that is, a square). Repeat with the pyramid pointing, top first, towards them. They should now draw the same square but with its two diagonals. Discuss what the diagonals represent and where the vertex of the pyramid is. Now repeat with two sideways views in turn: one face-on to the students and the other edge-on. They should firstly draw just a triangle and then draw a triangle with a line down its middle, to represent the edge of the pyramid.

Repeat with other 3D shapes. Include shapes with curved faces. Reassure students that they can ignore the curvature when viewing the cylinder and cone. Discuss the results which they draw on their mini-whiteboards.

Finally, ask students to imagine shapes 'in reverse'. Show them pairs of drawings of a top and a side view, and see if they can name the 3D shape.

Plenary

Show some commercially-produced 3D objects, such as boxes and tins. Ask students to draw the two views from the top and from the side. They need not draw the designs that they see on the labelling!

Exercise commentary

As with the previous exercise, this exercise too should be a resumé of much handling and discussion of a variety of 3D shapes.

Question 1 – This question is straightforward and students' answers can be appropriately coloured.

Questions 2 and **3** – These are more demanding. The slope of the pyramid can cause confusion, especially when viewed from the side. A cloth covering all but the required view is useful. Ask students about what they see using the language of 2D shapes.

Question 4 – Ask students to explain the reasoning behind their choices. They should easily be able to discount shape A as a possibility, and then notice that shape B is narrower than shape A, which matches the top and side views.

Question 5 – There is potential confusion about the views from the front, back and different sides. However, for these shapes, it is only in part **c** that the distinction is evident. In fact, students are asked for the side view, so it does not matter that the front view and back view are different.

Answers

1 a **b**

2 a **b**

3 a

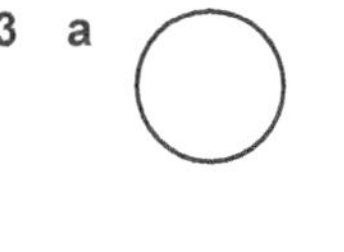

b

3 B

4 a

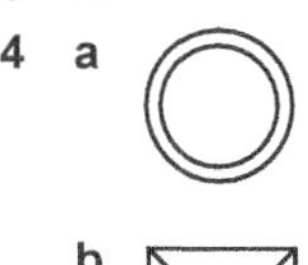

b

c

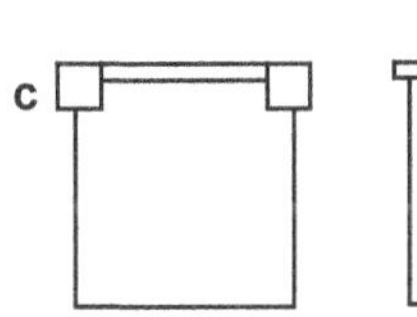

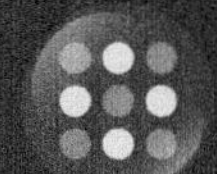

12e Measuring and drawing angles

Objectives	
• Measure and draw angles to the nearest degree (L5)	
Key ideas	**Resources**
1 A protractor must be in the correct position before measuring or drawing an angle. **2** Always line up a zero and count from that zero.	Measuring angles (1081) Protractors, both large class-size and students' size Rulers and pencils An orienteering-type compass An old-fashioned lady's fan
Simplification	**Extension**
Initially when measuring angles, provide angles which have one arm, at least 5 cm long, always horizontal across the paper and angles which are all measured clockwise using the outer scale from the same zero, on the left. Begin with acute angles. Once students are confident, continue to provide angles with a horizontal arm, but now measure anticlockwise, using the inner scale from the zero on the right. Finally, provide angles where neither arm is horizontal.	Provide students with a diagram of the route taken by army cadets as they walk across a stretch of moorland. The route is a series of straight lines forming a jagged line. The students should measure the angles at each point where there is a change in direction. Next, students can draw their own route and ask their partner to measure the angles involved.
Literacy	**Links**
The precision of the spoken language is important in order to describe, accurately and in sequence, how to position and use a protractor to measure an angle. Ensure that students can recall correctly which direction is clockwise, and which is anticlockwise. If in doubt, they should refer to a ticking clock or watch and observe the direction in which the hands move.	Although this is not a lesson on bearings, students could inspect a compass of the type used for map-reading and orienteering. They can turn the compass from north through a given angle. Ask how many degrees are needed to turn clockwise from north to east, south and west. (90°, 180°, 270°) Orienteering is a sport in which participants race each other to navigate around a series of places they have been instructed to visit, using a map and compass. There is more information about orienteering at www.britishorienteering.org.uk/

Alternative approach

Show students an old-fashioned lady's fan. Show it closed in a horizontal position pointing to the students' left. As the fan opens, it simulates the 'opening' of an angle on a protractor when students count clockwise from zero. Students could take turns at opening the fan through a series of given angles, first by estimating the size of the angle and then using a protractor to check.

Checkpoint

1 Draw several angles on paper. Measure the angle, specifying whether students should use the clockwise or anticlockwise scale on their protractor. For example

a 65° (clockwise) **b** 27° (anticlockwise)
c 113° (clockwise) **d** 142° (anticlockwise)

2 Use a protractor to draw an angle of 82°.

Starter – Quick fire

Ask students to respond on mini-whiteboards to a series of quick questions which recap previous work on angles and triangles. For example

- What is the name of an angle measuring between 90° and 180°? (Obtuse)
- If a triangle has angles of 40° and 60°, what is the size of its third angle? (80°)
- If a straight angle is in two parts and one part is 20°, how big is the other part? 160°)
- If a right-angled triangle has a 30° angle, what are the sizes of its other two angles? (90° and 60°)

Teaching notes

Remind students how to position a protractor correctly before using it to measure an angle. If necessary, refer back to the **Teaching notes** for lesson **5c**. In particular, ask students to count from the zero that they have lined up and to ignore the other zero.

For extra practice in measuring, provide angles where the arms of the angles are just over 5 cm long (the usual radius of a student's protractor) and where, initially, students use the same zero for angles measured clockwise using the outer scale. Only later have angles requiring the other zero and the inner scale.

When drawing an angle, students should follow the same instructions: position the protractor correctly; line up a zero; count from that zero.

Measuring angles in the context of maps adds interest. For example, if you stand on the top of Blackpool Tower looking towards Morecambe, or on the top of London's Shard looking down the Thames, what angle do you turn through if you then look towards the Isle of Man, or the BT Tower?

Plenary

Use a large class-size protractor. Ask students to take turns to demonstrate to the class how to measure a given angle and how to draw a given angle.
Ask them to agree on three 'top tips' that they would give to others to enable them to use a protractor and to draw angles correctly.

Exercise commentary

When measuring or drawing angles, the 'arms' should be drawn at least 5 cm long, which will make it much easier to work with a standard protractor.

Question 1 – Continually remind students to count from the zero which lies on one 'arm' of the angle. Ignore the other zero. A common error is to look only at the other 'arm' and read the outer scale whether it is the correct scale or not.

Question 2 – Students first need to find the correct zero to count from. Then, on the scale of that zero, they should count in 10s as far as is needed and then count in 1s. Some students will need to count in this way for every angle.

Question 3 – Having drawn a starting line, decide first at which end of the line the angle is to be drawn. The instructions in the second example in the student book are clear and easy to follow. If the angle is to be drawn at the other end of the line, follow the 'mirror image' of the instructions.

Question 4 – Students may need to guided in how to use the 'failed' attempts to help them suggest the correct angles for launching the balls of paper.

Question 5 – Students readily appreciate that 230° is 50° more than a straight angle but may not see how to place a protractor on the reflex angle to measure the 50°. When drawing the angle, students should first draw a long straight line, at an angle of 180° and work out how to add 50° to it.

Answers

1 **a** 25° **b** 35° **c** 130°

2 **a** A 25° B 48° C 66° D 104°
E 142° F 172°
b G 14° H 36° I 54° J 114°
K 136° L 168°

3 Students' drawings should be accurate to at least ±2°.

4 Possible estimates are
Bin 1 75° (must be > 60°)
Bin 2 45° (between 30° and 60°)
Bin 3 25° (must be < 30°)

5 There are a number of possible methods.
Measure the obtuse angle (130°) and subtract it from 360°.
'Reverse' the protractor and measure on from 180°; add the acute angle (40°) to 180°.
Use a 360° protractor.

Objectives	
• Use a ruler and protractor to construct a triangle given two sides and the included angle (SAS). (L5)	
Key ideas	**Resources**
1 Triangles can be constructed using a pencil, protractor, ruler, and information about the angle sizes and side lengths. **2** You do not need to know the sizes of all angles and sides in a triangle in order to draw it.	Constructing triangles (1090) Protractors Ruler and pencils Partly-drawn triangles Two drink cans, paper and coins
Simplification	**Extension**
Students who find this activity particularly difficult can be supported with partly-drawn triangles. They will work best where the angles to be drawn are multiples of 5 or 10 degrees.	Extend the more able students by requiring greater accuracy in their measurements, and include more examples of obtuse-angled triangles. Students can work in pairs to set each other challenging triangles to draw and then check each other's work.
Literacy	**Links**
The *base line* of a triangle is the horizontal line. The word 'construct' means 'build', and students can think of their ruler, protractor and pencils as the tools they need to create triangles on paper.	Bring in two drinks cans, some sheets of paper and some coins. Support a piece of paper at each end with the cans to make a bridge, and load it with coins until it collapses. Fold the paper in half lengthwise and try again. Try any folding techniques that the class suggests but do not move the cans closer together. Now fold the paper lengthwise like a fan (or concertina) to form a row of triangles. This gives the strongest bridge. Triangles are used in construction designs to make them strong.

Alternative approach

Interactive work on angles and protractors could be useful for students still needing to cement their understanding. There are various activities on angles at

www.resources.woodlands-junior.kent.sch.uk/maths/shapes/angles.html#Angles

MyMaths lesson 1090, 'Constructing Triangles', gives an animated demonstration of constructing a triangle from two sides and an angle.

Checkpoint

1 Show this triangle without labels (shown half size). Measure the lengths of the sides and the angles.

6.1 cm, 3.9 cm, 5 cm, 55°, 40°, 85°

2 Show an equilateral triangle of any size.

a Measure the length of one side and one angle. (Depends on diagram, 60°)

b Without measuring, what are the sizes of the other sides and angles? (All sides same length, all angles 60°)

Starter – Missing angles

Give students one angle in a triangle, and ask what the other angles could be. For example

- An isosceles triangle with an angle of 30°.
  (30° and 120°, or 75° and 75°)
- A right-angled triangle with an angle of 35°.
  (90° and 155°)

They should display their answers on mini-whiteboards.

Teaching notes

As in lesson **12e**, students may again need reminding of how to position a protractor correctly and of which scale to use when measuring or drawing an angle. Having decided which scale is correct, they should line up the zero of the protractor scale against the 'arm' of the angle and ignore the zero on the other scale.

Demonstrate the stages in drawing a triangle accurately as shown on p230 of the Student Book. All examples and questions in the Student Book use side lengths of at least 5 cm, which makes work with a standard protractor easier. Ensure that students work with sharpened pencils to improve the accuracy of their diagrams. Discuss with them that an error in just one angle or length will result in inaccuracies in the rest of the triangle.

Explain that you do not need to know the sizes of all the angles and sides in a triangle in order to draw it. Knowing the length of two sides and the angle between them, and triangles like this are often called SAS, 'side, angle, side', triangles.

Plenary

Give students the details of a triangle to be drawn. Students can work in pairs to check each other's drawings. One pair could be chosen to give a demonstration of their method and drawing to the whole class.

Exercise commentary

Question 1 – Some students may not realise that the size of an angle does not depend on the length of the lines used to draw it. Students should be asked to draw lines long enough to use the protractor. In part **c**, they need to use the anticlockwise scale.

Question 2 – Some angles and side lengths are missing from these triangles. Students need to start by drawing the base lines and aligning the protractor correctly, in order to draw the one given angle and second side. This will allow them to join the corners and draw the third line. For parts **b** and **c**, students then need to measure the missing angles and sides in order to identify their size. Triangle **v** poses more of a challenge. Students will need to recognise that it is an isosceles triangle so that two sides and two angles are equal. Angle y can then be calculated from the sum of the angles in a triangle. This gives the canonical SAS form.

Question 3 – Students will need support in understanding the wording of this question. They need to appreciate that the three friends are standing at the corners of an equilateral triangle. Students could then be asked if it matters how far apart the three friends are standing.

Answers

1 **a – c** Students' drawings should be accurate to at least ±2°.

2 **a** Accurate drawings will have the following measurements correct.

b **i** $q = 80°, r = 62°$ **ii** $s = 80°, t = 50°$
iii $u = 57°, v = 33°$ **iv** $w = 35°, x = 43°$
v $y = 132°, z = 24°$

c **i** $a = 3.8$ cm **ii** $b = 5.4$ cm
iii $c = 7.7$ cm **iv** $d = 8.6$ cm
v $e = 12.8$ cm, $f = 7$ cm

3 Yes, equilateral triangle.

Objectives

- Know the definition of a circle and the names of its parts. (L4)
- Use a pair of compasses and a ruler to construct a given circle. (L4)

Key ideas

1 Know the difference between radius and diameter and be able to measure them for a given circle.
2 Draw a circle of a given radius or diameter.

Resources

Compasses
Round objects such as cans
stiff card
rope

Simplification

Rather that the relatively complex diagrams in question **2**, ask students to draw isolated circles of given radii and diameters. Only once students have mastered the skill of drawing a single circle should you consider moving them on to creating more elaborate designs.

Extension

Question **3** can be extended by asking students to investigate more circles with different radii and collate the results in a table. Adding a separate column they could use a calculator to find

circumference ÷ diameter

With measurements accurate to ±1 mm, they should get answers in the range 2.9 – 3.4

Question **4** can be extended by asking students to copy other designs which heavily feature circles.

Literacy

The word circle comes from the Greek kirkos, meaning hoop, via the Latin circulus, meaning circus. A circus being an arena for chariot races, gladiatorial fights etc.

The word radius comes from the Latin word radius which means both ray and the spoke of a chariot wheel. Given its Latin origin the plural is radii, not radiuses. Other words with the i plural are rhombi and loci.

Links

In the solar system the planets follow orbits which are elliptical – the shape you get when you look at a circle from the side. However most of the ellipses are very nearly circular and moreover the ancient astronomers thought that circles were perfect shapes. So for a very long time solar models had planets travelling in circles, or combinations of circles, orbiting around the Earth (Ptolemy) or the Sun (Copernicus).

Alternative approach

Explain to students that they are going to copy this diagram.

Start by drawing a circle radius 4 cm. Then add a diameter line. Discuss the meaning of the words radius and diameter and check that studenst undertsand them. Ask, what is the radius of the two smaller circles? (2 cm)

Show students how to measure 2 cm from the edge of the circle, to mark a centre for a smaller circle, and add this to the drawing. Then leave students to add the second smaller circle themselves.

Once finished ask students to swap diagrams with a partner so that they can mark each others work. marks should be awarded for accuracy and roundness.

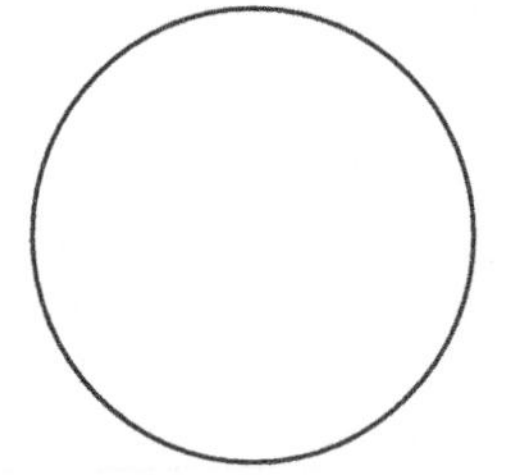

Drawn half size

Checkpoint

1 For this circle measure its

a radius (1.5 cm)

b diameter. (3 cm)

2 Draw a circle of diameter 4 cm.
(Check radius = 20 ± 1 mm)

Starter – Simon says compass turn

Ask students to stand up and clear a little space around them. Explain that the blackboard is always north. Issue the instructions 'Simon says turn to face east', 'Simon says turn to face south west' etc. As soon as the command is issued the students must act; those that are too slow or wrong must sit down. Increase the speed of instructions until one winner remains.

Teaching notes

This is a practical lesson, start by ensuring that students have the correct equipment: a ruler a pair of compasses and a sharp pencil. Remind students that they should have their own set of equipment.

Draw a circle on the board and ask students how they would describe it so that someone else in another room could draw a circle of the same size. Take suggestions and select answers corresponding to giving the radius or giving the diameter. Explain that mathematicians have special names for these distances.

Radius = the length of a line from the centre to the edge.

Diameter = the length of a line going from edge to edge that passes through the centre.

Check students understand these definitions by adding radii at different angles and asking are they all the same? Also add a 'diameter' that does not go through the centre and ask is this right? There is also potential to confuse the two words, one way to remember which is the Diameter is to think of the capital D which looks like half a circle and a diameter.

Next tell students that they have to draw a circle of radius 4 cm. Drawing an accurate circle requires some practice. There are a few tips

- Adjust the pencil so that both legs are the same length.
- Press the compass needle in firmly.
- Hold the compasses by the hinge, so as not to squash the legs.

Ask students to check one another's drawings giving marks out of four for accuracy of size and roundness.

Repeat asking for a circle of diameter 10 cm.

Plenary

Get students to stand up and move to a large open space. Select one student and ask the other students to stand 3 m from the selected students; use the rope to measure the distance. Once they have formed a circle ask the students what is its radius and diameter. Ask if the diameter is always twice the radius. (Yes)

Exercise commentary

Question 1 – Check that students measure the diameter along a line going through the centre of the circle and do not confuse diameter and radius. The answers to parts **a** and **b** involve multiples of 5 mm but part **c** involves a multiple of 2.5 mm. Some students may need reassurance that they are measuring accurately.

Question 2 – The diagrams are in increasing order of complexity but the most important point in each case is that the circles are accurately drawn. In part **b** it will help to start by drawing a mirror line on which the centres of the circles can be placed. Students could calculate that the centres need to be 8 cm apart or they could just set their compasses and see when the circles touch. In part **c**, it is intended that the triangle is isosceles (strictly the long side should be 8.8 cm long).

Question 3 – Students are likely to find it rather fiddly to measure the circumference of the circle in the student book. It will be easier for them to work with an actual solid object, such as, a tin can. An alternative is to draw and then cut out a 5 cm diameter (radius = 2.5 cm) circle on a piece of stiff card. Mark a point on the edge of the circle and draw a straight line at least 20 cm long. Starting with the point at the end of the line, roll the circle along the line and mark on the line where the point next touches it: the distance to this mark is the circumference.

Question 4 – Suggest students start by drawing a circle of radius 4 cm to which they add a diameter line with points marked at 2 cm and 6 cm from one end. They will then need to draw two semicircles of radius 2 cm and two smaller, full circles of radius, say 7 mm, using the marked points as centres.
Successful students could be asked to draw the same design but at a different size.

Answers

1 Distances should be accurate to ±1 mm.

a	i	15 mm	ii	30 mm
b	i	10 mm	ii	20 mm
c	i	17.5 mm	ii	35 mm

2 Check students' drawings for accuracy.

3 Estimates should be near 15.7 cm.

4 Check students' drawings for accuracy.

Key outcomes		Quick check
Recognise and name common 3D shapes	L3	**a** What is the mathematical name of this shape? (Triangular-based pyramid (tetrahedron)) **b** How many faces does it have? (4) **c** How many vertices does it have? (4) **d** How many edges does it have? (6)
Construct simple nets of 3D shapes	L4	Which net will fold to give the shape above? (B) **A** **B**
Use 2D representations to visualise 3D shapes	L4	Draw the shape above from **a** the top **b** the side. Top Side
Use a protractor to measure and draw angles	L5	**1** Draw this triangle. (Check using measurements.) 4 cm, 110°, 7 cm, $x°$, $y°$, z cm
Use a ruler and protractor to construct a triangle	L5	**2 a** Measure the size of the angles labelled $x°$ and $y°$. **b** Measure the length of the side labelled z. ($x = 46°$, $y = 24°$, $z = 9.2$ cm)
Know the parts of a circle	L4	**a** What is the diameter of this circle? (2.5 cm) **b** Draw a circle with twice the radius. (Same size)

Development and links
In book **2A**, the ability to accurately draw angles is utilized when creating pie charts and constructions are extended to include ASA triangles. Isometric drawings are introduced as an alternative 2D representation for a solid shape and nets are used to facilitate calculating the surface areas of cuboids. Measuring and drawing angles is a skill used in Geography when bearings need to be given or points found by triangulation. knowing how to create 2D representations of solid objects is important in design technology for product analysis and similar skills are drawn upon on in art.

MyMaths extra support

Lesson/online homework			Description
2D and 3D shapes	1229	L2	The second part of this lesson looks at identifying 3D shapes and their properties.
Measuring lengths	1146	L4	The first part of this lesson looks revises using a rule before looking at converting between units.

My Review

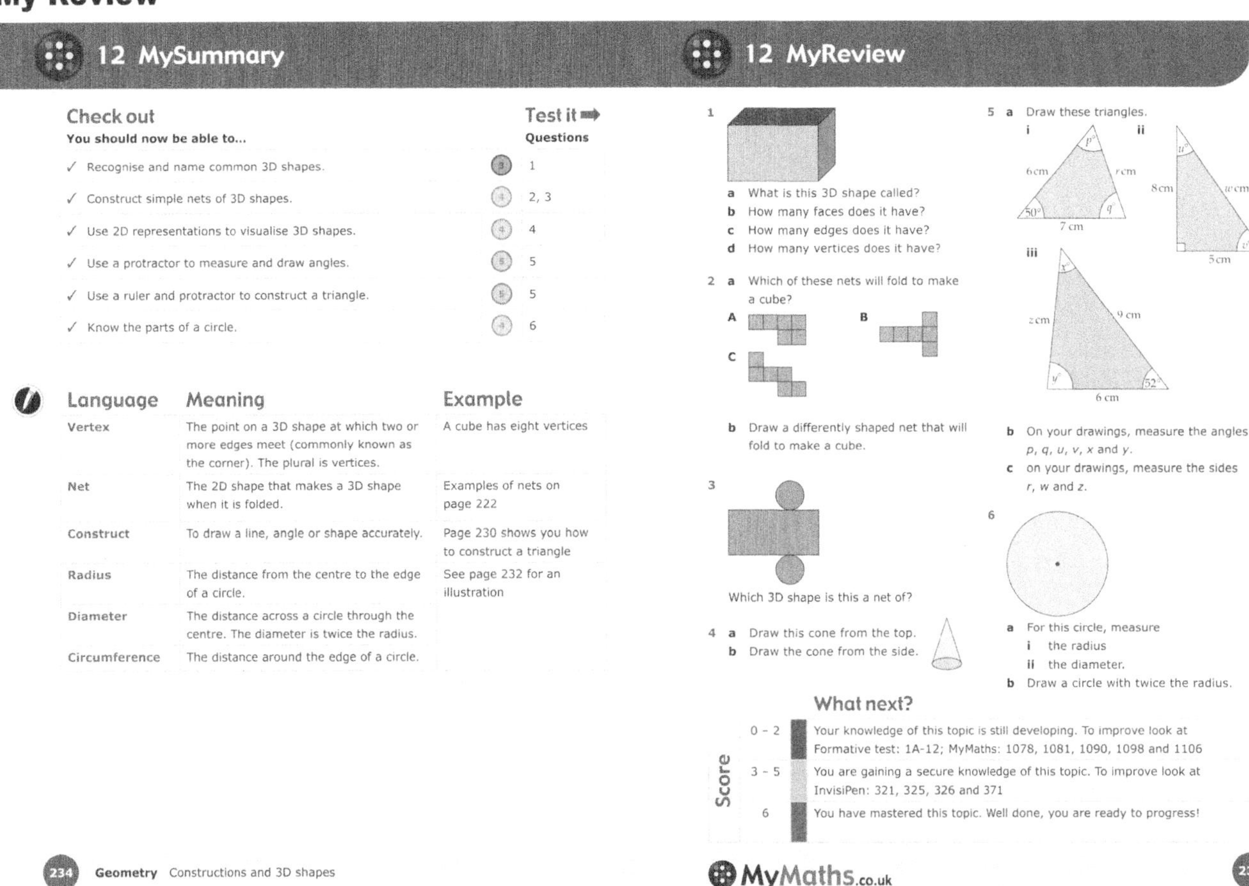

12 MySummary

Check out
You should now be able to...

	Test it ➡ Questions
✓ Recognise and name common 3D shapes.	1
✓ Construct simple nets of 3D shapes.	2, 3
✓ Use 2D representations to visualise 3D shapes.	4
✓ Use a protractor to measure and draw angles.	5
✓ Use a ruler and protractor to construct a triangle.	5
✓ Know the parts of a circle.	6

Language	Meaning	Example
Vertex	The point on a 3D shape at which two or more edges meet (commonly known as the corner). The plural is vertices.	A cube has eight vertices
Net	The 2D shape that makes a 3D shape when it is folded.	Examples of nets on page 222
Construct	To draw a line, angle or shape accurately.	Page 230 shows you how to construct a triangle
Radius	The distance from the centre to the edge of a circle.	See page 232 for an illustration
Diameter	The distance across a circle through the centre. The diameter is twice the radius.	
Circumference	The distance around the edge of a circle.	

234 Geometry Constructions and 3D shapes

12 MyReview

1
a What is this 3D shape called?
b How many faces does it have?
c How many edges does it have?
d How many vertices does it have?

2 a Which of these nets will fold to make a cube?
A B C
b Draw a differently shaped net that will fold to make a cube.

3 Which 3D shape is this a net of?

4 a Draw this cone from the top.
b Draw the cone from the side.

5 a Draw these triangles.
i ii iii

b On your drawings, measure the angles p, q, u, v, x and y.
c on your drawings, measure the sides r, w and z.

6
a For this circle, measure
i the radius
ii the diameter.
b Draw a circle with twice the radius.

What next?

Score	
0 – 2	Your knowledge of this topic is still developing. To improve look at Formative test: 1A-12; MyMaths: 1078, 1081, 1090, 1098 and 1106
3 – 5	You are gaining a secure knowledge of this topic. To improve look at InvisiPen: 321, 325, 326 and 371
6	You have mastered this topic. Well done, you are ready to progress!

MyMaths.co.uk 235

Question commentary

Students should have their own protractor, ruler and sharp pencil. Allow ± 2° and ± 2 mm on constructions.

Question 1 – (lesson **12a**) Beware of students who do not distinguish between cube and cuboid.

Question 2 – (lesson **12b**) Students should do this question by visualising folding up the cub; part **c** is most tricky.

Question 3 - (lesson **12c**) 'Circular prism' is also an acceptable answer. Check that students understand the difference between a prism and a pyramid.

Question 4 - (lesson **12d**) A circle and triangle should be drawn with no attempt to make them look 3D.

Question 5 - (lessons **12e** and **12f**) The answers to parts **b** and **c** will confirm, or not, the accuracy of the students' constructions. In triangle **ii**, check that students recognize the right angle symbol. All angles are acute, using the wrong scale on the protractor will give *incorrect* obtuse angles.

Question 6 - (lesson **12g**) Beware of students who confuse radius and diameter. In part **a ii**, ask how students could work out the diameter without measuring it.

Answers

1 **a** Cuboid **b** 6 **c** 12 **d** 8

2 **a** B and C

b There are nine other possible nets.

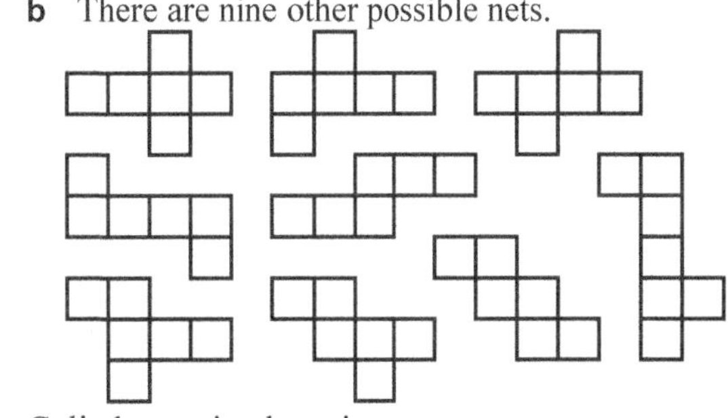

3 Cylinder or circular prism

4 **a** **b**

5 **a** Accurate drawings will have the following measurements correct.

b **i** $p = 74°, p = 56°$ **ii** $u = 32°, v = 58°$

iii $x = 42°, y = 86°$

c **i** $r = 5.6$ **ii** $w = 9.4$

iii $z = 7.1$

6 **a** **i** 1.5 cm **ii** 3 cm

b Check accuracy of circle, diameter 6 cm.

12 MyPractice

12a

1 Suggest possible 3D shapes from these descriptions.

a Six square faces

b Two faces, one of which is circular

c One face, no edges or vertices

12b

2 Which two nets will fold to make a cube?

12c

3 Draw a net of each of these solids. Draw your nets accurately.

12d

4 Draw the view from the top and side for each of these shapes.

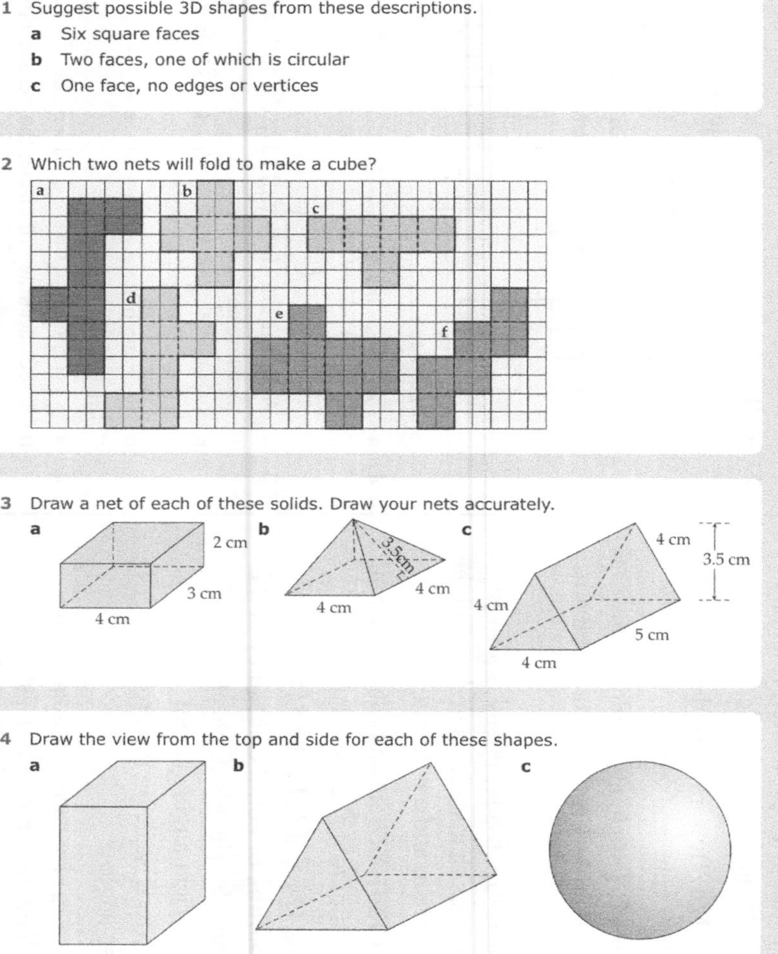

12e

5 Measure these angles accurately using a protractor.

6 Draw these angles using a protractor.

a 60° b 140° c 90° d 45° e 125° f 75°

12f

7 Draw these triangles accurately.

12g

8 For each circle measure **i** the radius **ii** the diameter.

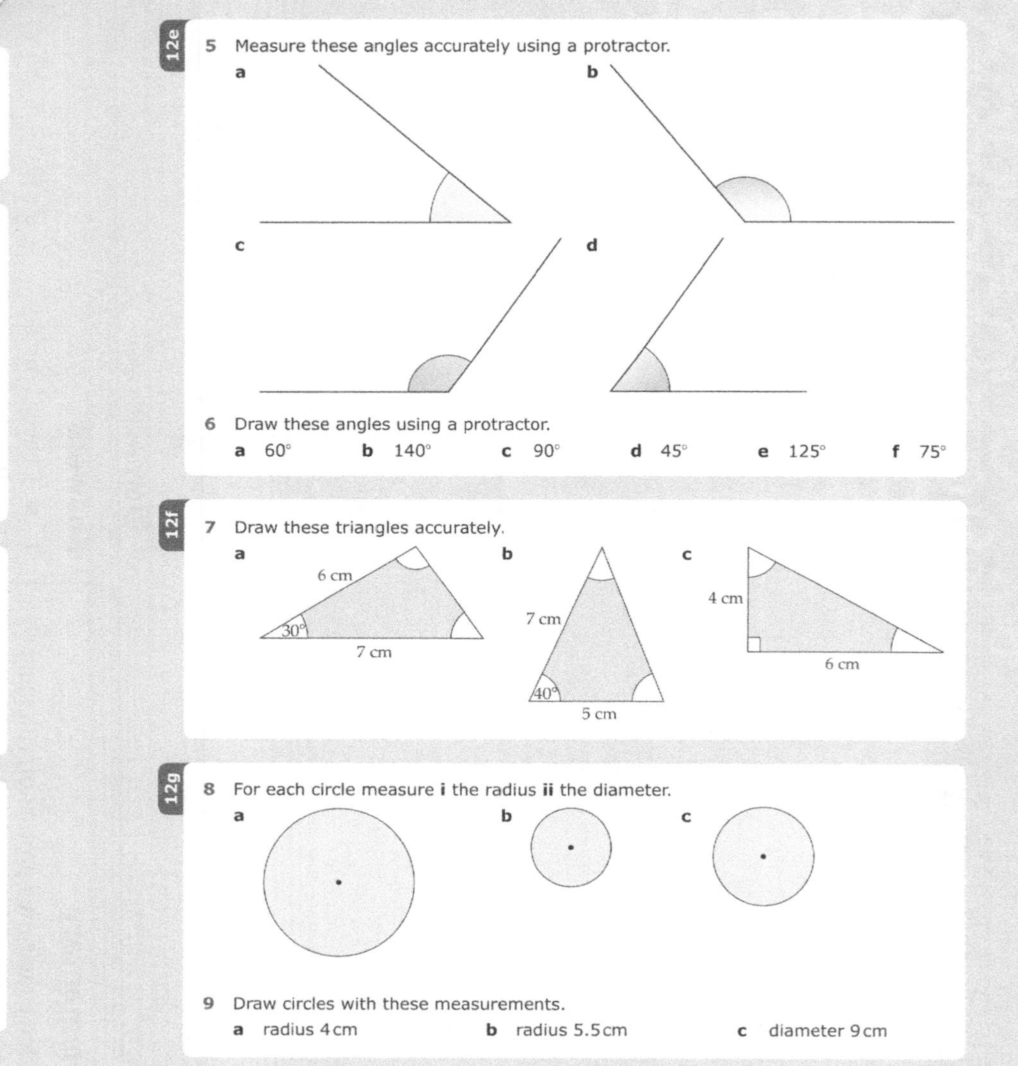

9 Draw circles with these measurements.

a radius 4 cm b radius 5.5 cm c diameter 9 cm

MyMaths.co.uk

Question commentary

Questions 1 – It may be necessary to have available models of the more common 3D shapes for students to handle; ideally these should not be labelled with their names. As required, discuss the meaning of the key vocabulary: face, edge, vertex/vertices etc.

Questions 2 – Be prepared to guide students thinking. How would you fold net **c**? What shape are the faces in nets **a** and **e**?/What are the shapes of the faces of a cube? How many faces does net **b** have?/How many faces does a cube have? If students can't conceptualise their thinking then provide, or ask them to create, the nets and see if they work.

Question 3 – Provide students with centimetre-square paper so that they can focus on the getting the shape of the net correct. If tabs are added to the nets students could create their own models.

Question 4 – In the first instance encourage students to visualise the shapes and then draw the views. Only if necessary should you provide physical models. If there is confusion over which is the side view then ask students which is the front view and then apply elimination.

Question 5 – The angles are all multiples of 5. Focus on whether students are using the correct scale on their protractors and whether the angle is acute or obtuse and therefore what range their answers should lie in.

Questions 6 – Again the main focus should be on using he correct scale and then on accuracy of drawing. Students should have their own equipment and a sharp pencil.

Question 7 – Once students have drawn their triangles ask them to swap with a partner who should measure the missing angles and length. Do they get the same answers, if not, where is/are the mistake(s)?

Question 8 – The most likely problem will be confusing radius and diameter. One way of remembering the meaning of diameter is to consider the shape of a capital D.

Question 9 – Students should have their own pair of compasses and a sharp pencil.

Answers

1 **a** Cube **b** Cone or half sphere (hemisphere)
c Sphere

2 **d** and **f**

3 Nets drawn quarter size.

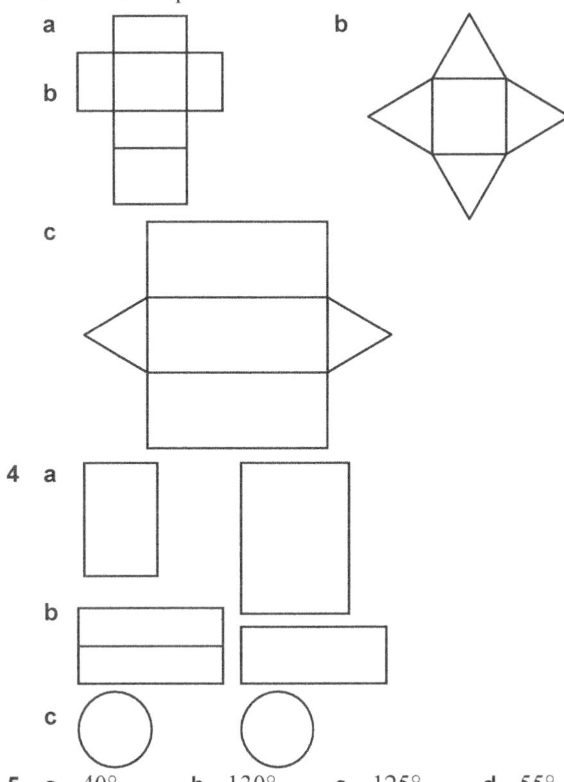

5 **a** 40° **b** 130° **c** 125° **d** 55°

6 **a – f** Students' drawings should be accurate to at least ±2°.

7 Accurate drawings will have the following missing angles and side measurements correct.

a 91°, 59° and 3.5 cm
b 95°, 45° and 4.5 cm
c 34°, 56° and 7.2 cm

8 Distances should be accurate to ±1 mm.

a **i** 15 mm **ii** 30 mm
b **i** 8 mm **ii** 16 mm
c **i** 10 mm **ii** 20 mm

9 Check students' drawings for accuracy; distances should be accurate to ±1 mm.

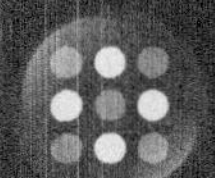

Case study 4: Labyrinths and mazes

Related lessons	Resources
	Pictures of hedge mazes Books with puzzle mazes Copies of the mazes in tasks **1**, **4** and **5** Centimetre square graph paper A long strip of paper
Simplification	**Extension**
Ensure that students have copies of the diagrams which they can draw on to trace routes. Produce a simpler version of the maze for task **4** which has fewer internal lines so that it is easier to imagine it being opened out.	Ask students to design two puzzle mazes: one where the hand on the wall method works and one where it doesn't work. They could swap with partners to try the mazes. Use photocopies to preserve the originals. Students could research mazes see **links**. Roman mazes are interesting in their use of rotation and symmetry to produce a single maze of four quarters. There is more information about Roman mazes at http://gwydir.demon.co.uk/jo/maze/roman/index.htm See also the suggestion in task **2**.

Links
When mazes are mentioned, people often think of hedge mazes or mazes in puzzle books. However, maze designs existed well before these relatively modern examples. Many early labyrinth patterns were spirals, as seen in this case study with Cretan labyrinths. Later puzzle mazes and hedge mazes often have multiple routes and dead ends. For more information about the history of mazes visit www.labyrinthos.net

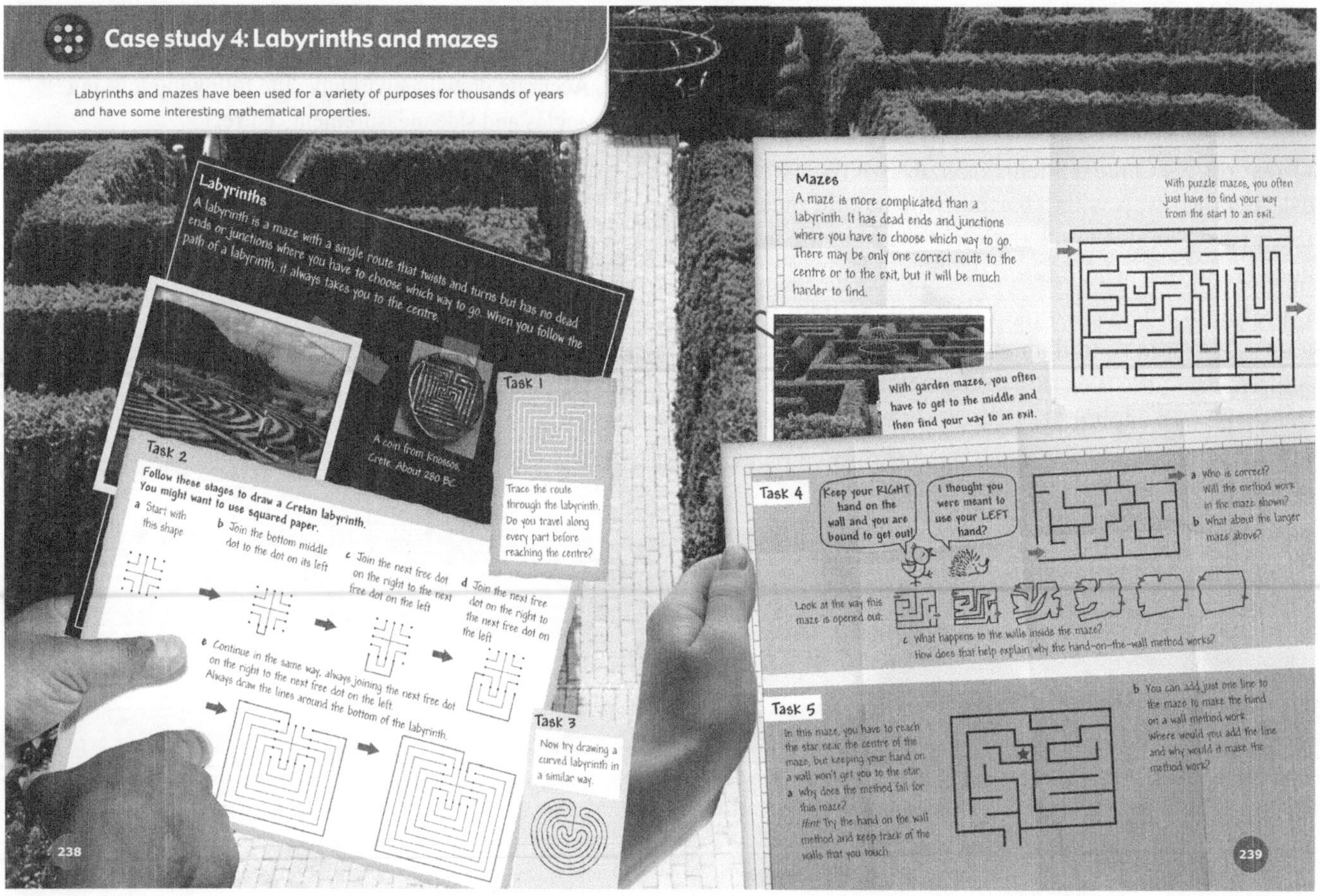

Case study 4: Labyrinths and mazes

Labyrinths and mazes have been used for a variety of purposes for thousands of years and have some interesting mathematical properties.

Labyrinths

A labyrinth is a maze with a single route that twists and turns but has no dead ends or junctions where you have to choose which way to go. When you follow the path of a labyrinth, it always takes you to the centre.

A coin from Knossos, Crete. About 280 BC

Task 1

Trace the route through the labyrinth. Do you travel along every part before reaching the centre?

Task 2

Follow these stages to draw a Cretan labyrinth. You might want to use squared paper.

a Start with this shape

b Join the bottom middle dot to the dot on its left

c Join the next free dot on the right to the next free dot on the left

d Join the next free dot on the right to the next free dot on the left

e Continue in the same way, always joining the next free dot on the right to the next free dot on the left. Always draw the lines around the bottom of the labyrinth.

Task 3

Now try drawing a curved labyrinth in a similar way.

Mazes

A maze is more complicated than a labyrinth. It has dead ends and junctions where you have to choose which way to go. There may be only one correct route to the centre or to the exit, but it will be much harder to find.

With puzzle mazes, you often just have to find your way from the start to an exit.

With garden mazes, you often have to get to the middle and then find your way to an exit.

Task 4

Keep your RIGHT hand on the wall and you are bound to get out!

I thought you were meant to use your LEFT hand?

a Who is correct? Will the method work in the maze shown?

b What about the larger maze above?

Look at the way this maze is opened out.

c What happens to the walls inside the maze? How does that help explain why the hand-on-the-wall method works?

Task 5

In this maze, you have to reach the star near the centre of the maze, but keeping your hand on a wall won't get you to the star.

a Why does the method fail for this maze? *Hint:* Try the hand on the wall method and keep track of the walls that you touch.

b You can add just one line to the maze to make the hand on a wall method work. Where would you add the line and why would it make the method work?

238 239

Teaching notes

Students may be familiar with the idea of mazes and labyrinths; start by discussing what they know about them and any examples that they have seen. Go on to explain that people now distinguish between a simple labyrinth and a more complex maze and that they shall look at both of them. They will also learn how they can use mathematics to always be able to get out of a maze.

Task 1

The coin shows the famous labyrinth at Knossos, Crete. Supposedly designed by the master inventor Daedalus it trapped the Minotaur, a half bull half human monster who demanded regular human sacrifice. That is until the Greek hero Theseus, helped by Ariadne who gave him a ball of thread, known as a 'klew', to retraces his steps with, killed him.

Tracing the route to the centre of the labyrinth is best done by drawing a continuous line on a copy of the diagram. Ask students how many lines are used to create the design, one or several? Point out the four ends of lines: two in the centre and two at the top. The pattern is basically the four arms of a cross spiralling around one another.

Task 2

Make available centimetre-square graph paper to help with making an accurate copy of the labyrinth. To start with it will help some students to do the first few steps together as a class. You can then concentrate your attention on those students who are struggling to follow the instructions.

To check their finished drawing they could ask a partner to see if they can trace a route to the centre.

More able students can be asked to create a set of instructions that a 'robot' could follow to get to the centre. Using squares as a distance unit, these could be 'south 3, east 4, south 8 …' or 'ahead 3, left 4, right 8, …'. If a large copy of the labyrinth was drawn in chalk on the floor then the instructions could be given to students to test out.

Task 3

The straight and curved labyrinths are the same in their essential details, that is, they are 'topologically equivalent'. Check that students can see this before introducing the idea of thinking of the walls as being deformable so that you can bend and straighten them out but not cut or stick them together which would change how walls are connected to one another.

Task 4

Challenge students to find a route through the large maze at the top of the right hand page. Once some students have an answer, ask them to try to explain how they did it. Several strategies are likely to be based on taking 'an overview of the maze'/'seeing ahead'. Ask students what they would do if they couldn't see the maze from above. For those methods that are not based on an overview, test to see if the methods work for the maze in task **4**.

Once students have tried out the left hand and right hand methods ask if they can explain how either method works and which is quicker. (For this maze, the right hand method takes 47 steps, the left hand 51.)

Use a long strip of paper to create a 'folded' version of the maze that can be opened out, as in the series of diagrams, to create an equivalent loop. The method then tells you to go along either the left or right hand walls until you reach the exit. Ask students to try to explain how the method gets you out of dead ends.

Task 5

Students should realise that the section of wall with the star is not connected to any of the outside walls, which contain the entrance: it is an island. Can students explain why the hand on a wall method fails? Can they explain by adding any piece of wall that connects the island to the outside wall will make the method work again? (Opened out the maze forms two disconnected 'loops' whilst adding the piece of wall joins them into a single loop.)

The maze at Hampton court maze contains an island.

Answers

1 Yes

2 Check student's drawings for accuracy.

3 Check student's drawings for accuracy.

4 **a** Both approaches work.

b Both approaches work.

c The walls open out to a square: the method takes you around the edge of the square to the exit.

5 **a** Student's explanations; these should include the fact that the central part is not connected to the rest of the maze.

b Any line that connects the central section with the outside section.

MyAssessment 3

These questions will test you on your knowledge of the topics in chapters 9 to 12.
They give you practice in the types of questions that you may see in your GCSE exams.
There are 50 marks in this test.

1 Look at these shapes. Copy or trace them and draw the lines of symmetry. (2 marks)

a b

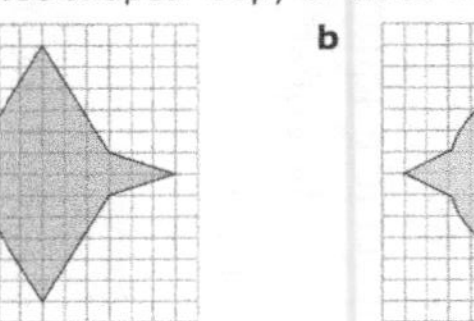

2 Look at these shapes. The dashed line is the position of the mirror line.
Copy each shape and mirror line onto squared paper.
Draw the reflection of each shape in the mirror line. (3 marks)

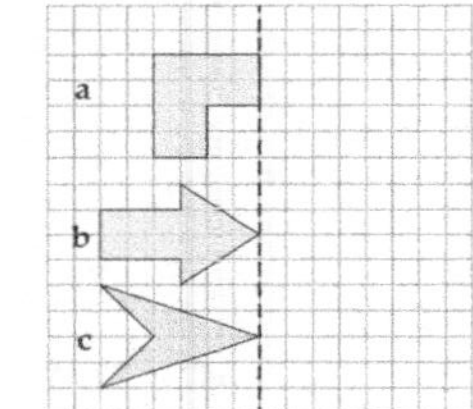

3 Copy this shape on squared paper.

a Translate the shape 5 to the right, then 5 down. (2 marks)

b Rotate this new shape about the dot 90° clockwise. (2 marks)

c Does this shape tessellate? (1 mark)

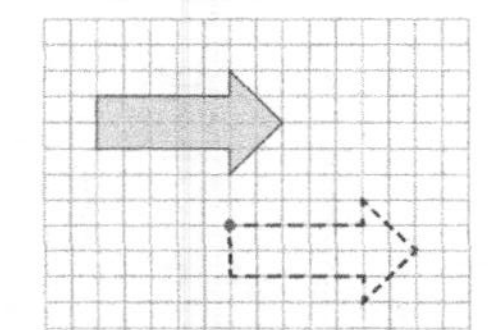
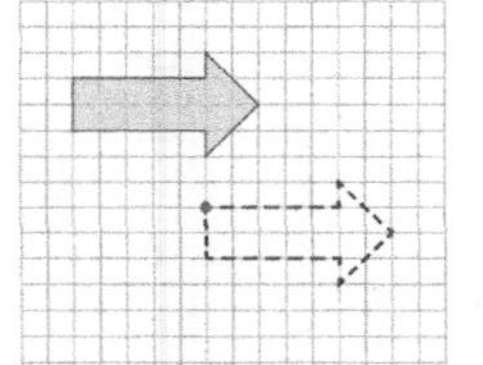

4 Work out the outputs for this function. (3 marks)

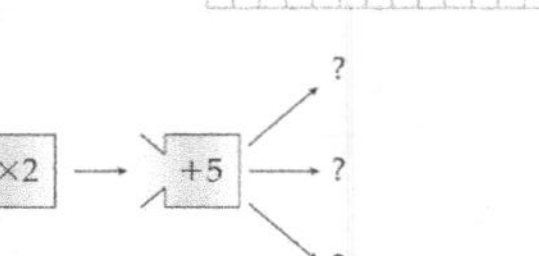

5 Copy and complete this function machine.
Replace the ? mark with the correct number and operation. (3 marks)

7 ⟶ ×3 ⟶ ?

7 ⟵ ? ⟵ ?

6 Find the value that makes each equation balance.

a $4 + y = 7$ (1 mark) b $t + 18 = 23$ (1 mark)

c $25 + n = 34$ (1 mark) d $4 + 9 = 6 + m$ (1 mark)

7 Use function machines to find the value of the letter in each equation.

a $w + 9 = 14$ (1 mark) b $8 \times p = 40$ (1 mark)

c $d - 8 = 4$ (1 mark) d $f \div 5 = 6$ (1 mark)

e $14 - g = 4$ (1 mark)

8 Fill in the missing factors for the number 12.
The factors of 12 are ☐, 2, ☐, 4, ☐, ☐ (2 marks)

9 Write down all multiples of four which are **less than** 30. (2 marks)

10 Here is a list of some square numbers. Copy and complete the list.

a $5^2 = 5 \times ? = 25$ (1 mark) b $8^2 = ? \times ? = ?$ (1 mark)

c $?^2 = 7 \times ? = ?$ (1 mark) d $?^2 = ? \times ? = 81$ (1 mark)

11 Which numbers from this group: 75, 550, 256, 349, 642, 123
cannot be **divided exactly** by at least one of the numbers 2, 3, 4, 5 or 10? (2 marks)

12 Name the shapes that have these properties.

a Circular base and top and no straight sides (1 mark)

b Six faces, twelve edges not all the same size and eight vertices (1 mark)

13 Here is a cube.
Draw this as a net on squared paper. (2 marks)

14 Here are the nets of some 3D objects. Identify the 3D objects in each case. (3 marks)

a b c

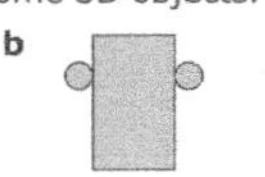
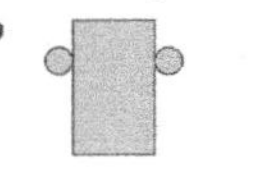
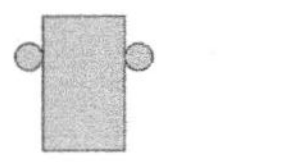

15 a Using a ruler, protractor or compasses, draw these shapes to scale. (4 marks)

b What are the lengths p, q and r? (3 marks)

c What size is the angle x? (1 mark)

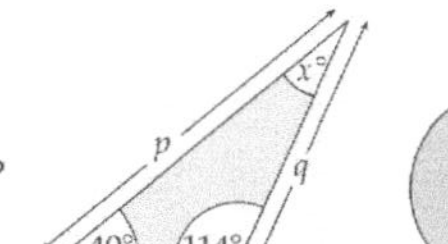

Mark scheme

Questions 1 – 2 marks (lesson **9a**)

a 1 2 lines of reflection symmetry: vertical and horizontal.

b 1 4 lines of reflection symmetry: vertical, horizontal and diagonally at 45°.

Questions 2 – 3 marks (lesson **9b**)

3 1 mark for each correct shape

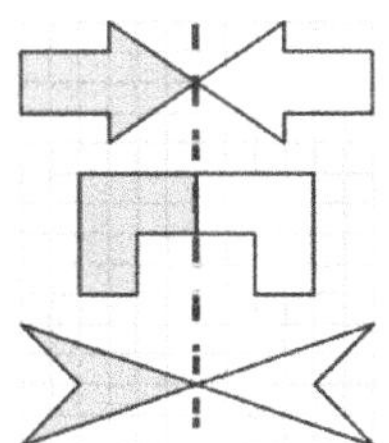

Questions 3 – 5 marks (lessons **9c**, **9d** and **9e**)

a 2 Arrow correctly translated

b 2 Arrow correctly rotated about dot; 1 mark for correct 90° rotation not about dot

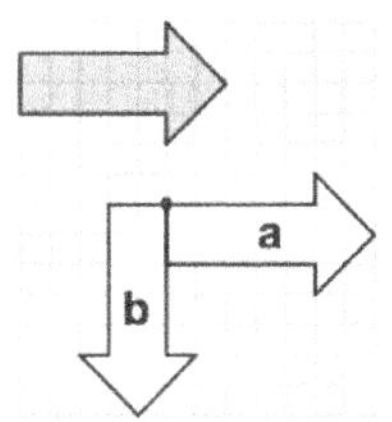

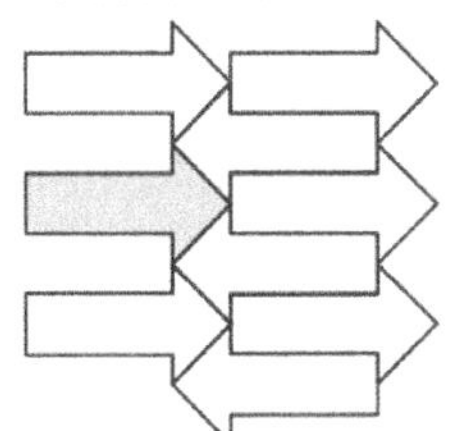

c 1 Yes

Questions 4 – 3 marks (lesson **10a**)

3 2 → 9, 6 → 17 and 7 → 19

Questions 5 – 3 marks (lesson **10b**)

3 Output is 21, input is 21 and operation is ÷3

Questions 6 – 4 marks (lessons **10c**, **10d** and **10e**)

a 1 $y = 3$ **b** 1 $t = 5$

c 1 $n = 9$ **d** 1 $m = 7$

Questions 7 – 5 marks (lessons **10c**, **10d** and **10e**)

a 1 $w = 5$ **b** 1 $p = 5$

c 1 $d = 12$ **d** 1 $f = 30$

e 1 $g = 18$

Questions 8 – 2 marks (lesson **11a**)

2 1, 3, 6, 12
– 1 mark each error or omission.

Questions 9 – 2 marks (lesson **11b**)

2 4, 8, 12, 16, 20, 24, 28
– 1 for each incorrect or omitted answer.

Questions 10 – 4 marks (lesson **11d**)

a 1 5

b 1 $8 \times 8 = 64$

c 1 $7^2 = 7 \times 7 = 49$

d 1 $9^2 = 9 \times 9$

Questions 11 – 2 marks (lesson **11c**)

2 349

Questions 12 – 2 marks (lessons **12a**)

a 1 Cylinder

b 1 Cuboid

Questions 13 – 2 marks (lesson **12b**)

2 Net drawn with squares, to make correct cube; there are eleven possible nets.

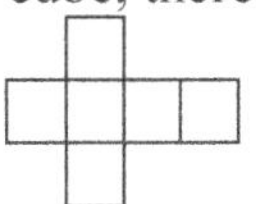

– 1 mark for each error

Questions 15 – 3 marks (lesson **12c**)

a 1 Square based pyramid

b 1 Cylinder

c 1 Triangular prism

Questions 16 – 8 marks (lessons **12e**, **12f** and **12g**)

a Check diagrams using answers to **b** and **c**

i 2 Correct construction of triangle, correct base length.

ii 2 Correct construction of circle, correct radius.

b 3 $p = 10.6$ cm, $q = 7.6$ cm, $r = 5.7$ cm; all ±2 mm

c 1 $x = 106° \pm 2°$

Levels

	Q1 – 3	Q4 – 7	Q8 – 11	Q12 – 15
	G & M	A	N	G & M
S 5		13 – 15		
D 5		9 – 12		17 – 20
M 4		5 – 8	8 – 10	13 – 16
S 4	8 – 10		4 – 7	9 – 12
D 4	4 – 7			5 – 8
FA	0 – 3	0 – 4	0 – 3	0 – 4

D developing S secure M mastery FA further assessment needed

Learning outcomes	
A2 Substitute numerical values into formulae and expressions, including scientific formulae.	(L4)
A14 Generate terms of a sequence from either a term-to-term or a position-to-term rule.	(L4)

Introduction

The chapter starts by introducing the concept of a mathematics sequence before going on to look at term-to-term rules. Sequences which include negative numbers are covered in the final spread.

The introduction discusses patterns in nature. Many patterns come about due to symmetry, or through the repetitive nature of time. One of the most remarkable types of pattern to occur in nature is linked to a very famous mathematical sequence, the Fibonacci Sequence. This sequence is formed by starting with two 1s and then adding up preceding pairs of terms to generate the next one:

$1 + 1 = 2$

$1 + 2 = 3$

$2 + 3 = 5$, etc.

This gives the sequence which continues 1, 1, 2, 3, 5, 8, 13,…

There are many naturally occurring phenomena that show the Fibonacci pattern. The spirals of seeds in the head of a sunflower, or the spikes on a pine cone go round in Fibonacci numbers. The breeding pattern of rabbits was where Fibonacci first noticed the sequence. The spiral nature of seashells is also linked to the Fibonacci sequence, as is the ratio of dimensions in many plane and solid figures such as pentagons and dodecahedrons.

A biography of Fibonacci can be found here.

http://www.maths.surrey.ac.uk/hosted-sites/R.Knott/Fibonacci/fibBio.html

Further details of the Fibonacci patterns in nature can be found here.

http://www.maths.surrey.ac.uk/hosted-sites/R.Knott/Fibonacci/fibnat.html

Prior knowledge

Students should already know how to…

- Do simple arithmetic
- Substitute positive whole numbers into simple formulae

Starter problem

The starter problem investigates different sequences that can be made from a total of 15 circles. Students are invited to describe the given sequence in words before investigating their own alternatives.

The given sequence goes 1, 5, 9 and could be described using term-to-term language: 'add 4' or by less formal methods such as by reference to the cross-like pattern formed.

There are many different sequences which could be formed, or the same sequence of numbers could be represented in different types of diagram.

As an extension to this problem, students could be invited to determine additional terms of the given sequence, or start with a different number of circles and generate further examples. If you are given 21 circles, for example, you could generate a sequence 2, 7, 12.

Resources

 **MyMaths**

Sequences	1173

Online assessment

Chapter test	1A–13
Formative test	1A–13
Summative test	1A–13

InvisiPen solutions

Sequences	281

Topic scheme

Teaching time = 4 lessons/2 weeks

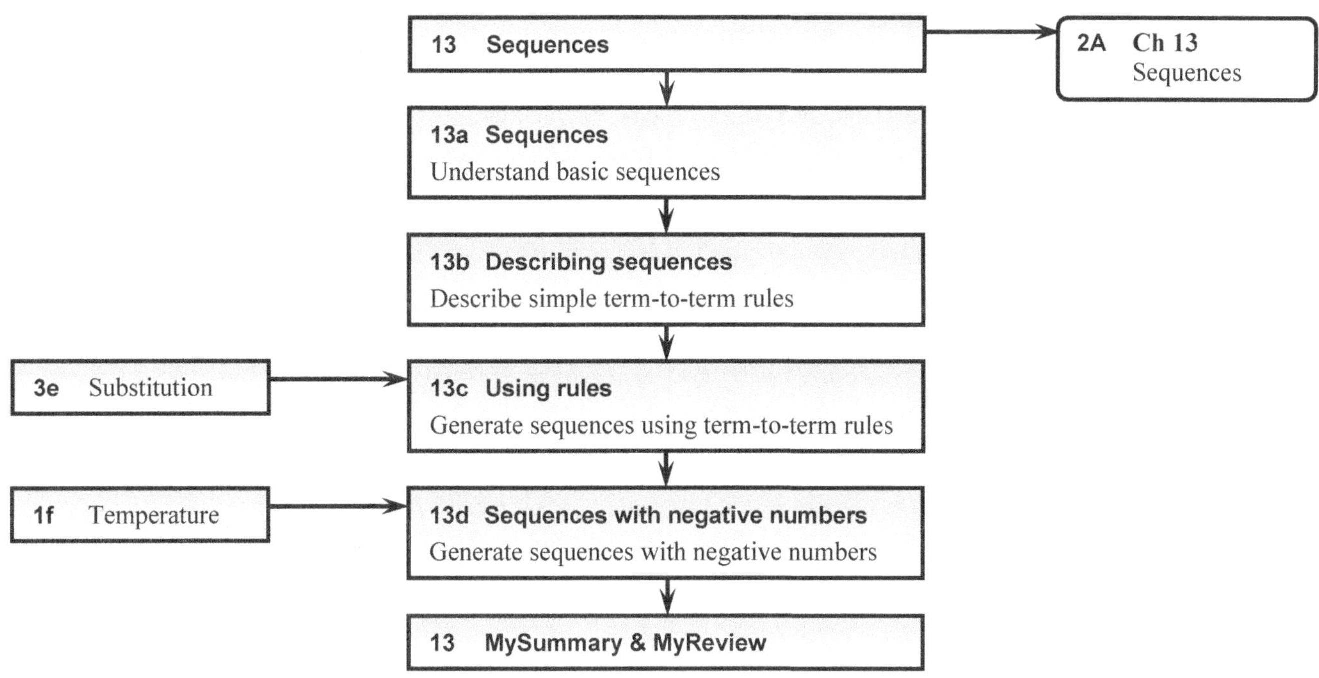

Differentiation

Student book 1A **242 – 255**

Understand basic sequences
Describing sequences
Using rules
Sequences with negative numbers

Student book 1B **246 – 259**

Understand basic sequences
Work with term-to-term rules
Work with position-to-term rules

Student book 1C **240 – 255**

Understand basic sequences
Sequence rules
Sequence notation
Finding a rule
Sequences of patterns

Objectives	
• Recognise and describe number patterns.	(L4)
• Find the next number in a sequence.	(L3)

Key ideas	Resources
1 Patterns grow and can be written as a sequence of numbers. **2** The next number in a sequence can be predicted by following the pattern.	Sequences (1173) Pegs and pegboards Tiles or counters of various shapes Large geoboards and rubber bands Dotted paper of various types Packs of 12 cards of shape sequences

Simplification	Extension
A practical approach using equipment of various kinds may be helpful. Students can begin by *either* creating their own patterns *or* building a given pattern, such as 3, 6, 9, 12, … using tiles or pegs.	Present students with more complicated sequences, such as 2, 5, 9, 14, 20, … ($T_{n+1} = T_n + n + 2$; 27, 35) 0, 1, 3, 6, 10, … ($T_{n+1} = T_n + n$; 15, 21) 28, 26, 23, 19, … ($T_{n+1} = T_n - n - 1$; 14, 8) Students should explain each number pattern and find the next two numbers in each sequence.

Literacy	Links
The word *sequence* has the general meaning of 'the following of one thing after another', such as a sequence of dance steps. In mathematics, the word is used for a series of numbers which arise from a pattern. The word comes from a Latin word meaning 'follow'.	There are some useful online tools which provide an opportunity for students to test their understanding of simple sequences. For example, the 'Spooky Sequences' games involve counting forwards and backwards in different increments. www.primaryhomeworkhelp.co.uk/maths/interactive/numbers.htm#Sequences The 'Domino Sequences' activity provides a good visual representation of sequences. www.nrich.maths.org/241

Alternative approach

Sequences can be explored and created electronically. Various approaches can be found in MyMaths lesson 1173 ('Sequences').

Checkpoint

1 Show this pattern of pattern coloured tiles/counters.

a How many tiles you would need in the next two stages of the pattern? (13, 16)

b What is the difference between each number in the sequence? (3)

c Write down the number sequence. (1, 4, 7, 10, 13, 16)

Starter – Consecutives

Ask students to give

- 2 consecutive integers with a sum of 15 (7, 8)
- 2 consecutive integers with a sum of 25 (12, 13)
- 3 consecutive integers with a sum of 30 (9, 10, 11)

Discuss strategies with the students.

Teaching notes

Geometric patterns (in shapes and objects, both man-made and in the natural world) can lead to numerical patterns. Ask students for examples, such as rows of houses having odd and even numbers on opposite sides of the street; the growth of cells in a bees' honeycomb; number of tiles on a bathroom wall depending on the shape and size of the tile. Discuss the word 'sequence', its general meaning as 'the following of one thing after another' and its numerical application to shapes and patterns as they grow.

Ask students to create growing patterns using

- pegs on a pegboard;
- various shapes of tile from commercial kits;
- dots on dotted square grids and isometric paper;
- rubber bands on geoboards.

In each case, they should write the numeric sequence and predict the next number.

A paired activity uses a pack of 12 cards. Four cards show an increasing pattern of triangles, four show an increasing pattern of squares and four show an increasing pattern of circles. Students separate the pack into the three sequences (different shapes) and write each sequence, such as 'The sequence is 2, 5, 8, 11'. They predict the next number in each sequence (14 in this case.)

Plenary

Have two cards numbered 5 and 11 and one card labelled with a question mark. Show the three cards 5, 11, ? to the class and ask for the missing number in this sequence. Students should answer on mini-whiteboards and give reasons for their answers. There will likely be more than one valid solution.
(In a linear sequence, ? = 17)

Repeat with the same cards in these orders 5, ?, 11 and ?, 5, 11.
(In linear sequences, ? = 8 and ? = -1)

Add an extra card. Show four cards 5, 11, ?, ? to the class and ask for the missing numbers.
(In a linear sequence, the numbers are 17 and 23)

Repeat for (5, ?, ? ,11), (?, 5, ?, 11) and (?, 5, 11, ?).
(In linear sequences, the numbers are 7 and 9; 2 and 8; -1 and 17))

Exercise commentary

Having a number line to refer to throughout this exercise would be useful.

Question 1 – Remind students that the same number has to be added (or, for part **d**, subtracted) repeatedly. Refer them to a number line if necessary.

Questions 3 and **4** – In Question **3**, the difference that is added, or subtracted, is found directly from the number line. In Question **4**, the difference is found by subtracting adjacent terms (or by referring to a number line) and, at the same time, noting whether the sequence is increasing or decreasing.

Question 6 – The numbers for this sequence are not in order and 9, 25, 37 and 45 are missing. Pairs of students could have cards for each number and each question mark to manipulate and so help to order them. It will help to start by putting the numbered cards in numeric order and look for a pattern of (almost) equal jumps.

Answers

1 **a** 31, 32, 33, 34, 35, 36, 37, 38
b 3, 5, 7, 9, 11, 13, 15, 17, 19
c 6, 9, 12, 15, 18, 21, 24, 27
d 41, 37, 33, 29, 25, 21, 17, 13

2 **a** 3, 5, 7, 9 **b** 2, 6, 10, 14
c 13, 10, 7, 4 **d** 4, 7, 10, 13

3 **a** **i** 13, 15, 17, 19, 21, 23, 25, ...
ii 75, 65, 55, 45, 35, 25, 15, ...
iii 4, 9, 14, ...
b **i** +2 **ii** −10 **iii** +5
c **i** 27 **ii** 5 **iii** 19

4 **a** 17, 20 **b** 31, 37 **c** 16, 12 **d** 32, 64

5 24, 35

4 1, 5, 9, 13, 17, 21, 25, 29, 33, 37, 41, 45

13b Describing sequences

Objectives	
• Describe integer sequences.	(L4)

Key ideas	Resources
1 A sequence needs a first term and a rule to get from one term to the next.	Sequences (1173) Collections of different shaped tiles A computer spreadsheet

Simplification	Extension
Make the activity practical by giving students small tiles with which to create terms/patterns in the sequence. As students make the second term/pattern from the first ask them, what did you do to make the next pattern? Then, will this work for the next term/pattern too?	Present students with more complicated sequences involving all four operations, such as 3, 6, 10, 15, 21,... ($T_{n+1} = T_n + n + 3$; 28, 36) 2, 6, 18, 54, 162,... ($T_{n+1} = 3 \times T_n$; 486, 1458) 50, 44, 38, 32, 26,... ($T_{n+1} = T_n - 6$; 20, 14) 320, 160, 80, 40,... ($T_{n+1} = T_n \div 2$; 20, 10) Students explain each number pattern and find the next two numbers in each sequence. Give students eight numbers; for example 1, 2, 4, 6, 7, 8, 10, 14. They choose four numbers from these eight, make a sequence and give its rule. They make three more different sequences by choosing four other numbers from these eight and give the rule each time.

Literacy	Links
Each number in a sequence is called a *term.* The sequence starts with the first term which is followed by the second term, and so on. The rule studied in this exercise lets a student find the next number of a sequence from the previous number. It is called a *term-to-term rule.*	In the Fibonacci sequence, each number is found by adding together the two numbers before it. So the first few terms are 0, 1, 1, 2, 3, 5, 8, 13, 21, 34...These numbers appear frequently in nature. The sequence is named after the Italian mathematician Fibonacci, also known as Leonardo of Pisa, who lived between about 1170 and 1250. There is more about the sequence at www.mathsisfun.com/numbers/fibonacci-sequence.html

Alternative approach

A spreadsheet can be set up to produce a sequence very quickly. Key the first number of the sequence into cell A1. Click on cell A2 and set up the rule by keying = A1 + 6 followed by the return key. This rule adds 6 onto the first term. Then drag the rule down the spreadsheet to create the sequence. Experiment with other rules.

Checkpoint

1 For the following sequences **i** What is the starting number? **ii** What is the rule?
- **a** 1, 3, 5, 7 (1, + 2)
- **b** 18, 6, 3, 1 (18, ÷ 3)

2 Another sequence has starting number 20 and the rule is – 4.
What are the first five numbers in the sequence? (20, 16, 12, 8, 4)

Starter – What comes next?

Ask students to give the next two terms in the following sequences, showing answers on their mini-whiteboards:

2, 3, 4, 5, …
2, 4, 6, 8, …
2, 4, 8, 16, …

Discuss strategies and rules with the students.

Teaching notes

Ask students what is needed to describe a sequence. Agree that the first term is needed and also a 'rule' to find the next term. Decide that the 'rule' can use any of the four basic operations: +, –, ×, ÷.

Use some small tiles to make a pattern. Show students the first pattern of tiles and ask what the first number of the sequence is. Add more tiles; ask for the second number of the sequence; ask for a possible rule. Repeat for the next pattern and ask if the rule is still working. Repeat again.

Now try the same process without tiles. Ask students to find the first three numbers of a sequence by giving them the first number and the rule. Use these examples.

- The first number is 4. You add 3 each time.
- The first number is 5. You add 2 each time.
- The first number is 26. You take away 4 each time.

Set a sequence in context. Say that you have a savings account, which started with £100 in it. Say that you save £15 each week to put into the account. Ask students to give the weekly amounts over time as a sequence.

Now suppose that it is not a savings account. Instead you start with £100 and spend £15 each week. Students give new weekly amounts as a sequence.

Plenary

Write the numbers 1, 2, 4 and 6 on separate cards. Ask students in groups of two or three to find as many different sequences of three numbers made from these cards. Arrange the numbers in ascending order.

For each of their sequences, ask the group to agree

- the next two numbers in the sequence;
- the rule for the sequence;
- which was the easiest sequence to devise and which was the most difficult?

Exercise commentary

Question 1 – Part **a i** could have a sequence which includes the red tile and another sequence that does not. This might be worth discussing as a class once students have attempted the question.

Question 2 –Students could copy the two lists side-by-side before drawing connecting lines to match the descriptions and sequences. A useful strategy is to start by pairing rules and numbers which a student is confident about as this eliminates possibilities from the more difficult considerations.

Question 3 – Each description needs both a first term and a rule for how to get from one term to the next.

Question 4 – Students could write out the sequence, with first term 1 and rule '+3'. They then need to check whether 17 appears in the sequence.

It is not intended to be a trick question with the original 18th plank now being the 17th due to the missing plank.

Question 5 – The most straightforward answer is by a direct demonstration. Students may (be encouraged to) notice that each term is 2 less than a multiple of 5; in which case they could say that zero is not 2 less than any multiple of 5.

Answers

1 **a** **i** 5, 9, 13 **ii** 15, 12, 9, 6
iii 2, 4, 8, 16 **iv** 18, 10, 2
c **i** Start at 5 and + 4 **ii** Start at 15 and – 3
iii Start at 2 and × 2 **iv** Start at 18 and – 8
e **i** 17, 21 **ii** 3, 0 **iii** 32, 64 **iv** -6, -14

2 **a** B **b** F **c** C **d** A
e D **f** E

3 **a** Start at 1 and × 2 **b** Start at 1 and × 3
c Start at 8 and + 3 **d** Start at 5 and × 5
e Start at 24 and ÷ 2 **f** Start at -9 and + 3
g Start at 19 and – 4 **h** Start at 2 and + 1.5

4 No (1, 4, 7, 10, 13, 16, 19 …)

5 **a** 3, -2, -7
b By writing out the terms.
c -2

13c Using rules

Objectives	
• Generate terms in a sequence given a simple term-to-term rule. (L4)	
Key ideas	**Resources**
1 To create a sequence, there needs to be a first term and a term-to-term rule.	Sequences (1173) Two sets of cards: one set gives first terms, the other set gives rules Counters and small tiles Number lines Dictionaries
Simplification	**Extension**
Some students may find access to practical equipment, such as tiles or counters, useful. Other students may prefer to use number lines, using arrowed jumps along the line from the first term.	A building has three lifts. They all start at floor 1. The first lift stops at floor 2 and then every second floor after that. The second lift stops at floor 3 and then every third floor after that. The third lift stops at floor 5 and then every fifth floor after that. Write a sequence of the floors that each lift stops at. (2, 4, 6, 8, 10, …; 3, 6, 9, 12, 15,…; 5, 10, 15, 20, 25,…) Which is the first floor (after 1) at which they all stop? (30) On which floors does no lift stop? (7, 11, 13, ...)
Literacy	**Links**
The word *term* has many meanings. Consider asking students to use a dictionary to find as many as possible. It derives from the Latin word 'terminus' which means 'end' or 'limit'. A 'school term' is for a limited time. We still use the word 'terminus' today to mean a railway station at the end of the line, such a Kings Cross or Paddington in London.	A time lapse video clip of a plant growing, 'rosette growth', can be viewed at plantsinmotion.bio.indiana.edu/plantmotion/vegetative/veg.html How many leaves does the plant have by the end of the video clip?

Alternative approach

A sequence set in context can provide a useful start to this exercise. For example, on cloudless sunny days, the solar panels on a house roof generate 12 kilowatts of energy. The meter reading at the start of a sunny spell read 3456. If the sunny spell lasted 5 days, what are the meter readings at the end of each day?
(3468, 3480, 3492, 3504, 3516)

Checkpoint

1 For the following sequences **i** What is the rule? **ii** What is the next term?

- **a** 20, 24, 28, 32 (+ 4, 36)
- **b** 3, 6, 12, 24 (× 2, 48)

2 Give the first four terms of these sequences.

- **a** Start at 40 and ÷2 (40, 20, 10, 5)
- **b** Start at 25 and –3 (25, 21, 18, 15)

Starter – Generations

Ask students to give, on their mini-whiteboards, the next three terms in sequences defined like these.

- The first term is 12; the rule is 'add 7' (12, 19, 26)
- The first term is 100; the rule is 'subtract 6' (100, 94, 88)
- The first term is 3; the rule is 'add 0.5' (3, 3.5, 4)
- The first term is $\frac{1}{4}$; the rule is 'double' ($\frac{1}{4}$, $\frac{1}{2}$, 1)

Teaching notes

In the previous exercise, students found the rule for a given sequence. In this exercise, they create the sequence for a given rule.

Start a whole-class activity by marking a number on a blank number line and giving a rule, such as '+ 4'. Ask students to draw a number line on their mini-whiteboards and mark the first four terms of the sequence with arrows labelled '+ 4' which jump from term to term.

Give pairs of students two sets of cards: one set has cards with a number on each one; the other set has an operation (such as '+ 3') on each one. Each student selects one card from each pack and gives it to their partner. They each write the first five terms of a sequence and exchange their answers for their partners to check.

A discussion can extend to comparing sequences with similar terms in different order, such as 3, 7, 11, 15, … and 15, 11, 7, 3, …

Plenary

Set sequences in context. Here are two examples.
David's grandparents retired to Spain in 2001. He has visited them every three years. Write the next four years when he went to Spain to see them.
Julia had £650 in her bank account in January. She draws out £110 each month. Write how much is in the account each month after January. When can she no longer carry on doing this?

Exercise commentary

Question 1 – Students should draw four diagrams, one for each term.

Question 2 – Students draw three plants. Ask whether the sequence can continue and why it cannot go into negative numbers.

Question 5 – The sequence cannot extend beyond 20, as there are only 20 floors.

Question 6 – Ask students whether they can see a pattern (a sequence) for the floors where both lifts stop.

Question 7 – Suggest that students draw the relevant part of a number line – starting at 109 – and count up in steps of 2. Check that they do not confuse left and right and therefor want to count down (to obtain 93).

The numbers on the house doors are increasing to the left which is the opposite of a conventional number line. Once a student has finished it may be useful to demonstrate the connection to turn their number line upside down so that it coincides with the house numbering.

In Britain the common convention is to have house numbers increase as you move away from a town centre with, as you look outward, odd numbers on the left hand side and even numbers on the right hand side of a street.

Answers

1 **a, b** Students answers; differences must be +3

2 **a** Check drawings for 8 leaves, 5 leaves, 2 leaves
b 11
c Start at 11 and – 3

3 **a** Start at 90 and – 5
b 75
c No; all terms are multiples of 5 and 24 is not.

4 **a** 6, 10, 14, 18, 22 **b** 80, 40, 20, 10
c 2, 6, 18, 54 **d** 25, 19, 13, 7
e 11, 18, 25, 32

5 2, 5, 8, 11, 14, 17, 20

6 **a** 1, 4, 7, 10, 13, 16, 19
3, 5, 7, 9, 11, 13, 15, 17, 19
b 7, 13, 19
c 2, 6, 8, 12, 14, 18, 20

7 133

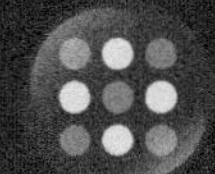

13d Sequences with negative numbers

Objectives	
• Use negative numbers in a sequence (L4)	
Key ideas	**Resources**
1 A sequence can contain negative numbers. **2** The sequence may start with a negative number.	Sequences (1173) Number lines labelled from -10 to +10
Simplification	**Extension**
Ensure that students are secure with positive numbers before encountering negative numbers. When adding to or subtracting from a negative number, the students should count the steps on a number line.	Give students a set of five numbers, such as 4, -2, -8, 1, -11. Say that these numbers are from a sequence but they are out of order, and there is one number missing. Ask the students to find the missing number and explain the rule of the sequence. Pairs of students can make up similar problems, exchange them, find the sequences and check their results.
Literacy	**Links**
One of the contexts for negative numbers relates to a bank account. Students may not know the words 'credit', 'debit' and 'balance'. They may not have met the phrases 'in the red' and 'in the black', which come from the days when red and black ink was used to show whether the account was in debt or not.	Charities rely on donations from members of the public. Nowadays, many people opt to pay a *direct debit* to the charity of their choice. They pay a small amount of money each month. A monthly donation of £2, for example, would show up on a bank statement as a sequence of 12 lots of -2 over the course of a year, where '-2' represents a payment of £2 being made.
Alternative approach	
The use of a speadsheet as in lesson **13b** is helpful here too.	
Checkpoint	
1 Without the aid of a number line **a** Start at 0 and count out loud in 2s up to 10 (0, 2, 4, 6, 8, 10) **b** Start at 0 and count out loud in 2s down to -10 (0, -2, -4, -6, -8, -10) **2** Imagine that you have borrowed £25 from a friend and you are paying back £5 a week. **a** Write this down as a sequence. (-25, -20, -15, -10, -5) **b** How long will it take you to pay back all of thc money? (5 weeks)	

Starter – Quick fire

Ask students to respond on mini-whiteboards to a series of quick questions which recap previous work on algebra and sequences in particular. Include questions such as:

Write the next three terms of these sequences.

- A first term of 7 and the rule '– 3'. (7, 4, 1, -2, -5)
- A first term of -2 and the rule '+ 2' (-2, 0, 2, 4)

Discuss questions when their answers indicate a need.

Teaching notes

A vertical number line labelled from -10 to +10 is useful, as are smaller number lines with the same range for each student.

Explore scenarios in context as in these examples.

- In a science experiment, the temperature of a liquid falls by 2 degrees every minute. Give the initial temperature and write the temperature every minute thereafter.
- A helicopter lowers a weight vertically on a wire. The weight starts 8 metres above sea-level and drops 3 metres every second. Write the height of the weight above sea-level for the next few minutes.
- A bank account is in credit, has the same amount withdrawn every day, and soon goes into debt. Write the starting sum and the balance every day thereafter.

Plenary

Ask students to draw a number line from -10 to +10 on their mini-whiteboards. Give them a first term and a rule for a sequence. They should then draw labelled arrows on their number line to show the sequence and write the first few terms of the sequence. Repeat with other sequences.

Define some sequences for students to write the first few terms without needing a number line.

Set some sequences in context.

Exercise commentary

A number line which includes negative numbers would be useful on display in the classroom.

Question 1 – Students should take care when working with negative numbers, and should notice that in part **a** the sequence involves addition, but in part **b** it involves subtraction.

Question 3 – Students need to write down the missing terms in the sequence as well as giving the rule.

Question 4 – This assumes that the temperature is rising at 4 degrees per minute over the entire 6 minutes.

Question 5 – There are two elements to the question. The first is repeatedly adding £10 to a negative amount. The second is stepping forward weekly on a calendar, which requires students to know that there are 31 days in July.

Answers

1 **a** -10, -8, -6, -4, -2, 0, 2, 4
 b -1, -3, -5, -7, -9, -11, -13, -15

2 3

3 **a** -10, -7, -4, -1, 2 Start at -10 and + 3
 b -15, -12, -9, -6, -3 Start at -15 and + 3
 c -5, -3, -1, 1, 3 Start at -5 and + 2
 d -8, -6, -4, -2, 0 Start at -8 and + 2
 e 2, 0, -4, -4, -6 Start at 2 and – 2
 f 4, 1, -2, -5, -8, -11, -14 Start at 4 and – 3

4

Time (min)	0	1	2	3	4	5	6
Temp (°C)	-10	-6	-2	2	6	10	14

5 13th August

Key outcomes	Quick check
Find patterns in sequences of numbers L3	**1** Draw the next two terms in this pattern and write it as a number sequence. (2, 4, 6, 8, 10, 12) **2** Find the next two terms in each sequence. **a** 7, 11, 15, 19, □, □ (23, 27) **b** 13, 24, 35, 46, □, □ (57, 68) **c** 78, 75, 72, 69, □, □ (66, 63) **d** 81, 72, 63, 54, □, □ (45, 36)
Describe a sequence using a rule to find the next term L4	Describe each sequence in words and find the next two terms. **a** 8, 13, 18, 23, □, □ (Start at 8, add 5; 28, 33) **b** 45, 38, 31, 24, □, □ (Start at 45, subtract 7; 17, 10) **c** 3, 6, 12, 24, □, □ (Start at 3, multiply by 2; 48, 96) **d** 70 000, 7000, 700, □, □ (Start at 70 000, divide by 10; 70, 7)
Generate terms in a sequence using a rule L4	Find the first four terms of these sequences. **a** Start at 11, add 3 (11, 14, 17, 20) **b** Start at 20, subtract 4 (20, 16, 12, 8) **c** Start at 3, multiply by 3 (3, 9, 27, 81) **d** Start at 400, divide by 2 (400, 200, 100, 50)
Use negative numbers in a sequence L4	**1** For each sequence **i** find the missing terms **ii** describe the sequence in words. **a** -15, -12, □, -6, □, (-9, -3; Start at -15, subtract 3) **b** -20, □, -14, -12, □ (-18, -10; Start at -20, add 2)

I

Development and links
The ability to generate repetitive patterns is used in some of the work on ratio and proportion in chapter **15**. In book **2A** sequences are used to describe real-life situations, position-to-term rules are used and the sequence of triangular numbers is introduced. People are very good at spotting patterns and numerical patterns often lead to sequences. It should not be surprising then that people have found lots of sequences around them and lots of ways to investigate and describe their structure.

MyMaths extra support

Lesson/online homework	Description
Negative numbers 1 1069 L3	This lesson revises the meaning of negative numbers, ordering them and finding differences involving them.

My Review

13 MySummary

Check out

You should now be able to ...

	Test it ➡ Questions
✓ Find patterns in sequences of numbers.	(5) 1, 2
✓ Describe a sequence using a rule to find the next term.	(4) 3, 4
✓ Generate terms in a sequence using a rule.	(4) 5
✓ Use negative numbers in a sequence.	(4) 6 – 8

Language	Meaning	Example
Sequence	A set of numbers that follow a rule.	1, 3, 5, 7, 9, ...
Rule	An operation to describe the link between two numbers that are next to each other in a sequence.	To get from 7 to 9, you apply the rule 'add 2'
Term	A number in a sequence. (The word 'term' is also used to mean part of an expression in algebra).	The second term is 3

13 MyReview

1 Write this pattern as a number sequence.

2 Find the next two numbers in each sequence.

a 3, 6, 9, 12, ..., ...
b 5, 9, 13, 17, ..., ...
c 8, 14, 20, 26, ..., ...
d 3, 15, 27, 39, ..., ...
e 50, 48, 46, 44, ..., ...
f 60, 52, 44, 36, ..., ...

3 Write a description for each sequence.

a 7, 17, 27, 37, ...
b 9, 16, 23, 30, ...
c 30, 27, 24, 21, ...
d 2, 4, 8, 16, ...
e 3, 12, 48, 192, ...
f 200, 100, 50, 25, ...

4 For each sequence

i describe the sequence
ii find the next two terms in the sequence.

a 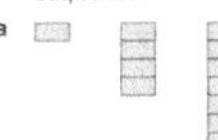 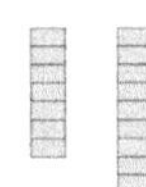

b

5 Work out the first four terms of the sequences with these descriptions.

a *Start at 3 and +5*
b *Start at 7 and +11*
c *Start at 50 and -9*
d *Start at 2 and ×5*
e *Start at 1 and ×6*
f *Start at 5000 and ÷10*

6 Find the missing terms of each sequence.

a -12, -8, ..., 0, ...
b -1, ..., -5, -7, ...
c -18, ..., -4, 3, ...

7 Write a description for each sequence.

a -17, -11, -5, 1, 7
b -5, -8, -11, -14, -17

8 Work out the first four terms of the sequences with these descriptions.

a *Start at 9 and -7*
b *Start at -14 and +8*
c *Start at -7 and -11*

What next?

Score	
0 – 3	Your knowledge of this topic is still developing. To improve look at Formative test: 1A-13; MyMaths: 1173
4 – 6	You are gaining a secure knowledge of this topic. To improve look at InvisiPen: 281
7 – 8	You have mastered this topic. Well done, you are ready to progress!

Question commentary

Questions 1 and **2** – (lesson **13a**) Test students understanding by asking them to give the term-to-term rules for each sequence: **1** +2, **2a** +3, **b** +4, **c** +6, **d** +12, **e** –2 and **f** –8.

Questions 3 and **4** – (lesson **13b**) Students must remember to state the start term as well as how to move from one term to the next. In part **ii**, the answers should be given as numbers and not as diagrams.

Question 5 – (lesson **13c**) Allow the use of a calculator for part **e**.

Question 6 – (lesson **13d**) Students need to work out the term-to-term rules by looking at the differences between neighbouring terms: **a** +4, **b** –2 and **c** +7

Questions 7 and **8** – (lesson **13d**) Students are likely to make mistakes with the negative numbers.

Answers

1 2, 4, 6, ...

2 **a** 15, 18 **b** 21, 25 **c** 32, 38 **d** 51, 63
e 42, 40 **f** 28, 20

3 **a** Start at 7 and add 10
b Start at 9 and add 7
c Start at 30 and subtract 3
d Start at 2 and double / multiply by 2
e Start at 3 and multiply by 4
f Start at 200 and halve / divide by 2

4 **a** **i** Start at 1 and add 3 **ii** 13, 16
b **i** Start at 26 and add subtract 3 **ii** 14, 11

5 **a** 3, 8, 13, 18 **b** 7, 18, 29, 40
c 50, 41, 32, 23 **d** 2, 10, 50, 250
e 1, 6, 36, 216 **f** 5000, 500, 50, 5

6 **a** -12, -8, -4, 0, 4 **b** -1, -3, -5, -7, -9
c -18, -11, -4, 3, 10

7 **a** Start with -17 and add 6
b Start with -5 and subtract 3

8 **a** 9, 2, -5, -12 **b** -14, -6, 2, 10
c -7, -18, -29, -40

13 MyPractice

13a

1 Write the missing terms in each sequence.

a 8, 10, __ , 14, 16 | b 0, __ , 14, 21, 28
c 21, 18, 15, 12, __ | d 2, 4, 6, __ , 10
e __ , 6, 18, 54, 162 | f 11, __ , 17, 20, __
g __ , 16, 14, __ , 10 | h 32, __ , 22, 17, __
i 8, __ , __ , 20, 24 | j __ , __ , 19, 15, 11

2 Jack is on his 'Space Hopper'. He is bouncing along a number line.

a

2 3 4 5 6 7 8 9 10 11 12 13 14 15 16 17 18 19 20

What is the next number Jack will land on? What is the rule?

b

2 3 4 5 6 7 8 9 10 11 12 13 14 15 16 17 18 19 20

What is the next number Jack will land on? What is the rule?

3 What is the next number in each sequence?

a 2, 4, 6, 8, __ | b 1, 4, 7, 10, __
c 3, 5, 7, 9, __ | d 2, 6, 10, 14, __
e 5, 10, 15, 20, __ | f 10, 20, 30, 40, __
g 9, 7, 5, 3, __ | h 15, 12, 9, 6, __
i 20, 16, 12, 8, __ | j 60, 50, 40, 30, __

13b

4 Match the sequences on the right with the statements on the left.

a	'Multiply by 3'
b	'Add 35'
c	'Divide by 4'
d	'Multiply by 5'
e	'Subtract 25'
f	'Divide by 6'

A	105, 80, 55, 30
B	45, 80, 115, 150
C	768, 192, 48, 12
D	25, 75, 225, 675
E	12, 60, 300, 1500
F	5400, 900, 150, 25

13b

5 Write the first four numbers in each sequence using the rule.

a The first number is 2. The rule is +4.
b The first number is 5. The rule is +3.
c The first number is 21. The rule is −3.
d The first number is 50. The rule is −10.
e The first number is 11. The rule is +5.
f The first number is 24. The rule is −4.

13c

6 Write out the first five terms for each sequence.

a Start at 4. The rule is +5. | b Start at 23. The rule is −3.
c Start at 0. The rule is +4. | d Start at 21. The rule is −4.
e Start at 30. The rule is +2. | f Start at 32. The rule is −5.

7 Copy and complete this description for each of these sequences:

Start at _____. The rule is _____.

a 1, 4, 7, 10, … | b 17, 14, 11, 8, … | c 9, 13, 17, 21, …
d 80, 70, 60, 50, …. | e 29, 24, 19, 14, … | f 8, 15, 22, 29, …

8 Copy and complete these statements for each of the sequences.

▶ The rule is ______.
▶ The next three terms are ______, ______, ______.

a 2, 5, 8, 11, … | b 2, 3, 4, 5, …
c 20, 18, 16, 14, 12, … | d 5, 7, 9, 11, 13, ….
e 2, 10, 18, 26, … | f 3, 6, 9, 12, 15, …
f 30, 26, 22, 18, 14, … | h 20, 30, 40, 50, …

13d

9 Use the number lines to help you find the missing terms.

a -22 -20 -18 -16 -14 -12 -10 -8 -6 -4 -2 0

-22, -18, -14, □, □, □

b -10 -9 -8 -7 -6 -5 -4 -3 -2 -1 0 1 2 3

□, -7, -4, □, □, □

c -10 -9 -8 -7 -6 -5 -4 -3 -2 -1 0 1 2 3

3, □, -5, □, □, □

Question commentary

Questions 1 – These are all linear sequences. Emphasise that a good first strategy is always to look at the differences between neighbouring terms; here all the differences are constant. Ask students to write out the full sequences, not just the missing terms, so that they can check that their answers follow the pattern they have found.

Questions 2 – In part **b**, check that students read the sequence in the direction of the arrows and don't simply read it from left to right.

Question 3 – These are all linear sequences; the last four parts include decreasing sequences. The question can be extended by asking students to write out the rule and starting number.

Question 4 – Some of these sequences are geometric. They can be identified by the fact that neighbouring terms differ by a constant multiplier or divisor. Consider organising students into small groups or pairs so that they can discuss their strategies for identifying the correct pairings. One simple strategy is to apply each given rule to the first term in each sequence and test if it generates the subsequent terms.

Questions 5 and **6** – These questions can be usefully extended by asking students to generate further sequences using the same rules but different starting values. Emphasise that both pieces of information need to be given in order to uniquely describe a sequence.

Questions 7 and **8** – All these sequences are linear. It may be helpful to do a few question parts together so that it becomes clear to students what they need to write once they have found the rule.

Questions 9 – Emphasise that the students should treat these questions just like the others, applying the same methods to identify the rules and find missing terms, in the hope that the negative numbers will be taken in their stride.

Answers

1 **a** 8, 10, 12, 14, 16 **b** 0, 7, 14, 21, 28
c 21, 18, 15, 12, 9 **d** 2, 4, 6, 8, 10
e 2, 6, 18, 54, 162 **f** 11, 14, 17, 20, 23
g 18, 16, 14, 12, 10 **h** 32, 27, 22, 17, 12
i 8, 12, 16, 20, 24 **j** 27, 23, 19, 15, 11

2 **a** 4 Start at 4 and + 3 **b** 3 Start at and – 5

3 **a** 10 **b** 13 **c** 11 **d** 18
e 25 **f** 50 **g** 1 **h** 3
i 4 **j** 20

4 **a** D **b** B **c** C **d** E
e A **f** F

5 **a** 2, 6, 10, 14 **b** 5, 8, 11, 14
c 21, 18, 15, 12 **d** 50, 40, 30, 20
e 11, 16, 21, 26 **f** 24, 20, 16, 12

6 **a** 4, 9, 14, 19, 24 **b** 23, 20, 17, 14, 11
c 0, 4, 8, 12, 16 **d** 21, 17, 13, 9, 5
e 30, 32, 34, 36, 38 **f** 32, 27, 22, 17, 12

7 **a** Start at 1. The rule is + 3
b Start at 17. The rule is – 3
c Start at 9. The rule is + 4
d Start at 80. The rule is – 10
e Start at 29. The rule is – 5
f Start at 8. The rule is + 7

8 **a** The rule is + 3 The next three terms are 14, 17, 20
b The rule is + 1 The next three terms are 6, 7, 8
c The rule is – 2 The next three terms are 10, 8, 6
d The rule is + 2 The next three terms are 15, 17, 19
e The rule is + 8 The next three terms are 34, 42, 50
f The rule is +3 The next three terms are 18, 21, 24
g The rule is – 4 The next three terms are 10, 6, 2
h The rule is + 10 The next three terms are 60, 70, 80

9 **a** -22, -18, 14, -10, -6 **b** -10, -7, -4, -1, 2, 5
c 3, -1, -5, -9, -13, -17

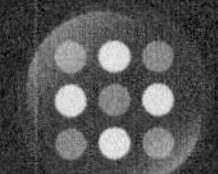

14 Multiplying and dividing

Learning outcomes	
N4 Use the 4 operations, including formal written methods, applied to integers, decimals, proper and improper fractions, and mixed numbers, all both positive and negative.	(L3/4)
N14 Use approximation through rounding to estimate answers and calculate possible resulting errors expressed using inequality notation $a < x \leq b$.	(L4)
N15 Use a calculator and other technologies to calculate results accurately and then interpret them appropriately.	(L4)

Introduction

The chapter starts by looking at multiplication using repeated addition and times tables. Multiplying by 10 and 100 is then covered before mental and written methods are looked at. Division is then covered, both in terms of mental strategies and formal written techniques. The final section covers calculator skills.

The introduction discusses Scott Flansburg, the 'human calculator' and explains that he uses a lot of strategies to do calculations very quickly in his head. You can 'meet' Scott and read about his amazing skill here.

http://thehumancalculator.com/

Using simple tricks to work out calculations quickly in your head can save a lot of time when shopping and working with money.

Some of those simple tricks are discussed in lessons **14c** and **14e** of the chapter. Splitting numbers into their factors, partitioning and the method of 'doubling and halving' are all discussed and used in these sections.

Prior knowledge

Students should already know how to…

- Multiply and divide single digit integers
- Add and subtract integers

Starter problem

The starter problem shows a neat arithmetic trick for multiplying numbers which have the same tens digit and where the units digits add up to 10. Students are invited to investigate this further and can change both the units digits (maintaining the sum to 10) to see it works for other pairs of numbers in the 50s. Using a different tens digit works as well. For example $82 \times 88 = 7216$.

Students could be invited to try and work out why the trick works by looking at the long multiplication sum that results from trying a formal method.

Resources

MyMaths

Money calculations	1014	Division chunking	1021	Doubling and halving	1023
Multiply single digit	1024	Multiplying by 10 and 100	1027	Long division	1041
Dividing	1228	Mixed tables 2 to 12	1367	Sharing	1391
Dividing by 10 and 100	1392				

Online assessment

Chapter test	1A-14
Formative test	1A-14
Summative test	1A-14

InvisiPen solutions

Multiplying and dividing by 10			114
Mental multiplication	122	Mental division	123
Written multiplication	126	Written division	127
Calculator methods	129	Estimating	135

Topic scheme

Teaching time = 8 lessons/3 weeks

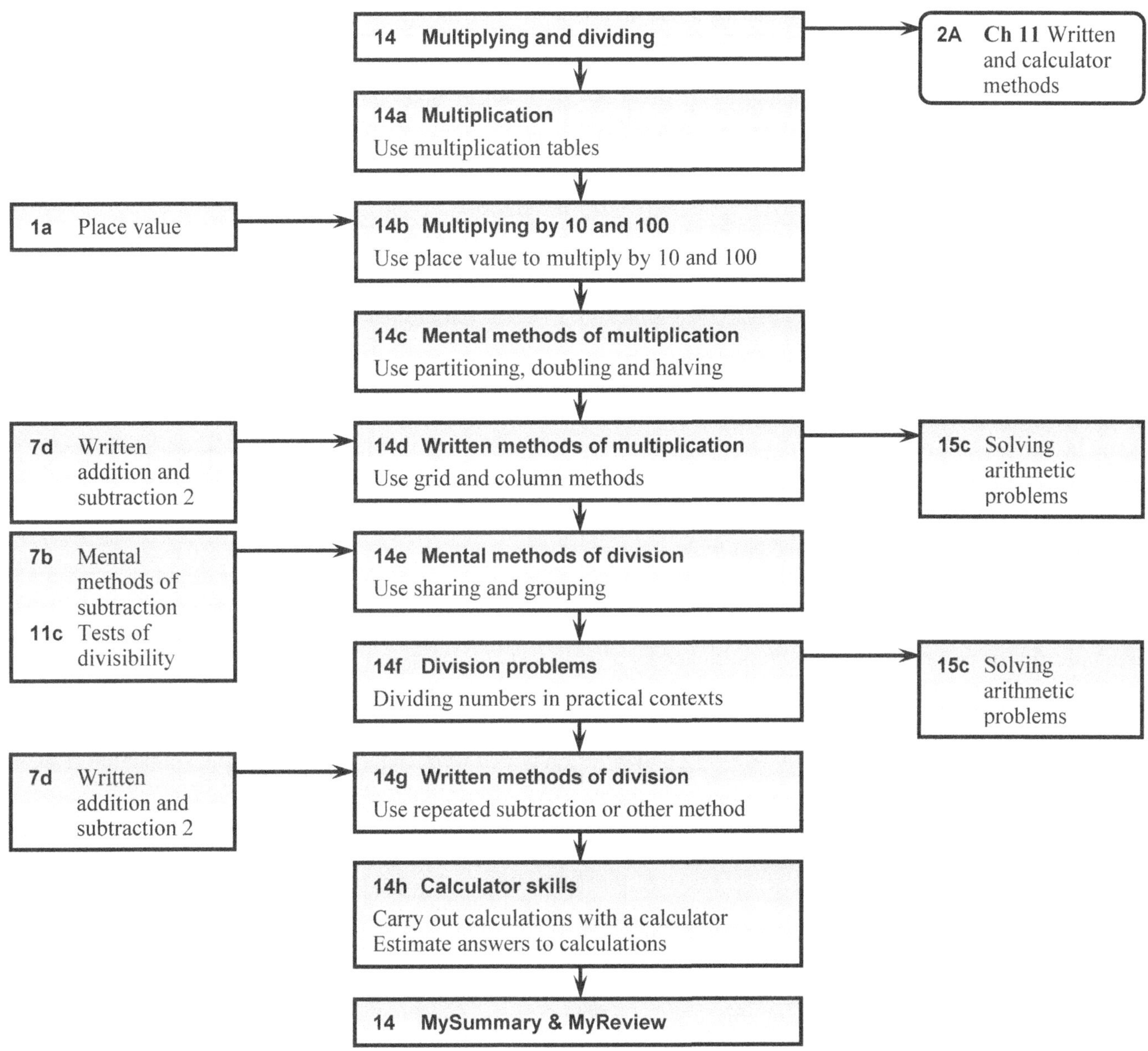

Differentiation

Student book 1A 256 – 277

Multiplication
Multiplying by powers of 10
Mental methods of multiplication
Written methods of multiplication
Mental and written methods of division
Division problems
Calculator methods

Student book 1B 260 – 273

Mental methods of multiplying and dividing decimals
Written methods of multiplying and dividing decimals
Using a calculator and interpreting the display

Student book 1C 260 – 273

Mental methods of multiplying and dividing decimals
Written methods of multiplying and dividing decimals
Calculator methods

14a Multiplication

Objectives

- Recall multiplication facts up to 12 × 12. (L4)
- Solve whole number problems including those involving multiplication. (L3)

Key ideas

1. Multiplication is repeated addition.
2. Multiplication is a commumative operation, that is, $a \times b = b \times a$.

Resources

Mixed tables 2 to 12 (1367)

Blank multiplication grid for students and display
Number lines, counting stick, mini-whiteboards

Simplification

Students who have difficulty recalling their times tables find the 1 times and 10 times tables straightforward. They can then progress to the 2 times table and 5 times table.

The 4 times table can be thought of as twice the 2 times table; for example, 4 × 7 is 'double 2 × 7' = 2 × 14 = 28. Students can then progress to the 3 times table. Use the pattern of the 9 times table; for example, 3 × 9 = 27 has digits 2 and 7 with 2 + 7 = 9. The 6, 7 and 8 times tables are usually learned last.

Extension

Give students a multiplication grid but label the columns and rows in a non-sequential order, say 8, 5, 3, 4, 7… rather than 1, 2, 3, 4… and ask students to complete the grid. This will hide the symmetry associated with swapping rows and columns and remove connections between neighbouring rows and columns. Completing the grid will be more of a test of memory and mental strategies.

Literacy

Multiplication facts can be spoken in various ways. For example, 7 × 6 can be expressed as '7 multiplied by 6', '7 times 6', '7 lots of 6' or '7 sixes'.

If students know that the order of the multiplication does not affect the answer, then it can also be thought of as '6 multiplied by 7' etc.

The expressions '7 lots of 6' and '7 sixes' also relate directly to repeated addition.

Links

The Scottish mathematician John Napier invented a calculating device in the early 1600s which was nicknamed 'Napier's bones' or 'Napier's rods'. It consisted of ten rods, made from ivory, wood or bone, on which were engraved the multiplication table. The device made the multiplication of a number by another one-digit number much quicker to carry out. There is more information about Napier at

www.johnnapier.com/

Alternative approach

Early work with multiplication derives from repeated addition; this suggests a progressive approach.

- Initially counting similar groups of objects as on p258 of the Student Book.
- Shading a number line using two colours for adjacent groups of a number; for example, the 7 times table has 1 – 7 shaded red, 8 – 14 shaded blue, 15 – 21 shaded red, etc. up to 70.
- Using a counting stick to count forwards and then backwards in groups of, say 7, while looking at the shaded number line and then without looking at it.

A student's ability to add (or subtract) to find an unknown fact from a known fact is important. For example, if 6 × 7 is not known, it can be found if 5 × 7 = 35 is known by adding an extra 7 to get 42. Readily known facts can include the more easily remembered tables (such as the 5 times table) and the square numbers. For example, 6 × 7 = 7 × 7 – 7= 49 – 7 = 42 or 6 × 7 = 6 × 6 + 6 = 36 + 6 = 42.

An alternative to chanting a times table in full (such as 'One 4 is 4; two 4s are 8; three 4s are 12; ...'), is just to chant answers ('4, 8, 12, ...') as an aid to concentration. Chanting in sight of a number line and then without a number line can build up confidence.

Checkpoint

1. What is the next multiple of 6 after 24? (30)
2. Can you write the next two multiples of 4 after 28? (32, 36)
3. If 5 × 8 = 40, what is 6 × 8? (48)

Starter – Jumbled products

Write a set of answers on the board: 28, 33, 40, 48, 54.

Ask students to work out what the multiplication questions to *four* of the answers could have been using the following numbers. 3, 4, 5, 6, 7, 8, 9, 11

($4 \times 7 = 28$, $3 \times 11 = 33$, $4 \times 7 = 28$, $5 \times 8 = 40$, $6 \times 9 = 54$)

Challenge students to make up questions for the extra answer.

($48 = 6 \times 8 = 4 \times 12$, 3×16, 2×24, 1×48)

Teaching notes

Note, the primary maths curriculum (England 2014) now includes the 11 times and 12 times tables. Check if some students have only been taught up to the 10 times table.

Ask students to find 3 + 3, then 3 + 3 + 3, then 3 + 3 + 3 + 3 + 3 etc. displaying their answers on their mini-whiteboards. You could go around the class one-by-one. Keep this fairly brief and lively. Then ask for an easier way of phrasing the additions. A cue may come from a student who asks, 'how many threes was that?' Reinforce the link between 3 + 3 + 3 + 3 + 3 + 3 and 'five lots of three'. Then ask, what would the later phrase look like as a calculation? (5×3)

Students should appreciate that multiplication is just repeated addition but that it is easier and quicker to say and write.

Have students write the answers to the 3 times table. Then display a blank multiplication grid, up to 12×12, and ask where the 3 times table can be entered. Now involve students in completing the whole table. Reinforce the patterns in each times table and encourage students to describe these patterns. For example, the 1 times table is just the numbers themselves, the 2 times table is the even numbers, the 5 times table ends 5, 0, 5, 0 etc. You might introduce an error and ask students to find it.

Explore the commutative property of multiplication; for example, '4 lots of 3' is the same as '3 lots of 4'. Point out that each row of the grid has an identical column.

Plenary

Ask contextual questions such as: A double decker sandwich uses three slices of bread. How many slices would you need for eight sandwiches? (24)

Use this example to expand the discussion to explore where students might use multiplication in their everyday lives, for example, finding the total cost of a number of identical items.

Exercise commentary

Question 1 – This question reinforces students' knowledge of the times tables. Part **b** includes parts of the eleven- and twelve-times tables.

Question 2– This requires students to recall multiplication facts in a non-systematic way; the largest example is 9×9. This question can be done with or without sight of a multiplication grid.

Students often find the 6, 7 and 8 times tables hardest to recall; there are various strategies which may help. For example, instead of 5×8 from the 8 times table, students could find 8×5 from the 5 times table. If students know the square numbers, then, for example, $7 \times 7 = 49$ allows you to find 8×7 as $49 + 7 = 56$ and 6×7 as $49 - 7 = 42$.

Question 3 – This tests knowledge of higher entries in the times tables. Students should start by matching pairs which they are confident about.

Question 4 to **6** – These involve using multiplication in simple contexts. Question 6 involves the 11 times table and students can explore the link between the 11 times and 10 times tables.

Further contextual questions could be asked orally with students showing their answers on mini-whiteboards.

Answers

1 **a**

×	1	2	3	4	5	6
1	1	2	3	4	5	6
2	2	4	6	8	10	12
3	3	6	9	12	15	18
4	4	8	12	16	20	24
5	5	10	15	20	25	30
6	6	12	18	24	30	36

b

×	7	8	9	10	11	12
7	49	56	63	70	77	84
8	56	64	72	80	88	96
9	63	72	81	90	99	108
10	70	80	90	100	110	120
11	77	88	99	110	121	132
12	84	96	108	120	132	144

2 **a** 8 **b** 15 **c** 14 **d** 32
e 25 **f** 21 **g** 9 **h** 40
i 18 **j** 81 **k** 16 **l** 56
m 20 **n** 56 **o** 28

3 $12 \times 3 = 36$, $12 \times 11 = 132$, $9 \times 7 = 63$, $11 \times 10 = 110$, $9 \times 9 = 81$

4 80

5 36

6 **a** 22 **b** 55

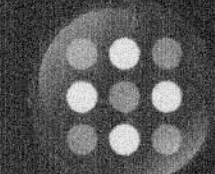

14b Multiplying by 10 and 100

Objectives	
• Multiply and divide integers by 10, 100 and 1000 and explain the effect. (L4)	
Key ideas	**Resources**
1 Multiplying by 10 moves digits one place to the left. **2** Multiplying by 100 moves digits two places to the left.	Multiplying by 10 and 100 (1027) Dienes blocks or equivalent apparatus Place value cards
Simplification	**Extension**
Ask students to write the headings Th, H, T, U, with a two or three-digit number underneath. Ask them to multiply the number by 10 and also 100, writing the answers under the same headings, so that the three numbers are in the appropriate column.	Get students to multiply decimals (with one decimal place) by 10, starting with decimals ending in 'point five'.
Literacy	**Links**
Remind students that they have met the words 'place value' before. A *place value* is the *value* of each digit in a number given to the digit because of its *place* in the number. So the 2 in 1325 has a different value from the 2 in 1235, because it is in a different place. Ask what the values of the 2s are – and also the values of the other digits.	Multiplying by (a power of) ten is easy because we write numbers using positional notation in *base ten*; that is, 1s, 10, 100, 1000s etc. The choice of ten could be based on the fact that we have ten fingers, or toes, to count on. However while it is the most popular base, ten is not the only possibility. For example, the Yuki Indians of California and the Pame Indians of Southern Mexico both use a base eight system because they count using the spaces between their fingers. It might be harder for them to multiply by ten but it is much easier for them to multiply by eight.

Alternative approach

Three approaches have been already offered: the use of Dienes blocks or equivalent apparatus; the use of 'place value' cards; the use of column headings Th, H, T, U. These three approaches are at their most effective when used together. They move from tactile to visual to symbolic representations.

Checkpoint

Use place value cards and ask the following questions.

1 a What does the digit 2 stand for in the number 126? (Twenty)
b Can you show me the 'place value' card for this 2? (20 card)

2 Can you give me the 'place value' cards for a number which is ten times bigger than 126? (1000, 200 and 60)

Starter – Place value revisited

Use the overlapping 'place value' cards to show the number 352 with the cards for 300, 50 and 2. Ask which card is used for the digit 5 (the 50 card). Repeat with other three-digit numbers.

As a whole-class session, ask one student to say a three-digit number, another student to select the correct cards, a third student to say what the number would be after adding 1 or 10 or 100 and a fourth student to supply the new card for that place value.

Teaching notes

The **Starter** above recalls the students' earlier work with place value. Build on it visually using Dienes blocks (or make your own from large squares showing a grid of 100 small squares, strips of 10 small squares, and single small squares). Show (say) two large squares, one strip and three small squares, ask students how many small squares there are altogether (213). Write 213 and ask what letters (T H U) could be written above them to indicate their sizes. Discuss and repeat with other three-digit numbers.

Show a two-digit number, such as 24, and say that you want to show ten times as many squares as these. Ask what you need to do. Discuss each digit in turn. Repeat with other two-digit numbers.

Follow the pattern of moving digits to the left when you ask what to do to make a three-digit number ten times bigger. This multiplication can be visually done if you have a 1000 cube from the Dienes blocks.

Return to multiplying 24. Multiply by 10, one shift left, and then by 10 again, another shift left, labelling using Th H T U. Link with multiplication by 100. Ask how multiplication by 100 be done 'in one move'.

Ask questions in context, such as, how many nails have you in 10 bags if there are 75 in one bag?, with students responding on mini-whiteboards.

At no time should students be told simply to 'add a 0' to multiply by 10. This rule does not work with decimal numbers and leads to misunderstandings in the future which are not easy to rectify.

Plenary

Give a series of quick fire questions for multiplying whole numbers by 10 and 100, including questions set in various contexts. For example, 'Multiply 46 by 10 and by 100. Write both answers' (460, 4600) and 'James drives 12 miles each to work and back. How far does he drive in 10 days and in 100 days?' (120 miles, 1200 miles) Ask students to respond on mini-whiteboards.

Exercise commentary

Questions 1 and **2** – These are straightforward applications with number of initial digits growing from one to three. In both questions, parts **h**, **i**, **l** and **m** may cause minor problems or confusion since the numbers end in zero.

For Questions **3** to **6**, check that students include the units, where appropriate.

Question 3 – This is a visual application of Questions **1** and **2**.

Question 4 – This is Question **3** without the diagrams.

Question 5 – Parts **a** to **c** require students to divide by ten; they should realise that this is the reverse of multiplying by ten. In part **d** the four bags, when full, weigh 40 kg. So simply subtract 3 from 40.

As a challenge, ask students how many bags would be required if you needed 35 kg. (4, which means that they will have 5 kg of cement left over at the end of the job.)

Question 6 – Part **d** involves converting ml to litres. More confident students could be given other examples of unit conversions, especially large units into small unit which involves multiplying. Metric units are introduced in lesson **2g**; metric unit conversions are introduced in Book 2A, lesson **2b**.

Answers

1	**a** 30	**b** 80	**c** 70	**d** 90
	e 160	**f** 170	**g** 190	**h** 200
	i 500	**j** 9710	**k** 6070	**l** 6700
	m 5000	**n** 7700		
2	**a** 300	**b** 500	**c** 1200	**d** 1500
	e 1700	**f** 2400	**g** 3500	**h** 6000
	i 9000	**j** 46 800	**k** 50600	**l** 38 000
	m 70 000	**n** 90 900		
3	**a** 30 m	**b** 50 m	**c** 70 m	**d** 100 m
4	**a** 90 m	**b** 110 m	**c** 190 m	**d** 230 m
	e 70 m	**f** 350 m	**g** 420 m	**h** 440 m
	i 200 m	**j** 1230 m	**k** 2400 m	**l** 3000 m
5	**a** 5	**b** 4	**c** 3	**d** 37 kg
6	**a** 400 ml	**b** 2200 ml	**c** 1500 ml	**d** 1.5 litres

14c Mental methods of multiplication

Objectives

- Multiply and divide integers by 10, 100 and 1000 and explain the effect. (L4)
- Recall multiplication facts up to 12 × 12. (L4)
- Use a range of mental methods of computation with all operations (L4)
- Solve whole number problems including those involving multiplication. (L3)

Key ideas	Resources
1 Multiplications can mentally be performed in parts which are then added together. **2** This process is called 'partitioning'.	Doubling and halving (1023) Materials to make two large posters Calculators

Simplification	Extension
Students who find partitioning and doubling methods difficult will need more practice with questions such 4 × 26, partitioning as 4 × 20 and 4 × 6, adding the answers together and comparing with 4 × 26 on a calculator. Written jottings for each part of the partition are useful as an intermediate position to a fully mental approach. With practice, students will see that any question such as 72 × 3 can be worked out as 70 × 3 + 2 × 3.	Develop the idea of the multiplication of a decimal by a single-digit number as an extension to the partitioning method. You may also want to introduce brackets, e.g. for 3.4 × 3, considering, as a start, 34 × 3 as (30 × 3) + (4 × 3). But this bracketed expression can create confusion and it may be better said than written. There are, of course, other ways of thinking of 3.4 × 3.

Literacy	Links
A balance has to be struck between what is said and what is written. A written approach to 34 × 3, such as (30 × 3) + (4 × 3), may be mathematically correct but visually difficult to understand. It is often better explained orally as 'three lots of thirty plus three lots of 4' which can then be written as 90 + 12.	'Population-doubling time' is the length of time it will take a population to double in size. It is often used as a measure by geographers and biologists to compare rates of growth of populations. The longer the doubling time, the slower the population is growing. The population of the world doubled from 3 billion in 1959 to 6 billion in 1999. What was the doubling time in 1959? The current doubling time for the world's population is about 61 years.

Alternative approach

The visual representation using a grid to partition numbers is often readily understood as a precursor to a fully mental method. For example, a rectangular grid for 4 × 26 is partitioned as two rectangles for 4 × 20 and 4 × 6.

Checkpoint

Ask students to answer these questions and to explain the method they use.

1 45 × 10 (450)
2 23 × 3 (69)
3 170 × 4 (680)

Starter – Partitioning

Write $10 \times 5 = 2 \times 5 + 8 \times 5$ on the board. Ask students to work out the answer.

Ask students to partition 10 in other ways and work out the answers. Emphasise that all the partitionings give the same answer as 10×5.

This can be differentiated by dictating the choice of numbers students should work with.

Teaching notes

Students need regular short practice with recall of simple multiplication facts. For many students at this level, it may be appropriate to work particularly on the 2, 3, 4, 5 and 10 times tables at first and then bring in larger times tables later.

As a starter for the lesson, consider multiplication questions involving × 2, × 4, × 8 by doubling. So 4×14 is seen as '2×14 doubled'; that is, $4 \times 14 = 2 \times 28 = 56$.

Introduce or revisit the concept of partition. Use this method, for example, for multiplying by 3.

So, 3×24 can be thought of as $2 \times 24 + 1 \times 24$ which is said rather than written as 'double 24 and add 24'. 'Double 24' itself is approached mentally as 'double 20 and double 4'. It may be useful to draw rectangles in a 'grid' as a visual representation. For example, reconsider 3×24 and draw

3 × 24 = 3 × | ? | ? | = | 3 × ? | 3 × ? |

= ? + ? = ?

Act as 'secretary' to the students, who should dictate what to replace the question marks by. The teacher can prompt and ask questions as needed.

Plenary

Ask students to work in pairs to find as many ways as possible to work out 4×46. They can contribute one of their methods to a large poster made by the whole class. For example,

$4 \times 46 = 2 \times$ 'double 46' $= 2 \times 92 = 184$;

$4 \times 46 = 46 + 46 + 46 + 46 = 194$;

$4 \times 46 = 4 \times 40 + 4 \times 6 = 160 + 24 = 194$.

Exercise commentary

Question 1 – This is effectively a test of the recall of multiplication tables.

Questions 2 and **3** – There are usually several ways of approaching each multiplication and a group or whole-class discussion to share methods may prove useful. For example, in part **f** of Question **2**, 15×4 could be done using partitioning: $10 \times 4 + 5 \times 4 = 40 + 20 = 60$ or doubling and halving: $15 \times 4 = 30 \times 2 = 60$. Remind students that multiplications can be written 'the other way round', so 20×5 can be thought of as 5×20.

Question 4 – Students may need to be reminded that there are two lots of 500 g in 1 kg (1 kg = 1000 g). It should then be clear what multiplication is required. Students should articulate their thinking.

Question 5 – These questions lend themselves to whole-class discussion with the emphasis as much on the mental methods as on the answers themselves. More of these can be undertaken.

Question 6 – The outcome of this question is a useful method for mentally checking the 9 times table in future. (A divisibility test for 9 is that the sum of the digits is a multiple of 9).

Question 7 – This is a variant of the previous question and the explanation is essentially the same. In this case the sum of the digits goes down by 1 (modulo 8) each time because '+ 1 – 2 = –1'. (In principle an 'add 10 subtract 3' rule works for the 7 times table but there are too many awkward cases for it to be useful.)

Answers

1 **a** 4 **b** 4 **c** 18 **d** 4
e 21 **f** 8 **g** 7 **h** 8

2 **a** 100 **b** 180 **c** 200 **d** 240
e 400 **f** 60 **g** 39 **h** 72
i 110 **j** 1800

3 **a** 70 **b** 78 **c** 430 **d** 530
e 520 **f** 600 **g** 147 **h** 168

4 24

5 **a** 'Digit shift', 130p = £1.30
b Partitioning, $120 \times 3 = 12 \times 3 \times 10 = 360$ = £3.60
c Partitioning, $6 \times 10 + 6 \times 4 = 60 + 24 = 84$

6 54, 63, 72, 81, 90 → 99, 108, 117, 126, 135, 144…
The pattern only works easily up until $10 \times 9 = 90$.
Then $11 \times 9 = (9 + 1) \times 10 + (0 - 1) = 100 - 1 = 99$, after which the pattern is again relatively straightforward.
The rule works because $9 = 10 - 1$

7 40 → 48, 56, 64, 72, 80, → 88, 96, 104, 112…
a Add 1 to the tens digit, subtract 2 from the units digit.
b Since $8 = 10 - 2$, adding 8 is the same as adding 10 and subtracting 2.

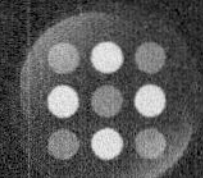

14d Written methods of multiplication

Objectives

- Use efficient written methods of short multiplication. (L4)

Key ideas	Resources
1 Partitioning a number requires a good understanding of the concept of place value.	Multiply single digit (1024) Blank partitioning trees and grids Square grid paper

Simplification	Extension
Multiply two-digit numbers by one-digit numbers, before using three-digit numbers. Blank trees for the partitioning method and blank grids for the grid method, on which students write their working, are a useful support. Students should have a multiplication square up to 10 × 10 to hand to help them. Asking for an initial estimate, for example, '52 × 4 is close to 50 × 4 = 200', reinforces knowledge of place value.	The exercise has been designed to only involve multiplying by numbers in the range 2 to 6. Questions can also be set that multiply by 7, 8 and 9. A further extension is to involve four-digit numbers and then, a greater challenge, to involve numbers with one decimal place, such as 3.5 and 4.2.

Literacy	Links
There are many other ways of multiplying two numbers than the three methods of this exercise. To be numerically literate, that is, numerate, the aim is for students to have a quick, efficient method and the standard column method is the ultimate goal of the National Curriculum. An understanding of 'place value' is essential, with students secure in knowing that the 'place' of a digit determines its 'value' in the number.	The partition of India took place in 1947. India had been ruled by Britain but achieved independence in 1947 and the country was partitioned (or divided) into two separate countries, Hindu India and Muslim Pakistan. Pakistan was in two parts, East and West Pakistan, with India between them. In 1971, East Pakistan became the independent state of Bangladesh. There is more information about the Partition of India at www.news.bbc.co.uk/hi/english/static/in_depth/south_asia/2002/india_pakistan/timeline/default.stm

Alternative approach

When using the standard column method, it is useful for students to have access to square grid paper. They then write only one digit in a square and so are more likely to keep their columns vertical. It may be useful initially to label the columns with H, T, U (hundreds, tens, units) to emphasise the 'place value' of each digit.

Two disadvantages of both the partitioning and grid methods are that the time taken to draw the trees and grids reduces the efficiency of finding the answer and that the need to find the final answer by the addition of parts introduces greater scope for errors.

Split the class into three parts, allocate each of the three methods to the three parts of the class, and time how long it takes for them to find the answers. Explore how long each method took and how many correct answers each method achieved. Ask students which one of the three methods they prefer. Discuss the reasons for their preferences.

Checkpoint

1 Calculate 78 × 5 (390)

- **a** What was your estimate? (80 × 5 = 400)
- **b** How does your answer compare to your estimate? (Should be close)

2 **a** When you calculate 142 × 3 (426), you have to carry a digit.
How do you know if you have written it in the correct column?
(3 × 40 = 120, the 1 goes in the 100s column)

- **b** What happens when you carry the digit for 142 × 3?
(Add the carry digit '1' to the '3' from 3 × 1 to give 4)

Starter – Doubling and halving

Ask students for the answer to 6×2.5 (15)

Discuss any answers and show the following method.

Double the decimal $6 \times 5 = 30$

Halve the answer $30 \div 2 = 15$

Give students more products to calculate, for example,

4×3.5 (14)

5×3.5 (17.5)

9×5.5 (49.5)

Teaching notes

Students are often requested to estimate an answer to a calculation before they do the calculation itself. In effect, they are being asked to get 'a feel' for the answer as a check on their calculated answer. Students need only use a rough approximation; for example, for 183×6 (1098), it is enough to estimate using the approximation 200×6 (1200) rather than 180×6 (1080).

Students may have experienced only limited success so far when multiplying two numbers. The two partitioning methods using the tree and the grid make the underlying structure of the methods very evident; both methods can be demonstrated simultaneously alongside each other.

The move to the standard column method can then be introduced alongside the tree and grid and all three methods performed simultaneously. Explain that the standard method is doing the addition of the parts as it goes along, whereas the tree and grid both need a final addition to get the answer.

To gain confidence with the methods and layout, keep all digits small so that students are using multiplication tables which they are confident with.

Plenary

Take feedback from students on their different approaches. For example, ask for different ways of working out 186×4. Ask for an estimate before any accurate calculation is done.

Compare the different methods, ask which methods were preferred (and why) and which method was the quickest.

Start subsequent lessons with a few simple multiplications to consolidate the standard column method. Provide homework for further practice (on squared paper), initially avoiding the larger digits.

Exercise commentary

Questions 1 – This revises partitioning and the students' understanding of place value (covered in lesson **1a**). Parts **f** – **h** involve numbers in which not all 'places' have a 'value'.

Question 2 – This applies partitioning to two-digit and then three-digit numbers multiplied by a one-digit number. In parts **i** and **j** students may need to be reminded that they can swap the order in multiplications, for example $4 \times 378 = 378 \times 4$.

Question 3 – This applies the grid method to two-digit and then three-digit numbers multiplied by a one-digit number. When students are confident in the layout of the method, further examples can be given requiring them to construct their own grid.

Questions 4 – This applies the standard column method to three-digit numbers multiplied by one-digit numbers. Carry digits occur in most cases; check that these are being handled correctly. For part **j**, students may be encouraged to notice that $5994 = 6000 - 6$ or $999 \times 6 = 1000 \times 6 - 6$ and a mental method is all that is needed.

Question 5 – This requires a mixture of experimentation and being systematic. Students should realise that they should place the higher value digits in the higher value places. The problem can be related to finding a rectangle with the largest area for a given perimeter.

Question 6 – The key is to realise that $5 \times \square + 4 = 39$. The problem can also be solved by division: $1395 \div 5 = 279$. Further 'missing digit' problems can be invented as appropriate.

Answers

1 **a** 200 + 60 + 4 **b** 300 + 50 + 7
c 100 + 50 + 8 **d** 300 + 30 + 3
e 700 + 90 + 6 **f** 600 + 9
g 800 + 50 **h** 700
i 900 + 90 + 9

2 **a** 92 **b** 172 **c** 156 **d** 370
e 378 **f** 708 **g** 1595 **h** 1710
i 1512 **j** 2775

3 **a** 120 + 8 = 128 **b** 250 + 15 = 265
c 80 + 28 = 108 **d** 1200 + 60 + 18 = 1278
e 1000 + 250 + 5 = 1255 **f** 1600 + 240 + 32 = 1872

4 **a** 372 **b** 426 **c** 975 **d** 435
e 1086 **f** 434 **g** 1620 **h** 1518
i 1125 **j** 5994

5 $93 \times 87 = 8091$

6 7

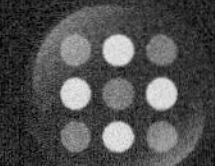

14e Mental methods of division

Objectives

- Multiply and divide integers by 10, 100 and 1000 and explain the effect. (L4)
- Recall multiplication facts up to 12 × 12 and quickly derive corresponding division facts. (L4)
- Use a range of mental methods of computation with all operations. (L4)

Key ideas

1. Division is the inverse of multiplication.
2. One multiplication fact has several other facts associated with it which use multiplication, division and fractions.

Resources

Dividing (1228)
Dividing by 10 and 100 (1392)

Multiplication grids to 10 × 10 and 12 × 12
Copies of the maze in Question **4**
Number lines, counters or cubes
Materials to makes small posters

Simplification

For those whose understanding of division is weak, take 4 groups of 3 counters and combine them into a rectangular array of 12. Say '4 lots of 3 are 12' and write '4 × 3 = 12'. Now do the opposite. Take the same array of 12 counters and divide them into 4 groups. Say '12 divided by 4 gives 3 in each group', and write '12 ÷ 4 = 3'. Students can use counters to write various multiplication facts and their associated division facts by making rectangular arrays.

Extension

Give able students the number 84 and ask them to write as many division problems as they can which start with this number, for example, '84 ÷ 2 = 42'. They could show all their answers on a small poster and then repeat with a number that they choose.

A further extension is to write division facts using fractions; for example, $\frac{1}{2}$ of 84 = 42.

Literacy

Division is the **inverse** of multiplication. The activity in the **Simplification** above demonstrates assembling and disassembling the rows of a rectangular array as a visual action representing multiplication and division. Students can be introduced to the words 'inverse' and 'opposite'.

Links

Armies are usually split into divisions, consisting of several thousand soldiers, and each division in the British Army is commanded by a major-general. A division is made up of three or four brigades, each of which is a collection of different regiments and supporting units. The exact composition of the brigade depends on the job it is designed to do, but usually contains infantry, cavalry and artillery regiments.

Alternative approach

An understanding of division can be developed by progressing through the various representations.

- Assembling and disassembling the rows of a rectangular array of counters.
  For example, 4 rows of 5 counters gives 4 × 5 = 20 and 20 ÷ 4 = 5.
- Forward and backward jumps on a number line.
  For example, 4 forward jumps of 5 from 0 lands on 20; 4 backward jumps of 5 from 20 lands on 0.
- Using a 10 × 10 multiplication grid to find 4 × 5 = 20 and discussing the inverse 20 ÷ 4 = 5.

A further progression leads to the language of fractions. For example, when disassembling the 20 counters in the rectangular array to illustrate 20 ÷ 4, the teacher can ask "Each of these rows is a quarter of the rectangle. So what is a quarter of 20?" The disassembly of the array thus leads not only to 20 ÷ 4 = 5 but also to $\frac{1}{4}$ of 20 = 5.

This thinking leads on to asking "What is a quarter of the way from 0 to 20 on the number line?" and "How can I find a quarter of 20 from the multiplication grid?"

So, for example, 3 × 6 = 18 leads to 18 ÷ 3 = 6 and $\frac{1}{3}$ of 18 = 6. If students know that 3 × 6 = 18 leads to 6 × 3 = 18, then further facts are 18 ÷ 6 = 3 and $\frac{1}{6}$ of 18 = 3.

Checkpoint

1 5 × 4 = 20. What other number facts does this multiplication give you?
(4 × 5 = 20, 20 ÷ 4 = 5, 20 ÷5 = 4 , $\frac{1}{4}$ of 20 = 5, $\frac{1}{5}$ of 20 = 4)

2 **a** What is 360 ÷ 10? (36) **b** What is 36 ÷ 10? (3.6)

Starter – Elevenses

Ask students to start with 300 and keep subtracting 11, writing down as many answers as possible in 1 minute. Have teams of students and a scoring system; for example,

- 10 points for 15 or more correct answers
- 5 points for 10 – 14 correct answers
- 3 points for 5 – 9 correct answers

Teaching notes

Students need to know that division is the inverse of multiplication. They need to practise their multiplication facts regularly and also be asked for related division facts. For example, when asked for 5 × 6, they could then be asked for 30 ÷ 5 and 30 ÷ 6. They then come to associate a multiplication fact with a division fact. For many students at this level, access to a 10 × 10 or 12 × 12 multiplication grid is useful. Ask students to use it to find division facts as well as multiplication facts.

As a starter to the lesson, present the class with 5 × 7 = 35, and ask students to write more facts using these three numbers. Answers should involve the symbols × and ÷. (7 × 5 = 35; 35 ÷ 5 = 7; 35 ÷ 7 = 5) Get students to work in pairs, with one student writing their own multiplication fact and their partner writing three or four associated facts.

Once secure, division facts can be discussed using the language of fractions; so 35 ÷ 5 is seen as $\frac{1}{5}$ of 35.

Remind students that multiplication can be represented by jumps upwards on the number line; for example, 7 × 4 is '7 lots of 4' or 7 leaps of 4 from 0 to 28. On the other hand, 28 ÷ 4 also involves leaps of 4 but, in this case, it is in the opposite direction and it needs 7 leaps of 4 from 28 to reach 0.

Plenary

Firstly, give students a multiplication such as 4 × 7 = 28 and ask them to re-write it as a multiplication, division or fraction in as many ways as they can.

Then give students six or seven numbers, for example, 48, 6, 8, 12, 4, 3, 2. Ask them to make as many division facts as possible using some of these numbers. Take feedback by asking students to articulate their thinking. Ask them to write their divisions facts using fractions.

Exercise commentary

Question 1 – Students may need to be shown how to use the multiplication grid. For 28 ÷ 7, they need to find 28 in either the 7 column and read along to see that it is in row 4 or find 28 row 7 and read up to find that it is in column 4.

Question 2 – Parts **a** to **c** can be found using the multiplication grid. The other parts require answers that are decimals and students need to have a secure knowledge of decimal place value.

Question 3 – This uses backward jumps on a number line to find answers. Students could be provided with blank number lines. In this lesson so far, students have experienced three ways of dividing: the multiplication square, the number line and, mentally, using decimal place value.

Question 4 – If students have copies of the maze, they can trace the path in pencil and correct any errors using an eraser. This is related to factors and multiples which were covered in Chapter **11**.

Question 5 – Those students who need extra support could use cubes or counters in envelopes to model the question. Having solved the question practically, they need to describe their method in writing in words and symbols. This problem is related to finding the mean average which is covered in book **2A**, lesson **8g**.

Answers

1 **a** 4 **b** 3 **c** 9 **d** 4
e 8 **f** 9 **g** 7 **h** 9

2 **a** 8 **b** 10 **c** 12 **d** 39
e 2.5 **f** 4.8 **g** 15 **h** 20

3 Check student's number lines.
The number of jumps down to 0 should be
a 3 **b** 2 **c** 4 **d** 7
e 3 **f** 6 **g** 3 **h** 3

4 3 → 15 → 30 → 21 → 18 → 12 → 9 **C**
7 → 14 → 35 → 21 → 28 → 42 → 70 **B**
6 → 30 → 12 → 24 → 18 → 60 → 36 **E**
5 → 30 → 10 → 25 → 15 → 35 → 40 **D**

5 45 ÷5 = 9 cups

14f Division problems

Objectives

- Recall multiplication facts up to 12 × 12 and quickly derive corresponding division facts. (L4)
- Use a range of mental methods of computation with all operations. (L4)
- Solve whole number problems including those involving division that may give rise to remainders. (L3)

Key ideas

1 The context defines nature of the answer to the division.

2 The same division may have different answers in different contexts.

Resources

Sharing (1391)
Dividing by 10 and 100 (1392)

Sets of five questions, some with incorrect answers
Cubes or counters

Simplification

Those students who need a practical approach can share cubes or counters. Questions **1** and **3** are suitable for this approach. Question **1** could also be attempted using backward jumps on a number line. In parts **b** and **c** of Question **3**, the notion of subtracting batches of 50 (10 groups of 5) is needed.

Extension

The more able students will be able to develop their division strategies using a standard written layout. For example

$\begin{array}{r} 32 \\ 4\overline{)128} \end{array}$ $\qquad$ $\begin{array}{r} 3\ 2\ \text{r}\ 3 \\ 5\overline{)16^{1}3} \end{array}$

Literacy

The context defines the nature of the answers to the questions in the exercise. Consider 15 ÷ 2. The answer may be

- exact and include a fractional or decimal answer, such as cutting a 15-metre plank into two equal pieces;
- an integer answer with a remainder, such as sharing 15 sweets between two children;
- an integer answer which doesn't allow a remainder, such as packing 15 dishes into boxes with no more than 2 dishes per box.

Students should learn to recognise the context of the question in order to give an appropriate answer.

Links

An egg box is a carton designed to carry eggs and protect them so that they do not get broken. It was invented in 1911 by a Canadian man named Joseph Coyle.

In the UK, egg boxes usually hold 6 eggs, but they can come in different sizes, holding up to 8, 10, 15, 18 or 20 eggs.

Alternative approach

Compile a list of scenarios to cover the three possibilities given in **Literacy**, above. Prepare students for these different types of solution by discussing the context in terms of "Does the question want an exact division? Will the question let you have any items left over? Does the question want to use up every item in the problem?" The aim, at this stage, is not so much to find the actual answer as to find the nature of the answer.

For example, the school minibus will seat 20 students. 68 students are going on a school trip using the minibus. How many trips will the minibus have to make? Ask whether it is acceptable to have students left over or whether the bus needs to make an extra journey to take the final few. Only then should you explore the actual number of trips needed by thinking of 68 ÷ 20. This is best thought of as a repeated addition: 20 + 20 + 20 + 8, so 4 trips are needed.

Checkpoint

1 I spend £7 on two identical bags. How much does each bag cost? (£3.50)

2 I have 7 pens and I give as many as possible equally to two friends.
How many do they each get and how many are left? (3 with 1 left)

3 My mother buys 7 bags of potatoes but I can only carry 2 bags at a time home from the corner shop.
How many trips do I have to make to get them all home? (4)

Starter – Sums and products

Ask students to find 2 numbers

- with a sum of 9 and a product of 20 (4 and 5)
- with a sum of 12 and a product of 35 (5 and 7)
- with a sum of 13 and a product of 36. (4 and 9)

Teaching notes

A simple introduction to the lesson could look at simple 'sharing' problems where the answers are small and there may be remainders (such as the example with the cakes on p268 of the Student Book). Develop this method in problems where the resulting solutions are greater than 10 and students practice the grouped 'take away' method shown in the necklace example.

There may be some students who are able to correctly use a standard written layout for division.

$4\overline{)\quad\quad\quad}$

Their use of this method should certainly not be discouraged (providing they are getting the solution correct). A good question to ask them is "In what way is this method the same as the one I am showing you on the board (the repeated subtraction method)? How is your method better than this?"

Extend the discussion to questions where measures such as length, volume and capacity are used and answers may have fractional parts, such as dividing a 5 litre tin of oil into four equal smaller tins to give $1\frac{1}{4}$ litres in each tin.

Plenary

Give students a set of approximately five questions to mark in pairs. Include two or three incorrect answers and ask students to explain to each other why some answers are wrong. Finally, as a whole class, discuss the answers to the questions and correct them where necessary.

Exercise commentary

Question 1 – These 12 short division questions all have remainders.

Question 2 – All the parts involve division by 3. Students should write their divisions in numbers, for (example, '39 ÷ 3') as well as their answers. There are no remainders.

Question 3 – These three contextual questions ask students to share items into equal amounts and find how many are left over, that is, the remainder. If a student finds these questions difficult, then allow the use of counters or cubes to share into groups.

Questions 4 and **5** – These questions involve larger numbers, and students should lay out their workings carefully. The method of grouped 'take away' can be used. In Question **4** a useful multiple of 6 to subtract (twice) is $60 = 10 \times 6$. In Question **5** a useful multiple of 5 to subtract is $50 = 10 \times 5$ or the square number $25 = 5 \times 5$. All divisions are exact.

Question 6 – These questions focus on how to handle a remainder. Once students have identified the calculation (13 ÷ 2 or 33 ÷ 4) and successfully found the answer (6 r 1 or **8** r 1) any discussion should focus on what happens to the remainder. Part **a** is a variant of Question 3, where the answers is 'rounded down', but with less scaffolding. Part **b** requires the answer to be 'rounded up'.

Answers

1 **a** 2 r 2 **b** 2 r 1 **c** 2 r 2 **d** 4 r 3
e 5 r 3 **f** 7 r 2 **g** 3 r 6 **h** 3 r 3
i 4 r 4 **j** 5 r 5 **k** 3 r 5 **l** 5 r 5

2 **a** 13 cm **b** 24 cm **c** 16 cm d 42 cm
e 36 cm

3 **a** 3 **b** 2 **c** 10 **d** 2
e 5 **f** 3

4 23 boxes

5 **a** 7 **b** 17 **c** 25

6 **a** 6 **b** 9

14g Written methods of division

Objectives	
• Use efficient written methods of short division.	(L4)

Key ideas	Resources
1 Written methods include repeated subtraction ('chunking') and the standard methods of short division and long division.	Division chunking (1021) Long division (1041) Number line, counters, mini-whiteboards Materials to make small posters

Simplification	Extension
Before attempting the written method, students should understand division using both a multiplication grid and a number line. When dividing by repeated subtraction, for example 188 ÷ 6, always have a number line so that the jumps on the number line (60, 60, 60 and 6) give a visual representation of the subtractions from 188. Students could check their final answers by using a calculator to find 31 × 6.	Further practice can be provided with both short and long division in the style of Question **4** for division by two-digit numbers. More questions such as Question **5** and **6** where the divisions occur in a variety of contexts can be provided, with students having first to decide on which method to use.

Literacy	Links
The numerate student has first to choose between a mental or written method when faced with a division. The mental method may be repeated subtraction or may use multiplication as the inverse of division. The written method may use repeated subtraction ('chunking') or the traditional methods of 'short' and 'long' division. The need for speed, accuracy and efficiency would encourage a traditional method.	Until the 1980s, sweets were generally not pre-packaged. Sweet shops had rows of jars of sweets on their shelves and the shopkeeper would weigh the sweets out using scales and wrap them in a paper bag. A 'quarter' of sweets weighed about 100 g. If sherbet pips cost 50p for 1 kg, and liquorice sweets cost 1p each, how much pocket money would Lisa need to buy a quarter of sherbet pips and three liquorice sweets? (8p)

Alternative approach

The simplest mental method where numbers are within the multiplication grid (< 100 or < 144) is to use the appropriate times table. For example, 38 ÷ 5 may be found from 7 × 5 = 35, giving an answer of 7 with a remainder of 38 – 35 = 3. The mental use of repeated subtraction may be used for examples such as 92 ÷ 30, where 90 – 30 - 30 – 30 in the head leaves a remainder of 2, giving an asnwer of 3 r 2.

In the second example on p270 of the Student Book, the written method of repeated subtraction ('chunking') is used on the left and 'long' division on the right . However, the overall aim should be for students to become confident with 'short' and 'long' division. Both have the same approach but their written layout is different. 'Short' division proceeds as follows.

$$4\overline{)9^{1}8} \quad \text{answer } 24$$

4 divided into the 9 of 98 gives 2 r 1. Write 2 in the answer and move the 1, written as a superscript, moves into the units column to make the 8 into an 18.

$$4\overline{)9^{1}8} \quad \text{answer } 24 \text{ r } 2$$

4 is now divided into the 18 to give 4 r 2. Write the 4 in the answer (to make 24) There is a remainder of 2 The answer is 98 ÷ 4 = 24 r 2.

For division by a single digit or by relatively easy two-digit numbers (such as 15 or 21), 'short' division is likely easier to master than 'long' division.

Checkpoint

1 Which is the best method to use for 52 ÷ 7?
What is the answer? (Inverse multiplication, 7 r 3)

2 Which is the best method to use for 635 ÷ 5?
What is the answer? (Short division, 127)

Other choices of method are valid but need convincing justifications.

Starter – Leap years

Leap year dates can be divided by 4. Which of the following events happened in a leap year?

- 1452 Leonardo da Vinci was born (Yes)
- 1544 William Shakespeare was born (Yes)
- 1840 Penny post started (Yes)
- 1953 Mount Everest was climbed (No)
- 1969 Man first stepped on the moon (No)
- 1994 Channel Tunnel was officially opened (No)

Teaching notes

Before introducing the written methods, students need to be able to use a multiplication grid in reverse for division and know how to represent division by backward jumps on a number line.

Ask students to find 42 ÷ 6 (7) using a multiplication grid; then ask them to work out 43 ÷ 6 (7 r 1) and 46 ÷ 6 (7 r 4) giving remainders as part of their answers. To find 50 ÷ 6, (8 r 2) they must search for the nearest multiple below 50, find 48, appreciate that there will be a remainder of 50 – 48 = 2, and answer with 8 r 2.

Now use prepared blank number lines to illustrate the same divisions by backward jumps. After this whole-class approach, students can use their mini-whiteboards to display answers to other divisions (both without and with remainders).

The first example of the written method to find 196 ÷ 6 can have a number line alongside the working to show the three backward jumps of 60, thereby linking the two approaches. Other examples will be needed (without and with remainders) such as 224 ÷ 7 (32) and 257 ÷ 8 (32 r 1). The disadvantages of this method, often called 'chunking', include that the use of many subtractions can lead to errors, that subtracting small 'chunks' leads to very lengthy working and that it is often time-consuming.

A balance needs to be struck on the emphasis given to this 'chunking' method of repeated subtraction and the subsequent more efficient standard methods of 'short' and 'long' division. Frequent practice, initially with small single-digit divisors, builds confidence.

Plenary

Ask students to collaborate in compiling a poster to calculate 67 ÷ 4. (= 16 r 3) It should show several different ways of finding the answer and give all necessary diagrams and working.

Exercise commentary

Question 1 – If necessary supply a 10 × 10 or 12 × 12 multiplication grid.

Question 2 – Some students may need prepared number lines, but most students should be expected to draw their own. Some students may realise that short cuts are possible. For example, for 35 ÷ 4, the backward jumps could start from the nearest multiple of 4 below 35, that is, start at 32. The jumps are then made more quickly as they land on the multiples of the 4 times table. The remainder is then the initial jump of 3 to reach 32.

Question 3 – All divisions are exact. They layout of 'short' division may be used as the most efficient method. Otherwise, if 'long' division is used, some students may find it helpful to see each subtraction as a backward step on a number line drawn alongside the written calculation.

Question 4 – There are a mix of exact divisions (**b** to **e, i** and **o**) and those with remainders. Later parts involve appreciably longer dividends and may not be suitable for less confident students. It is not necessary to attempt all question parts. Further easier divisions can be supplied.

Questions **5** to **7** involve straightforward divisions so the emphasis should be placed on identifying the necessary information, discussing the best method to use and interpreting the result.

Question 5 – Students should quickly identify the required calculation 134 ÷ 6 = 22 r 2.

Question 6 – There are two equivalent ways to approach this problem; either compare 78 with 6 × 12, or calculate 78 ÷ 12 and compare with 6.

Question 7 – There is the assumption that the five jars hold equal quantities of sweets. Students may not realise the links between the three parts of the problem.

Answers

1 **a** 6 **b** 3 **c** 3 **d** 4
e 8 **f** 4 **g** 2 **h** 7
i 3 **j** 8

2 **a** 8 r 3 **b** 8 r 3 **c** 7 r 3 **d** 6 r 6
e 7 r 4 **f** 8 r 3

3 **a** 41 **b** 31 **c** 44 **d** 26
e 31 **f** 33 **g** 51 **h** 32

4 **a** 24 r 2 **b** 15 **c** 32 **d** 14
e 45 **f** 24 r 2 **g** 24 r 3 **h** 62 r 2
i 68 **j** 28 r 5 **k** 32 **l** 44 r 4
m 448 r 1 **n** 647 r 1 **o** 691 **p** 622 r 3
q 12 643 r 2

5 23

6 Yes, 78 ÷ 12 = 6 r 6 > 6 or 6 × 12 = 72 < 78

7 **a** 8 **b** 16 **c** 32

14h Calculator skills

Objectives	
• Solve problems with or without a calculator	(L4)
• Enter numbers and interpret the display in different contexts	(L5)

Key ideas	Resources
1 An estimate is useful to compare with the calculator's answer. **2** The context of the problem is used to decide whether to round the calculator's answer.	Money calculations (1014) Blank number lines Calculators Materials to make A3 posters

Simplification	Extension
Students should be reminded of what they learned in lesson **1g**, 'Rounding and estimating'. Re-visiting the work of **Exercise 1g** is a useful introduction to this topic. Those who find rounding difficult need to have blank number lines available that they can write on.	Ask students why we need to round numbers. Can they find real-life situations where rounding is essential? Can they give numerical examples of the situations that they find?

Literacy	Links
The words 'rounding', 'approximating' and 'estimating' are often confused. To find an approximation to a number, it is usual to 'round' it. For example, 243.68 can be rounded down to one significant figure to give 200 and it can be rounded up to one decimal place to give 243.7. The word 'estimate' is used when finding an approximate answer to a calculation. For example, to estimate the answer to 243.68 × 3.21, use two approximations to give 200 × 3 and so get an estimate of 600.	In 2005, Turkey introduced the New Turkish Lira. 1 new lira was exchanged for 1 000 000 old lira. There are pictures of the new Turkish coins and notes at www.newlira.com/2004/11/new-turkish-lira-note-and-coin-designs.html Compare these with UK coins and notes. Which denominations are the same? Although no longer valid, old million lira notes can be redeemed in Turkish banks until 31 December 2015.

Alternative approach

This exercise uses rounding extensively. Before a calculator is involved, rounding is used to make an estimate of the answer. Refer to lesson **1g** at the start of this book and to the comments above under **Literacy**. The answer from the calculator is then compared with the estimated answer to see if they are both roughly in line with each other.

After the calculator has been used, rounding is again required to make sense of the answer on the display. For example, a display of 12.358 for a sum of money in £s has to be rounded to £12.36 to the nearest pence, £12.40 to the nearest 10p, or £12 to the nearest whole pound.

Preliminary revision of rounding numbers may well be beneficial before this exercise is started. Practice rounding numbers to the nearest ten/hundred/tenth, to one significant figure or to one decimal place.

Checkpoint

1 What is 643.78 rounded to
- **a** the nearest ten (640)
- **b** one significant figure (600)
- **c** one decimal place? (643.8)

2 Estimate the answer to
- **a** 389 + 114.7 (400 + 100 = 500)
- **b** 21.9 × 9.85 (20 × 10 = 100)

Starter – My calculator display shows ...

Write 31 on the board.

Ask students what the answer is if you multiply the number by 100.

Repeat using different starting numbers and multiplying by different powers of 10.

Extend the **Starter** by asking students what would happen if you divide 31 by 100.

Teaching notes

This exercise involves rounding and using the calculator. Many students will be comfortable rounding whole numbers to the nearest ten but they may be less confident when decimals are used. Build on what was achieved in lesson **7a** ('Mental methods of addition'). For example, 2.4 can be indicated by an arrow on a number line and then rounded to the nearest whole number to give 2.

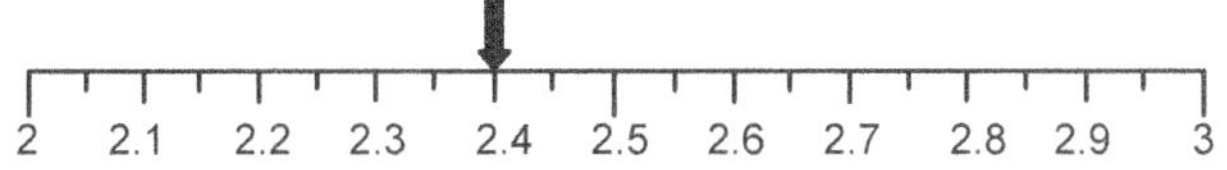

A more magnified number line can be used to show that 2.43 rounds to 2.4 to 1 decimal place.

When a calculator display gives an answer to many decimal places, students can be confused. However, if the display indicates a sum of money in pounds (£), students know that only two decimal places are allowed. In this case, rounding to one (or two) decimal place is rounding to the nearest 10p (or 1p). So, for example £20 ÷ 7 gives 2.857142 on the display, which is either £2.90 or £2.86 when rounded to 1 dp or 2 dp.

Plenary

Ask students, in pairs, to make a simple poster to explain how an estimate of the answer is made and how the calculator display is rounded.

The more able students may be asked to explain how to find the cost of one item if seven items cost £720, with the final answer rounded to two decimal places.

Less confident students can be asked to explain how to share £46 equally amongst three people.

Each group will need to use and display a decimal number line.

Exercise commentary

Questions 1 – Encourage students to approximate to two significant figures. In parts **b** and **d**, rounding to the nearest thousand will give zero as the estimate.

Question 2 – It may be helpful to pose these questions in terms of money, 3.4 stands for £3.40 etc., referring back to lessons **1d** and **1e**

Question 3 – Negative numbers were introduced in the context of temperature in lesson **1f**. Here the emphasis should be on entering negative numbers into a calculator. Different calculators may have different keys to do this.

Question 4 – A useful ploy is to draw a short vertical line in pencil after the second decimal place and then, by looking at what comes after the vertical line, answer the question 'Do I round up or round down?'

Question 5 – Since there are 100 pence in one pound, it only makes sense to quote two decimal places in answers. In money problems you should always round the answer to two decimal places.

Question 6 – Students should be reminded to pay attention to which operation is involved. Also with money calculations a calculator display of, for example, 5.8 (part **a**) should be written as £5.80.

Question 7 –In part **a**, ask students what a fair solution would be for the three friends. In part **b**, advise students to write down what calculation is required and any intermediate working as well as their final answer.

Answers

1 **a** ≈ 1200 + 1300 ≈ 2500 **b** ≈ 3500 – 3200 ≈ 300
c ≈ 1200 + 5700 ≈ 6900 **d** ≈ 3400 – 3200 ≈ 200

2	**a** 6		**b** 12.1		**c** 6.7		**d** 33	
	e 1.7		**f** 2.4		**g** 7		**h** 12.1	
3	**a** 13 °C		**b** 7 °C		**c** -5 °C		**d** -5 °C	
	e -12 °C							
4	**a** 0.14		**b** 0.64		**c** 6.13		**d** 2.03	
	e 1.38		**f** 4.24					
5	**a** £0.82		**b** £0.84		**c** £1.26		**d** £2.08	
	e £0.20		**f** £1.54		**g** £33.72			
6	**a** £5.80		**b** £6.40		**c** £8.80		**d** £1.70	
	e £15.90		**f** £1.40		**g** £29.90		**h** £6.40	

7 **a** No. They can have £13.33 each, but there is still a penny left over.

b 11 × 1 + 6 × 2 + 3 × 5 + 7 × 10 + 4 × 20 + 9 × 50 + 3 × 100
= 11 + 12 + 15 + 70 + 80 + 450 + 300 = 938
= £9.38

Key outcomes	Quick check
Consolodate multiplication facts up to 12 × 12. L3	Do these calculations in your head. **a** 5 × 6 (30) **b** 8 × 7 (56) **c** 7 × 7 (49) **d** 9 × 12 (108)
Multiply by 10 and 100. L4	**1** Multiply each number by **i** 10 **ii** 100 **a** 6 (60, 60) **b** 45 (450, 4500) **c** 342 (3420, 34 200) **d** 800 (8000, 80 000) **2** Edging tiles are 10 cm long. How many edging tiles are needed for a 2 m length of tiling? (20)
Multiply whole numbers using metal and written strategies. L4	**1** Do these calculations in your head. **a** 5 × 60 (300) **b** 40 × 6 (240) **c** 3 × 15 (45) **d** 12 × 120 (1440) **2** Do these calculations using a written method. **a** 4 × 32 (105) **b** 21 × 5 (105) **c** 6 × 88 (528) **d** 568 × 6 (3408)
Divide whole numbers using mental and efficient written strategies. L4	**1** Do these calculations in your head. **a** 230 ÷ 10 (23) **b** 28 ÷ 7 (4) **c** 48 ÷ 6 (8) **d** 121 ÷ 11 (11) **2** Do these calculations using a written method. **a** 280 ÷ 5 (56) **b** 875 ÷ 7 (125) **c** 58 ÷ 9 (6 r 4) **d** 348 ÷ 8 (43 r 4)
Use a calculator and interpret the display in different contexts, including money. L4	**1** Do these calculations using a calculator. **a** 6.7 + 7.5 (14.2) **b** 25.6 – 13.9 (11.7) **c** 2.1 × 2.3 (4.83) **d** 56.3 ÷ 14.5 (3.88 2 dp) **2** Do these calculations using a calculator. **a** £2.45 + £8.09 (£10.54) **b** £5.21 × 3.5 (£18.24) **c** Seven friends share £50, how much do they get each? (£7.14)

Development and links
These basic skills are developed and assumed throughout the course. Multiplying and dividing is extended to larger numbers and more involved problem solving scenarios in book **2A**. Calculator skills are also developed in book **2A**, to include multi-step calculations, handling fractions and interpreting the calculator display in context. In real life, mental arithmetic, together with approximating, is invaluable in making estimates and sense checking the results of a calculation. For example the change given at a checkout or a builder's estimate of costs. For more involved situations a calculator is likely to be used: this requires calculations to be entered correctly, answers to be sense checked and the result interpreted correctly.

MyMaths extra support

Lesson/online homework			Description
Mixed tables 3, 4, 6	1360	L3	A series of timed activities and games designed to help revise the 3, 4 and 6 times tables.
Mixed tables 7, 8, 9	1364	L4	A series of timed activities and games designed to help revise the 7, 8 and 9 times tables.

My Review

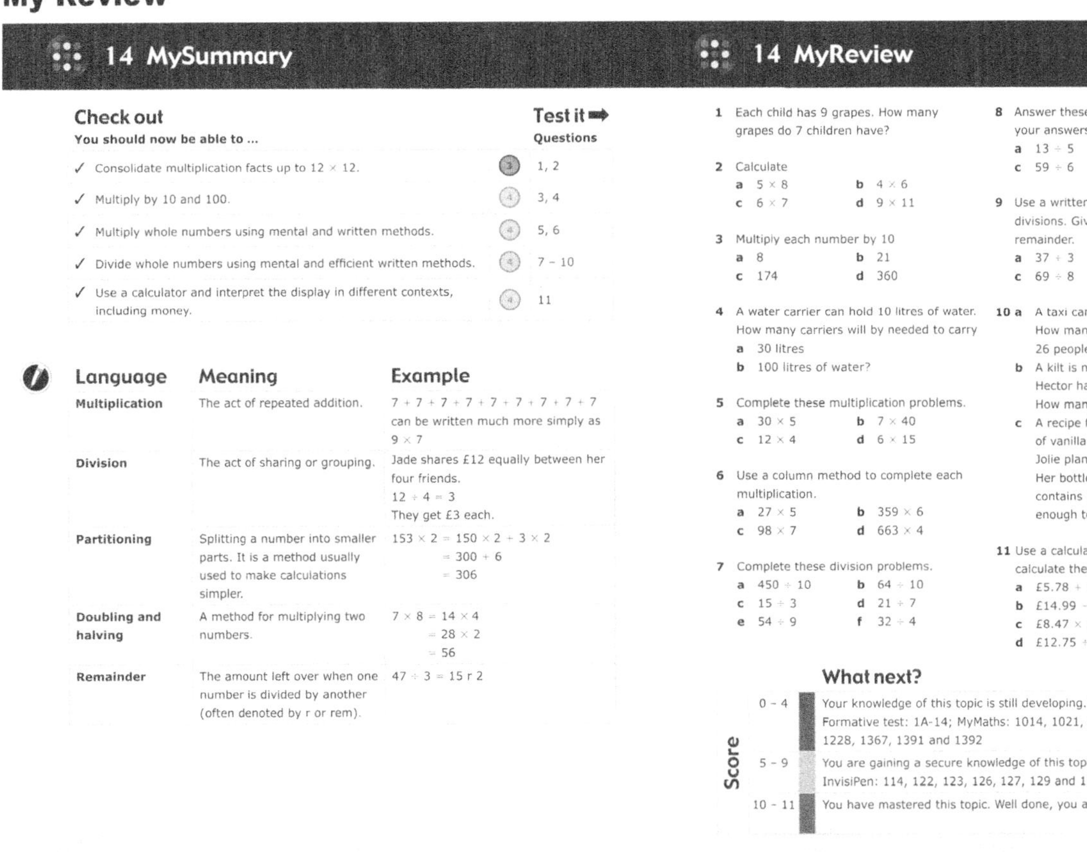

14 MySummary

Check out

You should now be able to ...

	Test it ➡ Questions
✓ Consolidate multiplication facts up to 12 × 12.	1, 2
✓ Multiply by 10 and 100.	3, 4
✓ Multiply whole numbers using mental and written methods.	5, 6
✓ Divide whole numbers using mental and efficient written methods.	7 – 10
✓ Use a calculator and interpret the display in different contexts, including money.	11

Language	Meaning	Example
Multiplication	The act of repeated addition.	7 + 7 + 7 + 7 + 7 + 7 + 7 + 7 + 7 can be written much more simply as 9 × 7
Division	The act of sharing or grouping.	Jade shares £12 equally between her four friends. 12 ÷ 4 = 3 They get £3 each.
Partitioning	Splitting a number into smaller parts. It is a method usually used to make calculations simpler.	153 × 2 = 150 × 2 + 3 × 2 = 300 + 6 = 306
Doubling and halving	A method for multiplying two numbers.	7 × 8 = 14 × 4 = 28 × 2 = 56
Remainder	The amount left over when one number is divided by another (often denoted by r or rem).	47 ÷ 3 = 15 r 2

274 **Number** Multiplying and dividing

14 MyReview

1 Each child has 9 grapes. How many grapes do 7 children have?

2 Calculate
a 5 × 8 **b** 4 × 6
c 6 × 7 **d** 9 × 11

3 Multiply each number by 10
a 8 **b** 21
c 174 **d** 360

4 A water carrier can hold 10 litres of water. How many carriers will by needed to carry
a 30 litres
b 100 litres of water?

5 Complete these multiplication problems.
a 30 × 5 **b** 7 × 40
c 12 × 4 **d** 6 × 15

6 Use a column method to complete each multiplication.
a 27 × 5 **b** 359 × 6
c 98 × 7 **d** 663 × 4

7 Complete these division problems.
a 450 ÷ 10 **b** 64 ÷ 10
c 15 ÷ 3 **d** 21 ÷ 7
e 54 ÷ 9 **f** 32 ÷ 4

8 Answer these division problems giving your answers with a remainder.
a 13 ÷ 5 **b** 21 ÷ 2
c 59 ÷ 6 **d** 238 ÷ 4

9 Use a written method to work out these divisions. Give your answers with a remainder.
a 37 ÷ 3 **b** 65 ÷ 4
c 69 ÷ 8 **d** 80 ÷ 9

10 a A taxi can carry 5 people. How many taxis are needed for 26 people?
b A kilt is made from 7 m of tartan. Hector has 40 m of material. How many kilts can he make?
c A recipe for a cake uses six drops of vanilla essence. Jolie plans to make 24 cakes. Her bottle of vanilla essence says it contains 150 drops. Will she have enough to make all the cakes?

11 Use a calculator or a written method to calculate these money problems.
a £5.78 + £18.92
b £14.99 − £2.45
c £8.47 × 5.5
d £12.75 ÷ 4

What next?

Score	
0 - 4	Your knowledge of this topic is still developing. To improve look at Formative test: 1A-14; MyMaths: 1014, 1021, 1023, 1024, 1027, 1041, 1228, 1367, 1391 and 1392
5 - 9	You are gaining a secure knowledge of this topic. To improve look at InvisiPen: 114, 122, 123, 126, 127, 129 and 135
10 - 11	You have mastered this topic. Well done, you are ready to progress!

MyMaths.co.uk 275

Question commentary

Questions 1 and **2** – (lesson **14a**) These should be done mentally using knowledge of times tables.

Question 3 – (lesson **14b**) Check students understanding of why the digits move.

Question 4 – (lesson **14b**) These are simple division problems. Ask students to write down the required calculation, 30 ÷ 10 and 100 ÷ 10, as an intermediate step.

Question 5 – (lesson **14c**) These should be done using mental methods. For example, **a** 3 × 5 × 10, **b** 7 × 4 × 10, **c** 12 × 2 × 2 and **d** 6 × 10 + 6 × 5. Discuss methods used by students.

Questions 6 – (lesson **14d**) Discourage the use of partitioning and the grid method.

Questions 7 – (lesson **14e**) These should be done mentally using knowledge of times tables.

Question 8– (lesson **14g**) These should be done by repeated subtraction or using a written method.

Question 9– (lesson **14g**) These should be done using a written method

Question 10 – (lesson **14f**) Require students to write out the calculation that they need to do: **a** 26 ÷ 5, **b** 40 ÷ 7 and **c** 24 × 6 or 150 ÷ 6. In each case students will need to decide how to handle the remainder.

Question 11 – (lesson **14h**) Answers should be rounded where necessary, parts **c** and **d**, to 2 dp and given in pounds, For example, **a** should not be £24.7

Answers

1	63			
2	**a** 40	**b** 24	**c** 42	**d** 99
3	**a** 80	**b** 210	**c** 174	**d** 36 000
4	**a** 3	**b** 10		
5	**a** 150	**b** 280	**c** 48	**d** 90
6	**a** 135	**b** 2154	**c** 686	**d** 2652
7	**a** 45	**b** 6.4	**c** 5	**d** 3
	e 6	**f** 8		
8	**a** 2 r 3	**b** 10 r 1	**c** 9 r 4	**d** 59 r 2
9	**a** 12 r 1	**b** 16 r 1	**c** 8 r 5	**d** 8 r 8
10	**a** 6	**b** 5	**c** Yes (144 < 150)	
11	**a** £24.70	**b** £12.54	**c** £46.59	**d** £3.19

14 MyPractice

14a

1 Work out:

a 7 × 6 **b** 6 × 8 **c** 4 × 9 **d** 6 × 9
e 5 × 6 **f** 9 × 8 **g** 10 × 7 **h** 11 × 4

2 Complete these multiplication grids.

a

×	3	8	2	7	5	11
4					20	
7			14			
10						
3						
8	24					
9						

b

×	2	4	8	10	9	12
6	12					
3			24			
5		20				
7						
8						
4						

14b

3 Connor has a pencil that is 10 cm long.
He uses his pencil to measure his desk and his classroom.
His table is 6 'pencils' wide, 12 'pencils' long and 7 'pencils' tall.

a What are these lengths in centimetres?

b What are they in metres?

His classroom is 85 'pencils' wide.

c What is this in metres?

4 A woodpecker is excavating a hole in a tree for his nest.
Each day he removes 100 g of wood.

a How much wood will be removed in a week?

b How much wood will be removed in 30 days?
Give your answer in kilograms.

14c

5 To multiply a number by 8, you can double it three times over.
for example, 14 × 8 ⟶ 14 × 2 = 28
× 2 = 56
× 2 = 112

Use doubling to work out these multiplications.

a 13 × 8 **b** 15 × 8 **c** 16 × 8
d 20 × 8 **e** 21 × 8 **f** 71 × 8

6 Use partitioning to work out these multiplications.

a 18 × 5 **b** 22 × 6 **c** 54 × 7
d 4 × 36 **e** 15 × 9 **f** 11 × 37

14d

7 Use a standard written method to work out these multiplications.

a 156 × 3 **b** 247 × 2 **c** 321 × 3
d 482 × 4 **e** 359 × 4 **f** 567 × 5
g 426 × 7 **h** 861 × 8 **i** 345 × 9
j 4116 × 5 **k** 6307 × 4 **l** 2643 × 7

14e

8 Work out these divisions in your head.

a 70 ÷ 10 **b** 90 ÷ 10 **c** 110 ÷ 10
d 500 ÷ 100 **e** 24 ÷ 6 **f** 77 ÷ 7
g 124 ÷ 4 **h** 132 ÷ 6 **i** 84 ÷ 12
j 88 ÷ 11 **k** 639 ÷ 3 **l** 248 ÷ 8

14f

9 A big dipper holds eight passengers.
Sixty-eight people are waiting to travel on the big dipper.
How many trips will be needed so that everyone has a ride?

14g

10 Use a standard written method to work out these divisions.

a 453 ÷ 3 **b** 621 ÷ 3 **c** 744 ÷ 4
d 856 ÷ 4 **e** 765 ÷ 5 **f** 873 ÷ 9
g 637 ÷ 7 **h** 4496 ÷ 8 **i** 2548 ÷ 7
j 2190 ÷ 6 **k** 3168 ÷ 9 **l** 14500 ÷ 4

14h

11 Use your calculator to work out these problems.

a 5.2 + 3.1 **b** 7.8 + 2.9 **c** 16.1 − 5.7
d £7.76 ÷ 8 **e** £10.29 ÷ 7 **f** £1.20 × 8

12 a Six friends win £20 in a raffle. They agree to share the money equally.
How much money do they get each?

b On Monday the temperature is -5°C.

i The temperature falls 3°C on Tuesday. What is the temperature on Tuesday?

ii The next Monday the temperature has risen 13°C. What is the temperature now?

Question commentary

Questions 1 – This could be done as an oral question with answers given on mini-whiteboards. The opportunity should be taken to allow students to explain how they remember the various times tables.

Questions 2 – Unlike the questions in exercise **14a** these tables are in a random order. This makes completing the tables more of a test of memory and reduces the scope for relying on patterns within the table.

Question 3 – The difficulty here is identifying the relevant information in the question. For part **c**, ask students why the answer is asked for in metres.

Question 4 – In part **b**, students should remember that 1 kg = 1000 g.

Question 5 and **6** – If a student can do these questions in their head then great, however explain that it is acceptable to use jottings to note intermediate results.

Questions 7 – Discourage the use of the grid or other partitioning method; rather encourage the use of a standard column procedure. For parts **a** and **c**, do the students answers satisfy the test for divisibility by three: sum of digits is a multiple of three.

Question 8 – This could be done as an oral question with answers given on mini-whiteboards. The opportunity should be taken to allow students to explain their methods for doing the various divisions. All the divisions are exact.

Question 9 – Check that students have abstracted the correct calculation, 68 ÷ 8, and obtained the correct answer, 8 r 4, before discussing how to handle the remainder. Emphasise that this always depends on the question and here it should be rounded up.

Questions 10 – Discourage the use of repeated subtraction or a chunking method; rather encourage the use of a standard column procedure. It may help to do the first few parts together to ensure that the correct layout of the workings is understood. All the divisions are exact.

Questions 11 – Unless a class set of calculators is supplied you should be aware of the possibility of small differences between students' calculators. In parts **d** to **f**, which involve money, check that students write their answers appropriately.

Questions 12 – In part **a**, ask students to check their answers. Can they explain that rounding down means there is a small amount, 1p, left over? In part **b**, in order to help in separating understanding/conceptual errors from practical calculator errors, get students to first write down the calculations that they need to do, that is, -5 – 3 and -5 + 13.

Answers

1 **a** 42 **b** 48 **c** 36 **d** 54
e 30 **f** 72 **g** 70 **h** 44

2 **a**

×	3	8	2	7	5	11
4	12	32	8	28	20	44
7	21	56	14	49	35	77
10	30	80	20	70	50	110
3	9	24	6	21	15	33
8	24	64	16	56	40	88
9	27	72	18	63	45	99

b

×	2	4	8	10	9	12
6	12	24	48	60	54	72
3	6	12	24	30	27	36
5	10	20	40	50	45	60
7	14	28	56	70	63	84
8	16	32	64	80	72	96
4	8	16	32	40	36	48

3 **a** 60 cm × 120 cm × 70 cm
b 0.6 m × 1.2 m × 0.7 m **c** 8.5 m

4 **a** 700 g **b** 3 kg

5 **a** 104 **b** 120 **c** 128 **d** 160
e 168 **f** 568

6 **a** 90 **b** 132 **c** 378 **d** 144
e 135 **f** 407

7 **a** 468 **b** 494 **c** 963 **d** 1928
e 1436 **f** 2835 **g** 2982 **h** 6888
i 3105 **j** 20 580 **k** 25 228 **l** 18 501

8 **a** 7 **b** 9 **c** 11 **d** 5
e 4 **f** 11 **g** 31 **h** 22
i 7 **j** 8 **k** 213 **l** 31

9 9

10 **a** 151 **b** 207 **c** 186 **d** 214
e 153 **f** 97 **g** 91 **h** 562
i 364 **j** 365 **k** 352 **l** 3625

11 **a** 8.3 **b** 10.7 **c** 10.4 **d** £0.97
e £1.47 **f** 15p

12 **a** £3.33 There is one penny left over.
b **i** -8 °C **ii** 8 °C

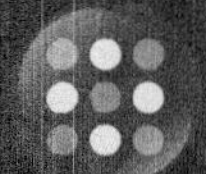

Case study 5: Electricity in the home

Related lessons		Resources
Ordering whole numbers	1b	Reading pie charts (1206)
Order of operations	1h	Data on electricity supply costs
Time	2c	Catalogues of domestic appliances with energy efficiency ratings
Fractions decimals and percentages	4h	
Reading lists and tables	8c	
Reading pie charts	8f	
Calculator skills	14h	

Simplification	Extension
Concentrate on tasks **1** and **3** where the imformation is more accessible and the required calculations more straightforward. Use discussion to guide students to an understanding of what they need to do.	In task **2** completing the table is naturally suited to being done using a spreadsheet. Ask students to create or complete a spreadsheet using the data in the student book. This can then be used to create their own pie chart. Students could also research other appliances and add them to their spreadsheet. Alternatively the results of this investigation can be used to create a poster encouraging people to save energy by switching appliances off or using energy efficient appliances.

Links

The Which? organisation provides an explanation of what is shown on an EU energy efficiency label.

www.which.co.uk/energy/saving-money/guides/energy-labels-explained/eu-energy-efficiency-labels/

The energy saving trust discusses how much energy the various types of domestic appliances use and things that you can do to reduce energy usage.

www.energysavingtrust.org.uk/Electricity/Products-and-appliances

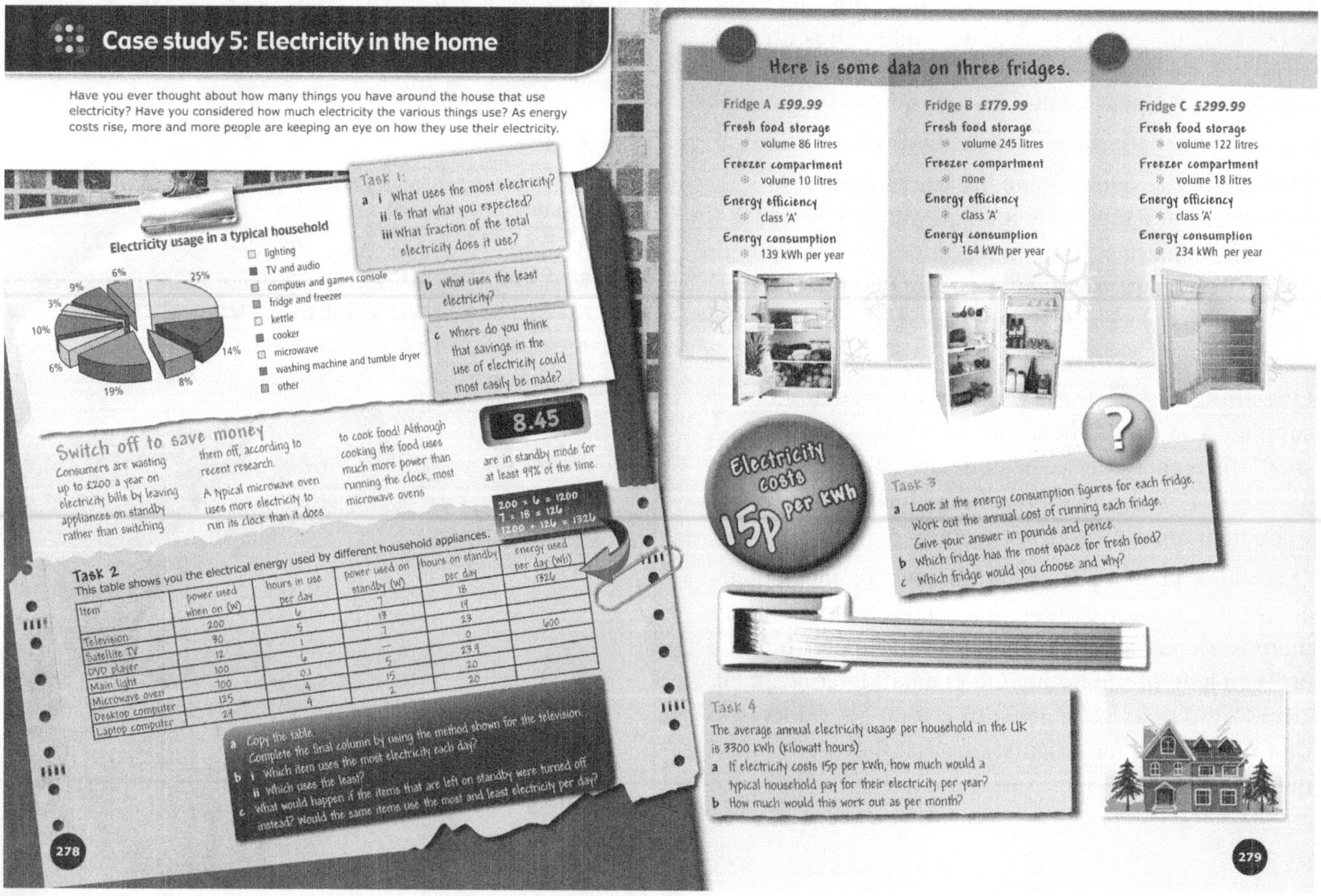

Case study 5: Electricity in the home

Have you ever thought about how many things you have around the house that use electricity? Have you considered how much electricity the various things use? As energy costs rise, more and more people are keeping an eye on how they use their electricity.

Electricity usage in a typical household

lighting; TV and audio; computer and games console; fridge and freezer; kettle; cooker; microwave; washing machine and tumble dryer; other

25%, 14%, 8%, 19%, 6%, 10%, 3%, 9%, 6%

Task 1:

a i What uses the most electricity?
ii Is that what you expected?
iii What fraction of the total electricity does it use?

b What uses the least electricity?

c Where do you think that savings in the use of electricity could most easily be made?

Switch off to save money

Consumers are wasting up to £200 a year on electricity bills by leaving appliances on standby rather than switching them off, according to recent research.

A typical microwave oven uses more electricity to run its clock than it does to cook food! Although cooking the food uses much more power than running the clock, most microwave ovens are in standby mode for at least 99% of the time.

8.45

200 × 6 = 1200
7 × 18 = 126
1200 + 126 = 1326

Task 2

This table shows you the electrical energy used by different household appliances.

Item	power used when on (W)	hours in use per day	power used on standby (W)	hours on standby per day	energy used per day (Wh)
Television	200	6	7	18	1326
Satellite TV	30	5	13	19	
DVD player	12	1	7	23	
Main light	100	6	—	0	600
Microwave oven	700	0.1	5	23.9	
Desktop computer	125	4	15	20	
Laptop computer	29	4	2	20	

a Copy the table.
Complete the final column by using the method shown for the television.

b i Which item uses the most electricity each day?
ii Which uses the least?

c What would happen if the items that are left on standby were turned off instead? Would the same items use the most and least electricity per day?

278

Here is some data on three fridges.

	Fridge A £99.99	Fridge B £179.99	Fridge C £299.99
Fresh food storage	volume 86 litres	volume 245 litres	volume 122 litres
Freezer compartment	volume 10 litres	none	volume 18 litres
Energy efficiency	class 'A'	class 'A'	class 'A'
Energy consumption	139 kWh per year	164 kWh per year	234 kWh per year

Electricity costs 15p per kWh

Task 3

a Look at the energy consumption figures for each fridge.
Work out the annual cost of running each fridge.
Give your answer in pounds and pence.

b Which fridge has the most space for fresh food?

c Which fridge would you choose and why?

Task 4

The average annual electricity usage per household in the UK is 3300 kWh (kilowatt hours).

a If electricity costs 15p per kWh, how much would a typical household pay for their electricity per year?

b How much would this work out as per month?

279

Teaching notes

The rising cost of electricity is a regular feature of news stories, as is the environmental impact of burning fossil fuels to produce the electricity. At the same time, many households have an increasing number of electrical appliances. Ask students to name appliances that they have at home and to suggest how much electricity they use. Which item uses the most? A cooker uses a lot but for a short time, how does this compare to a fridge which only uses a modest amount but is on all the time?

This case study looks at how to calculate the electricity consumption of household appliances. It raises awareness of how the amount of electricity used can be affected by choice of appliance and also by use, especially in terms of leaving appliances on standby rather than turning them off.

Task 1

Complimentary approaches can be used to answer parts **ai** and **b**. Students can look at the angles in the pie chart to identify the largest and smallest sector or they can place the given percentages in numerical order. Extend the question by asking for all the appliances to be listed in order. To find the relative order of washing machines, 9%, and computers, 8%, students will have to look at the numbers.

Check that students appreciate the difference between the 'power' of an appliance, how much electricity it uses in one unit of time, and its 'total energy use', which is the power multiplied by the time that it is on. A useful analogy would be a tap: fully open for five minutes versus dripping for a whole day. Ask, why does a kettle use so little electricity and light bulbs so much? (A kettle boils in minutes but lights can be on all day.)

Task 2

Allow students to look at the table and ask them to explain what the first five columns show. What is the difference between 'on' and 'on standby'? On standby means the appliances is idle but not switched off; it uses less electricity than when on but it still uses some.

Ask students to explain how to calculate 600 in the last column for main light. (100×6) Then ask them to explain how to calculate 1326 for television. ($200 \times 6 + 7 \times 18 = 1200 + 126 = 1326$) Allow students to use calculators so that they can focus on what to calculate rather than how to calculate. The first few calculations should be done together before students are encouraged to try to complete the table themselves.

It may help to add two extra columns: one for energy used when on and one for energy used when on standby, the final column is them the sum of these two columns. This will make answering part **c** much easier.

In part **c**, can students predict where the biggest savings will be made when switching off appliances? (For example, a DVD player is on standby a lot and then still uses a relatively large amount of electricity.)

The task can be extended by asking for the total electricity usage when appliances are on standby or switched off (3641.5 Wh, 2648 Wh,) What is the saving? (993.5 Wh) How many hours of television viewing is this equivalent to? (4 hrs 58 mins)

Task 3

A kWh = 1000 Wh. For part **a**, students need to do the calculations $139 \times 0.15 = £20.85$, etc. Discussing answers to part **c** provides an opportunity to test students understanding of the issues involved: purchase cost, running cost, capacity, etc.

Task 4

The calculation in part **a** is similar to that in task **3a**, allow students to try it without help. In part **b**, students need to know that there are 12 months in a year.

Answers

1 **a** **i** Lighting **ii** Students' answers

iii $\frac{1}{4}$

b Kettle

c Student's answers: could including turning off lights not leaving tv, computers, etc. on standby.

2 **a, c**

Item	Energy use per day (kWh)	Energy use, no standby (kWh)
Television	1326	1200
Satellite TV	397	150
DVD player	173	12
Main light	600	600
Microwave	189.5	70
Desktop	800	500
Laptop	156	116

b **i** Television **ii** Laptop

3 **a** A £20.85 B £24.60 C £35.10

b B

c Students' answers plus explanations. Answer could take into account purchase price, running costs, fresh/frozen storage capacity.

4 **a** £495 **b** £41.25

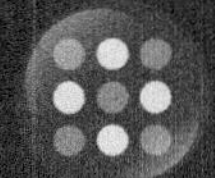

15 Ratio and proportion

Learning outcomes

R2 Use scale factors, scale diagrams and maps. (L5)

R3 Express 1 quantity as a fraction of another, where the fraction is less than 1 and greater than 1. (L5)

R4 Use ratio notation, including reduction to simplest form. (L5)

R5 Divide a given quantity into 2 parts in a given part : part or part : whole ratio; express the division of a quantity into 2 parts as a ratio. (L5)

R6 Understand that a multiplicative relationship between 2 quantities can be expressed as a ratio or a fraction. (L5)

R7 Relate the language of ratios and the associated calculations to the arithmetic of fractions and to linear functions. (L5)

Introduction

The chapter starts by looking at simple proportion expressed as both a fraction and a ratio. Ratio problems are then looked at before more general arithmetic problems. Scale drawing is covered in the final spread.

The introduction discusses how designers use ratio and proportion in their designs so that products are 'fit for purpose'. The main reference is to ergonomics, or the fitting of technology to the human body. Whenever a new product is being developed, ergonomics is considered along with many other things to ensure that the product works, is useful and safe. While it might seem secondary to things like the colour and feel, it is one of the most important things that designers consider because if the ergonomics are not right, people will not purchase the product, no matter how nice it looks.

Prior knowledge

Students should already know how to…

- Work with simple fractions
- Carry out simple calculations
- Convert between metric units

Starter problem

The starter problem gets students to measure their head-length and their height and investigate whether they are in the 'perfect' ratio, one tenth. These perfect ratios where set down by the Roman architect Vitruvius in about 15 BC. Leonardo da Vinci used these ratios to produce his drawing of a perfectly proportioned – Vitruvian – man. An introduction to this can be found here.

www.bbc.co.uk/science/leonardo/gallery/vitruvian.shtml

Students could be invited to test their own dimensions against many of the other features of the Vitruvian Man as well as the example given in the starter. For example, is the length of the outspread arms equal to the height? Is the distance from the elbow to the tip of the hand equal to a quarter of the height?

Resources

MyMaths

Proportion	1037	Ratio introduction	1052	Scale drawing	1117
Word problems	1393				

Online assessment

Chapter test	1A-15
Formative test	1A-15
Summative test	1A-15

InvisiPen solutions

Ratio	191	Ratio	192
Scale drawings	195		

Topic scheme

Teaching time = 4 lessons/2 weeks

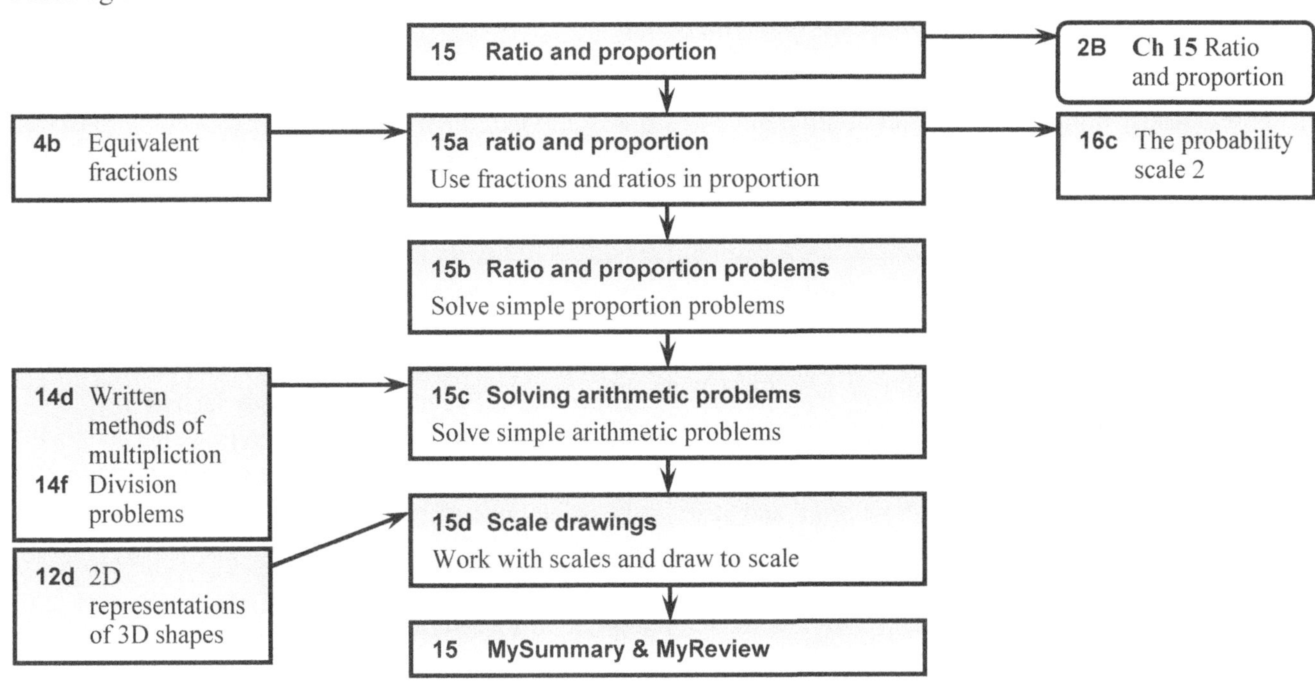

Differentiation

Student book 1A 280 – 293	Student book 1B 276 – 289	Student book 1C 272 – 28
Ratio and proportion Solving problems involving proportion Scale drawing	Work with simple proportion Covert from fractions to percentages Work with simple ratios Solve direct proportion problems	Fractions, decimals and percentages Direct proportion Ratio, dividing into given ratios Ratio and proportion Percentage problems

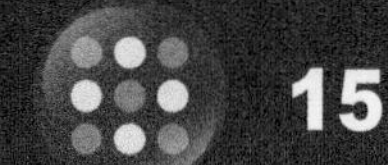

15a Ratio and proportion

Objectives	
• Begin to understand simple ratios.	(L4)
• Understand the relationship between ratio and proportion.	(L4)

Key ideas	Resources
1 A ratio deals with the relative sizes of different categories of items. **2** A proportion deals with the size of one category as a fraction of the total number of all items.	Ratio introduction (1052) A selection of different coloured beads and other items Cards the size of postcards

Simplification	Extension
Give students a card to write on. One side should be labelled 'Ratio' and has two questions: 'How many of this kind?' and 'How many of that kind?' as well as the sentence 'Write a ratio using this sign:' The other side should be labelled 'Proportion' and also has two questions: 'How many of this kind?' and 'How many in total?' as well as the sentence 'Write a proportion as a fraction.' For any problem involving ratio or proportion, the student should choose which side of the card they need to read, answer the questions on that side and write down the required ratio or proportion.	Students can explore problems involving ratios deriving from three categories; for example, mixes of three colours of paint. Ask questions such as, if a painter makes a colour by mixing yellow, red and blue in the ratio 4 : 2 : 1 respectively and they use 3 tins of blue paint, how many tins of yellow and red are needed? (12, 6) The meaning of the word 'respectively' needs exploring. What might happen if this word were not used?

Literacy	Links
The word *ratio* was first used in English with its mathematical meaning in the 1650s. It comes from Latin and had several meanings connected with 'reckoning' and 'reason'. The word *proportion* is an older word, similar to the word 'portion' which means 'a part of something'. A ratio is written using the colon (:), whereas a proportion is written as a fraction, which can then be converted into a decimal or percentage.	Computer printers use only cyan, magenta and yellow inks to create other colours. For example, a mix of cyan and yellow makes green. Pink is created by printing magenta dots close together but with white space between, thereby creating an optical illusion as the eye blends the red and white together. Changing the size of the dots and the amount of white space changes the shade of pink.

Alternative approach

There are a variety of activities in MyMaths lesson 1052 , 'Ratio Introduction', although some of them make rapid progress and may be better attempted later in the development of ratio.

Checkpoint

1 Consider a bag of marbles that contains 12 blue marbles and 6 green marbles.

- **a** What is the ratio of blue marbles to green marbles? (12 : 6 = 2 : 1)
- **b** How many marbles are there in total? (18)
- **c** What is the proportion of green marbles? (6 out of 18, which is $\frac{6}{18} = \frac{1}{3}$)
- **d** What is the proportion of blue marbles? (12 out of 18, which is $\frac{12}{18} = \frac{2}{3}$)

Starter – Odd one out

Ask students to find the odd one out in each of the following lists, and to explain why.

- 25%, $\frac{3}{12}$, $\frac{1}{2}$ of $\frac{1}{2}$, 0.004 (0.004)
- $\frac{1}{3}$ of 24, 10% of 80, $\frac{10}{80}$, 8 ($\frac{10}{80}$)
- 0.3, $\frac{1}{3}$, 30%, $\frac{3}{10}$ ($\frac{1}{3}$)

Teaching notes

The concepts of ratio and proportion can be confused and misunderstood. The key difference is that

- *Ratio* deals with how many there are in different categories; it is not concerned about the total number.
- *Proportion* deals with how many of the total are in a certain category and it is written as a fraction.

For example, if there are 13 boys and 11 girls in a class of 24 students, then the ratio of boys to girls is 13 to 11 and the proportion of boys in the class is $\frac{13}{24}$.

These concepts are best set in appropriate contexts. It is debatable whether it is best to discuss both concepts together in the same context or whether to study ratio first in several contexts before turning to proportion.

A variety of examples can be explored, for example,

- children and adults at a party
- the popularity of dogs and cats as pets
- Rovers and City supporters

For ratio, ask the questions, how many are in this category? How many are in that category?

For proportion, ask the questions, how many do you have altogether? How many of the total are in the category you are interested in?

For ratio, write the answer using a colon. For example, a ratio of 13 to 11 is written as 13 : 11.

For proportion, write the answer as a fraction of the total; for example, for 13 out of a total of 24, write $\frac{13}{24}$. Both can be simplified if there are common factors in the answers.

- For ratio, 4 : 8 = 1 : 2 after division by 4.
- For proportion, $\frac{12}{16} = \frac{3}{4}$ after division by 4.

A proportion can also be written as a decimal or a percentage because, for example, $\frac{3}{4} = 0.75 = 75\%$.

Plenary

Provide an example of beads on a necklace; say 4 red and 6 blue beads. Run through the basic ideas using questions which are answered on mini-whiteboards. For example, ask, what is the ratio of red to blue? Write your answer a simpler way. What is the proportion of red? Write your answer as a fraction. Now write it as a decimal and a percentage. Repeat for the proportion of blue.

Exercise commentary

Question 1 – The ratios and proportions do no need simplifying until parts **j** and **k**.

Question 2 – The order of the ratio matters. In the ratio 1 : 4, the 4 refers to yellow beads. So if there are 12 yellow beads, consider the equivalent ratio ? : 12. Access to coloured beads would be useful.

Questions 3 and **4** – Again, access to coloured beads is useful. When discussing the questions with students, a useful phrase is, for example, 'for every red, you need 3 yellow'.

Question 5 – The word 'proportion' should trigger the need for a fraction. Students need to recall finding equivalent fractions and simplifying.
The question could be extended by removing one column of the sweets (saying they have been eaten) and repeating parts **a**, **b** and **c**.

Answers

1 **a** **i** 1 **ii** 3 **iii** 1 : 3 **iv** $\frac{1}{4}$
v $\frac{3}{4}$
b **i** 3 **ii** 1 **iii** 3 : 1 **iv** $\frac{3}{4}$
v $\frac{1}{4}$
c **i** 1 **ii** 1 **iii** 1 : 1 **iv** $\frac{1}{2}$
v $\frac{1}{2}$
d **i** 2 **ii** 3 **iii** 2 : 3 **iv** $\frac{2}{5}$
v $\frac{3}{5}$
e **i** 2 **ii** 5 **iii** 2 : 5 **iv** $\frac{2}{7}$
v $\frac{5}{7}$
f **i** 3 **ii** 2 **iii** 3 : 2 **iv** $\frac{3}{5}$
v $\frac{2}{5}$
g **i** 1 **ii** 2 **iii** 1 : 2 **iv** $\frac{1}{3}$
v $\frac{2}{3}$
h **i** 1 **ii** 5 **iii** 1 : 5 **iv** $\frac{1}{6}$
v $\frac{5}{6}$
i **i** 1 **ii** 5 **iii** 1 : 5 **iv** $\frac{1}{6}$
v $\frac{5}{6}$
j **i** 4 **ii** 4 **iii** 4 : 4 = 1 : 1
iv $\frac{4}{8} = \frac{1}{2}$ **v** $\frac{4}{8} = \frac{1}{2}$
k **i** 3 **ii** 6 **iii** 3 : 6 = 1 : 2
iv $\frac{3}{9} = \frac{1}{3}$ **v** $\frac{6}{9} = \frac{2}{3}$

2 No, there will be one red bead left over.

3 **a** 1 : 3 **b** 6

4 **a** 1 : 2 **b** 6 **c** $\frac{1}{3}$

5 **a** $\frac{5}{20} = \frac{1}{4}$ **b** $\frac{5}{20} = \frac{1}{4}$ **c** $\frac{10}{20} = \frac{1}{2}$

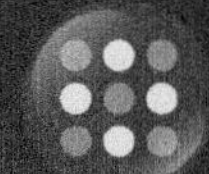

15b Ratio and proportion problems

Objectives

- Solve simple problems involving ratio and proportion using informal strategies. (L5)

Key ideas

1. Equivalent ratios can be found by multiplication or division.
2. Equivalent proportions can be found by multiplying or dividing the numerator and denominator

Resources

Proportion (1037)

Beads, counters or cubes of different colours

Copies of recipes

Simplification

Use four beads of two colours, say red and blue, to illustrate a simple ratio such as 1 : 3. Ask students to make a table with three columns labelled 'Red', 'Blue' and 'Ratio'. They enter '1', '3' and '1 : 3' in the columns.

Now double the red beads to 2 and match each red bead with three blue beads. Students should enter the data in the table as '2', '6' and '2 : 6'.

Repeat by increasing the red beads. Can students predict their results? Repeat with a different ratio.

Extension

Get students to divide quantities into three-part or four-part ratios. Ask them to write a model answer to a question of their own invention and include a justification of the processes they are using.

Literacy

Precision of spoken language helps students' understanding. Use wording such as:

- '.... four red beads for every blue bead'
- 'if you double the reds, you must double the blues'
- 'line up three red beads alongside each blue bead'

Links

One of the most famous cookery books ever published is *Mrs Beeton's Book of Household Management* which was published in 1861. As well as containing recipes, the book was a complete guide to running a Victorian household and included tips on caring for children and managing servants. Recipes included pigeon pie and barley gruel. The complete text of the book can be found at

www.mrsbeeton.com/

Alternative approach

Use the students of the class as data. Count the boys; count the girls; find the ratio of boys to girls. See if it can be simplified by division. Count those with surnames beginning with letters in the first half of the alphabet and those in the second half; find the ratio; simplify if possible. Repeat with those walking to school and those coming by some form of transport; those with siblings and those without; those who have only ever lived in the same house and those who have lived in more than one house.

Checkpoint

1. Provide a pile of beads containing 8 red and 16 blue.
   - **a** Separate the colours and count them.
   - **b** What is the ratio of red to blue? (8 : 16; see part **d**)
   - **c** If you line up the red beads wide apart, are there enough blue beads to place two beads alongside each red bead? (Yes)
   - **d** Can you simplify the ratio of red beads to blue? (Yes, 1 : 2)
   - **e** If you added 8 yellow beads, what would be the ratio of red to blue to yellow beads? (8 : 16 : 8 = 1 : 2 : 1)
   - **f** As a simple fraction, what proportion would be yellow? ($\frac{1}{4}$)

Starter – Pizzas!

Write the following ingredients needed to make pizza dough for four people.

300 g	flour
16 g	yeast
180 ml	water
20 ml	olive oil

Find how much of each ingredient is needed to make dough for 6 people? (450g, 24g, 270 ml, 30 ml)

Teaching notes

This lesson continues the work of the previous lesson by extending the use of ratios and proportions. The concepts and methods are the same; the variety of contexts in which they are applied is extended.

Alec's necklace in the student book is a good illustration of the notion of equivalence. The first two columns in each row of the table give the equivalent forms of the ratio of blue : red.

In its simplest form, the *ratio* is 2 : 3. Multiplication gives the same ratio in different ways, as in the other rows of the table.

So 2 : 3 becomes 4 : 6 when multiplied by 2
or 6 : 9 when multiplied by 3
or 8 : 12 when multiplied by 4, etc.

A discussion about the *proportion* of red beads also leads to equivalent forms found by multiplication. So, $\frac{2}{5}$ becomes $\frac{4}{10}$ or $\frac{6}{15}$ or $\frac{8}{20}$ etc.

A further example would be a recipe for making the crumble on top of an apple crumble. The ratio of butter : sugar : flour is 3 : 5 : 8. Ask, how much sugar and flour you need if you use 30 grams of butter and then 60 grams of butter?
(50 g sugar, 80 g flour; 100 g sugar, 160 g flour).

Plenary

Get students to use their mini-whiteboards to provide equivalent forms for ratios and proportions. For example, ask for:

- the missing number if 2 : 5 = 6 : □
- the ratio 6 : 8 in its lowest terms.

Questions can be set in context, such as, write the ratio of cows to sheep in its simplest form if a farmer has 50 cows and 150 sheep.

Exercise commentary

Question 1 – For part **c**, students watch for the number 15 appearing in the 'Total number' column. Parts **a** and **d** give a good indication of whether students have securely understood the concepts of ratio and proportion.

Question 2 – This can be answered by extending the table in questions **1** sufficiently.

Questions 3 and **4** – Students need to find the *total* number of parts first.

Question 5 – This introduces for the first time in this exercise, a ratio having more than two parts. Students could extend the question by designing their own stained glass window and answering similar questions. Do they know of examples of these windows in their local community?

Question 6 – This can be solved by creating a table with columns Hannah / Joe / Total and filling in successive rows 3 / 1 / 4, 6 / 2 / 8 etc. As an alternative, give students 20 beads and suggest students that they start by making four piles of five beads each. How could they share the beads in the ratio 3 : 1. Suggest sharing in other ratios such as 1 : 4, 2 : 3 or even 3 : 7 and see if students can work out for themselves how many piles to start with. (5, 5, 10).

Answers

1 **a** 1 : 2
b Next 3 rows are
4	8	12
5	10	15
6	12	18

c Green **d** $\frac{2}{3}$
2 **a** 10 **b** 20
3 **a** 10 **b** $\frac{6}{10} = \frac{3}{5}$ **c** $\frac{2}{10} = \frac{1}{5}$
4 **a** $\frac{1}{2}$ **b** $\frac{1}{8}$
c 25 butter, 10 water , 5 sugar
5 **a** 3 : 2 : 1 **b** $\frac{1}{2}$
6 Hannah £15, Joe £5

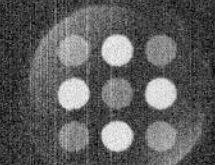

15c Solving arithmetic problems

Objectives

- Identify and obtain necessary information to carry through a task and solve mathematical problems. (L5)
- Develop own strategies for solving problems (L4)

Key ideas	Resources
1 Complex problems can be broken down into a series of simpler problems. **2** Simpler problems can be solved by deciding what data is needed and how you use it.	Proportion (1037) Word problems (1393) Cards describing various problem scenarios

Simplification	Extension
Present students with several one-stage problems set in a context which require students to chose one operation from +, – , × and ÷. Two-stage problems can follow later.	Present pairs of students with a scenario, such as planning a holiday or arranging a coach trip to a football match, within which various problems need addressing. Each pair should discuss the problem against the checklist given by Clara in the Student Book, draw up a strategy and then share their thinking with another pair of students who have the same problem.

Literacy	Links
Lengthy contextualised problems can be read in different ways. On a first meeting, the problem can be scanned quickly to get the gist of what is happening. Then the problem is read more slowly to take in the detail and to begin to see the different parts. An even slower reading is needed to select the numerical data and choose the arithmetic operations. Students should be encouraged to take great care when reading questions to ensure they do not miss key details.	Arithmetic is needed all the time in everyday life. The 'Math Hoops' activity on the Math Playground website provides lots of practice for word problems involving arithmetic in real-life contexts. www.mathplayground.com/MathHoops_Z1.html Note that the site is American and so US spelling and currency references are used.

Alternative approach

Rather than adopt a whole-class approach in the first instance, a complex scenario can be provided on cards which are given to pairs of students. They have a fixed time to absorb what is required to find a solution and arrange the cards in order, but they are not expected to do any calculations. Chosen pairs then report back to the whole class for everyone's comment and agreement.

Checkpoint

In each of these scenario ask students to articulate their thoughts when doing the calculation, stating what kind of problem it is, and showing their working when solving it.

1 There are five apples, six oranges and three pears in a fruit bowl.

a How many pieces of fruit are there in total? (Addition; $5 + 6 + 3 = 14$)

b If all of the apples are removed, how many pieces of fruit are left in the bowl? (Subtraction; $14 - 5 = 9$)

2 Bus tickets cost £1.50 for adults, and a child's ticket is half the price of an adult ticket.

a How much is a child's ticket? (Division; £1.50 ÷ 2 = £0.75 or 75p)

b How much does it cost for two adults and two children to travel on the bus?
(Multiplication and addition; 2 × £1.50 + 2 × £0.75 = £4.50)

Starter – Quick fire

Ask students to respond on mini-whiteboards to a series of quick questions which recap previous work on ratio and proportion. For example:

- If I have 2 oranges and 3 apples, what is the ratio of oranges to apples? (2 : 3)
- If there is one blue bead to every four red beads, what proportion of the beads are red? ($\frac{8}{10} = \frac{4}{5}$)
- Share £15 in the ratio 2 : 1. (£10 : £5)

Teaching notes

Give the whole class a multi-stage contextual problem to solve. For example, a car has a 1400 cc engine and its tank holds 30 litres of petrol when full. In urban traffic, it uses 1 litre every 7 miles. On the open road, it uses 1 litre every 9 miles. You take two hours to travel 41 miles, of which 14 miles is in towns. How many litres of petrol are used on this trip?

The arithmetic step-by-step is straightforward. The issue is how to grapple with so much information and what strategy to adopt. Students can refer to Clara's checklist in their book and discuss the problem to gain a good understanding of what is happening and what is needed.

Reject any unnecessary information, such as the engine size and the time taken for the trip. Break the problem into parts. Decide which arithmetical operation to use on which data. Answer the parts and bring them together to find the final answer. Ask if it is a sensible answer.
($14 \div 7 = 2$; $41 - 14 = 27$; $27 \div 9 = 3$; $2 + 3 = 5$ litres)

The exercise in the student book provides problems which are less complicated than the above.

Plenary

Ask students to articulate their thinking and their methods for the more involved problems in the exercise. Tell them that you are interested in their thought processes as much as in the actual calculations.

Exercise commentary

Questions 1 and **2** – These are straightforward.

Question 3 – Make it explicit that sometimes a problem provides more information than is needed. In this instance, the price of apples is given but is not needed.

Question 4 – This requires proportions, namely using division by 3. Some students, seeing a 400 g reduction in mince, may incorrectly want to subtract 400 g of spaghetti.

Question 5 – Students need to pay attention to the question, and could refer to Clara's checklist in their book.

Question 6 – Each operation from the red list is needed only once.

Answers

1 33 cm

2 **a** \$252 **b** £336

3 £4.50 ($2 \times 1.55 + 4 \times 0.35 = 3.10 + 1.40$)

4 **a** 300 g **b** 1

5 **a** £60 **b** £120

6 **a** + 5 **b** ÷ 2 **c** − 15 **d** × 10
e + 10 **f** − 12 **g** ÷ 4

Objectives

- Use and interpret scale drawings. (L5)
- Make scale drawings. (L5)

Key ideas

1. Scales are written as a ratio distance on drawing : distance in real life.
2. Scale drawings are the same shape as the real-life object but all lengths are reduced by the same scale factor.

Resources

Scale drawing (1117)

Centimetre square grid paper and scissors

Tape measure

Simplification

Repeatedly practice several conversions from scale drawing to real life and then from real life to scale drawings using the fixed scale 1 cm : 1 m. Repeat the same conversions using the new scale 1 cm : 2 m and then again using the scale 1 cm : 3 m.

Once students understand which calculations need to be done ask them to create a scale drawing of a 1 m by 2 m rectangle.

Extension

Students who grasp the principle of creating a scale drawing can be encouraged to create one of their classroom. They should start with major features, lengths of walls, positions of doors and windows, before starting to include items of furniture.

Such a scale drawing could form the basis of a classroom poster about scale drawings.

Literacy

A scale can be given in a number of ways.

One centimetre to two metres

1 cm : 2 m

1 : 200

1/200

0 4 m 8 m 12 m

Fractional scales are often quoted for models whilst graphic scales are usually given on a map.

Links

The idea of a scale drawing or model can be applied to some very large objects such as the solar system. This web site calculates the sizes of spheres need for the planets and their distances from the sun in a model of the solar system.

www.exploratorium.edu/ronh/solar_system/

Be warned, saying the sun should only be 14 mm across, a scale of 1 : 100 000 000 000, still means that Neptune, represented by a sphere less than half a millimetre across, should be orbiting at a distance of just over 45 m! Space is very empty indeed!

Alternative approach

Ask students to make a full size drawing of their calculator; agree that it can be represented by an 8 cm by 16 cm rectangle. Next ask them to do the same for their ruler. Ensure that some students have a 30 cm ruler so that there will be a problem. Take suggestions for what to do from the class and then agree that the ruler can be drawn half size so that, say, 30 cm by 4 cm ruler becomes 15 cm by 2 cm drawing. Suppose that the ruler was drawn quarter size, ask how big it should be. (7.5 cm by 1 cm) Next consider the reverse problem: draw a line 5 cm long beside the scale drawing and ask students to say what real-life length should be shown on the ruler. (10 cm or 20 cm)

Finally consider a much larger object, such, as a desk and together show how a scale of 1 cm : 1 m allows this to be drawn in an exercise book.

Checkpoint

In each question use the scale 1 cm : 2 m

1. These distances are measured on a scale drawing, how big are the distances in real life?
   a 1 cm **b** 2 cm **c** 4 cm (2 m; 4 m; 8 m)
2. These distances are measured in real life, how big are the distances on a scale drawing?
   a 2 m **b** 1 m **c** 4 m (1 cm; 0.5 cm; 2 m)

Starter – Square challenge

Ask students to draw, as accurately as they can, a square with sides 5 cm. When ready they should swap their drawing with a partner who should measure both diagonals in their partners drawing and write down what they find before returning the drawing.

In an accurate drawing both diagonals will be 7.1 cm.

Teaching notes

Ask students where they have seen scale drawings. Maps are a probable answer but press for more ideas: architects and engineers technical drawings, photographs, perhaps model toys. Emphasise that in every case the lengths in the drawings/models are all reduced by the same (scale) factor compared to the lengths in real life. This means that objects in the scale drawings keep the same shapes as the real-life objects.

Together say that you are going to create a scale drawing of the classroom door and that the scale will be 1 cm : 1 m. Explain that this is the same as 1 : 100 so that lengths in the drawing will be 100 times smaller than in real life. Get two students to measure the height and width of the door in centimetres, a chair might be needed to stand on. Next ask students to say how big the drawing should be and ask them to explain their reasoning. For example if the door is 2 m by 1 m then the drawing would be 2 cm by 1 cm. Ask students to make the scale drawing and label it with its actual size and the size of the door. Repeat the exercise with a new scale 2 cm : 1 m. This is 1 : 50 so the scale drawing will be 50 times smaller. The scale drawing of the door should now be 4 cm by 2 cm.

This exercise can be repeated for other objects such as a window or a student desk.

Finally return to the original scale drawing and ask students to add a line 1.5 cm long next to the door. Explain that this is the height of a man and ask how tall he would be in real life. (1.5 m) Repeat with the second scale drawing and say that the line now represents a child; they would be 75 cm tall.

Plenary

Show students a scale drawing of your desk, with dimensions in centimetres, and ask how they can work out the scale used in the drawing. Keep the numbers straightforward so that it is a test of reasoning and not arithmetic.

Exercise commentary

To check answers encourage students to think about the relative sizes of lengths in the scale drawing and in real life. For example if one length is twice another length then this will be true in the scale drawing and in real life. If one length lies between two others in real life then it will lie between the two others in a scale drawing.

Questions 1– All distances are to the nearest 5 mm or 0.5 m in the garden. The focus should be more on the correct conversion and less on the accuracy of the measurement. Refer students to the first example if they need help.

Questions 2– The scale is no longer 1 cm : 1 m, check that students use the correct scales. Refer students to the second example if they need help.

Question 3 – Make available one centimetre square grid paper so that students can concentrate on getting the correct dimensions, rather than drawing straight lines and right angles. Students must look at the measurements on the sketch, not the relative dimensions, as the diagram is distorted.

Question 4 – Students should choose their own scale; 2 cm : 1 m would be appropriate. A good approach would be to draw all the objects to scale and then cut them out before trying to arrange them to fit inside the outline of the bedroom again drawn to scale.

Not all the furniture will fit; the question can be extended by asking students to decide what furniture to leave out. Do they take into account that the door needs space to open inwards and that Mya will probably want some floor space to move around on.

Answers

1 **a** 8 m **b** 2.5 m **c** 0.5 m **d** 5 m **e** 1 m

2 **a** 4 m, 8 m **b** 9 m, 3 m **c** 18 m, 9 m

3 Drawing half scale size.

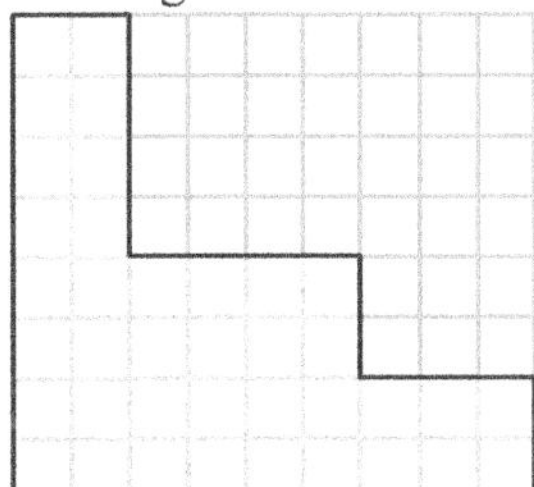

4 Not possible
(Area of objects = 7.75 m^2 > area of room = 7.5 m^2)

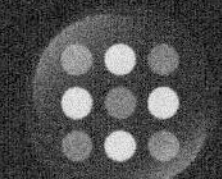

15 Ratio and proportion – MySummary

Key outcomes	Quick check
Write and use ratios and proportions. L4	For each drawing **i** write the ratio of black to white squares **ii** write the proportion of black squares **iii** write the proportion of white squares. **a** ■ ■ ■ □ $(3 : 1, \frac{3}{4}, \frac{1}{4})$ **b** □ ■ $(1 : 1, \frac{1}{2}, \frac{1}{2})$ **c** □ □ ■ □ □ ■ □ □ $(2 : 6, \frac{2}{8} = \frac{1}{4}, \frac{6}{8} = \frac{3}{4})$
Solve simple problems involving ratio and proportion. L5	**1** A necklace is made using two black beads for every three white beads. The finished necklace contains 30 beads ○●○●○ ○●○●○ **a** How many black beads are there in the finished necklace? (12) **b** What colour is the 17th bead? (Black) **2** Here is a recipe for eight pancakes. 1 egg 100 g flour 300 ml milk **a** How much of each ingredient do you need to make 24 pancakes? (3 eggs, 300 g flour, 900 ml milk) **b** If you start with 400 g of flour how much eggs and flour will you need? (4 eggs, 120 ml milk)
Solve arithmetic problems in context L5	A greengrocer sells oranges for 60 p each, four packs of pears for £1.20 and strawberries for £2 per 500 g. What is the cost of **a** 2 oranges and 8 pears (£3.60) **b** 4 kg of strawberries and an orange (£16.60) **c** 3 packs of pears and 5 oranges (£6.60)
Construct and interpret scale drawings L5	A drawing uses a scale 1 cm = 4 m **a** A distance on the map is 5 cm,. How far is this in real life? (20 m) **b** In real life a distance is 12 m. How far is this on the map? (3 cm)

Development and links
The idea of a probability as the proportion of successful outcomes in a set of possible outcomes is developed in chapter **16**. Work on ratio, proportion and problem solving is developed further in book **2A**, to include dividing in a given ratio and comparing proportions. Ratios and proportions occur whenever two or more things are mixed. For example, these can be the ingredients in a recipe or sand, cement and aggregate in a concrete mix or the colours cyan, magenta, yellow and black in colour printing. Scale drawings are used throughout geography, engineering and architecture.

MyMaths extra support

Lesson/online homework	Description
Simple equivalent fractions 1371 L4	This lesson revises finding fractions of a quantity, the meaning of a fraction and equivalent fractions.

My Review

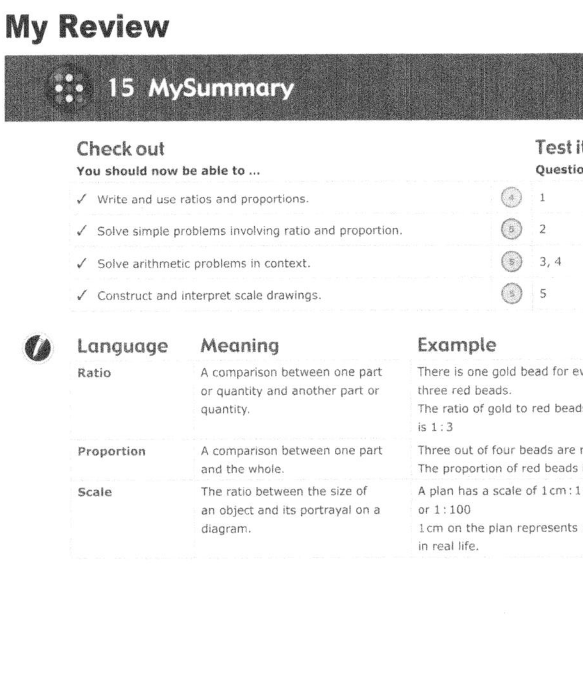

15 MySummary

Check out
You should now be able to ...

	Test it ➡ Questions
✓ Write and use ratios and proportions. (4)	1
✓ Solve simple problems involving ratio and proportion. (5)	2
✓ Solve arithmetic problems in context. (5)	3, 4
✓ Construct and interpret scale drawings. (5)	5

Language	Meaning	Example
Ratio	A comparison between one part or quantity and another part or quantity.	There is one gold bead for every three red beads. The ratio of gold to red beads is 1 : 3
Proportion	A comparison between one part and the whole.	Three out of four beads are red. The proportion of red beads is $\frac{3}{4}$.
Scale	The ratio between the size of an object and its portrayal on a diagram.	A plan has a scale of 1 cm : 1 m or 1 : 100. 1 cm on the plan represents 1 m in real life.

15 MyReview

1 In each drawing
 i write the ratio of squares to triangles
 ii write the proportion of squares.
 a ■■▲
 b ■■▲▲▲
 c ▲▲▲▲■

2 A necklace is made using 4 yellow beads to every 1 green bead.
 a What is the ratio of green beads to yellow beads?
 b How many yellow beads will be needed if there are 3 green beads?
 c How many green beads will be needed if there are 8 yellow beads?

3 The cost of a ticket to a basketball match is £20 for an adult. Children's tickets are half-price. What is the cost of
 a two adult tickets and a child ticket
 b 4 adult tickets and three child tickets
 c 10 adult tickets
 d 30 child tickets and 5 adult tickets?

4 Peaches cost £2.50 for a pack of four and plums cost 60p each. What is the cost of
 a 5 plums
 b 3 packs of peaches
 c 1 pack of peaches and 3 plums
 d 8 peaches
 e 16 peaches and 10 plums?

5 Write the length and width of each rectangle in real life
 a scale 1 cm : 1 m

 b scale 1 cm : 3 m
 c scale 1 cm : 4 m

6 A garden is a 10 m by 4 m rectangle. Draw a scale drawing of the garden using a scale of 1 cm : 2 m

What next?

Score		
0 – 2		Your knowledge of this topic is still developing. To improve look at Formative test: 1A-15; MyMaths: 1037, 1052, 1117 and 1393
3 – 5		You are gaining a secure knowledge of this topic. To improve look at InvisiPen: 191, 192 and 195
6		You have mastered this topic. Well done, you are ready to progress!

290 **Ratio and proportion** Ratio and proportion

MyMaths.co.uk

Question commentary

Question 1 – (lesson **15a**) Check that students write the ratios are the correct way around; 2 : 1 *not* 1 : 2 etc.

Question 2 – (lesson **15b**) In part **a**, check that the ratio is the correct way around. As necessary for parts **b** and **c**, encourage students to draw out the necklace.

Question 3 – (lesson **15c**) Check that students have correctly worked out that a child ticket costs £10.

Question 4 – (lesson **15c**) Students can answer in pounds or pence as long as they give the correct units. In part **b** do *not* accept £7.5 and in part **c** do *not* accept £4.3. Check that students correctly read the question: parts **b** and **c** ask for packs of peaches whilst parts **d** and **e** ask for individual peaches. Misreading the question would give the *wrong* answers: **b** £1.88, **c** £1.81, **d** £20 and **e** £46.

Question 5 – (lesson **15d**) The dimensions of the shapes are all multiples of 1 cm; accept answers accurate to ±10 cm, ±30 cm or ±40 cm respectively.

Question 6 – (lesson **15d**) The drawing should be accurate to ±2 mm.

Answers

1 **a** i 2 : 1 ii $\frac{2}{3}$ **b** i 2 : 3 ii $\frac{2}{5}$
 c i 1 : 4 ii $\frac{1}{5}$

2 **a** 1 : 4 **b** 12 **c** 2

3 **a** £50 **b** £110 **c** £200 **d** £400

4 **a** £3 **b** £7.50 **c** £4.30 **d** £5
 e £16

5 **a** 4 m by 2 m **b** 3 m by 15 m
 c 14 m by 16 m

6 Rectangle drawn 5 cm by 2 cm

15 MyPractice

15a

1 Express each of these ratios in its simplest form.

a 14:16 **b** 3:9 **c** 10:15 **d** 5:25 **e** 24:40 **f** 27:36

2 Coloured tiles are used to make a pattern.

a What is the ratio of yellow tiles to blue tiles?

b Write down the proportion of blue tiles as a fraction in its simplest form.

3 Coloured tiles are used to make another pattern.

a What is the ratio of red tiles to green tiles?

b As a fraction, what proportion of the finished tiling is red?

c As a fraction, what proportion of the finished tiling is green?

15b

4 Jo is making concrete using this mixture.

Gravel	5 parts
Cement	2 parts
Sand	4 parts
Water	1 part

a What is the ratio of sand to cement?

b What proportion of the concrete is

i cement **ii** sand?

c Jo has 12 units of sand to make concrete with.

i How much gravel is required?

ii How much water is required?

iii How much concrete will be made?

5 **a** Three sisters, Jean, Rita and Barbara, live in the same street. They decide to take their families to see their brother George. Their cars use petrol at different rates. During the journey Jean's car consumed 10 litres of petrol, Rita's consumed 12 litres and Barbara's consumed 14 litres. Express the figures as a ratio in its simplest form.

b The three sisters decide to take their families to see their other brother Tony, who lives further away than George. If Jean's car uses up 15 litres of petrol for this journey, how much is used up by

i Rita's car

ii Barbara's car?

15c

6 The school is organizing a trip to the theatre.
Childrens tickets cost £4.00, adult tickets cost £8.00.
There must be one teacher for every eight students on the trip.
The school is going to take 48 students.

a How much do the students' tickets cost?

b How many teachers need to go on the trip?

c What is the total cost of the trip?

7 Here is a recipe for pancakes.
Sam has 5 eggs.

Milk	300 ml
Eggs	1
Plain flour	100 g
Salt	pinch

a How much milk is required?
Give your answer in litres.

b How much flour is required?
Give your answer in Kilograms.

8 Apples are sold for £1.22 per kilogram.
Oranges are sold in bags of four £1.40.
Lemons cost 32p each.
What is the cost of

a 5 lemons

b 3kg of apples

c 4 bags of oranges

d 2kg of apples and 3 lemons

e 5kg of apples and 2 bags of oranges

f 12 oranges and 10 lemons?

15d

9 This is a scale drawing of Sam's garden. The scale is 1cm : 2m.

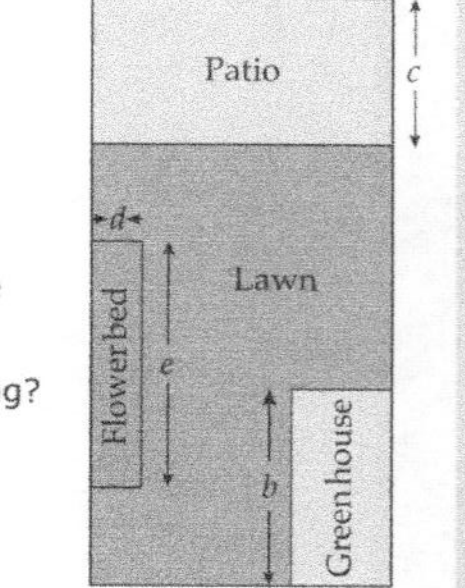

a How wide is the garden?

b How long is the greenhouse?

c How wide is the patio?

d How wide is the flower bed?

e How long is the flower bed?

10 Sam wants to add a pond to the drawing. The pond is to be rectangular with dimensions 3m by 2m.
What size rectangle should be drawn on Sam's scale drawing?

Question commentary

Question 1 – Students should be warned to check whether an answer can be simplified again; if it can it is not in its simplest form. It may be that the final answer is only found after a chain of simplifications. For example in part **e**, this might give 24 : 40 = 12 : 20 = 6 : 10 = 3 : 5. This could also be an issue in part **f**.

Questions 2 and **3** – Students may have difficulty remembering that ratio is part to part, written using a colon, and proportion is part to whole, written as a fraction (or percentage). Often, as here, the question gives a clue by saying 'as a fraction'. It may be helpful to discuss with students possible ways to remember the two definitions. In the two part **a**s, check that students appreciate that in a ratio the order matters: in general yellow : blue ≠ blue : yellow. In question **2**, ask students if they notice anything special about the answers to parts **b** and **c**. (The two proportions add up to 1, a whole.)

Question 4 – In part **c**, since 12 is exactly divisible by 4, then 'multiplying up' the quantities by 3 is likely to provide the most straightforward method.

Question 5 – This is a wordy question and some students may struggle to understand what they need to do and to identify the relevant information. A class discussion can be used to agree on the mathematical problem to be solved. In part **b**, students could multiply up the ratio written in its simplest form or they could argue that compared to the journey in part **a** it is half as much again. For example, the answer to part **b i** could be found as $12 + \frac{1}{2} \times 12 = 18$ litres. When appropriate, insist that students include units with their answers.

Questions 6 to **8** – Lesson **15c** starts by providing Clara's four top tips for solving problems. These can be used for framing any discussion of how to approach these problems. It may help weaker students' confidence to work in pairs. Calculators may also be allowed so that the focus can be placed on the more non-routine, problem solving aspects of the questions.

Questions 9 – It may help to do the first few parts together so that students understand what to do. All the measurements in the diagram are multiples of 0.5 cm. For parts **c** to **e** it may help to think of the scale as 0.5 cm : 1 m.

Questions 10 – Ask students to explain how they know that they should divide by two rather than multiply by two when finding the answers.

Answers

1 **a** 7 : 8 **b** 1 : 3 **c** 2 : 3 **d** 1 : 5
e 3 : 5 **f** 3 : 4

2 **a** 1 : 3 **b** $\frac{3}{4}$

3 **a** 2 : 3 **b** $\frac{2}{5}$ **c** $\frac{3}{5}$

4 **a** 2 : 1
b **i** $\frac{2}{12} = \frac{1}{6}$ **ii** $\frac{4}{12} = \frac{1}{3}$
c **i** 15 units **ii** 3 units **iii** 36 units

5 **a** 5 : 6 : 7
b **i** 18 litres **ii** 21 litres

6 **a** £4 **b** 6
c £240 (48 × 4 + 6 × 8 = 192 + 48)

7 **a** 1.5 litres **b** 0.5 kg

8 **a** £1.60 **b** £3.66 **c** £5.60 **d** £3.40
e £8.90 **e** £7.40

9 **a** 6 m **b** 4 m **c** 3 m **d** 1 m
e 5 m

10 1.5 cm by 1 cm

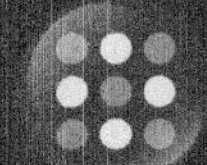

16 Probability

Learning outcomes	
P1 Record, describe and analyse the frequency of outcomes of simple probability experiments involving randomness, fairness, equally and unequally likely outcomes, using appropriate language and the 0-1 probability scale.	(L4)
P2 Understand that the probabilities of all possible outcomes sum to 1.	(L5)
P3 Enumerate sets and unions/intersections of sets systematically, using tables, grids and Venn diagrams.	(L4)

Introduction

The chapter starts by introducing the concept of probability before looking at the probability scale in terms of both 'likely' terminology and fractions of the whole. The final section looks at sorting with Venn diagrams.

The introduction discusses the appeal of games and the idea that many are a mixture of skill and chance. Understanding the concept of probability helps to ensure that the choices and decisions that are made when playing games involving chance are well thought out.

Venn diagrams were conceived by John Venn around 1880 and have been used ever since to show the relations between sets and to solve probability problems. Venn worked at around the same time as another famous mathematician, an Oxford don called Charles Dodgson. Dodgson developed a similar method for working with probability and his diagrams are called Carroll diagrams. The reason for this is that Charles Dodgson is actually the real name of the famous author of the Alice in Wonderland stories, Lewis Carroll. Biographies of Venn and Dodgson can be found here.

http://www-history.mcs.st-and.ac.uk/Mathematicians/Venn.html

http://www-history.mcs.st-and.ac.uk/Biographies/Dodgson.html

Prior knowledge

Students should already know how to…

- Work with simple fractions, decimals and percentages

Starter problem

The starter problem is a simple game which involves probabilities. The game is weighted in favour of the wolf since there are more numbers which move the wolf than the sheep. However, the sheep is closer to home. Since the probability is one third you move the sheep, and two thirds you move the wolf, it would seem that game is not fair, but since the sheep is less than half the distance from home as the wolf is, it should be possible to get the sheep home.

Students can be directed to try the game out a few times and record the results. Variations could include changing the numbers on the dice which move each animal, or changing the number of steps each can move. If the wolf moves two squares instead of one, does the game now remain fair?

Using probability in games like this is designed to mimic real-life. It is often referred to as *simulation*.

Resources

MyMaths

Probability intro	1209	Introducing data	1235		

Online assessment		**InvisiPen solutions**			
Chapter test	1A-16	Introducing probability	451	Sets	471
Formative test	1A-16				
Summative test	1A-16				

Topic scheme

Teaching time = 4 lessons/2 weeks

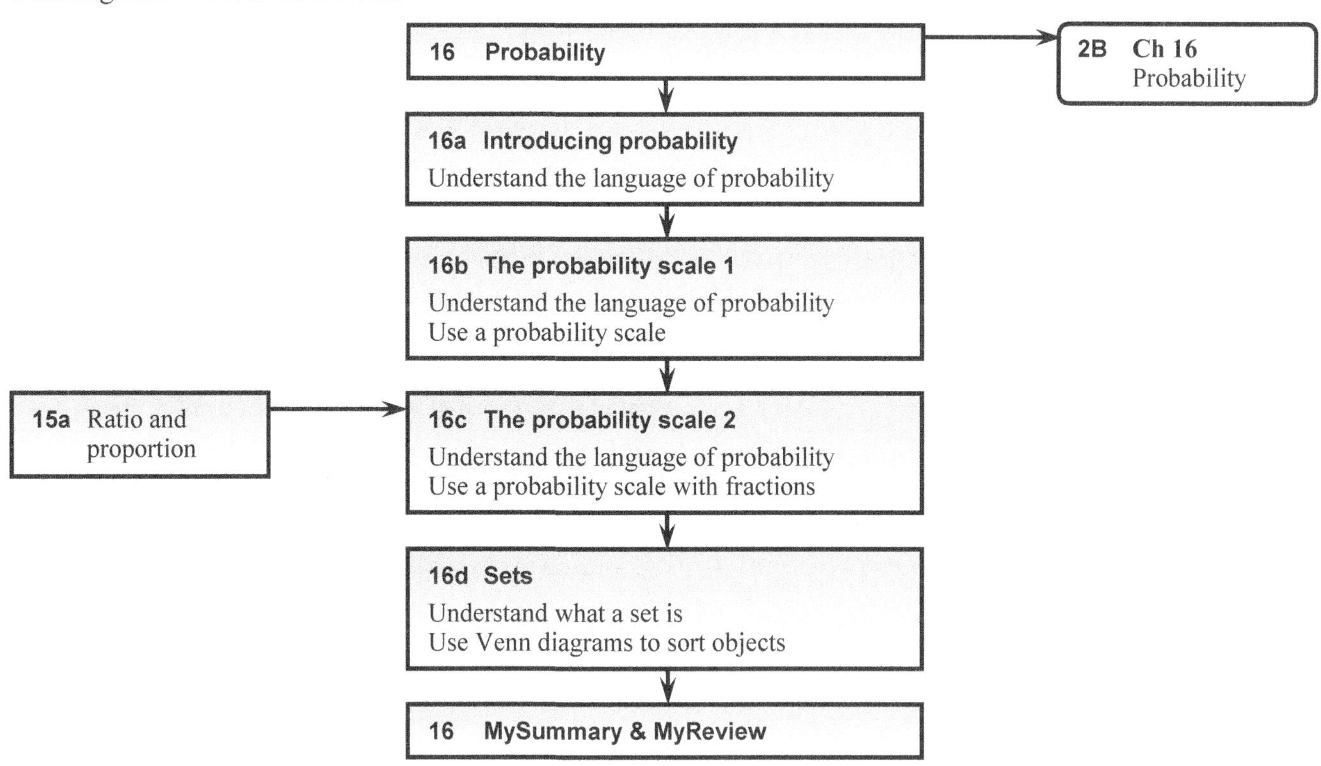

Differentiation

Student book 1A 294 – 307	Student book 1B 290 – 305	Student book 1C 290 – 307
Introducing probability	The probability scale	The probability scale
The probability scale	Listing outcomes	Equally likely outcomes
Sorting with Venn diagrams	Theoretical probability	Mutually exclusive outcomes
	Experimental probabilities	Experimental probability
	Sets and Venn diagrams	Comparing probabilities
		Sets and Venn diagrams

16a Introducing probability

Objectives	
• Use vocabulary and ideas of probability, drawing on experience. (L4)	
Key ideas	**Resources**
1 All events can be categorised as certain, uncertain or impossible. **2** There are various degrees of uncertainty.	Probability Intro (1209) A bag of coloured cubes Cards with events written on them
Simplification	**Extension**
Offer students a wide selection of examples of events to place in the three categories: 'certain', 'uncertain' and 'impossible'. Initially, list events where the choice of category is clearly defined and obvious.	Consider examples where the likelihood of certain events is not absolutely defined. It changes according to circumstance. For example, responses to 'Will you will fly from Heathrow next week?' depends on who is being spoken to and when the question being asked.
Literacy	**Links**
Many words in everyday use imply that life has many uncertainties. 'Only death and taxes' are certain, so it is said! Note that mathematics contrasts *impossible* with *certain*. Linguistically, the opposite of 'impossible' is 'possible', but a possible event is not necessarily certain, and the opposite of 'certain' is 'uncertain', but an uncertain event is not necessarily impossible. So mathematics uses these words in a very precise way.	People take out travel insurance when they go on holiday, so that they can claim money back if something goes wrong. For example, their flight is cancelled, or they need to visit a hospital abroad and pay medical fees. The cost of the travel insurance policy is calculated according to the likelihood of certain events happening, such as • bad weather causing a flight to be cancelled; • being pickpocketed and losing a wallet or mobile phone; • sports equipment being damaged, for example, on a skiing holiday. Look at a travel insurance policy, in a leaflet or online, and categorise events according to their likelihood.
Alternative approach	
Give pairs of students a pack of cards, where each card has an event, such as those in the student book, written on it. The students should place each card in one of three piles labelled 'certain', 'uncertain' and 'impossible'. Include three blank cards on which students can write their own events and place them, one each, on the three piles.	
Checkpoint	
1 Are the following events certain, uncertain or impossible? **a** It will rain tomorrow in London. (Uncertain) **b** Your cat will learn to write its own name. (Impossible) **c** Next week, the day before Sunday will be Saturday. (Certain) **d** The sun will be shining in the UK at midnight tonight. (Impossible) **e** Christmas Day will be on 25th December this year. (Certain) **f** You will get a 4 when you roll a dice. (Uncertain)	

Starter – What's in it for me?

Prepare a bag of coloured cubes with 50 red, 25 blue, 24 yellow and 1 green. Students do not know the numbers or colours of the cubes. Tell them that their aim is to find how many colours are in the bag, but they can only take one cube out at a time.

Ask for suggestions about how it can be done. Accept that a record has to be kept of each cube taken out and that the bag is shaken after the cube is replaced.

Repeat until students think they know what colours are in the bag. Ask if they are certain about their answers. If not, ask why not.

Tell them that there are 100 cubes in the bag. Can they say how many cubes of each colour there are? Can they be sure? Empty the bag to check.

Teaching notes

As an introduction to this chapter, invite students to develop the language of probability in the following ways.

- Answering questions such as, will it rain today? Will you swim the Atlantic tomorrow? Will you need food and drink to stay alive?
- Providing their own examples of events they perceive to be of varying likelihood.

Encourage the use of words such as 'certain', 'likely', 'probably', 'unlikely' and 'impossible'. List them for all to see.

This exercise develops the concept that some events are certain, some events are impossible, and some events are uncertain to various degrees. For example, whether it rains tomorrow and whether it snows tomorrow are both uncertain, but snow is more uncertain than rain.

Plenary

Ask students to write five events on their mini-whiteboards and then exchange their boards with a partner. Students should put each of their partner's events into one of three categories, 'certain', 'uncertain', 'impossible' by labelling them C, U, or I. Then they discuss their results in pairs and justify the outcomes.

Exercise commentary

Throughout the exercise, emphasise the meanings of the words 'certain', 'impossible', 'uncertain' by saying 'absolutely certain', 'totally impossible' and 'not sure'.

Question 1 – Part **f** and **h** are both 'uncertain'; ask students if one is less uncertain than the other.

Question 2 – This question is designed to allow a discussion of how likely a particular event is based on counting the number of 'successes'. For part **a**, you would be successful half the time, or 5 times out of 10, but in part **d** you would expect to be successful 9 time out of ten. In this way you can say event **d** is more likely than event **a**.

Question 3 –Part **b** deserves more than just the answer 'Yes'. Encourage discussion to provide examples of events with different levels of certainty.

Question 4 – Ask students to rank these three events in order of rising probability and to give their reasons. The discussion could be widen to include, for example, the probability of being involved in a natural disaster due to climate change, such as flooding, coastal erosion, water shortages, and their relative likelihoods.

Question 5 – Ask students to explain how they made their rankings. Is there anything that they could do to try and quantify the likelihood? For event **b**, students could roll a dice several times and see what fraction of the time they get an even number. For events **a** and **e**, students could look at historical data and see what fraction of the time the petrol price did not rise in a year or it did not rain in January.

Answers

1 Student answers and reasons; accept answers with a sensible reason.

a Unlikely **b** Certain
c Impossible **d** Impossible
e Likely **f** Uncertain
g Impossible **h** Uncertain
i Uncertain

2 **a** Certain **b** Impossible
c Uncertain, unlikely **d** Uncertain, likely

3–4 Student answers; require explanations for choices. Some possible answers are given.

3 **a** **i** Night will follow day.
ii England will win a world cup.
iii Pigs will fly.
b Yes

4 **a** Likely **b** Likely
c Unlikely

5 **c** (Certain), **a** (Likely), **b** (Even chance), **e** (Unlikely), **d** (Very unlikely?)

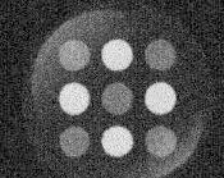

16b The probability scale 1

Objectives

- Use words to describe how likely an event might be (L4)

Key ideas	Resources
1 There is a range of words which describe the different likelihoods of events. 2 The words range from *impossible* to *certain*.	Probability intro (1209) Copies of the non-numeric scale in the student book Packs of cards, each labelled with one of the descriptions taken from the non-numeric scale Packs of twelve cards numbered 1 to 12

Simplification	Extension
Give students their own copy of the non-numeric scale and a list of events on a set of cards. Ask them to allocate each event to a description on the scale and discuss their results.	Give students a list of events, where each event on the list has a calculable probability, such as, rolling a 6 on a dice, tossing a head on a coin, choosing a vowel at random from the alphabet. Ask students to order the events in terms of increasing probability. Students should explain the reasons for their ordering but they are not expected to use, or be taught, any formal approach for calculating numerical probabilities.

Literacy	Links
The non-numeric scale has words in everyday use. Students might offer other suitable labels such as 'fifty-fifty' or 'odds-on' and discuss whereabouts they would best fit on the scale.	Weather forecasters, meteorologists, never know for certain what weather conditions will be like, but they can use scientific instruments to help them make sensible predictions about the conditions that will be most likely. In October 1987, a bad storm hit the UK and hurricane-force winds caused great damage. Weather reports from the day the storm hit failed to predict how severe it would be. The Met Office website gives reliable 5-day weather forecasts. www.metoffice.gov.uk/

Alternative approach

MyMaths lesson 1209, 'Introducing probability', leads several different approaches to probability.

In addition, the nrich website offers a simple activity which complements those in the MyMaths lesson.

www.nrich.maths.org/7245

Checkpoint

1 Explain in words how likely the following events are.

a	A coin will land on heads when you flip it.	(Even chance)
b	You will score an 8 when you roll a regular six-sided dice.	(Impossible)
c	You will have a PE lesson this week.	(Very likely)
d	You will win the lottery next month.	(Very unlikely)

Starter – Higher or lower

Recap work of previous chapters briefly, especially work on fractions, decimals and percentages. Ask rapid response questions with students replying on mini-whiteboards. Then introduce the following task.

A pack of twelve cards are numbered from 1 to 12. As a whole-class activity, choose one of the twelve cards without looking. Ask students whether they think the next card chosen will have a higher or lower number. Return the card to the pack. Select a second card. Students who predicted correctly score 1 point.

Repeat several times. Ask students if there is a strategy that would improve their points total. (If the chosen card is 6 or less, predict the next score to be higher; if the card is 7 or more, predict lower). Students explain their reason for this strategy. Does it work?

Teaching notes

Students have already met some of the language of probability: the words 'certain, 'uncertain' and 'impossible'. They already know that uncertain events have different probabilities depending on how likely they are. Some are more certain than others.

This exercise now develops the language more extensively and introduces a non-numeric scale of probability ranging from 'impossible' to 'certain'. A whole-class discussion explores and notes the different words we use when we talk about uncertain events. Create a list of these words, such as 'quite likely', 'very unlikely', 'almost certain', 'not at all probable', 'evens' and other words such as 'maybe', 'perhaps', 'iffy', 'odds-on'.

Give pairs of students a pack of nine cards with the seven descriptions of probabilities taken from the range given in the Student Book. Each pair of students has to arrange these seven cards in order of likelihood. The class discusses and agrees on the order. A further discussion ensues to allocate different events, such as 'rain tomorrow', to different positions on this scale.

Plenary

Various events can be suggested in turn to the whole class. Students should use mini-whiteboards to select from the seven descriptions and write the probability that best matches each event. A short discussion can reach a general agreement. The activity can be reversed so that a probability, such as 'almost certain', is offered and individual students suggest an appropriate event.

Exercise commentary

Take opportunities to discuss students reasoning when assigning probabilities or placing events in order of likelihood.

Question 1 – Students can copy these two lists and match events to probabilities with arrows.

Questions 2 and **3** – It is not expected that students calculate numerical probabilities as fractions – this is saved for a later date. However, they can choose from the words in boxes in Question **1**. More able students could be asked to give the expected number of successes if a dice where rolled six times and use these to order the events in terms of likelihood. (3, 3, 2, 1)

Question 4 – The discussion of the students' answers is more important than the answers themselves.

Question 5 – The order is likely to be different from one student to the next. Pairs of students can discuss the reasons for their order of events and explore if one list is ordered differently from the other list.

Answers

1 **a** Very likely (*but* student dependent).
 b Certain
 c Unlikely or likely (depending on time of year, geography, weather conditions etc.)
 d Very unlikely **e** Impossible

2 **a** Even chance **b** Even chance
 c Unlikely **d** Very unlikely

3 **a** Very unlikely
 b Quite unlikely (about a $\frac{1}{3}$ chance)
 c Impossible

4 Student answers; possible answers are
 a She will pick a number between 1 and 60 inclusive.
 b She will pick 61 (or any number outside 1–60).
 c She will pick a number from 1 to 59.
 d She will pick a 7 (or any other number in the range 0–60).

5 Student answers; require explanations for choices.

6 **a** **i** Even chance, $\frac{1}{2}$ **ii** Likely, $\frac{2}{3}$
 iii Unlikely, $\frac{1}{3}$
 b **i** Unlikely, $\frac{1}{4}$ **ii** Unlikely, $\frac{1}{4}$
 iii Even chance, $\frac{1}{2}$

Objectives	
• Understand and use the probability scale from 0 to 1. (L5)	
Key ideas	**Resources**
1 All probabilities lie between 0 and 1 and can be given as fractions, decimals or percentages. **2** A certain event has a probability of 1. An impossible event has a probability of 0.	Probability intro (1209) Lists of events to order on a probability scale
Simplification	**Extension**
Draw a probability scale with its two sets of labels: in words and in numbers, as in the student book. Add further words to the scale, such as 'quite likely', 'very likely', 'quite unlikely', 'very unlikely', 'almost certain' and 'almost impossible'. Students now have a greater selection when describing a numerical probability in words.	Use the opportunity to strengthen students' understanding of the equivalence of fractions, decimals and percentages. Provide a more demanding list of events for which the probabilities can be found. Ask students to write them in order, as decimals, from the lowest to the highest probability. Where a probability is found as a fraction, such as rolling a 6 on a dice, students should use a calculator to change the fraction to a decimal.
Literacy	**Links**
The words *random* and *bias* are commonly used with probabilities. When an event is 'biased', it means that the outcome is distorted because some results are more favoured than others and should not be. When an event is 'random', it means that there is no favouritism towards any particular outcome. If you choose something 'at random' like a card from a pack, you do not favour one card over another.	Throwing a dice may be random but it can be biased, for example if the dice is weighted off-centre. A random number generator (RNG) is a device that generates numbers without any discernible bias towards particular numbers. It is very difficult to determine whether or not the numbers are truly random, as the device has to be programmed to produce the numbers randomly in the first place! This website www.random.org/dice/?num=2 provides random results for several events, including rolling two dice.
Alternative approach	
Activities in MyMaths lesson 1210, 'Simple Probability', include using the probability scale from 0 to 1.	
Checkpoint	
1 If an event is certain, what is the probability it will happen? (1 or 100%) **2** There are 4 blue marbles and 4 red marbles in a bag. One marble is picked out at random. What is the probability that it is red? ($\frac{1}{2}$ or 0.5 or 50%) **3** What is the percentage probability that it will rain cats and dogs tomorrow? (0%)	

Starter – Quick fire

Ask students to respond on mini-whiteboards to a series of quick questions which recap previous work, giving particular emphasis to questions relating to fractions, decimals and percentages. For example

- Write 0.3 as a fraction. ($\frac{3}{10}$)
- What is 7% as a fraction? ($\frac{7}{100}$)
- Write 45% as a decimal. (0.45)

Discuss questions when their answers indicate a need.

Teaching notes

Recap the vocabulary of this chapter so far. Refer to the non-numeric scale. Discuss how to make the scale less vague and more precise. Decide on a numerical scale where 0 is the probability for 'impossible' and 1 is the probability for 'certain'. Draw the new numeric scale directly under the non-numeric scale. Discuss how the new scale can be labelled from 0 to 1. Label it three ways: 0.1 to 0.9, $\frac{1}{10}$ to $\frac{9}{10}$ and 10% to 90%.

Invite suggestions for a fraction, decimal or percentage to represent 'quite likely', 'almost impossible' and other worded labels.

Ask students to decide where to place the probabilities of given events on the numeric scale; for example

- tossing a heads with a coin;
- choosing a red cube from a bag containing 3 red and 7 blue cubes;
- rolling a score of 1 on a ten-sided dice;
- being set some maths homework this week.

Plenary

Give students a list of events and ask them to place them in order from the lowest to the highest probability. Find the probability of each event as a fraction, decimal or percentage. Discuss as a whole class and reach agreement.

Exercise commentary

Question 1 – This provides a quick test of whether students have made the connection between the numerical and descriptive probability scales. As necessary provide all numerical values as fractions to check that any problem does not lie with fraction-decimal-percentage conversions.

Question 2 – Students should place 30% on the scale 0 to 1 and then match the position with the non-numeric scale.

Question 3 – Students need to appreciate the difference between 'winning a prize'. on entry, and 'winning the game', at the end and presumably for a bigger and better prize. Students could discuss how such a game can make a profit if all the entries are given a prize.

Question 4 – Students count using the picture, find a fraction in tenths, and give the probability its value. Ask students for the total of all three answers and why they get the total they do.

Question 5 – Agree that we assume the dice is 'fair'; that is, that all faces are equally likely. A whole-class discussion leads into the probability of rolling a 6 and the number of 6s that could be expected from 100 throws.

Question 6 – Any surprise is likely to be due to the probability of '1 head, 1 tail' being twice the other event's probabilities. The reason is that no distinction is made between the two events 'first coin heads, second coin tails' and 'first coin tails, second coin heads'. That is there are two distinct ways to get '1 head, 1 tail'.

Answers

1 Impossible – 0   Very unlikely – 1%
Unlikely – 0.1   An even chance – 0.5
Quite likely – 65%   Certain – 100%

2 It is quite unlikely to rain tomorrow, although it would be best to still take some showerproof clothing!

3 It is certain that you will win something, that is, probability = 1. Of course, you may not win the prize you were hoping for!

4 **a** $\frac{1}{2}$ **b** $\frac{3}{10}$ **c** $\frac{2}{10} = \frac{1}{5}$ **d** 0
e $\frac{1}{2}$ **f** $\frac{8}{10} = \frac{4}{5}$ **g** 1

5 Student answers. Expectation is ≈ 17 times (100 ÷ 6), so probably not fair, that is, biased.

6 **a, b** Students' results.
c Expectations are 10, 20 and 10.

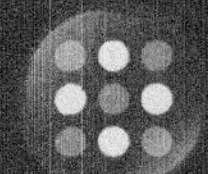

16d Sorting with Venn diagrams

Objectives	
• Continue to use Venn diagrams to record their sorting and classifying information. (L4)	

Key ideas	Resources
1 A group of objects can be sorted into different sets. **2** A Venn diagram visually represents how the elements are sorted. **3** You can draw Venn diagrams with numbers to show how many objects are each set.	Introducing data (1235) Blank Venn diagram templates Large rings and cut out shapes Chalk

Simplification	Extension
To help with grasping the basic sorting concept make this a practical activity. Use two large rings, hoola hoops or chalk drawn circles, to indicate the two overlapping sets and ask students to sort cards showing coloured shapes or numbers etc. into the two sets. Once students appreciate how to do the sorting discuss how to describe the number of items in the various regions 'in A but not in B', 'in B but not in A', 'in A and in B' and 'not in A and not in B'. Concentrate on questions **1** and **2** and further examples of this type.	Students are likely to agree that writing out the word descriptions of the various regions is time consuming. They could be introduced to set notation as an abbreviated way of writing, using ′ (prime) for 'not' and ∩ for 'and', that is $A \cap B'$ 'in A and not in B' $A' \cap B$ 'not in A and in B' $A \cap B$ 'in A and in B' $A' \cap B'$ 'not in A and not in B' Here the letters A and B are chosen to represent descriptions of the sets. Ask students to write their statements using this notation. Alternatively ask students to show how the four regions in a Carroll diagram map to the regions in a Venn diagram.

Literacy	Links
Check students understanding of the assumed vocabulary and clarify their meaining as necessary: 2D, 3D, multiple, factor and vowel (A, E, I, O & U)	Venn diagrams are often used in other subjects, such as English. This Venn diagram tool uses two overlapping circles to compare and contrast two ideas. www.readwritethink.org/files/resources/interactives/venn_diagrams/

Alternative approach

Find an open space and draw two large overlapping circles on the ground. Explain that one circle is for people with brown eyes and the other circle is for people with blond hair; ask students to work out where they should stand. Once they have settled down, ask how the various groups would describe themselves: 'not blond hair and brown eyes' etc. On the board make a Venn diagram copy of the overlapping circles and fill it withthe number of students in each area. Include a bounding rectangle for all people and put the number of students with 'not blond hair and not brown eyes' in the rectangle but outside the circles.

Repeat with other pairs of classifications: 'have a brother' and 'have a sister'; 'have a cat' and 'have a dog' etc. until the idea of how to use the diagram and name its parts is understood. Finally repeat with a more abstract example such as in question **1**.

Checkpoint

1 a Use a Venn diagram to sort the letters of the word DECIMALS into

- the set of vowels
- letters in the word PYRAMID.

b Use numbers to represent the number of letters in each set.

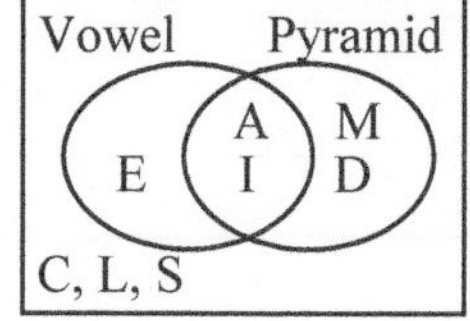

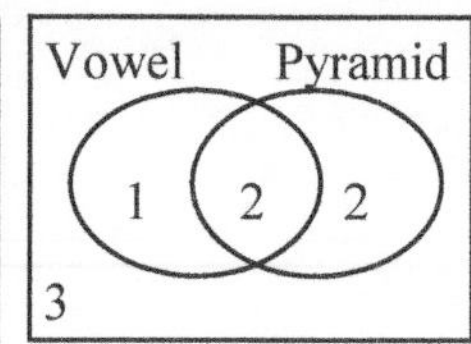

Starter – Sorting

Draw two circles on the board, label one circle 'even' and the other 'odd'. Ask students to sort the numbers from 1 to 10 into the circles.

Repeat with the circles 'odd' and 'multiples of 3'.

Ask students how they can alter the diagram to allow numbers to be placed in both circles and where to place numbers that do not belong to either circle.

Teaching notes

The lesson focuses on introducing how to draw and describe the regions of Venn diagrams.

Discuss the introduction in the student book, which sorts shapes into a Venn diagram. Discuss the benefits of using numbers to represent the number of objects in each region rather than the objects themselves.

Extend to a class activity by assigning each student with a different number using numbered cards or mini whiteboards. Draw a Venn diagram on the board that sorts the numbers into two sets. Ask students to hold up their card or board if they belong to a given region of the Venn diagram. Discuss any discrepancies. This can also be a good opportunity to revisit previous topics such as multiples and factors or properties of shapes.

Emphasise the importance of being able to describe each region of the Venn diagram in words.

Plenary

Ask students to invent their own version of question **4** in the student book and challenge a partner to match each group of objects with a Venn diagram.

Discuss how students can ensure that their objects do not result in the same Venn diagram.

Exercise commentary

Question 1 – Part **a** involves classifying objects into sets. Students may need to be reminded of the words *multiple* and *factor*. Part **b** involves writing descriptions of different regions of the Venn diagram. Students should be encouraged to use the example to help them write their answers.

Question 2 involves using numbers in Venn diagrams to represent the number of objects in each set. Encourage students to 'check off' each shape to avoid double counting or missing a shape. Weaker students may need to create a Venn diagrams with the objects themselves before writing the numbers.

Question 3 involves finding the number of elements in different regions. In part **c**, some students may make the mistake of not including the number in the intersection.

Question 4 involves matching Venn diagrams to three groups of objects. Encourage students to compare different regions on the diagrams with each set of cards rather than drawing Venn diagrams from scratch.

Answers

1 **i** **a**

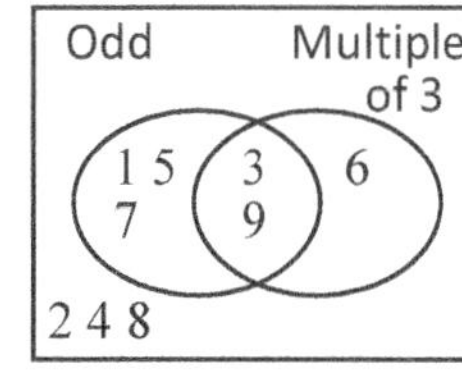

b Odd but not a multiple of 3.
Odd and a multiple of 3.
A multiple of 3 but not odd (even).
Not odd (even) and not a multiple of three.

ii **a**

5 or more | Even
5 7 9 | 6 8 | 2 4
1 3

b Five or more but not even.
Five or more and even.
Even but not five or more.
Not five or more and not even.

iii **a**

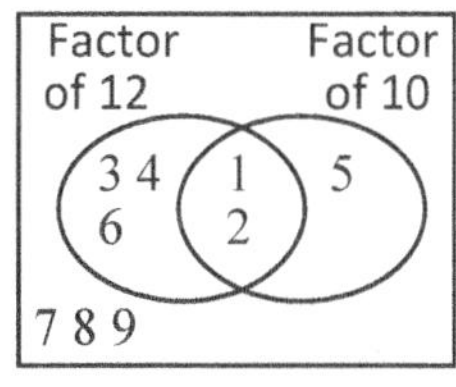

b A factor of 12 but not a factor of 10.
A factor of 12 and 10.
A factor of 10 but not a factor of 12.
Not a factor of 12 and not a factor of 10.

2

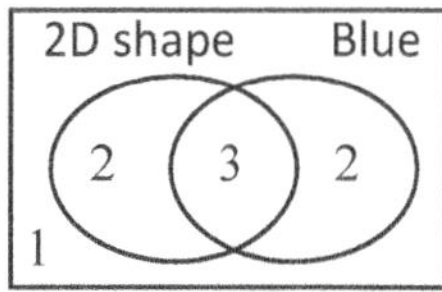

3 **a** 5 **b** 4 **c** 15

4 **a** 3 **b** 1 **c** 2

Key outcomes	Quick check
Use the vocabulary and ideas of probability, drawing on experience. L4	**1** Use words to describe the probability of these events. **a** The roll of a dice gives an odd number. (Even chance) **b** A persons birthday is 29th February. (Very unlikely) **c** There will be more sunny days in May than February. (Likely) **d** Three tosses of a coin give three heads. (Unlikely) **e** A persons birthday is 30th February. (Impossible)
Understand and use the probability scale from 0 to 1. L5	**1** A bag of marbles contains the following colours: 2 red, 4 white, 6 blue. Give the probability, as a fraction, that a randomly selected marble is **a** white $(\frac{4}{12}=\frac{1}{3})$ **b** red $(\frac{2}{12}=\frac{1}{6})$ **c** black (0) **d** red or white $(\frac{6}{12}=\frac{1}{2})$ **e** red, white or blue $(\frac{12}{12}=1)$ **2** Describe the probability of the events in question **1** using words. (**a** Unlikely **b** Very unlikely **c** Impossible **d** Even chance **e** Certain)
Sort objects using a Venn diagram. L4	**1** Place the numbers 1 to 10 into this Venn diagram. Factor of 12 Odd Factor of 12 Odd 2 4 6 | 1 3 | 3 5 7 8 10

Development and links

Probability is revisited in book **2A** where it is extended to include calculating probabilities, either theoretically by counting the fraction of successful outcomes as a fraction of equally likely outcomes or experimentally as the number of successful trials as a fraction of the total number of trials. Students also learn how to calculate probabilities from the numbers of entries in a Venn diagram.

The language of probability is often used in the news media making it important to understand what various statements mean or do not mean. Weather forecasters increasingly give predictions with probabilities: 'there is a 60% chance of rain tomorrow'. Knowing what this means could be the difference between staying dry or getting soaked!

MyMaths extra support

Lesson/online homework			Description
Lists and tables 2	1284	L2	This lesson allows students to build confidence in sorting shapes by colour and numbers by simple properties.

My Review

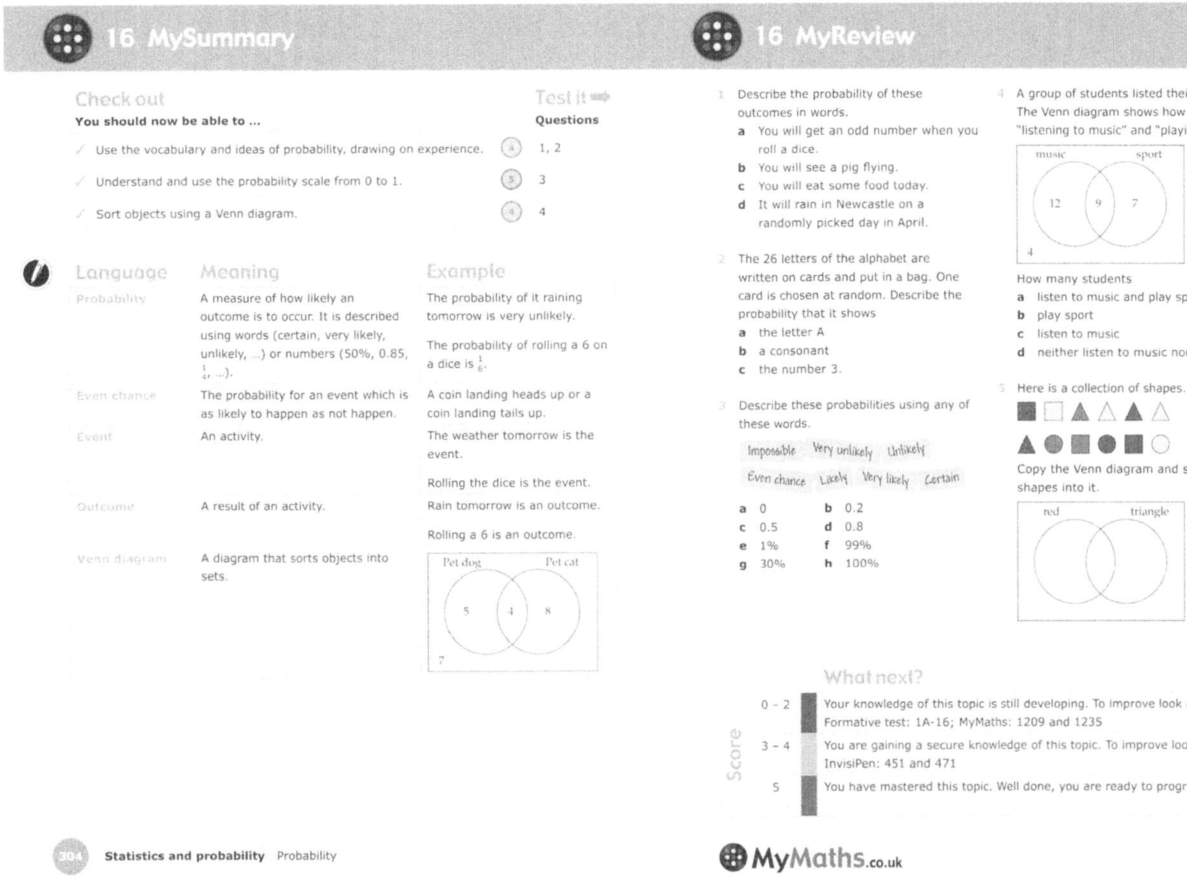

16 MySummary

Check out

You should now be able to ...

	Test it ➡ Questions
✓ Use the vocabulary and ideas of probability, drawing on experience. (4)	1, 2
✓ Understand and use the probability scale from 0 to 1. (5)	3
✓ Sort objects using a Venn diagram. (4)	4

Language	Meaning	Example
Probability	A measure of how likely an outcome is to occur. It is described using words (certain, very likely, unlikely, ...) or numbers (50%, 0.85, $\frac{1}{4}$, ...).	The probability of it raining tomorrow is very unlikely. The probability of rolling a 6 on a dice is $\frac{1}{6}$.
Even chance	The probability for an event which is as likely to happen as not happen.	A coin landing heads up or a coin landing tails up.
Event	An activity.	The weather tomorrow is the event. Rolling the dice is the event.
Outcome	A result of an activity.	Rain tomorrow is an outcome. Rolling a 6 is an outcome.
Venn diagram	A diagram that sorts objects into sets.	Pet dog, Pet cat: 5, 4, 8; 7

16 MyReview

1 Describe the probability of these outcomes in words.
a You will get an odd number when you roll a dice.
b You will see a pig flying.
c You will eat some food today.
d It will rain in Newcastle on a randomly picked day in April.

2 The 26 letters of the alphabet are written on cards and put in a bag. One card is chosen at random. Describe the probability that it shows
a the letter A
b a consonant
c the number 3.

3 Describe these probabilities using any of these words.
Impossible Very unlikely Unlikely Even chance Likely Very likely Certain

a 0	b 0.2	c 0.5	d 0.8
e 1%	f 99%	g 30%	h 100%

4 A group of students listed their hobbies. The Venn diagram shows how many said "listening to music" and "playing sport".
music, sport: 12, 9, 7; 4
How many students
a listen to music and play sport
b play sport
c listen to music
d neither listen to music nor play sport?

5 Here is a collection of shapes.
Copy the Venn diagram and sort the shapes into it.
red, triangle

What next?

Score	
0 – 2	Your knowledge of this topic is still developing. To improve look at Formative test: 1A-16; MyMaths: 1209 and 1235
3 – 4	You are gaining a secure knowledge of this topic. To improve look at InvisiPen: 451 and 471
5	You have mastered this topic. Well done, you are ready to progress!

304 Statistics and probability Probability

MyMaths.co.uk 305

Question commentary

Questions 1 to **3** – The event probability descriptions impossible, even chance and certain are unambiguous. Other descriptions, such as likely and very likely, are subjective and do not correspond to well defined probabilities. However their relative order should not be open to dispute.

Questions 1 – (lesson **16a**) Check students' idea of how likely they think a given event is as well as have they chosen the appropriate language to describe it.

As necessary provide students with the choice of words: impossible, (very) unlikely, even chance, (very) likely and certain.

Questions 2 – (lesson **16b**) In part **b**, check that students understand what consonant means and that there are 21 of them, compared to only 5 vowels.

Ask more able students if they can write their answers as fractions: **a** $\frac{1}{26}$, **b** $\frac{21}{26}$ and **c** 0.

Question 3 – (lessons **16c**) Check that students correctly distinguish between very (un)likely and (un)likely.

Question 4 – (lesson **16d**) In the answers to parts **b** and **c** heck that students include the nine students in the middle (the intersection), who enjoy both music and sport; failure to do so will give the *incorrect* answers **b** 7 and **c** 12.

Question 5 – (lesson **16d**) The Venn diagram can be drawn using either coloured shapes or the number of shapes in each region.

Answers

1 **a** Even chance **b** Impossible
c Certain **d** Likely

2 **a** Unlikely **b** Likely
c Impossible

3 **a** Impossible **b** Unlikely
c Even chance **d** Likely
e Very unlikely **f** Very likely
g Unlikely **h** Certain

4 **a** 9 **b** 16 **c** 21 **d** 4

5

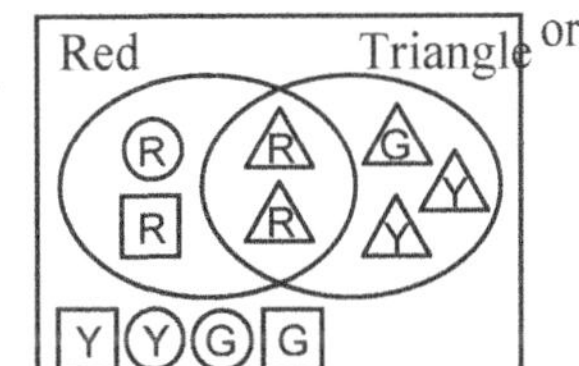

or

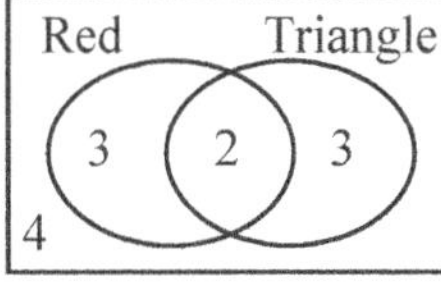

16 MyPractice

16a

1 Read each statement and choose a word from the list that describes the chance of it happening.

Certain
Likely
Unlikely Impossible
Equal chance

a
You will drink something before midnight.
b
An elephant will become Prime Minister.
c
The next person you phone will be a girl.
d
You are looking at this book.
e
You will walk on the sun tomorrow.
f
You will find treasure in the park.
g
It will snow in August.
h
You will learn to drive a car at some time in your life.

2 Use one of the words in the box to classify each of these events.

a If you keep running for long enough you will tire out.
b If you go out tonight after dark you will see a full moon.
c If you go out on a very cold morning you will see ice.
d If you arrive at a level crossing and the gate is closed, a train is coming.
e The year 2076 will be a leap year.
f The year 2077 will be a leap year.

Certain
Likely
Unlikely
Impossible
Uncertain

16b

3 If you are also able to choose from this list, can you give a better description for the events in question **2**?

Almost impossible
Quite unlikely
Even chance
Very likely
Almost certain

4 Use words to describe the probability of the points shown on this probability scale.

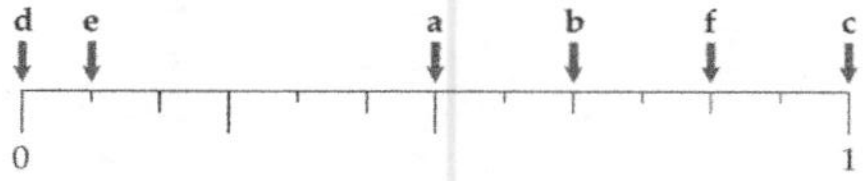
d
e
a
b
f
c
0
1

16b

5 Which statement best describes your chances of picking a red cube?

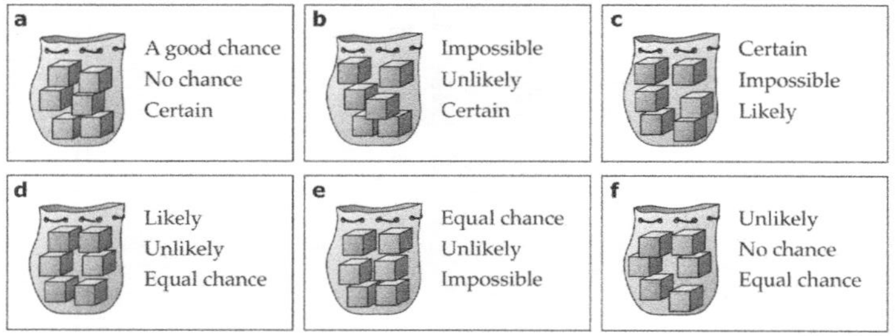
a
A good chance
No chance
Certain
b
Impossible
Unlikely
Certain
c
Certain
Impossible
Likely
d
Likely
Unlikely
Equal chance
e
Equal chance
Unlikely
Impossible
f
Unlikely
No chance
Equal chance

16c

6 The dominoes shown here are shuffled and placed upside down on a table.

If one is then picked up, find the probability that it will have

a 7 dots
b an odd number of dots
c an even number of dots
d a five on it
e a four on it
f a four *or* a five on it.

16d

7 The Venn diagram shows the numbers 1–10 organised into even numbers and multiples of 3.

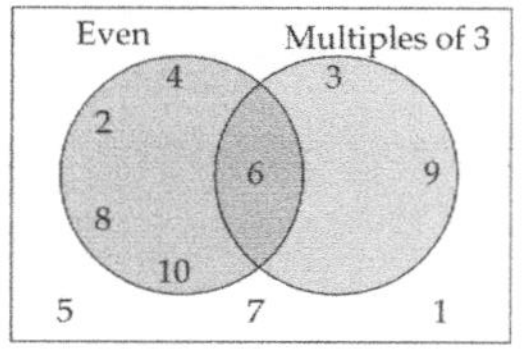
Even
Multiples of 3
4
2
8
10
6
3
9
5
7
1

a Write down the numbers that are multiples of 3 but not even.
b Write down the numbers that are even but not multiples of 3.
c Write down the numbers that are not multiples of 3 and not even.
d Copy the Venn diagram and expand it to include all the whole numbers up to 20.

Question commentary

Question 1 and **2** – As a way to ensure a separation between deciding how probably an event is from deciding the appropriate vocabulary to describe it, a classroom discussion may prove useful. Question **1c** could have quite different answers depending on whether the individual student is a boy or a girl. In question **2**, parts **e** and **f** students may need to be told the rule that a leap year is always divisible by four (but not by 100 unless a multiple of 400).

Questions 3 – Check that the answers to this question are compatible with the answers previously given in question **2**.

Question 4 – There is no ambiguity in the meaning of impossible, even chance and certain. Words like likely, quite likely and very likely and almost certain can't be given an absolute position on the probability line but it should be possible to achieve agreement on their relative positions.

Question 5 – This is can be extended by asking students to calculate the probabilities as fractions.

Questions 6 – For more able students, ask what do their answers to parts **b** and **c** add up to and can they explain why? The sum is one because all dominoes either have an odd or an even number of dots: they are the only possibilities and you can't be both. Then ask the students to add up their answers to parts **d** and **e** and compare this to their answer to part **f**. Is this what they expected? The sum is $1 > \frac{5}{6}$ and the reason for the discrepancy is that there is one domino with both a four and a five on it.

Questions 7 – Parts **a** to **c** could be done together to help with student understanding before allowing the students to do part **d** on their own. As an extension ask students to describe the numbers in the overlap region: numbers that are both even and multiples of 3 or simply even multiples of three.

Answers

1 Student answers; accept answers with a sensible reason.
- **a** (very) Likely **b** Impossible
- **c** Unlikely/Equal chance/Likely
- **d** Certain **e** Impossible
- **f** (very) Unlikely **g** (very) Unlikley
- **h** Likely

2 Student answers; accept answers with a sensible reason.
- **a** Certain **b** Unlikley/Likely
- **c** Likely **d** Likely
- **e** Certain **f** Impossible

3 **a**, **e** and **f** unchanged.
- **b** Quite unlikely/Very likely
- **c** Very likely
- **d** Very likely/Almost certain

4 **a** Even chance **b** Likely
- **c** Certain **d** Impossible
- **e** Very unlikely **f** Quite likely

5 **a** No chance **b** Certain
- **c** Likely **d** Likely
- **e** Evens chance **f** Unlikely

5 **a** $\frac{1}{2}$ **b** $\frac{4}{6} = \frac{2}{3}$ **c** $\frac{2}{6} = \frac{1}{3}$ **d** $\frac{2}{6} = \frac{1}{3}$
- **e** $\frac{4}{6} = \frac{2}{3}$ **f** $\frac{5}{6}$

6 **a** 3, 9 **b** 2, 4, 8, 10
- **c** 1, 5, 7
- **d**

Even — Multiple of 3

Even only: 2 4 8 10 14 16 20

Both: 6 12 18

Multiple of 3 only: 3 9 15

Outside: 1 5 7 11 13 17 19

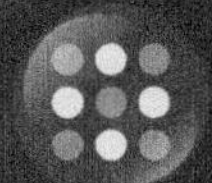

Case study 6: The school fair

Related lessons		Resources	
Decimals and money	1d	Probability intro	(1209)
Calculator skills	14h	Money calculations	(1014)
Solving arithmetic problems	15c	A five-sided spinner and coloured cards	
The probability scale 2	16c	Spare calculators	
		100-number cards	
		Dice, blank cards	

Simplification	Extension
Focus on tasks **1** to **3**. Supply students with a five-sided spinner and coloured cards so that they can play the game and undertsand how it works before attempting the questions. In task **2**, provide students with a preprepared table showing quantities, prices and cost (= quantity × cost), with one line completed, plus a row labelled total underneath the cost coloumn.	Supply students with dice and blank cards and ask them to design their own game of chance. They should decide what the prizes will be and calculate their cost. They should then calculate a cost to enter the game and what their profit will be after a fixed number of games. The game can then be played to test their ideas. Alternatively students could research the cost of cordial and packs of cups and plan their own drinks stall following the calculations in task **5**.

Links

A number of interactive spinners, with variable numbers of sectors, are available online.

shodor.org/interactivate/activities/BasicSpinner/
nlvm.usu.edu/en/nav/frames_asid_186_g_1_t_1.html?open=activities
illuminations.nctm.org/adjustablespinner/

A guide to planning a fete, including tombolas and raffles can be found here.

fundraisers-uk.co.uk/content/the-ultimate-guide-to-running-a-charity-fete.php

Case study 6: The school fair

A school is holding a fair to raise money. They need to make sure that they make a profit.

Task 1

a What is your chance of winning if you have the red card?
b What is your chance of losing if you have the blue card?
c Is the stall holder right to say "A prize every game"? Do you think it is misleading?

SPIN IT TO WIN IT!
To play the game, pay 50p and choose a coloured card.
The spinner will spin when all 5 colours have been bought.
The person with the colour the spinner stops at wins a prize!

a prize every game!

50p per go!

Task 2

Look at the notebook page entitled 'SPINNER GAME COSTS.' The total cost of prizes has been smudged out.
a Find the total cost of prizes for this game.
b How many games need to be played before the stall makes any profit?

Task 3

a Could the stall run out of the more expensive prizes before it makes a profit?
b Suggest how the stallholder could make the game fairer.

SPINNER GAME COSTS
3 cuddly toys @ £3.00 each
5 boxes of chocolates @ £2.20 each
10 key rings @ 20p each
10 cans of drink @ 25p each
Total cost of prizes:

DRINKS FOR SALE

Task 4

The tombola is filled with 100 tickets numbered from 1 to 100.
a Find the probability that the first person to buy a ticket wins a prize.
b Find the probability that the first person to buy a ticket does not win a prize.
c Find the probability that the first person to buy a ticket wins the watch.
d **(Challenge)** What is the largest profit that could be made from this game? How likely is that to happen?

Task 5 (Challenge)

Bethan is running a drinks stall.
She has bought 5 bottles of squash and 6 packs of cups.
Each bottle costs £1.80 and can make 30 cups of squash.
The packs of cups cost £2.20 each and there are 24 cups in a pack.
How much will Bethan need to charge per cup to ensure she makes a profit before she runs out of squash or cups?

50p per go

TOMBOLA
All tickets ending in 0 or 5 win a prize!

308 309

Teaching notes

Ask students if they have ever been to or been involved in a fund raising fair. What sorts of games were there? What do they think the organisers did to make sure that they made a profit? Ask students to suggest potential costs and sources of income for, say, selling drinks or a simple game of chance? How can they be sure that they make a profit? (income – costs > 0)

The main parts of this case study look at two sideshows that could be found at a typical school fair or similar occasion: a spinner game and a tombola. They have been chosen as they both appear to have a 1 in 5 chance of winning but actually behave differently to each other due to the non-replacement of tickets that have been picked out of the tombola.

Task 1

Ask students to explain to you how the game is played. Ask, how many cards do I need? How many sections should the spinner have? How many cards do I have to sell before the game starts? Have available a spinner and cards so that the game can be played for real.

In part **a**, ensure students to write their answer as a fraction, not, for example, as 'one in five'. Test their understanding by asking, does this mean I am sure to win if I play five games? (No) What is my probability of winning if I buy two coloured cards? ($\frac{2}{5}$)

In part **b**, suggest thinking of the question as asking, what is your chance of winning if you have a pink or red or yellow or green card?

In part **c**, this is an opportunity to warn against trickery and the dangers of gambling.

Task 2

These are typical of problems that need to be broken down into stages.

For part **a**, discuss with students what they need to calculate and then allow them to get on with it, only intervening as necessary. To avoid decimals do all calculations in pence. The calculations should be done using written methods and in stages: $3 \times 300 = 900$, $5 \times 220 = 1100$, $10 \times 20 = 200$, $10 \times 25 = 250$ and $900 + 1100 + 200 + 250 = 2450$. Avoid the use of calculators if possible.

For part **b**, again either discuss with students what needs to be calculated, before allowing them to get on with it, or allow small groups of students to decide for themselves. As a prompt ask, how much money is collected per game? (£2.50) In principle students need to calculate $24.50 \div 2.50$ and round up. However it will be easier to look for the first multiple of £2.50 which is greater than £24.50.

Task 3

This task tests students understanding of randomness. Their ideas for modifying the game will need to be assessed on an individual basis.

Task 4

Probabilities only need calculating for the first ticket drawn out of the initial one hundred. Unlike the spinner game, subsequent probabilities are not the same because tickets are not replaced.

As a prompt ask students how many tickets win/do not win a prize? (20/80) Weaker students could be given a 100-number square on which to count multiples of 5 and 10. Ask students to simplify the fractions in their answers. It may be helpful to point out that multiples of five are every five numbers and this gives rise to the 'one in five' probability.

Stronger students could be asked, what is the chance of winning at the second attempt? ($\frac{20}{99}$ or $\frac{19}{99}$ depending if the first ticket won.)

Part **d** relies on a very unlikely scenario. As a prompt ask, how many people could lose before someone must win? (80)

Task 5

This is quite a wordy question that needs breaking down into several parts. Students are likely to require guidance on how to proceed. The total cost is $5 \times 180 + 6 \times 220 = 900 + 1320 = 2220$. The number of cups is $6 \times 24 = 144$. The break even cost per cup is $2220 \div 144 = 15.4\ldots$ which will need rounding up. The final division will require a calculator and discussion of what to do with the answer but the other calculations should be done by hand, in pence to avoid decimals. This question could be done in small groups.

Answers

1 **a** $\frac{1}{5}$ **b** $\frac{4}{5}$
c One player wins a prize every game, not every player wins a prize.

2 **a** £24.50 **b** 10

3 **a** Yes **b** Choose prizes randomly

4 **a** $\frac{20}{100} = \frac{1}{5}$ **b** $\frac{80}{100} = \frac{4}{5}$ **c** $\frac{1}{100}$
d £40, when only eighty people play and all lose. Very, very unlikely (1.86×10^{-21})

5 16p or more.

MyAssessment 4

These questions will test you on your knowledge of the topics in chapters 13 to 16.
They give you practice in the types of questions that you may see in your GCSE exams.
There are 70 marks in total.

1 For these sequences
  - **a** find the next two numbers in each sequence (3 marks)
  - **b** say what is the difference between the numbers in each sequence. (3 marks)
    - **i** 24, 20, 16, 12, … **ii** 4, 6, 8, 10, … **iii** 4, 9, 14, 19, …

2 Write a description for each sequence using 'start at …. and …. each time'.
  - **a** 32, 16, 8, 4, … (2 marks) **b** -11, -7. -3, 1, … (2 marks)
  - **c** 17, 26, 35, 44, … (2 marks) **d** 3, -1, -5, -9, … (2 marks)

3 Here is a description for a sequence 'start at -3 and +7 each time'.
  - **a** Use this description to find the first three terms. (3 marks)
  - **b** Write down the first five terms of a sequence if the description is 'start at -4 and +7 each time'. (3 marks)

4 Use multiplication or division facts to calculate each answer.
  - **a** 9×7 (1 mark) **b** 8×5 (1 mark)
  - **c** $32 \div 4$ (1 mark) **d** $81 \div 9$ (1 mark)

5 Use multiplication facts to calculate each answer.
  - **a** 62×10 (1 mark) **b** 57×100 (1 mark)
  - **c** 17×100 (1 mark) **d** 23×10 (1 mark)

6 Use a number line and repeated subtraction to calculate each answer.
  - **a** $47 \div 5$ (1 mark) **b** $96 \div 6$ (1 mark)
  - **c** $63 \div 4$ (1 mark) **d** $29 \div 7$ (1 mark)

7 Use your calculator to answer these problems.
  - **a** £4.07 ÷ 5 (1 mark) **b** £9.64 × 6 (1 mark)
  - **c** £9.87 − £4.51 (1 mark)

8 Mortar is being made by adding 1 part cement to 5 parts sand.
  - **a** Write this as a ratio of cement to sand. (2 marks)
  - **b** If 2 kg of cement is used how much sand is needed. (1 mark)
  - **c** If 3 kg of cement is used how much mortar would you make. (2 marks)

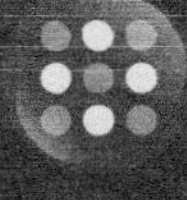

9 To make 10 blueberry muffins you need 200 g of flour, 100 g of butter and 80 g of blueberries.
  - **a** What is the ratio of flour to butter to blueberries? (2 marks)
  - **b** How much of each ingredient will you need to make
    - **i** 30 muffins **ii** 15 muffins? (4 marks)

10 Using the recipe in question **9**, flour costs 97 p per 100 g, butter £1.30 per 200 g and blueberries £2.00 per 80 g.
  - **a** How much does it cost for 200 g of flour? (1 mark)
  - **b** How much does it cost for 100 g of butter? (1 mark)
  - **c** How much does it costs to make 10 muffins? (2 marks)

11 Describe the likelihood of these events using the list of words below.

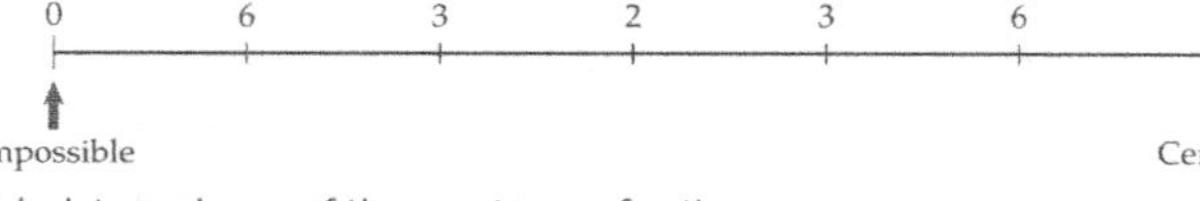

  - **a** It will rain tomorrow. (1 mark)
  - **b** Obtaining a Head when you toss a coin. (1 mark)
  - **c** The sun will rise tomorrow. (1 mark)

12 An ordinary six-sided dice is thrown.
Describe in words how likely it is to get a score
  - **a** exactly one (1 mark)
  - **b** an odd number (1 mark)
  - **c** more than four. (1 mark)

13 **a** For the dice thrown in question **12**, mark on the probability scale using the letters *a*, *b* and *c* the probability of these events occurring. (3 marks)

0   $\frac{1}{6}$ $\frac{1}{3}$ $\frac{1}{2}$ $\frac{2}{3}$ $\frac{5}{6}$ 1

Impossible   Certain

  - **b** Calculate each one of the events as a fraction. (3 marks)
  - **c** Write these probabilities as a percentage. (3 marks)

14 The numbers 1-10 are sorted into prime numbers and even numbers.
  - **a** Draw a Venn diagram to summarise this information. (3 marks)
  - **b** How many numbers are not prime and not even? (2 marks)

Mark scheme

Questions 1– 6 marks (lessons **13a**)

a i 1 8, 4; need both numbers for the mark
ii 1 12, 14; need both numbers for the mark
iii 1 24, 29; need both numbers for the mark
b i 1 -4
ii 1 2
iii 1 5

Questions 2 – 8 marks (lessons **13b** and **13d**)

a 2 Start at 32 and ÷2 each time
b 2 Start at - 11 and - 4 each time
c 2 Start at 17 and + 9 each time
d 2 Start at 3 and - 4 each time

Questions 3 – 6 marks (lessons **13c**)

a 3 -3, 4, 11
b 3 -4, 3, 10, 17, 24;
– 1 mark for each error or omission

Questions 4 – 4 marks (lessons **14a** and **14e**)

a 1 63
b 1 40
c 1 8
d 1 9

Questions 5 – 4 marks (lessons **14b**)

a 1 620
b 1 5700
c 1 1700
d 1 230

Questions 6 – 4 marks (lessons **14e**)

a 1 9 r 2
b 1 16
c 1 15 r 3
d 1 4 r 1

Questions 7 – 3 marks (lessons **14h**)

a 1 £0.81; answer must be to 2 dp.
b 1 £57.84
c 1 £5.36

Questions 8 – 5 marks (lessons **15a**)

a 2 1 : 5; colon needs to be shown for 1 mark.
b 1 1 kg
c 2 18 kg; 1 mark for 3 kg cement or 15 kg sand

Questions 9 – 6 marks (lessons **15b**)

a 2 200 : 100 : 80 or 10 : 5 : 4
b i 2 600 g flour, 300 g butter, 240 g blueberries
ii 2 300 g flour, 150 g butter, 120 g blueberries

Questions 10 – 4 marks (lessons **15c**)

a 1 £1.94
b 1 £0.65 or 65p
c 2 £4.59; 1 mark for correct sum seen

Questions 11 – 3 marks (lessons **16q**)

a 1 Likely; accept a number of responses here.
b 1 Even chance
c 1 Certain

Questions 12 – 3 marks (lessons **16b**)

a 1 One out of six
b 1 1, 3, 5 so three out of six
c 1 5, 6 so two out of six

Questions 13 – 9 marks (lessons **16c**)

a 3

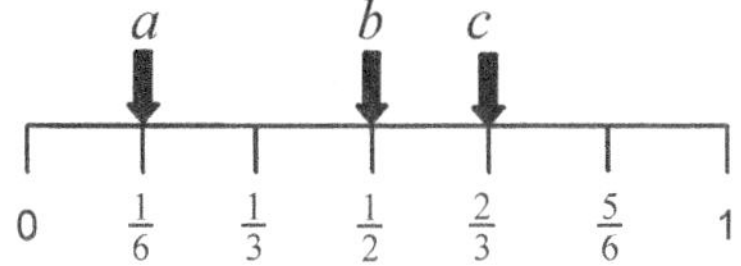

b 3 $\frac{1}{6}$, $\frac{3}{6}$ or $\frac{1}{2}$, $\frac{4}{6}$ or $\frac{2}{3}$
c 3 16.6%, 50%, 66.7%
Accept 17% and 67%

Questions 14 – 5 marks (lessons **16d**)

a 3 –1 mark for each error or omission.

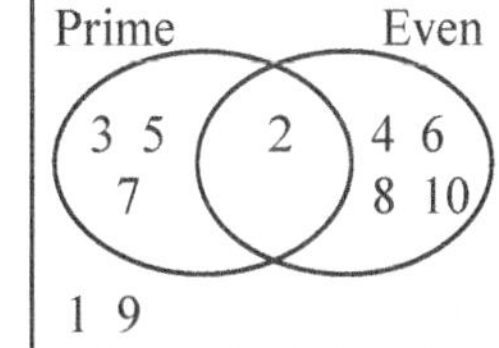

b 2 2

Levels

	Q1 – 3	Q4 – 7	Q8 – 10	Q11 – 14
	A	N	R & P	S & P
S 5			13 – 15	
D 5			9 – 12	17 – 20
M 4	17 – 20		5 – 8	13 – 16
S 4	13 – 16			9 – 12
D 4	9 – 12	13 – 15		5 – 8
M 3	5 – 8	9 – 12		
S 3		5 – 8		
FA	0 – 4	0 – 4	0 – 4	0 – 4

D developing S secure M mastery FA further assessment needed

17 Everyday maths

Learning outcomes	
DF2 Select and use appropriate calculation strategies to solve increasingly complex problems.	(L5)
DF5 Move freely between different numerical, algebraic, graphical and diagrammatic representations [for example, equivalent fractions, fractions and decimals, and equations and graphs].	(L5)
DF7 Use language and properties precisely to analyse numbers, algebraic expressions, 2D and 3D shapes, probability and statistics.	(L5)
RM1 Extend their understanding of the number system; make connections between number relationships, and their algebraic and graphical representations.	(L5)
RM2 Extend and formalise their knowledge of ratio and proportion in working with measures and geometry, and in formulating proportional relations algebraically.	(L5)
RM5 Begin to reason deductively in geometry, number and algebra, including using geometrical constructions.	
RM7 Explore what can and cannot be inferred in statistical and probabilistic settings, and begin to express their arguments formally.	(L5)
SP1 Develop their mathematical knowledge, in part through solving problems and evaluating the outcomes, including multi-step problems.	(L5)
SP2 Develop their use of formal mathematical knowledge to interpret and solve problems, including in financial mathematics.	(L5)
SP4 Select appropriate concepts, methods and techniques to apply to unfamiliar and non-routine problems.	(L5)

Introduction

The chapter consists of a sequence of five spreads based on the theme of the Swinley School swimming gala. This allows questions to cover a wide range of topics taken from algebra, statistics, geometry, number, and ratio and proportion. The questions are word-based and often do not directly indicate what type of mathematics is involved. Therefore students will need to work to identify the relevant mathematics and in several instances which of a variety of methods to apply before commencing. This approach is rather different from the previous topic based spreads and students may require additional support in this aspect of functional maths.

Prior knowledge

The chapter covers many topics; lessons which contain directly related material include

- 1b, c, d
- 2a, b, c, d, e, f, g
- 3a, e
- 5a, c, f, g
- 6a, d
- 7a, b
- 8b, c, e, g, h, i, j
- 9b
- 10c, e
- 11a
- 12c, e
- 14c, e, h
- 15a, b, c, d
- 16a, c

Using mathematics

The student book start of chapter suggests three areas of everyday life where aspects of the ability to apply mathematical ideas prove highly valuable.

Fluency: Fluency in arithmetic is vital in ensuring you manage your money effectively. Every time you use a checkout you rely on the person who programmed the till having done so correctly. How do you know that you get the correct change? Similarly, calculators can perform lots of amazing tasks, and can be a real help when working out hard sums. However their maths ability is only as good as the person who programmed them!

Mathematical reasoning: Working out the most efficient way of doing things often involves mathematical reasoning. An example would be the most efficient way to lay out a pattern on a piece of cloth. Similar problems have to be solved when arranging files on a hard drive so as to minimize wasted space or packing oranges in a box so as to reduce the need for packaging.

Problem solving: People use maths to solve problems in their daily working lives – not just mathematicans! Distribution centres face a difficult task in planning the best routes, loads and timetables. To guide them, they collect data on fuel costs, journey times, stock shortages, and so on. By carefully analyzing this data they can monitor and improve their performance.

Topic scheme

Teaching time = 5 lessons/2 weeks

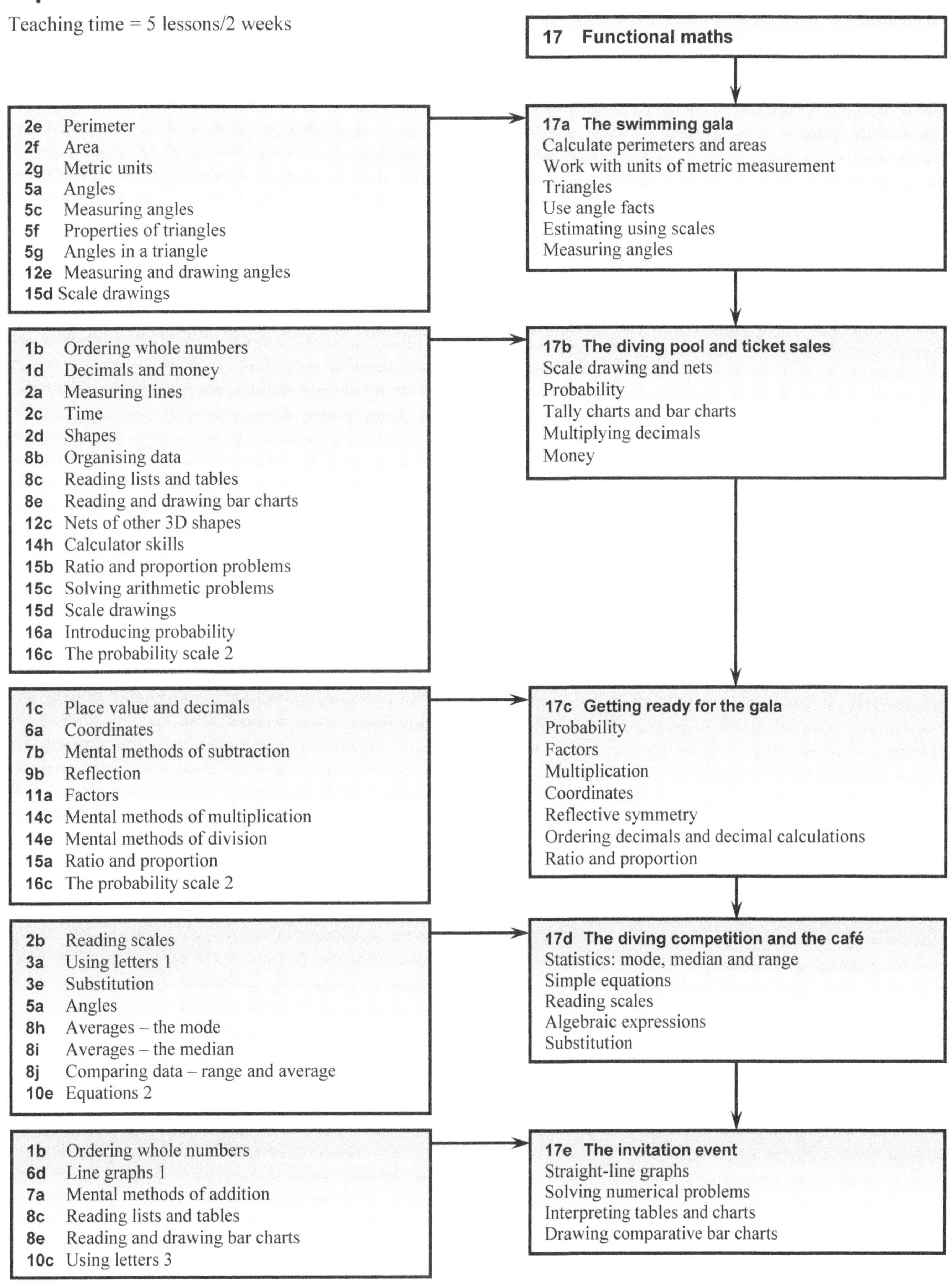

17 Functional maths
2e Perimeter
2f Area
2g Metric units
5a Angles
5c Measuring angles
5f Properties of triangles
5g Angles in a triangle
12e Measuring and drawing angles
15d Scale drawings
17a The swimming gala
Calculate perimeters and areas
Work with units of metric measurement
Triangles
Use angle facts
Estimating using scales
Measuring angles
1b Ordering whole numbers
1d Decimals and money
2a Measuring lines
2c Time
2d Shapes
8b Organising data
8c Reading lists and tables
8e Reading and drawing bar charts
12c Nets of other 3D shapes
14h Calculator skills
15b Ratio and proportion problems
15c Solving arithmetic problems
15d Scale drawings
16a Introducing probability
16c The probability scale 2
17b The diving pool and ticket sales
Scale drawing and nets
Probability
Tally charts and bar charts
Multiplying decimals
Money
1c Place value and decimals
6a Coordinates
7b Mental methods of subtraction
9b Reflection
11a Factors
14c Mental methods of multiplication
14e Mental methods of division
15a Ratio and proportion
16c The probability scale 2
17c Getting ready for the gala
Probability
Factors
Multiplication
Coordinates
Reflective symmetry
Ordering decimals and decimal calculations
Ratio and proportion
2b Reading scales
3a Using letters 1
3e Substitution
5a Angles
8h Averages – the mode
8i Averages – the median
8j Comparing data – range and average
10e Equations 2
17d The diving competition and the café
Statistics: mode, median and range
Simple equations
Reading scales
Algebraic expressions
Substitution
1b Ordering whole numbers
6d Line graphs 1
7a Mental methods of addition
8c Reading lists and tables
8e Reading and drawing bar charts
10c Using letters 3
17e The invitation event
Straight-line graphs
Solving numerical problems
Interpreting tables and charts
Drawing comparative bar charts

Related lessons		Resources	
Perimeter	2e	Measuring angles	(1081)
Area	2f	Angles in a triangles	(1082)
Metric units	2g	Area of rectangles	(1084)
Angles	5a	Perimeter	(1110)
Measuring angles	5c	Properties of triangles	(1130)
Properties of triangles	5f	Strips of paper	
Angles in a triangle	5g	Centimetre square graph paper	
Measuring and drawing angles	12e	Spare protractors	
Scale drawings	15d		

Background

This lesson sets the scene for the rest of the chapter which loosely revolves around the idea of a school swimming gala. The questions cover perimeter and area, name and measuring angles, identifying triangles and estimating distances in a scale drawing.

It may help to generate enthusiasm if, at the start, a little time is spent talking with the students about some of the issues that might arise when organising and competing in a gala: ticket pricing, scoring systems, catering, etc. Look ahead to see what topics will come up. If any students have direct involvement in a swimming gala or similar event then ask them to talk about their experience.

Simplification	Extension
Weaker students or those for whom the language may be an issue can be placed in pairs and encouraged to discuss what the question is asking, what information it provides or needs to be found and what calculation needs to be done.	Ask students to create their own designs for a diving platform. The design should include lots of triangles, which they should count and make a note of. They should then swap diagrams with a partner and challenge them to count the number of triangles. As a further challenge ask students to count the number of triangles of each type: right-angle, isosceles, scalene or equilateral.

Links

The oldest 'swimming pool' in the world is probably the 'great bath' at Mohenjo-daro, an ancient city in the Indus valley civilization located in what is now Pakistan. It dates to around 2500 bc. The pool is almost 12 m by 7 m and 2.5 m deep and made of mud bricks lined with bitumen to make it waterproof. A collection of photographs of the site can be found here, the bath and its drain appears in photos 25 to 32.

www.mohenjodaro.net/

A useful source of information on diving is the Great Britain Diving Federation

www.diving-gbdf.com/

Their site includes:

a history of diving	www.diving-gbdf.com/history.php
a list of UK swimming pools with diving boards	www.diving-gbdf.com/facilities.php
a list of local diving club	www.diving-gbdf.com/clubs.php

Teaching notes

Explain to students that this is the first of a new style of lesson, somewhat like the case studies, that each have a theme and have questions on a lot of topics not just one. They will be expected to decide what to do and where to find the necessary information to solve the questions themselves. That said, you should be ready to intervene, especially at the start, to get students going.

This is also the time to explain how you expect the students to approach the work. For example, as individuals, pairs or small groups, …., should they work at their own pace, start straight away, etc.

Once students have been given an overview it may be helpful to tackle the first few questions together as a way of modelling how students are intended to do the work. Read out load the text at the top of the left hand page, and then ask a student to read out question **1**. Discuss what the question is asking you to find and where any necessary information can be found: students need to look at the measurements on the diagram of the swimming pool. Agree the correct answer with the students and write it down for them to copy into their books.

Repeat with further questions until the majority of students are working independently of you. You can then focus your attention on students who are struggling.

Exercise commentary

Question 1 – (lesson **2g**) This first question is a straightforward exercise in reading information from the diagram of the pools in the student book. It can be used to check that students know what to do.

Question 2– (lesson **2e**) Since two of the pool's sides do not have lengths marked on them beware of students who just add 10 and 25 to get the *wrong* answer 35 m. It may help some students if you ask them to draw a sketch of the pool, a simple rectangle, and mark on all the side lengths.

Question 3 – (lesson **12e**) As with question **1** it will help students to sketch the diving pool and add on all the side lengths. These will need to be extracted from the sentence above the question. This is an opportunity to remind students to read all the information given and not to jump straight to the questions.

Question 4 – (lesson **2f**) The diagram in the student book is accurately drawn in that it shows 20 one metre-square tiles which students could count. Alternatively they could be given some centimetre square grid paper and asked to draw the wall, using a scale 1 cm: 1 m so that counting the number of squares gives the answer.

Question 5 – (lesson **15d**) The question ask for estimates so an accurate answer is not required. The simplest approach to this question is to give students a strip of paper which they can place beside Ellen and repeatedly mark of her height to create a 'ruler'. This will then need to be marked off in multiples of 1.5m (3 m, 4.5 m) or possibly multiples of 50 cm.

Alternatively students could measure Ellen's height, 3 cm, and deduce that the scale is 1 cm : 50 cm.

Question 6 – (lesson **5f**) Students will need to be systematic and may need prompting to include triangles that can be formed from two smaller triangles. There is one triangle on the left, two at the top, one at the bottom and eight (4 + 4) in the middle. It may be helpful to pair students and get them to compare totals.

Question 7 – (lesson **5a**) When trying to decide if an angle is greater than 90°, acute, or less than 90°, obtuse, students may find it helpful to rotate the book so that one arm of the angle is horizontal and then they can compare the other arm to the vertical.

Question 8 – (lessons **5c**, **5g** and **12e**) The angles are all multiples of 10° so that this becomes a test of whether students are using the correct 'starts at zero' scale. As a prompt ask them what type of angles are *r*, *s* and *t*? Then ask, what is the range of degrees for an acute angle? To measure angle RST students may find it helps to rotate the book or to hold the protractor vertically before making the measurement.

In part **b**, since individual angles should be measured to ± 1° the total should be within 180 ± 3°.

Answers

1 **a** 10 m **b** 25 m **c** 2 m

2 70 m

3 22 m

4 20 m^2

5 ≈ 3.25 m

6 12

7 **a** Acute **b** Obtuse **c** Right **d** Obtuse **e** Acute

8 **a** $r = 60°$, $s = 30°$, $t = 90°$ **b** 180°

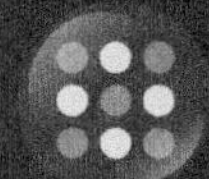

17b The diving pool and ticket sales

Related lessons		Resources	
Ordering whole numbers	1b	Money calculations	(1014)
Decimals and money	1d	Proportion	(1037)
Measuring lines	2a	Nets of 3D shapes	(1106)
Time	2c	Measuring lengths	(1146)
Shapes	2d	Scale drawing	(1117)
Organising data	8b	Frequency tables and bar charts	(1193)
Reading lists and tables	8c	Pictograms and bar charts	(1205)
Reading and drawing bar charts	8e	Probability intro	(1209)
Reading diagrams	8g	Ordering whole numbers	(1217)
Nets of other 3D shapes	12c	2D and 3D shapes	(1229)
Calculator skills	14h	Word problems	(1393)
Ratio and proportion problems	15b	Copies of the nets in question **3**	
Solving arithmetic problems	15c	Graph paper	
Scale drawings	15d	Spare calculators	
Introducing probability	16a		
The probability scale 2	16c		

Background

This lesson covers material on a diverse range of topics: measuring and scale drawing, 2D and 3D shapes, basic probability, proportional reasoning, tally charts, bar charts and arithmetic.

Ask if any students have been involved in an event for which tickets were sold in advance/on the door. If anyone has, invite them to explain what they did and how they kept track of how many tickets were sold and how much money was collected. Otherwise ask the class to think about how they would organise selling tickets.

Simplification

There are quite a large number of questions in this lesson and it may help to focus weaker students' attention on smaller sets of questions. Natural groupings are questions **1** to **3**, questions **4** and **5**, questions **8** to **10**, and questions **11** to **16**.

Avoid questions **6** and **7**

Extension

Students could use a spreadsheet to create a table containing the number of tickets sold by a group pf classes. Based on this table they could calculate the amount of money raised and create a bar chart or possible also a pie chart.

Links

3D models of polyhedral are a great way to spark students interest in maths and can make excellent classroom displays. There are a number of websites that make available nets for creating models.

www.senteacher.org/worksheet/12/NetsPolyhedra.html
www.korthalsaltes.com/

The Nrich organisation has a number of activities based around visualising 3D shapes and their nets. Particularly relevant are the videos of nets being folded up to see if they do form a solid.

nrich.maths.org/6307

Teaching notes

This lesson is packed with a diverse set of questions and a prompt start is advised; it may be necessary to take two lessons to cover the material.

Exercise commentary

Question 1 – (lessons **2a** and **15d**) Allow ± 2 mm uncertainty in the depth of the pool due to the choppy water line. Part **a** could be done collectively and then part **b** done by students on their own.

Question 2 – (lesson **2d**) Students should look at the diagram they just made the measurements on. Refer them to lesson **2d** if they need reminding of the names for 2D shapes. It may help to identify it as a trapezium if the page is turned through 90°.

Question 3 – (lesson **12c**) Have available copies of the nets if students cannot use reasoning alone. Alternatively students can make their own copies of the nets and see if they will fold into the pool shape.

Question 4 – (lesson **16c**) The question assumes that the lids have been swapped randomly and that only information on the lids is used to select the blue tin. If you look at the sides then you know that, as drawn, picking the blue lid will give green paint. For part **b**, students should think 3 out of 4 are not blue, rather than be expected to use $1 - \frac{1}{4} = \frac{3}{4}$.

Question 5 – (lesson **16a**) This is an opportunity to discuss the meaning of randomness with the class.

Question 6 – (lesson **15b**) This requires proportional reasoning in an unfamiliar context. Prompt students by asking, if one-fifth of the pool is painted in 20 mins, then how long does it take to paint two-fifths, then three-fifths…? (40 mins, 60 mins, …) Some students may need reminding that five-fifths is the same as the whole pool. Do *not* expect students to calculate $20 \text{ mins} \div \frac{1}{5}$.

Question 7 – (lesson **1b** and **2c**) This tests the need to use consistent units and that 60 minutes = 1 hour as well as ordering whole numbers.

Question 8 – (lesson **8b**) Students should only be reminded how to count the tallies for one class and be left to do the others on their own. Check the answers are correct before attempting questions **9** and **10**.

Question 9 – (lesson **8e**) It may help to do one bar as a whole class. Take the opportunity to check that scales are correctly drawn.

Question 10 – (lessons **8e** and **8g**) Answers can also be found using the table: this can be used as a cross-check.

Question 11 and **14** – (lessons **1d**, **4h** and **15c**) The multiplications are best done with a calculator, checking that the first two decimal places are understood as pence.

Question 12 – (lesson **8c**) Encourage the use of a written method for the addition.

Question 13 –This is similar to question **5**. As a prompt, ask, how many halves are there in a whole?

Question 16 – (lesson **15c**) This is the first place that subtraction is used; encourage using a written method.

Answers

1 **a** 6 m
  b **i** 6.5 m **ii** 5.5 m **iii** 2.5 m

2 Trapezium

3 **b** and **d**

4 **a** $\frac{1}{4}$ **b** $\frac{3}{4}$

5 Each colour is equally likely.

6 100 minutes = 1 hr 40 mins

7 No

8 7A = 30, 7B = 27, 7C = 18, 7D = 25

9

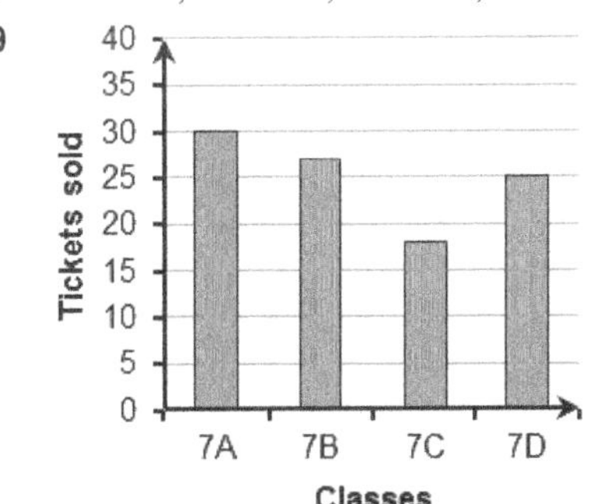

10 **a** Well done year 7. They sold a total of 100 tickets.
  b Class 7A sold the most tickets, selling 30 tickets altogether.
  c The range of sales is 12.

11

Class	Tickets sold	Total
7A	30	£45
7B	27	£40.50
7C	18	£27
7D	25	£37.50
	Total	£150.00

12 Year 7 collected a total of £150.

13 200

14 £250

15 The total money raised by the gala was £400.

16 £1950

Related lessons		Resources	
Place value and decimals	1c	Factors and primes	(1032)
Coordinates	6a	Ratio introduction	(1052)
Mental methods of subtraction	7b	Ordering decimals	(1072)
Reflection	9b	Coordinates	(1092)
Factors	11a	Lines of symmetry	(1114)
Mental methods of multiplication	14c	Probability intro	(1209)
Mental methods of division	14e	Mixed sums all numbers	(1345)
Ratio and proportion	15a	Graph paper	
The probability scale 2	16c	Coloured pencils	
		Coloured tiles	

Background

The lesson uses two themes, organising the seating and a swimming race in lanes, to cover elementary probability, factors, coordinates, reflective symmetry, arithmetic problems, ordering decimals and ratio and proportion.

Simplification	Extension
For question **4** supply students with a pre-labelled grid and a set of coloured tiles so that they can first copy the left hand side of the design and then create the right hand mirror image. The coloured tiles can also be used to recreate the pattern of floats refered to in questions **12** and **14**.	Challenge students to take the three incorrect answers in questions **7**, A, B & C, and reflect them to create three new, full seating plan designs. Pairs of students can then set one another questions to solve like those in questions **5** and **6**.

Links

Swimming has a very long history. There are paintings in the 'cave of the swimmers', south-west Egypt, believed to show people swimming 10 000 years ago when there is evidence a river ran through the area. Some photographs can be seen here

www.fjexpeditions.com/frameset/wsora.htm

Less ambiguous illustrations of people swimming can be seen in the artworks of more recent ancient civilisations such as those of the Babylonians, Minoans and Egyptians.

Competitive swimming is much more recent and started in England in the 1830s. In the beginning competitors only used breaststroke before a version of front crawl, copied from native south American swimmers, was introduced in 1873. Butterfly was only developed in the 1930s.

In England competitive swimming is regulated by the Amateur Swimming Association.

www.swimming.org/asa/

Teaching notes

Start the lesson by using a series of quick fire questions to test students' recall of the main topics that will be encountered in the lesson. use mini-whiteboards for the answers.

- What is the probability of rolling a 5 using a fair dice? ($\frac{1}{6}$)
- What are the factors of 12? (1, 2, 3,4, 6, 12)
- Draw the lines of symmetry on a kite?
- What is 30 – 17.5? (12.5)
- Put these numbers in ascending order: 4.4, 2.4, 4.2, 2.2? (2.2, 2.4, 4.2, 4.4)
- There are 6 black cards and 8 red cards what is the ratio of black to red? (6 : 8 = 3 : 4)
- What is the proportion of black cards? ($\frac{6}{14} = \frac{3}{7}$)

As necessary correct any mistakes and retest using further questions. Once students are reasonably confident ask them to start on the questions in the student book.

Exercise commentary

Question 1 – (lesson **16c**) Test students understanding by asking, what the probability would be if their where twice as many blue chairs as any other colour. It may help to clarify the meaning if you draw 2 blue squares, 1 red, 1 yellow and 1 green – as in the question. ($\frac{2}{5}$)

Question 2 – (lesson **14e**) Students will have to go back to the first sentence to see where the number of chairs, 160, is given.

Question 3 – (lesson **11a**) This question is essentially asking students to find the factors of 80.

Question 4 – (lesson **14c**) Students can count the number of chairs on the left but doing the multiplication 5 × 8 should be encouraged.

Question 5 – (lesson **6a**) This is a variant of the use of coordinates; emphasise that the coordinates label where the '*x*- and *y*-lines' intersect and not the spaces between the lines.

Question 6 – (lesson **6a**) A ruler will be needed to measure distances to (5, E), (4, F) or (3, F). Students are not expected to use Pythagoras!

Question 7 – (lesson **9b**) If students struggle to do this in their head then suggest that they copy the left hand half of seating plan onto squared paper and then reflect it in the dotted line. They can then match their image to one of the options A – D.

Question 8 – (lesson **7b**) Students need to do the subtractions 25 – 24, 25 – 20 etc. As necessary show what is required and where to find the information for one of the swimmers but then allow students to do the remainder themselves.

Question 9 – (lesson **7b** This can be done as 24 – 20 or, looking at distance left to go, 5 – 1.

Question 10 – (lesson **14c**) This should be done as a multiplication.

Question 11 – (lesson **1c**) Students need to think about the context here: the winner will have the shortest/smallest time and not the largest.

Question 12 – (lesson **14c**) Students should do their calculation assuming the five rope layout shown in the student book diagram.

Question 13 – (lesson **14c**) Ask students to compare this with their answer to question **10**; should they be the same? (Yes)

Question 14 – (lesson **15a**) Students should be encouraged to simplify their answers by cancelling down. They have not previously encountered a three term ratio. Ask students to suggest how this should be written before showing them.

Answers

1 **a** The chance of sitting in a blue chair is 40 out of 160.
   b $\frac{1}{4}$
2 80
3 Numbers of rows and columns can be swapped.

Number of chairs in a row	Number of rows	Total
8	10	8 × 10 = 80
4	20	4 × 20 = 80
2	40	2 × 40 = 80
16	5	16 × 5 = 80

4 40
5 **a** Red **b** (2, G)
6 (3, F)
7 D
8 From left to right: 1 m, 5 m, 8.5 m, 3.25 m
9 4 m
10 125 m
11 **a** Rio **b** Ahmed
12 **a** 50 **b** 20 **c** 10
13 125 m
14 **a** $\frac{2}{16} = \frac{1}{8}$ **b** 2 : 4 : 10 = 1 : 2 : 5

Related lessons		Resources	
Reading scales	2b	Simple equations	(1154)
Using letters 1	3a	Substitution 1	(1187)
Substitution	3e	Median and range	(1203)
Angles	5a	A scale with movable pointer	
Averages – the mode	8h	Sets of small cards	
Averages the median	8i		
Comparing data – range and average	8j		
Equations 2	10e		

Background

This lesson covers basic statistics, solving simple equations, reading scales, forming algebraic expressions and simple substitution.

Students are likely to have seen panels of judges give scores in game shows on television. If possible obtain real scores from one of these show and use the data to discuss how you could represent all the scores by a single average score; what could be the maximum possible score, etc.

Simplification

For question **1** give students a set of cards with the five scores on them to work with.

To make the algebra in questions **7** and **8** more real supply cards with 'cake / $a = 30$', 'tea / $b = 40$' etc written on them. Then to make the first order, soup, sandwich & pie, students can take the three cards 'soup / $c = 50$', 'sandwich / $e = 85$' and 'pie / $b = 40$'. Finally they can then use the cards to write '$c + e + b$' and '50 + 85 + 40' before completing the addition '50 + 85 + 40 = 175'.

Extension

Pair up students and ask each student to create their own version of question **4**. They should then swap questions and challenge their partner to find the missing score.

Show how a spread sheet can be used to evaluate the expressions such as those in questions **7** and **8** all at once. For example, in A1 write 'a =' and in B1 enter '30', in A2 write 'b =' and in B2 enter '40' etc. Then in D1 write '$c + e$' and in E1 enter '=B3+B5', in D2 write '$a + c$' and in E2 enter '=B1+B3', etc. Students should find that as soon as they hit return E1 contains 135, E2 contains 80, etc. More impressively students can change any of the prices in B1–5 and the cost of the orders in E1, E2, etc. will automatically update.

Links

Official diving competitions use a more elaborate scoring scheme than the one used in the student book. Each member of the panel of judges marks the dive out of ten, on criteria such as angle of entry, correct execution of moves, height of the dive etc. Two corrections are then applied. If there are five judges then the lowest and highest scores are discarded and the sum of the remaining 'middle three' score multiplied by $\frac{5}{3}$ (to correct back to a five judge score). This score is then multiplied by a 'Degree of Difficulty' factor which is determined by a combination of the moves involved, the position adopted in the attempted dive and its height. (In the 2012 Olympics there were seven judges and the top two and bottom two marks were eliminated with the sum of the remaining three again multiplied by $\frac{5}{3}$ and the DD.)

The governing body for diving is FINA, Federation Internationale de Natation; details of their rules and scoring system can be found here.

www.fina.org/H2O/docs/rules/FINAdvrules_20132017.pdf

Diving itself has a long history, at least 2500 years. The tomb of the diver found at Paestum, a town in Magna Graecia, Southern Italy, dated 470 BC clearly shows a man diving from a high platform.

www.paestum.org.uk/?page_id=303

Teaching notes

Start the lesson by using a series of quick fire questions to test students' recall of the main topics that will be encountered in the lesson. use mini-whiteboards for the answers.

- How many degrees are there in a right angle? (90)
- For the five integers 4, 6, 3, 2, 6 what is: the mode (6), the median (4) and the range? (4)
- What is the total of the five integers? (21)
- What is 5 + 7 + 2 + -4? (10)
- If 23 + □ = 30, what is □? (7)
- If 3 + 5 + 2 + 8 + □ = 27, what is □? (9)
- Show a scale with a pointer on it and ask for the 'reading'.
- What does the expression $x + x + y$ equal if $x = 4$ and $y = 5$? (13)

As necessary correct any mistakes and retest using further questions. Once students are reasonably confident ask them to work in pairs to do the questions in the student book. Explain that you will only help them if they are really stuck and that they should try to do the questions without any help.

When students ask for help, pose the problem to the whole class and see if another student can explain what to do.

Exercise commentary

Question 1 – (lesson **5a**) This could be extended to other multiples and fractions of 360°.

Question 2 – (lessons **1a**, **8h**, **8i** and **8j**) For parts **b** and **c**, students should be able to remember which is the mode average and which is the median average. In part **e** there are two ways to do the calculation: as 30 – total score, 22, or as the sum of individual differences (6 – 3) + (6 – 6) + … Do students get the same answer both ways. For part **f**, insist that students try to articulate the reason behind their choice of description.

Question 3 – This is a question that tests both written understanding and the ability to cope with a multi-step question: find the total score, find half the maximum and then compare the two.

Question 4 – (lesson **10e**) Suggest students call judge 5's score x and see if they can write an equation containing x: $6 + 2 + 3 + 5 + x = 16 + x = 24$.

Question 5 – (lesson **10e**) In part **b**, check that students add -4 to the answer from part **a**, 17 – 4, and do not repeat calculation the earlier calculation, 3 + … + 6 – 5. As necessary, point out which approach is the more efficient and less likely to be as error prone.

Question 6 – (lesson **2b**) Students may not have previously encountered the units bar and volt but any lack of familiarity should not be significant for the questions. (As a unit of pressure the bar is now deprecated and should be replaced by pascal.)

Question 7 – (lesson **3a**) In part **b**, ask students to collect any like terms in the algebraic expression.

Question 8 – (lesson **3e**) This is a more abstract version of the previous questions.

Answers

1 One complete turn.

2 **a** 3, 4, 4, 5, 6
b 4
c Amira's median average score was 4.
d 30 **e** 8
f Students' answers with reasons; a possible answer is Good as above halfway.

3 C

4 6

5 **a** 17 **b** 13

6 **a** The pressure is 3 bars.
b The electricity reading is 235 volts.
c There are 6.5 litres of water in the machine.
d The hot water temperature is 97 °C.
e The hot milk temperature is 45 °C.

7 **a** $b + c + e$ 40p + 50p + 85 p = 175p = £1.75
b $2a + b + d$ 30p + 30p + 40p + 60p= 160p = £1.60
c $a + c + d + e$ 30p + 50p + 60p + 85 p = 225p = £2.25

8 **a** £1.35 **b** 80p **c** 90p **d** £1.30
e £1.55 **f** £1.20 **g** £1.65

17e The invitation event

Related lessons		Resources	
Ordering whole numbers	1b	Simple equations	(1154)
Line graphs 1	6d	Pictograms and bar charts	(1205)
Mental methods of addition	7a	Ordering whole numbers	(1217)
Reading lists and tables	8c	A number line marked in tens up to 100	
Reading and creating bar charts	8e	Graph paper	
Using letters 3	10c	Sets of four cards labelled A, B, C and D	

Background

The questions focus on reading and creating graphs, interpreting data presented in tabular form and solving equations.

The first two questions look at how a handicapping system works. Some students may have competed in a handicap, if so ask them to explain how the system worked. It may also be possible to obtain data from a school wide event, perhaps from an athletics day, in which case look at how a handicap might allow you to compare the winners of the 100 m races for year 7, year 8, year 9 etc.

Simplification

To help with question **2**, provide students with a number line. Consider the sum of the ages of Mr Adams and Ms Brown: mark 27 and 51 on the number line and ask students what do you add to 27 to get to 51? (24) Next mark 24 and 56 and repeat to get Mrs court's age. (32).

In question **5** ask several 'who won event A' type questions until students have confidence interpreting the table. Then repeat these questions by turning them into a statement, 'X won event A' and asking if it is true or false. Finally extend the questions to include compound statements, 'X won even A and Y came second in event B'.

Extension

Ask pairs of students to each create a puzzle, like those in question **3**, which they can then swap and challenge their partner to solve. Is it possible to give less information in the puzzle and still be able to solve for everyone's age?

Alternatively issue students with four cards labelled A, B, C and D which they chose in a random order to determine the order in which four teams finish in an event. In this way they can create their own results table and repeat questions **4** to **8**.

Links

A number of sports use a system of handicapping to try to make competitions fairer for competitors with different levels of experience or age.

In British horse racing the majority of events are handicaps. One of the oldest systems, developed by Admiral Henry Rous around 1860, is called 'weight for age'. All horses in a race should carry a nominal weight but younger horses are given a reduction according to their age and the date of the race and the distance. This is to allow for the younger horses being less mature and having less stamina. The British horse racing association's weight allowances for flat races are given here

www.britishhorseracing.com/inside_horseracing/media/WFA_Flat.pdf

Teaching notes

Tell students that there is going to be a school swimming gala and that competitors of any age can enter: so that they might end up racing against sixth formers. Ask the students if this would be fair and if not what would they do to make it fairer? Introduce the idea of handicapping and look at questions **1** and **2**.

To introduce question **3**, tell the class that you have three numbers and some information. The first and second add up to 43 and the second and third add up to 35. Can they tell you what the numbers are? (No) If you then say the first number is 17 can they now give you the other two numbers? (Yes, 26 and 9) The numbers can also be found if the sum of the first and third number is given, 26, or if the total of the three numbers is given, 52, but these are much harder problems. better to ask students to calculate these two sums.

For questions **4** to **8** ask the whole class some questions that test their understanding of the table, especially the fact that '1' equates to loser and '4' to winner.

Exercise commentary

Question 1 – (lesson **6d**) Suggest that the fifteen year old's time was 24 seconds and together work through reading the graph and the calculation, $24 + 8 = 33$ s. Then let students attempt the question parts on their own or in pairs.

Question 2 – (lesson **1b**) Check students' answers to question **1** are correct before allowing them to proceed to this question. It may be interesting to discuss whether students think there should be a third place if there has been a joint second place.

Question 3 – (lesson **10c**) The information given suggests a series of 'equations': what number do you add to 27 to give 51? etc. The problem is over constrained in the sense that answers can be calculated in more than one independent way. For example, Mr Dean's age can be calculated as $32 + x = 96$ or $27 + x = 91$. Students could be challenged to try and find the ages in more than one way. They should also check that the sum of their answers is 147.

Question 4 – (lesson **7a**) A check is that the sum of the boys' totals and the sum of the girls' totals must both be 70; can students see why? (There are seven events and in each event 10 points, $1 + 2 + 3 + 4$, are awarded.)

Question 5 – (lesson **8c**) Students may need reminding that 1 indicates a loser and 4 a winner. If a statement is incorrect ask students to give the correct version.

Question 6 – (lesson **1b**) The winners will have the highest total.

Question 7 – (lesson **8c**) 'No winner' would not be a surprising result in reality but students might find it hard to accept in the context of a question.

Question 8 – (lesson **8e**) The axis labels are a little confusing in the sense that on the vertical axis the inter-line spaces are labelled whereas on the horizontal axis it is the lines which are labelled. Check that students label them correctly.

Question 9 – (lesson **1a**) To avoid argument/ambiguity you could add that the Olympic swimmer's birthday is at the end of the year, 31st December.

Answers

1 **a** 33 sec **b** 31 sec **c** 33 sec **d** 32 sec
e 32 sec

2 Grace (first), Rio & Eric (joint second),
Connor & Iman (joint fourth)

3 **a** 24 **b** 32 **c** 64

4 Boys: 7A 16, 7B 18, 7C 17, 7D 19
Girls: 7A 18, 7B 19, 7C 16, 7D 17

5 **a** Correct **b** Correct **c** Incorrect (Team B won)
d Correct **e** Incorrect (Team B won)

6 **a** 7B **b** 7D, 7C, 7A

7 Not awarded

8

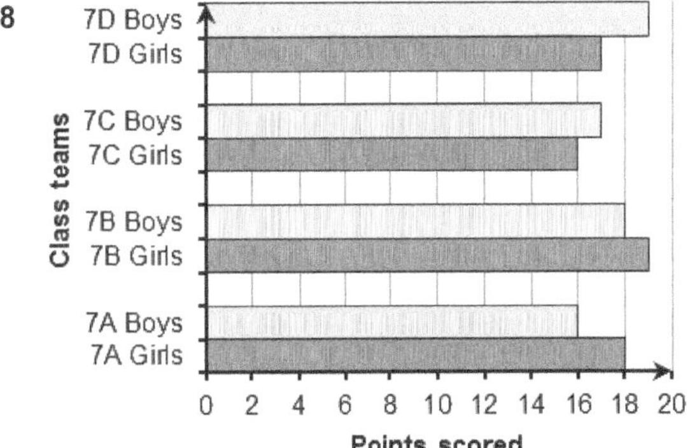

9 Assuming birthday not already passed:

2014	76	2015	77
2016	78	2017	79
2018	80	2019	81

Notes